Prospective Memory

Theory and Applications

Prospective Memory
Theory and Applications

Edited by

Maria Brandimonte
University of Trieste

Gilles O. Einstein
Furman University

Mark A. McDaniel
University of New Mexico

 LAWRENCE ERLBAUM ASSOCIATES, PUBLISHERS
1996   Mahwah, New Jersey

Lawrence Erlbaum Associates, Inc., Publishers
10 Industrial Avenue
Mahwah, New Jersey 07430

Cover design by Cheryl Minden

Library of Congress Cataloging-in-Publication Data

Prospective memory : theory and applications / edited by Maria Brandimonte, Gilles O.
    Einstein, Mark McDaniel.
        p.   cm.
    Includes bibliographical references and indexes.
    ISBN 0-8058-1536-8 (c)
        1. Memory. 2. Recollection (Psychology) 3. Memory—Age factors. I. Brandimonte,
    Maria. II. Einstein, Gilles O., 1950-   . III. McDaniel, Mark A.
    BF371.P76   1996   95-18844
    153.1'2—dc20   CIP

Books published by Lawrence Erlbaum Associates are printed on acid-free paper, and their
bindings are chosen for strength and durability.

Printed in the United States of America
10 9 8 7 6 5 4 3 2 1

Contents

Preface

In 1984, John Harris wrote an important review paper on prospective memory. This paper is noteworthy, not only for its clear and compelling organization of the existing knowledge in this nascent field, but also for its revelation that there had been little interest and few programmatic research efforts in prospective memory. The zeitgeist in contemporary cognitive psychology is becoming friendlier toward prospective memory research as recent developments in psychology are stimulating fresh interest in the subject. The rise in research activity on prospective memory corresponds nicely with heightened interest both in everyday memory and in the practical applications of memory research. As one indication of this increased interest, there were two paper sessions and one poster session devoted exclusively to prospective memory at the 1994 Practical Aspects of Memory Conference. Research programs by Park and Kidder (this volume) on medication adherence, by Camp, Foss, Stevens, and O'Hanlon (this volume) on effective strategies for improving prospective memory in persons with Alzheimer's disease, and by Vortac, Edwards, and Manning (in press) on prospective memory demands of air traffic controllers, provide ample evidence that prospective memory research has important applications for real-world memory problems.

Moreover, the processes and issues that are thought to be involved in prospective memory seem to have general relevance beyond that of prospective memory. One of the most salient features of prospective memory retrieval, for example, is that it often occurs spontaneously and without conscious attempts to interrogate memory (see Einstein & McDaniel, this volume). Thus, prospective memory may provide new and interesting avenues for examining issues related to implicit or nonconscious retrieval. Prospective memory research may also provide us with new and convenient paradigms to test theories of aging. As Maylor (this volume) points out, processes that are thought to be critical for good prospective memory (such as self-initiated retrieval, reality monitoring, and output monitoring) are thought to be highly sensitive to the effects of aging. Recent interest by neuropsychologists in the frontal lobes, which are thought to be involved in planning and inhibiting ongoing behavior, suggests that prospective memory might be a fruitful area for examining the effects of frontal lobe damage.

It is our belief that the psychological climate is now hospitable to prospective memory research and in fact, prospective memory research is starting to make its way into the major memory journals. New theoretical views, along with developing laboratory techniques, augur well for the future of prospective memory research. The goal of this book is to capture the recent interest in prospective memory and to organize the research and thoughts of the important contributors to the field into one comprehensive source. Our hope is that this volume will stimulate the thinking of active prospective memory researchers, provide a coherent organization of the area for the increasing number of people who are interested in prospective memory but who are not yet actively conducting research in the area, and serve as a book of readings for upper division seminars.

The book consists of 13 chapters organized into sections that cover (I) encoding, storage, and retrieval in prospective memory; (II) aging and prospective memory; (III) the neuropsychology of prospective memory; and (IV) the applications of prospective memory in real-world settings. We asked authors to focus on their own work, but also more generally to review existing research and to address where the methods and theories from the retrospective memory literature are useful and where they fall short. Each section is followed by at least one commentary, written by a prominent scholar in the field of memory. We asked the commentators to present a critical analysis of the chapters, but also to note ideas that they found particularly exciting and to use these ideas as a foundation or springboard on which to elaborate their own views of prospective memory. The chapters and summaries have served these purposes as we have come away from this project impressed with the richness of the current thinking on prospective remembering.

We would like to thank all the contributors of the chapters and commentaries. One of the interesting features of prospective memory is that the authors come from different parts of the world, and it is has been both a challenge (made so much easier by electronic mail) and a pleasure to engage in global communication. We are indebted to Judi Amsel at Lawrence Erlbaum Associates for encouraging us to go ahead with this project and for her good advice during all stages of the book's development. Lib Nanney's gracious help and wonderful organizational skills were invaluable in sorting through all the manuscripts and getting them to the right editors and commentators. We wish to thank Gus Craik for stimulating some of our earliest thinking about prospective memory and for his kind support over the years. We also thank the National Institute on Aging (Grant No. AG08436), which supported Gil Einstein and Mark McDaniel during the writing and editing of this book.

REFERENCES

Harris, J. E., (1984). Remembering to do things: A forgotten topic. In J. E. Harris & P. E. Morris (Eds.), *Everyday memory, actions, and absent-mindedness* (pp. 71–92). New York: Academic Press.

Vortac, O. U., Edwards, M. B., & Manning, C. A. (in press). Functions of external cues in prospective memory. *Memory*.

PART I

Encoding, Storage, and Retrieval in Prospective Memory

1

Prospective Memory or the Realization of Delayed Intentions: A Conceptual Framework for Research

Judi Ellis
University of Reading

As Neisser observed, ordinary language employs the word *remember* to reflect at least two different temporal perspectives: "remembering what we must do" or our future plans and "remembering what we have done" or events from the past (Neisser, 1982, p. 327). The former is termed *prospective,* and the latter, *retrospective* remembering, following Meacham and Leiman (1976).

The use of the term prospective remembering, or *prospective memory,* often carries an implicit assumption that one might be dealing with a distinct form of memory. Indeed, it is often contrasted with research on more extensively studied memory tasks described as examining retrospective memory, such as the free recall or recognition of previously learned word lists. In this chapter, however, I suggest that the term prospective memory may be a misleading or inadequate description of research on the formation, retention, and retrieval of intended actions or activities that cannot, for whatever reason, be realized at the time of initial encoding. Successful prospective remembering can be described, therefore, as processing that supports the realization of delayed intentions and their associated actions. As such, it is intimately associated with the control and coordination of future actions and activities.

The primary aim of this chapter is to develop this analysis of prospective memory tasks into a broad conceptual framework. It draws from research on a variety of cognitive processes and places prospective memory at the interface between memory, attention, and action processes. For this reason the description, *realizing delayed intentions,* is used here whenever it is appropriate to do so, in preference to the term, *prospective memory.* The final section

1

briefly examines the implications of this framework for future research questions and methodologies.

PHASES OF A PROSPECTIVE MEMORY TASK

The realization of a delayed intention and its associated action is described in terms of the following general phases,[1] illustrated in Fig. 1.1:

A. Formation and encoding of intention and action.
B. Retention Interval.
C. Performance Interval.
D. Initiation and Execution of Intended Action.
E. Evaluation of Outcome.

Phase A is concerned primarily with the retention of the *content* of a delayed intention. More precisely, it is concerned with the retention of an action (*what* you want to do), an intent (*that* you have decided to do something) and a retrieval context that describes the criteria for recall (*when* you should retrieve the intent and the action and initiate them). For example, the different elements of an intention to telephone a friend this afternoon may be encoded as follows: "I will" (that-element) "telephone Jane" (what-element) "this afternoon" (when-element). It is highly probable that planning and motivational operations that occur during this phase will influence the encoding and thus the eventual representation of the delayed intention.

Phase B refers to the delay between encoding and the start of a potential performance interval, whereas *phase C* refers to the performance interval or period when the intended action should be retrieved.[2] This distinction between retention and performance intervals is illustrated by the following example. An intention to visit a friend tomorrow morning may have been encoded 2 days ago. It would have, therefore, a retention interval of approximately 2 days and a performance interval of approximately 3 hours (9:00 a.m.–12:00 p.m.). The duration of retention and performance intervals will vary considerably and a delayed intention may be remembered at any point during either of these two phases. The successful realization of an intention, however, requires that it be retrieved on at least one occasion during a performance interval and on the occurrence of the following events. First, an appropriate situation must be recognized as an occasion that is (a) a retrieval context and (b) associated with a particular intention to do something: retrieval of the when- and that-elements. Second, the action that was encoded with these elements must be retrieved—recall of the what element. *Phases D* and *E* are concerned with the initiation and execution of an intended action, and the evaluation of the re-

---

[1]Cf. Brandimonte (1991); Einstein & McDaniel (1990); Ellis (1991).
[2]Cf. Harris and Wilkins' (1982) description of a *window of opportunity*.

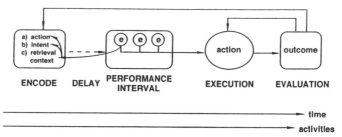

FIG. 1.1. Schematized view of the phases involved in the realization of a delayed intention. Note. e = event, and so forth, to signal retrieval context.

sultant outcome, respectively. Moreover, some form of record of an outcome is necessary either to avoid an unnecessary repetition of a previously satisfied delayed intention or to ensure the future success of a postponed or failed delayed intention.

Einstein and McDaniel (1990) proposed that we can usefully discriminate between two components of a prospective memory task. The first retrospective memory component refers to the retention of the action and "target event" or retrieval context. The second prospective memory component refers to the retrieval of the action "at the appropriate time or in response to the appropriate event" (p. 725). These two components correspond broadly to operations postulated to occur during phases A and C, respectively (see Fig. 1.1). To facilitate a more comprehensive and componentially neutral analysis of the task of realizing a delayed intention, these components are referred to here as *retrospective* (phase A) and *prospective* (phases B through to E). The exclusion of the term *memory* is a deliberate step designed to avoid a potential bias toward only considering "pure" memory processes.

TOWARD A CONCEPTUAL FRAMEWORK: COMPONENTS AND PROCESSES

The Retrospective Component

This consists of the what- (action), that- (intent), and when- (retrieval context) elements that together form the content of a delayed intention. These elements are considered briefly here and examined in more detail at a later point.

The *action* or what-element will vary with respect to its overall complexity and the origin of this complexity. It may describe, for example, a physical or mental activity that varies from the relatively routine or well-learned to the relatively nonroutine or novel.[3] The less routine the action, or part of that action

---

[3]The term *routine* describes an action that is well-learned and highly integrated such that its constituent elements are performed in a consistent order on each occasion.

is, the more likely it becomes that planning processes, concerned with how the action is to be performed (what-realization), will be required (see also, Ellis & Shallice, 1993). The application of these planning processes is likely to result in a more detailed encoding of constituent action components for a non-routine action (see, e.g., Kolodner, 1983; Schank, 1982).

Complexity may be also derived from a requirement to either carry out several relatively independent enabling actions prior to the intended action, or execute several constituent actions in the pursuit of a particular extended activity. For example, in order to carry out an action such as photocopying a journal article, you may need to carry out enabling actions such as discovering the library that stocks that journal and/or completing an interlibrary request form. Alternatively, photocopying may describe an activity that requires the performance of more than one action, such as making more than one type of copy of the article (e.g., a double-sided version and a reduced-size copy). In general, as the number of these enabling and/or constituent actions increases, the demands of that action in terms of encoding and retention will also increase. However, these demands will be mediated by the temporal or causal connections either between constituent actions or between enabling actions and the initially intended action (see, e.g., Schank, 1982). Finally, the action may require the transmission of information. Here, as before, the number of items to be relayed or requested, the degree to which they have been learned previously, their semantic relations, and so on, will all exert an influence on encoding demands (see, e.g., Mandler, 1967; Tulving, 1962).

The *intentional status* of a delayed intention (or that-element) refers to a decision or readiness to act—the notion of "something to do" at a future moment (see, for further discussion, Kvavilashvili & Ellis, this volume). It incorporates motivational forces that reflect one's degree of commitment to the realization of that intention. The intentional status of an intention may vary from a *wish* or *want* to a *must, ought,* or *will* (see, for further discussion, Kuhl, 1985). This "strength" of an intention may reflect not only its personal importance, but also the potential benefits of realizing it as well as the costs of failure. Although these three dimensions (personal importance, benefits, and consequences) are highly correlated in naturally occurring intentions (Ellis, 1988a, 1988b) there are occasions on which they appear to be in conflict. For example, a personally important intention, such as buying a new item of clothing, may confer a high degree of personal benefit but relatively low consequences if one fails to satisfy it. The strength of a delayed intention, moreover, is likely to be influenced further by (a) its origin or primary source (oneself or another person), (b) its primary direction or beneficiary (self or other), and (c) the status, in relation to oneself, of a relevant other person (for further discussion, see Meacham, 1988). For example, an intention to buy flowers for a visitor's room may have low personal importance—unless the visitor happens to be your mother-in-law! In summary, it is clear that the intentional status or

TABLE 1.1.
Examples of general (categorized) and specific retrieval contexts.

Type of Retrieval Context	General	Specific
Event	A leisure period at work	The first coffee break
Activity	Domestic work	Cleaning the bathroom
Person	A secretary	Your personal secretary
Object	A postbox	Your local postbox
Time	In the morning	At 10:00 a.m.
Location	A garage	The garage next to your office

strength of a delayed intention will be strongly affected by the relations between that intention and other, longer term intentions, aims, and personal themes (see, e.g., Barsalou, 1988; Conway, 1992; Ortony, Clore, & Collins, 1988).

Finally, the *retrieval context* (or when-element) describes some characteristics of a future occasion that should prompt the retrieval of a delayed intention. Several potentially distinct types of context can be identified—events, activities, times, persons, objects, or locations (see, e.g., Einstein & McDaniel, 1990; Harris, 1984). The relationships between these retrieval context types are examined by Kvavilashvili and Ellis (this volume). A retrieval context that is defined in terms of only one of the above types is described as a *pure* retrieval context (e.g., telephone John at 10:00 a.m. [pure, time] or telephone Mary when you are in your office [pure, location]). A pure retrieval context may be either relatively *general* or categorized (e.g., a set of possible events or time period) or relatively *specific* (e.g., a particular event or particular time). Examples of both specific and general, pure retrieval contexts are provided in Table 1.1. Frequently however, for naturally occurring intentions at least, a retrieval context may be described in terms of more than one context type (e.g., an intention to see John at 10:00 a.m. before you go to a meeting refers to both a time and an event). These multiple-type or *combined* retrieval contexts can vary from the general to the specific.

Both pure and combined retrieval contexts may differ with respect to their opportuneness. This refers to the frequency with which a context occurs within a given performance interval (e.g., give Mary a message this morning when Mary usually enters your room several times during the morning), or number of performance intervals (e.g., give John a message this week when John comes into work on three mornings). The generality of a retrieval context may reflect, in some instances, the potential number of opportunities for performing an intended action. For example, an intention to telephone someone today may have a general retrieval context because one anticipates, at encoding, several potentially appropriate occasions during the day when a telephone will be readily available. Similarly, a specific retrieval context may reflect a restricted set of opportunities (e.g., you have several meetings that day). It is also possible, however, that multiple opportunities will be encoded in the form of separate specific retrieval contexts rather than a general one (Einstein, personal communication, February 18, 1995). The implications of these different distinctions for the outcome of a delayed intention are considered later in the discussion on retrieval.

Representation of Retrospective Component

Clearly the various elements outlined above, which together constitute the content of a delayed intended action, are not necessarily independent of one another. For example, the application of planning processes that are directed towards action- or what-realization may increase the strength of an intention, whereas the latter may influence the specificity of a retrieval context. How, though, are these elements related and represented within a cognitive system? In an *action–trigger–schema* (ATS) framework, developed by Norman (1981) and Norman and Shallice (1986) and extended by Rumelhart and Norman (1982), actions are represented by action schemas that at any given time have a level of activation together with trigger conditions. A schema is selected once its activation level exceeds a certain threshold and initiated once its trigger conditions have been satisfied. The activation value is important primarily in the selection of an action, and the extent of the match between existing conditions and an action's trigger conditions influences the amount of activation received by that action. For example, Rumelhart and Norman suggested that a well-learned action sequence such as typing a word can be represented by a set of schemas. The occurrence of a perceptual event (e.g., the handwritten word), and processing of this event (by, e.g., a parser) activates the schema for that word which in turn activates subschemas for particular key presses. The perceptual event, together with other more specific conditions as appropriate, provides the trigger conditions for the initiation of the schema and the selection of the appropriate motor movements (see Rumelhart & Norman, 1982, for further details).

The retrieval context of a delayed intention can be seen as providing the trigger conditions for the future retrieval of its encoded action whereas its intentional status or strength might be expected to exert an influence on the activation level of that action. Activation (and inhibition) can spread to other related action + goal structures (*schemas*) which, in turn, may influence the intentional status and thus the activation level of the initial encoded action. Activation levels, however, are temporary and short-lived, and thus unlikely to reflect the more durable and pervasive aspects of many motivational states. It is suggested, therefore, that variations in intentional status are likely to be reflected in the threshold value associated with a particular action schema. This means of representing delayed intentions forms the basis of the conceptual framework that is elaborated in the following discussion.

The Prospective Component

This includes the elements described in phases B through to E, described previously and illustrated in Fig. 1.1. It includes also other relevant events, such as recollections, that occur during either retention or performance intervals. The term *recollection* refers to occasions on which a delayed intention is remembered prior to the occurrence of a retrieval context during a performance interval.

Recollections of a delayed intention may be prompted by any one of variety of factors. Some recollections may occur as a result of a direct or deliberate act that originates either from oneself (e.g., after noticing a previously planned memory such as a memo to oneself) or from another person (e.g., following a direct reminder from a colleague); see, for further discussion, Harris (1980). Others may occur with apparent "spontaneity," in the absence of a direct or deliberate reminder. These recollections—their occurrence and the frequency and rate at which they occur—may play a role in the eventual outcome of a delayed intention.

There is some indication, from laboratory tasks, that failures to carry out a delayed intention are associated both with a low frequency of recollections during a short (3- to 15-min.) retention interval and the absence of a recollection close to the appearance of a retrieval context during a performance interval (Einstein & McDaniel, 1990; Einstein, McDaniel, Cunfer, & Guynn, 1991; Harris & Wilkins, 1982). Kvavilashvili's (1987) findings, moreover, suggest that the occurrence *per se* of a recollection during a short retention interval increases the likelihood of a successful outcome. Studies of naturally occurring intentions, with much longer retention intervals (hours, days), indicate that the occurrence rather than the frequency of recollection is associated with success on these intentions (Ellis, 1988a, 1988b).

The precise role of recollections in the performance of delayed intentions is as yet unknown. One possibility is that they function as a means of refreshing or strengthening the content of the intention by, for example, increasing its activation level. If a recollection functions in this manner and it occurs close to a potential retrieval context, then it should increase the likelihood of selecting the intended action. Recollections, therefore, within a comparatively brief retention interval would be expected to have—as empirical observations suggest—a beneficial effect on performance.[4] An alternate explanation is that

---

[4]This situation may also lead to errors. A recently activated (recollected) intention may be selected when there is only a partial overlap between the presented and encoded context; that is, on an inappropriate occasion.

recollections represent occasions on which the memory trace of that intention is reformulated or altered in some beneficial way. The recollection of a delayed intention, perhaps particularly during an extended retention interval, may prompt awareness of the vulnerability of that intention to failure; this situation could result in changes to the encoded content of the delayed intention. Such recoding could include, for example, increases in the specificity of the retrieval context (more specific trigger conditions) and/or increases in intentional strength (lower threshold value). Recent research indicates that both greater specificity and higher importance (part of intentional strength) increase the likelihood of satisfying delayed intentions (see, e.g., Einstein et al., 1991; Ellis, 1988a; Ellis & Milne, 1992a; Kvavilashvili, 1987).

The aforementioned discussion indicates the possibility of more than one effect of a recollective experience, one that results in a temporary increase in the activation level of an intended action and another that prompts replanning and a change in threshold or trigger conditions. These effects are not necessarily mutually exclusive. For example, a recollection that increases the activation level of a delayed intention may facilitate the occurrence of a subsequent recollection at which replanning processes may be applied. Indeed, activation may be a fixed outcome of recollection, and replanning an optional one. It is further possible that the circumstances that precede a recollection (deliberate reminder, etc.) and the current situational demands (attentional requirements or importance of a current activity) will influence the nature and extent of any processing that is carried out on these occasions (see, for further discussion, Ellis & Nimmo-Smith, 1993). These variations would be compatible with observations derived from current (retrospective) memory research, suggesting more than one type of recollective experience (see, e.g., Kelley & Jacoby, 1993; Mandler, 1980, 1986). Finally, in the dynamic and partially unpredictable environment of our everyday lives, recollections can facilitate opportunistic behaviors. A delayed intention may be satisfied—when appropriate—at an unintended moment. For example, you may have encoded an intention to telephone a colleague tomorrow afternoon. The recollection of that intention in the morning, when you are near a telephone, have some free time and expect that your colleague will be available, may result in a (successful) attempt to contact him or her.

Retention Intervals can vary considerably, both in their duration and in their content. In traditional (retrospective) memory research, different mechanisms have been postulated to underlie observed variations in patterns of retention over different time periods. These periods typically vary from several seconds to several minutes or even days, although some research has addressed retention over several years (see, e.g., Bahrick, 1984; Conway, Cohen, & Stanhope, 1991). It may be appropriate to apply a similar distinction to delayed intentions. Baddeley and Wilkins (1984), for example, suggested that delayed intentions may be usefully classified as either shorter or longer term, and that each may rely on the operation of different processes. They argued that shorter term tasks may have to be maintained in "conscious awareness" (p. 13) for the duration of a retention interval in order to ensure a successful outcome. In a similar vein, Meacham and Leiman (1976) suggested that over brief retention intervals "remembering to carry out an action . . . may be no different than the problem of maintaining one's vigilance or attention" (p. 328). In contrast, McDaniel and Einstein (1993) argued that conscious awareness may be relevant only during a performance interval. They also suggested that its role may depend on the nature of a retrieval context: It may be more critical for a time-based task than for an event-based one (see Einstein & McDaniel, this volume). There is some indication also that the character of a retention interval may be as important as its relative duration. Recent research suggests that the nature of one's activity, for example, may influence the recollection of both longer (Ellis & Nimmo-Smith, 1993) and shorter term delayed intentions (Kvavilashvili, 1987), and the eventual outcome of shorter term ones (Brandimonte & Passolunghi, 1994).

It was suggested that classifications used to describe longer term (retrospective) memory, such as the episodic–semantic distinction (Tulving, 1972, 1983), may be usefully applied to prospective memory (Baddeley & Wilkins, 1984). Baddeley and Wilkins pointed out that although many longer term delayed intentions are episodic (e.g., they refer to specific encoding events), they rely on accessing, activating, and executing action plans that are essentially semantic. Ellis and Shallice (1993; see also Ellis, 1988b) argued that planning processes that operate on these action plans, particularly those toward retrieval at an appropriate moment (when-realization), also exert an important influence on performance. These planning processes are thought to be highly dependent on and interactive with the representation of regularly executed routine-based actions and activities. An intention to visit a friend this evening, for example, may require rescheduling of one's typical evening activities (dinner, walking the dog, etc.). These points are developed further in the following discussion on retrieval in a performance interval.

Retrieval in a Performance Interval relies on recognition that a particular situation presents a potential retrieval context that is associated with an intention to do something (when and that elements) and on the retrieval of the appropriate action. It could be described, therefore, as an example of a production rule such that *When [context] Then [do x]*. Using the action–trigger–schema (ATS) framework, outlined earlier, this rule becomes slightly more complex :

When [activation level reaches threshold]
Then [select schema].

And When [trigger conditions satisfied]
Then [initiate action].

A number of different factors are likely to influence the probability of successfully activating, triggering, and selecting the relevant intended action at an appropriate moment. First, there is the closeness of the match between an encoded retrieval context and the current situation. Determination of this overlap is similar to the general problem of pattern or feature matching that is said to occur in, for example, category membership judgments (see, e.g., Anderson, 1983; Smith, Shoben, & Rips, 1974). Thus, the features of an encoded retrieval context, such as its type (person, location, etc.) and its specificity (particular person, or any one of a class of persons), are compared with the features of a particular situation. Sufficient overlap between these two sets of features (encoded and currently perceived) may result in a form of recognition in which a particular situation is perceived as familiar and related to a previous experience (cf. Mandler, 1986). Consider, for example, an intention to relay a message when you enter the general office tomorrow morning and see Jane. Entering the office and seeing Jane on the following morning (whenelements of the intention) may elicit a feeling of familiarity (recognition of the when-element). However, the associated encoded intent—the decision to act at this time—may not be retrieved. A second factor in the successful selection of an intended action, therefore, is the strength of the processing links between the encoded retrieval context and its associated intent: the links between the decision to act in a certain way and the circumstances under which this decision should be enacted.

The phenomenological experience of "something to do" is a common one in everyday life (see, e.g., Reason, 1984). In many instances, it is associated with a premature exit from the retrieval process associated with delayed intentions—when a retrieval context and intent are recalled but the associated action is not retrieved at that moment.[5] Retrieval of the correct (associated) action will depend not only on the processing links between a retrieval context and the intended action, but also on the number and relative strength of other (same) context-to- (alternate) action mappings. The episodic[6] nature of many delayed intentions suggests that the particular context + intent-to-action relations they describe are not ones that are likely to be intrinsically or typically elicited by the occurrence of those contexts. In a given situation, other, more regularly executed and well-learned actions will tend to be associated with the retrieval context of a given delayed intention. Consider, for instance, the earlier example of an intention to convey a message to Jane when you enter the office tomorrow morning. Your entry into the office may typically be associated with the performance of other actions, such as picking up your mail or

---

[5] On other occasions it may result from the retrieval of an incorrect context-to-intent mapping.
[6] With respect to a particular context-to-action relation.

asking whether or not there are any telephone messages. Therefore, the triggering and execution of the "correct" (intended) action, at an appropriate moment, will often require the inhibition of other unwanted but strongly associated actions.

Meacham and Leiman (1976) drew attention to a relevant issue in their distinction between *habitual* and *episodic* remembering of delayed intentions. They relate habitual remembering to the execution of Routinely[7] performed tasks, such as remembering to clean one's teeth before going to bed, and contrast this with episodic remembering, which is related to tasks performed "infrequently or on an irregular basis . . . such as stopping for bread on your way home" (p. 328). Meacham and Leiman argued that habitual tasks are easier to retrieve than episodic ones because performance of the former is guided by cues "in the immediate environment or . . . from preceding activities" (p. 328). (As I discuss later, it is the *relative strength* of the connections between environmental cues and a preceding activity on the one hand, and an intended action on the other, that distinguishes habitual tasks from episodic ones.) Meacham and Leiman noted that one strategy for facilitating the successful outcome of a delayed intention (episodic task) is to "integrate the desired activity into the stream of our daily activities [habitual tasks]" (p. 328). Examples of the effectiveness of this strategy have been reported by, for example, Ellis (1988b) and Maylor (1990).

How might this integration of a delayed intention into Routine or habitual actions and activities be achieved? One explanation of these processes was proposed by Shallice and Burgess (1991). They suggested that the performance of nonRoutine (episodic) actions requires the setting up of a provisional plan in which *markers* are encoded and used to interrupt activity at some future time. A marker is a message that a particular event or behavior is not simply Routine but should serve as a cue for a particular, additional or substitute action. So, for example, when you leave the house tomorrow morning, this event should serve as a cue to go to the post office rather than to take your usual walk in the opposite direction, to the railway station. Using the analysis developed in this chapter, these markers would serve to identify a retrieval context and intent associated with a nonRoutine action that is not normally performed when that context occurs. Shallice and Burgess suggested that triggering an appropriate marker should lead to an interruption of ongoing activity and the recall of a particular delayed intention.

The processes Shallice and Burgess outlined (goal articulation [of intention], plan formulation, marker creation, and triggering) are undertaken by the *Supervisory System*. The latter is one of two proposed modes or levels of

---

[7]*Routine* is used here to describe an action or activity that is frequently and regularly performed at a particular time or in response to a particular situation, for example, having a coffee break at a particular time each day. Note that Routine actions can also be routine in the sense described earlier (Footnote 1).

processes thought to be involved in the cognitive control of action and thought operations (Norman & Shallice, 1986; Shallice, 1988). The Supervisory System is required when a task cannot be carried out by the normal operations of the other, second mode of processes—*contention scheduling*. It is necessary when well-learned triggering procedures are not sufficient to ensure an intended outcome. For example, contention scheduling alone would normally be sufficient to ensure the relatively error-free performance of a well-learned action such as brushing one's teeth. If, however, you had received instructions from your dentist to incorporate a particular, novel procedure into this action then some modification of that action would need to occur. This modification would require the operation of the Supervisory System.

The Supervisory System operates by activating or inhibiting particular schemas and thus modulating contention scheduling. It is critical for the performance of a particular (delayed intended) action rather than one more routinely associated with a particular retrieval context. It is necessary when, for example, we want to telephone someone after watching a television program, instead of carrying out one of a set of actions, such as reading the newspaper, that is more frequently performed in that context. Even if these typical actions are successfully inhibited, however, the retrieval of the correct delayed intention will clearly depend also on the strength of associative links in the relevant context–intent–action mapping. For example, I may correctly recall that I wish to telephone someone after an evening program, but call the wrong person, or I may recall that there is something I want to do, but retrieve the wrong— in that context—action (e.g., carry out a different delayed intention that was also designated for that evening). Finally, it may be necessary to take account of the potentially different requirements for action coordination—between a delayed intended action and a typically executed action—following marker identification. At least four different types of requirements can be identified: (a) inhibit current action (do not go for coffee when you enter work), (b) inhibit current action and insert a substitute (get a sandwich instead of coffee), (c) insert an additional action into a current activity (pick up your mail when you get some coffee), and (d) inhibit current action and insert a modification of it (get a cup of tea instead of coffee). Although any alteration of a routinely executed action is likely to be attentionally demanding (see, e.g., Reason, 1984), the inhibition of such an action may be more difficult to achieve without error, than the insertion of an additional action into an otherwise unmodified action sequence.

Shallice and Burgess (1991) described one means of retrieving delayed intentions at an appropriate moment for performance and of how associations between Routine (regularly performed) and nonRoutine actions might facilitate these retrieval processes. Research on naturally occurring intentions, however, suggests the operation of at least two types of retrieval processes (Ellis & Shallice, 1993). The first, *hierarchical retrieval*, occurs through a hierarchy of activities, whereas the second, *brute retrieval,* operates by means of the marker system suggested by Shallice and Burgess. Tulving (1983) proposed a complimentary two route process of retrieval in retrospective memory suggesting that ". . . an item can be retrieved on its own merits [cf. brute retrieval] or through items in its higher-order (subjective) unit [cf. hierarchical retrieval]. . . ." (p. 200). As far as the proposed hierarchical process is concerned, entities higher up in a hierarchy would be more easily accessible than those lower down (cf. Kolodner's proposals on the retrieval of E–MOPs; Kolodner, 1983).

For delayed intentions designated for realization during the course of a particular day, Ellis and Shallice suggested that the hierarchical process operates by means of a structured representation (virtual or real) of one's normal Routine daily activities. The latter forms the basis of a *Daily Routine* that reflects the organization and temporal characteristics of these activities. A Daily Routine has a hierarchical organization and a central structure formed by *anchor-point* activities. Anchor-points are activities that are defined in time (they occur around the same clock time each day) and signal a change from one superordinate level of activity to another (e.g., from domestic to leisure activities); for further details, see Ellis and Shallice (1993). Planning directed toward the retrieval of a delayed intention at an appropriate moment (when-realization) is said to consist of the processes of forming insertions or modifications to a Daily Routine. These processes vary with the nature of a retrieval context. Naturally occurring intentions designated for a particular day have variable temporal requirements for successful retrieval and performance: specific and general time-based retrieval contexts (Ellis, 1988a, 1988b). Under a proposed classification scheme, these intentions were described as either *Pulses, Intermediates,* or *Steps,* to reflect the decreasing specificity of these requirements. A Pulse has a specific point for retrieval (e.g., a meeting at 2:00 p.m.), whereas a Step has a wider, more general time period (e.g., meeting Mary sometime today). Intentions with temporal requirements that lie between these two classes are described as Intermediates (e.g., seeing Mary during a lunch break); for further details, see Ellis (1988a); Ellis and Nimmo-Smith (1993).

In brief, Ellis and Shallice argued that the accommodation of the (more specific) temporal demands of a retrieval context for a Pulse is more likely to result in the reorganization of a Daily Routine into a temporary representation or Day Plan. Thus, delayed intentions such as Pulses, which more frequently result in greater changes to a Daily Routine at the superordinate level of activity, are more easily retrieved at an appropriate moment by the proposed hierarchical process than are either Steps or Intermediates.[8] The latter, we sug-

---

[8]The temporally determinate properties of a Pulse tend to form a break or boundary within the typical organization of a Daily Routine. In many instances, this creates the potential for the formation of a temporary categorical change in activity at this boundary, thus producing a temporary anchor-point.

gest, would need to make more use of the second, brute or marker mechanism. We argue, therefore, that the retrieval of episodic delayed intentions is contingent on the interrelations between these intentions and other habitual or Routine tasks. These proposals thus develop and further specify the links and variations in retrieval demands between Meacham and Leiman's (1982) habitual (Daily Routine) and episodic (delayed intentions) tasks. They illustrate the potential importance of considering (a) the nature, organization, and structure of the activities in which a delayed intention should be realized, (b) individual variations with respect to the organization, and so on, of these activities, (c) planning processes directed toward the retrieval of delayed intentions, and (d) variations in the characteristics of retrieval contexts.

Initiation and Execution.   The successful initiation and execution of a delayed intention are important to its eventual realization. However, the theoretical issues raised by these events are well-documented in research on, for example, action and attention and action-slips (Heckhausen & Beckmann, 1990; Norman, 1981; Norman & Shallice, 1986; Reason, 1984). There are few issues in this domain that are directly relevant to the performance of delayed intentions. There are some events, however, pertinent to the successful outcome of delayed intentions, such as distraction (by an external or internal event) during task performance or a failure to complete a task due to unforeseen extraneous circumstances. An intention to telephone a colleague, for example, may either be initiated but then interrupted by the arrival of an important visitor or fail because the colleague is either absent or engaged. In both situations it would be necessary to re-establish or replan the intention for a further attempt (e.g., encode a new or revised retrieval context). It is possible that, under these conditions, the partial completion of a delayed intention will impose qualitatively different processing demands for an eventual successful outcome. It is unclear, however, whether or not these would act to increase the likelihood of later recall (cf. Mäntylä, this volume; Seifert & Patalano, 1991; Zeigarnik, 1927) or to decrease it (cf. errors in reality monitoring, Johnson, 1988). A further related issue arises with occasions on which the actions of another person preempt the performance of a delayed intention (e.g., a friend may telephone you before you call him or her). In studies of naturally occurring intentions, these occasions are often distinguished by subjects spontaneously recording such tasks as satisfied but not directly by themselves (Ellis, 1988b). It is possible that on these occasions some vestige of the content of the task remains active, for example, the subjective feeling that one has to telephone someone this evening. Here the object of an action would have been cancelled whereas the encoded retrieval context may continue to trigger recall of intent and action schema.

Evaluation of Outcome.   This implies, as noted earlier, the application of a comparative process between the retrospective content of a delayed intention and the effects of an executed or nonexecuted action. In problem-solving terminology, this would be described as examination of the match or mismatch between an encoded *goal state* and *current state* (see, e.g., Newell & Simon, 1972). Logically, three different outcomes are possible: The content (or goal state) may be fully satisfied, partially satisfied, or unsatisfied. Full satisfaction corresponds to a sufficient overlap between content (what you planned to do) and outcome (what actually happened); examples of partial satisfaction were considered in the immediately preceding discussion. An unsatisfied delayed intention is one that is not carried out during the appropriate (encoded) performance interval. Where recovery from error is possible, the intention may be regarded as a "late" intention, with respect to its performance. (The degree of lateness that is acceptable before an intention is regarded as a failed one will vary between naturally occurring intentions.) Although failures are often described in research articles as well as in everyday language as "forgotten" intentions, this description could be misleading. Some of these intentions, for example, may have been recalled during a performance interval, but at an inappropriate moment for action; it is not, therefore, a forgotten intention in an absolute sense. It may be theoretically helpful to distinguish between these situations and others in which the intention is never recalled during a performance interval, or indeed, shortly afterwards, without the assistance of a direct reminder.

Reasons of efficiency alone suggest that some form of record of outcome is necessary in order to either prevent the unnecessary repetition of a satisfied intention or to ensure a future attempt to recover from an earlier failure. The work of Koriat and his colleagues is particularly noteworthy in drawing attention to this aspect of delayed intentions (Koriat & Ben-Zur, 1988; Koriat, Ben-Zur, & Druch, 1990; Koriat, Ben-Zur, & Sheffer, 1988) . One proposal, consistent with the framework outlined in this chapter, is proffered for consideration.

Koriat employed the term *output monitoring* to describe the processes concerned with recording which acts have been performed and which are still to be performed (Koriat & Ben-Zur, 1988). He also made a distinction between output monitoring that marks the ". . . completion of a planned act on-line . . ." and those which ". . . rely on a retrospective judgement that it was carried out . . ." (p. 203). *Online processes* occur when an act has been completed and either delete the representation of a delayed intention or in some way mark it as executed. *Retrospective processes,* by contrast, occur when an occasion (retrieval context) for executing a delayed intention (re-)appears. Errors may occur, depending on the (largely unknown) nature of these retrospective processes, through either inappropriate deletion or inappropriate tagging of the relevant representation. Retrospective processing therefore appears to be dependent, at least in part, on the operation of online processing.

Both the brute (marker) and the hierarchical (Day Plan) modes of planning and retrieval proposed earlier suggest that representations of delayed intentions are "tagged" in some way. Most delayed intentions have retrieval contexts that usually provide trigger conditions for the performance of other, more Routinely executed actions. In both types of retrieval processes, then, the trigger conditions (retrieval context) for a particular action schema, or set of possible action schemas, are associated with an episodic record of processing that should signal and index an alternate course of action. Hierarchical retrieval processes are further assisted by the operation of the currently active Day Plan. Online processes, when successful, should result in the removal of this marker; that is, in the deletion (or possibly decay, if unrefreshed) of an episodic association between the relevant retrieval context, intent and action. If these associations constitute an active (to be realized) delayed intention, then their removal or weakening should preclude unnecessary repetitions. In addition, for intentions such as Pulses that tend to be represented at a superordinate and thus more accessible level in a Plan, the guiding function of the Day Plan on performance provides information on one's current "place" in one's daily activities, thus potentially decreasing the likelihood of repetition errors. Errors of omission, on the other hand, if the intention is subsequently recalled and the error is recoverable will generally necessitate re-planning/re-encoding as described in the discussion on action execution.

Any outcome, successful or otherwise, obviously constitutes an episodic event and thus any decision on (re-)executing a delayed intention depends not only on the operation of online processing, but also on retrospective processing (Koriat & Ben-Zur, 1988). In addition to the results of online processing, other sources of information or evidence of past action are potentially available to these retrospective processes (e.g., an episodic trace together with internal or external evidence of action). The retrieval of the appropriate Day Plan would also provide information on the (retrospective) outcome of delayed intentions. If Pulse intentions are more likely to be integrated in these Plans, Pulses should be more accessible to retrieval from a Plan than either Steps or Intermediates. Some evidence for this proposal comes from a recent study of the retrieval of the fate of previously documented intentions (Ellis & Milne, 1992b).

SUMMARY OF FRAMEWORK

The conceptual framework that emerged from the preceding discussion is offered as a means of identifying and drawing together, the different processing requirements in the realization of delayed intentions. It is briefly summarized here.

At encoding, an action schema is associated with a context for retrieval (which provides the trigger conditions for that action) and with an intent that receives its strength (expressed in the threshold value of that action) primarily through its associations with other action + goal structures and higher level personal themes and aims (see, e.g., Barsalou, 1988; Conway, 1992; Schank, 1982; for discussion of the latter). The action schema may be retrieved directly from existing processing structures or indirectly through modifications and/ or elaborations. In common with most recent theories of action representation and execution, an action is represented at the highest possible level of description (see, e.g., Kolodner, 1983; Kuhl, 1985; Schank, 1982; Young & Simon, 1987). Planning processes directed toward what- and when-realization may be applied at encoding with concomitant effects on the characteristics, specification, and content of an action schema and its trigger conditions. The association between an action schema, retrieval context, and intent signals that a particular future situation should be regarded as nonRoutine. It thereby provides either an individual marker (Shallice & Burgess, 1991) or a revised section of a Daily Routine (Ellis & Shallice, 1993): A form of "tagging" occurs.

Encoding of the delayed intention is followed by a retention interval and by one or more performance intervals. During these periods, and prior to an opportunity for performance, recollections of delayed intentions may occur and have the effect of either raising the activation level of the action (a temporary effect) and/or prompting (re-) planning processes. These planning processes—primarily concerned with when- and what-realization—will have effects on the original encoding that are either direct (e.g., alter trigger conditions) or indirect (e.g., alter action specification, increasing strength and changing threshold value). As with other memory phenomena, the level of awareness that accompanies a recollection, and possibly its effects on subsequent processing, may vary as a consequence of the causal chain underlying that event and the processing demands of the current situation.

At some point during a performance interval at least one situation should arise that represents an appropriate opportunity for performance of the delayed intention. Successful realization requires that the presented and perceived situation correspond to the encoded retrieval context and thus activate the intent and trigger initiation of the correct action. Many errors are possible, including those that result either from faulty encoding (of context, etc.) or from the misapplication of attentional resources (e.g., failure to modify current activity). These may result in either partial (late or incomplete action) or complete (omission) failures to realize the delayed intention. Moreover, recovery of the delayed intention can result in cancellation (if circumstances have changed from those anticipated at encoding) or replanning (postponement). If the intended action is initiated and executed, some form of evaluation and record of these events is required in order to prevent unnecessary future repetition or to permit a further attempt, where possible. Evaluation requires a comparative processing between the encoded and actual action, intent, and context whereas a record is suggested to take the form both of an episodic trace and the removal or decoupling of the action–intent–context association. Repetition errors may thus arise from incorrect decoupling of this association, a weak or inaccessible episodic trace, or from the absence of other external evidence of a previous action.

IMPLICATIONS OF FRAMEWORK FOR RESEARCH QUESTIONS AND METHODS

The conceptual framework I describe in this chapter illustrates the variety of processing requirements for realizing delayed intentions. It suggests that the task of realizing these intentions is not solely dependent on the operation of memory processes in the conventional sense (the retention and retrieval of past experiences). Although these are necessary for successful performance, other processes are also implicated: for example, intention formation; plan creation, retrieval, and modification; attentional modes of action control. The skills and knowledge underlying the realization of delayed intentions require examination, empirical and theoretical, of the interface between memory, attention, and action. Shallice and Burgess (1991), for example, described the creation and realization of intentions as part of a set of *bridge processes* between motivational and special purpose or retrospective memory processes. They suggested that these processes are controlled by the Supervisory System. Baddeley (1986) adopted this system as a model of the regulatory and control functions of the central executive in his conceptualization of working memory (Baddeley, 1986; Baddeley & Hitch, 1974). The processing requirements for the realization of delayed intentions outlined in this chapter suggest that research on this topic offers an important means of exploring that interface between memory, attention, and action, that the Supervisory System/central executive is designed to address.

Throughout this chapter, I prefer the use of the phrase "realizing delayed intentions" to the more commonly used term prospective memory to describe research on this topic. This is not simply a matter of personal whimsy but rather reflects a concern, detailed in this chapter, that the prospective memory description places too great an emphasis on the contribution of memory to the exclusion of other relevant cognitive processes. This analysis has implications for the development of research questions and methods of investigation in this area: We need to design or exploit situations that allow the expression and utilization of these different processes. Although any one series of empirical studies will focus on examining a particular aspect of the topic, current experimental designs are limited in this regard. The typical focus is one that examines the operation of variables known to affect performance on conventional or retrospective memory tasks in a prospective memory task (but see, for exceptions, Ellis & Nimmo-Smith, 1993; Goschke & Kuhl, 1993). Moreover, particular consideration is given to the examination of retrieval rather than encoding demands (but see Mäntylä, 1993, for an exception).

Current tasks tend to prescribe the performance of either a "single" or a "repeated" context-to-action mapping (see, also, Kvavilashvili, 1992). Single-task designs require the execution of one action in response to a single retrieval context (e.g., Kvavilashvili, 1987). Repeated-task designs require repetition of a single action in response to either multiple presentations of a single context (e.g., McDaniel & Einstein, 1993) or multiple presentations of two or more contexts (e.g., Einstein, Holland, McDaniel, & Guynn, 1992). In both variations of the latter design the action remains constant. Multiple-task designs, by contrast, require the performance of a particular action in response to a particular context when multiple and distinct context-to-action relations are prescribed (e.g., Ellis & Williams, 1990; Mäntylä, 1993). Multiple-task designs, which are more closely related to naturally occurring intentions, may be a necessary development if we wish to explore, in detail, the operation of planning processes.

A related point concerns the nature of a concurrent activity—the task in which the delayed intention should be retrieved and realized. Findings from research on naturally occurring intentions suggest that planning processes directed at when-realization are intimately dependent on the (previously experienced) characteristics of the circumstances (concurrent activity) in which they should be realized. We may need to develop more complex background activities with varying structure and semantic relations to enable a full exploration of planning processes (see Shallice & Burgess, 1991, for an example). In the absence of these, and given the necessary practical limitations of laboratory studies with regard to manipulating the extent of a retention interval, we may need to focus attention on the development of satisfactory techniques for the investigation of longer term, naturally occurring intentions (see, e.g., Ellis & Nimmo-Smith, 1993; see also Kvavilashvili & Ellis, this volume).

As Shallice and Burgess (1991) pointed out, the realization of delayed intentions relies not only on retrospective memory processes but also on processes concerned with the ". . . creation and maintenance of goals and intentions (and) of their realization at appropriate times . . ." (p. 736). Baddeley and Wilkins (1984) also suggested that "we suspect that the theoretical development of this area [prospective memory] will depend on the integration of theories of memory with theories of action." (p. 14). To progress in our understanding of this topic we therefore need to examine questions and theories that extend beyond those normally considered in many established areas of memory research. Of course there are other existing areas that explicitly recognize this need: for instance, autobiographical memory (see, e.g., Conway,

1993; Shallice, 1988) and implicit or indirect memory (see, e.g., Jacoby, 1991). As researchers in these areas have demonstrated, such a move can lead to considerable theoretical and methodological progress (e.g., Jacoby, 1991).

ACKNOWLEDGEMENTS

The preparation of this chapter benefited from discussions with several colleagues, most notably Debra Bekerian, Paul Burgess, Martin Conway, and Alan Milne. The final version benefited considerably from constructive comments by Gil Einstein and Mark McDaniel.

REFERENCES

Anderson, J. R. (1983). *The architecture of cognition.* Cambridge, MA: Harvard University Press.
Baddeley, A. D. (1986). *Working memory.* Oxford, England: Oxford University Press.
Baddeley, A. D., & Hitch, G. J. (1974). Working memory. In G. A. Bower (Ed.), *Recent advances in learning and motivation,* (Vol. 8, pp. 47–90). New York: Academic Press.
Baddeley, A. D., & Wilkins, A. J. (1984). Taking memory out of the laboratory. In J. E. Harris & P. E. Morris (Eds), *Everyday memory, actions and absent-mindedness.* New York: Academic Press.
Bahrick, H. P. (1984). Semantic memory content in permastore: Fifty years of memory for Spanish learned in school. *Journal of Experimental Psychology: General, 113,* 1–29.
Barsalou, L. W. (1988). The content and organisation of autobiographical memory. In U. Neisser & E. Winograd (Eds.), *Remembering reconsidered: Ecological and traditional approaches to the study of memory* (pp. 193–243). Cambridge, England: Cambridge University Press.
Brandimonte, M. A. (1991). Ricordare il futuro. *Giornale Italiano di Psicologia, 3,* 351–374.
Brandimonte, M. A., & Passolunghi, M. C. (1994). The effect of cue-familiarity, cue-distinctiveness and retention interval on prospective remembering. *Quarterly Journal of Experimental Psychology, 47,* 565–588.
Conway, M. A. (1992). A structural model of autobiographical memory. In M. A. Conway, D. C. Rubin, H. Spinnler, & W. A. Wagenaar (Eds.), *Theoretical perspectives on autobiographical memory* (pp. 167–194). Dordrecht, The Netherlands: Kluwer Academic Publishers.
Conway, M. A. (1993). Impairments of autobiographical memory. In H. Spinnler & F. Boller (Eds.), *Handbook of neuropsychology,* (Vol. 8, pp. 175–191). North Holland: Elsevier Science.
Conway, M. A., Cohen, G., & Stanhope, N. (1991). On the very long-term retention of knowledge acquired through formal education: Twelve Years of cognitive psychology. *Journal of Experimental Psychology: General, 120,* 395–409.
Einstein, G. O., Holland, L. J., McDaniel, M. A., & Guynn, M. J. (1992). Age-related deficits in prospective memory: the influence of task complexity. *Psychology and Aging, 7,* 471–478.
Einstein, G. O., & McDaniel, M. A. (1990). Normal aging and prospective memory. *Journal of Experimental Psychology: Learning, Memory, & Cognition, 16,* 717–726.
Einstein, G. O., McDaniel, M. A., Cunfer, A. R., & Guynn, M. J. (1991, November). *Aging and time- versus event-based prospective memory.* Paper presented at the meeting of the Psychonomic Society, San Francisco, CA.
Ellis, J. A. (1988a). Memory for future intentions: Investigating pulses and steps. In M. M. Gruneberg, P. E. Morris, & R. N. Sykes (Eds.), *Practical aspects of memory: Current research and issues* (Vol. 1, pp. 371–376). Chichester, England: Wiley.

Ellis, J. A. (1988b). *Memory for naturally-occurring intentions.* Unpublished doctoral dissertaion, University of Cambridge.

Ellis, J. A. (1991, July). *An eclectic approach to the study of prospective memory tasks.* Paper presented at the International Conference on Memory, Lancaster, UK.

Ellis, J. A., & Milne, A. B. (1992a, July). *The effects of retrieval cue specificity on prospective memory performance.* Paper presented at the meeting of the Experimental Psychology Society, York. Manuscript submitted for publication.

Ellis, J. A., & Milne, A. B. (1992b, December). *Memory for naturally-occurring intentions: remembering what you have done and what you have to do.* Paper presented at the London meeting of the British Psychological Society, City University.

Ellis, J. A., & Nimmo-Smith, I. (1993). Recollecting naturally-occurring intentions: a study of cognitive and affective factors. *Memory, 1,* 107–126.

Ellis, J. A., & Shallice, T. (1993). *Memory for, and the organisation of, future intentions.* Manuscript submitted for publication.

Ellis, J. A. & Williams, J. M. G. (1990, April). *Retrospective and prospective remembering: Common and distinct processes.* Paper presented at the Experimental Psychology Society, Manchester.

Goschke, T., & Kuhl, J. (1993). Representation of intentions: Persisting activation in memory. *Journal of Experimental Psychology: Learning, Memory & Cognition, 19,* 1211–1226.

Harris, J. E. (1980). Memory aids people use: Two interview studies. *Memory and Cognition, 8,* 31–38.

Harris, J. E. (1984). Remembering to do things: A forgotton topic. In J. E. Harris & P. E. Morris (Eds.), *Everyday memory, actions and absent-mindedness* (pp. 71–92). London, England: Academic Press.

Harris, J. E., & Wilkins, A. J. (1982). Remembering to do things: A theoretical framework and an illustrative experiment. *Human Learning, 1,* 123–136.

Heckhausen, H., & Beckmann, J. (1990). Intentional action and action slips. *Psychological Review, 97,* 36–48.

Jacoby, L. L. (1991). A process dissociation framework: Separating automatic from intentional uses of memory. *Journal of Memory and Language, 30,* 513–541.

Johnson, M. K. (1988). Discriminating the origin of information. In T. F. Oltmans & B. A. Maher (Eds.), *Delusional beliefs: Interdisciplinary perspectives* (pp. 34–65). New York: Wiley.

Kelley, C. M., & Jacoby, L. L. (1993). The construction of subjective experience: Memory attributions. In M. Davies & G. W. Humphreys (Eds.), *Consciousness: Psychological and philosophical essays* (pp. 74–89). Oxford, England: Blackwell.

Kolodner, J. A. (1983). Maintaining organisation in a dynamic long-term memory. *Cognitive Science, 7,* 243–280.

Koriat, A., & Ben-Zur, H. (1988). Remembering that I did it: Processes and deficits in output monitoring. In M. M. Gruneberg, P. E. Morris, & R. N. Sykes (Eds.), *Practical aspects of memory Current research and issues* (Vol. 1, pp. 203–208). Chichester, England: Wiley.

Koriat, A., Ben-Zur, H., & Druch, A. (1990). The contextualization of input and output events in memory. *Psychological Research, 53,* 260–270.

Koriat, A., Ben-Zur, H., & Sheffer, D. (1988). Telling the same story twice: Output monitoring and age. *Journal of Memory and Language, 27,* 23–39.

Kuhl, J. (1985). Volitional mediators of cognitive-behaviour consistency: Self-regulatory processes and actions versus state orientation. In J. Kuhl & J. Beckmann (Eds.), *Action control: From cognition to behaviour* (pp. 101–128). New York: Springer.

Kvavilashvili, L. (1987). Remembering intention as a distinct form of memory. *British Journal of Psychology, 78,* 507–518.

Kvavilashvili, L. (1992). Remembering intentions: A critical review of existing experimental paradigms. *Applied Cognitive Psychology, 6,* 507–524.

McDaniel, M. A., & Einstein, G. O. (1993). The importance of cue familiarity and cue distinctiveness in prospective memory. *Memory, 1,* 22–42.

Mandler, G. (1967). Organisation and memory. In K. W. Spence & J. T. Spence (Eds.), *The psychology of learning and motivation* (Vol. 1, pp. 327–372). New York: Academic Press.

Mandler, G. (1980). Recognizing: The judgement of previous occurrence. *Psychological Review, 87,* 252–271.

Mandler, G. (1986). Reminding, recalling, recognizing: Different memories? In F. Klix & H. Hagendorf (Eds.), *Human memory and cognitive capabilities: Mechanisms and performance* (pp. 289–297). North Holland: Elsevier Science.

Mäntylä, T. (1993). Priming effects in prospective memory. *Memory, 1,* 203–218.

Maylor, E. A. (1990). Age and prospective memory. *Quarterly Journal of Experimental Psychology, 42A,* 471–493.

Meacham, J. A. (1988). Interpersonal relations and prospective remembering. In M. M. Gruneberg, P. E. Morris, & R. N. Sykes (Eds.), *Practical aspects of memory: Current research and issues* (Vol. 1, pp. 354–359). Chichester, England: Wiley.

Meacham. J. A., & Leiman, B. (1982). *Remembering to perform future actions.* In U. Neisser (Ed.), *Memory observed: Remembering in natural contexts* (pp. 327–336). San Francisco: Freeman.

Neisser, U. (Ed.). (1982). *Memory observed: Remembering in natural contexts.* San Francisco: Freeman.

Newell, A., & Simon, H. A. (1972). *Human problem-solving.* Englewood Cliffs, NJ: Prentice-Hall.

Norman, D. A. (1981). Categorisation of action slips. *Psychological Review, 88,* 1–15.

Norman, D. A. & Shallice, T. (1986). Attention to action: Willed and automatic *control of behaviour.* In R. J. Davison, G. E. Schwartz, & D. Shapiro (Eds.), *Consciousness and self-regulation* (Vol. 4, pp. 1–18). New York: Plenum.

Ortony, A., Clore, G. L., & Collins, A. (1988). *The cognitive structure of emotions.* Cambridge, England: Cambridge University Press.

Reason, J. T. (1984). Lapses of attention. In W. Parasuraman, R. Davies, & J. Beatty (Eds.), *Varieties of attention* (pp. 515–549. New York: Academic Press.

Rumelhart, D. E., & Norman, D. A. (1982). Simulating a skilled typist: A study of skilled cognitive-motor performance. *Cognitive Science, 6,* 1–36.

Schank, R. C. (1982). *Dynamic memory: A theory of reminding and learning in computers and people.* Cambridge, England: Cambridge University Press.

Seifert, C. M., & Patalano, A. L. (1991). Memory for incomplete tasks : A re-examination of the Zeigarnik effect. *Proceedings of the Thirteenth Annual Meeting of the Cognitive Science Society* (pp. 114–119). Chicago, IL.

Shallice, T. (1988). *From neuropsychology to mental structure.* Cambridge, England: Cambridge University Press.

Shallice, T., & Burgess, P. (1991). Deficits in strategy application following frontal lobe damage in man. *Brain, 114,* 727–741.

Smith, E. E., Shoben, E. J., & Rips, L. J. (1974). Structure and process in semantic memory: A featural model for semantic decision. *Psychological Review, 81,* 214–241.

Tulving, E. (1962). Subjective organisation in free recall of "unrelated" words. *Psychological Review, 69,* 344–354.

Tulving, E. (1972). Episodic and semantic memory. In E. Tulving & W. Donaldson (Eds.), *Organisation of memory.* New York: Academic Press.

Tulving, E. (1983). *Elements of episodic memory.* New York: Oxford University Press.

Young, R. M., & Simon, T. (1987). Planning in the context of human-computer interaction. In D. Diaper & R. Winder (Eds.), *People and computers Volume 3.* Cambridge, England: Cambridge University Press.

Zeigarnik, B. (1927). Das Behalten erledigter und unerledigter Handlungen. *Psychologische Forschungen, 9,* 1–85.

2

Varieties of Intention:
Some Distinctions and Classifications

Lia Kvavilashvili
University of Wales College of Cardiff

Judi Ellis
University of Reading

Mook (1989) recently noted that "the explosion of interest in everyday memory has enormously enriched the field. Entire areas of investigation that were unknown a few years ago — prospective memory, for instance, — are boiling with ideas and findings" (p. 25). It is, of course, encouraging to hear that an ardent defender of artificial laboratory experiments (see Mook, 1983) holds such an enthusiastic view about the accomplishments of everyday memory research (cf. Banaji & Crowder, 1989). In our opinion, however, this view tends to be slightly exaggerated, at least with respect to prospective memory. It is difficult to describe an area of research as boiling with ideas and findings when approximately only 45 papers were published over the past 20 years (see Fig. 2.1). This means two papers are published on average per year, or if one takes into account only experimental work, this figure drops to about one paper per year. However, this is great progress compared to a 40-year period preceding the early 1970s[1] when, to our knowledge, only three relevant studies appeared, one experimental (Birenbaum, 1930) and two theoretical (Lewin, 1926/1951; Miller, Galanter, & Pribram, 1960). An enhanced interest toward this important but unjustly neglected area of research is also reflected in the fact that recent and forthcoming conferences on memory have started to devote one symposium, among many others, solely to prospective memory. Finally, the publication of the present volume can be said to mark an important milestone in prospective memory research.

---

[1]Although the term *prospective* was not in use until 1975 (Meacham & Leiman), the first study of prospective memory by a cognitive psychologist was conducted by Loftus in 1971.

Studies on Prospective Memory

Questionnaire Studies	Diary Studies	Theoretical and Review Papers	Experimental Studies	Case Studies
Meacham & Kushner, 1980	Ellis, 1988a	Miller, Galanter, & Pribram, 1960	Birenbaum, 1930	McKitrick et al., 1992
Kreutzer et al., 1982	Andrzejewski et al., 1991	Meacham, 1982	Loftus, 1971	Sohlberg et al., 1992a
Andrzejewski et al., 1991	Ellis & Milne, 1992b	Harris, 1984	Meacham & Leiman, 1975	Sohlberg et al., 1992b
Herrmann & Neisser, 1978	Ellis & Minno-Smith, 1993	Wilkins, 1986	Meacham & Dumitru, 1976	Cockburn, 1994
Harris & Sunderland, 1981	Crovitz & Daniel, 1984	Meacham, 1988	Meacham & Singer, 1977	Shallice & Burgess, 1991
Cavanaugh et al., 1983	Terry, 1988	Winograd, 1988b	Wilkins & Eaddeley, 1978	
Cohen & Faulkner, 1984	West, 1984	Cohen, G., 1989	Meacham & Colombo, 1980	
Martin, M., 1986		Brandimonte, 1991	Harris & Wilkins, 1982	
Dobbs & Rule, 1987		Ellis, 1991	Poon & Schaffer, 1982	
Mateer et al., 1987		Kvavilashvili, 1992b	Somerville et al., 1983	
Devolder et al., 1990		McDaniel & Einstein, 1992	Wichman & Oyasato, 1983	
Lovelace & Twohig, 1990		Morris, P. E., 1992	Ceci & Brorfenbrenner, 1985	
		Maylor, 1993a, 1993b	Dobbs & Rule, 1987	
			Kvavilashvili, 1987	
		Lewin, 1926/1951	Ceci et al, 1988	
		Baddeley & Wilkins, 1984	West, 1988	
		Levy & Loftus, 1984	Einstein & McDaniel, 1990	
		Mateer & Sohlberg, 1988	Ellis & Williams, J. M. G., 1990	
		Payne, 1993	Maylor, 1990	
			Cockburn & Smith, P. T., 1991a	
			Cockburn & Smith, P. T., 1991b	
			Einstein et al., 1991	
			Einstein et al., 1992	
			Ellis & Milne, 1992a	
			Blackburn et al., 1993	
			Kvavilashvili, 1993	
			Mäntylä, 1993	
			Maylor, 1993a	
			McDaniel & Einstein, 1993	
			Patton & Mei, 1993	
			Sellen et al., 1993	
			Brandimonte & Passolunghi, 1994	
			Cockburn & Smith, P. T., 1994	
			Studies in medical compliance, e.g.	
			Shepard & Moseley, 1976	
			Levy, 1977	
			Levy & Claravall, 1977	
			Levy & Clark, H., 1980	

FIG. 2.1. Studies of prospective memory arranged in five groups according to the type of study reported (questionnaire, diary, theoretical–review, experimental, or case study). The studies in the boxes refer to articles in which prospective memory is examined either in context of medical compliance or only as one of several topics under investigation/review. (Several experimental papers, particularly the more recent ones, are conference papers.)

When one starts to investigate a new and unexplored phenomenon, its proper description and measurement is of paramount importance. Although various aspects of these issues are addressed in previous papers and throughout this volume, there is still much more to be said on the topic. For example, it is now well acknowledged that prospective memory is always embedded in people's everyday actions and activities (see, e.g., Baddeley & Wilkins, 1984; Cohen, 1989; Ellis, this volume; Harris, 1984; Meacham, 1982; Morris, 1992). People, however, often commit a variety of errors and mistakes while performing these actions (see, e.g., Norman, 1981; Reason, 1979, 1984). It seems necessary, therefore, to develop a taxonomy that will allow us to differentiate instances of prospective memory failure from other forms of error. Second, there appears to be agreement that a variety of intentions occur in everyday life. This is stressed in a number of papers and some potentially important distinctions have been drawn (see, e.g., Einstein & McDaniel, 1990; Ellis, 1988a; Harris, 1984). The observation and analysis of naturally occurring intentions, however, indicate that further distinctions are possible. The classificatory scheme we propose attempts to identify the more important of these distinctions for research and to capture the relationships between the potentially different types of intentions that emerge from this analysis. Finally, a number of different research methods and paradigms are employed by prospective memory researchers. It is important, therefore, to consider the appropriateness of a particular method in relation to a particular type of intention. In addressing these three questions, this chapter aims to demonstrate the complex nature of prospective memory, the difficulties of its investigation, and the possibilities for studying a wide variety of intentions despite these difficulties.

PROSPECTIVE REMEMBERING AND INTENTIONS

Prospective memory is defined either as remembering to do something at a particular moment in the future or as the timely execution of a previously formed intention. Because prospective memory refers to remembering *intentions,* we should pause to briefly consider the nature of intentions. For example, it is important to know what kind of phenomenon an intention is, how it is related to human behavior and the types of intention people usually form and carry out in their everyday lives. Answers to these questions may substantially enhance our understanding of prospective memory and its underlying mechanisms.

The most important feature of intentions is their intrinsic relation to the actions and activities that we perform in our everyday lives. Indeed, some philosophers define human behavior as events caused by intentions (Brand, 1984; Harré, 1982). Gauld and Shotter (1977), however, suggested that it is almost impossible to provide a single definition of an intention that could encompass the great variety of naturally occurring intentions people usually carry out. Although this is true to some extent, in general, an intention can be defined as a person's readiness to act in a certain way in the future, where *what* has to be done and *when* it has to be done are defined with more or less clarity. This readiness to act in a certain way in the future can be described as the *that* aspect of an intention (see Ellis, this volume; Gauld & Shotter, 1977). Of course, there are other aspects of intentions, such as who, where, and how (see, e.g., Cohen, 1989; Fishbein & Ajzen, 1975; I. James, 1990, cited in Morris, 1992). In many respects, however, the latter are not as central to the realization of an intention as are the *what* and *when* aspects. For example, how an action is effected (its *component action sequence*) can be regarded as a further specification of the what aspect. Similarly, who (i.e. to, with, or for whom) and where are often closely connected with a specification of the when aspect (for further discussion see Ellis, this volume).

Searle (1983) distinguished two broad types of intentions, namely, *prior intentions* and *intentions-in-action*. A prior intention is one in which the intention is formed prior to action, whereas an intention-in-action is not associated with a prior intention. (One example of an intention-in-action would be a spontaneous action, such as picking up an umbrella you see on your way out of the house). An important feature of a prior intention is that it always occurs as a result of a conscious decision to act in a certain way (see, e.g., Brand, 1984; Heckhausen & Kuhl, 1985; Nuttin, 1987). If no such decision has been made, then no relevant prior intention can exist.

On many occasions, people begin to carry out their prior intentions immediately after a decision has been made. We can call these *immediate intentions* and distinguish them from *delayed intentions* (cf. Gauld & Shotter, 1977). The fulfilment of a delayed intention is, by definition, always postponed and it is possible to realize the intention only at some designated moment in the future. The term *prospective memory* appears to be used to describe the processes associated with the retrieval and satisfaction of these delayed intentions. Moreover the difficulty of prospective remembering—the timely retrieval of an intention—arises only with these delayed intentions. For any one of a variety of reasons, one may miss this prearranged moment and thus fail to satisfy an intention.

PROSPECTIVE MEMORY FAILURES, ABSENT-MINDED ERRORS AND OTHER MEMORY LAPSES

Prospective memory failures are common in everyday life (see, e.g., Crovitz & Daniel, 1984; Einstein & McDaniel, this volume; Terry, 1988; West, 1984). However, they are not the only source of failures that occur during the performance of our everyday activities. It is important, therefore, to try to distinguish prospective memory failures from other forms of action errors.

Absent-Minded Errors

A distinction should be drawn between *prospective memory failures* and *absent-minded errors* (see Cohen, 1989). The latter constitute a broad class of different failures and lapses, and are usually described as *action-slips* (Heckhausen & Beckmann, 1990; Norman, 1981), *actions-not-as-planned* (Reason, 1979), or *strong habit intrusions* (James, 1890). Although these errors take a variety of forms, they all describe failures that occur during the execution or performance of an intended action. Prospective memory errors, in contrast, take the form of a failure to retrieve an intended action at all, at an appropriate moment (cf. Cohen, 1989). The most typical absent-minded errors are ones in which a person carries out an unintended action instead of the intended one. For example, we may start to remove some tomatoes from the refrigerator instead of the eggs or tidy up a room instead of fetching a book we had left there. Because these errors occur when an unintended action is substituted for an intended one, we refer to them here as *action substitution* errors.

Another type of absent-minded error includes occasions when we start to carry out an intended action but suddenly realize (usually within a few seconds or minutes) that we no longer know what we had set out to accomplish. This type of error occurs when, for example, someone opens the refrigerator or enters a bedroom only to discover that he or she cannot recall what was needed (a *what am I doing here* experience; Reason, 1984). This form of forgetting cannot be characterized as a prospective memory failure (but see, for an alternate view, Einstein & McDaniel, this volume). Rather, it refers to the loss of the contents—the action or what aspect—of an immediate intention during the performance of the intended activity.

Finally, there is a class of absent-minded errors[2] that appears to result from an incorrect assessment of one's current place in a sequence of actions. These errors, sometimes referred to as *place-losing* ones (Reason, 1984), usually take the form of either omissions or repetitions of a particular action in the sequence. A failure to switch the kettle on after filling it, for example, would be classified as an omission error, whereas an attempt to fill an already filled kettle would be an example of a repetition error. In both instances, the error occurs during the performance of an intended action and its occurrence is not connected with a failure to retrieve the intention to carry out that action. It cannot, therefore, be regarded as a failure of prospective remembering.

A crucial difference between absent-minded slips or errors and prospective memory failures is that the former occur in relation to either immediate intentions whose performance has been initiated or to intentions-in-action, and

---

[2]There are, of course, many other types of absent-minded errors that have been documented by, for example, Heckhausen and Beckmann (1990), Norman (1981), Reason (1979, 1984). However, the ones considered here are thought to be most vulnerable to be misattributed as failures of prospective memory.

the latter in relation to delayed intentions. Once a delayed intention is initiated, however, it is transformed into an immediate one and any of the different types of absent-minded errors outlined previously may be committed. If these errors are not corrected, they may contribute to the overall failure of the prospective memory *task,* but they are not attributable to a failure to retrieve the delayed intention. For example, if you forgot to telephone a friend at 8:00 p.m., as arranged, this would be an example of a prospective memory failure. If, however, you recalled the intention at this time and had even started to carry it out (e.g., moved toward the hall) the delayed intention would be transformed into an immediate one and would be potentially vulnerable to any one of the absent-minded errors outlined. For example, you may either dial the number of a different friend (substitution error), enter the hall but forget why you wanted to go there (loss of action content), dial only part of the telephone number (omission), or dial the number twice in succession (repetition error).

Output Monitoring

Some omission and repetition errors differ from their absent-minded counterparts in that they usually occur in relation to delayed intentions; they are, therefore, more closely related to failures of prospective remembering. These errors constitute a broad and interesting class that Koriat and his colleagues refer to as *failures in output monitoring* (see Koriat & Ben-Zur, 1988; Koriat, Ben-Zur, & Sheffer, 1988). Suppose, for example, that someone has formed the intention to take a pill after breakfast. Errors of output monitoring could occur if one either subsequently forgets that a pill has already been taken and takes an additional pill (repetition error), or falsely remembers having taken it and thus ends up taking no pill at all (omission error). In both of these cases, the intention to take a pill is not forgotten. In the former, it is actually remembered twice, and in the latter, it is remembered but not carried out. Although repetition errors tend to result in inefficient behaviors (the risk of overdose, for example), omission errors are likely to contribute to failure on prospective memory *tasks* (taking no pill at all). Neither of these errors, however, are prospective memory failures because they do not result from the failure to remember an intention at an appropriate moment. Rather, they arise from the faulty encoding or retrieval of an actual (repetition error) or imagined (omission error) action.

Forgetting the Content of Delayed Intention

Some errors occur during the course of remembering a delayed intention and are therefore closely related to failures of prospective remembering. Nonetheless, they should not be regarded as prospective memory failures because they refer only to the partial loss of the what or when aspects of the content of a delayed intention. Suppose, for example, that one had decided to buy some food, such as eggs, cheese, and bread from a shop on the way home. Returning home without stopping at the shop would be a clear and typical example of a prospective memory failure. Omitting to buy one of the food items, however, could be regarded as a failure to retrieve part of the what aspect of the delayed intention and thus would be classified as a failure of retrospective memory (see, for further discussion, Einstein & McDaniel, this volume).[3] Similarly, one may remember the what aspect of intention (like having an appointment with a friend on that day) but no longer remember accurately or completely the when aspect or exact time when this intention should be carried out (e.g., whether it is 1:00 p.m. or 2:00 p.m.).

Finally, there are paradoxical cases of successful prospective remembering that are accompanied by a complete loss of the what aspect of a delayed intention. These are occasions on which we have a feeling of something to do in response to a particular place, time, and so on, but are unable to recall what it is that we should be doing (see, for further discussion, Einstein & McDaniel, this volume; Ellis, this volume). Although a delayed intention may be remembered at an appropriate moment (retrieval of *when* aspect) it is clearly impossible to complete a prospective memory task unless the action (*what* aspect) is also recalled. Phenomenologically, however, the experience that accompanies such an occasion may be similar to ones associated with the temporary loss of an immediate intention—a what am I doing here experience, described earlier in the section on absent-minded errors.

Additional Sources of Error

As the previous discussion illustrates, it would be erroneous to assume that all failures to carry out an intention are errors of prospective memory. Failures of output monitoring or forgetting the contents (what and when) of a delayed intention are not, however, the only reasons why a delayed intention may be remembered but not performed. One obvious reason for nonperformance is that a person may simply decide that they no longer wish to carry out the intention. In these cases, the intention may be either postponed, with revised *when* and possibly *what* conditions, or cancelled (cf. Ellis, this volume).

Other instances of action failure, which might mistakenly be categorized as prospective memory failures, highlight the importance of the presence or absence of an initial decision to act in a certain way (the *that* aspect of an intention). For example, many failures to carry out a clearly necessary action or

---

[3]Classification depends on the nature of the original encoding—whether one or more intentions were formed. In other words, was the original intention to go to a particular shop to buy food, with some passing consideration of possible items, or were separate intentions formed to buy cheese, bread, and eggs? Caution is advisable without knowledge of the initial decision(s) or, in a laboratory study, the experimental instructions.

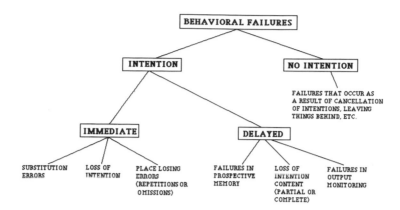

FIG. 2.2.   A classification of behavioral failures according to the presence or absence of an intention and the type of to-be-performed intention (immediate or delayed).

activity in a particular situation are not associated with such a decision and, as a result, no relevant delayed intention can be said to have been formed. A common example of this kind of failure is leaving behind objects, and occasionally even animals or children; for example, leaving an umbrella in a post office. It is unlikely that people in these situations typically make a conscious decision not to leave the umbrella or jacket behind. Rather, we assume that there will be sufficient situational cues available at an appropriate moment to support the performance of these actions. Repeated failures, however, may lead to the formation of a positive decision and thus to the encoding of a delayed intention.

In summary, people tend to perform a variety of errors in their everyday lives (see Fig. 2.2). Some occur as a result of making decisions and forming intentions (immediate or delayed) whereas others occur in the absence of these prior intentions (e.g., leaving things behind). For immediate intentions, different kinds of absent-minded errors are possible (e.g., substitution errors, temporary loss of intention, and place-losing errors). For delayed intentions, these errors may be due to either prospective memory failures, partial or complete loss of the content of an intention, or failures of output monitoring.

A VARIETY OF INTENTIONS

A great variety of delayed intentions can be classified in relation to the following four main phases of information processing—encoding, retention, retrieval, and performance. Although successful retrieval in most retrospective memory tasks almost always results in performance (production of the retrieved event) this is not necessarily true in prospective memory. For example, an intention may be retrieved at an appropriate moment but not be carried out. For this reason, we consider the retrieval and performance phases separately; cf. Brandimonte and Passolunghi, 1994; Ellis, 1991; Ellis, this volume.

Encoding

The following distinctions can be drawn in relation to the processes that operate during the initial encoding phase of prospective memory—simple or difficult decision, self- or other-generated, important or unimportant, and pleasant, neutral, or unpleasant.

Intentions Based on Simple or Difficult Decisions. The first refers to the type of decision that precedes the formation of an intention. Intentions may be formed as a result of either a simple, often momentary decision or a difficult, often time-consuming one (cf. Kvavilashvili, 1992a). Suppose, for example, that a friend asks you to go to the cinema with him or her this evening. If you have no particular plans for the evening, then you may agree almost immediately. On the other hand, if you wanted to complete a particular task then it may take some time and thought before you decide to postpone the task and watch the movie. Although in both cases the resulting intention is to go to the cinema, these intentions may be psychologically different. Several factors suggest that, other things being equal, the likelihood of forgetting an intention preceded by a simple decision may be higher than that of forgetting one preceded by a difficult decision. For instance, as the examples provided here illustrate, simple decisions are often less time-consuming than difficult ones. A difficult decision may require, for example, the reorganization of one's activities, prioritization of these activities, and/or the examination of future opportunities for performing alternate actions. The planning processes evoked by such considerations are likely to result in more elaborate and distinctive processing for intentions preceded by difficult decisions than for those preceded by simple decisions.

Self- or Other-Generated Intentions. At an encoding phase, intentions can be divided further into ones that are formed as a result of a personal need to do something and ones that are formed as a result of a request from someone else. The former can be described as *self-generated intentions* and the latter as *other-generated intentions* (Cohen, 1989; Ellis & Nimmo-Smith, 1993; Kvavilashvili, 1992b). Self- and other-generated intentions differ mainly in terms of the needs that they satisfy or that they originate from. Other-generated intentions are based on extrinsic needs (e.g., to comply with certain norms, obligations, etc.). Self-generated intentions, on the other hand, are based on intrinsic needs (see, e.g., Tuomela, 1977, on the distinction between extrinsic and intrinsic needs). Thus far, experimental tasks have studied only other-generated intentions, formed as a result of a request from an experimenter. In contrast, diary studies of naturally occurring intentions are likely to include examples of both self- and other-generated intentions. Unfortunately, these studies have not examined possible variations in retrieval between these two types of intentions (Andrzejewski, Moore, Corvette, & Herrmann, 1991; Ellis, 1988a; Ellis & Nimmo-Smith, 1993).

To what extent might the origin of an intention influence the encoding and likely outcome of that intention? Certainly, research on the generation effect in retrospective memory indicates that self-generated intentions should be better retained and recalled than other-generated ones (e.g., Slamecka & Graf, 1978). McDaniel, Waddill, and Einstein (1988) suggested that a generation task induces consistent relational or distinctive processing (or both) of the material to be remembered. If retrieval requires the use of either or both of these processes, then a positive generation effect should be observed. However, it may not be possible to draw a direct parallel between self- and other-generated intentions and self- and other-generated information to be learned. In the case of the former, a request from another person has to induce an extrinsic need to comply with that request. Only after such a need has been formed can it be transformed into a delayed intention.[4] This, however, requires some degree of personal commitment to the performance of that intention, and thus, processing and transformation of the requested material has to occur. This would not necessarily differ from the processing that occurs with self-generated intentions. Relational and elaborate encoding of the what, when, and that aspects is equally likely for both types of intention—irrespective of the type of need from which they originate.

We would therefore not expect to observe a "prospective generation effect" —that is, a difference in the probability of retrieving self- as opposed to other-generated intentions. Some preliminary support for this conjecture comes from the results of a questionnaire study we conducted as part of a larger scale study on individual differences in prospective remembering. Subjects in this study were asked to rate how frequently they forget to pass a message (other-generated intention) and to tell someone something (self-generated intention). There was no significant difference in the forgetting rate of these intentions. If anything, subjects reported to forget self-generated intentions slightly more often than other-generated intentions ($t[59] = -1.90$, p = .06, two-tailed). Moreover, those who performed well on self-generated tasks tended to perform well on other-generated tasks, and vice versa ($r[58] = .45$, p < .001).

Important or Unimportant Intentions.   As suggested, delayed intentions

---

[4]If there is no desire to pass on a message, for example, then no relevant intention is formed even if one formally agrees to comply with that request.

can also be distinguished with reference to their importance. Having formed an intention we can usually state whether or not it is important for us to carry it out. Clearly, the information that enables us to make this assessment can be derived from several sources, such as the consequences of failure or the benefits of success for oneself or for another person, associated with an intention.

A distinction between important and unimportant intentions was drawn by Freud (1901), who suggested that people are highly unlikely to forget genuinely important intentions unless they suffer from a serious psychological or psychiatric problem. If correct, this observation suggests that the phenomenon of forgetting intentions is more likely to occur with relatively unimportant intentions than with relatively important ones. Empirical support for this conjecture has been demonstrated in a wide variety of situations (real-world and laboratory), in both adults and children (Ellis, 1988a, 1988b; Kvavilashvili, 1987; Meacham & Singer, 1977; Somerville, Wellman, & Cultice, 1983).

The level of importance that is attributed to a delayed intention is probably derived from the links between that intention and other intentions, and more general goals, aims, desires, and so on (see, e.g., Baars & Mattson, 1981). The encoding of a relatively important intention, therefore, is likely to attract more integrative and organizational processing with respect to these other intentions than a less important one. The resultant associations may also provide additional cues for the retrieval of a particular delayed intention by, for example, the retrieval or performance of these other, associated intentions. Attributions of importance, however, are likely to cut across the self- versus other-generated distinction. Self-generated intentions are not necessarily more personally important than other-generated ones. The critical feature is likely to be the strength and character of the associative links between a particular delayed intention (self or other-generated) and other intentions, aims, and so on. The importance of a delayed intention, therefore, may have a more critical influence on its outcome than does the origin of that intention.

Pleasant, Neutral, or Unpleasant Intentions. Another potentially interesting distinction was also drawn a long time ago, and refers to the emotional tone of a to-be-remembered intention: *pleasant, unpleasant,* or *neutral* (Birenbaum, 1930). Unpleasant intentions, for example arranging a visit to the dentist, may be remembered as often as pleasant ones, but tend to be either cancelled or postponed more often. The postponement of a dental appointment, for example, may provide a temporary resolution of a conflict between a perceived need to satisfy that intention and a basic desire to avoid painful experiences (see, e.g., Oatley & Johnson-Laird, 1987). Alternatively, the construct of Freudian repression would predict that unpleasant intentions may be more likely to be forgotten (not recalled) than pleasant ones (see, for further discussion, Meacham & Kushner, 1980).

Experimental studies have thus far investigated only the remembering of neutral intentions. However, a questionnaire study conducted by Meacham and Kushner (1980) suggests that intentions reported as remembered but not executed (i.e., postponed or cancelled) were described as more uncomfortable to carry out than those either remembered and satisfied or not remembered at all. A more extensive investigation of the outcome of pleasant and unpleasant intentions may prove to be a fruitful line of inquiry.

In summary, we can draw at least four distinctions between delayed intentions with reference to processes that operate during an encoding phase. So far, only one of these—the importance of an intention—has been investigated. One reason for this might be that self-generated, pleasant–unpleasant intentions based on difficult decisions are not easy to experimentally manipulate, either in the laboratory or in the field. This is especially true of self-generated intentions, although a distinction between self- and other-generated intentions may not be as functionally important as, for example, the corresponding distinction in retrospective memory. The distinctions between pleasant and unpleasant intentions and between intentions based on either simple or difficult decisions are then theoretically more interesting. One possibility is that the ease with which a decision is made is dependent not only on circumstantial constraints (e.g., time, competing tasks) but also on individual differences in decision-making strategies or style (e.g., action- vs. state-orientation; see Goschke & Kuhl, 1993; Kuhl, 1985).[5] Another possibility is that factors shown to influence the retention and recall of pleasant and unpleasant information in retrospective memory research (e.g., positive and negative mood effects), may exert comparable influences on the recall of pleasant and unpleasant intentions. At present, however, the only means of exploring the theoretical importance of these distinctions is to study naturally occurring intentions, using either a questionnaire or a structured diary (see, e.g., Andrzejewski et al., 1991; Ellis, 1988a, 1988b; Ellis & Nimmo-Smith, 1993).

Retention

All delayed intentions, however they are differentiated at encoding, can be distinguished during a retention phase only in terms of the delay between their formation and the designated moment for retrieving and carrying out the intended action. As Baddeley and Wilkins (1984) suggested, they can be divided into short and long term intentions. Such a distinction is central to research on retrospective memory, and Baddeley and Wilkins argued that it may be appropriately applied to prospective memory. The processing necessary to sup-

---

[5]For example, it may be the case that action-oriented subjects tend to form their future intentions mostly on the basis of simple decisions, whereas state-oriented participants are more likely to form their intentions on the basis of difficult decisions.

port the timely retrieval of, for example, an intention to telephone someone in 5 min may be qualitatively different from that required to support an intention to telephone the person in 5 days (see Ellis, this volume, for further discussion). Laboratory studies of prospective memory have examined only the remembering of shorter term delayed intentions. Longer term intentions have been investigated in a natural context, using either diary studies or field experiments. To our knowledge, there are no reported studies that directly compared performance on short and long term delayed intentions that are equivalent in all major respects other than the extent of their retention intervals.[6]

The importance of considering also the nature of one's activities during this interval was highlighted in a study on shorter term intentions by Brandimonte and Passolunghi (1994). Their findings suggest that prospective memory failures occur because of interference from interpolated activities (see also, Ellis & Nimmo-Smith, 1993; Wichman & Oyasato, 1983). These effects, moreover, may be moderated by the importance of the delayed intention. Kvavilashvili (1987), for example, observed a reliable effect of the character of an intervening period (either unfilled or filled with an interesting–uninteresting activity) on the performance of a relatively unimportant intention, whereas no such effect was present for an important intention.

Retrieval

It is during this phase that an appropriate opportunity for carrying out an intention occurs. The retrieval phase is a critical one, therefore, in that it is here that an intention is either recalled or forgotten. All delayed intentions have to be remembered and carried out in response to particular occasions (defined by the when aspect). The nature of these occasions, however, varies in a number of different ways.

Event-, Time-, or Activity-Based Intentions. If we consider the basic nature of a retrieval occasion, several potentially different types can be identified—activities, locations, persons, objects, events, times, or time periods. We might wish to describe delayed intentions, therefore, as either time-based or activity-based or object-based, and so on. Kvavilashvili (1990), however, described three distinct types of prospective remembering based on the differences between events, times, and activities. Einstein and McDaniel (1990; this volume), on the other hand, draw a distinction between time- and event-based intentions only, whereas Harris (1984) differentiated between *appointment-*

---

[6]Einstein, Holland, McDaniel, and Guynn (1992) examined the effects of 15- and 30-minute delays on prospective remembering. Although no reliable differences in performance were observed, this manipulation does not really capture the difference between the shorter (minutes) and longer term (hours) delays under consideration here.

keeping intentions (time-based) and intentions to *do one thing before or after another* (activity-based).

To what extent can these different types of retrieval occasions be subsumed under the more general descriptions of time- versus event-based or time- versus activity-based intentions? An event is an occurrence relatively independent of a particular person. We speak, for example, of "attending an event," "an event happening," and so on. In this sense, persons, locations, and objects could all be classed as different types of event-based intentions—for example, when you see John, when you are in the kitchen, when you see a telephone. Activities, however, usually refer to something in which the individual engages. (Although one may observe another person's activity, a retrieval occasion that is defined with respect to that person's activity could be described as an event; for example, Mary has finished photocopying). An activity-defined retrieval occasion (such as taking a pill before or after dinner) requires the identification of our own actions rather than something that is independent of those actions. Finally, time-defined retrieval occasions (e.g., turn the oven off at 5:00 p.m.) appear to be different from both activity- and event-defined ones because time is a process independent of our activity and events.

A distinction between time-, activity- and event-based intentions may represent a reasonably coherent classification of different types of retrieval occasions. However, are these distinctions psychologically important? Are these different types of intentions, for example, associated with different processing requirements? Einstein and McDaniel (1990) suggested that whereas, in event-based intentions, the event provides an external cue for remembering those intentions, the same is not true of time-based intentions; the latter, they suggested, are more reliant on self-initiated retrieval processes. Thus, following Craik (1986), they argued that time-based intentions are more difficult for elderly persons to retrieve than are event-based ones and presented evidence in support of this conjecture (see Einstein and McDaniel, this volume).

With regard to the presence or absence of external cues, event- and activity-based intentions seem to be broadly similar to one another. After all, finishing an activity (e.g., a meal) may be regarded as an external cue in the same way that seeing a friend is a cue in an event-based task. Thus, both Brandimonte and McDaniel (personal communication, January, 1994) have argued that there is no need to distinguish activity-based intentions from event-based ones. However, there is another important dimension along which these intentions may differ. The retrieval of both event- and time-based intentions usually requires the interruption of an ongoing activity. For example, in order to buy some food on the way home, we have to interrupt a journey, and in order to keep an appointment, we have to interrupt writing an essay. The interruption of an ongoing activity is likely to place particular demands on current attentional resources. Retrieval of an activity-based intention, on the other hand, does not require such an interruption. In the latter case, we have to do something after finishing or before starting another activity—to do something during the gap between two consecutive activities.

If we take account of the presence–absence of an external cue and the interruption–noninterruption of an ongoing activity, then a three-way distinction between activity-, event-, and time-based delayed intentions is a theoretically valid proposal. The following predictions follow from this analysis. First, activity-based intentions are probably the easiest to remember at an appropriate moment, as they do not require the interruption of an ongoing activity and they benefit from the presence of external cues. (These cues, however, may be less distinctive than those associated with event-based intentions). Second, time-based intentions are probably the most difficult to remember because no obvious external cues are necessarily associated with the various times and our current activity must be interrupted in order to carry out an intention. Event-based intentions are likely to occupy an intermediate position in terms of ease of recall, because they share some features with both time- and activity-based ones; both event- and time-based intentions require interruption of an ongoing activity, whereas both event- and activity-based ones benefit from the presence of an external cue. These predictions, however, are based on an assumption that the presence or absence of an external cue and the necessity to interrupt our activity are of equal importance in determining the effects of different retrieval occasions on the outcome of delayed intentions. This assumption clearly requires empirical examination.

The potential differences and similarities between the remembering of activity-, event-, and time-based intentions have not been studied systematically. To our knowledge, there are only two experiments that attempted to compare subjects' performance on event- and time-based tasks. In one, a field study conducted by Sellen, Louiel, Harris, and Wilkins (1993), participants were asked to press the button of electronic badges (carried with them for 2 weeks during working hours) during each of several 5-minute intervals spaced 2 hours apart (time-based task) and whenever they were in a particular room (event-based task). In the other, a 30-min computer-based laboratory task (Richardson, cited in Einstein & McDaniel, this volume), some participants were asked to press a designated key once every 5 min (time-based), whereas others were asked to press the same key whenever they saw a question about a president (event-based). Both studies, despite considerable variations in design, produced converging evidence in support of a distinction between event- and time-based intentions and thus point to the importance of this distinction. Unfortunately, however, there are no experiments in which the distinctions between activity- and time-based and, more importantly, between activity- and event-based intentions were directly compared.

Pure or Combined Intentions. Retrieval occasions in everyday life, can occur in either a relatively pure form (activity- or time-based, for example) or in combination—pure and combined intentions (cf. Ellis, this volume). Although laboratory studies typically define and investigate only pure intentions, naturally occurring intentions often take a compound form. For example, they may be a combination of event and time (give a message to a partner when he or she comes home at 6:00 p.m.), event and activity (give a message to a partner when you have finished writing a letter), or time and activity (telephone someone at 8:00 p.m. when you have finished watching a television program). On the whole, combined intentions may be more easily remembered at an appropriate moment than pure ones because the former provide more cues for retrieval (cf. West, 1988). Some support for this conjecture comes from a study conducted by Loftus (1971) in which participants were asked to convey their place of birth at the end of a verbally administered questionnaire (pure, activity-based intention). However, half of the subjects were also informed about the content of the final question (combined, activity + event-based task). As expected, those in the combined intention condition were more likely to relate their birthplace at the correct moment than were those in the pure intention condition.

Episodic or Habitual Intentions. A further distinction refers to the frequency and regularity with which a retrieval occasion occurs and its associated intention should be remembered and executed. Meacham and Leiman's (1975/1982) distinction between episodic and habitual intentions was made with reference to these dimensions. They suggested that episodic intentions refer to actions that are performed either infrequently and/or on an irregular basis, such as buying bread on your way home from work, whereas habitual ones refer to actions that are carried out in a regular or routine manner, such as brushing teeth or buying a newspaper on the way to work. They argued that habitual intentions are easier to remember than episodic ones, as the former provide additional cues from both the environment and preceding activities (see Ellis, this volume, for further discussion).

Episodic intentions, if defined in terms of frequency, can be divided further into single and repeated intentions (Kvavilashvili, 1992b). A single intention is one that has to be remembered on only one occasion in response to a single retrieval occasion (e.g., telephoning one's mother this evening). A repeated intention, on the other hand, is one that has to be remembered several times in response to a recurring occasion (e.g., telephoning one's mother every evening this week). Interestingly, repeated intentions seem to be a necessary intermediate stage in transforming a single episodic intention into a habitual one (e.g., telephoning one's mother every evening for the rest of the year). Like all habitual intentions, a repeated intention does not require one to make a new decision prior to each retrieval occasion. The intention is formed once only but, unlike a single intention, it has to be retrieved on more than one occasion. Although naturally occurring intentions are usually instances of either single–episodic or habitual intentions, repeated intentions are useful and important in experimental research because they enable the collection of quantitative measures of prospective remembering (see, for further discussion, Kvavilashvili, 1992b).

Relatively few studies have attempted to investigate the distinction between episodic and habitual intentions, and one of these, an early field experiment by Meacham and Singer (1977), failed to reveal any reliable variation in the performance of the two types of intentions. However, as Harris (1984) pointed out, their experimental manipulation (participants had to post a card either every Wednesday or on a variable day each week) did not really capture the complexity of the distinction they described.[7] In contrast, a diary study conducted by Andrzejewski et al. (1991), reported findings in support of an episodic–habitual distinction—the likelihood of remembering to keep an appointment was positively related to the frequency of making such appointments. Some care, however, is clearly required in drawing a distinction between habitual and episodic intentions because it includes a possible confound between the regularity with which an action is carried out and the frequency with which it is carried out. An intention to attend a monthly seminar, for example, can be described as a regularly but infrequently performed action (see also Harris, 1984). Is this intention, therefore an episodic or a habitual one? Andrzejewski et al.'s study suggests that the frequency with which an intention has to be carried out may have a greater influence on performance than the regularity with which it is carried out. In fairness, Andrzejewski et al.'s study was not designed to clearly dissociate between regularity and frequency; moreover, in everyday life the two variables are likely to be correlated.

Pulse, Intermediate, or Step Intentions.   Finally, retrieval occasions can be distinguished with regard to the temporal specification of a retrieval occasion (Ellis, 1988a; see also Harris and Wilkins' (1982) notion of a *window of opportunity*). Although some intentions have to be remembered within a very narrow time interval (such as a telephone call at 4:00 p.m.), others are associated with much longer time periods (such as a telephone call this evening). One of us introduced a broad classification scheme in which the former (narrow interval) intentions were described as *pulse intentions* and the latter as *step intentions;* intentions with temporal requirements that lie between are referred to as *intermediates* (see Ellis, 1988a, 1988b; Ellis and Nimmo-Smith, 1993). This scheme was constructed using information collected from a series of diary studies on naturally occurring intentions and refers primarily to time-based intentions. However, both event- and activity-based intentions may also

---

[7]It is extremely difficult to experimentally study habitual intentions. Indeed, Meacham and Singer (1977) were actually studying repeated intentions in both of their experimental conditions while varying only the regularity of to-be-performed action.

be described within the pulse–step classification scheme. For example, we may have to relay a message to a colleague whom we are likely to either meet briefly in the corridor (pulse, event-based), or see during a coffee break (intermediate) or attend a dinner with this evening (step). Similarly, we may need to take a medication either immediately (pulse, activity-based), within the next 15 min (intermediate) or any time after having our breakfast (step).

One obvious prediction that arises as a result of the pulse-step distinction is that step intentions may be easier to remember on time than are either pulses or intermediates; the relatively long time intervals associated with steps are likely to afford more opportunities for remembering. This is supported by a study conducted by Maylor (1990) who asked her subjects to telephone her either within a certain time interval each day (step) or at the same exact time each day (pulse). Maylor reported that those in the pulse condition performed worse than those in the step condition, both in terms of the number of calls they made and the number of errors or memory failures associated with those calls (e.g., calling outside the prescribed times). On the other hand, Ellis (1988a) reported a diary study on naturally occuring intentions in which pulses were less likely to be forgotten than were steps. Pulse intentions were rated as more important than steps, which could account for the discrepancy between the two sets of findings. However, further analyses of these data, together with the findings from a second diary study, suggest that both personal importance and the pulse–step distinction exert independent and reliable influences on the outcome of naturally occuring intentions (Ellis, 1988b; Ellis & Milne, 1992b).

One reason for the discrepancy between the field (Maylor) and diary (Ellis) investigations may arise from the type of mnemonic strategies that Maylor's participants claimed to have employed. Maylor reported that those in both the pulse and step conditions performed equally well if they used the same type of cue. Thus participants in both conditions who used conjunction cues (e.g., replanning the day for the call or tying it to a routine event) or external cues (e.g., external memory aid, such as a memo) performed better than those who used internal cues (i.e., reliance on memory alone). Those in the step condition who used conjunction cues might have been transforming a step into a pulse intention. Indeed, the operation of this strategy can be seen in naturally occuring intentions following a failure to carry out a step intention (Ellis, 1988b, this volume). Other differences between intentions in the two studies, such as single versus repeated, regular versus irregular intentions, may also be relevant to explanations of the observed variations in performance.

Finally, the results of Andrzejewski et al.'s (1991) diary study indicate that the effects of some pulse–step intentions may be mediated by the importance of these intentions. When participants have to keep important appointments, they report satisfying pulses slightly more often than steps, whereas for unimportant appointments more steps than pulses are successfully carried out (Andrzejewski et al., 1991). Further investigation is necessary to study differences in pulse and step intentions. As we pointed out earlier, in everyday life retrieval occasions are often combined (e.g., time + event) rather than pure. It may be more appropriate, therefore, to study the possible effects of the pulse–step distinction in the laboratory where both pure and combined intentions are easier to define and where a greater degree of experimental control is possible (for further discussion, see Ellis, this volume).

In summary, a total of four distinctions can be drawn at a retrieval stage of prospective remembering. An important difference between these and the previous distinctions is that each of the former have been examined in at least one experimental study. This situation is probably due to a particular interest, from researchers, in the processes that operate during the retrieval phase of prospective remembering. Moreover, unlike most of the previous distinctions, these four are potentially amenable to experimental investigation. The only exception is probably the episodic–habitual distinction. As suggested earlier, it is almost impossible to simulate habitual intentions not only in the laboratory but also in a field experiment. At present, the only way to experimentally study this distinction is to define repeated intentions and to vary the frequency and regularity with which these intentions have to be carried out (Meacham & Singer, 1977; Wichman & Oyasato, 1983). An alternative is to study naturally occuring habitual intentions using diaries and questionnaires.

PERFORMANCE

In common with many researchers, we suggest that the primary characteristic of prospective remembering appears to be the retrieval of an intention at an appropriate moment (for further discussion, see Einstein & McDaniel, this volume). Although performance of the intended action does not seem as crucial for prospective remembering as the retrieval phase, it may have some impact on retrieval. Two aspects of the performance phase that might be relevant in this regard are discussed here:

Momentary, Short, or Long Intentions.   Delayed intentions can be distinguished with reference to the amount of time that is required to carry out the intended action. Although some may be executed within a few seconds or minutes (e.g., conveying a message), others may occupy several hours (e.g., going shopping) . The former can be referred to as *momentary intentions,* and the latter as *long* or *time-consuming intentions,* whereas intentions that require more than few minutes but less than an hour (such as a phone call) can be classified as *short intentions.* It is clearly difficult to decide upon an exact criterion for distinguishing intended actions that lie between the two extremes (min vs. hours). However, it seems likely that intentions associated with actions that take either a few seconds, 20 min or several hours will have different processing demands. One possibility is that more time-consuming intentions will tend to elicit more elaborative processing at encoding. Satisfaction of these intentions is more likely to require, for example, greater reorganization of normal activities and thus the application of planning processes in order to accommodate them into a particular time period. Relatively time-consuming intentions may also be more likely to require the performance of other, enabling actions (e.g., checking the refrigerator and making a shopping list prior to going to the shops). Thus it is possible that, as a result of the effects of these variables on encoding, long or time-consuming intentions may be less vulnerable to failure than either short or momentary ones.

One- or Two-Stage Intentions.   A second distinction refers to the number of times one has to remember an intention in order to complete a prospective memory task. Consider, for instance, one-stage and two-stage intentions (although there may be three- and even multi-stage ones). In the former, only one act of remembering is necessary (e.g., to convey a message to a colleague when you see her in the coffee room), whereas in the latter, two acts are necessary (e.g., to take a letter when setting out to work and to post it on your way to work). Theoretically, two opposite but equally plausible predictions can be made about the relative likelihood of completing one- and two-stage intentions. According to Lewin (1926/1951), for example, remembering the first step of a two-stage intention should result in the partial discharge of tension associated with that intention, and this may result in a failure to remember the second step. On the other hand, extrapolation from more recent models of action control (e.g., Norman, 1981; Reason, 1984) suggests that remembering the first step should enhance the activation level of action schemata associated with that intention and thus increase the probability of remembering the second step. The likelihood of this facilitation effect, however, will clearly depend on the degree to which the two action stages are integrated at encoding (for further discussion, see Ellis, this volume). Although it would be interesting to test these two hypotheses, it may be difficult to model two-stage intentions in the laboratory. Field experiments, diaries, and questionnaires may provide a more appropriate vehicle for examining a one- versus two-stage distinction.

In summary, two possible distinctions emerge at the final performance phase of prospective remembering. These distinctions are both practically and theoretically important. To our knowledge, however, no relevant research has been conducted on these distinctions, nor have they been identified as a potentially interesting area of prospective memory research. This is probably due to an insufficient emphasis on the role of performance phase in prospective remembering. However, carefully controlled field experiments, diaries, and questionnaires could provide us with important information on these distinctions.

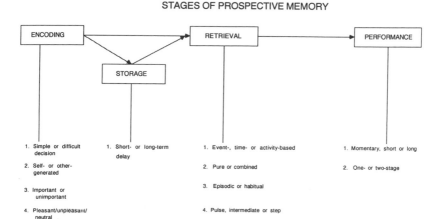

STAGES OF PROSPECTIVE MEMORY

FIG. 2.3.   Illustrating possible types of delayed intentions, classified according to variations at the encoding, storage, retrieval, and performance phases of prospective memory.

CLASSIFICATION OF EXISTING EXPERIMENTAL PARADIGMS

In this chapter, we try to show that the great variety of intentions people have to remember and carry out in their life can perhaps be best classified with regard to processing that occurs during each of the four main stages of prospective remembering. This classification scheme is summarized in Fig. 2.3. Naturally, this scheme is by no means exhaustive—one may easily continue to draw new and finer grained distinctions. However, the intention types outlined here seem to be the most obvious and potentially important for future prospective memory research. We also try to demonstrate that this research can actually be conducted using a variety of research methods. If a certain intention type does not render itself to experimental manipulations then it is always possible to employ a nonexperimental method, such as structured diaries or questionnaires.[8] Although the latter are popular in everyday memory research, few are used to directly investigate prospective remembering.

As Fig. 2.1 illustrates, most prospective memory studies have employed an experimental method. In some experiments participants are asked to perform an action during a laboratory task (e.g., pressing a key on a computer keyboard) whereas in others, they are asked to carry out an action in the course

---

[8]These methods are particularly relevant for studying intentions preceded by difficult decisions, self-generated intentions, pleasant–unpleasant intentions, two-stage intentions and long or time-consuming intentions.

of their everyday activities (e.g., post a letter)—laboratory and field experiments, respectively. Both types can be further divided according to the character of the task the participants have to remember at a designated moment. Tasks can either be artificial or similar to those encountered in everyday life— artificial and natural tasks. The advantages and limitations of the four experimental paradigms emerging from this alternative classification scheme proposed by one of us, were discussed elsewhere (Kvavilashvili, 1992b). A possible weakness of this classification is that it is not always easy to decide whether a certain prospective memory task is artificial or natural (cf. Winograd, 1988a). Moreover, a distinction between artificial and natural tasks may not be critical for empirical research. Kvavilashvili (1992b), for example, suggested that the problem of obtaining ceiling effects was more likely to occur when artificial tasks were prescribed. However, recent laboratory experiments using artificial tasks (e.g., pressing a response key when a certain target word occurs), consistently managed to avoid ceiling effects (see, e.g., Brandimonte & Passolunghi, 1994; Einstein & McDaniel, 1990; Mäntylä, 1993; McDaniel & Einstein, 1993). In contrast, the classificatory scheme presented in this chapter (see Fig. 2.3) captures a theoretically motivated set of distinctions. It enables us to focus both on the processes underlying prospective remembering and the appropriateness of different research methods in relation to a particular research question.

If we examine existing experimental studies of prospective remembering with respect to the distinctions illustrated in Fig. 2.3 then all have investigated the following—neutral, relatively unimportant, episodic, pure, pulse, mostly one-stage, momentary intentions, generated by other people (usually an experimenter), and formed as a result of simple decisions. Some experiments, however, have examined the remembering of short-term delayed intentions, and others have investigated longer term ones. These studies can be further divided according to the type of retrieval occasion—event-, time-, and activity-based intentions. If we focus only on these last two distinctions, then all existing experimental studies in prospective remembering easily fall within one of the six experimental paradigms that emerge (see Fig. 2.4). In Fig. 2.4, it can be seen that all experiments on short-term delayed intentions have taken place within the laboratory, whereas long-term delayed intentions have been investigated using field experiments. Event- and activity-based intentions have usually been studied in the laboratory, whereas time-based intentions have mainly been investigated in the field. (Diary studies and questionnaires tend to examine event-, time-, and activity-based, longer term delayed intentions).

This classificatory scheme reveals an interesting pattern with respect to the remaining distinctions we discuss in this chapter. For example, all short-term delayed intentions (whether event-, time-, or activity-based) studied in the laboratory are examples of pure, pulse, one-stage, momentary intentions, whereas there is no such uniformity with long-term delayed intentions. Indeed, some of the latter (field) experiments investigated pulses (Levy & Clark, 1980; Maylor, 1990; Moscovitch & Minde, 1982 [cited in Moscovitch, 1982]; Poon & Schaffer, 1982; Wilkins & Baddeley, 1978), and others examined either intermediates (Levy, 1977; Maylor, 1990; Sellen et al., 1993) or steps (Meacham & Leiman, 1975/1982; Meacham & Singer 1977; West, 1988). Some of these experiments examined performance on momentary intentions (e.g., pressing the button of an electronic badge), whereas others required the execution of either short or more time-consuming intentions (e.g., making a telephone call or keeping an appointment, respectively). Finally, some field studies of longer

	Short-Term Delayed	Long-Term Delayed
Event-Based	Dobbs & Rule, 1987 Cockburn & Smith, P. T., 1991b Einstein & McDaniel, 1990 Einstein et al., 1992 Mäntylä, 1993 Maylor, 1993a McDaniel & Einstein, 1993 Brandimonte & Passolunghi, 1994	Somerville et al., 1983
Time-Based	Harris & Wilkins, 1982 Wichman & Oyasato, 1983 Ceci & Bronfenbrenner, 1985 Patton & Meit, 1993 (Exp. 1)	Meacham & Leiman, 1975 Meacham & Singer, 1977 Wilkins & Baddeley, 1978 Moscovitch & Mindes, 1982 　(cited in Moscovitch, 1982) West, 1988 (Exp. 1) Maylor, 1990 Patton & Meit, 1993 (Exps. 1 & 3) And all studies in compliance 　(see Fig. 2.1)
Activity-Based	Birenbaum, 1930 Loftus, E., 1971 Meacham & Dumitru, 1976 Meacham & Colombo, 1980 Kvavilashvili, 1987 West, 1988 (Exp. 2) Cockburn & Smith, P. T., 1991b	Somerville et al., 1983 Dobbs & Rule, 1987

FIG. 2.4. Classification of published experimental studies into one of six categories defined by the length of the retention interval for an intention (short or long) and the type of retrieval occasion (event, time, or activity) on which the intention has to be recalled. (Some studies fall into more than one category because participants were asked to perform more than one type of intention.)

term intentions investigated pure time-based ones (e.g., Wilkins & Baddeley, 1978), and others probably combined ones (e.g., Meacham & Leiman, 1975/ 1982).

CONCLUSIONS

In this chapter, we draw attention to some of the distinctions and possible classificatory schemes that may be important for future prospective memory research. We show that a variety of everyday behavioral errors and failures can be classified in terms of the type of intention (immediate or delayed) that is formed, and that absent-minded slips and errors occur in relation to immediate intentions, whereas prospective memory failures are always associated with delayed intentions. We demonstrate also that the great variety of intentions people usually have to remember and carry out in their everyday lives can perhaps be best classified in relation to the encoding, storage, retrieval and performance phases of prospective memory.

A total of eleven distinctions are drawn with respect to these four phases (see Fig. 2.3). Some of these distinctions are theoretically more important than others. The four that refer to the retrieval phase of prospective remembering, for example, may be of paramount importance given the critical role of this phase in the successful completion of a prospective memory task. We also suggest that some of the distinctions outlined in the study can be easily investigated in the laboratory, whereas it may be appropriate to study others using either field experiments or diaries and questionnaires. Finally, the distinctions between short- and long-term delayed intentions and event-, time-, and activity-based intentions, and the six experimental paradigms that result from these distinctions, appear to provide a useful means of organizing existing experimental studies. The latter classification indicates that most published experiments on short-term delayed intentions actually studied event- and activity-based intentions only, in the laboratory, whereas experiments on longer-term delayed intentions examined mainly time-based intentions outside of the laboratory.

ACKNOWLEDGMENTS

The preparation of this chapter was supported by a postdoctoral fellowship awarded by The Royal Society to Lia Kvavilashvili for joint research with Judi Ellis at U.W.C.C. Cardiff, U.K. The chapter has benefitted from constructive comments by Maria Brandimonte, Mark McDaniel, and Ken Markham.

REFERENCES

Andrzejewski, S. J., Moore, C. M., Corvette, M., & Herrmann, D. (1991). Prospective memory skill. *Bulletin of the Psychonomic Society, 29,* 304–306.

Baars, B. J., & Mattson, M. E. (1981). Consciousness and intentions: A framework and some evidence. *Cognition and Brain Theory, 4,* 247–263.

Baddeley, A. D., & Wilkins, A. (1984). Taking memory out of the laboratory. In J. E. Harris & P. E. Morris (Eds.), *Everyday memory, actions and absent-mindedness* (pp.1–17). London, England: Academic Press.

Banaji, M. R., & Crowder, R. G. (1989). The bankruptcy of everyday memory. *American Psychologist, 44,* 1185–1193.

Birenbaum, G. (1930). Das vergessen einer vorahme. *Psychologische Forschung, 13,* 218–284.

Blackburn, A. B., Lockhart, R. S., & Li, K. (1993, July). *Developing a cued prospective memory task to study involuntary recollection.* Paper presented at the meeting of the Experimental Psychology Society, Toronto.

Brand, M. (1984). *Intending and acting: Toward a naturalised action theory.* Cambridge, MA: MIT Press.

Brandimonte, M. (1991). Ricordare il futuro. *Giornale Italiano di Psicologia, 3,* 351–374.

Brandimonte, M. A., & Passolunghi, M. C. (1994). The effect of cue familiarity, cue-distinctiveness, and retention interval on prospective remembering. *The Quarterly Journal of Experimental Psychology.*

Cavanaugh, J. C., Grady, J. G., & Perlmutter, M. (1983). Forgetting and use of memory aids in 20 to 70 year olds' everyday life. *International Journal of Aging and Human Development, 17,* 113–122.

Ceci, S. J., Baker, J. G., & Bronfenbrenner, U. (1988). Prospective remembering, temporal calibration, and context. In M. M. Gruneberg, P. E. Morris, & R. N. Sykes (Eds.), *Practical aspects of memory: Current research and issues,* (Vol. 1, pp. 360–365). Chichester, England: Wiley.

Ceci, S. J., & Bronfenbrenner, U. (1985). "Don't forget to take the cupcakes out of the oven": prospective memory, strategic time-monitoring, and the context. *Child Development, 56,* 152–164.

Cockburn J. (1994). Task interruption in prospective memory: A frontal lobe function? *Cortex, 31,* 87–97.

Cockburn, J., & Smith, P. T. (1991a, July). *Differential performance on tests on prospective memory by elderly people living in the community and in residential care.* Paper presented at the International Conference on Memory, Lancaster, U.K.

Cockburn, J., & Smith, P. T. (1991b). The relative influence of intelligence and age on everyday memory. *Journal of Gerontology: Psychological Sciences, 46,* 31–36.

Cockburn, J., & Smith, P. T. (1994). Anxiety and errors of prospective memory in elderly people. *British Journal of Psychology, 85,* 273–282.

Cohen, G. (1989). *Memory in the real world.* Hillsdale, NJ: Lawrence Erlbaum Associates.

Cohen, G., & Faulkner, D. (1984). Memory in old age: "Good in parts". *New Scientist, 11 October,* 49–51.

Craik, F. I. M. (1986). A functional account of age differences in memory. In F. Klix & H. Hagendorf (Eds.), *Human memory and cognitive capabilities: Mechanisms and performances (Part A)* (pp. 409–422). Amsterdam: Elsevier Science.

Crovitz, H. F., & Daniel, W. F. (1984). Measurements of everyday memory: toward the prevention of forgetting. *Bulletin of the Psychonomic Society, 22,* 413–414.

Devolder, P. A., Brigham, M. C., & Pressley, M. (1990). Memory performance awareness in younger and older adults. *Psychology and Aging, 5,* 291–303.

Dobbs, A. R., & Rule, B. G.(1987). Prospective memory and self-reports of memory abilities in older adults. *Canadian Journal of Psychology, 41,* 209–222.

Einstein, G. O., Holland, L. J., McDaniel, M. A., & Guynn, M. J. (1992). Age-related deficits in prospective memory: The influence of task complexity. *Psychology and Aging, 7,* 471–478.

Einstein, G. O., & McDaniel, M. A. (1990). Normal aging and prospective memory. *Journal of Experimental Psychology: Learning, Memory and Cognition, 16,* 717–726.

Einstein, G. O., McDaniel, M. A., Cunfer, A. R., & Guynn, M. J. (1991, November). *Aging and time- versus event-based prospective memory.* Paper presented at the 32nd annual meeting of the Psychonomic Society, San Francisco, CA.

Ellis, J. A. (1988a). Memory for future intentions: Investigating pulses and steps. In M. M. Gruneberg, P. E. Morris, & R. N. Sykes (Eds.), *Practical aspects of memory: Current research and issues* (Vol.1, pp. 371–376). Chichester, England: Wiley.

Ellis, J. A. (1988b). *Memory for naturally occuring intentions.* Unpublished doctoral dissertaion, Cambridge University.

Ellis, J. A. (1991, July). An eclectic approach to the study of prospective memory tasks. Paper presented at the International Conference on Memory, Lancaster, U.K.

Ellis, J. A., & Milne, A. B. (1992a, July). *The effects of retrieval cue specificity on prospective memory performance.* Paper presented at the meeting of the Experimental Psychology Society, York. Manuscript submitted for publication.

Ellis, J. A., & Milne, A. B. (1992b, December). *Memory for naturally-occuring intentions: Remembering what you have done and what you have to do.* Paper presented at the London meeting of the British Psychological Society, City University.

Ellis, J. A., & Nimmo-Smith, I. (1993). Recollecting naturally occurring intentions: A study of cognitive and affective factors. *Memory, 1,* 107–126.

Ellis, J. A. & Williams, J. M. G. (1990, April). *Retrospective and prospective remembering: common and distinct processes.* Paper presented at the Experimental Psychology Society, Manchester. Manuscript in preparation.

Fishbein, M., & Ajzen, I. (1975). *Belief, attitude, intention, and behavior: An introduction to theory and research.* Reading, MA: Addison-Wesley.

Freud, S. (1901). *The Psychopathology of everyday life.* London, England: Penguin.

Furst, C. (1986). The memory derby: Evaluating and remediating intention memory. *Cognitive Rehabilitation, 4,* 24–26.

Gauld, A., & Shotter, J. (1977). *Human action and its psychological investigation.* London, England: Routledge.

Goschke, T., & Kuhl, J. (1993). Representation of intentions: Persisting activation in memory. *Journal of Experimental Psychology: Learning, Memory and Cognition, 19,* 1211–1226.

Harré, R. (1982). Theoretical preliminaries to the study of action. In M. von Cranach & R. Harré (Eds.), *The analysis of action: Recent theoretical and empirical advances* (pp. 5–34). Cambridge, England: Cambridge University Press.

Harris, J. E. (1984). Remembering to do things: A forgotten topic. In J. E. Harris & P. E. Morris (Eds.), *Everyday memory, actions and absent-mindedness* (pp. 71–92). London, England: Academic Press.

Harris, J. E., & Sunderland, A. (1981). Effects of age and instructions on an everyday memory questionnaire. *Bulletin of the British Psychological Society, 35,* 212.

Harris, J. E., & Wilkins, A. J. (1982). Remembering to do things: A theoretical framework and an illustrative experiment. *Human Learning, 1,* 123–136.

Heckhausen, H., & Beckmann, J. (1990). Intentional action and action slips. *Psychological Review, 97,* 36–48.

Heckhausen, H., & Kuhl, J. (1985). From wishes to action: The dead ends and short cuts on the long way to action. In M. Frese & J. Sabini (Eds.), *Goal-directed behavior: Psychological theory and research on action* (pp. 134–160), Hillsdale, NJ: Lawrence Erlbaum Associates.

Herrmann, D., & Neisser, U. (1978). An inventory of everyday memory experiences. In M. M. Gruneberg, P. E. Morris, & R. N. Sykes (Eds.), *Practical aspects of memory* (pp. 52–60). New York: Academic Press.

James, W. (1890). *The principles of psychology*. New York: Holt, Rinehart & Winston.

Koriat, A., & Ben-Zur, H. (1988). Remembering that I did it: Processes and deficits in output monitoring. In M. M. Gruneberg, P. E. Morris, & R. N. Sykes (Eds.), *Practical aspects of memory: Current research and issues* (Vol. 1, pp. 203–208). Chichester, England: Wiley.

Koriat, A., Ben-Zur, H., & Sheffer, D. (1988). Telling the same story twice: Output monitoring and age. *Journal of Memory and Language, 27*, 23–39.

Kreutzer, M. A., Leonard, C., & Flavell, J. H. (1982). Prospective remembering in children. In U. Neisser (Ed.), *Memory observed: Remembering in natural contexts* (pp. 343–348). San Francisco: Freeman.

Kuhl, J. (1985). Volitional mediators of cognition-behavior consistency: Self-regulatory processes and action versus state orientation. In J. Kuhl & J. Beckmann (Eds.), *Action control: From cognition to behavior* (pp. 101–128). Berlin: Springer-Verlag.

Kvavilashvili, L. (1987). Remembering intention as a distinct form of memory. *British Journal of Psychology, 78*, 507–518.

Kvavilashvili, L. (1990). *Remembering/forgetting intention as a distinct form of memory and the factors that influence it*. Tbilisi, Russia: Metsniereba.

Kvavilashvili, L. (1992a). Intention, set and volitional behaviour. *MATSNE: Series in Philosophy and Psychology, 1*, 40–68.

Kvavilashvili, L. (1992b). Remembering intentions: A critical review of existing experimental paradigms. *Applied Cognitive Psychology, 6*, 507–524.

Kvavilashvili, L. (1993, December). *Remembering intentions: Testing a new method of investigation*. Paper presented at the London Conference of the British Psychological Society, London.

Levy, R. L. (1977). Relationship of an overt commitment to task compliance in behavior therapy. *Journal of Behaviour Therapy and Experimental Psychiatry, 8*, 25–29.

Levy, R. L., & Claravall, V. (1977). Differential effects of a phone reminder on patients with long and short between-visit intervals. *Medical Care, 15*, 435–438.

Levy, R. L., & Clark, H. (1980). The use of an overt commitment to enhance compliance: A cautionary note. *Journal of Behavior Therapy and Experimental Psychiatry, 11*, 105–107.

Levy, R. L., & Loftus, G. R. (1984). Compliance and memory. In J. E. Harris & P. E. Morris (Eds.) *Everyday memory, actions and absent-mindedness* (pp. 93–112). London, England: Academic Press.

Lewin, K. (1951). Intention, will, and need. In D. Rapaport (Ed. and Trans.), *Organization of and pathology of thought*. New York: Columbia University Press. (Original work pulished 1926)

Loftus, E. (1971). Memory for intentions: The effect of presence of a cue and interpolated activity. *Psychonomic Science, 23*, 315–316.

Lovelace, E. A., & Twohig, P. T. (1990). Healthy older adults' perceptions of their memory functioning and use of mnemonics. *Bulletin of the Psychonomic Society, 28*, 115–118.

Mäntylä, T. (1993). Priming effects in prospective memory. *Memory, 1*, 203–218.

Martin, M. (1986). Aging and patterns of change in everyday memory and cognition. *Human Learning, 5*, 63–74.

Mateer, C. A., & Sohlberg, M. M. (1988). Paradigm shift in memory rehabilitation. In H. Witaker (Ed.), *Neuropsychological studies of nonfocal brain damage* (pp. 202–225). New York: Springer-Verlag.

Mateer, C. A., Sohlberg, M. M., & Crinean, J. (1987). Perceptions of memory functions in individuals with closed head injury. *Journal of Head Trauma Rehabilitation, 2*, 74–84.

Maylor, E. (1990). Age and prospective memory. *Quarterly Journal of Experimental Psychology, 42A*, 471–493.

Maylor, E. (1993a). Aging and forgetting in prospective and retrospective memory tasks. *Psychology and Aging, 3*, 420–428.

Maylor, E. (1993b). Minimized prospective memory loss in old age. In J. Cerella, J. Rybash,

W. Hoyer, & M. L. Commons (Eds.), *Adult information processing: Limits on loss* (pp. 529–551). San Diego. CA: Academic Press.

McDaniel, M. A., & Einstein, G. O. (1992). Aging and prospective memory: Basic findings and practical applications. In T. E. Scruggs & M. A. Mastropieri (Eds.), *Advances in learning and behavioral disabilities: Vol. 7* (pp. 87–105). Greenwich, CT: JAI Press.

McDaniel, M. A., & Einstein, G. O. (1993). The importance of cue familiarity and cue distinctiveness in prospective memory. *Memory, 1,* 23–41.

McDaniel, M. A., Waddill, P. J., & Einstein, G. O. (1988). A contextual account of the generation effect: A three-factor theory. *Journal of Memory and Language, 27,* 521–536.

McKitrick, L. A., Camp, C., & Black, F. W. (1992). Prospective memory intervention in Alzheimer's disease. *Journal of Gerontology: Psychological Sciences, 47,* 337–343.

Meacham, J. A. (1982). A note on remembering to execute planned actions. *Journal of Applied Developmental Psychology, 3,* 121–133.

Meacham, J. A. (1988). Interpersonal relations and prospective remembering. In M. M. Gruneberg, P. E. Morris, & R. N. Sykes (Eds.), *Practical aspects of memory: Current research and issues* (Vol. 1, pp. 354–359). Chichester, England: Wiley.

Meacham, J. A., & Colombo, J. A. (1980). External retrieval cues facilitate prospective remembering in children. *Journal of Educational Research, 73,* 299–301.

Meacham, J. A., & Dumitru, J. (1976). Prospective remembering and external retrieval cues. *Catalog of Selected Documents in Psychology, 6,* No. 65 (Ms. No. 1284).

Meacham, J. A., & Kushner, S. (1980). Anxiety, prospective remembering, and performance of planned actions. *Journal of General Psychology, 103,* 203–209.

Meacham, J. A., & Leiman, B. (1975). *Remembering to perform future actions.* Paper presented at the meeting of the American Psychological association. Chicago, September. Also in U. Neisser (Ed.), *Memory observed* (pp. 327–336). San Francisco: Freeman.

Meacham, J. A., & Singer, J. (1977). Incentive effects in prospective remembering. *Journal of Psychology, 97,* 191–197.

Miller, G. A., Galanter, E., & Pribram, K. H. (1960). *Plans and structure of behavior.* New York: Holt.

Mook, D. G. (1983). In defence of external invalidity. *American Psychologist, 38,* 379–387.

Mook, D. G. (1989). The myth of external validity. In L. W. Poon, D. C. Rubin, & B. A. Wilson (Eds.), *Everyday cognition in adulthood and late life* (pp. 25–43). Cambridge, England: Cambridge University Press.

Morris, P. E. (1992). Prospective memory: Remembering to do things. In M. Gruneberg & P. Morris (Eds.), *Aspects of memory: Vol. 1,* (pp. 196–222). London, England: Routledge.

Moscovitch, M. (1982). A neuropsychological approach to memory and perception in normal and pathological aging. In F. I. M. Craik & S. Trehub (Eds.), *Aging and cognitive processes* (pp. 55–78). New York: Plenum.

Norman, D. A. (1981). Categorization of action slips. *Psychological Review, 88,* 1–15.

Nuttin, J. R. (1987). The respective roles of cognition and motivation in behavioral dynamics, intention and volition. In F. Halisch & J. Kuhl (Eds.), *Motivation, intention and volition* (pp. 309–321). Berlin: Springer-Verlag.

Oatley, K., & Johnson-Laird, P. L. (1987). Towards a cognitive theory of emotions. *Cognition and Emotion, 1,* 29–50.

Patton, G. W. R., & Meit, M. (1993). Effect of aging on prospective and incidental memory. *Experimental Aging Research, 19,* 165–176.

Payne, S. J. (1993). Understanding calendar use. *Human-Computer Interaction, 8,* 83–100.

Poon, L. W., & Schaffer, G. (1982, August). *Prospective memory in young and elderly adults.* Paper presented at the meeting of the American Psychological Association, Washington, DC.

Reason, J. T. (1979). Actions not as planned: The price of automatisation. In G. Underwood & R. Stevens (Eds.), *Aspects of consciousness: Vol. 1,* (pp. 67–90). London, England: Academic Press.

Reason, J. (1984). Absent-mindedness and cognitive control. In J. E. Harris & P. E. Morris (Eds), *Everyday memory, actions and absent-mindedness* (pp. 113–132). London, England: Academic Press.

Searle, J. R. (1983). *Intentionality: An essay in the philosophy of mind*. Cambridge, England: Cambridge University Press.

Sellen, A., Louiel, G., Harris, J. E., & Wilkins, A. J. (1993, July). *Thinking about and remembering intentions*. Paper presented at the meeting of Experimental Psychology Society, Toronto.

Shallice, T., & Burgess, P. (1991). Deficits in strategy application following frontal lobe damage in man. *Brain, 114*, 727–741.

Shepard, D. S., & Moseley, T. A. (1976). Mailed vs. telephoned appointment reminders to reduce broken appointments in a hospital outpatient department. *Medical Care, 14*, 268–273.

Sinnott, J. D. (1989). Prospective/intentional memory and aging: Memory as adaptive action. In L. W. Poon, D. C. Rubin, & B. A. Wilson (Eds.), *Everyday cognition in adulthood and late life* (pp. 352–372). Cambridge, England: Cambridge University Press.

Slamecka, N. J., & Graf, P. (1978). The generation effect: Delineation of a phenomenon. *Journal of Experimental Psychology: Human Learning and Memory, 4*, 592–604.

Sohlberg, M. M., White, O., Evans, E., & Mateer, C. (1992a). Background and initial case studies into effects of prospective memory training. *Brain Injury, 6*, 129–138.

Sohlberg, M. M., White, O., Evans, E., & Mateer, C. A. (1992b). An investigation of the effects of prospective memory training. *Brain Injury, 6*, 139–154.

Somerville, S. C., Wellman, H. M., & Cultice, J. C. (1983). Young children's deliberate reminding. *Journal of Genetic Psychology, 143*, 87–96.

Sunderland, A., Watts, K., Baddeley, A. D., & Harris, J. E. (1986). Subjective memory assessment and task performance in elderly adults. *Journal of Gerontology, 41*, 376–384.

Terry, W. S. (1988). Everyday forgetting: Data from a diary study. *Psychological reports, 62*, 299–303.

Tuomela, R. (1977). *Human action and its explanation: A study on philosophical foundations of psychology*. Dordrecht: Reidel.

Vortac, O. U., Edwards, M. B., Fuller, D. K., & Manning, C. A. (1993). Automation and cognition in air traffic control: An empirical investigation. *Applied Cognitive Psychology, 7*, 631–651.

West, R. L. (1984, August). *An analysis of prospective everyday memory*. Paper presented at the meeting of the American Psychological Association, Toronto.

West, R. L. (1988). Prospective memory and aging. In M. M. Gruneberg, P. E. Morris, & R. N. Sykes (Eds.), *Practical aspects of memory: Current research and issues* (Vol. 2, pp. 119–125). Chichester, England: Wiley.

Wichman, H., & Oyasato, A. (1983). Effects of locus of control and task complexity on prospective remembering. *Human Factors, 25*, 583–591.

Wilkins, A. J. (1986). Remembering to do things in the laboratory and everyday life. *Acta Neurologica Scandinavica, 74 (Suppl. 109)*, 109–112.

Wilkins, A. J., & Baddeley, A. D. (1978). Remembering to recall in everyday life: An approach to absent-mindedness. In M. M. Gruneberg, P. E. Morris (Eds.), *Practical aspects of memory* (pp. 27–34). New York: Academic Press.

Winograd, E. (1988a). Continuities between ecological and laboratory approaches to memory. In U. Neisser & E. Winograd (Eds.), *Remembering reconsidered: Ecological and traditional approaches to memory* (pp. 11–20). Cambridge, England: Cambridge University Press.

Winograd, E. (1988b). Some observations on prospective remembering. In M. M. Gruneberg, P. E. Morris, & R. N. Sykes (Eds.), *Practical aspects of memory: Current research and issues* (Vol.1, pp. 348–353). Chichester, England: Wiley.

3

Remembering What to Do: Explicit and Implicit Memory for Intentions

Thomas Goschke
Julius Kuhl
University of Osnabrück

When we form an intention like the one to mail an important letter, usually the intended activity cannot be executed immediately. Instead, most of our intentions have to be postponed until an adequate opportunity for their execution occurs. As Freud put it, "the intention slumbers on in the person concerned until the time for its execution approaches. Then it awakes and impels him to perform the action" (1952, p. 79). However, the intuitive plausibility of this metaphorical description can hardly conceal the fact that very little is known about the representation of intentions in memory and the conditions that determine their activation and retrieval. Despite an increasing interest in *prospective memory* for future actions, of which the present volume gives testimony, the field is still aptly described by a quote from Morris (1979, p. 161), who noted more than a decade ago that "our knowledge of how we remember what we intend doing is virtually non-existent." There is a particular lack of controlled experiments on the representation of intentions and integrative theoretical frameworks for organizing the empirical findings.

The successful execution of intentions, especially when they have to be postponed for longer durations, involves at least two memory skills: we must remember at the right moment or in response to the right cue that we have to do something, and we have to recall what has to be done, that is, a representation of the intended activity has to be retrieved. We may speak of a *prospective* and a *retrospective* component of intention memory (cf. Einstein & McDaniel, 1990; Ellis & Williams, 1990; Kvavilashvili, 1987). Research on prospective memory to date primarily focuses on the prospective aspect of intention memory, that is, on the question of whether or not participants remember to perform an activity at the right time or in response to the right cue. We focused on the retrospective aspect, that is, on the representation of the content of intentions.

In this chapter, we summarize some results of a research program in which we made attempts to investigate memory for intentions under laboratory conditions and to develop a theoretical framework to integrate research on intention memory in a more general theory of action control (see Goschke, in press-a, in press-b; Kuhl, 1983, 1986, 1992, 1994b; Kuhl & Goschke, 1994b; Kuhl & Kazén-Saad, 1988, for more comprehensive expositions of our theoretical framework). We focus on three questions:

1. Are memory representations of intentions characterized by a special persistence, that is, by an increased or more sustained level of activation as compared to other memory contents?
2. Do intentions facilitate the subsequent processing of intention-related information even if the representation of the intention is not consciously recollected?
3. Are there systematic individual differences that moderate the representation and activation of intentions in memory?

INTENTIONS AND THEIR MENTAL REPRESENTATION

Prospective Memory and Intentional Action

Prospective memory is intimately related to the concept of intentional action. Ever since James' famous chapter on the will, numerous theorists have stressed that willed or intentional action involves an "anticipation of the movement's sensible effects, resident or remote" (James, 1890, p. 521; cf. Kimble & Perlmuter, 1970; Münsterberg, 1889; von Holst & Mittelstaedt, 1950). The ability to mentally represent effects and outcomes of actions is what distinguishes intentional action from reflex behavior and simpler forms of motivated or goal-directed behavior (cf. Brand, 1984; Bratman, 1987; Gallistel, 1985; Goschke, in press-b; Hershberger, 1989; Kuhl, 1986). Internal representations of intended actions are the basis for the ability to choose among mentally represented action alternatives and to recombine skills into new action plans by means of mental simulation.

When we speak of memory for intentions, it is presupposed that having an intention involves an internal representation of the intended action, and that this representation plays a specific role in the causation of behavior. For instance, when I intend to raise my arm, I have a mental representation with the semantic content "the arm raises," and this representation has the functional or causal role of an intention (in contrast to a belief or a wish). In this context, intentions are often distinguished from other mental states by referring to the fact that the individual is committed to the execution of a particular course of action (as opposed to merely wishing or desiring a goal state; cf. Brand, 1984; Heckhausen & Kuhl, 1985; Klinger, 1987; Kuhl, 1983).[1]

Intentions may exert their causal effects on the control of actions in different ways. When an intended action can be realized by automatized routine skills, and when all parameters of the intended activity are sufficiently specified, a stimulus may trigger the action without the intervening retrieval of a conscious representation of the intention (Ach, 1935; Goschke, in press-b; Neumann, 1989). For instance, choice reaction experiments showed that simple intended actions (e.g., to press the right or the left key depending on which of two stimuli is flashed on the monitor) can be be triggered by the stimulus without mediation of a conscious recollection of the intention (Neumann & Klotz, 1994). Such cases can be explained by assuming that the intention directly sets stored action schemas or skills into a state of readiness, such that they will be automatically activated when their trigger conditions are satisfied (cf. Norman & Shallice, 1986). Intentions thus establish a transient coupling of specific connections between execution conditions and action schemas (Neumann & Prinz, 1987; cf. Ach's, 1910, 1935, concept of a *determining tendency;* see also Anderson, 1983, for a similar view of intentions as condition–action–rules). In terms of the popular distinction between automatic and controlled processes (e.g., Posner & Snyder, 1975; Schneider & Shiffrin, 1977) the action is performed automatically. However, in contrast to the traditional definition of automaticity, many actions, even if they are directly triggered by a stimulus, nevertheless depend on the prior formation of an intention. For example, even for a skilled piano player sitting in front of a piano, the perception of a partitur will not trigger finger movements in a reflexive manner, if he or she does not have the intention to perform the piece. Thus, most automatic actions are dependent on prior intentions, that is, they are not uncontrolled,

---

[1]This analysis presupposes a particular philosophical view of intentional terms in general. According to this view, to be in an intentional state (e.g., to have a belief, desire, or intention) means that one has a mental representation that plays a specific functional or causal role in the causation of behavior or other mental states. In other words, intentional states are explained in terms of concrete, causally efficacious, internal states with a specific semantic content. Unfortunately, this view raises a number of intricate philosophical problems surrounding the concept of mental representation, the nature of propositional attitudes, and the semantic content of internal states (e.g., Cummins, 1989; Dennett, 1987; Fodor, 1987; Goschke & Koppelberg, 1991). In particular, some philosophers argued against such a realistic view of intentional terms. They argued that intentional terms should better be conceived of as interpretative ascriptions, which we make from a third-person perspective in order to render the observed behavior of others meaningful, but do not necessarily correspond to concrete internal representational states (cf. Dennett, 1987). Due to space limitations, we cannot discuss these problems in more detail in the present chapter.

but controlled in a specific way (Bargh, 1989; Goschke, in press-a, in press-b; Logan, 1988; Neumann, 1984). We speak of *procedural intentions* in such cases.

The situation is quite different when the execution of an intention has to be postponed for longer durations, and concrete parameters of the intended action cannot be specified in advance, or when the intention cannot be realized by already stored skills (for instance, when one intends to write a book chapter next month). In such cases, the intention cannot directly set concrete action schemas in a state of readiness, but its realization requires that details of the concrete actions are specified by further planning or problem solving (cf. Neumann, 1987, 1989). Consequently, an abstract representation of the intention will be stored in declarative memory, and this representation will have to be retrieved before concrete actions can be performed. We speak of *declarative intentions* in such cases.

Kuhl (1983, 1986; cf. Dörner, 1986) proposed a propositional network model in which representations of intentions in declarative memory consist of four components: A subject node represents the agent of the action ("I"); a context node represents the execution conditions of the action; an object node represents the action plan; an relation node represents the intentional modus of the action ("I will" in contrast to "I wish" or "I can").

In the experiments to be described, we focus on intentions, represented in declarative memory in the form of *verbal instructions*. Ach (1910) concluded on the basis of introspective evidence, that the content of what he called *primary acts of the will* often consist of inner speech. The eminent significance of verbal regulation of action was stressed by Luria (1961) and Vygotski (1962), according to whom the ability to control one's actions by internalized verbal instructions is a crucial step in the development of intentional action (see Diaz & Berk, 1992). The emergence of linguistic representations of goals and intentions is a precondition for the ability to persist in pursuing long-term goals and to decouple actions from immediate stimuli and internal need states (cf. Kuhl & Kraska, 1989).

The fact that intentions can be represented in declarative memory like other knowledge has the additional important implication that the selection and execution of actions does not always depend on explicit decision processes. Rather, the probability that a stored intention will be retrieved depends, like that of other memory structures, on the presence of adequate retrieval cues and on the current activation of the intention representation. The more the execution conditions of an intention match with the current stimulus situation, or the more strongly the activational strength of an intention becomes, the higher the probability that the intention will be retrieved. Consequently, a previously formed intention in declarative memory may be activated by retrieval cues and then guide the current selection of actions, even if the individual does not engage in an explicit decision-making process of weighing values and expectancies. In other words, by storing intentions in declarative memory, the results of a prior decision can constrain the later selection of actions in the absence of a novel decision process. This implies an important qualification of the assumption inherent in many motivational theories, that at any point an individual will perform the action alternative that is associated with the maximal subjective utility (cf. Atkinson, 1957; Feather, 1982; Heckhausen, 1977). In our view, the selection of action is determined both by the outcome of explicit, prior decision processes and by the currently present retrieval cues. Motivational theories like Atkinson's (1957) risk-taking model have primarily focused on situations in which participants had to choose from a number of action alternatives on the basis of explicitly defined values and expectancies, and in which they had to immediately execute the chosen action alternative. By contrast, the longer the time interval between the formation of an intention and its execution, the stronger becomes the impact of memory mechanisms that are unrelated to the motivational strength of action alternatives.

The adaptive value of such a memory-based selection of actions becomes obvious if we take into account that individuals have to select and execute actions in a world in which it is not possible to perform, at each point in time, an exhaustive weighing of all action alternatives on the basis of the subjective values and probabilities of all of their anticipated consequences. Because decision making costs time and resources, it is necessary to terminate decision processes at some point and to commit to the chosen course of action (Goschke, in press-a; Kuhl, 1983). To a certain degree "intention resists reconsideration: it has a characteristic *stability* or *inertia*" (Bratman, 1987, p. 16).[2]

That intentions may have a special functional status in memory was stressed in motivational psychology in a number of new theories of volition, explicitly containing the assumption that the effects of intentions on subsequent information processing and behavior are partially independent from the values and expectancies that initially led to the formation of the intention (Kuhl, 1982, 1983, 1986; cf. Gollwitzer, 1989; Heckhausen & Kuhl, 1985). This brings us directly to the central topic of the present chapter—the specific persistence of intentions.

Persistence of Intentions

One frequently noted property of intentions is their persistence. Lewin (1926) used the term *tension system* to describe the observation that intentions attach valences ("Aufforderungsgehalte") to objects in the environment that persist until the intended goal has been attained. If the execution of an intended

---

[2]This does not, of course, imply that it is impossible to revise an intention when this is demanded by changes in the situation or in our goal hierarchy (see Dibbelt, 1993; Goschke, in press-b, for a discussion of the problem of maintenance versus revision of intentions).

action is interrupted, the tension cannot discharge, producing a tendency to resume the activity if possible (Ovsiankina, 1928). Most important for the present topic, Lewin (1926) assumed that the persisting *task tension* should also show up in better recall of unfinished in contrast to completed activities (see also Mäntylä, this volume).[3] This hypothesis was put to empirical test by Lewin's coworker Zeigarnik (1927) in her well-known task interruption experiments. Zeigarnik demonstrated that participants who had been working on a series of simple activities showed superior recall of activities that were interrupted prior to completion as compared to completed actions. Although these results seemed to provide clear evidence for the assumption that incomplete intentions produce a persisting task tension, task interruption research was critized for conceptual and methodological shortcomings. In fact, the numerous studies that were performed in order to replicate the original findings of Zeigarnik produced a remarkably inconsistent pattern of results (for reviews see Butterfield, 1964; Hörmann, 1964; Ryan, 1970; van Bergen, 1968). The frustration expressed in these reviews has probably been responsible for the almost total decline of task interruption research.

On the other hand, more recent research on memory for intentions, which has been carried out under the heading of prospective memory, almost exclusively focused on what we termed the prospective aspect of intention memory at the beginning of this chapter. The major question was whether or not participants remember to perform an activity at the right time or in response to an adequate cue. Thus, the dependent variables in typical prospective memory studies were the frequency or punctuality with which individuals perform simple activities like mailing postcards at the right time (for review see Baddeley & Wilkins, 1984; Cohen, 1989; Harris, 1984). Although this is an interesting and important question, these studies tell us little about the representation and activation of the content of the intention during the retention interval. In fact, there is almost no research on how the declarative content of intentions is represented and whether or not representations of intentions may be characterized by special dynamic properties. This research bias towards the prospective aspect of intention memory reflects a widespread assumption among memory researchers, according to which "mechanisms responsible for the forgetting of names, faces, nonsense syllables, words, and other material traditionally studied in the laboratory are also responsible for the forgetting of intentions" (Loftus, 1971, p. 316).

One notable exception was a study by Koriat, Ben-Zur, and Nussbaum (1990), who made a more direct attempt to investigate memory for the content of intentions. They found that simple activities that had been learned for later per-

---

[3]The concept of tension systems and the analogy between intentions and (quasi-)needs was critized on conceptual and methodological grounds (see Goschke, in press-a; Kuhl, 1983; Miller, Galanter, & Pribram, 1960; Ryan, 1970; van Bergen, 1968; for discussions). We return to the conceptual issues surrounding the term persistence in the final part of this chapter.

formance, were better recalled in an unexpected memory test than activities that had been learned for later recall. This effect can be attributed to different encoding strategies, because subjects were informed before the study phase whether they had to perform or to recall an activity. Thus, the question remains open whether the superior recall of to-be-performed activities reflects an intrinsic dynamic property of intentions or whether it is due the voluntary use of encoding strategies.

In conclusion, the available evidence on task interruption and prospective memory leaves open several questions about memory for the content of intentions. When starting our own research program on intention memory, we focused on four issues, to be dealt with in the following sections of this chapter.

1. Are representations of intended activities characterized by a higher or more sustained level of activation as compared to representations of nonintended activities, and if so, does this persisting activation result from the voluntary use of memory strategies, or does it reflect an intrinsic property of intentions to function as source nodes (Anderson, 1983; section 3)?

2. Do intentions facilitate the retrieval and processing of intention-related material, even if the intention is not consciously recollected? This question, derived from ideas in older theories of volition in the Würzburg school (e.g., Ach, 1910, 1935), was investigated with an implicit memory paradigm (section 4).

3. Are there systematic individual differences with respect to the activation and persistence of intentions? In particular, we focused on a personality disposition towards *action* versus *state orientation* (Kuhl, 1984, 1985, 1994b; Kuhl & Beckmann, 1994; section 5).

4. Finally, we performed two studies to investigate the spontaneous recall of real-life intentions and wishes in order to investigate the effect of variables like realizability, importance, and urgency on the recall of everyday intentions and wishes (section 6).

In the next sections, we first describe empirical findings pertinent to each of these questions. In our final discussion, we discuss the mechanisms and functions of implicit and explicit forms of intention memory and try to integrate our empirical results into a more general theoretical framework.

EXPLICIT MEMORY FOR INTENTIONS

The main purpose of the studies described in this section was to measure the activation of representations of intentions during the retention interval between the formation of the intention and the execution of the intended activity. These experiments were based on the assumption that—other factors being equal—the activation of a memory structure is directly related to the time it takes to match a probe item to the corresponding structure in long-term memory (cf. Anderson, 1983; Ratcliff & McKoon, 1978). If representations of uncompleted intentions are characterized by a more sustained or higher level of subthreshold activation in long-term memory (see also Einstein & McDaniel, this volume), intention-related material should be recognized faster than neutral material. This should hold even when the use of controlled rehearsal strategies is prevented.

The Postponed-Intention Paradigm

In order to investigate the activation of intention-related memory contents under controlled conditions, we developed a *postponed-intention paradigm* (Goschke, in press-a; Goschke & Kuhl, 1993). In a study phase, subjects had to learn a pair of two short texts describing two simple actions to a fixed learning criterion (e.g., setting a dinner table, cleaning up a messy desk, removing garbage, dressing up for leaving). Each of these "scripts" consisted of four component actions (e.g., light the candles). Before the study, subjects were informed that their memory for words from both scripts would be tested in a recognition test.

Secondly, depending on the experimental condition, subjects received one of two instructions. In the execution condition, subjects were informed that they would have to execute one of the scripts later, whereas in the observation condition they were instructed to observe the experimenter performing one of the scripts and to register possible mistakes. That is, in the execution condition one of the learned scripts was made the object of an intention to execute the corresponding action sequence. The second script of a given pair served as a control in both conditions. We call the to-be-executed or the to-be-observed script the *prospective script,* and the control script, that had to be remembered only, the *neutral script.* Note that subjects were instructed *before* the study phase that their recognition memory for both scripts would be tested irrespective of whether a script had to be executed, to be observed, or merely to be remembered. Each subject went through an execution and an observation condition. The order of conditions, the assignment of the script pairs to each condition, and the assignment of a script as the prospective versus the neutral one was counterbalanced across subjects.

Thirdly, immediately after the execution or observation instruction, a word recognition test started. In this test, subjects were presented a list of words, one at a time, on the computer screen and they had to decide for each word, whether it had appeared in one of the two studied scripts. One half of the words were taken from the study scripts, whereas the other one half were new words. One half of the distractor words were semantically related to either the prospective or the neutral script. Thus, it was not possible to discriminate old and

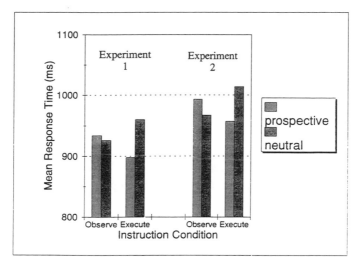

FIG. 3.1. Mean recognition latencies for prospective and neutral words in the observation and execution conditions of Experiments 1 and 2.

new words simply on the basis of their semantic relatedness to the study scripts, but subjects had to engage in genuine fact retrieval (cf. Reder, 1982).

Finally, after the recognition test, subjects had to actually execute or observe the prospective script. Subjects were not reminded as to which script was to-be-executed or to-be-performed and only subjects who correctly remembered the prospective script were included in the analyses.

Our major prediction was that if intention representations persist in a state of high activation, recognition latencies for words from the to-be-executed script should be shorter than words from the to-be-remembered script. In the observation condition, in which subjects did not have to execute a script by themselves, no such difference was expected, because in this condition the representation of the prospective script was not the object of an execution intention.[4]

The Intention-Superiority Effect

In our first two experiments with the postponed-intention paradigm, 30 and 60 undergraduates from the University of Osnabrück served as subjects, respectively. Figure 3.1 shows mean recognition latencies for correct responses

---

[4]The prospective script in the observation condition might nevertheless have been the object of an intention, namely to observe someone else performing the activity. However, our point is that it makes all the difference whether or not an action representation is the object of an intention to execute the activity by oneself. Only in the former case did we expect higher activation of the script representation in memory.

to neutral and prospective words in the execution and observation condition. In both experiments there were virtually no differences in response times for neutral and prospective words in the observation condition. By contrast, in the execution condition, prospective (i.e., intention-related) words were recognized reliably faster than were neutral words. This pattern of results was confirmed in an analysis of variance (ANOVA), which yielded a reliable interaction of script (prospective vs. neutral) and instruction (execution vs. observation). Planned comparisons revealed that in both experiments, the only reliable difference was between neutral and prospective words in the execution condition. An analysis of the nonparametric discriminability index A' (Pollack, 1970; Pollack & Norman, 1964) yielded analogous results: In the execution condition, intention-related words were recognized with higher sensitivity than neutral words.

In summary, in our first two experiments, words from action scripts that had to be executed at a later time were recognized faster and more accurately than words from scripts that had to be memorized only. By contrast, the instruction to observe someone else executing a script had no reliable effects on recognition latencies or error rates. Under the assumption that recognition latencies reflect the level of activation of concepts in memory (cf. Anderson, 1983), these results indicate that the representation of an intended action persists in a state of heightened subthreshold activation for a longer duration as compared to neutral material (see also Einstein & McDaniel, this volume).[5]

In our third experiment (Goschke & Kuhl, 1993), we investigated the time course of intention activation over a longer duration.[6] We extended the duration of the recognition test by repeating the whole set of test items up to eight times in different random orders. This way, we could measure recognition performance over a period of approximately 10 to 15 min (depending on the subject's speed in responding). The general procedure was identical to that of the previous experiments, with the exception that subjects were not explicitly cued as to when to stop the recognition test and when to start with the execution or observation of the prospective script. They were instructed to interrupt the recognition test by themselves when they felt that 15 min had passed.

For each subject, we computed mean response times for an equal number

---

[5]Note, that by persisting activation we mean higher or more sustained activation of intention-related memory contents relative to other, equally well-learned contents in a given condition. This relative advantage of intention-related contents could in principle be due to either heightened activation of intention-related contents, inhibition of unrelated material, or a mixture of both activation and inhibition. It is difficult to tell from the data which possibility is correct. As there was both a slowing of responses to neutral items as well as faster responses to prospective items in the execution condition, it may be both activation and inhibition. However, as we do not know whether the execution and observation condition were—for whatever reason—associated with different baselines, we prefer to interpret primarily the relative differences between neutral and prospective words in both conditions.

[6]This experiment was performed by Arno Fuhrmann as part of his diploma thesis.

TABLE 3.1

Mean Recognition Latencies for Prospective and Neutral Words
From the Initial, Center and Final List Interval in
the Execution and Observation Conditions

	List interval		
Condition	Initial	Center	Final
Execution			
prospective	937	807	756
neutral	1012	818	803
Observation			
prospective	951	809	791
neutral	951	837	811

of neutral and prospective words from the beginning, the center, and the end of the recognition test list. These means are shown separately for the execution and observation conditions in Table 3.1. Recognition latencies dramatically decreased as a function of the test interval, attributable to the fact that the same pool of test items was repeated several times. As in our previous experiments, there were virtually no differences between neutral and prospective words in the observation condition. By contrast, in the execution condition, subjects recognized prospective words in the first list interval reliably faster than neutral words. In the center interval, prospective and neutral words did not differ from each other. However, at the end of the test list, that is, immediately before subjects initiated the intended activity, intention-related words were again recognized faster than neutral words.

On a descriptive level, this pattern of results indicates that intention-related memory contents initially have a heightened level of activation, but nevertheless decay (albeit at a slower rate than neutral contents) until they reach a resting level not different from that of neutral items. Intention-related items were again recognized faster than neutral items in the final list interval. This suggests that the activation of the intention representation rises again shortly before the subject actually initiates the intended activity.[7]

This description of results should be taken with caution, however, because in an ANOVA computed for the execution condition, only the main effect of

---

[7]It may be noteworthy that this pattern of latencies at different points during the retention interval resembles the overt time-monitoring behavior of subjects observed in some prospective memory studies (e.g., Ceci et al., 1988; Harris & Wilkins, 1982). Subjects who had to perform simple activities at prespecified times made most time checks at the beginning of the retention interval and immediately before executing the activity. Whether or not there is a causal relation between overt time-monitoring and internal activation of the intention (e.g., whether or not external time monitoring behavior reflects increases in the activation of the internal intention representation), is an interesting but open question.

script (neutral vs. prospective) was reliable, whereas the interaction between list interval and script was at best marginally reliable. Thus, if one prefers a more conservative interpretation, the results of our third experiment support the reliability of the intention-superiority even over a markedly longer retention interval. The interpretation of the specific time course of the intention activation, however, is merely suggestive at present.

Automatic Persistence or Voluntary Rehearsal of Uncompleted Intentions?

A number of methodological advantages of our postponed-intention paradigm as compared to the task interruption methodology (Zeigarnik, 1927) are noteworthy. We did not interrupt our subjects while they were performing an activity, but tested memory performance after the induction and before the execution of an intention. We thus unconfounded the specific effect of the intentional status of an action from unspecific effects of an interruption on subjects' arousal and attention. By having subjects first learn scripts to a fixed criterion, we controlled the content of the intentions and the amount of initial learning. By using reaction time as the dependent variable we measured the activation of intention-related memory structures in a sensitive and nonreactive way (cf. Ratcliff & McKoon, 1978). As our subjects were not aware during study as to whether or not a given script was to be executed, effects of the intention induction cannot be attributed to differential encoding strategies.

Despite these methodological advantages, the results from our first two experiments leave open the important question of whether the recognition advantage for intention-related words is an automatic effect (LaBerge & Samuels, 1974; Posner & Snyder, 1975), or whether it is due to the selective use of voluntary memory strategies. In particular, two skeptical challenges may be raised against the assumption of a special dynamic status of intentions in memory.

First, the crucial difference between the observation and execution conditions may not be whether or not subjects form an intention to execute the prospective script. Rather, the two conditions may differ with respect to the test expectancies induced in our subjects. More specifically, the instruction to perform a script may have been interpreted as the announcement of a free recall test, whereas the instruction to observe someone else performing the script in order to detect mistakes may have induced the expectation of a recognition test. Subjects may consider a free recall test to be more difficult than a recognition test (cf. d'Ydewalle, 1981), and thus would be more motivated to use rehearsal or imagery.

Secondly, even if test expectancies were not an important variable in our experiments, the instruction to perform an activity may have motivated subjects to selectively rehearse or imagine the to-be-executed script more than did the instruction to observe someone else performing the script. Although our subjects could not anticipate during the study phase which script would turn out to be the prospective one, subjects may have selectively rehearsed or imagined the to-be-executed script after they had received the execution instruction. Even partial attempts to rehearse the prospective script after the study phase may have been sufficient to produce the observed latency differences.

Therefore, we performed a further experiment in order to directly investigate the role of test expectancies and selective imagery (Goschke & Kuhl, 1993, Exp. 4). The postponed-intention paradigm was modified in two respects. First, identical test expectancies were induced for both scripts by instructing subjects prior to the learning phase that they would have to recall both the neutral and the prospective script at the end of an experimental block. If the intention-superiority effect was merely due to the fact that the instruction to execute the prospective script leads subjects to expect a free recall test, we would expect no differences between neutral and prospective scripts when subjects expect a recall test for both scripts.

Secondly, we manipulated the use of poststudy rehearsal and imagery. After subjects received the instruction to execute the prospective script, they either had to imagine both the to-be-executed and the neutral script for 1 min (imagery condition), or they had to carry out a demanding visuospatial distractor task requiring spoken responses, designed to prevent both imagery and rehearsal (blocking condition). Thus, in both the imagery and blocking conditions, subjects were prevented from selectively rehearsing or imagining the to-be-executed script at the cost of the neutral script.

The most important result of this experiment was that we nevertheless obtained an intention-superiority effect, that is, intention-related words were again recognized reliably faster and yielded higher discriminability indices than neutral words. Because subjects expected a recall test for both types of items, the intention-superiority effect obtained in our previous experiments cannot be accounted for by the mere expectancy of a recall test for the prospective script in the execution condition. The interaction of delay task (blocking vs. imagery) and item type (neutral vs. intention-related) was not even marginally reliable. This indicates that the persisting activation of intention-related memory contents was an automatic effect that did not depend on the use of controlled memory strategies. (It is unlikely that subjects rehearsed the to-be-executed script during the recognition test itself, given the fast-paced presentation of test items.) This conclusion was corroborated by an analysis of subjects' postexperimental ratings, in which they indicated whether or not they had used various memory strategies. The degree of self-reported, selective poststudy rehearsal or imagery of the prospective script did not significantly correlate with the magnitude of the intention-superiority effect (i.e., the difference between recognition latencies for neutral and intention-related words).

A final noteworthy point is that there were virtually no performance differences between neutral and executed scripts in the final free recall test. Given

that free recall performance is especially sensitive for the effects of test expectancies and strategic operations (e.g., d'Ydewalle, 1984; Eysenck, 1982),
this finding constitutes converging evidence that the intention-superiority effect is not due to the selective rehearsal of the intended script, but reflects an
automatic and temporary enhancement of the activation level of intention-
related memory contents.

In summary, the whole pattern of findings summarized so far provides evidence that the intention-superiority effect is not due to the selective allocation
of voluntary memory strategies to the to-be-executed script, and that the effect cannot be reduced to the mere expectancy of a recall test. Rather, intention-related information persists in a state of increased subthreshold activation
longer than neutral material, even if both types of material have been learned
equally well (see also Einstein & McDaniel, this volume).

IMPLICIT MEMORY FOR
INTENTION-RELATED INFORMATION

Determining Tendencies as Implicit Memory

In the experiments summarized so far, we used an *explicit* recognition test, in
which subjects had to refer back to the study episode and to decide whether
or not a word had appeared in one of the studied scripts. In other words, we
investigated the conscious recollection of intention-related contents. Thus, in
using the term *persistence* to this point, we always referred to the sustained
subthreshold activation of an *episodic* intention representation, presumably
mediating an increased accessibility of a conscious representation of the intended activity.

However, when early theorists of will psychology discussed the functional
properties of intentions, they assumed that intentions may facilitate the processing of intention-related information even if the intention itself is not consciously recollected. In particular, Lewin (1926) suggested that intentions increase the perceptual readiness to process intention-related information even
in the absence of a conscious recollection of the intention. Lewin used the
example of a person who intends to mail a letter and shows an increased perceptual sensibility for yellow mailboxes, even though he or she is not constantly
having conscious thoughts about the intention. Ach (1910, 1935), a further
prominent protagonist of early will psychology, arrived at a similar conclusion
despite his critical attitude toward the concept of tension systems. Ach (1935,
p. 143) was impressed by the observation that intentions influence the subsequent processing of information "in the sense of the goal image." He used the
term *determination* to describe the coherence and goal-directedness of men-

tal processes caused by an intention. Ach also stressed that determining tendencies can have their facilitative effects "without a conscious recollection of the task or the instruction" (1935, p. 150).

From a different theoretical vantage point, unconscious influences of experiences on the subsequent processing of information attracted considerable interest in research on *implicit memory* (for reviews see Richardson-Klavehn & Bjork, 1988; Roediger, 1990; Schacter, 1987). In typical implicit memory tests, the instruction for the subject does not require conscious recall or recognition of the study stimuli, but implicit memory for the study episode is inferred from repetition priming effects, that is, from the fact that a previous encounter with the stimulus facilitates later processing of the same stimulus. For example, in a perceptual identification task, tachistoscopically presented words are identified at lower thresholds when they were read before (Jacoby & Dallas, 1981), or in a word-fragment completion task, reading words increases the probability that they will be correctly completed when they are later presented in fragmented form (e.g., Tulving, Schacter, & Stark, 1982). Various dissociations were reported between performance in priming or *indirect* memory tasks and explicit or *direct* memory tasks. For instance, fragment-completion performance was shown to be stochastically independent from performance in a recognition test (Hayman & Tulving, 1989; Tulving et al., 1982; but see Hintzman & Harty, 1990, for critical remarks). In addition, encoding variables like depth of processing or elaboration, which improve recall and recognition performance (Craik & Tulving, 1975), usually have no or even reverse effects on indirect memory tests (at least when so-called *data-driven* tests are considered; cf. Roediger & Blaxton, 1987). Finally, amnesic patients with lesions of medial–temporal or diencephalic brain structures show almost normal repetition priming effects in indirect memory tests, although they are severely impaired on explicit memory tests (Warrington & Weiskrantz, 1970; for review see Shimamura, 1986; Squire, 1992; Tulving & Schacter, 1990).

Despite the different theoretical traditions of both research programs, there are interesting analogies between the rationale underlying implicit memory tasks and the characterization of intention effects in older theories of the will. Lewin and Ach assumed that a prior episode (i.e., the formation of an intention to perform an activity) facilitates the perception or processing of information related to that intention, even if the intention is not consciously recollected. That is, a prior intention implicitly primes the processing of intention-related information. To our knowledge, no attempts were made to investigate the effects of intentions within the framework of implicit memory. In particular, most of the experiments on memory for interrupted activities that were carried out to test Lewin's (1926) persistence hypothesis (e.g., Zeigarnik, 1927; see van Bergen, 1968, for review), as well as most prospective memory studies, used explicit memory tests.

TABLE 3.2
Proportion of Correctly Solved Word-Fragments From the Neutral and
the Prospective Script (Means and Standard Deviations)

	Script	
Condition	Neutral	Prospective
Experiment 1		
Observe	53.5 (19.4)	55.1 (20.2)
Execute	48.8 (21.1)	58.6 (16.7)
Experiment 2		
Recall	66.1 (19.8)	64.1 (17.1)
Execute	60.9 (15.4)	70.8 (14.6)

Priming Effects of Intentions on
Word-Fragment Completion

On the basis of these considerations, we performed a series of experiments in order to investigate whether or not an intention to perform an activity facilitates the processing of information related to that intention in an implicit memory test. To this end, we combined the postponed-intention paradigm with a word-fragment completion test (Goschke & Kuhl, 1994). In a first experiment, 36 undergraduates served as subjects. After subjects had memorized two scripts, they received the instruction either to execute or to later observe one of the scripts. After this instruction, a word-fragment completion test started. Forty-eight word-fragments (e.g., T-BL- for TABLE) appeared on the computer monitor. There were 12 fragments from the prospective script, 12 fragments from the neutral script, and 24 new fragments. Subjects were told they should feel free to solve fragments in any order they preferred, that they should start with simple fragments and return to difficult ones later, and that they should complete fragments with the first word that came to mind. Subjects were not told that the fragment completion task was a memory test, but that we were interested in "verbal fluency." After 12 min, the fragment completion task was interrupted by an alarm clock and subjects had to execute or to observe the prospective script.

The first part of Table 3.2 shows the mean proportion of correctly solved neutral and prospective fragments in the execution and observation conditions. There were virtually no differences between prospective and neutral fragments in the observation condition. By contrast, in the execution condition, a reliably larger proportion of prospective as compared to neutral fragments were solved.

In a replication study with 16 subjects, we introduced a different control condition. Instead of instructing subjects to observe the prospective script, they were told they would have to recall the prospective script in verbatim form

after the fragment completion test. If the advantage of intention-related fragments in the completion test was due to the fact that the to-be-executed script
also had to be recalled, we should expect the same advantage for fragments related to a to-be-recalled script. As can be seen in the second part of Table 3.2,
the intention-superiority effect appeared only in the execution condition. Although subjects recognized more prospective than neutral fragments in the execution condition, there were no reliable differences in the recall condition.
This shows that the intention-superiority effect is specific for items refering to
a script that actually has to be executed.

Dissocations Between Implicit and
Explicit Intention Memory

The crucial question concerning these results is whether or not they actually
reflect implicit effects of the intention on the processing of intention-related
information. Subjects may have treated the completion test as an explicit cued-
recall test, and they may have completed some of the fragments on the basis
of explicitly retrieved words from the studied scripts (cf. Perruchet & Baveux,
1989; Schacter, Bowers, & Booker, 1989). Even if only some subjects solved
some fragments on the basis of explicit recollections of script words, it would
be unjustified to attribute the intention-superiority effect to the implicit priming of intention-related information. Rather, the superior completion performance for word-fragments from the to-be-executed script may have been caused
by the fact that words from the to-be-executed script were more often explicitly recalled during the completion test.

To examine this possibility, we carried out a further experiment in which
subjects first received a word-fragment completion and then a recognition test
for the same items (see Goschke & Kuhl, 1994, for details). This way, it was
possible to investigate whether both memory tests were related or whether
they would dissociate. It is a difficult methodological problem to show that performance on an indirect memory test was not contaminated by explicit recollections, because there are presumably no process-pure memory tasks tapping
exclusively implicit or explicit memory (Jacoby, 1991). We therefore used various pieces of evidence as converging support for the implicit nature of the intention-superiority effect. None of these pieces of evidence is in itself sufficient
to prove that no contamination with explicit recollections occurred, but in conjunction they constitute suggestive support.

Tables 3.3 and 3.4 show the results for the recognition and the fragment
completion test. Because the present experiment included the imagery and
blocking manipulations that were described in relation to our recognition
memory experiments, the results are shown separately for both conditions. An
intention-superiority effect was obtained in both conditions and both memory
tests. Words from a later to-be-executed script were recognized faster than neu-

TABLE 3.3

Recognition Latencies for Prospective and Neutral Words in the Imagery
and Blocking Conditions (Means and Standard Deviations)

	Script	
Condition	Neutral	Prospective
Blocking	1103 (261)	1052 (223)
Imagery	1095 (232)	1049 (241)

TABLE 3.4

Proportion of Correctly Solved Word-Fragments From the Neutral and
the Prospective Script in the Imagery and Blocking Conditions
(Means and Standard Deviations)

	Script	
Condition	Neutral	Prospective
Blocking	67.6 (21.8)	72.7 (19.1)
Imagery	63.1 (26.3)	70.8 (20.8)

tral words and fragments of words from the prospective script were completed
more frequently than neutral word-fragments. This was the case although subjects in this experiment were instructed that they would receive a final free recall test for both the neutral and the to-be-executed script. Thus, the intention-
superiority effect cannot be attributed to the expectancy of a free recall test.
Moreover, if the intention-superiority effect were due to the selective processing of the prospective script at the expense of the neutral script, we would have
expected no difference between neutral and prospective items in the imagery
condition in which both scripts were imagined to an equal degree after the execution instruction. Likewise, we would have expected no difference between
neutral and prospective items in the blocking condition, in which poststudy rehearsal and imagery were prevented. By contrast, in both the imagery and the
blocking conditions, prospective items were recognized reliably faster and
completed more frequently than neutral words.

   The main theoretical motivation for the present experiment was to investigate whether the intention-superiority effect in the fragment completion test
was independent from the explicit recollection of script words. Three pieces of
evidence suggest that the intention-superiority effect in the fragment completion task did not depend on conscious recollections.

   First, we computed Pearson correlations across subjects between the intention-superiority effect in the fragment completion test (i.e., the difference between the proportions of solved neutral and prospective items) and the effect

in the explicit recognition test (i.e., the difference between response times for neutral and prospective words). This correlation did not differ reliably from 0.

Second, we asked subjects in a postexperimental questionnaire whether they had tried to explicitly recall script words in order to solve them in the fragment completion test, or whether they had solved the fragments with the first words that came to mind. The intention-superiority effect for subjects who reported that they had tried to solve word-fragments by explicitly remembering script words (approximately one half of the sample), was not larger than for subjects who reported they had solved the word-fragments implicitly, that is, with the first word that came to mind. To the contrary, the difference between the proportions of correctly solved prospective and neutral word-fragments was even larger in the implicit group (10.2%) than in the explicit group (4.9%).

Third, if the intention-superiority effect in the fragment completion test was due to items that had been solved on the basis of the explicit recollection of script words, the effect should have been stronger for items for which both tests were stochastically dependent. This follows from the assumption that word-fragments completed primarily on the basis of explicit recollections should show a higher probability of being correctly recognized in the explicit recognition test. If, on the other hand, the intention-superiority effect was independent from the explicit recollection of script words, the advantage of intention-related fragments should be identical for items for which fragment completion and recognition tests are stochastically dependent, and for items for which both tests are independent (cf. Flexser & Tulving, 1978; Hayman & Tulving, 1989; Tulving et al., 1982; Tulving & Schacter, 1990). We thus determined for each item and each subject whether or not it had been correctly solved in the word-fragment completion test and whether or not it had been correctly recognized. On the basis of the resulting 2×2 contingency table, we computed Yule's Q as a measure of stochastical dependency between both tests (see Hayman & Tulving, 1989).[8] This analysis showed that the fragment completion and recognition tests were reliably dependent with respect to verbs ($Q = .52$; $p < .001$), whereas both tests were unreliably related for nouns ($Q = .19$; $p > .20$). Whatever the cause may be for this difference between verbs and nouns, the intention-superiority effect in the word-fragment completion test did not reliably differ for verbs and nouns. In fact, on a descriptive level, the intention effect (that is, the difference between the proportions of correctly solved prospective and neutral fragments) was even larger for nouns (7.8%) as compared to verbs (5.1%). Thus, although a contamination by explicit recollection was

---

[8]Stochastic independence between direct and indirect tests was sometimes interpreted as evidence for separate memory systems (e.g., Hayman & Tulving, 1989; Tulving et al., 1982). This interpretation as well as the general rationale underlying the use of measures of stochastic dependence in memory research was challenged on theoretical and methodological grounds (e.g., Hintzman & Harty, 1990). Therefore, we make no commitments as to whether stochastic independence implies multiple memory systems.

more likely for verbs (for which both tests were stochastically dependent) than for nouns (for which both tests were independent), the intention-superiority effect was stronger for nouns than for verbs. This interpretation rests on the assumption that stochastic independence constitutes evidence that performance in both tests was mediated by different underlying processes. We are, however, aware of the severe methodological problems inherent in the logic of stochastic independence as an index for different underlying processes (e.g., Hintzman & Harty, 1990; Howe, Rabinowitz & Grant, 1993). Thus, we should interpret the above results not in isolation, but consider them as a pattern, which in our view provides suggestive evidence for the implicit nature of the intention-superiority effect in the fragment completion test.

In summary, although being far from conclusive, these findings suggest that the intention to execute an activity may facilitate the processing of intention-related information even in the absence of a conscious recollection of the explicit intention representation. This conclusion fits with Ach's (1910) suggestion that an intention establishes a determining tendency that modulates subsequent information processing according to the goal representation, even if the goal representation is not explicitly retrieved (see also Gollwitzer, in press, for related findings). Given the severe methodological problems in excluding contamination of indirect memory performance by explicit retrieval processes, it remains to be seen whether or not our present interpretation will stand the test of further experiments, in which we try to rule out such contaminations more strictly. We are currently performing experiments in which we try to separate implicit and explicit intention effects in a more compelling way by applying Schacter et al.'s (1989) *retrieval intentionality criterion*. Despite these reservations, we consider the findings from our fragment completion experiments as support for the fruitfulness of our general attempt to bring research on implicit memory for intentions in closer contact with theoretical perspectives developed in older will psychology. We discuss some implications of the distinction between explicit and implicit intention memory at the end of this chapter.

INDIVIDUAL DIFFERENCES IN
THE PERSISTENCE OF INTENTIONS

So far, we discuss intention memory solely in terms of general effects holding for all subjects. However, in her task interruption studies, Zeigarnik (1927) stressed the importance of individual differences as moderators of the persistence of intentions in memory. For instance, the Zeigarnik-effect was apparently larger for more "ambitious" subjects (cf. van Bergen, 1968). In our own research, we focused on a particular personality disposition that is termed *state* versus *action orientation* and that is closely related to differences in volitional competence and self-regulatory efficiency (Kuhl, 1983, 1984, 1994b; Kuhl & Beckmann, 1994). State orientation is characterized as a tendency to experience involuntary intrusions concerning past failures or future goals. These intrusions may impair the ability to carry out intended activities, especially in conflict situations demanding self-regulation and the suppression of interfering thoughts about currently irrelevant goals. For instance, Kuhl (1981) showed that individuals scoring high on state orientation found it more difficult than did action-oriented subjects to inhibit intrusive thoughts about a past failure, even though they were motivated to cope with a novel task (see also Beckmann, 1994). In a related study, Kuhl and Helle (1986) informed their subjects that they would have to perform a simple task later in the experiment. Although this future task was currently irrelevant, state-oriented subjects were impaired on a subsequent short-term memory task and reported more thoughts related to the future task than in a control condition. From these and related findings the hypothesis emerged that, in state-oriented individuals, a declarative representation of an intention involuntarily persists in a state of high activation even if the intention has to be postponed and one can rely on external trigger cues. By contrast, action-oriented individuals are supposed to deactivate the declarative representation of a postponed intention, when external trigger cues are available and one can rely on being reminded of the intention even without constantly thinking of it. Because in most of our experiments, the initiation of the postponed intention was externally prompted, we expected state-oriented subjects to show a larger intention-superiority effect than action-oriented subjects.

We classified subjects as action- or state-oriented depending on whether their scores on the subscale for Prospective Action Orientation of Kuhl's Action Control Scale (ACS; Kuhl, 1994a) were above or below the median of the respective samples. This subscale assesses the disposition to engage in overly exhaustive decision making, and to ruminate excessively about unrealistic or currently irrelevant future goals. The scale describes a number of concrete situations (e.g., "when there are two things I really want to do, but I can't do both"), for which subjects have to choose between two response alternatives. One alternative describes an instrumental activity (e.g., "I quickly begin one thing and forget about the other thing"), whereas the other describes ruminations about future goals (e.g., "It's not easy for me to put the thing that I couldn't do out of my mind"; see Kuhl, 1994a, for psychometric properties of the scale; see Kuhl & Beckmann, 1994, for validation studies with the ACS).

Table 3.5 shows the differences between recognition latencies for neutral and prospective words in the execution condition (i.e., the intention-superiority effect), separately for action- and state-oriented subjects from three experiments, in which the postponed-intention paradigm was used in conjunction with an explicit recognition test. State-oriented subjects showed a larger intention-superiority effect than action-oriented subjects. Analyses of variance

TABLE 3.5

Differences Between Recognition Latencies for Neutral and Prospective Words
in the Execution Condition for Action-Oriented (AOP)
and State-Oriented (SOP) Subjects

	Exp. 1	Exp. 2	Exp. 3
AOP	10	44	5
SOP	116	71	63

Note. A positive difference represents an intention-superiority effect).

TABLE 3.6

Differences Between Completion Rates for Prospective and
Neutral Word-Fragments in the Execution Condition for
Action-Oriented (AOP) and State-Oriented (SOP) Subjects

	Exp. 1	Exp. 2	Exp. 3
AOP	13.5	9.4	7.1
SOP	6.5	10.4	5.7

Note. A positive difference represents an intention-superiority effect.

showed that in all three experiments, the difference between neutral and prospective words in the execution condition was reliable for state-oriented subjects only.

Thus, action-oriented subjects appear to deactivate intention-related material relatively fast and to focus their attention on the current task, at least when the timely initiation of the intention is prompted by an external cue.[9] In contrast, in state-oriented subjects the explicit, episodic representation of a postponed intention persisted in an active state even if external cues were available and active maintenance of the intention was not necessary. Both groups of subjects did not differ with respect to the actual performance of the intended actions after the recognition test. This shows that continuous activation of an intention in explicit memory is not necessary for its execution when external retrieval cues are available (see Einstein & McDaniel, 1990; Meacham & Colombo, 1980, for further discussion of the role of retrieval cues in prospective remembering).

The analogous analyses of our fragment-completion experiments yielded a different picture. As can be seen in Table 3.6, in three experiments we found no evidence for individual differences between action- and state-oriented indi-

---

[9]In one of our experiments in which the timely execution of the intention had to be self-initiated in the absence of external cues, both action- and state-oriented subjects showed a reliable intention-superiority effect.

viduals with respect to the completion rates of neutral and intention-related word-fragments. In both groups, intention-related fragments were solved more frequently than were neutral fragments in the execution condition.

In summary, both action- and state-oriented subjects showed an increased readiness to process intention-related cues in an implicit test. By contrast, in an explicit memory test, only state-oriented subjects showed a reliable intention-superiority effect. This pattern of results is consistent with the assumption that state-oriented individuals show a form of over-maintenance of the explicit representation of an uncompleted intention. Although persisting activation of a declarative intention representation may be adaptive when there are no external trigger cues and we have to engage in some form of explicit time-monitoring, persisting activation is not necessary in situations in which the action will be externally prompted. In fact in such situations, persisting activation of an explicit intention representation can even deteriorate performance in an ongoing task because it may reduce working memory resources (cf. Kuhl, 1983, 1994b; Kuhl & Goschke, 1994a; Kuhl & Helle, 1986).

These findings suggest an important theoretical distinction between two different aspects of the concept of *persistence,* namely the activation of explicit declarative intention representations and the procedural readiness to process intention-related information.

FREE RECALL OF EVERYDAY
INTENTIONS AND WISHES

The experiments described so far have produced converging evidence for an intention-superiority effect in both explicit and implicit memory tests. How do these findings generalize from our rather artificial laboratory setting to the retrieval of peoples' "real" goals and intentions in everyday life? In order to answer this question, we performed two studies, in which a "free goal recall" paradigm was used to investigate the retrieval of everyday intentions (Goschke, in press-a; see also Kuhl & Kazén, 1994). Subjects were instructed to spontaneously recall any incomplete wishes, intentions, and obligations that came to mind within 3 min, and to write down one or two keywords as a shorthand for a given goal. There were no constraints as to the kind of material to be produced, apart from the fact that it should refer to "something uncompleted," be it a wish, an intention, an utopic long-term goal, or a profane obligation. Subjects were encouraged to let their minds wander freely without a specific set and without paying much attention to how important or realistic a given goal was. After the goal recall, subjects rated each of the retrieved goals on scales assessing various motivational variables (e.g., importance, urgency, expectancy of success, subjective competence). In addition, they had to categorize each goal as a wish (something desired even if it is unrealistic), an intention (something we are committed to do), or an external obligation (something we must do, even if we do not like to).

Our main question was whether the intention-superiority effect is specific for intentions, or whether it simply reflects an unspecific retrieval advantage for any kind of motivationally relevant or subjectively important memory contents. We focused on the distinction between intentions and wishes. Following Heckhausen and Kuhl (1985; cf. Kuhl, 1983), we assumed that a wish gains the status of an intention when its subjective realizability exceeds a certain threshold. Although we may wish impossible things (e.g., eternal youth), we usually intend to do things only when we believe that they can be realized by our own actions. Thus, if the intention-superiority effect is indeed specific for intentions, realistic goals that have the mental status of intentions or obligations should be retrieved faster from memory than unrealistic wishes.[10]

Two goal recall studies were performed which differed only with respect to the recall instruction. In the first study, subjects were instructed to recall as many goals as spontaneously came to mind within 3 min. In the second study, no time limits were imposed, but subjects had to recall exactly 15 goals as fast as possible. For each subject, output percentiles were computed for each retrieved goal (Bjork & Whitten, 1974). This was done by dividing the rank position at which a given goal had been recalled by the total number of recalled goals, and then multiplying the resulting value with 100. Means of the output percentiles were then computed separately for each of the three goal categories (intentions, obligations, wishes). These means are shown in Table 3.7. In both studies, there was a reliable intention-superiority effect. Goals that were categorized as either self-chosen intentions or externally determined *intentions* (i.e., obligations) were recalled reliably earlier than wishes. Most importantly, this recall advantage of both types of intentions as compared to wishes remained reliable even after the effect of the subjective importance or urgency of the goals on their recall order had been statistically removed in an analysis of covariance (Goschke, in press-a).

The general recall advantage of intentions as compared to wishes received additional support from multiple regression analyses with the output percentiles of goals as the criterion variable and the self-rated realizability, importance, and urgency as predictor variables. Given that our assumption is correct, that the crucial difference between intentions and wishes consists in their different degree of subjective realizability (Heckhausen & Kuhl, 1985; Kuhl, 1983), we expected subjective realizability to be the major predictor of recall position. Consistent with this assumption, in both studies multiple regression

---

[10]This conceptual analysis of the difference between wishes and intentions was validated by an analysis of subjects' ratings of their recalled goals. In both goal-recall studies, discriminant analyses showed that subjects' classification of goals as wishes versus intentions was predicted solely on the basis of the subjective realizability of the goal. The resulting discriminant function was characterized by high loadings of ratings for subjective probability and competence to realize the goal.

TABLE 3.7
Mean Output Percentiles for Intentions, Obligations,
and Wishes in the Free Goal Recall Studies

	Goal Category		
	Intention	Obligation	Wish
Study 1	50.8	41.6	59.6
Study 2	48.7	47.3	58.7

analyses revealed subjective realizability as the only reliable predictor of recall position. The more realistic a goal was rated, the earlier it was recalled on average. By contrast, the importance or urgency of the goals did not reliably add to the proportion of explained variance of the recall positions (see Goschke, in press-a, for details).

In summary, both goal recall studies yielded a clear intention-superiority effect and thus support the generalizability of our laboratory findings to the recall of everyday goals. Realistic intentions were not only recalled reliably faster than unrealistic wishes, but this retrieval advantage of intentions was independent from possible confounding variables like the motivational importance and the urgency of the goals. This is consistent with our interpretation of the laboratory findings in that the intentional status of a goal (i.e., whether it is represented as an intention or as a wish) has an effect on the activation level of the goal representation, independent from the motivational significance of the goal.

Various methodological problems may be raised with respect to the use of self-report data and correlational analyses in the goal recall studies. For instance, one might suspect that self-ratings are not valid indicators of the "real" importance of goals, but rather reflect subjective theories about their motivational states that may be false (cf. Dennett, 1987; Ericsson & Simon, 1980; Nisbett & Wilson, 1977). In addition, the correlational nature of the data prohibits causal interpretations. Although it is plausible that intentions were recalled earlier than wishes because the former were more highly activated in long-term memory, we cannot exclude the reverse causal relationship—that highly accessible goals will be rated as more realistic because of their high accessibility. Various reasons speak against this possibility (see Goschke, in press-a, for a more detailed discussion), but further studies are needed to remedy this concern. Note, however, that the interpretation of the goal recall studies was based on a priori hypotheses that were derived from our laboratory findings. All correlational results reported were replicated in both studies as well as in randomly chosen subsamples of subjects within each study. Therefore, if viewed in conjunction with our laboratory findings, we consider the results from our goal recall studies as converging evidence for a special dynamic status of everyday-intentions in memory.

THEORETICAL PROSPECTS:
INTENTION MEMORY AND ACTION CONTROL

Summary of experimental findings

Let us summarize the main findings of the research program described in this chapter. First, intention-related memory contents were characterized by a heightened and more sustained level of activation as compared to other memory contents in an explicit memory test. In four experiments, words referring to an activity that had to be executed later were recognized faster and more accurately than words from an equally well learned script that was to be remembered only. In a control condition in which subjects were instructed to observe someone else performing the activity, no such differences were obtained. These results provide clear support for Lewin's (1926) persistence hypothesis.

Secondly, word-fragments constructed from words of a script that had to be executed later were completed more frequently than were fragments from an equally well-learned script that was not to be executed. In control conditions in which subjects were instructed to observe someone else performing the activity or to recall the script, no such difference was found. There was suggestive evidence that performance in implicit and explicit tasks was in fact independent. Although further research is needed to establish this conclusion more convincingly, the present findings are consistent with the assumption that intentions facilitate the processing of intention-related information even if the episodic representation of the intention is not consciously recollected.

The memory advantage of intentions was further confirmed in two goal recall studies, showing that everyday intentions were recalled reliably earlier than wishes, irrespective of their motivational importance or temporal urgency.

Systematic individual differences were obtained with respect to explicit intention memory. State-oriented subjects, who are characterized by frequent intrusions about unfulfilled goals or previous failures, showed a markedly stronger persistence of explicit intention representations than did action-oriented subjects. In contrast, no such differences were obtained in the implicit memory experiments.

In our final discussion, we focus on possible mechanisms accounting for the intention-superiority effect, on the role of voluntary strategies and individual differences in intention memory, and on the functional role of intention memory for the control of action.

Mechanism Underlying the Intention-Superiority Effect

As we argued, the intention-superiority effect cannot be attributed to the fact that our subjects have selectively encoded or rehearsed the to-be-executed script. First, subjects could not anticipate during encoding which script they would have to execute. Secondly, an intention-superiority effect was obtained even if subjects expected a free recall test for both the neutral and the to-be-performed script, and even when selective post-study processing of the to-be-executed script was prevented either by having subjects imagine both scripts or by blocking imagery and rehearsal by a distractor task. In conclusion, the intention-superiority effect is not the result of selective encoding or rehearsal, but appears to reflect the intrinsic property of representations of intentions to decay more slowly than representations of nonintended activities. Thus, in terms of Anderson's (1983) ACT* theory, intentions may be considered as source nodes in memory, which sustain activation without rehearsal. However, whereas in ACT* only those goals are source nodes that are currently in working memory and that control immediate action, our findings suggest that representations of postponed intentions also decay more slowly than do neutral contents.

The assumption that postponed intentions are subthreshold source nodes in long-term memory explains why intention-related words were recognized faster than neutral words. How can such an increased activation of intention representations account for the intention-superiority effect in the fragment completion task? What may seem puzzling at first sight is how a clearly conceptual process (i.e., the formation of an intention) may exert priming effects on word-fragment completion, usually regarded as a *data-driven* or *perceptual* test. Data-driven tests are strongly influenced by changes in perceptual surface features of the study material (Jacoby & Dallas, 1981; Jacoby & Hayman, 1987; Kirsner, Milech & Standen, 1983), but are relatively immune to conceptual influences like depth or elaboration of processing (e.g., Blaxton, 1989; Roediger, Weldon, & Challis, 1989; cf. Roediger, 1990; Roediger & Blaxton, 1987). On the other hand, priming effects on word-fragment completion were frequently reported to be larger after conceptual, elaborative encoding than after shallow encoding (Challis & Brodbeck, 1992; Chiarello & Hoyer, 1988; Graf, Squire, & Mandler, 1984; Hamann, 1990), and small but reliable cross-modal priming effects on fragment completion were obtained that plausibly must have been conceptually mediated (Bassili, Smith, & MacLeod, 1989; Graf, Shimamura, & Squire, 1985; Hirshman, Snodgrass, Mindes, & Feenan, 1990). These findings indicate that word-fragment completion is sensitive to both lexical and conceptual-semantic factors (Weldon, 1991). It is thus a viable possibility that conceptual intention representations exert top-down influences on the activation of associated lexical units in the mental input lexicon. Such a lexical activation may occur independently from the activation of a conceptual representation of the *episodic context* in which the intention was formed. Thus, persisting activation of an intended activity may enhance the activation level of corresponding lexical units without producing an explicit recollection of the intention. As a result of the higher activation of intention-related word units, they will be more easily accessed when a word-fragment is provided as a cue (cf. Besner & Smith, 1992, for evidence for top-down influences from conceptual to lexical representations).

Individual Differences in Intention Memory

As we predicted from our theory of action control (e.g. Kuhl, 1994b; Kuhl & Goschke, 1994b), there were systematic individual differences with respect to the activation of intention representations in an explicit memory test. State-oriented subjects showed a larger intention-superiority effect in the recognition test as compared to action-oriented subjects. In contrast, both groups of subjects showed an equally large intention-superiority effect in the implicit word-fragment completion test. How can we account for this dissociation between recognition and fragment-completion with respect to action- and state-oriented subjects?

In a recognition test, subjects have to decide whether or not a test item has appeared in the study episode. The intention-superiority effect in the recognition test can thus be explained by assuming that in state-oriented subjects, a representation of the intention together with the episodic context in which the intention was formed remain active. This idea fits with the general conceptualization of state orientation as a mode of processing in which attention is primarily focused on the analysis of past (and future) episodes (cf. Kuhl & Beckmann, 1994). The tendency of state-oriented subjects to frequently experience intrusive thoughts about currently irrelevant past or future states associated with unfulfilled goals may thus be a consequence of the persisting activation of episodic intention representations.

By contrast, action-oriented individuals deactivate the episodic context in which the intention was formed and rather maintain an increased readiness to respond to intention-relevant cues. Such a readiness does not require activation of the episodic context of the intention and thus need not be associated with frequent conscious thoughts about the intentions. It rather suffices that the representation of the execution conditions of the intended activity persist in an active state. This should increase the probability of detecting intention-related information (which shows up in priming effects in implicit memory tasks, not requiring reference to the study context), but it should not necessarily improve performance in a recognition test in which subjects have to explicitly decide whether or not a cue item appeared in the study list.

Intention Memory, Action Control, and Different Forms of Persistence

We would like to conclude with some more speculative remarks about the different functional roles of implicit and explicit forms of intention memory in the control of intentional action (cf. Goschke, in press-a, in press-b; Kuhl, in press-a, in press-b; Kuhl & Goschke, 1994a; Kuhl & Kazén-Saad, 1988). We began by refering back to Lewin's (1926) characterization of intentions as persisting tension systems. On the basis of the results summarized in this chapter, we think it is theoretically important to distinguish between different forms of persistence and different types of intention representations. The following taxonomy of different forms of intention memory is based on three distinctions: (a) Is an intention represented in procedural or declarative form? (b) Is the intention associated with external cues or not? (c) Is the intention consciously retrieved or not?

Procedural Persistence. As we noted in our introduction, when an intended action can be realized by automatized routine skills and when all parameters of the intended activity can be specified in advance, the intention can be implemented in terms of a transient activation of specific connections between execution conditions and action schemas (*procedural intention;* cf. Neumann & Prinz, 1987; Norman & Shallice, 1986). With respect to such intentions, the term *persistence* refers to the enduring readiness of procedural action schemas, that is, it denotes the fact that these schemas have an increased probability of being triggered when their execution conditions are fulfilled (*procedural persistence;* cf. Goschke, in press-a; Kuhl, in press-b; Kuhl & Goschke, 1994b). This fits with Ach's (1935) idea that objects in the environment may acquire *teleological qualities* (finale Qualitäten), that is, that they can directly trigger an intended activity without prior conscious retrieval of the intention.

Implicit Respondent Persistence. When concrete parameters of an intended action cannot be fully specified in advance, the intention has to be stored in a declarative, presumably linguistic format. A second meaning of persistence relates to the priming of a declarative intention representation in the absence of a conscious recollection of the intention. In our experiments, this form of *implicit persistence* showed up in priming effects on the completion of intention-related word fragments. Implicit persistence is not associated with the continuous maintainance of an intention representation in consciousness. It may be established by what Prinz (1983) termed *relevance markers* that are tagged to the representation of the execution conditions of an intention. The function of relevance markers is to increase the probability of detecting execution conditions or intention-related cues, thereby increasing the probability that the intention will be retrieved in the right moment (see also Mäntylä, 1993, this volume). This suggests that implicit priming of intention-related information should primarily concern the execution conditions of an intended activity, but not necessarily the representation of the action. Consistent with this assumption, in all of our experiments the intention-superiority effect in the fragment completion task was larger for nouns (representing the objects and thus the execution conditions of the intended activities) than for verbs (representing the intended activities).

The main difference between procedural and implicit persistence concerns the specificity of execution conditions and action schemas. We speak of procedural persistence of an intention when specific action schemas are set into readiness, and we use the term implicit persistence when an abstract, declarative representation of the intention is primed. Both procedural and implicit forms of intention memory have in common that control over the triggering of intentions is passed to external cues (cf. Gollwitzer, in press). Reliance on a cue-based or *respondent* initiation of intentions should be particularly adaptive when an intention is associated with high probability of success, does not require further planning or problem solving, and is associated with clearly defined external trigger conditions (cf. Goschke, in press-a; Kuhl, in press-b).

Explicit Operant Persistence.   Cue-based or respondent intentions can be contrasted with time-based (Einstein & McDaniel, 1990) or *operant* intentions that are not associated with external trigger cues, but that have to be retrieved in a self-initiated manner (e.g., when one intends to take the cake out of the oven after 20 min without setting an alarm clock; cf. Ceci, Baker, & Bronfenbrenner, 1988). In such cases, it should be adaptive to retrieve a conscious, episodic representation of the intention at more or less regularly spaced points in time. It was shown that the frequency of thoughts about a time-based intention was positively correlated with the probability that the intention was remembered at the right time (Einstein, McDaniel, Cunfer, & Guynn, 1992; Harris & Wilkins, 1982; Kvavilashvili, 1987). We speak of *operant persistence* to denote the increased tendency to occasionally retrieve an explicit intention representation. Whereas we described implicit respondent persistence as a priming of the representation of the *execution conditions* of an intention (which should increase the probability of cue-based retrieval of the intention), explicit operant persistence is mediated by the sustained subthreshold activation of the declarative representation of the intended *action*. This sustained activation was presumably responsible for the intention-superiority effect in our recognition memory experiments and should increase the probability that the episodic representation of the intention is occasionally retrieved even in the absence of external cues. Operant persistence will often be related to intentions that are not linked to specific cues or concrete action schemas and that are represented in an abstract form allowing for flexibility in the face of changing situational conditions.

Involuntary Explicit Persistence.   Finally, persistence of an intention can denote an enduring, involuntary tendency to maintain an intention representation in consciousness. This kind of persistence shows up phenomenologically in the form of intrusive thoughts and frequent rumination about the intention.

We assume that this form of persistence is related to situations in which the execution of an intention is difficult or risky, requires planning and reflection, or is associated with the anticipation of fear or punishment.

Kuhl (in press-b) suggested that the anticipation of reward and punishment associated with an intention determines the preferred form in which the intention is maintained in memory. Intentions that are associated with high expectancy of success and the anticipation of reward will be associated either with procedural persistence (when concrete action parameters can be specified in advance), or with implicit respondent persistence (when the intention is represented in declarative form, but is associated with external trigger cues), or with explicit operant persistence (when there are no external trigger cues). These three forms of persistence should increase the probability of executing the intention in the right moment. By contrast, intentions that are associated with fear of failure or punishment are presumably associated with increased physiological arousal, vigilance, and a tendency towards continuous conscious representation, whereas at the same time the readiness of procedural action schemas is inhibited. Evidence for such a *behavioral inhibition system* can be found in the animal literature (Gray 1987), as well as in experiments with human subjects (Patterson & Newman, 1993). This configuration of behavioral inhibition and conscious activation of an intention representation may be adaptive when an intended action is associated with fear of failure, because in such cases the automatic triggering of premature actions has to be prevented in favor of planning, reflection, or an analysis of the situation. However the continuous maintenance of a conscious intention representation can become dysfunctional, because it demands working memory resources and may thus impair the execution of other important activities (Kuhl, 1984; Kuhl & Helle, 1986). State-orientation is an extreme form of an originally adaptive mode of processing in which conscious planning and reflection degenerate to involuntary rumination and preoccupation (e.g., when thoughts about taking the cake out of the oven interfere with preparing for an exam, even if one has set an alarm clock to remind one of the cake, and even if the action is neither difficult nor risky; cf. Kuhl & Goschke, 1994a; Martin & Tesser, 1989; Uleman & Bargh, 1989).

Dissociations Between Different Forms of Persistence. We all know from everyday experience that different aspects of intention memory can dissociate. For instance, we may find ourselves in front of the open refrigerator being unable to consciously recall what it was that we were intending to take out (procedural persistence in the absence of an explicit recollection of the intention). We may find ourselves ruminating intensively about a long-standing intention like the one to prepare an important talk without succeeding in initiating the necessary actions (persistence of a conscious intention in the absence of procedural action readiness). We may be sensitive for intention-related cues without a corresponding conscious intention, for example, when attention is captured by mailboxes even if the letter has already been mailed (implicit respondent persistence without conscious maintenance of the intention). We may reliably perform an intention when confronted with appropriate cues (e.g., taking the cake out of the oven when the alarm clock rings), but fail to do so in the absence of external cues (respondent without operant persistence).

Consistent with such anecdotal observations, Kvavilashvili (1987) found that the probability of explicitly remembering what one has to do was uncorrelated with the probability of actually remembering to carry it out at the right moment (cf. Einstein & McDaniel, 1990; Ellis & Williams, 1990; see Goschke, in press-a, for review of the relations between different aspects of intention memory). We obtained preliminary evidence for a dissociation between conscious maintenance of intentions and procedural persistence in one study (Kuhl & Goschke, 1994a), in which subjects were instructed at the beginning of the experiment to execute a simple intention at the end (reminding the experimenter of a phone call). Although state-oriented subjects had faster recognition latencies for intention-related words (i.e, showed a high degree of explicit persistence), they nevertheless forgot more often than action-oriented subjects to carry out the intention at the right time. Thus, high activation of an explicit intention representation does not always guarantee that the intended activity will be executed at the right time.

Thus, in addition to the distinction between explicit and implicit forms of intention memory, which is the primary focus of this chapter, it is important to differentiate within the category of *explicit* intention memory different forms of persistence. We distinguish between the tendency to occasionally retrieve a conscious representation of an intention (which should promote the execution of time-based intentions and is presumably typical for intentions associated with success or reward), and the involuntary rumination and overmaintenance of conscious intentions characteristic for state-oriented individuals (who at the same time show increased behavioral and volitional inhibition; cf. Kuhl, in press-b).

Kuhl (in press-b) suggested that involuntary rumination about uncompleted intentions (state orientation) and procedural and operant persistence of intentions may be antagonistically coupled. This hypothesis received indirect support from recent experiments using a brain imaging technique (PET) to isolate brain systems involved in attention (for review see Posner & Rothbart, 1992). It was observed that during the maintenance of a vigilant state an area of the right lateral midfrontal cortex showed a higher metabolic activation, whereas the anterior cingulate gyrus in the midprefrontal cortex was most active during a target detection task. Interestingly, metabolic activation of the vigilance system was accompanied by reduced activation of the anterior cingulate. If one assumes that the anterior cingulate is involved in maintenance of a procedural action readiness (e.g., in a target detection task), whereas the vigilance system is related to the inhibition of behavior in favor of an analysis of the current situation, these brain imaging results are consistent with the idea of an antagonistic coupling between the procedural persistence of a current intention and state orientation. Although this must remain speculative at present, it seems tempting to relate this finding to the observation that state-oriented subjects show an impairment in the self-initiated execution of intended activities despite an increased tendency to consciously ruminate about past and future goals (see Kuhl & Beckmann, 1994, for pertinent studies; see also the chapters in the neuropsychology section of this volume for additional ideas concerning the neuropsychology of prospective memory).

Although many of the conjectures in this final section are speculative, we hope that we have succeeded in showing that it is important and fruitful to differentiate between procedural, implicit, and explicit forms of intention memory: Different forms of intention memory have different antecendent conditions (e.g., action vs. state orientation and the anticipation of success or failure), serve different functions in the control of intentional action, and are associated with different costs and merits, depending on the conditions under which intentions must be retrieved (e.g., time-based or cue-based). It is of major theoretical significance in future work on prospective memory to further investigate the mechanisms and functions of implicit and explicit intention memory within a theory of adaptive action control.

ACKNOWLEDGMENTS

The research reported in this article was supported by Grants Ku 377/6–2 and 377/6–3 from the German Science Foundation (DFG) to Julius Kuhl. We thank Arno Fuhrmann, Ulla Klerx, Elisabeth Kuhl, Wilma Maschmeier, Karin Schröder, and Birgit Stürmer for their assistance in running the experiments the results. Parts of this chapter contain modified versions of parts from Goschke and Kuhl (1993) and Kuhl and Goschke (1994a).

REFERENCES

Ach, N. (1910). *Über den Willensakt und das Temperament* (On will and temperament). Leipzig: Quelle & Meyer.

Ach, N. (1935). *Analyse des Willens* (Analysis of the will). In E. Abderhalden (Ed.), *Handbuch der biologischen Arbeitsmethoden* [*Handbook of biological working methods*] *(Vol. 6)*. Berlin: Urban & Schwarzenberg.

Anderson, J. R. (1983). *The architecture of cognition.* Cambridge, MA: Harvard University Press.

Atkinson, J. W. (1957). Motivational determinants of risk-taking behavior. *Psychological Review, 64,* 359–372.

Baddeley, A. D. & Wilkins, A. J. (1984). Taking memory out of the laboratory. In J. E. Harris & P. E. Morris (Eds.), *Everyday memory and absent-mindedness* (pp.1–18). London: Academic Press.

Bargh, J. A. (1989). Conditional automaticity: varieties of automatic influences in social perception and cognition. In J. S. Uleman & J. A. Bargh (Eds.), *Unintended thought* (pp. 3–51). New York: Guilford.

Bassili, J. N., Smith, M. C. & MacLeod, C. M. (1989). Auditory and visual word-stem completion: Separating data-driven and conceptually-driven processes. *Quarterly Journal of Experimental Psychology, 41A,* 439–453.

Beckmann, J. (1994). Volitional correlates of action and state orientation. In J. Kuhl & J. Beckmann (Eds.), *Volition and personality. Action versus state orientation* (pp. 155–166). Toronto: Hogrefe.

Besner, D., & Smith, M. C. (1992). Models of visual word recognition: When obscuring the stimulus yields a clearer view. *Journal of Experimental Psychology: Learning, Memory, and Cognition, 18,* 468–482.

Bjork, R. A., & Whitten, W. B. (1974). Recency-sensitive processes in long-term free recall. *Cognitive Psychology, 6,* 173–189.

Blaxton, T. A. (1989). Investigating dissociations among memory measures: Support for an transfer-appropriate processing framework. *Journal of Experimental Psychology: Learning, Memory, and Cognition, 15,* 657–668.

Brand, M. (1984). *Intending and acting. Toward a naturalized action theory.* Cambridge, MA: MIT Press.

Bratman, M. E. (1987). *Intention, plans, and practical reason.* Cambridge, MA: Harvard University Press.

Butterfield, E. C. (1964). The interruption of task: Methodological, factual, and theoretical issues. *Psychological Bulletin, 62,* 309–322.

Ceci, S. J., Baker, J. G., & Bronfenbrenner, U. (1988). Prospective remembering, temporal calibration, and context. In M. M. Gruneberg, P. E. Morris, & R. N. Sykes (Eds.), *Practical aspects of memory: Current research and issues* (pp. 360–365). Chichester, England: Wiley.

Challis, B. H., & Brodbeck, D. R. (1992). Level of processing affects priming in word fragment completion. *Journal of Experimental Psychology: Learning, Memory, and Cognition, 18,* 595–607.

Chiarello, C., & Hoyer, W. J. (1988). Adult age differences in implicit and explicit memory: Time course and encoding effects. *Psychology and Aging, 3,* 358–366.

Cohen, G. (1989). *Memory in the real world.* Hillsdale, NJ: Lawrence Erlbaum Associates.

Craik, F. I. M., & Tulving, E. (1975). Depths of processing and the retention of words in episodic memory. *Journal of Experimental Psychology: General, 104,* 268–294.

Cummins, R. (1989). *Meaning and mental representation.* Cambridge, MA: MIT Press.

Dennett, D. C. (1987). *The intentional stance.* Cambridge, MA: MIT Press.

Diaz, R. M. & Berk, L. E. (1992). *Private speech. From social interaction to self-regulation.* Hillsdale, NJ: Lawrence Erlbaum Associates.

Dibbelt, S. (1993). *Wechseln und Beibehalten als Grundfunktionen der Handlungskontrolle* [Shifting and maintaining intentions as basic function of action control]. Unpublished manuscript, University of Osnabrück.

Dörner, D. (1986). Intention memory and intention regulation. In F. Klix & H. Hagendorf (Eds.), *Human memory and cognitive capabilities. Mechanisms and performances: Part B* (pp. 929–940). Amsterdam: Elsevier.

d'Ydewalle, G. (1981). Test expectancy effects in free recall and recognition. *Journal of General Psychology, 105,* 173–195.

d'Ydewalle, G. (1984). Motivation and information processing in learning experiments. *Australian Journal of Psychology, 36,* 149–160.

Einstein, G. O., & McDaniel, M. A. (1990). Normal aging and prospective memory. *Journal of Experimental Psychology: Learning, Memory, and Cognition, 16,* 717–726.

Einstein, G. O., McDaniel, M. A. Cunfer, A. R., & Guynn, M. J. (1992). *Aging and prospective memory: Examining the influence of self-initiated retrieval processes and mind wandering.* Unpublished manuscript, Furman University.

Ellis, J., & Williams, M. (1990). *Retrospective and prospective remembering: Common and distinct processes.* Manuscript submitted for publication.

Ericsson, K. A., & Simon, H. A. (1980). Verbal reports as data. *Psychological Review, 87,* 215–251.

Eysenck, M. W. (1982). Incidental learning and orienting tasks. In C. R. Puff (Ed.), *Handbook of research methods in human memory and cognition* (pp. 197–228). New York: Academic Press.

Feather, N. T. (Ed.) (1982) *Expectations and actions.* Hillsdale, NJ: Lawrence Erlbaum Associates.

Flexser, A. J., & Tulving, E. (1978). Retrieval independence in recognition and recall. *Psychological Review, 85,* 153–171.

Fodor, J. (1987). *Psychosemantics. The problem of meaning in the philosophy of mind.* Cambridge, MA: MIT Press.

Freud, S. (1952). *Psychopathology of everyday life.* New York: Mentor. (Original work published 1909)

Gallistel, C. R. (1985). Motivation, intention, and emotion: Goal directed behavior from a cognitive-neuroethological perspective. In M. Frese & J. Sabini (Eds.), *Goal directed behavior: The concept of action in psychology* (pp. 48–66). Hillsdale, NJ: Lawrence Erlbaum Associates.

Gollwitzer, P. (1989). Action phases and mind-sets. In E. T. Higgins & R. M. Sorrentino (Eds.) (1990). *Handbook of motivation and cognition: Foundations of social behavior* (Vol. 2, pp. 53–92). New York: Guilford.

Gollwitzer, P. (in press). Goal achievement: the role of intentions. In W. Stroebe & M. Hewstone (Eds.), *European Review of Social Psychology* (Vol.4). Chichester, England: Wiley.

Goschke, T. (in press-a). *Gedächtnis für Absichten* [Memory for intentions]. Göttingen: Hogrefe.

Goschke, T. (in press-b). Wille und Kognition. Zur funktionalen Architektur der intentionalen Handlungssteuerung. (Will and cognition. The functional architecture of intentional action control). In H. Heckhausen & J. Kuhl (Eds.), *Enzyklopädie der Psychologie Serie IV, Band 4: Motivation, Volition und Handeln.* Göttingen: Hogrefe.

Goschke, T., & Koppelberg, D. (1991). The concept of representation and the representation of concepts in connectionist models. In W. Ramsey, D. E. Rumelhart, & S. Stich (Eds.), *Philosophy and connectionist theory* (pp.129–162). Hillsdale, NJ: Lawrence Erlbaum Associates.

Goschke, T., & Kuhl, J. (1993). The representation of intentions: Persisting activation in memory. *Journal of Experimental Psychology: Learning, Memory, and Cognition, 19,* 1211–1226.

Goschke, T., & Kuhl, J. (1994). *Implicit memory for intentions: priming of intention-related information in word-fragment completion.* Manuscript submitted for publication.

Graf, P., Shimamura, A. P., & Squire, L. R. (1985). Priming across modalities and priming across category levels: Extending the domain of preserved function in amnesia. *Journal of Experimental Psychology: Learning, Memory, and Cognition, 11,* 385–395.

Graf, P., Squire, L. R. & Mandler, G. (1984). The information that amnesic patients do not forget. *Journal of Experimental Psychology: Learning, Memory and Cognition, 10,* 164–178.

Gray, J. A. (1987). *The psychology of fear and stress* (2nd ed). Cambridge, England: Cambridge University Press

Hamann, S. B. (1990). Level-of-processing effects in conceptually driven implicit tasks. *Journal of Experimental Psychology: Learning, Memory, and Cognition, 16,* 970–977.

Harris, J. E. (1984). Remembering to do things: a forgotten topic. In J. E. Harris & P. E. Morris (Eds.), *Everyday memory, actions and absent-mindedness* (pp. 71–92). New York: Academic Press.

Harris, J. E., & Wilkins, A. J. (1982). Remembering to do things: A theoretical framework and an illustrative experiment. *Human Learning, 1,* 123–136.

Hayman, C. A. G., & Tulving, E. (1989). Contingent dissociation between recognition and fragment completion: The method of triangulation. *Journal of Experimental Psychology: Learning, Memory, and Cognition, 15,* 228–240.

Heckhausen, H. (1977). Achievement motivation and its constructs: A cognitive model. *Motivation and Emotion, 1,* 283–329.

Heckhausen, H., & Kuhl, J. (1985). From wishes to action: The dead ends and short cuts on the long way to action. In M. Frese & J. Sabini (Eds.), *Goal-directed behavior: Psychological theory and research on action* (pp. 134–160). Hillsdale, NJ: Lawrence Erlbaum Associates.

Hershberger, W. A. (1989). *Volitional action. Conation and control.* Amsterdam: North-Holland.

Hintzman, D. L. & Harty, A. L. (1990). Item effects in recognition and fragment completion: Contingency relations vary for different subsets of words. *Journal of Experimental Psychology: Learning, Memory, and Cognition, 16,* 955–969.

Hirshman, E., Snodgrass, J. G., Mindes, J., & Feenan, K. (1990). Conceptual priming in fragment completion. *Journal of Experimental Psychology: Learning, Memory, and Cognition, 16,* 634–647.

Hörmann, H. (1964). Die Bedingungen für das Behalten, Vergessen und Erinnern. [The conditions of remembering, forgetting, and retrieving]. In R. Bergius (Ed.), *Handbuch der Psychologie, I.2* (pp. 225–283). Göttingen: Hogrefe.

Howe, M. L., Rabinowitz, F. M., & Grant, M. J. (1993). On measuring the (in)dependence of cognitive processes. *Psychological Review, 100,* 737–747.

Jacoby, L. L. (1991). A process dissociation framework: Separating automatic from intentional uses of memory. *Journal of Memory and Language, 30,* 513–541.

Jacoby, L. L., & Dallas, M. (1981). On the relationshup between autobiographical memory and perceptual learning. *Journal of Experimental Psychology: General, 110,* 306–340.

Jacoby, L. L., & Hayman, C. A. G. (1987). Specific visual transfer in word identification. *Journal of Experimental Psychology: Learning, Memory, and Cognition, 1,* 456–463.

James, W. (1890). *Principles of psychology.* New York: Holt.

Kimble, G. A., & Perlmuter, L. C. (1970). The problem of volition. *Psychological Review, 77,* 361–384.

Kirsner, K., Milech, D., & Standen, P. (1983). Common and modality-specific processes in the mental lexicon. *Memory & Cognition, 11,* 621–630.

Klinger, E. (1987). Current concerns and disengagement from incentives. In F. Halisch & J. Kuhl (Eds.), *Motivation, intention, and volition* (pp. 337–349). Berlin: Springer.

Koriat, A., Ben-Zur, H., & Nussbaum, A. (1990). Encoding information for future action: Memory for to-be-performed tasks versus memory for to-be-recalled tasks. *Memory & Cognition, 18,* 568–578.

Kuhl, J. (1981). Motivational and functional helplessness: The moderating effect of state versus action orientation. *Journal of Personality and Social Psychology, 40,* 155–170.

Kuhl, J. (1982). The expectancy-value approach within the theory of social motivation: Elaborations, extensions, critique. In: N. T. Feather (Ed.), *Expectations and actions* (pp. 125–159). Hillsdale, NJ: Lawrence Erlbaum Associates.

Kuhl, J. (1983). *Motivation, Konflikt und Handlungskontrolle* (Motivation, conflict, and action control). Heidelberg: Springer.

Kuhl, J. (1984). Volitional aspects of achievement, motivation, and learned helplessness: Toward a comprehensive theory of action control. In B. A. Maher (Ed.), *Progress in Experimental Personality Research, Vol.13* (pp. 99–170). New York: Academic Press.

Kuhl, J. (1985). Volitional mediators of cognitive-behavior consistency: Self-regulatory processes and actions versus state orientation. In J. Kuhl & J. Beckmann (Eds.), *Action control: From cognition to behavior* (pp. 101–128). Heidelberg: Springer.

Kuhl, J. (1986). Motivation and information processing: A new look at decision making, dynamic change, and action control. In R. M. Sorrentino & E. T. Higgins (Eds.), *Handbook of motivation and cognition: Foundations of social behavior* (pp. 404–434). Chichester, England: Wiley.

Kuhl, J. (1992). A theory of self-regulation: Action versus state orientation, self-discrimination, and some applications. *Applied Psychology: An International Review, 41,* 95–129.

Kuhl, J. (1994a). Action versus state orientation: Psychometric properties of the action-control scale (ACS–90). In J. Kuhl & J. Beckmann (Eds.), *Volition and personality: Action versus state orientation* (pp. 47–59). Toronto: Hogrefe.

Kuhl, J. (1994b). A theory of action and state orientation. In J. Kuhl & J. Beckmann (Eds.), *Volition and personality: action versus state orientation* (pp. 9–46). Toronto: Hogrefe.

Kuhl, J. (in press-a). Motivation and volition. In G. d'Ydewalle, Bertelson & Eelen (Eds.), *International perspectives on psychological science* (Vol. 2, pp. 311–340). Hillsdale, NJ: Lawrence Erlbaum Associates.

Kuhl, J. (in press-b). Wille und Freiheitserleben: Formen der Selbststeuerung [Volition and self-determination: Forms of self-regulation]. In J. Kuhl & H. Heckhausen (Eds.), *Enzyklopädie der Psychologie Serie IV, Band 4: Motivation, Volition und Handeln.* Göttingen: Hogrefe.

Kuhl, J. & Beckmann, J. (Eds.) (1994). *Volition and personality: Action versus state orientation.* Toronto: Hogrefe.

Kuhl, J., & Goschke, T. (1994a). State orientation and the activation and retrieval of intentions in memory. In J. Kuhl & J. Beckmann (Eds.), *Volition and personality: Action versus state orientation* (pp. 127–153). Toronto: Hogrefe.

Kuhl, J., & Goschke, T. (1994b). A theory of action control: Mental subsystems, modes of control, and volitional conflic-resolution strategies. In J. Kuhl & J. Beckmann (Eds.), *Volition and personality: action versus state orientation* (pp. 93–124). Toronto: Hogrefe.

Kuhl, J. & Helle, P. (1986). Motivational and volitional determinants of depression: The degenerated-intention hypothesis. *Journal of Abnormal Psychology, 95,* 247–251.

Kuhl, J., & Kazén, M. (1994). Volitional aspects of depression: State orientation and self-discrimination. In J. Kuhl & J. Beckmann (Eds.), *Volition and personality: action versus state orientation* (pp. 297–315). Toronto: Hogrefe.

Kuhl, J., & Kazén-Saad, M. (1988). A motivational approach to volition: Activation and de-activation of memory representations related to unfulfilled intentions. In V. Hamilton, G. H. Bower, & N. H. Frijda (Eds.), *Cognitive perspectives on emotion and motivation* (pp. 63–85). Dordrecht, The Netherlands: Martinus Nijhoff.

Kuhl, J., & Kraska, K. (1989). Self-regulation and metamotivation: Computational mechanisms, development, and assessment. In R. Kanfer, P. L. Ackerman, & R. Cudeck (Eds.), *Abilities, motivation, and methodology: The Minnesota Symposium on individual differences* (pp. 343–374). Hillsdale, NJ: Lawrence Erlbaum Associates.

Kvavilashvili, L. (1987). Rembering intention as a distinct form of memory. *British Journal of Psychology, 78,* 507–518.

LaBerge, D., & Samuels, S. J. (1974). Towards a theory of automatic information processing in reading. *Cognitive Psychology, 6,* 293–323.

Lewin, K. (1926). Vorsatz, Wille und Bedürfnis [Intention, will, and need]. *Psychologische Forschung, 7,* 330–385.

Loftus, E. F. (1971). Memory for intentions. *Psychonomic Science, 23,* 315–316.

Logan, G. D. (1988). Toward an instance theory of automatization. *Psychological Review, 95,* 492–527.

Luria, A. R. (1961). *The role of speech in regulation of normal and abnormal behavior.* London: Pergamon.

Mäntylä, T. (1993). Priming effects in prospective memory. *Memory, 1,* 203–218.

Martin, L. L., & Tesser, A. (1989). Toward a motivational and structural theory of ruminative thought. In J. S. Uleman & J. A. Bargh (Eds.), *Unintended thought* (pp. 307–326). New York: Guilford.

Meacham, J. A., & Colombo, J. A. (1980). External retrieval cues facilitate prospective remembering in children. *Journal of Educational Research, 73,* 299–301.

Miller, G. A., Galanter, E., & Pribram, K. H. (1960). *Plans and the structure of behavior.* New York: Holt, Rinehart, & Winston.

Morris, P. E. (1979). Strategies for learning and recall. In M. M. Gruneberg & P. E. Morris (Eds.), *Applied problems in memory.* London: Academic Press.

Münsterberg, H. (1889). *Beiträge zur Experimentellen Psychologie, Heft 1* [Contributions to experimental psychology]. Freiburg: Mohr.

Neumann, O. (1984). Automatic processing: a review of recent findings and a plea for an old theory. In W. Prinz & A. F. Sanders (Eds.), *Cognition and motor processes* (pp. 255–294). Berlin: Springer.

Neumann, O. (1987). Beyond capacity: A functional view of attention. In H. Heuer & A. F. Sanders (Eds.), *Perspectives on perception and action* (pp. 361–394). Hillsdale, NJ: Lawrence Erlbaum Associates.

Neumann, O. (1989). Kognitive Vermittlung und direkte Parameterspezifikation. Zum Problem mentaler Repräsentation in der Wahrnehmung. *Sprache & Kognition, 8,* 32–49.

Neumann, O., & Klotz, W. (1994). Motor responses to nonreportable, masked stimuli: where is the limit of direct parameter specification? In M. Moscovitch & C. Umiltá (Eds.), *Attention & Performance XV: Conscious and unconscious information processing* (pp. 124–150). Cambridge, MA: MIT Press.

Neumann, O., & Prinz, W. (1987). Kognitive Antezedenzien von Willkürhandlungen [Cognitive antecedents of voluntary actions]. In H. Heckhausen, P. M. Gollwitzer, & F. E. Weinert (Eds.), *Jenseits des Rubikon: Der Wille in den Humanwissenschaften* [Beyond the Rubicon: The will in the humanities] (pp. 195–215). Berlin: Springer.

Nisbett, R. E., & Wilson, T. D. (1977). Telling more than we can know: Verbal reports on mental processes. *Psychological Review, 84,* 231–259.

Norman, D. A., & Shallice, T. (1986). Attention to action: willed and automatic control of behavior. In R. J. Davidson, G. E. Schwartz, & D. Shapiro (Eds.), *Consciousness and self-regulation: Advances in research* (Vol. 4, pp. 1–18). New York: Plenum.

Ovsiankina, M. (1928). Die Wiederaufnahme unterbrochener Handlungen [The resumption of interrupted tasks]. *Psychologische Forschung 11,* 302–379.

Patterson, C. M., & Newman, J. P. (1993). Reflectivity and learning from aversive events: toward a psychological mechanism for the syndrome of disinhibition. *Psychological Review, 100,* 716–736.

Perruchet, P., & Baveux, P. (1989). Correlational analyses of explicit and implicit memory performance. *Memory & Cognition, 17,* 77–86.

Pollack, I. (1970). A nonparametric procedure for evaluation of true and false positives. *Behavior Research Methods and Instrumentation, 2,* 155–156.

Pollack, I., & Norman, D. A. (1964). A non-parametric analysis of recognition experiments. *Psychonomic Science, 1,* 125–126.

Posner, M. I., & Rothbart, M. K. (1992). Attention and conscious experience. In A. D. Milner & M. D. Rugg (Eds.), *The neuropsychology of consciousness* (pp. 94–112). London: Academic Press.

Posner, M. I., & Snyder, C. R. R. (1975). Attention and cognitive control. In R. L. Solso (Ed.), *Information processing and cognition: The Loyola symposium* (pp. 55–85). Hillsdale, NJ: Lawrence Erlbaum Associates.

Prinz, W. (1983). *Wahrnehmung und Tätigkeitssteuerung* [Perception and action control]. Berlin: Springer.

Ratcliff, R., & McKoon, G. (1978). Priming in item recognition: evidence for the propositional structure of sentences. *Journal of Verbal Learning and Verbal Behavior, 17,* 403–417.

Reder, L. M. (1982). Plausibility judgment versus fact retrieval: Alternative strategies for sentence verification. *Psychological Review, 89,* 250–280.

Richardson-Klavehn, A., & Bjork, R. A. (1988). Measures of memory. *Annual Review of Psychology, 39,* 475–543.

Roediger, H. L. (1990). Implicit memory. Retention without remembering. *American Psychologist, 45,* 1043–1056.

Roediger, H. L., & Blaxton, T. A. (1987). Effects of varying modality, surface features, and retention interval on priming in word fragment completion. *Memory & Cognition, 15,* 379–388.

Roediger, H. L., Weldon, M. S., & Challis, B. H. (1989). Explaining dissociations between implicit and explicit measures of retention: A processing account. In H. L. Roediger & F. I. M. Craik (Eds.), *Varieties of memory and consciousness: Essays in honour of Endel Tulving* (pp. 3–41). Hillsdale, NJ: Lawrence Erlbaum Associates.

Ryan, T. A. (1970). *Intentional behavior: An approach to human motivation.* New York: Ronald Press.

Schacter, D. L. (1987). Implicit memory: History and current status. *Journal of Experimental Psychology: Learning, Memory, and Cognition, 13,* 629–639.

Schacter, D. L., Bowers, J., & Booker, J. (1989). Intention, awareness, and implicit memory: The retrieval intentionality criterion. In S. Lewandowsky, J. C. Dunn, & K. Kirsner (Eds.), *Implicit memory. Theoretical issues* (pp. 47–66). Hillsdale, NJ: Lawrence Erlbaum Associates.

Schneider, W., & Shiffrin, R. W. (1977). Controlled and automatic human information processing: I. Decision, search, and attention. *Psychological Review, 84,* 1–66.

Shimamura, A. P. (1986). Priming effects in amnesia: Evidence for a dissociable memory function. *Quarterly Journal of Experimental Psychology, 38A,* 619–644.

Squire, L. R. (1992). Memory and the hippocampus: A synthesis from findings with rats, monkeys, and humans. *Psychological Review, 99,* 195–231.

Tulving, E., & Schacter, D. L. (1990). Priming and human memory systems. *Science, 247,* 301–305.

Tulving. E., Schacter, D. L., & Stark, H. A. (1982). Priming effects in word-fragment completion are independent of recognition memory. *Journal of Experimental Psychology: Learning, Memory, and Cognition, 8,* 336–342.

Uleman, J. S., & Bargh, J. A. (Eds.) (1989). *Unintended thought.* New York: Guilford.

van Bergen, A. (1968). *Task interruption.* Amsterdam: North-Holland.

von Holst, E., & Mittelstaedt, H. (1950). Das Reafferenzprinzip [The reafference principle]. *Naturwissenschaften, 37,* 464–476.

Vygotski, L. S. (1962). *Thought and language.* Cambridge, MA: MIT Press.

Warrington, E. K., & Weiskrantz, L. (1970). Amnesic syndrome: Consolidation of retrieval? *Nature, 228,* 629–630.

Weldon, M. S. (1991). Mechanisms underlying priming on perceptual tests. *Journal of Experimental Psychology: Learning, Memory, and Cognition, 17,* 526–541.

Zeigarnik, B. (1927). Über das Behalten von erledigten und unerledigten Handlungen [On remembering finished and unfinished activities]. *Psychologische Forschung, 9,* 1–85.

4

Activating Actions and Interrupting Intentions: Mechanisms of Retrieval Sensitization in Prospective Memory

Timo Mäntylä
University of Stockholm, Sweden

This chapter focuses on one of the most characteristic features of prospective memory (PM), namely, on the spontaneous experience when a planned action suddenly "pops in to mind" while we are engaged in other activities:

> If I form an intention in the morning which is to be carried out in the evening, I may be reminded of it two or three times in the course of the day. It need not however become conscious at all through the day. When the time of for its execution draws near, it suddenly springs to mind and causes me to make necessary preparations for the proposed actions. (Freud, 1901, p. 152).

The point of departure of this chapter is the notion that successful prospective remembering is, at least in part, determined by the individual's preparedness, or sensitivity, to identify a given event as a PM cue for the planned action. Retrieval sensitivity is assumed to reflect effects of and interactions among (a) the level of activation of the underlying event representations (referred as the *trace-dependent* component of PM), (b) the characteristics of the cue event for triggering the planned action (*cue-dependent* component), and (c) the individual's attentional resources for task monitoring and self-initiated retrieval operations (*capacity-dependent* component).

Assume that a person is making shopping plans and he or she has planned to buy tea and other items. Whether or not the person remembers to buy tea may be trace-dependent in the sense that the planning facilitates prospective remembering due to an increased activation of the underlying event representation. That is, the fact that the person made shopping plans heightened the activation level of the "grocery" representation that increased his or her sensitivity to recognize the target item as a functional cue for the planned action.

Prospective remembering may be *cue-dependent* in that successful performance is determined by the properties of the target event (e.g., distinctiveness, familiarity). According to one view of PM, target events that are salient are more efficient reminders of the planned action than are nonsalient target events (McDaniel & Einstein, 1993). Thus, the person remembers to buy tea, not because this intention is sustained in the memory, but because, for example, a distinctive package of tea catches his or her attention, and thereby reminds him or her that "something" should be purchased (cf., tying a string around a finger).

Finally, because retrieval information is implicit in most PM tasks, memory for future actions is not only guided by the properties of the target event. Instead, whether or not the person remembers to buy tea may be capacity-dependent in that successful performance requires self-initiated operations during the retention interval and at the time of retrieval (Craik, 1983, 1985). Especially under conditions in which the to-be-performed actions are infrequent or irregular, as compared to routine activities, the demands on self-initiated retrieval operations are high in most PM tasks because the rememberer has to recognize a given event as a target for the planned action.

When considering PM research from the perspective outlined here, past research focused on the cue- and capacity-dependent components of PM. The latter component was especially central in the context of aging, including the notion that aging disrupts self-initiated retrieval processes (see Maylor, 1993; McDaniel & Einstein, 1992, this volume, for reviews), whereas most retrieval-related studies focused on (a) the type of memory aids people use in (everyday) memory tasks (e.g., Harris, 1980; Harris & Wilkins, 1982; Intons-Peterson & Fournier, 1986; Maylor, 1990; Meacham & Colombo, 1980; Meacham & Singer, 1977; Wilkins & Baddeley, 1978), and (b) the optimal characteristics of these memory aids for triggering a planned action (e.g., Brandimonte & Passolunghi, 1994; Ellis & Milne, 1992; Einstein & McDaniel, 1990; Einstein, McDaniel, Cunfer, & Guynn, 1991; Kvavilashvili, 1987; McDaniel & Einstein, 1992; Meacham & Leiman, 1982)

By contrast, there is little published research focusing on the trace-dependent component of prospective remembering. This lack of research is surprising considering that the "spontaneous" characteristic of PM was emphasized in the literature. For example, Einstein and McDaniel (1990; Einstein et al., 1992; McDaniel & Einstein, 1992, 1993, see also this volume) considered PM as composing of processes that are both similar to and different from those of a standard retrospective memory (RM) task. Based on their componential analyses of PM,[1] McDaniel and Einstein (1992) stated that "the unique feature

---

[1]Einstein and McDaniel's (1990; Einstein et al., 1992; McDaniel & Einstein, 1992, 1993; see

of a prospective memory task is that the memory must be spontaneously or automatically activated at the appropriate time; there is (usually) no request for remembering the designated time, as in retrospective memory tasks" (p. 100).

ACTIVATING ACTIONS: PRIMING EFFECTS IN PROSPECTIVE MEMORY

In the present conceptualization of prospective remembering (see also Män-tylä, 1993, 1994), operations related to planning and task monitoring are assumed to facilitate PM by increasing the level of activation of the individual's knowledge representation that increases his or her sensitivity to identify the target item.

Prospective remembering due to an increased activation of knowledge structures may be related to retrieval and to earlier stages of processing. At the time of retrieval, the cue event may evoke retrieval implicitly by increasing activation from some resting level to a level that is above a hypothetical threshold. Using the shopping example mentioned earlier, even a relatively automatic encoding of the items displayed in the grocery store may reactivate the original shopping plan, and thereby induce a retrieval mode that increases the individual's sensitivity to perform the planned action.

Furthermore, the individual's self-initiated operations while performing other activities ("What should I remember to remember?") may maintain or even increase the activation level of the planned action. For example, while buying groceries, the person may remind himself or herself of an earlier plan to pick up a dress from the dry cleaner, and subsequently, due to an increased activation level of the "dry cleaner" representation, the probability that the person remembers to stop at the dry cleaner is increased.

Concerning research on the trace-dependent component of PM, Goschke and Kuhl (1993) and Koriat, Ben-Zur, and Nussbaum (1990) examined the nature of the representations underlying memory for future actions. Koriat et al. studied memory for to-be-performed tasks by presenting subjects with a series of verbal commands describing simple activities (e.g., "touch the stone," "lift the ashtray;" see also Bäckman & Nilsson, 1984; Cohen, 1983; Kausler & Hakami, 1983). Subjects memorized the minitasks either for later recall or actual performance, and were subsequently tested by verbatim recall or enactment. Koriat et al. found that subjects who were instructed to perform a task

---

also this volume) componental approach, PM is similar to retrospective cued-recall tasks because successful performance requires remembering the contents of the planned action as well as its association with the target event. Because of this similarity, Einstein and McDaniel labelled this aspect of PM the *retrospective component.* Another component, labelled the *prospective component,* is not shared with retrospective memory tasks.

showed better memory performance than subjects who were expecting a free recall task, regardless of which mode of report was actually required. Koriat et al. attributed this effect to differences in encoding strategies, rather than to differences in the level of activation of the underlying representations. Because the subjects were informed before the study phase whether they had to perform or to recall and activity, they used more efficient encoding strategies (symbolic enactment, imagery) when expecting task performance than verbal recall (see also Bäckman & Nilsson, 1984; Helstrup, 1986).

However, Goschke and Kuhl (1993, see also this volume) reported similar findings even under conditions in which the use of encoding strategies was limited. In their study, subjects memorized verbal descriptions of two different activities (e.g., setting the dinner table and clearing a messy desk). After the study phase, subjects were informed they would later have to either execute one of the scripts or to observe the experimenter executing the action and to register possible mistakes. The second script in each condition was neither executed nor observed, but the subjects were informed that their memory for both scripts of a pair would be tested. Immediately after the execution or observation instructions, the subjects received a recognition test for words for both scripts.

Goschke and Kuhl reasoned that if intention-related concepts are characterized by a higher level of activation than nonintention-related concepts, the recognition latencies for words from the to-be-executed script should be faster than words from the to-be-remembered script. The results of their study supported this prediction by showing an intention-superiority effect even when the use of strategies was limited. However, in a control condition in which the subjects had to observe someone else executing a script, latencies for words from the to-be-observed script did not differ from neutral words.

Although these findings indicate that intention-related concepts are characterized by a heightened and more sustained level of activation than other memory contents, they do not necessarily justify the conclusion that the intention-superiority effect underlies successful prospective remembering. In other words, although the to-be-performed actions were better remembered than the to-be-recalled actions in Koriat et al.'s (1990) study, and intention-related concepts were recognized faster than nonintention-related concepts in Goschke and Kuhl's (1993), the question remains open as to whether or not an increased activation of intention representation also facilitates subsequent prospective memory performance (i.e., memory for intent as compared to content). Thus, it is possible that although planned actions are represented at a heightened level of activation, measured in terms of different retrospective memory tasks, these dynamic properties may have minimal or nonexistent effects on remembering that one has to do something as compared to what has to be done.

Mäntylä (1993) provided more direct support for the hypothesis that in-

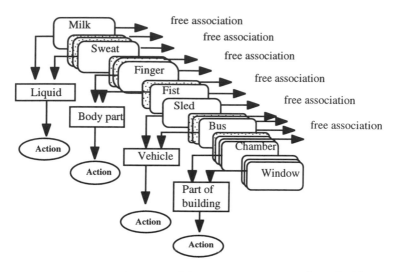

FIG. 4.1.   A schematic illustration of the prospective memory task used by Män-tylä (1993).

creased activation at the time of planning–encoding facilitates memory for fu-ture actions. In this study, level of semantic activation was manipulated by giv-ing subjects a category fluency task for one half of the target categories used in the subsequent PM task. The basic idea underlying Mäntylä's study was that the category fluency task would increase subjects' sensitivity to perform an ac-tion when a primed target item was encountered.

Subjects were given a background task in which they generated associations to auditorily presented words (see Fig. 4.1). Parallel with this free association task,[2] the subjects were instructed to perform an action whenever they heard an instance of the categories *liquids, parts of human body, vehicles,* and *parts of building,* respectively. Thus, the subjects were supposed to remember to per-form an action when they heard, for example, the words *milk,* or *bus.*

To manipulate level of semantic activation, the association and PM tasks were preceded by a category-fluency task in which the subjects generated, for example, as many liquids and vehicles as possible, whereas the two remaining target categories were not included in the fluency task. Effect of priming was

---

[2]The dual-task characteristic of the paradigm used (namely, remembering to make the re-quired action while generating an association) resembles everyday PM in that the cue event oc-curs while the individual is involved in some other activity (e.g., remembering a new route while listening to the car radio). The free association technique was considered as an appropriate sec-ondary task because subjects are involved in a continuous activity that is relatively demanding, but has certain personal relevance to the individual. Furthermore, most younger and older adults find the task interesting; and subjects' own associations can be used as cues in a subsequent ret-rospective recall test (see also Mäntylä, 1986; Mäntylä & Nilsson, 1988).

determined by comparing each subject's PM performance on target items that were instances of the categories used in the fluency task (primed targets) with those not used in the fluency task (nonprimed targets). To the extent that the category fluency task facilitates PM performance, better performance was expected for primed than for nonprimed targets.

Furthermore, based on the notion that optimal PM is also determined by cue- and capacity-dependent factors, the effects of activation on PM were examined under conditions in which the individual's capacity for self-initiated operations were assumed to be reduced due to aging, and the degree of retrieval support was limited by using target items that were only peripherally related to the prospective target criterion.

Young and older subjects were presented with primed and nonprimed target items that were typical or atypical members (*milk* vs. *sweat*) of a given semantic category (*liquids*). Target items that were relatively closely related to the task criterion were expected to provide more retrieval support (and require less self-initiation) than were atypical targets that were more peripheral members of a given category (see also Mäntylä, 1994).

The manipulation of item typicality might be compared to a real-world task in which a person is supposed to remember to buy a loaf of bread on the way home. There are several places where bread can be found (e.g., bakery, grocery store, deli, shopping center). However, these alternatives are not equal in terms of demands for self-initiated retrieval operations. In some cases, the target event serves as an explicit reminder of the planned action with minimal requirements for self-initiated retrieval (a bakery ⇒ bread: buy a loaf), whereas in other conditions successful performance requires more extensive retrieval operations (a shopping center ⇒ groceries ⇒ bread: buy a loaf).

The results of the study showed that the category fluency task improved subsequent prospective remembering in that the subjects performed planned actions more frequently when instances of the semantic categories used in the fluency task were presented as targets than when instances from the excluded categories were presented as targets (i.e., primed vs. nonprimed targets). Although the younger and older subjects showed comparable overall effects of priming, these effects were limited to certain levels of retrieval support. As can be seen in Fig. 4.2, the magnitude of priming interacted with age and item typicality, so that the younger subjects showed priming effects for atypical targets only, whereas an opposite pattern of results was obtained for older adults. Thus, the young showed reliable effects of priming when the demands for self-initiated retrieval operations were increased (i.e., atypical targets), whereas the old, who were assumed to have reduced resources for self-initiation, revealed significant effects of priming also under condition in which the degree of retrieval support was high. However, priming effects were not observed when the individual's resources for self-initiation and the degree of retrieval support were low. This pattern of results indicates that the effects of priming are de-

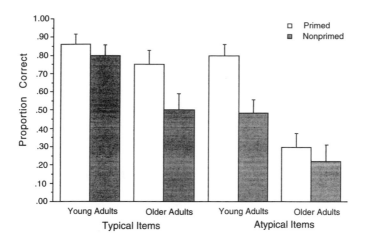

FIG. 4.2.   Prospective memory as a function of age, item typicality, and priming in Mäntylä (1993).

pendent rather than independent of retrieval-related factors in prospective remembering.

It should be noted that the priming effects observed in Mäntylä's (1993) study were not related to the number or type of category instances generated. That is, older subjects might have shown reduced priming effects for atypical items because they generated fewer category instances in the fluency task than the younger subjects, which may have reflected a less extensive activation of the underlying representation. Subsequent analyses showed minimal correlations between the fluency and priming scores, suggesting that the observed age difference in priming was not related to quantitative differences in category fluency. Also, qualitative analyses of the fluency data supported this conclusion, showing that the two age groups generated relatively similar category instances, measured both in terms of typicality and distinctiveness of generation.

Related to these analyses, younger adults may have shown greater priming effects for atypical items because they produced more atypical targets in the category fluency task than did older adults. However, subsequent analyses showed that the probability of generating an atypical target was low for both age groups. (Of the total of 430 responses, the younger subjects generated 2 atypical targets, and 1 of the older subjects' responses occurred as an atypical item in the PM task.)

In a subsequent study, we (Mäntylä & Jonzon, 1994) attempted to manipulate semantic activation by varying the duration of the category fluency task. The primary purpose of this study was to examine whether or not a manipulation of the level of activation also would affect subsequent PM performance. To manipulate level of activation, subjects generated category instances either during 60 sec (high-activation condition, as in Mäntylä's, 1993 study) or during 20 sec (low-activation condition). In a subsequent PM task, the subjects were given two target categories, one of which was included in the category fluency task (high vs. low primed target), whereas the remaining target category was not included in the category fluency task (nonprimed targets).

Although the results of the study showed better memory for primed than nonprimed targets, replicating Mäntylä's (1993) findings, there were no reliable differences between the high-activation and low-activation conditions. However, these findings should be interpreted with caution because only two levels duration (20 sec vs. 60 sec) were used in the fluency task, and each subject's performance was based on two target items (of which one was a primed and the other a nonprimed target). In Mäntylä's (1993) study, subjects were presented with a total of eight PM targets.

The results of our studies suggest that memory for future actions is not only determined by retrieval-related factors, but that an increased activation at the time of planning–encoding facilitates the individuals' sensitivity to perform a planned action. Expressing these findings in relation to Anderson's (1983) adaptive control of thought (ACT*) model, the category generation may have produced automatic spreading of activation from the semantic-memory nodes of its lexical constituents to those of other related items, including a memory trace of the target items used in the subsequent PM task. Consequently, although this activation may have been weak (or below a threshold for complete access), it may have sensitized subjects for future occurrences and thereby facilitated the detection of potential target items at the time of prospective retrieval.

INTERRUPTING INTENTIONS: PROSPECTIVE REMEMBERING AS "UNRESOLVED GOAL TENSION"

The research summarized supports the hypothesis that operations related to planning and task monitoring facilitate subsequent PM performance by increasing the activation level of the underlying knowledge representation. Although these notions were expressed in terms of contemporary terminology (prospective priming, spread of activation, retrieval sensitization), the basic ideas are similar to those formulated by Lewin (1926/1961) years ago.

Apart from Freud (1901), Lewin (1926/1961, p. 1234) was the first psychologist who considered "the influence of time on the effect of intention" (which was the subtitle of his classic paper *Intention, will, and need*). According to Lewin, intentional actions are composed of three main phases: First, a motivation process, characterized by a "vigorous struggle of motives," followed by an act of choice during the second phase, and finally, either after a short or long interval, the "consummatory" intentional action itself.

A central question, according to Lewin (1926/1961), was "how does the act of intending bring about the subsequent action, particularly in those cases in which the consummatory action does not follow immediately the act of intending . . . what are the further characteristics of this after-effect of the act of intending" (pp. 1234–1235). Lewin argued that the aftereffect of intention is a force, or a "goal tension" that produces a "quasi-need" to carry out the planned action. Lewin stated that the clearest subjective experience of this force occurs in the resumption of interrupted tasks, "when after completing the interrupting activity, a general pressure—that 'there is something I should do'—appears" (p. 1251).

Lewin and his collaborators experimentally examined these notions by presenting subjects a series of concrete tasks, such as threading beads or drawing a vase. Although the tasks were relatively simple, Lewin observed that subjects showed considerable reluctance to obey when they were told to stop before they had finished the task assigned them. Furthermore, when a second activity, interrupting the first one, was completed, there appeared a strong desire to resume the unfinished task.

A central concept in Lewin's interruption studies was the principle of homeostasis: Systems under tension tend toward a state of equilibrium, at the lowest possible level of tension, with the neighboring regions. A task, as long as it is unfinished, is considered as a system under tension, whereas completion of the task releases tension. However, if the activities that lead to towards tension discharge are blocked, the system remains under tension. According to Lewin, task interruption has effects on various phenomena like resumption, memory, and substitute activities (see e.g. Boring, 1957; Tolman, 1948, for more detailed discussions of Lewin's work).

Zeigarnik, Lewin's student in his Berlin laboratory, examined the memorial consequences of interrupting actions. In her study (Zeigarnik, 1927; see also Ovsiankina, 1928), subjects were allowed to complete one half of the tasks, whereas the remaining tasks, interspersed throughout the series, were interrupted by the experimenter before subjects could complete them. Immediately following the completion of the series, subjects were given an unexpected free recall test in which they were asked to recall the names of the tasks. The result of the study showed that subjects consistently recalled more of the interrupted than completed tasks.

According to Boring (1957), there is an anecdotal story related to Zeigarnik's experiment:

> Lewin and his friends were in a restaurant in Berlin, in the sort of prolonged conversation which always surrounded Lewin. It was long time they had ordered and the waiter hovered in the distance. Lewin called him over, asked what he owed, was told instantly and paid, but the conversation went on. Presently Lewin had an insight. He called the waiter back and asked him how much he had been paid. The waiter no longer knew. When his tension was relieved by having the bill paid, the memory was no longer kept alive. (p. 734)

Although the Zeigarnik effect is an interesting (but inconsistent) empirical phenomenon, the primary purpose of this chapter is not to discuss the adequacy of the Gestalt psychological explanation of the effect (but see van Bergen, 1968; Butterfield, 1964; Pachauri, 1935, for reviews). Instead, the focus of the following section is to examine the effects of task interruption in relation to prospective remembering.

ZEIGARNIK-LIKE EFFECTS IN PROSPECTIVE MEMORY

Although Lewin (1926/1961) was one of the first psychologists to discuss prospective remembering in everyday life, including the pioneering experimental work of his student, Birenbaum (1930), it should be noted that the Zeigarnik effect deals with *retrospective* remembering. That is, subjects are presented a series of tasks, some of which are completed and others interrupted, and following the study phase, subjects are given explicit instructions to recall the names of the tasks.

However, the phenomenon is interesting in the context of PM, and especially in relation to the notion of retrieval sensitization discussed earlier (including Lewin's notion of goal tension), because task interruption might facilitate retrieval in the absence of explicit agents that prompt the execution of planned actions. In other words, interrupted or temporarily suspended items might maintain a higher level of activation than completed tasks, and consequently, the effects of interruption might facilitate performance on the subsequent PM task.

To explore this notion, we (Mäntylä & Sgaramella, 1993) used the same procedure as Mäntylä (1993), except that the category fluency task was replaced by an anagram task. To this end, we followed Baddeley's (1963) study, in which subjects were presented with anagrams of common 5-letter nouns. In his study, task interruption was based on each subject's ability to solve a given item within 1 min. If a subject failed to solve an anagram within the time limit, the experimenter told the correct solution of the uncompleted item. Baddeley found that subjects recalled more unsolved than solved anagrams, independently of solving time.

The basic strategy underlying our experiment was to manipulate the level of activation by including (some of) the PM targets in the anagram task. To the extent that a form of residual activation, or *unresolved goal tension*, contributes to the spontaneous characteristic of PM, interrupted targets were expected to produce better PM performance than completed targets.

In the first phase of the experiment, subjects were given a list of 30 anagrams that were based on five-letter (Italian) nouns, taken from six semantic categories (e.g., liquids). If the subject solved a given item (e.g., TLETA) within

30 sec, the response time was noted, and the next item was presented by the experimenter. If the subject failed to solve the anagram within the time limit, the experimenter told the correct (and unique) solution (LATTE) before presenting the next item.

Immediately after the anagram task, subjects were given a free association task in which they generated associations to auditorily presented words. Parallel with this background task, the subjects were instructed to perform an action whenever they heard an instance of the categories *liquids, body parts* or *vehicles*. Thus, as in Mäntylä's (1993) study, subjects were supposed to remember to perform an action when they heard, for example, the words *milk* [latte], or *train*. The total of six targets (two items per category) were included in the PM task. Four of these targets were included in the anagram task (primed targets), whereas the remaining two items were not included in the first phase of the experiment (nonprimed targets). The subjects solved one half of the targets included in the anagram task (primed completed), whereas the solutions of the remaining items were interrupted (primed interrupted). Each target occurred equally often as a primed–nonprimed and completed–interrupted item in the anagram and PM tasks. Finally, because the experimenter gave correct solutions for the unsolved items, it was possible to examine Zeigarnik-like effects in RM. The subjects were first given a free recall test in which they were asked to recall the solutions of the anagrams they studied earlier. The free-recall test was followed by a yes–no recognition test in which the study words were presented along with comparable distractors.

To summarize, the present experiment was designed to test three hypotheses. First, to the extent that a prior activation facilitates subsequent PM performance, target items included in the anagram task were expected to produce higher levels of PM than excluded targets (primed vs. nonprimed targets). Secondly, to the extent that task interruption facilitates prospective remembering, unsolved PM targets were expected to show better performance than targets that were solved in the anagram task (primed completed vs. primed interrupted), and finally, to the extent that task interruption facilitates subsequent RM performance, recall and recognition of uncompleted anagrams were expected to be better than those of completed anagrams.

The results of the study supported the first hypothesis by replicating Mäntylä's (1993) findings in that primed targets (items included in the anagram task) showed better PM performance than nonprimed targets (excluded items). Concerning the second hypothesis, the results showed somewhat, but not significantly, better PM performance for interrupted than completed targets. However, the interpretation of the Zeigarnik effect in PM was complicated by the fact that the level of performance for primed (but not for nonprimed) targets was close to ceiling. That is, the subjects showed relatively high levels of performance whether an item was completed or interrupted in the anagram task. Concerning Zeigarnik-like effects in RM (i.e., when subsequently asked

to remember the words presented in the anagram task), the subjects both recalled and recognized interrupted items significantly better than completed
items.

Baddeley's study (1963) and the present experiment showed Zeigarnik-like
effects in RM performance, although the interrupted items were completed by
the experimenter. This result is difficult to interpret in the light of Lewin's tension system theory (i.e., a task is considered as a system under tension only
as long as long it is unfinished, and completion of the task means tension re-
lease). The effects of interruption should have been reduced because the task
was finished by the experimenter. Thus, as Baddeley (1963) concluded "it
seems . . . that interruption is the crucial factor, though how it facilitates recall is by no means clear either in the present situation or with the Zeigarnik
effect in general" (p. 64).

However, according to Zeigarnik (1927), the crucial factor is not the objective of completion or interruption, but the subjective feeling of having finished or of being still unsatisfied:

> A quasi-need persists if the task has not been completed to the subject's own sat-
> isfaction regardless of whether this is equivalent to what may seem from another
> person's inspection to constitute "finished" or "unfinished." Tasks with whose
> solution the subject is not content will function in his memory as "unfinished"
> even though the experimenter may have classified them as completed, and vice
> versa. (p. 85; but see also van Bergen, 1968)

To further examine the effects of interruption on PM, we carried out a second experiment in which the manipulation of interruption and completion was
more closely related to the PM task (and also more similar to Zeigarnik's original study). Instead of using free associations as a background task, the PM
task was included in the anagram task. Specifically, subjects were presented
with 54 anagrams, with each item having a two-digit random number printed
on the upper corner of the response sheet (see Fig. 4.3).

Furthermore, four anagrams (cue items) differed from the remaining study
items in that the third letter of each item was underlined. The subjects were
instructed that, in addition to the anagram task, they should decide whether
a subsequent (target) anagram contained the same or a different third letter
as the underlined letter of the cue item. The identity of each target item was
determined by the two-digit number printed on the response sheet of the underlined cue item, which was the same (#65) for all and four items, and the
cue-target interval varied between 8 to 10 items.

In the first phase of the experiment, subjects were given a practice session
in which they solved a list of 10 anagrams. To obtain an equal number of completed and uncompleted items in the subsequent main task, we calibrated each
subject's solving time on the basis of his or her performance on the practice
items. Also, to reduce practice and item-specific effects, the experimenter

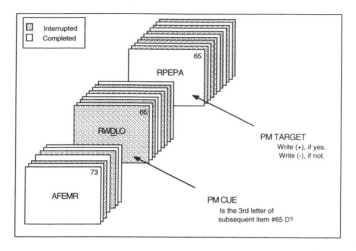

FIG. 4.3.   A schematic illustration of the prospective memory task used by Mäntylä and Sgaramella (1993).

monitored subjects' performance on each trial, and attempted to interrupt subjects relatively late while they were solving to-be-interrupted items.

Thus, after the practice session, subjects solved anagrams, and when, for instance, the anagram RWDLO [world] was presented, with the number 65 printed on the upper corner of the response sheet, they were supposed to remember to decide whether "D" was the third letter of the subsequent anagram #65. When responding, the subjects wrote a plus sign (+) on the response sheet if the anagram contained the same third letter as the cue item, and a minus sign (−) if it was different. The subjects were also told that if they could not remember the letter (i.e., the content of the PM task), they should write a circle (o) on the response sheet. The subjects solved one half of the anagrams, in random order, whereas the solution of the remaining items was interrupted by the experimenter (who always gave the correct solution for the interrupted anagram). Also, two of the four prospective cue events were completed and the remaining two were interrupted (but the prospective targets were always completed). Furthermore, items completed by one half of the subjects were interrupted items for the remaining subjects, and vice versa. After the anagram task, the subjects were given a free-recall test in which they were asked to recall the correct solutions of the anagrams they studied earlier. The free-recall test was followed by a recognition test in which the study words were presented along with comparable distractors.

The results of the experiment showed that interrupted items produced better PM performance than completed items. As can been seen from the upper section of Table 4.1, a correct response (i.e., +/− sign) was given more frequently following a PM instruction that was associated with interrupted than

TABLE 4.1
Prospective and Retrospective Memory Performance as a
Function of Item Type (in Mäntylä & Sgaramella, 1993)

Type of Task	Prospective Memory		Retrospective Memory			
			Free Recall		Recognition	
Type of Item	M	SD	M	SD	M	SD
Experiment 2						
Completed	.58	.24	.39	.11	.64	.20
Interrupted	.74	.29	.51	.15	.71	.26
Experiment 3						
70% Completed	.32	.33	.15	.10	.52	.16
30% Interrupted	.59	.37	.24	.09	.79	.18
30% Completed	.23	.26	.16	.09	.58	.21
70% Interrupted	.42	.39	.19	.08	.64	.21

completed anagrams. A more lenient scoring criterion (i.e., the subjects wrote a circle on the response sheet) showed a similar pattern of results, although this effect was only marginally significant ($p < .10$).

Concerning RM performance, interrupted items were again better recalled and recognized than completed items. Thus, although the study time for completed items was longer than that for interrupted items, and a correct solution was always given after the interruption, the subjects both recalled and recognized interrupted items better than they did completed items.

Finally, in Experiment 3, we replicated and extended these findings by increasing the number of study items, extending the interval between the prospective cue and target items, and varying the proportion of interrupted and completed items. The purpose of the latter manipulation was to test the hypothesis that interrupted items produced better PM performance than completed items in Experiment 2, because task interruption increased *distinctiveness* (rather than level of activation) of the cue item (Hunt & McDaniel, 1993; Jacoby & Craik, 1979).

To examine this notion, the number of interrupted and completed items was varied, so that one half of the subjects completed 70% of the anagrams and 30% were interrupted, whereas the remaining subjects completed 30% of the anagrams and 70% were interrupted. If cue distinctiveness produced Zeigarnik-like effects in the previous experiment, these effects should be reduced when the proportion of interrupted items was increased (and attenuated when the level of interruption was increased).

As in the previous experiment, the subjects solved anagrams, and were instructed to decide whether or not the target anagram contained the same third letter as the previously presented cue item (the cue–target interval was between 18–20 items). Again, the subjects solved one half of the anagrams, whereas the solution of the remaining items was interrupted by the experimenter. In contrast to Experiment 2, in which the identity of the target item was based on the same number (#65), each cue–target pair was now defined by different two-digit numbers. Each number occurred equally often for completed and interrupted items. In the final phase of the experiment, subjects were given free-recall and recognition tests on the correct solutions of the anagrams they studied earlier.

The results of Experiment 3 are summarized in the lower section of Table 4.1. Although the overall levels of performance were somewhat lower than those of Experiment 2, Zeigarnik-like effects were observed both in prospective and retrospective memory performance. As can be seen from Table 4.1, interrupted items produced nearly twice as high PM performance than completed items, and in contrast to the previous experiment, both the strict and lenient scoring criteria produced statistically significant effects.

Furthermore, the manipulation of the ratio of completed to interrupted items had no reliable effects on PM performance. The mean difference between the two item types was .27 when the completed items were more frequent than the interrupted items, and .19 in the opposite condition. However, as can be seen from Table 4.1, the manipulation of set size had larger effects on RM performance. Although the interactions between set size and item type were not reliable, a series of planned comparisons confirmed this observation by showing Zeigarnik effects only in when the completed items were more frequent than the interrupted items. Thus, although PM performance was not affected by the manipulation of set size, additional research is needed before the effects of distinctiveness on task interruption can be evaluated.

CONCLUDING REMARKS

The point of departure for this chapter is the notion that successful prospective remembering is determined by the individual's sensitivity to identify a given event as a PM cue for the planned action. Activities related to planning, subsequent task monitoring, and evaluation–updating are assumed to increase the activation level of underlying intention representation, and thereby facilitate the individual's preparedness to remember a planned action.

The notion that an initial activation–planning increases the individual's sensitivity to recognize a target event in a subsequent PM task is similar to Yaniv and Meyer's (1987) explanation of the *incubation effect* in problem solving (i.e., extra work on unsolved problems may lead to improvement if the new work is delayed rather than undertaken immediately after initial solution attempts; see e.g., Posner, 1973; Smith & Blankenship, 1989, Woodworth & Schlosberg, 1954).

Yaniv and Meyer (1987) studied the activation of inaccessible information by using a modified tip-of-the-tongue paradigm (e.g., Brown & McNeill, 1966) and different criterion tasks (lexical decision, feeling-of-knowing ratings, and yes–no recognition). Subjects first attempted to recall some rare target words in response to a series of definitions meant to cue retrieval from long-term semantic memory. For the words that could not be recalled initially, subjects rated their feelings of knowing, followed by a lexical decision task in which the target words and other control items were presented. Yaniv and Meyer found priming of initially unretrieved words, as evidenced by performance on the lexical decision task.

Yaniv and Meyer (1987) interpreted this as evidence in support of their *memory sensitization* hypothesis, which states that partial activation resulting from the initial unsuccessful attempt makes the activated target more accessible to subsequent attempts. The initial unsuccessful attempts to recall target words activated stored, but currently inaccessible, memory traces (cf., the category fluency task used in Mäntylä's 1993 study). During a subsequent intervening period of other endeavors, "the activation sensitized a person to chance encounters with related external stimuli that raise the critical traces above threshold" (p. 200).

As mentioned earlier, and related to Yaniv and Meyer's memory sensitization hypothesis, Goschke and Kuhl (1993) and Koriat et al. (1990) showed that intention-related items were better recalled and recognized than nonintention related items, suggesting that representations of intended actions differ in their dynamic properties from other (retrospective) memory contents. The experiments summarized here extend these findings by showing that prior activation is not only beneficial for the memory of the content, but also the execution of postponed intentions was facilitated when prior activation was increased by means of a category fluency task or task interruption.

Although these experiments support the idea that planning and task monitoring activities facilitate PM by influencing the level of activation of the underlying intention representation, planning and task monitoring also may have additional effects on PM performance. The task-interruption and category-fluency tasks were useful methods for manipulating those aspects of planning that were related to the activation of knowledge structures, but they were not designed to explore other potential effects of planning on PM performance.

Planning in most everyday situations is a dynamic and complex activity that, in addition to activation of knowledge structures, includes different types of organizational and elaborative operations (e.g., integration and spatiotemporal sequencing; see also Gärling, Säisä, Böök, & Lindberg, 1986; Hayes-Roth & Hayes-Roth, 1979). Thus, different planning activities (e.g., long-term vs. short-term planning, familiar vs. unfamiliar plans) may have differential effects both on the level and type of activation (e.g., a high level of activation of some central attributes of the plan), and different planning operations may produce intention representations that vary in their structure and complexity.

Extensive planning (i.e., thinking and imaging about the specific elements of the plan, actions to be performed, their consequences for other relevant plans, etc.), may not only increase the activation or strength of the intention representation, but may also produce a more differentiated representation as compared to a situation in which planning is less elaborated. Consequently, a more differentiated (but equally active) intention representation may facilitate prospective remembering by increasing the number of potential cues that could trigger a planned action at the time of retrieval.

To illustrate this notion, compare a hypothetical situation in which a person plans to make a phone call after lunch, with a situation in which the person plans to make a phone call after lunch, but before returning to his or her office, and to use a phone booth that is located close to his or her parking lot. Furthermore, we assume that the person also thinks about the contents of the phone call and the interlocutor's reactions in both situations, making them comparable in terms of activation. However, the latter example, in which the person made more elaborated plans, may produce better PM performance because there are more potential cues for triggering the action. In addition to the event "after lunch," which is a potential cue in both situations, the person may also remember to make the phone call because the additional events (leaving the restaurant, phone booth, and parking lot) are potential cues for the planned action.

Thus, instead of assuming that planning influences prospective remembering by merely increasing the level of activation of the intention representation, a more reasonable position is to assume that operations performed at the time of planning facilitate prospective remembering by increasing the level of activation and the number of potential cues for activating the action. An important avenue for future research on prospective remembering is to examine the effects of different types of planning activities, varying from a relatively automatic activation of the intention representation to complex encoding operations that produce a rich and detailed memory representation. Furthermore, these trace-dependent components of PM may interact with the cue-dependent components, so that certain types of planning activities are optimal only in combination with specific retrieval conditions.

The spontaneous characteristic of prospective retrieval is probably the most central difference between a retrospective and prospective memory task. Although this aspect of PM is emphasized here, it is not necessarily a unique feature of prospective remembering. Instead, retrospective remembering may be spontaneous and involuntary (Ebbinghaus, 1885/1913; Fulgosi & Guilford, 1968; Murray & Denny, 1969; Salaman, 1970; Yaniv & Meyer, 1987). For example, Ebbinghaus (1885/1913) divided recollective experiences between voluntary and involuntary remembering: "Often, even after years, mental states once present in consciousness return to it with apparent spontaneity and without any act of the will; that is, they are reproduced involuntarily" (pp. 1–2).

Instead of assuming that the spontaneous retrieval is a unique component of prospective remembering, a more general view for conceptualizing the two temporal dimensions of episodic remembering is to assume that both prospective and retrospective retrieval are always cued (cf., Jones, 1978; Tulving & Madigan, 1970; Watkins, 1979). Thus, although episodic retrieval was labelled as cued or noncued (Tulving & Pearlstone, 1966), or prompted or unprompted (Bahrick, 1970), and PM was termed as *uncued* (Levy & Loftus, 1984) or *self-cued* (Wilkins & Baddeley, 1978), some aspects of the individual's physical and/or cognitive environment initiate and influence the process of retrieval both in retrospective and prospective memory tasks (cf., Tulving, 1983). From this perspective, both prospective and retrospective retrieval are considered as cue-dependent, but the functional retrieval cues are more invisible (cf., Eich, 1980) in a PM task than in a typical RM task. Consequently, because cue-dependency is de-emphasised in memory for future actions, the spontaneous experience when a planned action suddenly pops to mind becomes the most prominent feature of prospective remembering.

ACKNOWLEDGMENTS

This research was supported by a grant from the Swedish Council for Research in the Humanities and Social Sciences. The chapter was written while the author was a visiting researcher at the University of Padua, Italy.

REFERENCES

Anderson, J. R. (1983). *The architecture of cognition*. Cambridge, MA: Harvard University Press.
Baddeley, A. D. (1963). A Zeigarnik-like effect in the recall of anagram solutions. *Quarterly Journal of Experimental Psychology, 15*, 63–64.
Bäckman, L., & Nilsson, L.-G. (1984). Aging effects in free recall: An exception to the rule. *Human Learning, 3*, 53–69.
Bahrick, H. P. (1970). Two-phase model of prompted recall. *Psychological Review, 77*, 215–222.
Birenbaum, G. (1930). Das Vergessen einer Vornahme. *Psygologische Forschung, 13*, 218–284.
Boring, E. G. (1957). A history of experimental psychology (2nd ed.). New Englewood Cliffs, NJ: Prentice-Hall.
Brandimonte, M. A., & Passolunghi, M. C. (1994). The effect of cue familiarity, cue-distinctiveness, and retention interval on prospective remembering. *Quarterly Journal of Experimental Psychology, 47*(A), 565–587.
Brown, R., & McNeill, D. (1966). The "tip of the tongue" phenomenon. *Journal of Verbal Learning and Verbal Behavior, 5*, 325–337.
Butterfield, E. C. (1964). The interruption task. Methodological, factual, and theoretical issues. *Psychological Bulletin, 62*, 309–322.

Cohen, R. L. (1983). The effects of encoding variables on the free recall of words and action events. *Memory & Cognition, 11*, 575–582.

Craik, F. I. M. (1983). On the transfer of information from temporary to permanent storage. *Philosophical Transactions of the Royal Society of London, 302*, 341–359.

Craik, F. I. M. (1985). Human memory paradigms. In L.-G. Nilsson & T. Archer, (Eds.), *Perspectives on learning and memory* (pp. 197–221). Hillsdale, NJ: Lawrence Erlbaum Associates.

Ebbinghaus, H. (1913). *Über das Gedächtnis* [Memory]. (H. Ruyer & C. E. Bussenius, Trans.). New York: Teacher's College, Columbia University. (Original work published 1885)

Eich, J. E. (1980). The cue-dependent nature of the state-dependent retrieval. *Memory and Cognition, 8*, 37–55.

Einstein, G. O., Holland, L. J., McDaniel, M. A., & Guynn, M. J. (1992). Age-related deficits in prospective memory: The influence of task complexity. *Psychology and Aging, 7*, 471–478.

Einstein, G. O., & McDaniel, M. A. (1990). Normal aging and prospective memory. *Journal of Experimental Psychology: Learning, Memory, and Cognition, 16*, 717–726.

Einstein, G. O., McDaniel, M. A., Cunfer, A. R., & Guynn, M. J. (1991). *Aging and prospective memory: Examining the influence of self-initiated retrieval processes and mind wandering.* Unpublished manuscript, Furman University.

Ellis, J. A., & Milne, A. B. (1992). *The effects of retrieval cue specificity on prospective memory performance.* Unpublished manuscript, University of Wales, College of Cardiff.

Freud, S. (1901). *The psychopathology of everyday life.* London: Hogarth Press.

Fulgosi, A., & Guilford, J. P. (1968). Short-term incubation in divergent production. *American Journal of Psychology, 81*, 241–246.

Gärling, T., Säisä, J., Böök, A., & Lindberg, E. (1986). Spatiotemporal sequencing of everyday activities in the large-scale environment. *Journal of Environmental Psychology, 6*, 261–280.

Goschke, T., & Kuhl, J. (1993). Representation of intentions: Persisting activation in memory. *Journal of Experimental Psychology: Learning, Memory, and Cognition, 19*, 1211–1226.

Hayes-Roth, B., & Hayes-Roth, F. (1979). A cognitive model of planning. *Cognitive Science, 3*, 275–310.

Harris, J. E. (1980). Memory aids people use: Two interview studies. *Memory & Cognition, 8*, 31–38.

Harris, J. E., & Wilkins, A. J. (1982). Remembering to do things: A theoretical framework and an illustrative experiment. *Human Learning, 1*, 123–136.

Helstrup, T. (1986). Separate memory laws for recall of performed acts. *Scandinavian Journal of Psychology, 27*, 1–29.

Hunt, R. R., & McDaniel, M. A. (1993). The enigma of organization and distinctiveness. *Journal of Memory and Language, 32*, 421–445.

Intons-Peterson, M. J., & Fournier, J. (1986). External and internal memory aids: How often we use them. *Journal of Experimental Psychology: General, 115*, 267–280.

Jacoby, L. L., & Craik, F. I. M. (1979). Effects of elaboration of processing at encoding and retrieval: Trace distinctiveness and recovery of initial context. In L. S. Cermak & F. I. M. Craik (Eds.), *Level of processing in human memory* (pp. 1–21). Hillsdale, NJ: Lawrence Erlbaum Associates.

Jones, G. W. (1978). A fragmentation hypothesis of memory: Cued recall of pictures and sequential position. *Journal of Experimental Psychology: General, 105*, 277–293.

Kausler, D. H., & Hakami, M. K. (1983). Memory for activities: Adult age differences in intentionality. *Developmental Psychology, 19*, 889–894.

Kvavilashvili, L. (1987). Remembering intention as a distinct form of memory. *British Journal of Psychology, 78*, 507.

Koriat, A., Ben-Zur, H., & Nussbaum, A. (1990). Encoding information for future actions: Memory for to be-performed tasks versus memory for to-be-recalled tasks. *Memory & Cognition, 18*, 568–578.

Levy, R. L., & Loftus, G. R. (1984). Compliance and memory. In J. E. Harris and P. E. Morris (Eds.), *Everyday memory, actions, and absent-mindedness* (pp. 93–112). New York: Academic Press.

Lewin, K. (1961). Intention, will, and need. In T. Shipley (Ed. and Trans.), *Classics in psychology* (pp. 1234–1288). New York: Philosophical Library. (Original work published 1926)

Mäntylä, T. (1986). Optimizing cue effectiveness: Recall of 500 and 600 incidentally learned words. *Journal of Experimental Psychology: Learning, Memory, and Cognition, 12*, 66–71.

Mäntylä, T. (1993). Priming effects in prospective memory. *Memory, 1*, 203–218.

Mäntylä, T. (1994). Remembering to remember: Adult age differences in prospective memory. *Journal of Gerontology: Psychological Sciences, 49*, 276–282.

Mäntylä, T., & Jonzon, E. (1994). *The effects of semantic activation on prospective remembering.* Unpublished manuscript, University of Stockholm.

Mäntylä, T., & Nilsson, L.-G. (1988). Cue distinctiveness and forgetting: Effectiveness of self-generated cues in delayed recall. *Journal of Experimental Psychology: Learning, Memory, and Cognition, 14*, 502–509.

Mäntylä, T., & Sgaramella, M. T. (1993). *Interrupting intentions: Zeigarnik-like effects in prospective memory.* Unpublished manuscript. University of Stockholm.

Maylor, E. A. (1990). Age and prospective memory. *Quarterly Journal of Experimental Psychology, 42A*, 471–493.

Maylor, E. A. (1993). Minimizing prospective memory loss in old age. In J. Cerella, W. Hoyer, J. Rybash, & M. L. Commons (Eds.), *Adult information processing: Limits and loss* (pp. 529–551). Orlando, FL: Academic Press.

McDaniel, M. A., & Einstein, G. O. (1992). Aging and prospective memory: Basic findings and practical applications. *Advances in Learning and Behavioral Disabilities, 7*, 87–105.

McDaniel, M. A., & Einstein, G. O. (1993). Relations between prospective and retrospective memory: The importance of cue-familiarity and cue-distinctiveness. *Memory, 1*, 23–42.

Meacham, J. A., & Colombo, J. A. (1980). External retrieval cues facilitate prospective remembering. *Journal of Educational Research, 73*, 299–301.

Meacham, J. A., & Leiman, B. (1982). Remembering to perform future actions. In U. Neisser (Ed.), *Memory observed: Remembering in natural contexts* (pp. 327–336). San Francisco: Freeman.

Meacham, J. A., & Singer, J. (1977). Incentive effects in prospective remembering. *Journal of Psychology, 97*, 191–197.

Murray, H. G., & Denny, J. P. (1969). Interaction of ability level and interpolated activity (opportunity for incubation) in human problem solving. *Psychological Reports, 24*, 271–276.

Ovsiankina, M. (1928). Die Wiederaufnahme unterbrochener Handlungen. *Psychologische Forschung, 11*, 302–379.

Pachauri, A. R. (1935). A study of gestalt problems in completed and interrupted tasks. *British Journal of Psychology, 25*, 447–457.

Posner, M. I. (1973). *Cognition: An introduction.* Glenview, IL: Scott & Foresman.

Salaman, E. (1970). *A collection of moments.* London: Longman.

Smith, S. M., & Blankenship, S. E. (1989). Incubation effects. *Bulletin of Psychonomic Society. 27*, 311–314.

Tolman, E. C. (1948). Kurt Lewin 1890–1947. *Psychological Review, 55*, 1–4.

Tulving, E. (1983). *Elements of episodic memory.* New York: Oxford University Press.

Tulving, E., & Madigan, S. A. (1970). Memory and verbal learning. *Annual Review of Psychology, 21*, 437–484.

Tulving, E., & Pearlstone, Z. (1966). Availability versus accessibility of information in memory for words. *Journal of Verbal Learning and Verbal Behavior, 87*, 1–8.

van Bergen, A. (1968) *Task interruption.* Amsterdam: North-Holland.

Watkins, M. J. (1979). Engrams as cuegrams and forgetting as cue overload: A cuing approach to the structure of memory. In C. R. Puff (Eds.), *Memory organization and structure* (pp. 347–351). New York: Academic Press.

Wilkins, A. J., & Baddeley, A. D. (1978). Remembering to recall in everyday life: An approach to absentmindedness. In M. M. Gruneberg, P. E. Morris, & R. N. Sykes (Eds.), *Practical aspects of memory* (pp. 27–34). London: Academic Press.

Woodworth, R. S., & Schlosberg, H. (1954). *Experimental psychology.* New York: Holt, Rinehart & Winston.

Yaniv, I., & Meyer, D. E. (1987). Activation and metacognition of inaccessible information: Potential bases for incubation effects in problem solving. *Journal of Experimental Psychology: Learning, Memory, and Cognition, 13,* 187–205.

Zeigarnik, B. (1927). Über das Behalten von erledigten und underledigten Handlungen. *Psychologische Forschung, 9,* 1–85.

5

Retrieval Processes in Prospective Memory: Theoretical Approaches and Some New Empirical Findings

Gilles O. Einstein
Furman University

Mark A. McDaniel
Purdue University

Prospective memory is memory for actions to be performed in the future, such as remembering to return a library book, give someone a message, perform your back exercises, and pick up the children at school. Despite the fact that researchers only recently began to study prospective memory, it is a type of memory that is prevalent in everyday life. In informal surveys of our classes, when asked to list "the last thing you remember forgetting," over one half of our students (including older students enrolled in an elderhostel class) listed memory failures that are prospective in nature. Moreover, good prospective memory is critical for normal functioning. Problems in remembering to turn off the oven and to take medication, for example, threaten independent living.

Although we tend to characterize memory tasks as either prospective or retrospective, prospective memory tasks contain components of retrospective memory tasks as well as components that do not appear in most laboratory retrospective memory tasks. For example, remembering to give a message to a friend requires that we remember the message and the friend to whom it is to be given. This aspect of a prospective memory task seems indistinguishable from that found in many retrospective memory tasks (e.g., cued-recall tasks) and we refer to this as the *retrospective component* of a prospective memory task. Remembering only the retrospective memory component of a prospective memory task, however, will not produce successful prospective memory. One must in addition remember to perform this task in the appropriate context, or in this case, when we see the friend. We label this the *prospective component*.

Many prospective memory failures occur because of problems in remembering the retrospective memory component (Einstein, Holland, McDaniel, & Guynn, 1992), especially because many of our prospective memory tasks are complex in nature (e.g., over one third of older people take three or four medications daily, Park, 1992; see also Park & Kidder, this volume). The retrospective memory component is even occasionally forgotten in simple prospective memory tasks, such as when we walk into a room and sometimes forget what we are supposed to do there. We suspect that the abundant theoretical views in the retrospective memory literature will prove useful for understanding memory for the retrospective component of a prospective memory task.

Everyday experience tells us that we often forget to perform a task despite complete retrospective memory for that task. This type of forgetting is rarely studied in the laboratory, and it is unclear how existing memory theories can be used to understand how we go about remembering to remember. In this chapter, we focus on developing and evaluating theoretical views concerning memory for the prospective component of a prospective memory task. This was a strategy in our research and accordingly, we have for the most part developed laboratory tests of prospective memory in which the retrospective memory component is simple and not easily forgotten. This approach allows us to attribute prospective memory forgetting to the prospective memory component of the task.

Unlike with retrospective memory, we are rarely externally prompted to initiate a controlled search of memory when the appropriate context occurs (i.e., the sight of the friend). Instead, successful remembering requires that the appearance of the friend spontaneously reminds us (i.e., without an external cue or prompt to initiate a directed search of memory) of the prospective memory. Remembering in prospective memory situations is difficult because it requires that the prospective memory interrupt our flow of thoughts and come to mind while we are involved in some ongoing activities. In retrospective memory situations, this interruption is externally prompted. Thus, although students can count on tests from their psychology professors to cue searches of memory for knowledge of course content, they cannot rely on this kind of prompting to remember to give their roommate a telephone message or to remember to attend a meeting with their faculty adviser at 9:00 a.m. on Tuesday (at least this is the case when not using external cueing devices like alarms). In these situations, a person must recognize that his or her roommate is a cue to give a message (in addition to being a friend with whom to have a conversation) or that the hour of 9:00 a.m. is a cue for a meeting (and not just a time to carry on with whatever he or she happens to be engaged in).

Ste-Marie and Jacoby (1993) captured this distinction in contrasting *directed* and *spontaneous remembering*. Directed remembering, which involves consciously controlled processing, is what we typically study in laboratory tests of memory. This is the kind of remembering that takes place when we search memory in response to direct questions or prompts and involves the calling of "memories into consciousness by an act of will" (p. 777). Prospective remembering, by contrast, often involves what Ste-Marie and Jacoby called *spontaneous remembering*, which seems to be an automatic process that occurs when memories arise in consciousness involuntarily and without direct prompts to interrogate memory.

Our chapter focuses on retrieval similarities and differences between prospective and retrospective memory. We present and evaluate models of information processing that can account for how people remember to perform actions under the appropriate conditions. This focus on retrieval processes does not deny the possibility (indeed, likelihood) that prospective and retrospective memory differ in other ways as well. In fact, several studies suggest different encoding processes and storage characteristics for prospective and retrospective memory. Koriat, Ben-Zur, and Nussbaum (1990) presented impressive evidence showing encoding differences for to-be-performed and to-be-recalled tasks. They found better memory (on both performance and recall tasks) for subjects who expected to perform a set of tasks relative to subjects who expected to recall that same set of tasks. Koriat et al. suggested that encoding and rehearsal of to-be-performed actions involves internal visualization or enactment of the task, thereby creating a multimodal representation (i.e., visual and motor codes in addition to a verbal code). They further suggested that this multimodal representation is what accounts for better memory for the content of to-be-performed tasks and may also be useful for enhancing the likelihood that the prospective memory will be cued or activated in the appropriate contexts. The additional features associated with visual and motor codes make it more probable that the retrieval conditions will activate the memory representation. Goschke and Kuhl (1993; see also this volume) suggested that there are special storage properties associated with prospective memory. Their finding of faster recognition latencies for prospective memories relative to retrospective memories suggests that prospective memories may be stored in a more highly activated state. This higher level of activation would be adaptive given the special cueing problems (i.e., the lack of external prompts to initiate searches of memory) inherent in prospective memory tasks.

DISTINGUISHING BETWEEN TYPES OF PROSPECTIVE MEMORY TASKS

Our initial research in the special retrieval characteristics of prospective remembering was focused in the aging arena because it provided a convenient and theoretically rich forum for examining these retrieval characteristics. Although the aging and memory literature is clear in showing that memory declines with age (Light, 1991), it is also clear that age-related deficits are larger on some tasks than they are on others. An interesting question then is how best to explain this variability in age-related declines on memory tasks. A currently influential theory, that of Craik (1986), suggests that older adults have particular difficulty performing self-initiated retrieval processes. From this perspective, memory tasks that provide subjects with little external or environmental support for retrieval (i.e., high in self-initiated retrieval) should show large age-related decrements relative to memory tasks that provide subjects with a good deal of environmental support (i.e., low in self-initiated retrieval). Craik and others (Craik, 1986; Craik & McDowd, 1987) provided support for this view by finding larger age-related decrements on free-recall and cued-recall tasks relative to recognition tasks. Craik further assumed that successful prospective memory depends highly on self-initiated retrieval processes, even more so than free recall. This is because in contrast to free recall, where at least at some point the experimenter prompts a subject to initiate a search of memory, subjects must remember to remember on their own. Based on this analysis, we expected large age differences on a prospective memory task.

To test these ideas, we developed a laboratory task in which we busily engaged subjects in a task while at the same time asking them to remember to perform an activity in the future (Einstein & McDaniel, 1990; Einstein et al., 1992). We told subjects that we were primarily interested in their ability to improve their short-term memory capacity. After receiving detailed instructions and practice on the short-term memory trials, they were told that we had a secondary interest in their ability to remember to do something in the future. Subjects were asked to press a response key on the computer whenever a certain target word appeared (e.g., *rake*) during the short-term memory task. After a delay of approximately 15 min in which subjects were tested for free recall and recognition, they received 42 short-term memory trials, during which the target word appeared three times. Prospective memory performance was measured by the proportion of the three trials on which subjects remembered to press the designated key and by the latency with which subjects pressed the key.

To our surprise, in three different experiments, we failed to find age deficits on the prospective memory task—at least this was the case with simple prospective memory tasks in which both younger and older subjects remembered the content or retrospective memory component of the prospective memory task (see Einstein et al., 1992, for further information and see Maylor, this volume, for a review of studies that found age differences). This failure to find age differences in prospective memory occurred despite finding reliable age differences on the retrospective memory tasks of free recall and recognition. Moreover, our failure to find age differences in prospective memory was not the result of using an insensitive task for studying prospective memory, as other manipulated variables (the availability of an external aid and the familiarity of the target event) affected prospective memory performance (Einstein & McDaniel, 1990).

These surprising findings suggest either that Craik's (1986) theory of the type of processing that is most affected by age is wrong or that the original assumption that all prospective memory tasks are high in self-initiated retrieval is wrong.

Given the success of the self-initiated retrieval theory in explaining aging results obtained from retrospective memory tasks, we thought it more parsimonious to explore the latter alternative. What we conjectured was that prospective memory tasks, like retrospective memory tasks, differ in terms of their retrieval dynamics. Consider the difference between time-based and event-based prospective memory tasks (Einstein & McDaniel, 1990; Einstein, McDaniel, Richardson, Guynn, & Cunfer, in press; McDaniel & Einstein, 1992). Event-based tasks (remembering to perform an action when some external event occurs, such as remembering to give a message to a colleague or remembering to press a key when a target word occurs) have external cues that can support or guide remembering, whereas time-based tasks (remembering to perform an action at a certain time or after a certain amount of time has elapsed such as remembering an appointment at 3:00 p.m.) do not. By this analysis, there are fundamental differences between event-based and time-based prospective memory tasks, with time-based tasks more dependent on self-initiated monitoring or retrieval processes than event-based tasks. Thus, our failure to find age differences in event-based prospective memory is understandable. Moreover, this differentiation between event-based and time-based tasks has implications for the retrieval conditions and theoretical mechanisms involved in successful prospective memory, and we discuss these two types of tasks separately in the pages that follow.

This distinction does not fully capture all the important dimensions along which prospective memory tasks vary. For example, distinctions have been made between habitual (routine) and episodic (infrequently performed) prospective memory tasks (Harris, 1983), single-activity and dual-activity prospective memory tasks (Harris, 1983), simple and complex prospective memory tasks (Einstein et al., 1992), and short- and long-term prospective memory tasks. The particular characteristics of these different type of prospective memory tasks are also likely to have implications for prospective memory retrieval. For example, remembering to turn off the microwave in 10 sec may be solved by keeping the prospective memory task active in working memory until the appropriate time occurs. By contrast, remembering to take the turkey out of the oven in 3 hours may involve more complex processes associated with monitoring long-term memory. Analyses of the changing retrieval dynamics of different types of prospective memory tasks could lead to greater understanding of particular patterns of decline in prospective remembering for special populations (e.g., Fahy & Schmitter, 1991, reported that head injured patients showed difficulties on dual-activity but not single-activity prospective memory tasks).

EVENT-BASED PROSPECTIVE MEMORY

Our general analysis of an event-based prospective memory task is that it is structurally similar to a retrospective cued-recall task. For example, the prospective memory task of remembering to give a message to a friend is similar to the retrospective memory task of remembering that the word *dog* is paired with *yard*. In both cases, successful remembering requires that the cue and the target information (or action in the case of prospective memory) be associated and that aspects of that association be reinstated at retrieval. As discussed earlier, a potentially important difference in the two kinds of tasks is that in retrospective memory situations, the experimenter (or some external agent) prompts the subject to initiate a directed search of memory. In contrast, in prospective memory situations, there is typically no external agent to prompt a directed search of memory and, instead, successful prospective memory requires that subjects spontaneously recognize the event or cue as a stimulus for performing an action.

We suspect that this spontaneous remembering component, which appears to be present in event-based prospective memory tasks but not in explicit retrospective memory tasks, accounts for the consistent failure to obtain reliable correlations between prospective memory tasks and free recall, recognition, and short-term memory tasks (Brandimonte & Passolunghi, 1994; Einstein & McDaniel, 1990; Einstein et al., 1992; McDaniel & Einstein, 1993). The failure to find positive correlations between retrospective memory tasks and simple prospective memory tasks should be interpreted cautiously as experimenters have tended to compare prospective memory and retrospective memory tasks that differ on dimensions other than the kind of memory task (e.g., length of the retention interval, time given for encoding), and it is not clear that two prospective memory tasks or two retrospective memory tasks would significantly correlate under these conditions. Nonetheless, these results do suggest basic differences between prospective memory and explicit retrospective memory tasks. Although preliminary, there is also the interesting suggestion that prospective memory is positively correlated with performance on indirect memory tests (word-fragment completion, McDaniel & Einstein, 1993). This association makes sense in light of current thinking that word fragment completion tests also involve the spontaneous use of previously encountered information or performed processes (Jacoby & Kelley, 1991). We further discuss this possibility in a later section.

Our view that event-based tasks are externally cued assumes that successful prospective memory will depend heavily on the ease of identifying the cue or target event. We (Einstein et al., in press) recently tested this idea by varying instructions concerning the target events. Subjects were presented with individual words in the center of a computer screen for 2 sec each. Occasionally, at intervals that were not predictable to subjects, subjects were stopped and asked to recall as many of the last 10 items as possible. The demands of this task required subjects to pay close attention to the words. We embedded a prospective memory task within this recall task, and we varied the specificity of the subjects' instructions concerning the prospective memory target events. Some subjects were asked to press a designated key on the keyboard whenever the items *leopard, lion,* and *tiger* occurred (specific instructions) and others were asked to press a key whenever any animal occurred (general instructions). Regardless of condition, each of the three target events (*leopard, lion,* and *tiger*) occurred once. We also varied age in this study, comparing a group of college students to a group of older adults (M = 69.13 years). As expected from our view that subjects are externally cued on event-based prospective memory tasks, both younger and older subjects were more likely to press the designated key in the specific (M proportion correct responses were .85 and .83 for the younger and older subjects, respectively) condition than in the general (mean proportion responses were .56 and .47 for the younger and older subjects, respectively) condition. This result supports our view that variables that affect the ease of identifying the target cue will have important effects on the success of event-based prospective remembering.

We (McDaniel & Einstein, 1993, Exp. 2) also showed that prospective memory performance will be affected by the properties of the target event. In this study, subjects were presented with 42 short-term memory trials in which they were asked to learn and then immediately recall a set of words on each trial. Additionally, subjects were asked to press a response key on the keyboard whenever a particular target event or word occurred. The target word occurred three times across the 42 trials, and our measure of prospective memory was the proportion of times that subjects remembered to press the key when the target word occurred. The critical variables in this experiment were the familiarity and distinctiveness of the target word or cue. One half of the subjects were given a familiar target event (*fuse* or *movie*) and the others were given an unfamiliar item as the target event (*sone* or *yolif*). For one half of the subjects, the majority of nontarget words were either similar in familiarity (nondistinctive condition) or dissimilar in familiarity (distinctive condition) to the prospective memory target word. The results showed that unfamiliar target events benefit prospective memory performance as do target events that are distinctive relative to the local context. These effects on performance were large with mean proportion correct being .55 and .95 for the familiar and unfamiliar conditions, respectively, and .60 and .89 for the nondistinctive and distinctive conditions, respectively (see also Brandimonte & Passolunghi, 1994, for similar results).

These results indicate that the properties of the target cues or events affect performance on an event-based prospective memory task, and we now develop two theoretical views for how cues in the environment can remind subjects of to-be-performed actions. Both models (a Simple Activation model and a Noticing + Search model) account for the spontaneous remembering processes that we assume are involved in prospective memory.

Simple Activation Model

According to the *Simple Activation* framework, when a subject is given a prospective memory task, he or she forms an associative encoding of the cue–action pairing. When a subject then begins to perform other intervening activities, the activation of the cue-action coding subsides to levels below conscious awareness. This subthreshold activation continues to dissipate over time, unless there is some additional activation as a consequence of external exposure to the target cue or internally initiated thoughts about activities to be performed (such as might be the case when one reviews his or her plans or activities for the day). As activation decreases, the probability of reactivating the prospective memory into awareness when the target event appears also decreases. Activities that raise activation levels (such as rehearsal of the cue–action association) make it more likely that subsequent exposure to the target cue at the time of intended remembering will raise activation above threshold and in so doing, elicit prospective remembering. Further it should be noted that activation levels of the cue–action association can fluctuate below the level of conscious awareness (see Yaniv & Meyer, 1987), such that prospective remembering will depend on the activation level of the cue–action association at the time the target event occurs. Another important factor is the extent to which the target event is processed when it occurs. Processing of the target event should influence the degree to which the cue–action association is activated, which determines whether or not the cue–action association enters consciousness.

This model explains our finding of higher prospective memory with specific instructions by assuming that subjects form different cue–action pairings in the specific and general conditions (*lion-press key* vs. *animal-press key*, respectively). Given that it is specific items that later occur as target events (i.e., *lion*), it is more likely that the specific cue–action pairing receives sufficient activation than the general cue-action pairing (where activation is dependent on spreading activation from the specific item to the category superordinate). We further assume that presentation of a stimulus item produces activation of that item's node in an associative network (e.g., Anderson, 1983). Activation then spreads to associated items, increasing the activation levels of these items. The degree to which these related items are activated, however, will be inversely related to the number of associations emanating from the presented item (i.e., the *fan of associations*). Thus, as a result of less fan for an unfamiliar target item, it is more likely that the targeted action with which the unfamiliar item is associated will receive increments and activation necessary to raise it above threshold level. The familiarity effects in prospective memory (e.g., McDaniel & Einstein, 1993) are closely related to the fan effects reported for recognition (see Anderson, 1983). This view also directly handles the benefits of cue distinctiveness. If distinct cues attract more processing (Schmidt, 1991), then the greater, longer levels of activation for the target cue will increase the probability that the to-be-performed action will receive sufficient activation.

Noticing + Search Model

We have developed an alternative model for how prospective memories are retrieved—a two-stage Noticing + Search model. In successful prospective memory, encounter with the prospective memory target event may automatically elicit feelings of familiarity, perceptual fluency, or other kinds of internal responses that cause the target event or cue to be noticed. This noticing might then stimulate a further probe of memory (*directed search*) to determine what it is that the cue might signify. This analysis is similar to the processes assumed in problem solving in which current problems can cause prior problems stored in memory to be noticed and, with further probing, aspects of the prior problem might then be retrieved to facilitate solution of the current problem (Ross, 1987). This view is also consistent with Jacoby and Kelley's (1991; see also Jacoby & Whitehouse, 1989) view that experiences of perceptual fluency (thought to automatically evoke feelings of familiarity) can be followed by controlled retrieval processes that attempt to attribute the familiarity to some source.

An even more direct parallel of the current formulation is Mandler's (1980) analysis for a hypothetical case of context-free recognition in which you see a man on a bus and you are certain that you "know" him—that you have seen him before. You then attempt to search for contextually associated information (where could I know him from?) to eventually determine that the man is the butcher from the supermarket. The assumption here is that the two separate processes involved in this example (familiarity and retrieval or search) operate separately and sequentially. Mandler, however, viewed the sequential nature of these processes (illustrated in this hypothetical example) as occurring infrequently, and accordingly focused on directed recognition tests in which these processes operate conjointly. Our analysis suggests that prospective remembering may reflect a typical and frequent memory task that involves processes found in directed recognition but that differ in terms of their operational dynamics. In sum, the Noticing + Search view assumes two stages, with the initial stage (dependent on noticing) being relatively automatic and the directed search stage relying more on controlled processes.

According to the Noticing + Search view, good prospective memory depends on the success of the directed search process. Whether or not this search is initiated, however, depends on the extent to which the presentation of the target cue elicits feelings of familiarity, perceptual fluency, or "noticing." As such, this view straightforwardly accounts for our results showing that the specificity of the instructions, familiarity, and distinctiveness of the target cue can affect prospective memory performance. Clearly, specific instructions in which the precise target event (*leopard, lion,* and *tiger*) are indicated will lead to greater feelings of familiarity when these items actually occur relative to a general category name (*animal*).

Our familiarity effects can be understood by assuming that exposure to an unfamiliar item (e.g., during prospective memory instructions) leads to greater increments in intraitem integration than exposure to a familiar item. Thus, later occurrence of an unfamiliar target event during a prospective memory task will produce greater feelings of familiarity. or noticing, relative to familiar items. The logic here borrows from that used by Mandler (1980) to explain the finding that low-frequency or unfamiliar items are better recognized than high-frequency items. According to Mandler, presentation of an item leads to increments in occurrence information or item integration (organization of the perceptual features of an item), which is what produces the phenomenal experience of familiarity. Moreover, increments in intraitem integration are thought to be inversely related to the baseline level of familiarity for that item. Thus, when an item appears again, say on a recognition test or as a target item for a prospective memory task, subjects are likely to experience stronger feelings of familiarity and greater noticing for unfamiliar items. The finding that events that are distinctive relative to local contexts produce better prospective memory could be explained by assuming that the increased attention or orienting that is thought to be associated with distinctive presentations (see Schmidt, 1991) would play a role in helping subjects notice the familiarity of the target event. In summary, we assume that the three cue manipulations we found to influence prospective memory (specificity of instructions, familiarity, and distinctiveness) do so by enhancing noticing of the target cue.

From the perspective of both of these models, several classes of variables should affect prospective memory. These include the nature of the target event, the type of processing and extent of processing of the target event (and target event–action association) at encoding, the length and nature of the retention interval (Brandimonte & Passolunghi, 1994), rehearsal, and the type of processing and extent of processing of the target event at retrieval. According to these models, activation of the prospective memory or noticing of the target event should be more likely when the target event occurs in the focal task (i.e., something that we are attending to) than when it occurs in a peripheral task. In a similar vein, it seems that the nature of the ongoing activities will influence prospective remembering with resource demanding activities, making it less likely that the occurrence of the target event is noticed or making it more difficult to sufficiently activate the prospective memory.

The demands of the ongoing task are also likely to influence the degree to which subjects rehearse the prospective memory task. Ellis and Shallice's (1993) subjects reported planning and reviewing intended activities throughout the day, particularly during breaks. Ellis and Nimmo-Smith's (1993) subjects, from structured diaries, reported that thoughts of prospective memories "sprang to mind" more often when they were involved in tasks that required less concentration. Kvavilashvilli (1987) reported a reliable correlation between the number of these thoughts during the retention interval and remembering. Taken together, these results suggest that subjects are more likely to think of or rehearse the prospective memory task during times that are less resource demanding and that such rehearsal benefits prospective memory. Beyond factors associated with the characteristics of the ongoing task, other variables are likely to affect rehearsal of a prospective memory task, such as the perceived importance of the task and personality variables (the role of personality in affecting prospective memory performance is amplified when discussing time-based prospective memory).

Both models capture the spontaneous remembering characteristic of event-based tasks in that they explain how the presentation of a target event can lead to memory for the target action, without the presence of a special external prompt to initiate a search of memory. The models differ in the degree to which they rely on automatic versus directed retrieval processes, with the Simple Activation model relying exclusively on automatic processes (i.e., without intervening controlled retrieval processes) and the Noticing + Search model relying on both processes. At this time, given the limited research on prospective memory and the fact that these theories can explain the available results, it is difficult to evaluate them. These models do, however, make different predictions regarding the influence of certain variables and may serve as useful heuristics for guiding further research.

For example, these models have implications for understanding aging and prospective memory. According to the Simple Activation view, because only automatic processes are involved in prospective memory retrieval and because automatic processes are relatively unaffected by aging (Light, 1991), there should be few effects of aging on event-based prospective memory. By the Noticing + Search view, variables that affect familiarity (an automatic process thought not to be affected by aging) should not differentially affect younger and older subjects, whereas variables that increase the difficulty of the directed search (a process thought to decline with age) should produce more disruption in performance for older relative to younger subjects (Dywan & Jacoby, 1990; see also Light, 1991). These models also make different predictions about the kinds of rehearsal that might benefit prospective memory. According to the Simple Activation view, effective encoding and rehearsal will be that which strengthens the association between the target event and the target action. By the Noticing + Search view, other kinds of rehearsal will also be effective, particularly rehearsal that increases the probability that the target event will be noticed. Thus, by this view, priming of the target event—even in a different context and prior to the presentation of the prospective memory instructions—should improve prospective remembering (see Mäntylä, 1993, and Mäntylä's chapter in this volume for evidence of priming effects on prospective memory).

Although these models are presented here as contrasting accounts of spontaneous retrieval, it is possible that both models are correct. Just as recognition decisions are sometimes thought to be based on a quick familiarity decision and at other times on a more extended retrieval check (Mandler, 1980), it may be that the processes involved in prospective memory are not invariant across situations. That is, it is likely that in some situations, perhaps when there is a strong association between the target event and target action, subjects may become consciously aware of the prospective memory task without the occurrence of a directed retrieval search (as described by the Simple Activation model). Consistent with this idea, subjects often report to us that the thought of performing an action seems to pop into mind when the target event occurs. In other situations, however, the two-stage model may more accurately describe the retrieval process.

Linkages Between Prospective Memory and Indirect Memory

Another potential lead in illuminating retrieval mechanisms that underlie event-based prospective memory is the report that prospective memory performance correlated with performance on an indirect memory test using word-fragment completion (McDaniel & Einstein, 1993). This finding prompts the observation that there are tantalizing similarities between patterns of performance on prospective memory tasks and indirect memory tasks. Indirect memory tests, like simple event-based prospective memory tasks, tend not to produce age-related deficits (e.g., see Einstein & McDaniel, 1990, for prospective memory; Mitchell, 1989, for implicit memory). Additionally, prospective memory performance can be primed through prior activation of the target event in an unrelated task that is performed prior to the prospective memory instructions (Mäntylä, 1993). This is similar to priming that is produced on an indirect test by prior presentation of the target on a task unrelated (at least in the subject's view) to the indirect test. If prospective memory and indirect memory are associated, then the theoretical work on the mechanisms involved in indirect memory performance might be fruitfully applied to prospective remembering. Accordingly, some of our current research has been directed at establishing the extent to which retrieval in prospective memory shares features that are similar to those that operate in indirect memory performance.

One feature that sets most indirect memory tests apart from most direct retrospective tests is that retrieval in indirect memory tests tends to be data driven (see Roediger & McDermott, 1993, for discussion of exceptions). Data-driven retrieval relies on perceptual information more so than on conceptual information. This data-driven property of indirect tests was demonstrated by showing that priming (enhanced performance relative to that obtained when the target is not previously presented) is attenuated or eliminated when the sensory features of the initial presentation do not match those of the test presentation. For example, one line of work showed that changing from pictures to words (or vice versa) from the initial presentation to the test presentation disrupts priming on a variety of indirect memory tests (e.g, Brown, Neblett, Jones, & Mitchell, 1991; Roediger & Weldon, 1987). That is, word–word and picture–picture presentations produce more priming than do picture–word and word–picture presentations. In contrast, because direct retrospective tests rely on conceptually driven retrieval, changing the format from study to test (e.g., pictures to words) has less impact than the quality of initial processing of the target. For such tests, picture presentations (at study) confer an advantage over word presentations regardless of the format used at test (termed the *picture superiority effect*). In short, the absence of the picture superiority effect can be taken as a hallmark of a data-driven process typically found in many indirect memory tests with verbal cues (Roediger & Weldon, 1987).

Bridget Robinson (1992) in a masters thesis conducted at Purdue University examined whether or not a picture superiority effect would emerge in prospective memory. Robinson factorially manipulated the format of the prospective memory target (word, picture) at encoding and test. The prospective memory task was embedded in a sentence verification procedure in which subjects were required to verify the truth-value of a set of sentences (e.g., "A hard swing of a bat could lead to a home run"). At the outset, several example sentences were presented, with the last example sentence containing the prospective memory target. In the word-encoding condition, the target (e.g., "bat") appeared as a word, and in the picture-encoding condition the target appeared as a line drawing placed in the sentence in lieu of the word. Subjects were instructed that if they later saw the item (bat) in any subsequent sentence, they should remember to press a particular key on the keyboard. After filler activities, subjects were given the set of sentences for truth verification (regardless of the retrieval condition, all subjects saw some sentences that were composed entirely of words and some with pictures inserted for words). For one half of the subjects, the target item always appeared as a word (there were four presentations of the target) and for one half of the subjects, the target item always appeared as a picture.

Prospective memory performance showed a clear picture superiority effect. Successful prospective remembering occurred 91% of the time when the target was encoded as a picture and only 47% of the time when the target was encoded as a word. Critically, the advantage of picture encoding was found even when the test presentation was a word. Specifically, the picture–word subjects remembered to respond 81% of the time, whereas the word–word subjects responded 58% of the time (a statistically significant difference). This just-mentioned pattern corresponds to that found for conceptually driven direct memory tests, but is the reverse of that found on indirect tests relying on data-driven processes (e.g., Brown et al., 1991).

To gather convergence for the idea that prospective memory depends on conceptually driven retrieval, we (along with Robinson) manipulated the level of processing given to the prospective memory target at encoding. We reasoned that to the extent that retrieval in prospective memory is conceptually based, a level-of-processing effect should emerge. Additionally, the experiment focused on the issue of whether or not prospective remembering required attentional resources. To the degree that it does so, it may have more processes in common with direct retrospective retrieval processes than indirect processes.

Briefly, the method incorporated the following main features. For the prospective memory encoding phase, two targets were embedded in a list of words for which one half of the subjects performed a semantic orienting task (adjective generation) and the other one half performed a nonsemantic orienting task (rhyme generation). Subjects were informed that those two words would appear in a subsequent list for which pleasantness ratings would be collected, and that they should press a particular key on the keyboard upon encountering those words in the pleasantness rating task. After three distractor activities (processing different lists of words with various orienting tasks), the list of words was presented for which subjects were instructed to perform pleasantness ratings (each of the two target words appeared twice in the list). To implement the divided attention condition, one half of the subjects in each prospective memory encoding group (semantic, nonsemantic) were required to monitor an audio presentation of numbers for three consecutive odd numbers while they were performing the pleasantness ratings (see Jacoby, Woloshyn, & Kelley, 1989).

There were main effects of the levels of processing manipulation ($p < .08$) and the attentional manipulation ($p < .05$), with no interaction. Semantic processing of the prospective memory cues (at encoding) led to a higher proportion of prospective memory responses (.42) than did nonsemantic processing of the cues (.29). This result adds weight to the suggestion (prompted by the picture superiority effect) that retrieval in prospective remembering is conceptually mediated. With regard to the influence of the focus of attention on successful retrieval, full attention to the pleasantness rating task resulted in more prospective memory responding (.45) than did divided attention (.19). This preliminary result implies that prospective remembering has a component that requires attentional resources, perhaps in the service of the kinds of conscious, directed search processes implicated in direct retrospective tests.

We started this section by noting possible links between indirect memory and prospective memory. Our current research clarified some boundary conditions regarding these possible linkages. First, prospective remembering exhibits the hallmarks of a conceptually driven task. Its retrieval processes would thus differ from those involved in data-driven indirect memory tasks, although perhaps not differ from processes in conceptually driven indirect tasks. Second, retrieval in a prospective memory task appears to require attentional resources. Not much research has been conducted on this issue for indirect memory tasks, but the general view is that retrieval (priming) in indirect memory is an automatic process (see Roediger & McDermott, 1993, for a review). It may be the case, however, that in other contexts prospective memory involves more automatic processes. For instance, in the experiment described, in the target task (pleasantness rating) there were words that had appeared in the experiment before. Thus, making a distinction between the prospective memory targets and these "lures" may have demanded attention. In our other experimental contexts, none of the words except the prospective memory targets appeared in other parts of the experiment. It would be informative to test the effects of attentional resources on prospective memory levels to see if prospective remembering might be more automatic in these situations.

TIME-BASED TASKS

The distinguishing feature of a time-based prospective memory task is that the appropriateness of the action is determined by the passage of time rather than by the occurrence of an event. Examples of time-based tasks include remembering to turn off the burner on the stove in 2 min and remembering to take medication at 6:00 p.m. Two time-based tasks that are frequently used in research are mailing something to the experimenter on a designated day(s) (Dobbs & Rule, 1987; Meacham & Leiman, 1982; Meacham & Singer, 1977) and remembering to telephone the experimenter at a designated time(s) (Maylor, 1990; West, 1988). Subjects may convert time-based tasks into event-based tasks (e.g., reconceptualizing the task of calling in at 6:00 p.m. to calling in when the evening news starts; see Maylor, 1990) but in this section we focus on time-based tasks that have no obvious external cue. Prospective remembering in the models described in the previous section is initiated by the presence of an external target event or stimulus, and therefore they cannot account for how remembering occurs in more purely time-based tasks where external cues are absent. In these situations, subjects must rely on internal processes, and Harris and Wilkins (1982) developed a specific model of the processes that are necessary to successfully perform a time-based prospective memory task.

Harris and Wilkins' (1982) model is based on Miller, Galanter, and Pribram's (1960) Test–Operate–Test–Exit (TOTE) model for solving problems that require monitoring or checking the current status of a task until an appropriate end state is reached (e.g., hammering a nail). Harris and Wilkins' model, called the Test–Wait–Test–Exit (TWTE) model, proposes that subjects initially encode a prospective memory task and then wait for a period of time until a check or test of memory seems appropriate. They then wait for another period of time until another check seems appropriate. They continue looping through these test–wait cycles until a test is made during a critical period (i.e., a period in which it is appropriate to respond). At this point, they exit the loop and perform the action. According to this model, successful remembering is critically dependent on monitoring or checking the time during a critical period, a process that seems to be mainly self-initiated.

To test this view, Harris and Wilkins (1982) asked subjects to carefully watch a movie. They also gave subjects a stack of cards to hold, with a time written on each one (either 3 min or 9 min). Subjects were asked to hold up each card at the appropriate time and to display it to a video camera that was recording their actions. Thus, if a subject's first three cards indicated 3, 9, and 3 min, respectively, they were to wait 3 min and hold up the first card, wait 9 min and hold up the second card, and wait 3 min before they held up the third card. Subjects monitored the time by turning to look at a clock on the wall behind them and this enabled the experimenters to record the number of monitors. Harris and Wilkins tabulated the number of on-time responses, defining an on-time response as one that occurred within 15 sec of a target time. They found that monitoring of the clock was closely related to the latency of responding, with shorter latencies associated with a greater rate of monitoring, especially during the period immediately preceding the target time. Persons who were late tended to monitor the clock very infrequently during the period immediately preceding a target time (see also Ceci & Bronfenbrenner, 1985, for similar results using 10- and 14-year-old children).

Borrowing from procedures used by Harris and Wilkins (1982), we tried to provide further tests of this model. One possible problem in the Harris and Wilkins study is that subjects held the stack of cards (with the intervening times written on them) and this would seem to serve as an external aid. Because of the availability of this external cue, the focus of the study seemed to be more on how subjects monitored a clock, rather than whether or not they remembered to do so. Consistent with this view, only about 12% of the responses were over 15 sec late. In the studies described here, we tried to eliminate obvious external cues. In addition, we varied age in an effort to determine if age differences emerge on these kinds of tasks. To the extent that time-based tasks rely heavily on self-initiated retrieval processes and to the extent that aging disrupts these processes, age differences should occur on these kinds of prospective memory tasks.

Our first study (conducted with Cunfer and described in detail in Einstein et al., in press) was a time-based analog of the study described earlier in which we found that specific instructions concerning the target events (i.e., *lion, leopard,* and *tiger* vs. *animals*) produced better memory than general instructions.

To remind the reader, the background activity of this experiment involved subjects in a continuous recall task in which they were presented words one at a time in the center of a computer screen for 2 sec each. At unpredictable times, subjects were interrupted and asked to recall the last 10 items that had been presented. In the time-based version of the experiment, instead of asking subjects to press a key whenever they saw an animal, we asked subjects to press a designated key on the keyboard after 10 min had elapsed, and again after 20 min. After giving subjects these instructions, a digital clock was started, and subjects could use this clock to monitor the time. The clock was located behind the subjects so that it did not serve as an external cue and so that we could record subjects' monitoring behavior.

Because we stressed to subjects that they should press the response key at exactly 10 min and 20 min, we scored a response as "on time" if it occurred at the 10th or 20th min (i.e., within 1 min of the target time). Analysis of these scores showed that younger subjects ($M = .91$) had a greater proportion of on-time responses than did older subjects ($M = .62$). (This same conclusion emerged when we used a latency-based measure of performance.) We also examined monitoring or checking of the clock as a function of 2-min periods preceding a target time. As can be seen in Fig. 5.1, subjects tended to monitor the clock more often as the target time approached. Moreover, there was a reliable interaction between age and periods, indicating that younger subjects monitored the clock more often than older subjects only in the 2-min period immediately preceding a target time. Importantly, there were high and reliable correlations between monitoring frequency and prospective memory perfor-

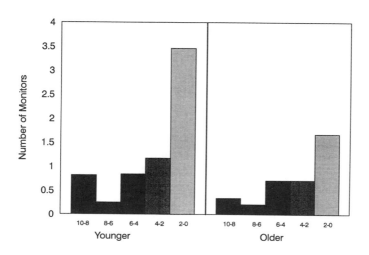

FIG. 5.1. Mean number of monitors during the five 2-min periods preceding a target time (averaged over two trials) for younger and older subjects.

mance. These correlations were particularly high when using monitoring frequency from the last 2-min period most proximal to the target time.

These results strongly support Harris and Wilkins (1982) model of prospective memory, showing that monitoring frequency, especially monitoring close to the target time or critical period, is highly related to prospective memory performance. These results also contrast sharply with our previous results with simple event-based prospective memory tasks in which we consistently failed to find age differences. Our analysis of the emergence of age differences in this experiment is that performance on a time-based task is heavily dependent on monitoring and that monitoring is primarily a self-initiated activity. Older subjects then, who are assumed to have difficulty with self-initiated retrieval processes, should have difficulty with these types of tasks.

Several factors suggest that these results should be interpreted cautiously. First, this is the first laboratory study that we know of that has compared younger and older subjects on a time-based task. Second, our analysis of age effects across time-based and event-based tasks involves cross-experimental comparisons, using different experimenters and different numbers of target event–times. Third, it was suggested that the lower monitoring rates (and hence, the poor prospective memory performance) by older subjects could be due to their physical limitations and annoyances involved in straining to look back at the clock. For these reasons, the aforementioned conclusions must be considered preliminary.

Sarah Richardson recently finished a study at Furman University in which she varied age and type of prospective memory task (time-based, event-based) in the same study (Einstein et al., in press). Younger and older subjects in this experiment were told that we were interested in their ability to answer questions that would be presented to them on a computer one at a time. These four-choice questions tested knowledge for facts, trivia, and problem-solving skills. To adjust for cognitive slowing of older subjects, each question was presented for 9 sec for younger subjects and 12 sec for older subjects. To engage subjects in this task, they were presented with feedback indicating the correct answer and their cumulative percentage correct after each question. For the time-based task, subjects were asked to press a designated key on the keyboard every 5 min. Our monitoring response, designed not to be physically demanding and therefore not biased against older subjects, involved pressing another designated key on the keyboard. Subjects were told that they could keep track of the time by pressing this key, which would cause the elapsed time (the "clock") to appear on the computer monitor. The question answering task lasted 32 min and there were six target times across the experimental session. Subjects in the event-based prospective memory condition were asked to press a designated key on the keyboard whenever they received a question about a president. There were six target questions, programmed to occur approximately every 5 min, and the word *president* appeared in each of the target questions.

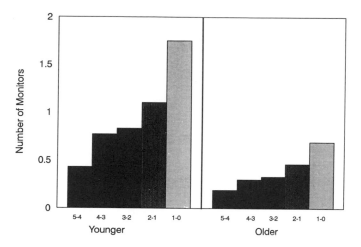

FIG. 5.2.   Mean number of monitors during the five 1-min periods preceding a target time (averaged over six trials) for younger and older subjects.

We tested 36 younger subjects (18 in the event-based condition and 18 in
the time-based condition) and 24 older subjects (13 in the event-based condition and 11 in the time-based condition). For both event-based and time-
based tasks, we scored responses as correct if they occurred within 1 min of
the target–time. Thus, proportion correct in both conditions was based on a
possibility of six correct responses. For subjects in a time-based task, we also
scored responses as correct if they were early by as much as 15 sec. (A few subjects in this experiment thought that early responses were acceptable.) An
analysis of these results revealed lower performance on the time-based task
($M = .62$) relative to the event-based task ($M = .90$), as might be expected by
the lack of external cues in the former condition. Importantly, there was no effect of age on the event-based task ($Ms = .93$ and $.86$ for the younger and older
subjects, respectively), but younger subjects remembered more often on the
time-based task ($Ms = .72$ and $.45$ for younger and older subjects, respectively).
These memory differences were related to monitoring behavior. Figure 5.2
shows monitoring frequency for 1-min periods preceding a target time. As can
be seen, subjects tended to monitor the clock more often in the periods immediately preceding a target time. There was a reliable interaction between
age and periods such that younger subjects tended to monitor more often than
older subjects in the periods most proximal to the target time. Finally, consistent with our previous results, monitoring frequency, particularly during the
period closest to the target time, was correlated with performance.

Generally, these data offer support for the idea that there are basic differences between time-based and event-based tasks, with time-based tasks being

more dependent on self-initiated retrieval. Subjects who monitor or check the clock more often perform better on time-based prospective memory tasks. Moreover, presumed problems with self-initiated retrieval such as those thought to occur with older adulthood, were associated with lower monitoring rates and lower prospective memory. The view here is that self-initiated thoughts such as thinking about the prospective memory task and monitoring, occur less often in older adults, with the result that this causes problems on tasks that do not have external cues (i.e., time-based tasks).

On the view that self-initiated thoughts about the prospective memory task in monitoring are critical to successful performance on a time-based prospective memory task, an interesting question concerns the factors that lead us to have these self-initiated thoughts (cf. Dobbs & Reeves, this volume). One possibility is that these thoughts are not really self-initiated, but rather occur in response to sometimes direct and sometimes subtle cues in the environmental context. Perhaps there were cues in our questions (e.g., questions involving time or references to time or clocks) that triggered thoughts about the prospective memory task. Consistent with this possibility, about one third of Harris and Wilkins' (1982) subjects reported that events in the film reminded them of the prospective memory task (e.g., discussions of time, visual views of clocks). (See also Morris, 1993, for evidence of subjects reporting this kind of reminding.) From this view, age differences on time-based tasks may reflect differential sensitivity or processing of incidental details in the environmental context (see Light, 1991). Another possibility is that thoughts about monitoring time are truly self-initiated and based on judgments of time derived from biological and/or cognitive clocks (Coren & Ward, 1989). Perhaps subjects are somehow able to "set" an internal clock for the purpose of checking plans or activities that are yet to be performed. If so, then prospective memory performance might be expected to be related to time estimation ability, an ability that may be affected by age. Craik and Hay (1994) presented evidence showing that older subjects' judgments tend to underestimate the amount of time that has passed. One interpretation of this finding is that aging "slows down" an internal clock and this would be consistent with the poorer performance by older subjects on a time-based prospective memory task.

There are a host of other variables that are likely to affect the rate of monitoring. To the extent that monitoring requires attentional resources, the cognitive demands of the ongoing task (i.e., the extent to which a person is busily engaged with a task) should affect monitoring rates and hence, prospective remembering (see Ellis & Nimmo-Smith, 1993, Ellis & Shallice, 1993, and Kvavilashvilli, 1987 for suggestions along these lines). Another possibility is that monitoring levels might be related to internal distraction (i.e., mind wandering) and this may be especially problematic for older adults because of a deficient inhibitory mechanism (Hasher & Zacks, 1988). Ideally, this inhibitory mechanism functions to keep thoughts that are irrelevant to one's cognitive goals out of working memory. However, if this mechanism fails to suppress or dampen off-task thoughts, then these thoughts begin to occupy attentional resources and interfere with processing of the task at hand. For example, while listening to a lecture, a student may start to think about his or her weekend plans. These internal distractions might also be expected to interfere with monitoring of a prospective memory task. It often seems that prospective memory failures occur when we get distracted by internal thoughts and/or other activities.

Another likely possibility is that noncognitive factors, such as personality, play an instrumental role in prospective memory. According to Winograd (1988) and Meacham (1988), an important distinction between prospective and retrospective memory is that variables other than purely cognitive ones are thought to affect performance. It seems particularly likely that personality variables such as compulsiveness and conscientiousness would affect the degree to which subjects initiated thoughts about a to-be-performed prospective memory task. Consistent with this idea, Goschke and Kuhl (1993) presented evidence that subjects who have a state orientation (relative to an action orientation and measured by the Action Control Scale) are more likely in certain prospective memory situations to keep intentions for to-be-performed activities in a highly activated state. According to Goschke and Kuhl, state-oriented subjects are those who tend to experience more "ruminations concerning unfulfilled intentions" (p. 1212).

ENVIRONMENTAL CONTEXT AND PROSPECTIVE MEMORY

In prospective memory situations, there is no external agent prompting the rememberer to try to retrieve information encoded in the past. Current views of retrieval (when considered in terms of retrospective memory) hold that retrieval is accomplished by conscious, directed, strategic reinstatement of the initial encoding context (e.g., Masson & MacLeod, 1992). For prospective remembering, however, reinstatement of the initial encoding context may not be accomplished through strategic processes (McDaniel & Einstein, 1993). Instead, the context reinstatement may be spontaneously prompted at retrieval by the target event and features of the retrieval environment. To the extent that retrieval in prospective remembering relies on spontaneous retrieval, it seems likely that prospective remembering would be especially sensitive to the match of features present at encoding and retrieval. One such set of features would be the environmental context in which the intended action is encoded and in which the action is eventually performed. Though environmental context has limited mnemonic effects in direct retrospective tests (e.g., McDaniel, Anderson, Einstein, & O'Halloran, 1989), for the reasons outlined, environmental context may play a more prominent role in prospective remembering.

Robinson (1992) performed an initial experiment examining the influence of environmental context on prospective memory. The prospective memory task was embedded in the sentence verification procedure described in a preceding section of this chapter (in which picture or word targets were embedded in sentences that were responded to on the basis of truth value). Environmental context was manipulated with two laboratory rooms (a spacious room with stark white walls and a small room with brightly colored posters on the wall). In the same-environment group, subjects remained in the same room throughout all phases of the experiment. In the different-environment group, subjects were given the prospective memory instruction and an intervening retrospective memory task in one room. After completing the retrospective memory task, these subjects were taken to the other experimental room for the remainder of the experiment (including the prospective memory trials).

The effects of environmental context depended on the initial encoding of the prospective memory target. When the target was encoded as a picture (presumably affording a more elaborate encoding), changing rooms produced no decrement in prospective remembering (same room = .83; different room = .98). When the prospective memory target was encoded as a word (perhaps supporting a less elaborate encoding), changing the room from study to test significantly disrupted prospective remembering (same room = .65; different room = .29).

This pattern of environmental context effects is not unlike those reported with recall; for example, McDaniel et al. (1989) found environmental reinstatement effects unless the target materials were processed using elaborative orienting tasks (imagery, organization, self-referent encoding). The magnitude of the context effects, however, is unlike that typically obtained with retrospective memory tasks. In contrast to environmental reinstatement effects with retrospective memory tasks, which tend to produce modest influences on memory (Fernandez & Glenberg, 1985), Robinson's (1992) results show dramatic effects of changing environmental contexts (at least for verbal encoding of the target). These environmental effects may show up even more prominently on a time-based task where, in the absence of a specific target event, retrieval may be more dependent on general environmental features. Our preliminary results with environmental context effects, along with our analysis that even larger environmental context effects may occur on time-based tasks, offer some promising avenues for further research.

EPILOGUE

Successful prospective memory requires that a person not only remember what action has to be performed and when it has to be performed (retrospective memory component) but also to remember to perform the action when the appropriate event or time occurs (prospective memory component). We have argued that this latter component, which seems not to be present in most laboratory tests of retrospective memory, is typically accomplished through spontaneous remembering. That is, successful prospective memory requires that the occurrence of the appropriate event or time activates the memory without the benefit of a specific external prompt to initiate a controlled search of memory at the time of remembering. Consistent with this interpretation, prospective memory failures are often the result of a failure to recognize a cue or a time as a signal for performing an action, despite clear retrospective memory for the cue, time, and action.

We have also proposed what we see as a critical distinction between event- and time-based prospective memory tasks. Event-based tasks have external target events that signal when it is appropriate to perform an action, and our view is that they provide greater environmental support (i.e., require less self-initiated retrieval) than do time-based tasks. Consistent with this view, populations thought to have difficulty with self-initiated retrieval (older adults) show relatively greater forgetting on time-based tasks than on event-based tasks. We develop two very different models of how spontaneous remembering processes might be initiated by external cues present in event-based tasks. We also present Harris and Wilkins' (1982) model of the remembering processes involved in tasks in which there are no external cues (i.e., time-based tasks). Partly because of the current lack of research in the area of prospective memory research, these models are presented only in general terms, with the hope that they will serve a useful function in guiding future research. As testament to their potential, we suggest a number of variables that according to the models should have important effects on prospective memory.

We add two general impressions of prospective memory. One is that, like others (Meacham, 1988; Mullin, Herrmann, & Searleman, 1993; Winograd, 1988), we see prospective memory as operating within a broader context than was traditionally acknowledged for retrospective memory (see also the Ellis, Dobbs & Reeves, and Park & Kidder chapters in this volume for amplification of this theme). With the obvious importance of planning for prospective memory performance, and because prospective memories are by definition tied to actions, it seems clear that noncognitive variables like those associated with motivation and different personality constructs will have marked effects on prospective memory. Second, we think that the spontaneous remembering processes (as opposed to directed searches of memory) that we assume are involved in prospective memory are highly representative of the kind of remembering that occurs in everyday retrospective memory situations. When we use our knowledge and experiences, for example to solve problems or to carry on conversations, it seems that memories often (perhaps, most often) come to mind spontaneously.

We close with a reminder of Ebbinghaus' distinctions made over 100 years ago. He (1885/1964) discussed three types of memories: (a) voluntary production, or the kind of remembering involved in direct memory tasks like free and cued recall when "we call back into consciousness by an exertion of the will . . . the seemingly lost states" (p. 1); (b) unconscious influences of prior states that indirectly provide evidence of their lasting effects (i.e., the kind of remembering that current researchers investigate with indirect memory tests); and (c) spontaneous appearance of a mental state "without any act of the will" (p. 2) that is recognized as previously experienced or what might be described as a memory popping into consciousness (Roediger, 1985, also noted the applicability of Ebbinghaus' observations to today's memory research). The first 100 years of research on memory focused on the first category of memory situations, and research since the 1980s demonstrates great interest in the second category of memory tasks. Thus far, there has been little attention given to spontaneous remembering processes either in prospective memory situations or in other memory situations (i.e., Ebbinghaus' third category). We propose that prospective memory may provide a meaningful paradigm for studying an important kind of memory that is pervasive in everyday life.

ACKNOWLEDGMENTS

The writing of this paper was supported by National Institute on Aging Grant AG08436 to the authors.

REFERENCES

Anderson, J. R. (1983). *The architecture of cognition.* Cambridge, MA: Harvard University Press.

Brandimonte, M. A., & Passolunghi, M. C. (1994). The effect of cue familiarity, cue distinctiveness, and retention interval on prospective remembering. *Quarterly Journal of Experimental Psychology, 47,* 565–587.

Brown, A. S., Neblett, D. R., Jones, T. C., & Mitchell, D. B. (1991). Transfer of processing in repetition priming: Some inappropriate findings. *Journal of Experimental Psychology: Learning, Memory, and Cognition, 17,* 514–525.

Ceci, S. J., & Bronfenbrenner, U. (1985). "Don't forget to take the cupcakes out of the oven": Prospective memory, strategic time-monitoring, and context. *Child Development, 56,* 152–164.

Coren, S., & Ward, L. M. (1989). *Sensation and perception* (3rd ed). Orlando, FL: Academic Press.

Craik, F. I. M. (1986). A functional account of age differences in memory. In F. Klix & H. Hagendorf (Eds.), *Human memory and cognitive capabilities: Mechanisms and performances* (pp. 409–422). Amsterdam: Elsevier.

Craik, F. I. M., & McDowd, J. M. (1987). Age differences in recall and recognition. *Journal of Experimental Psychology: Learning, Memory, and Cognition, 13,* 474–479.

Craik, F. I. M., & Hay, J. F. (1994, April) *The effects of aging and task demands on subjective time judgments.* Paper presented at the 1994 meeting of the Cognitive Aging Conference, Atlanta, GA.

Dobbs, A. R., & Rule, B. G. (1987). Prospective memory and self-reports of memory abilities in older adults. *Canadian Journal of Psychology, 41,* 209-222.

Dywan, J., & Jacoby, L. L. (1990). Effects of aging and source monitoring: Differences in susceptibility to false fame. *Psychology and Aging, 5,* 379-387.

Ebbinghaus, H. (1964). *Memory: A contribution to experimental psychology.* New York: Dover. (Original work published 1885; translated 1913)

Einstein, G. O., & McDaniel, M. A. (1990). Normal aging and prospective memory. *Journal of Experimental Psychology: Learning, Memory, and Cognition, 16,* 717-726.

Einstein, G. O., Holland, L. J., McDaniel, M. A., & Guynn, M. J. (1992). Age related deficits in prospective memory: The influence of task complexity. *Psychology and Aging, 7,* 471-478.

Einstein, G. O., McDaniel, M. A., Richardson, S. L., Guynn, M. J., & Cunfer, A. R. (in press). Aging and prospective memory: Examining the influences of self-initiated retrieval. *Journal of Experimental Psychology: Learning, Memory, and Cognition.*

Ellis, J. A., & Nimmo-Smith, I. (1993). Recollecting future intentions: A study of cognitive and affective factors. *Memory,* 107-126.

Ellis, J. A., & Shallice, T. (1993). *Memory for, and the organization of, future intentions.* Unpublished manuscript.

Fahy, J. F., & Schmitter, M. E. (1991). Current issues in memory research: What is prospective memory? *Journal of Head Injury, 11,* 38-41.

Fernandez, A., & Glenberg, A. M. (1985). Changing environmental context does not reliably affect memory. *Memory & Cognition, 13,* 333-345.

Goschke, T., & Kuhl, J. (1993). Representation of intentions: Persisting activation in memory. *Journal of Experimental Psychology: Learning, Memory, and Cognition, 19,* 1211-1226.

Harris, J. E. (1983). Remembering to do things: A forgotten topic. In J. E. Harris & P. E. Morris (Eds.), *Everyday memory, actions, and absent-mindedness* (pp. 71-92). New York: Academic Press.

Harris, J. E., & Wilkins, A. J. (1982). Remembering to do things: A theoretical framework and an illustrative experiment. *Human Learning, 1,* 123-136.

Hasher, L., & Zacks, R. T. (1988). Working memory, comprehension, and aging: A review and a new view. In G. H. Bower (Ed.), *The psychology of learning and motivation* (Vol. 22, pp. 193-225). San Diego: Academic Press.

Jacoby, L. L., & Kelley, C. M. (1991). Unconscious influences of memory: Dissociations and automaticity. In A. D. Milner & M. D. Rugg (Eds.), *The neuropsychology of consciousness* (pp. 201-233). Boston: Academic Press.

Jacoby, L. L., & Whitehouse, K. (1989). An illusion of memory: False recognition influenced by unconscious perception. *Journal of Experimental Psychology: General, 118,* 126-135.

Jacoby, L. L., Woloshyn, V., & Kelley, C. (1989). Becoming famous without being recognized: Unconscious influences of memory produced by dividing attention. *Journal of Experimental Psychology: General, 118,* 115-125.

Kvavilashvili, L. (1987). Remembering intention as a distinct form of memory. *British Journal of Psychology, 78,* 507-518.

Koriat, A., Ben-Zur, H., & Nussbaum, A. (1990). Encoding information for future action: Memory for to-be-performed tasks versus memory for to-be-recalled tasks. *Memory & Cognition, 18,* 568-578.

Light, L. L. (1991). Memory and aging: Four hypotheses in search of data. *Annual Review of Psychology, 42,* 333-376.

Mandler, G. (1980). Recognizing: The judgment of previous occurrence. *Psychological Review, 87,* 252-271.

Mäntylä, T. (1993). Priming effects in prospective memory. *Memory, 1,* 203-218.

Masson, M. E. J., & MacLeod, C. M. (1992). Reenacting the route to interpretation: Enhanced perceptual identification without prior perception. *Journal of Experimental Psychology: General, 121,* 145–176.

Maylor, E. A. (1990). Age and prospective memory. *The Quarterly Journal of Experimental Psychology, 42A,* 471–493.

McDaniel, M. A., Anderson, D. C., Einstein, G. O., & O'Halloran, C. M. (1989). Modulation of environmental reinstatement effects through encoding strategies. *American Journal of Psychology, 102,* 523–548.

McDaniel, M. A., & Einstein, G. O. (1992). Aging and prospective memory: Basic findings and practical applications. In T. E. Scruggs & M. A. Mastropieri (Eds.), *Advances in learning and behavioral disabilities* (Vol. 8, pp. 87–105). Greenwich, CT: JAI Press.

McDaniel, M. A., & Einstein, G. O. (1993). The importance of cue familiarity and cue distinctiveness in prospective memory. *Memory, 1,* 23–41.

Meacham, J. A. (1988). Interpersonal relations and prospective remembering. In M. M. Gruneberg, P. E. Morris, & R. N. Sykes (Eds.), *Practical aspects of memory* (Vol. 1, pp. 354–359). Chichester, England: Wiley.

Meacham, J. A., & Leiman, B. (1982). Remembering to perform future actions. In U. Neisser (Ed.), *Memory observed: Remembering in natural contexts* (pp. 327–336). San Francisco: Freeman.

Meacham, J. A., & Singer, J. (1977). Incentive effects in prospective remembering. *The Journal of Psychology, 97,* 191–197.

Miller, G. A., Galanter, E., & Pribram, K. H. (1960). *Plans and the structure of behavior.* New York: Holt, Rinehart & Winston.

Mitchell, D. B. (1989). How many memory systems? Evidence from aging. *Journal of Experimental Psychology: Learning, Memory, and Cognition, 15,* 31–49.

Morris, P. E. (1993). Prospective memory: Remembering to do things. In M. M. Gruneberg and P. E. Morris (Eds.), *Aspects of memory: Practical Aspects,* (Vol. 1, pp. 196–221). London: Routledge.

Mullin, P. A., Herrmann, D. J., & Searleman, A. (1993). Forgotten variables in memory theory and research. *Memory, 1,* 1–22.

Park, D. C. (1992). Applied cognitive aging research. In F. I. M. Craik & T. A. Salthouse (Eds.), *The handbook of aging and cognition* (pp. 51–110). Hillsdale, NJ: Lawrence Erlbaum Associates.

Robinson, M. B. (1992). *Contextual effects in prospective memory.* Unpublished masters thesis, Purdue University.

Roediger, H. L. (1985). Remembering Ebbinghaus. *Contemporary Psychology, 30,* 519–523.

Roediger, H. L., & McDermott, K. B. (1993). Implicit memory in normal human subjects. In F. Boller & J. Grafman (Eds.), *Handbook of Neuropsychology* (Vol. 8, pp. 63–131). Amsterdam: Elsevier.

Roediger, H. L., & Weldon, M. S. (1987). Reversing the picture superiority effect. In M. A. McDaniel & M. Pressley (Eds.), *Imagery and related mnemonic processes: Theories, individual differences, and applications* (pp. 151–174). New York: Springer-Verlag.

Ross, B. H. (1987). This is like that: The use of earlier problems and the separation of similarity effects. *Journal of Experimental Psychology: Learning, Memory, and Cognition, 13,* 629–639.

Schmidt, S. (1991). Can we have a distinctive theory of memory? *Memory & Cognition, 19,* 523–542.

Ste-Marie, D. M., & Jacoby, L. L. (1993). Spontaneous versus directed recognition: The relativity of automaticity. *Journal of Experimental Psychology: Learning, Memory, and Cognition, 19,* 777–788.

West, R. L. (1988). Prospective memory and aging. In M. M. Gruneberg, P. E. Morris, & R. N. Sykes (Eds.), *Practical aspects of memory* (Vol 2, pp. 119–125). Chichester, England: Wiley.

Winograd, E. (1988). Some observations on prospective remembering. In M. M. Gruneberg, P. E. Morris, & R. N. Sykes (Eds.), *Practical aspects of memory* (Vol. 1, pp. 348–353). Chichester, England: Wiley.

Yaniv, I., & Meyer, D. E. (1987). Activation and metacognition of inaccessible stored information: Potential bases for incubation effects in problem solving. *Journal of Experimental Psychology: Learning, Memory, and Cognition, 13,* 187–205.

6

COMMENTARY

The Trouble with Prospective Memory: A Provocation

Robert G. Crowder
Yale University

Of course I am not here recommending the abandonment of this new and attractive (if small; see Kvavilashvili & Ellis, this volume) subdiscipline of psychology. We collectively can and should continue to examine memory for *intended actions,* as Ellis (this volume) calls them, or *intention memory* in the words of Goschke and Kuhl (this volume). And as virtually everybody whose work is represented among these chapters is careful to stipulate, some components of such intended actions are necessarily examples of retrospective memory. Goschke and Kuhl (this volume) explicitly aim in this retrospective direction with their own work. (Although their commentary on the field is perhaps the most sensitive, among these chapters, to the mixture of memory psychology and motivational psychology within the specialty.) It is the other nonretrospective components I am talking about: Einstein and McDaniel (this volume) refer to these as *noncognitive factors.* I see no excuse for calling such components prospective memory.

Just as all remembering is inherently retrospective (look at the morphological derivation of the word), so is all intention necessarily prospective: Ellis' stages (Ellis, this volume) must apply to all planned actions however brief the intervals B, D, and perhaps C might be. Intentions, therefore, must be forward-looking and memory must be backward-looking. Conflating these concepts with a term like prospective memory is misleading if not downright careless thinking. Accordingly, a term such as Mäntylä's (this volume) *memory for future actions* is an oxymoron.

I speculate that if we had a specialty in psychology called "performance of

planned actions," or perhaps, "carrying out delayed intentions," it would be indistinguishable from what is under discussion in this book, despite failing to
enjoy as catchy a title as prospective memory. All would agree that there are
some components that depend on memory and others on more motivational
and situational factors, such as whether the intention is perceived as important or unimportant. These latter seem to be the targets of the detailed taxonomy by Kvavilashvili and Ellis (this volume). The loss of the term prospective memory would leave us better off, not impoverished.

Early in the chapter by Einstein and McDaniel (this volume), the issue is
raised in distinguishing prospective and retrospective memory:

> Remembering only the retrospective component of a prospective memory task,
> however, will not produce successful prospective memory. In addition, one must
> remember to perform this task in the appropriate context. . . .

I suggest the words "remember to" in the second sentence here are not
needed. We could say

> Remembering only the retrospective component of a prospective memory task,
> however, will not produce successful prospective memory. In addition, one must
> . . . perform this task in the appropriate context. . . .

with no loss of meaning. Remembering an intention is a necessary condition
for carrying it out later on cue, but the remembering and the carrying-out are
arguably based on different psychological principles. Later, Einstein and Mc-
Daniel write

> Everyday experience, however, tells us that we often forget to perform a task de-
> spite complete retrospective memory for that task.

Substitute "fail to perform" for "forget to perform" and the same point is made.

Nor are all of the authors in this volume convinced that the term prospective memory is a good one, which shows that it is not simply my own cranki-
ness that led to such a title for the present chapter. Ellis writes,

> In this chapter, however, I suggest that the term *memory* may be a misleading or
> inadequate description of research on . . . intended actions.

Later she speaks of

> . . . a concern, detailed in this chapter, that the description "prospective mem-
> ory" places too great an emphasis on the contribution of memory to the exclu-
> sion of other relevant cognitive processes.

Do certain theoretical principles apply to remembered intentions that are
different from those established for other remembered events? The automatic
retrieval criterion (see Mäntylä, this volume; who believes this is the "most central" though not unique, aspect) surely cannot be the deciding factor, for as
Mäntylä observes in his own chapter, automatic retrieval of memory was noted
as early as the writing of Ebbinghaus. As Einstein and McDaniel observe in

their chapter, many retrospective memory experiments (and classroom examination situations) rely on deliberate searches of memory, whereas performing
delayed intentions often depends on automatic interruptions of activities in
progress. But who is to say that natural retrospective memory is not equally
characterized by automatic and passive retrieval—the déja vu and "reminding"
situations? These deliberate searches may be the ecologically exceptional
strategies whether for facts or for intentions.

Even the noneffect of activation time found in the study by Mäntylä and Jonzon (1994) described in Mäntylä's chapter has precedent in the literature on
maintenance rehearsal (Woodward, Bjork, & Jongeward, 1973) and in the literature on priming effects as affected by word repetition (Roediger & Challis,
1992). Likewise, the priming of intended actions by ostensibly unrelated background tasks (Mäntylä, this volume) is not a new and different memory principle applying only to prospective memory (Roediger, 1990).

If anything, the work of Goschke and Kuhl (this volume) identifies an intention superiority effect that gives modern meaning to the classic von Restorff
phenomenon and thereby to qualify as a new principle of memory. Their careful exclusion of encoding factors from their experiments allows us to attribute
the effect to intended actions and not to some routine encoding factor. Can
this phenomenon be a new and unsuspected feature of prospective memory?
Perhaps not, because as Mäntylä (this volume) observes, this is truly a retrospective memory phenomenon, albeit perhaps with special relevance for prospective memory. Thus, the intention superiority effect should probably take
its place among other important and powerful manipulations of level of processing.

I was first alerted to the new area called prospective memory by the Einstein and McDaniel (1990) experiment in which subjects were given verbal targets requiring some kind of a response during a background memory task. The
striking result in that report was an absence of an age effect upon their task,
in contrast to virtually all studies of retrospective memory. That year, I passed
along this information to my undergraduate class on memory, with the suggestion that here was a form of memory that seemed to obey different laws
than we had expected from the available literature. In the chapter by Einstein
and McDaniel (this volume) we learn of new studies by Cunfer and Richardson that seem to rationalize this situation with respect to the distinction between time-based and event-based cues. The underlying factors seem to be
sensitivity to different types of cues, along with, perhaps, differences in time
perception. It was not the prospective nature of the task in Einstein and Mc-
Daniel (1990) that led to the unexpected results, but rather age differences in
sensitivity to different types of situational cues. So, here again, what appeared
at first to be unexpected principles that apply to prospective but not retrospective memory, turn out to be special cases of what we knew to be well-
established principles.

Some will say that both the common language and everyday experience are replete with examples and failures of prospective memory. I do not deny this for a moment: One morning recently, I forgot to do some shopping before dinnertime and on another night, I forgot to take the garbage out for the weekly trash collection in our town. Calling these occurrences "forgetting" doesn't make them such, however. The common language is full of words and expressions that have a precise technical meaning within the field and much less precision in informal usage. Examples are *reminiscence, recall, recognition, reward, rehearsal,* and *decay.*

Intentions, like other mental events, can be remembered or forgotten afterwards. Creeping into this literature is another criterion, however—whether or not the action is actually carried out under the specified cueing situation. Mäntylä's repeated insistence (this volume) on performance of the intended action is a typical example from among these chapters. It is ecologically important for us to understand when and why intentions are later carried out. From the basketball court to foreign policy, we are constantly making these predictions. But actual performance of the action is an unrealistic criterion for studying how and whether that intention is remembered. Kvavilashvili (1987) first showed that explicitly remembering an intention is uncorrelated with actually doing it at the prescribed moment. To appreciate the inappropriateness of a performance criterion for the remembering of intended actions, we have only to consider *impossible intentions* (squaring the circle, finding an exact value of *pi,* constructing a Graeco-Latin square of dimension four, and so on). Those impossible intentions can be remembered, but they cannot be accomplished, ever. Thus, as I said earlier, memory for the intention is a necessary condition for its later performance, but it must not be considered sufficient. The chapter by Goschke and Kuhl grapples most directly with the various criteria we can have for memory of intentions; they conclude that these different criteria are tapping different, definable aspects of intention memory, possibly even related to different memory systems and motivational reward systems. As they guardedly conclude, these ideas go beyond available data and must be examined in further research programs.

I began my comments by affirming the value of examining the subject matter of this book. It is an advance over common sense to recognize that memory for intentions plays a role in these prospective situations. The activation and cueing of remembered intentions are well-studied and increasingly understood among these chapters. Calling the whole area a field of memory is a step backward, for it renames a specialty for one of its constituent processes.

ACKNOWLEDGMENTS

Heidi Wenk and Mahzarin Banaji were kind enough to read and comment on an earlier version of this chapter.

REFERENCES

Einstein, G. O., & McDaniel, M. A. (1990). Normal aging and prospective memory. *Journal of Experimental Psychology: Learning, Memory and Cognition, 6,* 717–726.

Kvavilashvili, L. (1987). Remembering intention as a distinct form of memory. *British Journal of Psychology, 78,* 507–518.

Mäntylä, T., & Jonzon, E. (1994). The effects of semantic activation on prospective remembering. *Stockholm Psychological Reports,* University of Stockholm, Department of Psychology.

Roediger, H. L. III. (1990). Implicit memory: Retention without remembering. *American Psychologist, 45,* 1043–1056.

Roediger, H. L., & Challis, B. H. (1992). Effects of exact repetition and conceptual repetition on free recall and primed word-fragment completion. *Journal of Experimental Psychology: Learning, Memory and Cognition, 18,* 3–14.

Woodward, A. E., Bjork, R. A., & Jongeward, R. H. (1973). Recall and recognition as a function of primary rehearsal. *Journal of Verbal Learning and Verbal Behavior, 12,* 608–617.

7

COMMENTARY

Prospective Memory and Episodic Memory

Henry L. Roediger, III
Rice University

The study of prospective memory is booming. As Kvavilashvili and Ellis (this volume) note, psychological meetings have whole sessions devoted to the topic, papers on it appear regularly in the journals, and now an entire book is devoted to it. They also point out that the actual number of empirical and review papers is still rather small—they count about 45. Even assuming that by the time this book is published the number will have increased to, say, 60 or so, the amount of information would still be manageable, relative to a number of other topics in cognitive psychology. A person could still spend 2 weeks in the library and master the extant literature. As most of the authors in this section point out, although the study of prospective memory enjoyed a promising beginning, much (even most) remains to be learned on this topic. Researchers in this area are beginning to understand the topic, but are in no danger yet of completing the job. The aim of the present commentary is to assess the progress made to this point. On balance, it is impressive, with researchers developing new paradigms and with interesting findings arising from them.

The study of prospective memory has really taken off in the past decade, but it is not the only new trend. Another topic that has seen an explosion of interest in our field since the mid-1980s is the study of implicit memory, where researchers are interested in the unintentional retrieval of past events (Roediger & McDermott, 1993; Schacter, 1987). Implicit memory measures are contrasted with explicit measures, those in which subjects are asked to recall or to recognize events from their pasts. In implicit tests, retrieval of the past is incidental to performance of some task, but may nonetheless aid or prime that performance. Like the explicit–implicit division, the distinction between retro-spective and prospective memory tasks contrasts a set of tasks that have been studied for a long time (i.e., retrospective memory tasks) with ones that are new (i.e., prospective memory tasks). Indeed, retrospective memory tests are ex-plicit memory tests. It is prospective tasks and implicit tests that are the excit-ing new ones to which attention is devoted, although the aims of researchers using implicit and prospective tests differ.

Implicit memory tests assess the incidental (Roediger & McDermott, 1993) or automatic (Toth, Reingold, & Jacoby, 1994) retrieval of past experiences, which can be accomplished even by brain-damaged subjects rendered amnesic (e.g., Warrington & Weiskrantz, 1970). Prospective memory tests assess the accomplishment of intended actions in the future, which require conscious processes that are not automatic, require capacity, and are severely impaired in patients with memory disorders. So it is clear (and no surprise to anyone) that the processes involved in prospective memory tests are quite different from those underlying implicit memory tests. Of course, Goschke and Kuhl (this volume) do show a parallel effect of intentions on episodic recognition and primed word fragment completion for words related to that intention, but even then they attribute the effect to common aspects between the tests.

The energy fueling the study of implicit memory is different from that sus-taining prospective memory research. The grail for which researchers inter-ested in implicit memory strive is dissociations or differences between implicit and explicit tests. These researchers are never so happy as when they can ma-nipulate an independent variable or subject variable and observe different pat-terns of performance on explicit and implicit tests, thereby indicating that the laws of the two are different. An independent variable such as level of pro-cessing (a graphemic, phonemic or semantic orienting task during study) often has a great effect on an explicit test, but little or no effect on an implicit test with degraded perceptual cues (Graf & Mandler, 1984; Jacoby & Dallas, 1981; Roediger, Weldon, Stadler, & Riegler, 1992). Other variables such as modality (auditory or visual presentation) create the opposite pattern of ef-fect: On visual implicit memory tests with degraded cues, there are large ef-fects of this variable, but on long-term recall and recognition tests, there are usually no effects (e.g., Jacoby & Dallas, 1981; Roediger & Blaxton, 1987). Fi-nally, the most interesting pattern is when the same manipulation produces opposite effects on the two types of test. For example, generating words from conceptual clues (e.g., producing a synonym to the clue *avaricious-g*____), relative to reading the words (*greedy*), generally enhances recall and recogni-tion on explicit memory tests but creates less priming on perceptual implicit memory tests (Blaxton, 1989; Jacoby, 1983). Similarly, study of pictures pro-duces higher rates of performance than does study of words on most explicit tests, but words produce greater priming than do pictures on verbal implicit tests with perceptually degraded cues (Weldon & Roediger, 1987; Weldon,

Roediger, Beitel, & Johnston, 1995). These are the sorts of findings that titillate researchers of implicit memory and about which their theories revolve. Dissociations or differences between explicit and implicit tests abound and are greeted with excitement; similarities between tests generally draw yawns.

The situation in the study of prospective memory is quite different. As I read the chapters, I was struck at how many findings from the study of prospective memory are of the same general kind as from studies of retrospective memory. Let us consider some examples. Einstein and McDaniel note that retrieval cues aid recall of intentions in prospective tasks, that distinctive and specific encodings aid later performance, that performing prospective tasks requires mental capacity, and that one must consider both trace dependent and cue dependent processes (Tulving, 1974) for a good understanding of prospective memory phenomena. These are all factors that play critical and similar roles in retrospective memory tests. In a similar vein, Mäntylä (this volume) maintains that both encoding and retrieval factors are important to understanding prospective memory and that Zeiganrnik effects and "spontaneous" retrieval processes occur in both prospective and retrospective tasks. Kvavilashvili and Ellis (this volume) note that important intentions are better remembered than unimportant ones, that a short-term–long-term distinction is critical in understanding prospective memory, and that forgetting of intentions may be caused by interference from interpolated activities. All doubtless true conclusions, but none is different from generalizations drawn from studying retrospective memory.

At least in the chapters under review here, there are no cases of principles emerging that would cause us to change our thinking about how memory works or to believe that prospective tasks fundamentally differ from retrospective tasks. The manipulated variables generally have parallel effects on prospective and retrospective tests. There is nothing wrong with this state of affairs, and we may even take comfort that what we have learned in one domain (studies of retrospective memory) extends so well to a new domain (prospective memory tasks). But, more critically, we can ask: If retrospective memory (in its usual laboratory manifestation) is the study of lists of events from subjects' pasts, is the study of prospective memory any more than the study of "lists of things to do" in the future? Is prospective memory just another form of episodic memory? If so, it would be no surprise that the normal study of episodic (i.e., retrospective) memory has led to the same principles as studies of prospective memory, because the two are really the same, or at most, slight variations on the same entity. If prospective memory is the mental equivalent of a person's list of "things to do," then why get excited about this new way of studying episodic memory?

Now I hasten to add several provisos here. First, some differences were reported. Koriat, Ben-Zur, and Nussbaum (1990) showed that tasks subjects expected to perform were remembered better than tasks they only expected to recall. This is similar to Goschke and Kuhl's (this volume) finding that words from scripts that subjects expected to act out were recognized more quickly than were words from control scripts. However, in both these cases the difference between events to be recalled and those to be performed was a main effect that could be interpreted as showing better encoding, storage, or retrieval of information. Because no interactions were shown between prospective (to-be-performed) and retrospective (to-be-recalled) items, the simplest interpretation of the difference is in terms of encoding or storage differences.

Second, as already discussed, researchers are just starting the study of prospective memory and the surprises may lie in the future. The early studies used variables familiar from past (retrospective memory) research and they generalize well, so far, to prospective memory research. But other variables, as yet unexplored, may produce differences (or dissociations) between prospective and retrospective memory tasks. As Ellis (this volume) and Kvavilashvili and Ellis (this volume) note, the range of approaches to the study of prospective memory has thus far been rather narrow. As the latter authors characterize the situation, "it would appear that all [studies of prospective memory] have investigated the following: neutral, relatively unimportant, episodic, pure, pulse, mostly one-stage, momentary intentions, generated by other people (usually an experimenter) and formed as the result of simple decisions." Kvavilashvili and Ellis describe many interesting variables that seem likely to be important to the understanding of prospective memory, but unfortunately most have not been studied by them or by anyone else. In some cases, it is difficult to imagine how the variables Ellis discusses can be studied, but we feel sure that clever researchers will do so in the future. This future research may turn up the interesting new principles that have thus far eluded researchers in this area.

If differences between prospective and retrospective memory are not fueling the spate of research in this area, what is? My guess is that, in part, the problem seems so new and different, even if the research has not yet shown it to be. Prospective memory tasks are representative of everyday memory functioning. We all have commitments to remember in our lives, whether externally or internally imposed—people to call, meetings to attend, pills to take, papers to review, and on and on. These things to do in the future do seem different from the things that happened in the past, and, as Koriat et al. (1990) showed, they are remembered well. Therefore, the study of prospective memory is on firm ground whether or not new principles emerge from its study.

Ellis (this volume) eschews use of the term prospective memory as being too narrow. She prefers to write of "realizing delayed intentions" as being broader and covering more territory. Current study of prospective memory usually involves subjects accomplishing tasks the experimenter told them to do in the future, at certain times or at the appearance of certain cues. The researcher measures whether or not (and how accurately) subjects accomplish what they are told to do. Ellis notes that people's intentions often go far beyond such mundane obligations to perform. Delayed intentions include things we should or must do—what researchers study now—but also include things we want to do, hope to do, wish we might do, and so on. If we take this broad view, then not surprisingly memory processes become less important and many other cognitive processes (such as planning and problem solving) become more crucial. In addition, the study of motivation and emotion becomes as critical, or more critical, than the study of memory.

As I gaze over to my bookcase in my home office, I spot at least 30 books sitting on the shelves, waiting to be read. Surely when I purchased those books I intended, at some level, to read them. Is the fact that they are unread a failure of prospective memory? After all, I did not follow through on my intention to read the books I bought. Similarly, for years I planned to write a grant proposal with one of the editors of this book. We even outlined two proposals that, so far, remain unwritten. Once again, we failed to realize intentions. But I suspect that these failures and many others are common occurrences, and agree with Ellis (this volume) that it would be wrong to construe them as failures of prospective memory. We remember the commitment, but have not executed it.

This issue—the breadth of the area of inquiry—leads us back to the problem of definition: How should the definition of prospective memory be circumscribed? I do not claim to be an expert in solving this problem, but my guess is that it is best to start with a narrow definition (as has so far been the case) and then gradually expand it. I would limit the study of prospective memory to those tasks that a person feels compelled to do, the ones he or she must do. If people accomplish these tasks on cue, we can clearly judge them correct and if they do not, we can mark them for an error. This definition has been the one to guide most past research and it has created an interesting body of work. If all intentions are included in the study of prospective memory, however—hopes and wishes and dreams—then the study goes beyond that of prospective memory and may have little in common with it, as we narrowly defined it.

I do not believe I am disagreeing with Ellis in any major way in the previous remarks. Certainly the study of how people plan their futures—what their intentions are and how they are or are not realized—is a fascinating one and little studied, at least by cognitive psychologists. And I would agree with Ellis that it cannot be covered under the rubric of prospective memory. Such studies would likely draw as much or more on social psychology than on cognitive psychology. It would seem wise to keep such studies distinct from experiments on prospective memory, as typically defined.

Goschke and Kuhl (this volume) are among the first to study a factor that probably occurs to everyone reading about prospective memory: Are there individual differences among people (besides age) in carrying out intended tasks? Their questionnaire sorting people into state-oriented and action-oriented types impressively correlated with at least their recognition results. How is this personality measure related to other psychological tests, such as those measuring intelligence or need for achievement or various other personality scales or pathologies (e.g., obsessive–compulsive disorder). In our daily experiences we all know that some people carry through and do what they say they will do, whereas others, seeming to believe their commitments at the time, seldom follow through. What variable or variables predict those who are good at prospective memory and those who are not, assuming the tasks are ones to which people have committed themselves? Of course, along with Ellis, we suspect that memory variables are not the only relevant ones in explaining some of these differences, but rather social–personality factors control the variance.

The study of prospective memory may still be in its infancy, or at least in its toddler period, with basic definitions, methods, and terminology still unresolved. I would like to end by making one strong recommendation, which should resonate with psychologists who study learning and memory and who know about retroactive and proactive interference. People should be forbidden from referring to prospective memory by the abbreviation PM (as in some of the chapters under review). The initials PM already have a standard meaning in our field, primary memory. Unless researchers interested in prospective memory want to create havoc in the minds of older readers—anyone in the field in the 1970s—they should abandon the practice of referring to prospective memory as PM. The same is true of those who would refer to retention interval as RI, because using RI in this way creates RI in the original sense. In fact, it seems surprising that anyone—but particularly psychologists studying memory—would suggest PM and RI as abbreviations for terms besides primary memory and retroactive interference. However, psychologists in our field have a long history of creating names of tasks or phenomena, and acronyms for them, that are unfortunate. Remember MMFR for modified modified free recall? Surely a bad name for the task—it was not even free recall, for one thing—and the name created a bad acronym. But we do not need to create interference by deliberating picking new abbreviations that already have a standard meaning. Recall the lesson of levels of processing and interference theory research—give terms deep, meaningful names, but ones that are not already in use. However, my favorite example of terminological problems grows out of the levels of processing work. Craik and Lockhart (1972) imbued in us the need for deep, meaningful processing and they distinguished two types of processing. What names did they give them? Type 1 and Type 2! So there is a long history of poor choices of terminology in our field. But let us stick our finger in the dike over PM for prospective memory.

ACKNOWLEDGMENTS

The author appreciates the comments of Gil Einstein, Mark McDaniel, and Kathleen McDermott. Preparation of this chapter was supported by AFOSR Grant F49620–92–J–0437.

REFERENCES

Blaxton, T. A. (1989). Investigating dissociations among memory measures: Support for a transfer-appropriate processing framework. *Journal of Experimental Psychology: Learning, Memory and Cognition, 15,* 657–668.

Craik, F. I. M., & Lockhart, R. S. (1972). Levels of processing: A framework for memory research. *Journal of Verbal Learning and Verbal Behavior, 11,* 671–684.

Graf, P., & Mandler, G. (1984). Activation makes words more accessible, but not necessarily more retrievable. *Journal of Verbal Learning and Verbal Behavior, 23,* 553–568.

Jacoby, L. L. (1983). Remembering the data: Analyzing interactive processes in reading. *Journal of Verbal Learning and Verbal Behavior, 22,* 485–508.

Jacoby, L. L., Dallas, M. (1981). On the relationship between autobiographical memory and perceptual learning. *Journal of Experimental Psychology: General, 110,* 306–340.

Koriat, A., Ben-Zur, H., & Nussbaum, A. (1990). Encoding information for future action: Memory for to-be-performed tasks versus memory for to-be-recalled tasks. *Memory & Cognition, 18,* 568–578.

Roediger, H. L., & Blaxton, T. A. (1987). Retrieval modes produce dissociations in memory for surface information. In D. Gorfein & R. R. Hoffman (Eds.), *Memory and cognitive processes: The Ebbinghaus centennial conference* (pp. 349–379). Hillsdale, NJ; Lawrence Erlbaum Associates.

Roediger, H. L., & McDermott, K. B. (1993). Implicit memory in normal human subjects. In J. Grafman & F. Boller (Eds.), *Handbook of neuropsychology: Vol. 8* (pp. 63–131). Amsterdam: Elsevier.

Roediger, H. L., Weldon, M. S., Stadler, M. L., & Riegler, G. L. (1992). Direct comparison of two implicit memory tests: Word fragment and word stem completion. *Journal of Experimental Psychology: Learning, Memory and Cognition, 18,* 1251–1269.

Schacter, D. L. (1987). Implicit memory: History and current status. *Journal of Experimental Psychology: Learning, Memory and Cognition, 13,* 501–518.

Toth, J. P., Reingold, E. M., & Jacoby, L. L. (1994). Towards a redefinition of implicit memory: Process dissociation following elaborative processing and self-generation. *Journal of Experimental Psychology: Learning, Memory and Cognition, 20,* 290–303.

Tulving, E. (1974). Cue-dependent forgetting. *American Scientist, 62,* 74–82.

Warrington, E. K., & Weiskrantz, L. (1970). Amnesic syndrome: Consolidation or retrieval. *Nature, 228,* 628–630.

Weldon, M. S., & Roediger, H. L. (1987). Altering retrieval demands reverses the picture superiority effect. *Memory and Cognition, 15,* 269–280.

Weldon, M. S., Roediger, H. L., Beitel, D. A., & Johnston, T. R. (1995). Perceptual and conceptual processes in implicit and explicit tests with picture fragment and word fragment cues. *Journal of Memory and Language, 34,* 268–285.

8

COMMENTARY

Representations May Be Restrictive: Where is the Feeling of Prospective Memory?

R. Reed Hunt
Rebekah E. Smith
University of North Carolina at Greensboro

The research presented in the previous chapters holds exciting prospects for the study of memory. Not all memory research is motivated by a phenomenon whose existence outside the laboratory is beyond dispute, but the validity of prospective memory is without question. This validity assures not only that the research will be of some practical advantage, but also that the data obtained from studies that do mirror nonlaboratory prospective memory provide a valid criterion against which to assess extant concepts. Can we use existing ideas to some advantage in understanding prospective memory, and if not, is it because the phenomemon is different or because those ideas are inadequate for their current application? The attempt to distinguish prospective and retrospective memory will provide such information, because the tools of memory theory were forged from studies of retrospective memory, yet the implicit assumption is that prospective memory is a different psychological process. Evaluation of this assumption entails not only demonstrating the inadequacy of current concepts as exhaustive explanations of prospective memory, but will also produce new information about retrospective memory.

Why is it so intuitively plausible that prospective memory is different from retrospective memory? The most obvious answer is the temporal dichotomy of future versus past, but this operational distinction is only symptomatic of a deeper intuition. After all, the only conceivable adaptive function of retrospective memory is to preserve past experience for future use. Rather, the intuitive plausibility of the distinction may rest on a feeling. We suggest this difference in feeling is real and that it is the subjective experience of intentionality. Especially at the time of encoding the to-be-remembered experience, prospective memory is accompanied by a feeling of intentionality that is different than that of retrospective memory. The difference lies in part in the fact that the encoding for retrospective memory outside of the laboratory is usually not with intent to remember, but rather with intent to perceive and comprehend the current experience. Prospective memory always occurs under intent for future action. The centrality of intent to the analysis of prospective memory is recognized in the research of this volume, and given the fundamental importance of the concept to understanding the mind, the concern with intentionality is a good reason to be excited about the developments in research on prospective memory.

We shall examine the general theoretical framework used by the authors of the preceding chapters to describe prospective memory, paying particular attention to their descriptions of the interface between intent and memory. Our goal is to evaluate the success of the proposed theoretical analyses in capturing differences between prospective and retrospective memory with a constant eye cast to the conceptualization of intentionality. Evaluation of these frameworks will begin with a description of the structuralist approach that is used by the authors and some of the possible limitations of using this approach to direct investigations of prospective memory. In the end, we suggest an alternative framework from which to approach these matters and discuss the implications of this approach for empirical work on prospective memory.

THE STRUCTURALIST APPROACH

Although there are differences in wording, the preceding chapters share a conceptualization of memory that includes the concepts of representation and activation of the representation. In order to evaluate this framework, two questions must be addressed. How is intentionality described? Does this account of intentionality distinguish prospective and retrospective memory? The first question is answered in two different ways.

Goschke and Kuhl (this volume) suggest that future intent is represented in declarative memory as a proposition. The proposition contains a relational node that represents the intentional status of the action. Intent is theoretically described as part of the content of a representation, for example, "I must remember to buy beer on the way home from work." The to-be-done aspect of the prospective memory is included as an additional node in the collection of nodes that is the representation of the memory. Although Goschke and Kuhl do not discuss the representation of a retrospective memory, it is reasonable to assume that the same structural system would be invoked. An event would be represented in propositional form in the network. Suppose that event is a joke I intend to remember. The representation would be something like, "I must remember this joke," which includes a to-be-remembered node.

In this account, there is only one important difference in the content of the representations of prospective and retrospective memory. In prospective memory, the intent is to remember to act, and in retrospective memory, the intent is to remember to remember. Is this simply a difference in memory for motor action versus verbal content? Brooks and Gardiner (1994) asked subjects to study verbal phrases describing a simple action, and subsequently to either verbally recall the phrases or to perform the actions described by the phrases. Subjects knew the test condition at the time of study. Memory was not different for verbal report versus motor action. Thus, even though the subjects intended to perform the action in one case and to remember the verbal description in the other, performance was equivalent. The results suggest that the difference between intent to act versus intent to remember is not critical to subsequent retention. It should be noted that Koriat, Ben-Zur, and Nussbaum (1990) did obtain an advantage when subjects were informed at study that they would have to perform an action versus verbally recall the action at test. Brooks and Gardiner noted the discrepancy between their data and those of Koriat, Ben-Zur, and Nussbaum, but the source of this discrepancy is unclear and the issue bears further research. In the interim, there is no principled reason to suggest that intent to act should benefit memory more than would intent to remember, with the possible exception that intent to act involves more detailed processing, an issue we address shortly.

The second and more prevalent theoretical description of intentionality in these chapters is the concept of activation. Intention confers a state of readiness (Goschke & Kuhl, this volume), or a readiness to act (Ellis, this volume), or a sensitivity due to heightened activation (Mäntylä, this volume) of the representation. Each of the authors appeals to higher or more sustained activation of representations of intended activities. Intentionality is an energized representation in that the resting level of activation exceeds some theoretical base rate and is thus more easily activated into full awareness by appropriate cues.

Using this metaphor, one can readily interpret Goschke and Kuhl's recognition latency data and draw a parallel between prospective memory and priming interpretations of indirect memory performance (Einstein & McDaniel, this volume, and Mäntylä, this volume). If we assume that implicit memory is the result of priming, we have adopted the stucturalist paradigm in that a representation must already exist to be primed and the concept of priming is the activation metaphor. The function of intent is one of priming a permanently existing representation—an important reason that research is converging on the relationship between prospective and indirect memory. On the other hand, reason exists to question this model of the role of intentionality.

First is the issue of distinguishing retrospective and prospective memory. If intent is theoretically described as heightened activation of a representation, then intentional retrospective memory becomes theoretically indistinguishable from prospective memory. Both are described as activated representations, keeping in mind that we had to invoke activation because the content of the representations was insufficient to capture important differences.

A second matter concerns the concept of priming as the metaphor for intentionality. If future intent corresponds to a primed representation, then the only plans we can make are those that already exist as a permanent memory. That is, a new plan or course of action can not be primed because there is nothing to prime. If activation by priming is the metaphor for intent, all of the interesting instances of episodic prospective memory are excluded. One might complain that this observation is too harsh in that a representation of unique plans is formed and the intent primes those representations. Acceptance of this argument still leaves the problem of the previous paragraph unaddressed.

The activation metaphor also appears to neatly fit the Zeigarnik effect, an often mentioned phenomenon in the preceding chapters. Interrupting a task prior to completion seems to enhance memory for that task, an effect readily interpreted as heightened activation of the representation of the interrupted task. The connection between the Zeigarnik effect and prospective memory presumably rests on the assumption that a future action has not been completed and is therefore analogous to an interrupted task. Mäntylä (this volume) reports a series of three experiments that encourage the connection between task interruption and prospective memory. Interrupted tasks corresponding to subsequent prospective memory cues yielded more accurate prospective performance than did completed tasks. What are the implications of these results for our two questions?

First, as Mäntylä (this volume) points out, the effects on prospective memory parallel those of the Zeigarnik effect—retrospective memory. If prospective memory is analogous to an interrupted task, then the memory mechanisms of prospective and retrospective memory appear to be the same, at least as reflected in this variable.

Second, are these effects captured by an activation metaphor describing interrupted intent? Subsequent to the preparation of Mäntylä's chapter, Pantalano and Seifert (1994) reported a study of retrospective memory as a function of the proportion of tasks that were or were not completed. Contrary to Mäntylä's results, Pantalano and Seifert discovered that memory for incomplete tasks was a function of the proportion of those tasks. When the number of incomplete tasks exceeded the number of complete tasks, the incomplete tasks were more poorly remembered than were the complete tasks. Whatever the correct interpretation of this finding may be, the results pose a problem for the activation account of memory for incomplete tasks.

Further, as Mäntylä notes, his subjects received the correct answer to the interrupted anagrams and in that sense, the tension associated with an incomplete task should not exist. Pantalano and Seifert's (1994) preparation was different in that the subjects' incomplete task was an impasse in problem solving and the subjects were not given the solution, a situation that should lead to the activation of an interrupted intent. Perhaps by providing the subjects with solutions to anagrams they had solved, Mäntylä subtly induced additional processing of those items and that would account for the superior memory as well as the discrepancy between his results and those of Pantalano and Seifert. However this may be, research on Zeigarnik effects does not dissociate retrospective and prospective memory, nor does an activation explanation of incomplete task effects account for all of the data.

Finally, the activation model of intent is difficult to reconcile with research comparing intentional and incidental retrospective memory. Studies of incidental memory repeatedly showed that intent to remember confers no advantage over an incidental orienting task focused on semantic aspects of the material (e.g., Hyde & Jenkins, 1969; Mandler, 1967).Indeed, the principle points of levels-of-processing (Craik & Lockhart, 1972) are that memory is a by-product of perception and thought, and retention is a function of the qualitative nature of these processes. Momentary intent may influence memory by influencing the encoding processes, but from that point, retention is due to the quality of those processes in conjunction with the conditions of retrieval. In short, future intent may influence subsequent memory only insofar as it affects current processing. The explanatory burden then rests squarely on analysis of the mental processes underlying prospective memory, not on the analysis of permanent representations or on the concept of activation. We suggest that the proceduralist analysis of the mental processes involved in prospective memory offers a productive alternative the structuralist approach.

THE PROCEDURALIST APPROACH

The analysis we have in mind requires a shift from the structural metaphors favored in the preceding chapters to an explicit procedural model of mental functioning (Kolers & Roediger, 1984). Rather than focus on a permanently existing representation that is activated by intent to act, the content of prospective memory is theoretically carried by mental processes engaged by current task requirements. Memory is transfer from prior processing to a current task requiring the same processes, an assumption expressed in the principle of transfer appropriate processing (Bransford, Franks, Morris, & Stein, 1979). That is, if the processing requirements of the current task overlap with previous processing, positive transfer will occur.

The initial processing corresponding to the intended act is provoked by some cue situation, ranging, for example, from noticing that only one bottle of beer remains, to someone instructing you to buy beer, to remembering that there is only one bottle of beer. Leaving aside the motivational issue of why I want beer at all, plans are made to buy beer at some point in the future, these plans corresponding to a mental process.

At future times, processing requirements may occur that reinstate the prior processing, in which case memory for the intended action has occurred. The cues may be anything that corresponds to all or part of the original processing. For example, I may hear a song on the radio on my way home that reminds me of my undergraduate days, which reminds me of beer—the processing now overlaps with the original intent. Or, I may simply notice a store on my way home and that processing reengages the original processing. Regardless, it is the overlap between the current processing and the prior processing that reinstates that prior processing.

To this point, nothing here distinguishes prospective from retrospective memory. The perception and comprehension of a prior experience correspond to particular mental processes in the same way that planning corresponds to particular mental processes. The reinstatement of the mental processes operates by the same principle of transfer appropriate processing. One might expect, however, potential differences in the particular processes involved.

For example, prospective memory may involve more detailed processing than is normally the case with retrospective memory. If the action requires detailed planning, the processing may be more extensive than is the processing required to perceive and comprehend events that become the content of retrospective memory. Kolers (1973) showed that sentences presented in inverted typography were better remembered than the identical sentences presented in standard typography. He attributed this effect to the detailed processing required to read the inverted sentences. This processing could not be in reference to meaning, because the same sentences were presented in both cases. At some point in each of the preceding chapters, the authors allude to potential differences between detailed versus superficial plans and speculate that prospective memory may differ in favor of the detailed plan. The data and general principles from proceduralism are consistent with this speculation in that detailed processing offers more opportunities for future processing to overlap. Notice, however, that the proceduralist position does not place a premium on semantic content (e.g., Kolers' effect of typography), opening a wider range of potential cues to remind us of the prior processing. Prospective memory also does not necessarily differ from retrospective memory on this principle, and the same effects of detailed processing would be expected in retrospective memory.

Another important practical difference between prospective memory and retrospective memory concerns the intent at the time of encoding. Much of retrospective memory is encoded incidentally to memory, whereas prospective memory is intentional to memory. We mentioned that this difference does not control subsequent retention, except insofar as it influences the current processing. Intent to remember in practical situations may have important effects on behavior, ranging from the subtlety of more detailed processing to the more obvious strategy of generating external cues. Again, however, intentional retrospective memory does not differ, in principle, from prospective memory.

The distinction between incidental and intentional memory can also be raised at retrieval, where we may characterize the difference as conscious versus automatic use of prior experience. Goschke and Kuhl (this volume) distinguish procedural and declarative prospective memory on the basis of whether or not we are conscious of the intent prior to acting. The distinction is whether a conscious representation of the intention must be retrieved prior to the action, or whether the intention directly sets stored action schemas or skills into a state of readiness, such that they will be automatically activated when their trigger conditions are satisfied.

The principle of transfer appropriate processing suggests that the successful execution of a prior intent always entails engaging that prior processing. However, I may or may not be aware of the prior processing when the action is executed. Jacoby (e.g., Jacoby & Kelley, 1987) offered a useful metaphor of memory as a tool and memory as an object. Used as a tool, prior experience guides action in service of current intent (e.g., problem solving), but there is no sense of conscious recollection. When current intent is focused on the past, however, memory is the object and the effects of prior experience will be attributed to memory. The subjective experience of remembering requires something in addition to the concept of activating the representation, because the representation often guides behavior with no subjective experience of remembering. But in order to guide the behavior, the representation must have been activated.

At this point, Kelley and Jacoby's (1990) account of subjective experience is pertinent. Subjective experience is constructed from inferences about performance, and in the case of memory, the inference is based on the combination of fluent processing and current intent. The metaphor of fluency of processing is invoked to describe the effect of prior processing on the current task. That is, on repetition, a mental process operates more fluently. A process of unconscious inference attributes this fluency to some source. The attribution is determined by current intent. For example, if my current intent is to recognize items from a prior list, the prior study of the list will enhance the fluency of processing (e.g., just in reading the item) and that fluency will give rise to a feeling of familiarity. The feeling of familiarity can then be the basis for calling the item "old" because familiarity is interpreted in the context of my current intent. If, on the other hand, I currently intend to judge how frequently a given word appears in the language, the feeling of familiarity that arises from recent exposure to the word might be misattributed to frequency rather than to the prior processing.

A number of interesting instances of misattribution were reported, one of the most convincing of which is a simple perceptual illusion (Toth & Hunt,

1990; Witherspoon & Allen, 1985). Suppose you are asked to simply read a list of words. Then you are shown words on the monitor at a very rapid rate followed immediately by a pattern mask. Your task is to identify the words, some of which were in the original list you read and some of which are new. Your accuracy will be better for the old list words than for the words you did not read at study. This is the priming effect in perceptual identification. The subjective experience, however, is not one of remembering or of familiarity. Subjects, when asked, reliably report that the words were on the screen longer. Futhermore, the phenomenon is not subject to conscious control. Even if you know that the old words are better identified than the new ones because of their prior presentation, you will still literally see a difference in the duration of test item presentation. The fluency of processing is misattributed to presentation duration, presumably because the current intent is to read highly degraded words. Perhaps a similar interaction of current intent and prior experience may produce differences in subjective experience that form the basis of a distinction between prospective and retrospective memory.

Jacoby's ideas point to this possible difference in principle between retrospective and prospective memory, namely, a real difference in feeling. Retrospective memory is accompanied by a subjective experience of pastness that we call *memory*, whereas prospective memory, at least until the time of actual event performance, is accompanied by a feeling of future that is usually labelled *intent*. In concert with Jacoby's ideas, both memory and intent are subjective experiences constructed from the combined influences of prior experience and current intent. In what follows, we sketch this difference between retrospective and prospective memory as a function of conscious and unconscious retrieval.

Reinstatement of prior processing is essential to success for either retrospective or prospective memory, and at least in that sense, prospective memory entails retrospective memory. When this retrospective memory of the prior event is conscious, what is reinstated in prospective memory is the prior processing corresponding to planning. The prior processing associated with prospective memory originally occurred under current intent of future action. Conscious recollection of that prior processing then reinstates the subjective experience of future, namely, intentionality. Conscious recollection from retrospective memory includes contextual details identifying the event as past and producing a subjective experience of memory.

Kelley and Jacoby (1990) distinguished intention, as the context for attributions, from intention, as the product of attribution. As the context for attribution, intention biases the inference about the source of processing in accord with the momentary goal of processing. This is the function of current intent described in the preceding paragraph and is the basis for misattributions of prior processing to sources in the current task. Intention as a product of attribution and inference is the constructed experience of intention. In the case of prospective memory, we speculate that the current intent serves as the context for producing the subjective experience in that the current intent is focused on the future and the processing that occurs in that context is experienced as intentionality.

Conscious recollection may have been initiated by current intent to remember or it may be spontaneous in the context of some other current intent. If the reinstatement is due to current intent to remember, the intent would be for retrospective memory in both prospective and retrospective memory. For example, I can stop at the end of the day and try to remember what I need to do, or I can stop at the end of the day and try to remember what I did last night. Thus, both prospective and retrospective memory involve intentional retrospective memory, but in the case of prospective memory, the intent is to use retrospective memory as a tool for future action. The reinstated processes corresponding to prior planning would be interpreted in the context of this current intent and thus be experienced as intent rather than memory. When the planning processes corresponding to buy beer on the way home are reinstated, the constructed subjective experience is one of future intent, not memory. Reference to the prospective memory is accompanied by a feeling of futurity.

In order to avoid confusion about the subjective experiences that accompany the conscious recollections involved in prospective and retrospective memories, let us consider the similarities and differences in subjective experience among intentional retrospective, incidental retrospective, and prospective memory at the points of initial encoding, intermediate retrieval, and final retrieval. The subjective experience that accompanies each of three kinds of memories at each of these points is what distinguishes prospective and retrospective memories.

At the time of encoding, the subjective experience of intentional retrospective and prospective memory is similar and both involve future intent, but as described earlier, they are distinguished by intent to recall versus intent to act. Incidental retrospective memory is not accompanied by a feeling of futurity, but carries the subjective experience appropriate to the comprehension and responses determined by the task at the time.

Sometimes there is intermediate retrieval, as in the preceding description of remembering to buy beer. At this stage, an individual may recall an incidental retrospective event and the subjective experience would be one of pastness. This same subjective experience would occur at final retrieval. as well, assuming that the initial experience is recalled in a context that allows attribution to the past. At the intermediate stage of retrieval, intentional retrospective memory would also be accompanied by a feeling of pastness as would prospective memory, but unlike incidental retrospective memory, both would carry an additional feeling of intent. At this point, both kinds of memory would be reminders for the future.

It is the final stage of retrieval or execution at which intentional retrospective and prospective memory become distinguishable on the basis of subjective experience, and both kinds of retrospective memory become similar. Whether the retrospective memory was intentional or incidental to the task at hand at the time of encoding, both now carry a feeling of pastness when the final recall of the event occurs. Prospective memory no longer carries a feeling of pastness or futurity, but one of currency. Prospective memory, unlike either type of retrospective memory, now takes on the subjective experience of current action. In this way, the three types of memory can be distinguished according to the accompanying subjective experience that is constructed from the context.

In the case of spontaneous retrieval, which we wish to distinguish from unconscious influences, a thought "popping" into mind is followed by an attempt to identify its source. Unconscious influences of prior experience are not accompanied by subsequent conscious recollection. The reason such spontaneous retrieval may appear more common in prospective memory is that action based on that retrieval must be justified. If I find myself standing in front of the grocery store, I want to know why. Justification can be provided by conscious recollection of prior experience—in this case, retrospective memory of my plan to buy beer. Again, however, this reinstatement of prior processes is experienced as intent not as memory. "Mind popping" or reminding from retrospective memory may engage the same processes of justification, but now the current intent is likely to be matching current cues with some past experience to answer the question of why I am having this thought. When the answer appears, it will be in the context of the current intent to recover the past and, even though the mechanisms are essentially the same as those of prospective memory, the subjective experience will be of remembering, not intent.

The case of automatic or unconscious retrieval is different. Here, prior processing is reinstated without conscious recollection of the prior event. Processing of the cues or materials required to perform some current task overlaps with the prior processing and the current processing is thus fluent. The fluency will be attributed to some source and this attribution is the subjective experience. Attribution of the fluency will be determined by the current task, and under circumstances of unconscious retrieval, prior processing may be misattributed to some other source. In short, reinstatement of the prior processing in the absence of conscious recollection may or may not give rise to the appropriate feeling of memory or intent.

In summary, the proceduralist analysis leads to a different perspective on the relationship between prospective and retrospective memory and a different view of intent than does the foregoing structuralist position. Rather than being distinguished by the presence or absence of intention nodes or by heightened levels of activation, in the proceduralist analysis, both prospective and retrospective performance are grounded in the reinstatement of prior processing. The mechanisms of prospective and retrospective memory are identical. The distinction between the two rests in the different subjective experiences that each carries, and depends on the combined influences of prior processing and current intent. Given these points of identity and discrimination, the sketch of a proceduralist account offered here directs attention to research designed to demonstrate associations between retrospective and prospective use of prior experience, and to demonstrations of dissociations between the subjective experiences of memory and intent.

IMPLICATIONS

We can easily imagine several lines of empirical work that would follow from the preceding account of prospective memory. For example, the differences between detailed versus less detailed prospective memory tasks should show an advantage for the detailed task, assuming the subjects seriously engaged detailed planning processes. However, we would also include comparable retrospective conditions on the prediction that the variable of detailed processing would have the same effect on prospective and retrospective performance. Further, the proceduralist account predicts no difference in the retrospective and prospective tests. To control for extraneous factors, the conditions of the tests should be identical, except that one is retrospective and the other is prospective. A simple implementation would be to first have subjects plan (either in an elaborate or in a nondetailed fashion), several tasks to be performed in the future. Both types of plans would include the appropriate cues for each task. All subjects would perform this same initial task followed by a stage in which cues are presented for one half of each kind of task (elaborate and less detailed planning). In a final stage, subjects would then be asked to recall those tasks that had already been completed and to perform the remaining tasks. The recall of the performed tasks provides a measure of retrospective memory and the performance of the remaining tasks provides a measure of prospective memory. The experiment would show how the two kinds of memory are affected by the planning manipulation. The retrospective memory test represents what happens in most incidental, real world memory situations in that a person plans to do something and then later may try to recall what happened at the time of performance.

Event and Time-Based Prospective Memory

Other less obvious implications from the proceduralist account include an analysis of time- versus event-based tasks. *Event-based prospective memory* is operationally defined by the presence of an external cue in the test, whereas *time-based* tests require the subject to generate the performance at the correct time. We see a parallel with Roediger's (e.g., Roediger & McDermott,

1993) distinction between *data-driven* and *conceptually driven processing*. Roediger's ideas are in the proceduralist tradition because memory is conceived as the transfer of prior processing. On a broad dichotomy, processes can be initiated or driven by sensory processes (data-driven) or by thoughts (conceptually driven). Event based prospective memory corresponds to data-driven processing, whereas time-based corresponds to conceptually driven processing.

With this analogy, Roediger's framework yields staightforward predictions. For example, event-based tasks should benefit from data-driven study tasks, whereas time based tests would show greater transfer from conceptually driven study tasks. A simple example of a data- versus conceptually driven manipulation is the standard generate versus read comparison. We might then expect better event-based performance if the prospective cue were read at study and better time-based performance if the cue were generated at study.

Another possiblity is to manipulate the overlap of study and test processing. Roediger's research program showed that data-driven processes are affected by surface feature variations of the cues between study and test. For example, a modality change from auditory to visual presentation of the cues at study and test disrupts data-driven tests, but has little effect on conceptually driven tests. Comparable manipulations could be performed using event-based and time-based tests.

Attributions to Memory and Intent

Our speculated application of Jacoby's analysis of subjective experience to memory and future intent leads to experiments in which we attempt to dissociate the effects of prior experience and subjective experience. Two lines of attack follow from the distinction between intent as context and intent as attribution (Kelley & Jacoby, 1990).

Current intent is crucial to the interpretation of automatic influences in Jacoby's theory. If we have no conscious recollection of a prior event, the fluency of processing will be attributed to some source in the current situation—that is, the effects of prior experience will be misattributed to the current context. Current intent forms an important part of the current context and, therefore, we would predict that the unconscious influence of prior experience will likely be attributed to the current intent. These premises lead to derivations concerning predictable confusion between retrospective and prospective memory.

Suppose subjects are given a long list of things to do. The situation is set up such that we can be sure that subjects will not remember to perform all of the tasks. Following a long retention interval, the subjects are given a recognition memory test for the original list of tasks, including distractor items that are plausible from the original context. Then the subjects are asked to return to the original task, now set up so that it includes the possiblity of performing on the items used as distractors in the recognition test. One group is told to redo the tasks they successfully did before, whereas a second group is told to do only the tasks they did not previously complete. The former instruction focuses attention on retrospective memory for completed tasks, and the second group is focused on the uncompleted tasks. The primary prediction concerns the tasks that subjects failed to recognize in the recognition memory test. These tasks were not consciously recollected but should be subject to unconscious influences due to the original study processing. If so, those influences should be interpreted in the context of the current intent. That is, the nonrecognized tasks are likely to be treated as previously completed tasks in the first group and as uncompleted tasks in the second group, regardless of their actual status. Any intrusions from the distractors of the recognition test should follow the same pattern, but fewer of these types of errors would be expected. In one case, the current intent contributes to the construction of the subjective experience of memory and in the other, it contributes to the construction of a subjective experience of intent.

To demonstrate intent as an attribution, we can imagine an experiment modeled on Jacoby and Kelley (1987). In their task, subjects were asked to rate the difficulty of anagrams. Prior to the rating, subjects read words that corresponded to the solution to the anagrams. The anagrams were rated as less difficult than they were objectively known to be, presumably because the prior reading increased the availablity of the solution. This fluency from the prior experence was misattributed to the difficulty of the anagram. Suppose subjects were asked to solve a list of anagrams with a 1-min time limit for each. The anagrams vary in difficulty so that we know some of them will not be solved. Later, the subjects are given a second list of anagrams that contains the previously unsolved items and an equal number of new anagrams. One half of the new anagrams are easy to solve and one half are difficult. The subjects are instructed to proceed through this second list and write the solutions for only those they failed to solve in the first test. As Jacoby and Kelley suggested, decisions about the anagrams are most likely to be based on an attempt to solve them. The gambit in this experiment is that new anagrams that are easy to solve will be falsely judged to be from the original list because the fluency of processing will be misattributed. In some sense, the ease of anagram solution will be misattributed to intent to solve.

Using this example as a guide, the basic experimental paradigm suggested to compare retrospective and prospective memory could be altered to investigate the role of intent as an attribution in prospective memory. One possible experiment could begin in the same fashion, but the second stage would include additional task descriptions and corresponding cues. These additional task descriptions would sometimes overlap with tasks from the original planning stage, but in both cases would be performed during this phase. The final stage would require subjects to respond to cues by performing actions that had not been performed, recalling the action that had been performed, or recalling, but not performing actions that had been described only during the second stage of the experiment. If enough different actions were involved, it may be possible to have subjects mistakenly attribute the increased fluency of the repeated descriptions to an intent to perform that action.

SUMMARY

The experiments we outline are intended to provide a flavor of the direction we might take by adopting a proceduralist account of prospective memory. The potential advantage of this change in direction is its focus on subjective experience. We suggest that on neither the structural nor procedural account are there obvious differences between prospective or retrospective memory qua memory mechanisms. We further speculate that real psychological differences in the two situations may lie in subjective experience. Unfortunately, the structural metaphor for memory offers little insight into questions of subjective experience, and the concept of activation does not distinguish prospective and retrospective memory. Drawing largely on Jacoby's ideas, we sketch an alternative to the structural approach. Pursuit of this alternative will provide different types of information about the relationship between prospective and retrospective memory, and may provide further understanding of intentionality.

REFERENCES

Bransford, J. D., Franks, J. J., Morris, C. D., & Stein, B. S. (1979). Some general constraints on learning and memory research. In L. S. Cermak & F. I. M. Craik (Eds.), *Levels of processing in human memory* (pp. 331–354). Hillsdale, NJ: Lawrence Erlbaum Associates.

Brooks, B. M., & Gardiner, J. M. (1994). Age differences in memory for prospective compared with retrospective subject performed tasks. *Memory & Cognition, 22,* 27–33.

Craik, F. I. M., & Lockhart, R. S. (1972). Levels of processing: A framework for memory research. *Journal of Verbal Learning and Verbal Behavior, 11,* 671–684.

Hyde, T. S., & Jenkins, J. J. (1969). The differential effects of incidental tasks on the organization of recall of a list of highly associated words. *Journal of Experimental Psychology, 82,* 472–481.

Jacoby, L. L., & Kelley, C. M. (1987). Unconscious influences of memory for a prior event. *Personality and Social Psychology, 13,* 314–336.

Kelley, C. M., & Jacoby, L. L. (1990). The construction of subjective experience: Memory attributions. *Mind and Language, 5(1),* 49–68.

Kolers, P. A. (1973). Remembering operations. *Memory & Cognition, 1,* 347–355.

Kolers, P. A., & Roediger, H. L., III. (1984). Procedures of mind. *Journal of Verbal Learning and Verbal Behavior, 23,* 425–449.

Koriat, A., Ben-Zur, H., & Nussbaum, A. (1990). Encoding information for future action: Memory for to-be-performed tasks versus memory for to-be recalled tasks. *Memory & Cognition, 18,* 568–578.

Mandler, G. (1967). Organization of Memory. In K. Spence & J. Spence (Eds.), *The psychology of learning and motivation* (pp. 327–372). New York: Academic Press.

Pantalano, A. L., & Siefert, C. M. (1994). Memory for impasses during problem solving. *Memory & Cognition, 22,* 234–242.

Roediger, H. L., III, & McDermott, K. B. (1993). Implicit memory in normal human subjects. In F. Boller & J. Graham (Eds.), *Handbook of Neuropsychology: Vol. 8* (pp. 63–131). Amsterdam: Elsevier.

Toth, J. P., & Hunt, R. R. (1990). Effect of generation on a word-identification task. *Journal of Experimental Psychology: Learning, Memory, and Cognition, 16,* 993–1003.

Witherspoon, D., & Allen, L. G. (1985). The effects of a prior presentation on temporal judgements in a perceptual identification task. *Memory & Cognition, 13,* 101–111.

PART II

Aging and Prospective Memory

9

Does Prospective Memory Decline With Age?

Elizabeth A. Maylor
MRC Applied Psychology Unit, Cambridge, England

Articles on prospective memory traditionally begin with some everyday examples of prospective remembering, and this one is no exception. Remembering to pay an electricity bill on time, to take medicine every 4 hours, and to pass a message on to a friend, would generally be regarded as prospective memory tasks. These contrast with retrospective memory tasks, such as recognizing a familiar face, recalling the details of an accident, or retrieving the name of a country's capital city. The psychological literature is dominated by studies of retrospective memory. However, both prospective and retrospective memory abilities are required for successful functioning in everyday life, and this is no less true of the elderly (at least those living independently) than of the young.

WHY ARE THERE SO FEW
PROSPECTIVE MEMORY STUDIES?

There are probably many reasons why prospective memory was rather neglected as an area of investigation. For example, an emphasis in the past on laboratory controlled studies made it impractical to address questions such as whether or not subjects would remember to perform an action at some distant point in the future (bill-paying or pill-taking analogues). However, it is now acknowledged that more naturalistic studies conducted outside the laboratory can be informative (see Gruneberg, Morris, & Sykes, 1988; Poon, Rubin, &

173

Wilson, 1989), and some recent examples on aging are reviewed later. Another explanation for the existence of few prospective memory studies in the literature is that it may have been assumed that prospective and retrospective memory are not qualitatively different and that similar principles apply to both (see Hitch & Ferguson, 1991; McKitrick, Camp, & Black, 1992). Evidence for dissociations (e.g., in terms of the effects of aging) would obviously question this assumption. (Note that evidence from aging was used as support for multiple systems within retrospective memory; e.g., Mitchell, 1989.)

Perhaps the most significant factor in accounting for the small prospective memory literature is the difficulty in designing tasks that provide pure measures of prospective memory, uncontaminated by other factors such as compliance (Levy & Loftus, 1984), or motivation (Meacham, 1982). If we consider the everyday examples mentioned earlier, it is clear that a number of components are involved in prospective memory tasks (see Brandimonte, 1991; Brandimonte & Passolunghi, 1994; Payne, 1993). First, there is an encoding phase during which a future intention is formed. This may include the setting-up of a cue, either internal or external (Harris, 1980; Intons-Peterson & Fournier, 1986). The necessary information (task content) must then be retained until the appropriate moment or occasion arrives for performing the task. Note that the content of the task comprises what has to be done, and when (or in response to what). Successful performance depends on the retention of both elements, and this must be achieved while carrying out other activities. When the specified time or situation occurs, it must be recognized as such (i.e., associated with the original intention) and then acted upon (retrieval and execution). Finally, there is a cancellation phase in which some record of having performed the task is stored so that it is not repeated. Again, this could include the use of an external aid.

MEMORY FOR INTENTION AND MEMORY FOR CONTENT

If prospective memory is defined as remembering at some point in the future that something has to be done, without any prompting in the form of explicit instructions to recall, then it should be apparent from the previous analysis that a person could fail a prospective memory task for any number of reasons, only some of which would be considered as pure failures of prospective memory. Compliance and motivation were already mentioned as other possible factors (e.g., one may remember that the electricity bill is due but have insufficient money to pay). However, a more significant complication is probably that of retrospective memory. It is important to distinguish between remembering that something has to be done (*prospective memory*), and remembering what has to be done and when or where (*retrospective memory*). In other words, the contrast is between memory for intention and memory for content (see Kvavilashvili, 1987). To take the example of passing a message on to a friend, it is possible to remember (a) both the intention and the content, (b) the intention but not the content (by meeting the friend but getting the message wrong), (c) the content but not the intention (by failing to pass the message on until prompted by the friend's question, "Was there a message for me?"), and (d) neither the intention nor the content.

This discussion suggests that performance in prospective memory tasks may not necessarily be informative about the functioning of the prospective memory component itself. For example, poor performance could be due to a lack of compliance or to a failure of retrospective memory, whereas good performance could be achieved by enlisting the help of another person to act as a reminder, thus eliminating the prospective memory component. Nevertheless, the results from studies in which components other than prospective memory may play a role still have practical relevance. Obviously some caution is necessary in interpreting the evidence.

AGING AND PROSPECTIVE MEMORY

A simple answer to the question, "Does prospective memory decline with age?" is unlikely, not only for the reasons already outlined, but also because of enormous differences between prospective memory tasks (see Kvavilashvili, 1992; Reeves & Dobbs, 1992). For example, the three tasks described earlier differ in terms of the "conditions for action" (a particular date, a particular time, and meeting a particular friend, respectively), whether or not the task must be repeated, the retention interval, and so on. Age-related changes in retrospective memory are determined by many factors, including the method and parameters of testing (e.g., see Wiggs, 1993, on direct vs. indirect tests; Craik & McDowd, 1987, on recognition vs. recall; Craik, 1977, on primary vs. secondary memory), and this may also be the case for prospective memory.

SOME PARADIGMS EXCLUDED
FROM THIS REVIEW

A prospective memory task is defined here as one that contains a prospective memory component, that is, the requirement to remember to perform an action at some point in the future (thereby interrupting ongoing activity), in the absence of any prompting by the experimenter. This excludes from the present discussion a number of studies in the literature. For example, Sinnott (1986) tested subjects aged 23 to 93 as part of a longitudinal study of aging. Her conclusion was that age adversely affected retrospective memory but had no significant effect on prospective memory. However, the prospective items examined memory for information such as knowing the date of the next visit to the research center, rather than whether or not subjects actually turned up for their next appointment. Similarly, Hitch & Ferguson's (1991) study of students' memory for films they intended to see and films they had already seen is not regarded in the present definition as a comparison of prospective and retrospective memory.

Tasks in which subjects are presented with phrases describing actions to be performed after some retention interval ("lift the ashtray," "touch the cup," etc.) are not considered here if recall is explicitly requested by an instruction such as, "Now perform all the assignments you remember" (Koriat, Ben-Zur, & Nussbaum, 1990, p. 574; see also Brooks & Gardiner, 1994). Another case for exclusion is that of "remembering to deliver a message" from the Rivermead Behavioural Memory Test (RBMT; Wilson, Cockburn, & Baddeley, 1985). This item was used as a measure of prospective memory in studies of aging (Cockburn & Smith, 1988, 1991), brain damage (Cockburn, 1993), and dementia (Huppert & Beardsall, 1993). The testing procedure is as follows: The experimenter asks the subject to "watch what I do, and when I have finished, do the same thing." He or she then traces a short path around the room, describing each action en route ("I am going to start from this chair, and take this envelope with me. From here I am going over to the door. And from the door to the window. From the window to the table. I am going to leave this envelope on the table, and from here I am going back to the chair.").

The subject's performance is scored in terms of (a) remembering to take and deliver the message (i.e., picking up the envelope at the start and placing it down at the end), and (b) remembering each stage of the route in the correct order (i.e., chair, door, window, table, chair). As noted, several authors adopted the former as a measure of prospective memory and the latter as a measure of retrospective memory. For example, Huppert and Beardsall (1993) found that the difference between mildly demented patients and controls was greater for the message than for the route and therefore concluded that "prospective memory tasks are particularly sensitive to the early stages of dementia" (p. 805). However, remembering to take and deliver the message is not strictly a prospective memory task because the subject is prompted by the experimenter's instruction to recall. Moreover, there are no logical grounds for distinguishing between the prospective and retrospective elements of the task, which could alternatively be described as a serial recall test of retrospective memory for a list of actions, some of which may simply be more difficult to remember than others.

Finally, there is the issue of whether or not the literature on sustained attention, or vigilance, is relevant to prospective memory. In a vigilance task, subjects are required to monitor an information source for the infrequent occurrence of a specified target event—for example, double jumps of a clock hand

TABLE 9.1

Summary of Craik's Functional Account of Age Differences in Memory Tasks (adapted from Craik, 1986, p. 412). Reprinted with permission.

Task	Environmental Support	Self-Initiated Activity	Age-Related Decrement
Prospective memory	Low	Maximal	Large
Free recall				
Cued recall				
Recognition				
Relearning				
Priming	High	Minimal	Small

that moves once per second (Mackworth Clock test). Although there may be an element of vigilance in some prospective memory tasks, particularly in recent laboratory paradigms (Einstein & McDaniel, 1990; Maylor, 1993a), the vigilance literature is not included in this discussion for a number of reasons. First, vigilance is a single task that does not involve the interruption of other activities whenever a target event occurs. Second, a failure to detect a target in a vigilance study is usually perceptual–attentional in origin, whereas a failure to respond to a target in a prospective memory study is usually attributable to a memory lapse. Thus when questioned later about misses, subjects in prospective memory tasks rarely claim that the target event did not occur (as they would in vigilance tasks)—instead, they report that they "simply forgot" (Einstein & McDaniel, 1990). Third, the possible influence of vigilance can probably be ignored in the present context in view of evidence that suggests that vigilance is actually unaffected by aging (see Giambra, 1993, for a summary). For example, Giambra & Quilter (1988) used the Mackworth Clock test with targets occurring approximately every 3 min. There was no overall effect of age on target detection. Although the likelihood of detection decreased over the course of 1 hr, this vigilance decrement was the same for all age groups.

PREDICTIONS FROM CURRENT MODELS

Before reviewing the evidence in detail, it is worth considering why we might or might not expect age-related changes, both in the purely prospective memory component and also more broadly in prospective memory tasks, on the basis of current models of aging. First, of most relevance to the prospective memory component itself is Craik's (1986) framework as summarized in Table 9.1. In this account, performance is determined by an interaction between external factors such as cues and context, and the type of operation required. Functions and processes are emphasized rather than structures or systems. The claim is that self-initiated mental activities become more difficult to execute with increasing age. However, age-related deficits are reduced in situations in which environmental support is high. Table 9.1 presents the resulting hierarchy of memory tasks, "drawn up on an intuitive basis" (Craik, 1986, p. 411), with prospective memory and priming at opposite ends of the scale (large and small age-related decrements, respectively).

By definition, prospective remembering places a heavy demand on self-initiated retrieval processes. Nevertheless, it is recognized that some prospective memory tasks may place heavier demands than others (see Einstein & McDaniel, 1990; McDaniel & Einstein, 1992). For example, compare the task of remembering to take medicine in 4 hrs' time with that of passing a message on to a friend. In the former case, successful performance may be entirely dependent on self-initiated activity (such as looking at the clock every few minutes), whereas in the latter case, seeing the friend may act as a trigger for remembering. These can be described as time-based and event-based prospective memory tasks, respectively. A clear prediction is that age-related impairments should be more apparent in time-based tasks than in event-based tasks (which contain environmental support in the form of some external cue event).

It is generally assumed that aging is associated with a reduction in processing resources (see chap. 8 of Salthouse, 1991, for a summary). This is viewed in terms of limitations on speed (Cerella, 1985), working memory capacity (Salthouse, 1992), and attention (Hartley, 1992). Several components of prospective memory tasks would therefore be expected to decline with increasing age as a result of reduced processing resources. First, consider the encoding phase during which the requirements of the task are presented and a future intention is formed. Under timed conditions, older adults would be less able to perform elaborative encoding, such as forming a mental image of the target in an event-based task. Second, the content of an intention is obviously more likely to exceed the working memory capacity of an older adult than of a younger adult. Third, a prospective memory task must be "kept in mind" until the appropriate moment for action; in the meantime, other activities must be performed. In other words, the retention interval can be regarded as a divided attention or dual task situation. There is clear evidence for age-related impairments under such conditions (see Hartley, 1992, and Madden & Plude, 1993, for reviews). Most cognitive tasks become more demanding in terms of attentional resources with increasing age. If older and younger adults are asked to perform the same intervening activities, then the elderly's performance on the prospective memory task would be expected to suffer more as a consequence. (See Brandimonte & Passolunghi, 1994, on the detrimental effects of demanding interpolated activity on prospective memory performance; also Ellis & Nimmo-Smith, 1993, on the reduction in spontaneous recollections of a prospective memory task when concentrating on concurrent activity.)

A further possibility is that there are age-related deficits, not only in attentional capacity, but also in attentional allocation. For example, the central executive of working memory (Baddeley, 1986) or the supervisory attentional system involved in the control and coordination of tasks (Shallice, 1982) may be compromised in old age as a result of frontal deterioration (Moscovitch & Winocur, 1992). This would make it particularly difficult to switch attention from the intervening activity to the prospective memory task. However, recent evidence argued against this because older adults appear to be no worse at performing tasks concurrently than would be expected on the basis of an overall increase in task complexity (e.g., McDowd & Craik, 1988; Somberg & Salthouse, 1982). In other words, the elderly are impaired in dual task situations, but not disproportionately so.

There are two further deficits associated with aging that have implications for performance in prospective memory tasks. The first is in *reality monitoring* (Johnson & Raye, 1981), that is, the ability to distinguish between real and imagined events (or perceived vs. generated memories). Thus, older adults may fail a prospective memory task as a result of mistaking the memory of an intention to perform an action for the memory of performing that action, leading to an omission error (see Cohen & Faulkner, 1989). The second deficit is in *output monitoring*, that is, memory for subject-initiated activity. A study by Koriat, Ben-Zur, & Sheffer (1988) concluded that the elderly are more likely than the young to forget that a planned action has already been performed and therefore repeat it, leading to a commission error.

With the possible exception of event-based tasks, the predictions so far are not encouraging for the elderly. But are there any grounds for taking a more optimistic view of the effects of aging in prospective memory tasks? Perhaps an obvious point to note is that as people get older, they gain more experience in using prospective memory in everyday life. This is often accompanied by useful feedback on performance (see Rabbitt, 1990, on the importance of awareness of errors). For example, failing to pay an electricity bill on time results in a final demand. Thus the ideal conditions exist for the development of compensatory strategies (Salthouse, 1990) or cognitive support systems (Bäckman, 1989) to overcome possible deficits in ability.

If older people do indeed use their experience and feedback to develop effective strategies that can compensate for failing prospective memory ability, then at least three predictions follow:

1. Reliance on external memory aids to solve prospective memory tasks outside the laboratory should increase with age.
2. Self-rated ability in everyday prospective memory tasks should not decline with age.
3. Performance in prospective memory tasks conducted outside the laboratory should be unimpaired by age.

However, based on the earlier arguments, prospective memory tasks conducted under laboratory conditions should produce age deficits (prediction 4), particularly if they are time-based, rather than event-based, tasks. The evidence relating to each of these predictions is now reviewed.

AGING AND THE USE OF CUES

A distinction is often drawn between internal and external cues for remembering future intentions (Harris, 1980, 1984). Internal cues involve the internal manipulation of information and include encoding mnemonics (e.g., imagery) and retrieval strategies (e.g., alphabetic search). External cues involve the external manipulation of the environment, such as writing notes in diaries or setting alarm clocks. However, the distinction may not be so clear. For example, the activity required in producing an external cue may influence the internal representation of the intention (Conway & Gathercole, 1990; Intons-Peterson & Fournier, 1986). Also, the effectiveness of an external cue may depend on an internal strategy to remember to consult it. For present purposes, it is sufficient to note that benefits from adopting external rather than internal cues were repeatedly demonstrated (Maylor, 1990; McEvoy & Moon, 1988; Meacham & Colombo, 1980; Meacham & Leiman, 1982).

If the elderly are aware of their failing cognitive abilities, they should rely less on internal cues and more on external cues, in comparison with the young. Indeed, this was found to be the case in a study by Jackson, Bogers, & Kerstholt (1988) in which students and older adults were questioned about their use of memory aids in everyday prospective memory tasks. The older subjects reported that they relied more on external cues than on internal cues, whereas the students reported the opposite. Similarly, Lovelace & Twohig (1990) reported an increase with age in the "subjective frequency of using external aids, most notably writing notes to oneself and placing items where they will be seen to trigger memory" (p. 118). Finally, a study by Moscovitch & Minde (described in Moscovitch, 1982) concluded that the elderly's superior performance in a task in which subjects were asked to telephone the experimenter was due to using mnemonic devices. In contrast, the young simply relied on their memory.

Others, however, failed to observe an effect of age on cue choice. Patton & Meit's (1993) older subjects did not use external aids significantly more frequently than did their younger subjects in a mailing task. A diary study by Cavanaugh, Grady, and Perlmutter (1983) found no difference between old and young subjects in their reported use of external and internal cues for remembering. In experiments to be described in more detail later, both Einstein & McDaniel (1990) and Maylor (1990) noted that older subjects were no more likely to construct an external cue than were younger subjects.

Finally, two studies suggest that the elderly rely less on external cues than the young, contrary to prediction. First, Dobbs & Rule (1987) asked volunteers aged 30 to 99 to rate their "use of memory aids" on a 7-point scale ranging from 1 (always) to 7 (never). The greatest use was reported by those in their 40s (who may have had more to remember). Second, West (1988) found that younger subjects used external cues more than did older subjects in a task requiring them to make a telephone call and mail a postcard. (Unfortunately, information on cue use was not available for all subjects, particularly in the older group.)

This confusing picture is probably the result of several factors, including small sample sizes in some studies and missing data in others. More importantly, consistent results are unlikely to emerge from asking questions such as, "How often do you use a memory aid?," without defining either the task or the memory aid. Even subtle differences between prospective memory tasks, such as whether an action must be performed at an exact time (9:18) or between two times (8:00–12:00), were shown to influence the choice of cue (see Ellis, 1988; Maylor, 1990). It is therefore worth emphasizing the results of a preliminary study by Reeves and Dobbs (1992). Subjects were presented with everyday examples of four types of prospective memory task. These were either time-based or event-based, and either episodic (infrequent) or habitual (frequent). For example, remembering to "pass a message on to someone next time you see them" was defined as an event-based episodic task, whereas remembering to "take out the garbage every Monday night" was defined as a time-based habitual task. For each scenario, subjects were asked to indicate which method they would typically use to remember to perform the task, from a list that included both internal cues (e.g., "rehearse instructions") and external cues (e.g., "mark on calendar").

First, the results demonstrated that the choice of cue was determined by the type of prospective memory task. For example, external cues were preferred for time-based episodic tasks, whereas internal cues were preferred for event-based habitual tasks. Second, there was no difference between older and younger subjects in their choice of cue for both time-based episodic and event-based habitual tasks. However, older subjects were significantly more likely than were younger subjects to select external cues for event-based episodic and time-based habitual tasks. Although there is no obvious explanation for this precise pattern, the results provide at least partial support for the prediction that the reliance on external cues to solve everyday prospective memory tasks should increase with age.

SELF-RATED PROSPECTIVE MEMORY ABILITY

In memory questionnaires, subjects are often asked to rate themselves in absolute terms on prospective items such as "How often do you forget appointments?." There is no evidence that self-rated prospective memory ability measured in this way declines with increasing age (see Maylor, 1993b, for a review). Studies demonstrated either no effect of aging (Cohen & Faulkner, 1984; Dobbs & Rule, 1987), or even improvement (Harris & Sunderland, 1981, as reported in Harris, 1984; Martin, 1986; Rabbitt & Broadbent, as reported in Maylor, 1993b). The data are therefore consistent with the argument that self-rated ability in everyday prospective memory tasks is preserved in old age due to an increased reliance on external memory aids. But, of course, other interpretations are possible (see Abson & Rabbitt, 1988; Rabbitt & Abson, 1990; on the limitations of questionnaire studies in cognitive aging). For example, older adults may forget fewer appointments because they have fewer appointments to forget. We must turn instead to experimental studies in which older and younger subjects are required to perform the same prospective memory task.

"NATURALISTIC" PROSPECTIVE MEMORY STUDIES

Experiments conducted outside the laboratory usually involve time-based telephone or mailing tasks in which subjects are free to adopt their own strategy for remembering. To summarize the evidence on aging: Older adults are at least as good as younger adults (and sometimes better) at remembering to mail postcards or questionnaires back to the experimenter as requested (Maylor, 1990; Patton & Meit, 1993; West, 1988; Woolf, 1993). With just one exception (see later), the same is true of remembering to telephone the experimenter at particular times and on specified dates (Kerr, 1992; Moscovitch & Minde, as reported in Moscovitch, 1982; Poon & Schaffer, 1982; West, 1988). An examination of attendance records at a research laboratory by Martin (1986) revealed that older subjects are less prone to miss appointments unexpectedly than are younger subjects (no surprise to researchers involved in aging studies!).

The largest naturalistic study of aging and prospective memory was by Maylor (1990) who tested 222 subjects, aged 52 to 95. They were selected from a well-documented panel of middle-aged and elderly volunteers participating in a longitudinal study of cognitive aging. Subjects were women, most of whom were living alone; all had previously expressed a willingness to be included in further studies. Thus there was good reason to suppose that the influence of social and motivational factors was minimal (see Meacham, 1982, 1988; Patton & Meit, 1993).

Subjects were required to telephone the experimenter once a day from Monday to Friday, either between two times or at an exact time. At the end of the week, they had to complete a questionnaire and mail it back as soon as possible. One of the questions asked subjects to describe how they remembered to make the telephone calls. Another asked them to indicate why they thought they forgot to make a telephone call (if indeed they did).

The most important influence on performance in the telephone task was the method chosen for remembering. Consistent with the implications of Craik's (1986) model, the best performance was from subjects (n = 30) who essentially converted the task from a time-based to an event-based task. Thus they telephoned either in conjunction with another routine event ("Tied it in with an after-breakfast coffee") or engaged in some form of advanced planning of the daily schedule ("Normally I start getting tea ready around 4:45 p.m., so waited until after making the telephone call"). These were termed *conjunction cues*. The worst performance was from subjects (n = 57) who used *internal cues* ("I tried to condition myself to remember without any aid"). Finally, performance was intermediate from those who used *external cues* (n = 135) such as notes or diary entries. As already noted, the three groups did not differ significantly in age (means of 70, 71, and 69, respectively).

A weak but positive effect of age was observed on performance in both the telephone and mailing tasks (in sharp contrast with significant negative effects of age on retrospective memory measures such as digit span). However, the effect of age in the telephone task was influenced by the type of cue. For subjects using internal cues, those who forgot were slightly older than those who remembered, whereas for subjects using conjunction and external cues, those who forgot were slightly younger than those who remembered.

Prospective memory studies conducted outside the laboratory are therefore consistent in showing no age-related impairments, with the exception of internal cue-users in Maylor's (1990) study. (There remains the question of why these subjects did not adopt a more effective strategy, but note that they produced significantly lower scores on an intelligence test than did the external cue users.) Superior performance by the elderly in naturalistic prospective memory studies is usually attributed to their greater probability of using external cues compared with the young (Moscovitch, 1982). But Maylor (1990) observed positive effects of age even within groups of subjects apparently using the same cues. Older subjects may be better at using external or conjunction cues than are younger subjects, perhaps because they are more practiced (see Martin, 1986). However, each category of cue covered a variety of different methods, some probably more helpful than others. In other words, the positive effect of age could be the result of older subjects choosing more effective cues within either the conjunction or external cue category. Individuals vary enormously in the way they use identical cues (see Payne, 1993).

Although these prospective memory studies conducted outside the laboratory have several advantages over self-rated questionnaires, including control over the task required of subjects, there is still the problem of possible age differences in intervening activity. Older adults tend to be engaged in less demanding activities outside the laboratory than are younger adults. Prospective memory performance is influenced by the demands of the tasks carried out in the period between forming and executing an intention (Brandimonte & Passolunghi, 1994; Wichman & Oyasato, 1983; Kvavilashvili, 1987). Note that in Maylor's (1990) study, the younger subjects using conjunction and external cues were more likely to give being absorbed or distracted by other activities as their excuse for forgetting than were the older subjects using internal cues.

LABORATORY-CONTROLLED
PROSPECTIVE MEMORY STUDIES

Although the study of behavior in context is important, it cannot be a replacement for the systematic study of behavior under laboratory conditions (Ceci & Bronfenbrenner, 1991). This section therefore reviews in detail the experimental evidence on aging and prospective memory. To summarize, there is not a single laboratory study in the literature in which the elderly significantly outperformed the young, although there are some studies in which older and younger subjects did not differ. In contrast, there are several reports of age-related impairments.

A common paradigm is the single observation event-based prospective memory task embedded within an interview or a battery of tests. Dobbs & Rule (1987) instructed subjects early in the testing session that they would be asked later to draw a circle and a cube, at which point they should ask for a red pen. Subjects in their 30s, 40s, 50s, and 60s performed at or near ceiling, whereas subjects in their 70s were significantly worse at remembering to ask for the red pen. Cockburn & Smith (1991) administered the Rivermead Behavioural Memory Test to 94 subjects aged 70 to 93 and found significant age-related decline on the two items that fit the present definition of prospective memory, namely, remembering to ask about the next appointment when an alarm clock went off, and remembering to ask for the return of a hidden belonging when told that the session was over. (Note that in neither case were subjects explicitly prompted to recall, in contrast to remembering to deliver a message, as discussed earlier.) West (1988) asked subjects to remind the experimenter to check her tape recorder and take a pen out of a folder when prompted by the verbal cue: "That is the end of the passage recall test." Students were more successful at remembering the prospective memory task within 2 min of the verbal cue than were elderly subjects, that is, 81% compared with 31%. Finally, Woolf (1993) observed age deficits among subjects aged 18 to 92 in a number of tasks, such as remembering to write down their town of birth after proofreading a passage of text.

To date, there is just one study of aging and prospective memory using a single observation time-based paradigm. Patton & Meit (1993) asked 24 students and 17 elderly volunteers to view a film on videotape and note the scene in which there was a Dalmatian dog (though, in fact, no such dog appeared). Subjects were also required to stop the videotape after 30 min, using a clock located behind them to monitor the time (cf., Ceci, Baker & Bronfenbrenner, 1988; Harris & Wilkins, 1982). Contrary to the prediction that age impairments should be more apparent in time-based than in event-based tasks, there was no significant effect of age on performance. Unfortunately, the mean deviations from the target time of 30 min were less than 30 sec for both age groups, so ceiling effects cannot be ruled out.

Age-related decline can be demonstrated in single observation prospective memory tasks (if ceiling effects are avoided), despite only trivial demands on retrospective memory. However, single observation paradigms are criticized for their unreliability. So what of multiple observation paradigms? In an experiment by Schonfield & Shooter (reported by Welford, 1958), subjects had to remember to press a particular key before providing each response in a perceptual judgment task. The probability of failing to press the key prior to responding steadily increased from teenage to elderly subjects.

Mäntylä (1993) presented subjects with single words at a rate of 10 sec per item. The task was to write down one association to each word that would later enable subjects to recall the originally presented word when given their own association as the cue. The prospective memory component was to mark with a cross the corresponding page of the response booklet whenever a word belonging to one of four semantic categories was presented (*liquids, parts of the body, vehicles,* and *parts of buildings;* two from each category). Students (n = 16; M age = 26) marked significantly more of the eight targets than older subjects (n = 16; M age = 72)—73% vs. 44%. Students (n = 16; M age = 72)—73% vs. 44%. It could be argued that the elderly performed poorly because they forgot the target categories (i.e., retrospective memory failure). However, in a final unexpected recall test, all subjects in both age groups were able to name the four categories.

A similar task was used by Maylor (1993a) in which middle-aged and elderly subjects were repeatedly presented with slides of 30 famous faces, at a rate of 10 sec per item. They were asked to name each celebrity and also to respond to two targets (a beard and a pipe) by marking the trial number on the response sheet. In contrast to Mäntylä's (1993) design, the same two targets each appeared four times during the session. Younger subjects (n = 43; M age = 57) marked significantly more of the eight targets than older subjects (n = 43; M age = 75)—83% vs. 69%.

Perhaps the most influential laboratory paradigm for investigating prospective memory is that of Einstein and McDaniel (1990). In their study, subjects were presented with lists of words that they had to recall (short-term retrospective memory task). Some time before the task began, they were instructed to press a response key whenever a specified word (a single prospective memory target event) appeared in the list. In their first experiment, Einstein and McDaniel (1990) examined the effects of age (24 students, 24 elderly volunteers) and the opportunity to form an external aid using two conditions—no aid (in which subjects simply were told to press the response key whenever they saw the target word) and external aid (in which subjects were allowed to construct a memory aid out of material provided, such as paper and pens). As expected, the younger subjects performed significantly better than did the older subjects on the nonprospective memory task (which was also the case in the studies by Mäntylä, 1993, and Maylor, 1993a). Performance in the prospective memory task was not at ceiling (M number of responses to the target's three occurrences = 1.8). Although there was a significant benefit in using a memory aid, there was no effect of age, and no interaction.

In their second experiment, Einstein and McDaniel (1990) again examined the effect of age, but also manipulated target event familiarity (see McDaniel & Einstein, 1993, for further investigations on the latter). Performance was nearly three times better when the target event was an unfamiliar word than a familiar word. As in the first experiment, neither an effect of age nor an interaction with target event familiarity were seen. Thus Einstein and McDaniel demonstrated the absence of an age effect on prospective memory, in the context of both significant effects of other manipulations (memory aid and target event familiarity) and a significant negative effect of age on retrospective memory. Their conclusion was that "prospective memory seems to be an exciting exception to typically found age-related decrements in memory" (p. 724).

This surprising result was replicated in a further study by Einstein, Holland, McDaniel, and Guynn (1992). There were two prospective memory conditions: Subjects were asked to respond either to a single target word (which occurred three times) or to four target words (only three of which actually appeared). As before, no significant effect of age was found in the single-target condition. However, older subjects were significantly worse than students in the four-target condition. When prospective memory was conditionalized on retrospective memory for the target events (from a final recall test of the targets), this age deficit disappeared. In other words, "age-related performance differences, when they occurred, were associated with poorer retrospective memory for the target events" (p. 471).

An unpublished study by Einstein, McDaniel, Cunfer and Guynn (1991; described in McDaniel & Einstein, 1992) directly compared the effects of age in time-based and event-based prospective memory tasks. These were embedded in a running retrospective recall task in which words were presented at a rate of 2 seconds per item. When the stream was interrupted by a beep, subjects were required to recall as many of the last 10 words as possible. In the time-based version, the prospective memory task was to press a key after 10 and 20 min had elapsed; to keep track of the time, subjects had to turn around to look at a clock positioned behind them. In the event-based task, subjects had to press a key whenever they encountered a particular word. Older subjects were significantly less accurate than were younger subjects in the time-based prospective memory task, and this was associated with age differences in clock-monitoring frequency (see also Kerr, 1992). In contrast, there was no significant effect of age in the event-based prospective memory task. Similar results were obtained in a study by Richardson as reported by Einstein and McDaniel (this volume). These preliminary data are therefore consistent with the prediction that age deficits should be greater for time-based than for event-based prospective memory tasks, because the former require more self-initiated activity than the latter.

The conclusion emerging from these laboratory-controlled studies is that age-related deficits in prospective memory were clearly demonstrated, with the exception of event-based tasks by Einstein and colleagues. An obvious question to ask is what is different about their particular methodology that could account for the discrepancy? There may be several possibilities, but perhaps the most crucial is the fact that they deliberately reduced the cognitive demands of the nonprospective task for the older subjects, at least in their published studies. Thus the difficulty of the short-term memory task was equated across age groups by manipulating the number of items in each word list. Their results are therefore interpreted here as suggesting that the elderly can perform as well as the young in event-based prospective memory tasks, if they have equivalent processing resources available to them.

FURTHER ANALYSIS OF REPEATED PROSPECTIVE MEMORY TASKS

In this section, data from two of the studies, in which subjects were required to repeat the same prospective memory task on several occasions, are considered in more detail. The argument is as follows: Performance on the first occasion is presumably determined by whether or not the intention was sufficiently well-encoded and stored, by whether or not the target time or event is recognized as such (i.e., associated with the original intention), and by whether or not the appropriate action is retrieved and executed. If performance is successful, then an episodic trace of actually carrying out the task is formed in retrospective memory. On the next occasion, performance may still be affected as before by factors at encoding and so on, but there may be an additional influence of this episodic memory. In other words, the trigger for performance this time may be not so much the recall of the intention but more the recall of what was done on the previous occasion.

Consider, for example, the study described earlier in which subjects were repeatedly presented with the same set of famous faces (Maylor, 1993a). The task on each occasion was to name the faces and to mark the trial number if a beard or a pipe appeared. There are several possible strategic responses to the instructions for the prospective memory task that could determine whether or not performance is successful on the first occasion, including subvocal rehearsal of the words *beard* and *pipe*, generation of a visual image of a bearded man smoking a pipe, covert rehearsal of the action to-be-performed, and so on. Assuming a subject succeeds at least once in performing the prospective memory task as instructed, then memory for the action itself (rather than an abstract verbal description of it) can be stored, together with the context of the action. In the present example, the motor act of marking the trial number of the pipe is remembered and also associated with recognizing the face as that of the ex-Prime Minister, retrieving his name, and so on. Next time, if prospective memory fails to be triggered by the pipe, it could still be triggered by some other aspect of the action's context, such as writing *Harold Wilson*.

These considerations lead to at least three predictions:

1. Retrospective memory should be less strongly associated with whether or not performance is successful on the first occasion than with whether or not performance continues to be successful on subsequent occasions.

2. Because age is known to affect retrospective memory for actions (see Kausler, 1991, for a summary) and context (e.g., McIntyre & Craik, 1987), the same should apply to the effect of aging.

3. There should be other factors, perhaps those associated with encoding, that are more strongly associated with initial performance than with subsequent performance.

In Maylor's (1993a) face-naming study, there were four blocks of trials, with two prospective memory targets (*beard* and *pipe*) per block. Figure 9.1 shows the data broken down by age group and block. Clearly there was no effect of age group in the first block; thereafter, hits increased for the younger group but remained constant for the older group. In further analyses, *forgetting* was

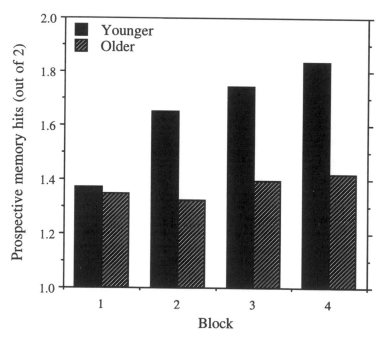

FIG. 9.1. Mean numbers of prospective memory hits as a function of age group and block (data from Maylor, 1993a).

TABLE 9.2
Summary of the Results of Six Analyses of Variance From a
Laboratory-Controlled Prospective Memory Task (Maylor, 1993a)

	Initial Performance (0, 1 or 2 hits)	Subsequent Forgetting (Present or Absent)
Retrospective memory[a]	No difference between groups	Present worse than absent
Age	No difference between groups	Present older than absent
Coding recall	0 and 1 worse than 2	No difference between groups

[a]Maylor (1993a) combined fluid intelligence, speed, and retrospective memory to produce a general ability factor. The results for retrospective memory were qualitatively identical to those reported for general ability.

Note. The entries shown are the effects of the independent variables (initial performance and subsequent forgetting) on the dependent variables (retrospective memory, age, and coding recall).

defined as success followed by failure on consecutive blocks, and *recovery* was defined as failure followed by success. For example, if a subject responded to the beard in blocks 1, 2, and 4, and to the pipe in blocks 2, 3, and 4, this was scored as one instance of forgetting (beard: block 2 → 3) and two instances of recovery (beard: block 3 → 4; pipe: block 1 → 2). Analysis of the data in terms of such instances of forgetting and recovery indicated that the pattern shown in Fig. 9.1 was attributable to equivalent recovery in the two age groups but greater forgetting in the older group than in the younger group.

Two separate sets of analyses were then performed. In the first set, subjects were categorized on the basis of their *initial performance* (number of hits in the first block: 0, 1, or 2). In the second set, they were categorized in terms of the presence or absence of at least one instance of *subsequent forgetting* (success in one block followed by failure in the next). (A third set of analyses, based on recovery, is not of interest here.) The resulting groups formed the independent variable in analyses of variance, with various measures as the dependent variable including age, retrospective memory (e.g., picture recognition), and coding recall (an unexpected test of memory for the code after completing a letter–letter substitution task). Table 9.2 summarizes the findings. It can be seen that subjects grouped on the basis of their initial performance did not differ significantly in terms of either retrospective memory or age. As predicted, the presence of subsequent forgetting was associated with lower retrospective memory scores and greater age. In contrast, coding recall was associated (positively) with initial performance, but was unrelated to subsequent forgetting.

Coding recall may partly reflect an active strategy of committing informa-

TABLE 9.3
Summary of the Results of a Naturalistic Prospective Memory Task (Reanalysis of Maylor, 1990)

	Initial Performance (Failure or Success)	Subsequent Forgetting (Present or Absent)
Proportion of Internal cues	Failure higher than success	No difference between groups
Age	No difference between groups	Internal cues: Present older than absent[a] Conjunction or external cues: Present younger than absent
Coding recall	Failure better than success	Present worse than absent[a]

[a]Marginal effect ($p < .06$)

Note. Subjects were grouped according to initial performance and subsequent forgetting. The entries shown are the differences between these groups in terms of the proportion of subjects using internal cues (χ^2 analyses), age, and coding recall (ANOVAs).

tion to memory rather than passively consulting external sources. It could therefore be related to prospective memory at encoding when the verbal instruction is perhaps converted into a visual image of the target event. This would be important when it is first encountered, but less so on subsequent occasions. To summarize, the evidence so far is consistent with the suggestion that retrospective memory and age should be less strongly associated with initial performance than with subsequent forgetting, and that another variable (possibly more indicative of encoding behavior) should produce the opposite result.

Maylor's (1990) telephone task was then examined in a similar way, that is, in terms of initial performance (subjects who failed vs. subjects who succeeded in telephoning on the first day of the study) and subsequent forgetting (subjects with vs. subjects without at least one instance of forgetting, again defined as success then failure on consecutive days). Table 9.3 summarizes these analyses. The actual results with respect to age and type of cue are presented in Table 9.4. First, it can be seen that subjects who failed initially did not differ in age from those who succeeded initially, regardless of the type of cue used. Second, for subjects using conjunction and external cues, those who subsequently forgot were younger than those who did not forget. In contrast, for subjects using internal cues, those who subsequently forgot tended to be older than those who did not forget. Again, there is the difficulty in explaining why it was the younger subjects using conjunction and external cues who forgot. However, the pattern for those using internal cues is consistent with the predictions regarding age. Third, it is clear from the number of subjects in each cell of Table 9.4 that cue-type influenced initial performance ($\chi^2[1, N =$

TABLE 9.4

Mean Ages, Standard Deviations, and Numbers of Subjects in Maylor's (1990) Study, Categorized in Terms of Cue (Conjunction and External vs. Internal), Initial Performance (Failure or Success), and Subsequent Forgetting (Present or Absent)

| | Initial Performance | | |
	Failure	Success	Difference
Conjunction and external cues			
M age	69.7	69.2	$F(1, 163) = 0.03$, p > .10
SD	11.9	7.1	
N	8	157	
Internal cues			
M age	72.0	71.2	$F(1, 55) = 0.08$, p > .10
SD	10.9	7.7	
N	14	43	

| | Subsequent Forgetting | | |
	Present	Absent	Difference
Conjunction and external cues			
M age	64.5	70.1	$F(1, 163) = 14.39$, p < .0005
SD	6.1	7.2	
N	27	138	
Internal cues[a]			
M age	75.6	70.5	$F(1, 54) = 3.90$, p = .053
SD	8.6	8.0	
N	13	43	

[a]1 subject, who telephoned only on the final day of the study, is missing.

222]=18.44, p < .001), but not subsequent forgetting ($\chi^2[1$, N = 221]=1.32, p > .10). In other words, setting up an external or conjunction cue was beneficial to performance on the first day, but was no longer important once a telephone call had been made.

Coding recall data were available for only 164 of the 222 subjects. However, the results from 2-way analyses of variance (cue-type being the second independent variable) are intriguing. For initial performance, coding recall was significantly higher for those who failed ($M = 6.9$, $SD = 3.7$, $n = 15$) than for those who succeeded ($M = 4.8$, $SD = 3.8$, $n = 149$)—$F(1, 160) = 5.49$, p < .05. This effect did not interact with cue-type ($F < 1.00$). For subsequent performance, coding recall tended to be lower for subjects who forgot ($M = 4.1$, $SD = 3.4$, $n = 31$) than for those who did not forget ($M = 5.2$, $SD = 3.8$, $n = 132$)—$F(1, 159) = 3.63$, p < .06. Again, there was no interaction with cue-type—$F(1, 159) = 2.14$, p > .10.

Note the contrast between the negative effect of coding recall on initial performance in this naturalistic study (Table 9.3) and the positive effect in the previous laboratory-controlled study (Table 9.2). How can this be explained? It was suggested that coding recall is partly an indication of the extent to which a subject develops an active internal strategy in preference to relying on external sources for information. Within the confines of the laboratory, where subjects are forced to rely on their own memories, an active internal response to the prospective memory instructions (such as imagining what the target might look like) could be expected to improve performance, at least initially. However, deliberately committing the task to memory would not necessarily be the best policy outside the laboratory where relying on the use of external cues such as alarm clocks, memos, and so on, is perhaps more sensible. Although higher coding recall scores were associated with initial failure in the telephone task, they tended to be associated with the absence of subsequent forgetting. Combined with the fact that cue-type significantly affected initial performance but not subsequent forgetting, subjects may have shifted from initially relying on external sources to subsequently relying on their own memories.

Clearly, these explanations are speculative and post-hoc. Nevertheless, the preliminary observations summarized in Tables 9.2 and 9.3 are consistent with the general predictions based on the analysis of possible components involved in repeated prospective memory tasks. It was argued that performance on a particular occasion should be influenced by different factors depending on whether the task is being performed for the first time (in which case, behaviour at encoding may predominate) or has already been performed (in which case, memory for the earlier occasion and its context may play an additional role). Thus two factors, coding recall and cue-type, were found to have stronger effects on initial performance than on subsequent forgetting, whereas two other factors, retrospective memory and age, were found to have stronger effects on subsequent forgetting than on initial performance. These latter results may help to explain why age and retrospective memory produced inconsistent effects in previous studies of prospective memory (see Maylor, 1993b).

CONCLUSIONS

The ability to perform successfully in prospective memory tasks, such as those listed at the beginning of this chapter, is obviously essential for independent living. It therefore is surprising that, until recently, prospective memory was a neglected area of research within cognitive psychology. There are probably both practical and theoretical reasons for this, including the problem of distinguishing between memory failures and lack of compliance, or between prospective and retrospective components of a task, and so on. Indeed, several studies were excluded from this chapter because they did not correspond to my definition of a prospective memory task.

With regard to age, the elderly would not be expected to perform as well as the young because of their reduced processing resources (e.g., Craik, 1986). In particular, deficits in processes such as self-initiated retrieval, reality monitoring, and output monitoring would be detrimental to performance in prospective memory tasks. However, experience and feedback accumulate with age, providing the opportunity for the elderly to develop compensatory strategies to overcome their cognitive deficits. Preliminary evidence suggests that the use of external memory aids increases with age in some conditions. This could account (at least partly) for the striking absence of age deficits in self-rated ability in everyday prospective memory tasks, and in "naturalistic" prospective memory studies conducted outside the laboratory. As Hunt (1993) commented, "learned habits of personal record keeping and adoption of an orderly life . . . may have overridden changes at the biological and information processing levels" (p. 590).

Consistent with their declining cognitive abilities, the elderly are less able to perform as well as the young under laboratory conditions (where the use of external memory aids is either excluded or controlled by the experimenter). The effect of age is particularly evident in time-based prospective memory tasks in which environmental support is low and self-initiated activity is high. Age deficits are less apparent in event-based tasks (greater environmental support available and less self-initiated activity required), and may be absent altogether if some allowance is made for the elderly's depleted processing resources by reducing the cognitive demands of the background activity accordingly.

Finally, the analysis of data from repeated prospective memory tasks in terms of initial performance, subsequent forgetting, and also subsequent recovery (although not dealt with here) may prove to be a useful approach in the future. The preliminary analyses presented in this chapter suggest that there are factors (including age) that have differential effects on initial and subsequent performance in repeated prospective memory tasks. Both the practical and theoretical significance of this remain to be explored.

ACKNOWLEDGMENTS

I am grateful to Alison Jones at the Age and Cognitive Performance Research Centre, University of Manchester, for assistance with data analysis, and to Alan Baddeley, Maria Brandimonte, and Gil Einstein who provided helpful comments on an earlier version of this chapter.

REFERENCES

Abson, V., & Rabbitt, P. (1988). What do self rating questionnaires tell us about changes in competence in old age? In M. M. Gruneberg, P. E. Morris, & R. N. Sykes (Eds.), *Practical Aspects of Memory: Current Research and Issues. Volume 2: Clinical and Educational Implications* (pp. 186–191). Chichester, England: Wiley.

Bäckman, L. (1989). Varieties of memory compensation by older adults in episodic remembering. In L. W. Poon, D. C. Rubin, & B. A. Wilson (Eds.), *Everyday Cognition in Adulthood and Late Life* (pp. 509–544). Cambridge, England: Cambridge University Press.

Baddeley, A. D. (1986). *Working Memory*. Oxford, England: Oxford University Press.

Brandimonte, M. A. (1991). Ricordare il futuro. *Giornale Italiano di Psicologia, 18,* 351–374.

Brandimonte, M. A., & Passolunghi, M. C. (1994). The effect of cue-familiarity, cue-distinctiveness and retention interval on prospective remembering. *Quarterly Journal of Experimental Psychology, 47A,* 565–587.

Brooks, B. M., & Gardiner, J. M. (1994). Age differences in memory for prospective compared with retrospective subject-performed tasks. *Memory & Cognition, 22,* 27–33.

Cavanaugh, J. C., Grady, J. G., & Perlmutter, M. (1983). Forgetting and use of memory aids in 20 to 70 year olds' everyday life. *International Journal of Aging and Human Development, 17,* 113–122.

Ceci, S. J., Baker, J. G., & Bronfenbrenner, U. (1988). Prospective remembering, temporal calibration, and context. In M. M. Gruneberg, P. E. Morris, & R. N. Sykes (Eds.), *Practical Aspects of Memory: Current Research and Issues. Volume 1: Memory in Everyday Life* (pp. 360–365). Chichester, England: Wiley.

Ceci, S. J., & Bronfenbrenner, U. (1991). On the demise of everyday memory. *American Psychologist, 46,* 27–31.

Cerella, J. (1985). Information processing rates in the elderly. *Psychological Bulletin, 98,* 67–83.

Cockburn, J. (1993). Dissociations in performance on tests of retrospective and prospective memory after cerebral infarction. Abstract in *Journal of Clinical and Experimental Neuropsychology, 15,* 387.

Cockburn, J., & Smith, P. T. (1988). Effects of age and intelligence on everyday memory tasks. In M. M. Gruneberg, P. E. Morris, & R. N. Sykes (Eds.), *Practical Aspects of Memory: Current Research and Issues. Volume 2: Clinical and Educational Implications* (pp. 132–136). Chichester, England: Wiley.

Cockburn, J., & Smith, P. T. (1991). The relative influence of intelligence and age on everyday memory. *Journal of Gerontology: Psychological Sciences, 46,* 31–36.

Cohen, G., & Faulkner, D. (1984). Memory in old age: 'good in parts'. *New Scientist, 11 October,* 49–51.

Cohen, G., & Faulkner, D. (1989). The effects of aging on perceived and generated memories. In L. W. Poon, D. C. Rubin, & B. A. Wilson (Eds.), *Everyday Cognition in Adulthood and Late Life* (pp. 222–243). Cambridge, England: Cambridge University Press.

Conway, M. A., & Gathercole, S. E. (1990). Writing and long-term memory: Evidence for a "translation" hypothesis. *Quarterly Journal of Experimental Psychology, 42A,* 513–527.

Craik, F.I.M. (1977). Age differences in human memory. In J. E. Birren & K. W. Schaie (Eds.), *Handbook of the Psychology of Aging* (2nd ed., p. 384–420). New York: Van Nostrand Reinhold.

Craik, F.I.M. (1986). A functional account of age differences in memory. In F. Klix & H. Hagendorf (Eds.), *Human Memory and Cognitive Capabilities: Mechanisms and Performances* (pp. 409–422). North-Holland: Elsevier Science.

Craik, F.I.M., & McDowd, J. M. (1987). Age differences in recall and recognition. *Journal of Experimental Psychology: Learning, Memory & Cognition, 13,* 474–479.

Dobbs, A. R., & Rule, B. G. (1987). Prospective memory and self-reports of memory abilities in older adults. *Canadian Journal of Psychology, 41*, 209–222.

Einstein, G. O., Holland, L. J., McDaniel, M. A., & Guynn, M. J. (1992). Age-related deficits in prospective memory: The influence of task complexity. *Psychology and Aging, 7*, 471–478.

Einstein, G. O., & McDaniel, M. A. (1990). Normal aging and prospective memory. *Journal of Experimental Psychology: Learning, Memory and Cognition, 16*, 717–726.

Einstein, G. O., McDaniel, M. A., Cunfer, A. R., & Guynn, M. J. (1991). *Aging and prospective memory: Examining the influences of self-initiated retrieval processes and mind wandering.* Unpublished manuscript, University of Furman.

Ellis, J. A. (1988). Memory for future intentions: Investigating pulses and steps. In M. M. Gruneberg, P. E. Morris, & R. N. Sykes (Eds.), *Practical Aspects of Memory: Current Research and Issues. Volume I: Memory in Everyday Life* (pp. 371–376). Chichester, England: Wiley.

Ellis, J. A., & Nimmo-Smith, I. (1993). Recollecting naturally-occurring intentions: A study of cognitive and affective factors. *Memory, 1*, 107–126.

Giambra, L. M. (1993). Sustained attention in older adults: Performance and processes. In J. Cerella, J. Rybash, W. Hoyer, & M. L. Commons (Eds.), *Adult Information Processing: Limits on Loss* (pp. 259–272). San Diego, CA: Academic Press.

Giambra, L. M., & Quilter, R. E. (1988). Sustained attention in adulthood: A unique, large-sample, longitudinal and multicohort analysis using the Mackworth Clock-test. *Psychology and Aging, 3*, 75–83.

Gruneberg, M. M., Morris, P. E., & Sykes, R. N. (Eds.) (1988). *Practical Aspects of Memory: Current Research and Issues.* Chichester, England: Wiley.

Harris, J. E. (1980). Memory aids people use: Two interview studies. *Memory and Cognition, 8*, 31–38.

Harris, J. E. (1984). Remembering to do things: A forgotten topic. In J. E. Harris & P. E. Morris (Eds.), *Everyday memory: Actions and absentmindedness* (pp. 71–92). London: Academic Press.

Harris, J. E., & Sunderland, A. (1981). Effects of age and instructions on an everyday memory questionnaire. Abstract in *Bulletin of the British Psychological Society, 35*, 212.

Harris, J. E., & Wilkins, A. J. (1982). Remembering to do things: A theoretical framework and an illustrative experiment. *Human Learning, 1*, 123–136.

Hartley, A. A. (1992). Attention. In F. I. M. Craik & T. A. Salthouse (Eds.), *The Handbook of Aging and Cognition* (pp. 3–49). Hillsdale, NJ: Lawrence Erlbaum Associates.

Hitch, G. J., & Ferguson, J. (1991) Prospective memory for future intentions: Some comparisons with memory for past events. *European Journal of Cognitive Psychology, 3*, 285–296.

Hunt, E. (1993). What do we need to know about aging? In J. Cerella, J. Rybash, W. Hoyer, & M. L. Commons (Eds.), *Adult Information Processing: Limits on Loss* (pp. 587–598). San Diego, CA: Academic Press.

Huppert, F. A., & Beardsall, L. (1993). Prospective memory impairment as an early indicator of dementia. *Journal of Clinical and Experimental Neuropsychology, 15*, 805–821.

Intons-Peterson, M. J., & Fournier, J. (1986). External and internal memory aids: When and how often do we use them? *Journal of Experimental Psychology: General, 115*, 267–280.

Jackson, J. L., Bogers, H., & Kerstholt, J. (1988). Do memory aids aid the elderly in their day to day remembering? In M. M. Gruneberg, P. E. Morris, & R. N. Sykes (Eds.), *Practical Aspects of Memory: Current Research and Issues. Volume 2: Clinical and Educational Implications* (pp. 137–142). Chichester, England: Wiley.

Johnson, M. K., & Raye, C. L. (1981). Reality monitoring. *Psychological Review, 88*, 67–85.

Kausler, D. H. (1991). *Experimental Psychology, Cognition, and Human Aging (2nd ed.).* New York: Springer-Verlag.

Kerr, S. A. (1992, April) *Prospective memory and aging: Older subjects burn their breakfast in a simulated cooking task*. Poster presented at the Fourth Biennial Cognitive Aging Conference, Atlanta, Georgia.

Koriat, A., Ben-Zur, H., & Nussbaum, A. (1990). Encoding information for future action: Memory for to-be-performed tasks versus memory for to-be-recalled tasks. *Memory & Cognition, 18,* 568–578.

Koriat, A., Ben-Zur, H., & Sheffer, D. (1988). Telling the same story twice: Output monitoring and age. *Journal of Memory and Language, 27,* 23–39.

Kvavilashvili, L. (1987). Remembering intention as a distinct form of memory. *British Journal of Psychology, 78,* 507–518.

Kvavilashvili, L. (1992). Remembering intentions: A critical review of existing experimental paradigms. *Applied Cognitive Psychology, 6,* 507–524.

Levy, R. L., & Loftus, G. R. (1984). Compliance and memory, In J. E. Harris & P. E. Morris (Eds.), *Everyday memory: Actions and absentmindedness* (pp. 93–112). London: Academic Press.

Lovelace, E. A., & Twohig, P. T. (1990). Healthy older adults' perceptions of their memory functioning and use of mnemonics. *Bulletin of the Psychonomic Society, 28,* 115–118.

Madden, D. J., & Plude, D. J. (1993). Selective preservation of selective attention. In J. Cerella, J. Rybash, W. Hoyer, & M. L. Commons (Eds.), *Adult Information Processing: Limits on Loss* (pp. 273–300). San Diego, CA: Academic Press.

Mäntylä, T. (1993). Priming effects in prospective memory. *Memory, 1,* 203–218.

Martin, M. (1986). Ageing and patterns of change in everyday memory and cognition. *Human Learning, 5,* 63–74.

Maylor, E. A. (1990). Age and prospective memory. *Quarterly Journal of Experimental Psychology, 42A,* 471–493.

Maylor, E. A. (1993a). Aging and forgetting in prospective and retrospective memory tasks. *Psychology and Aging, 3,* 420–428.

Maylor, E. A. (1993b). Minimized prospective memory loss in old age. In J. Cerella, J. Rybash, W. Hoyer, & M. L. Commons (Eds.), *Adult Information Processing: Limits on Loss* (pp. 529–551). San Diego, CA: Academic Press.

McDaniel, M. A., & Einstein, G. O. (1992). Aging and prospective memory: Basic findings and practical applications. In T. E. Scruggs & M. A. Mastropieri (Eds.), *Advances in Learning and Behavioral Disabilities: Vol. 7* (pp. 87–105). Greenwich, CT: JAI Press.

McDaniel, M. A., & Einstein, G. O. (1993). The importance of cue familiarity and cue distinctiveness in prospective memory. *Memory, 1,* 23–41.

McDowd, J. M., & Craik, F.I.M. (1988). Effects of aging and task difficulty on divided attention performance. *Journal of Experimental Psychology: Human Perception and Performance, 14,* 267–280.

McEvoy, C. L., & Moon, J. R. (1988). Assessment and treatment of everyday memory problems in the elderly. In M. M. Gruneberg, P. E. Morris, & R. N. Sykes (Eds.), *Practical Aspects of Memory: Current Research and Issues. Volume 2: Clinical and Educational Implications* (pp. 155–160). Chichester, England: Wiley.

McIntyre, J. S., & Craik, F.I.M. (1987). Age differences in memory for item and source information. *Canadian Journal of Psychology, 41,* 175–192.

McKitrick, L. A., Camp, C. J., & Black, F. W. (1992). Prospective memory intervention in Alzheimer's disease. *Journal of Gerontology: Psychological Sciences, 47,* 337–343.

Meacham, J. A. (1982). A note on remembering to execute planned actions. *Journal of Applied Developmental Psychology, 3,* 121–133.

Meacham, J. A. (1988). Interpersonal relations and prospective remembering. *Practical Aspects of Memory: Current Research and Issues. Volume 1: Memory in Everyday Life* (pp. 354–359). Chichester, England: Wiley.

Meacham, J. A., & Colombo, J. A. (1980). External retrieval cues facilitate prospective remembering in children. *Journal of Educational Research, 73,* 299–301.

Meacham, J. A., & Leiman, B. (1982). Remembering to perform future actions. In U. Neisser

(Ed.), *Memory Observed: Remembering in Natural Contexts* (pp. 327–336). San Francisco: Freeman.

Mitchell, D. B. (1989). How many memory systems? Evidence from aging. *Journal of Experimental Psychology: Learning, Memory and Cognition, 15,* 31–49.

Moscovitch, M. (1982). A neuropsychological approach to memory and perception in normal and pathological aging. In F. I. M. Craik & S. Trehub (Eds.), *Aging and Cognitive Processes* (pp. 55–78). New York: Plenum Press.

Moscovitch, M., & Winocur, G. (1992). The neuropsychology of memory and aging. In F.I.M. Craik & T. A. Salthouse (Eds.), *The Handbook of Aging and Cognition* (pp. 315–372). Hillsdale, NJ: Lawrence Erlbaum Associates.

Patton, G.W.R., & Meit, M. (1993). Effect of aging on prospective and incidental memory. *Experimental Aging Research, 19,* 165–176.

Payne, S. J. (1993). Understanding calendar use. *Human-Computer Interaction, 8,* 83–100.

Poon, L. W., Rubin, D. C., & Wilson, B. A. (Eds.) (1989). *Everyday Cognition in Adulthood and Late Life.* Cambridge, England: Cambridge University Press.

Poon, L. W., & Schaffer, G. (1982, August). *Prospective memory in young and elderly adults.* Paper presented at the meeting of the American Psychological Association, Washington, DC.

Rabbitt, P.M.A. (1990). Age, IQ and awareness, and recall of errors. *Ergonomics, 33,* 1291–1305.

Rabbitt, P.M.A., & Abson, V. (1990). 'Lost and found': Some logical and methodological limitations of self-report questionnaires as tools to study cognitive ageing. *British Journal of Psychology, 81,* 1–16.

Reeves, M. B., & Dobbs, A. R. (1992, October) *The utilization and evaluation of prospective memory aids by younger and older adults.* Poster presented at the 21st Annual Scientific and Educational Meeting of the Canadian Association on Gerontology, Edmonton, Alberta.

Salthouse, T. A. (1990). Cognitive competence and expertise in aging. In J. E. Birren & K. W. schaie (Eds.), *Handbook of the Psychology of Aging* (3rd ed., pp. 310–319). London: Academic Press.

Salthouse, T. A. (1991). *Theoretical Perspectives on Cognitive Aging.* Hillsdale, NJ: Lawrence Erlbaum Associates.

Salthouse, T. A. (1992). *Mechanisms of Age-Cognition Relations in Adulthood.* Hillsdale, NJ: Lawrence Erlbaum Associates.

Shallice, T. (1982) Specific impairments of planning. *Philosophical Transactions of the Royal Society of London B, 298,* 199–209.

Sinnott, J. D. (1986). Prospective/intentional and incidental everyday memory: Effects of age and passage of time. *Psychology and Aging, 1,* 110–116.

Somberg, B. L., & Salthouse, T. A. (1982). Divided attention abilities in young and old adults. *Journal of Experimental Psychology: Human Perception and Performance, 8,* 651–663.

Welford, A. T. (1958). *Ageing and Human Skill.* London: Oxford University Press.

West, R. L. (1988). Prospective memory and aging. In M. M. Gruneberg, P. E. Morris, & R. N. Sykes (Eds.), *Practical Aspects of Memory: Current Research and Issues. Volume 2: Clinical and Educational Implications* (pp. 119–125). Chichester, England: Wiley.

Wichman, H., & Oyasato, A. (1983). Effects of locus of control and task complexity on prospective remembering. *Human Factors, 25,* 583–591.

Wiggs, C. L. (1993). Aging and memory for frequency of occurrence of novel, visual stimuli: Direct and indirect measures. *Psychology and Aging, 8,* 400–410.

Wilson, B. A., Cockburn, J., & Baddeley, A. D. (1985). *The Rivermead Behavioural Memory Test.* Titchfield, England: Thames Valley Test Co.

Woolf, M. J. (1993). *Age difference in prospective memory in everyday life.* Unpublished masters thesis, University of Liverpool, England.

10

Prospective Memory: More Than Memory

Allen R. Dobbs
M. Barbara Reeves
University of Alberta

Although researchers have been interested in remembering to carry out future actions for at least 100 years (cf. Colegrove, 1898), there was little research reported on the topic until the 1970s. From an historical perspective, this is not surprising given that prospective remembering is a complex task that did not fit easily within the associationistic tradition that dominated much of the research on human memory. However, with the shift toward cognitive psychology, and especially with the renewed interest in everyday memory, a substantial body of research on prospective remembering is accumulating. Nevertheless, even among the studies that have been reported, there is less advancement than one might have expected, both in terms of the development of experimental paradigms and in the extent and sophistication of the conceptual analyses.

One reason that progress has been slow may be because remembering to carry out an action in the future was often associated with a type of memory rather than a type of remembering. Treating prospective remembering as a type of memory led researchers to contrast prospective and retrospective *memory*, designing and conducting studies to examine the relationship between the two types of memory abilities (e.g., Einstein & McDaniel, 1990; Loftus, 1971; Maylor, 1993; Wilkins & Baddeley, 1978).

Unfortunately, treating prospective remembering as a type of memory leaves the impression that it is unidimensional. Remembering to complete a future action is, however, far from a unidimensional task. Prospective remembering potentially involves a wide variety of qualitatively different types of mental processes. In this sense, it would have been more fruitful to ask what aspects of prospective remembering bear a relationship to particular aspects of retrospective remembering. However, that approach requires a more complete analysis of prospective remembering than was previously accomplished.

Using one or another prospective memory task to investigate possible deficits of brain injured or disease groups illustrates the problem of treating prospective remembering as though it were a type of memory. The finding that a brain injured or diseased group performs more poorly than a control group on a prospective memory task would not justify a claim that prospective *memory* was compromised in that group. The poor performance of the pathology group could have resulted from a number of qualitatively different types of dysfunctions. For example, the dysfunction could have resulted in planning deficits that precluded the appropriate setting of memory aids, attentional processes could have been altered such that monitoring was impaired, memory could have been compromised so that the person forgot what to do even if he or she knew when to act, personality could have been altered such that the person was less compliant, or any combination of these or other deficits could have been responsible for the lowered performance.

Prospective Memory: More than Memory

As the title of this chapter suggests, our position is that prospective memory is not a type of memory. Instead, the label *prospective memory* is merely a label that loosely categorizes a set of tasks in which a necessary though not sufficient attribute is that a defined action is to be accomplished in the future. In this sense, the term *prospective memory* is no different than *retrospective memory* which refers to a collection of diverse tasks for which remembering information from the past is a dominant but not defining attribute.

To date, there have been a number of investigators who proposed that prospective remembering involves different components (e.g., Harris, 1984; Levy & Loftus, 1984; Meacham, 1982, but see Brandimonte & Passolunghi, 1994; Einstein & McDaniel, and Ellis chapters of this book). However, because of the goals of the study or the orientation of the researcher, most often only a few possible components were mentioned in any one study, and these differed from report to report. This is unfortunate, because prospective remembering is a multidimensional task that can involve a wide variety of processes. The specific nature of the task will determine which types of processes are emphasized, de-emphasized, or even omitted. This makes for vast opportunities to alter and study different processing attributes. However, the potential array of different tasks makes comparisons among them difficult or perhaps even inappropriate if the task differences have processing implications.

Moreover, if the person *knows* on the basis of prior knowledge that he or she is likely to fail at one or another aspect of a prospective remembering task, the person may completely change the nature of the task (e.g., by setting an alarm, thereby eliminating the necessity of monitoring time). Being able to compensate for potentially poor performance on one aspect of a prospective remembering task by altering this or another aspect of the same task is not a trivial point. The importance of the point is well-illustrated by comparing prospective remembering in young and old adults. Older persons are often found to outperform younger people. Interestingly, it also is the case that older adults are more likely than younger adults to alter the demands of the task (e.g., by using external memory aids, Moscovitch & Minde, cited in Moscovitch, 1982). When a task is altered by one group but not the other, it is no longer a study of possible differences in the ability to perform *that* task. People often do alter prospective memory tasks, making comparisons between groups difficult. For this and other reasons, it would be helpful if there was a general framework that catalogued the different components that might be involved in prospective remembering. This framework could be used to analyze any specific task as an aid to exploring what needs to be measured or controlled, and for comparing among different tasks. Our goal in this chapter is to explore the multi-dimensionality of prospective remembering using a framework that we found useful in guiding our own thinking.

Overview of Framework

The task of remembering to complete an action in the future potentially involves a variety of qualitatively different components. The person may have prior knowledge about the task and his or her abilities, use this knowledge to construct some plan as to how to remember, monitor for the appropriate time or event that signals when the action is to be performed, recall the action, comply and actually perform the action, and remember that the action was or was not completed. We have labelled these steps as *metaknowledge* (knowledge about the specific task demands), *planning* (the formulation of a plan to facilitate performance) *monitoring* (intermittently recalling that the task needs to be completed and evaluating whether or not the designated circumstances are current), *content recall* (remembering the action that is to be carried out), *compliance* (the person's willingness to carry out the action at the appropriate time), and *output monitoring* (remembering if the action was carried out). We do not presume that any one of these components is unitary or that there may not be some overlap in the individual processes that make up the components. The manner in which one component is accomplished will often affect the processing demands of other components. The framework is not put forward as a theory explicating the full extent of processing within components nor the *interactions* between components. Nor do we assume that all components will be accomplished or even necessary in all tasks. But, from our point of view, even the omission of any one of these components because of the nature of the task or the competence of the individual may have important implications. The framework is meant as a heuristic to segment the task in order to facilitate the generation of hypotheses about individual processes and variables that may be central. We will consider each of these components separately and discuss the relevant research.

In addition, prospective memory tasks vary and different tasks alter the cognitive demands. Because of this, it is important that the nature of the demands be well-articulated in studies of prospective remembering. It may be helpful if the tasks could be catalogued along some restricted number of dimensions. Such a taxonomy could be useful in at least defining the nature of the components that are typical of that task and this could facilitate developing paradigms and measurements, and aid in comparing performance between and among tasks. As a step toward this goal, we will discuss dimensions that may be important in developing a taxonomy.

We turn now to a discussion of six components of prospective remembering tasks. Each component will be described and some of the evidence we interpreted as being relevant to understanding the nature of the component will be presented, along with suggestions for future research. Following this discussion, we will describe four dimensions that may be useful for categorizing prospective remembering tasks.

COMPONENTS OF PROSPECTIVE REMEMBERING

Metaknowledge

The terms *metacognition* and *metamemory* have been used in a variety of ways (e.g., Brown, 1978; Brown, Bransford, Ferrara, & Campione, 1983; Cavanaugh, 1989, Cavanaugh & Perlmutter, 1982; Dixon, 1989; Flavell, 1971; Flavell & Wellman, 1977). We opted to use the term metaknowledge because it is theoretically more neutral than either metacognition or metamemory, and because here we are interested in the domain of knowledge restricted to prospective remembering. Our use of the term metaknowledge refers to the general knowledge one has about tasks of prospective remembering and personal knowledge about one's own abilities and behaviors. At the general level, the metaknowledge includes information about the nature of the task demands, task attributes, strategies that could optimize or impede performance in general, and beliefs about the abilities and motivations of others. The personal metaknowledge is specific to the individual. It would include beliefs about his or her own abilities, obstacles to successful performance, the personal utility of performance enhancers and how likely he or she is to use them, and related idiosyncratic information. There is no suggestion that metaknowledge about prospective remembering is any more accurate than is metaknowledge about any other topic. It only refers to the belief system people hold about prospective remembering.

Relatively little is known about this metaknowledge. This is unfortunate because metaknowledge about prospective remembering can be at least as important a determinant of performance as is knowledge about the effectiveness of rehearsal for remembering information in short-term memory, or the facilitatory effect of imagery or organizational strategies for learning. Research directed toward understanding the structure of this belief system, how it develops, the accuracy of various aspects of those beliefs for different groups or individuals, and how and when it is accessed are all empirically answerable questions that could provide information useful for both design considerations and the interpretation of findings.

Although only the most basic information is available, it is clear that there are individual differences in this metaknowledge. As one example, there are developmental trends both for knowing the importance of reducing the demands of monitoring for when an action should be carried out and for knowing the effectiveness of different plans. Istomina (1986) and Kreutzer, Leonard, and Flavell (1975) reported that young children do not see the need for setting plans and Beal (1985, 1988) showed that there is a developmental trend for children to recognize the components of a good plan.

In one of our own investigations, we were interested in whether or not there were adult age differences in the ability to recognize a good plan. We presented young and old adults with scenarios describing a variety of different kinds of prospective memory tasks along with several types of internal and external cues that could be used to facilitate performance. We asked each person to indicate for each task which method would be the best to use "if it was absolutely essential to remember to carry out the action" and which method they typically would use to perform that task. The tasks fell into several categories created by crossing two of the dimensions from the taxonomy we present later in this chapter. There were some differences between types of tasks, but of particular interest was the change in the pattern of responding from the absolutely essential or best method to the "typical" method for that person. Although both groups rated external cues as best in the *must* situation, their reported typical use of external cues was much lower, with this difference being especially large for the young adults. This finding suggests that at the general level, the metaknowledge for the effectiveness of different types of cues may be similar for young and older adults. However, having the knowledge is not a sufficient condition for its use. Task situations (type of task, importance) and personal beliefs about one's own abilities may determine if and when this knowledge is put into play.

Personal knowledge about one's own prospective remembering abilities have been studied by several investigators. The findings from self-ratings indicate that older people give themselves higher ratings on prospective remembering than do younger adults (e.g., Martin, 1986). Similarly, both McMillan (1984) and Bennett-Levy and Powell (1980) found that their participants believed that performance on returning a borrowed item and giving messages increased with age. These studies do not, however, indicate why older people give themselves higher ratings. There is a need to study not only that different groups rate themselves differently on accomplishing prospective remembering tasks, but why they give these differential ratings. Within the context of the present chapter, that would entail whether or not the groups would accomplish the tasks in the same way, and if not, in what ways they would alter the various components.

The relationship between self-perceptions of prospective remembering abilities and actual performance was studied by Devolder, Brigham, and Pressley (1990). Older adults were found to rate their own ability on an appointment keeping task more highly than did younger adults, and the personal performance predictions and postdictions of the older adults were more accurate. In contrast, Dobbs and Rule (1987) were unable to find a relationship between rated ability and performance for any of the adult age groups studied. The same null result was obtained in a more recent study comparing self-rated ability and actual performance on prospective memory tasks by mild head-injured and whiplash patients (Dobbs, Reeves, & Rule, 1995). Although we consistently failed to find a relationship between rated ability and measured performance, both of our studies involved ratings taken across several representative tasks rather than of predictions about the specific performance task, as was done by Devolder et al. (1990). Given the wide variation in the type of tasks and a corresponding variation in the types of processing demands, perhaps the lack of a relationship is understandable. On the other hand, Zelinski, Gilewski and Anthony-Bergstone (1990) reported that even people's general memory complaints can be a good predictor of prospective remembering failures. In any case, people's beliefs about the tasks, the ways in which the tasks can be altered to maximize performance, and their own abilities can be the basis for substantially altering the task demands and types of processing that are required.

The structure and content of prospective memory metaknowledge needs to be better articulated than is presently the case. We suspect that advancement is most likely if research instruments are developed specifically to investigate metaknowledge relevant to prospective remembering. As a starting point, the questionnaire could be directed toward both general and personal knowledge, with the components outlined in this chapter serving as the topic areas for individual questions. As the knowledge base accumulates, this information can be incorporated in the designs of experimental studies to address questions about its use and, if the study of other components is of interest, to more appropriately ensure that all participants are approaching the task in similar ways. This latter point is especially important in studies comparing different groups. Deficits in one type of processing could be accommodated or accentuated by good or poor knowledge of the tasks or personal abilities and lead to failures to show differences where they exist or lead to overestimates of the extent of dysfunctions in other cases.

Planning

The planning component of prospective memory concerns not people's knowledge of the efficacy of different plans (metaknowledge), but the construction and actual implementation of plans in prospective remembering tasks. This distinction between the construction and implementation of plans (planning) and knowledge about plans (metaknowledge) is important. Metaknowledge about prospective remembering is a necessary but insufficient condition for planning. This was suggested by our findings in which old and young persons revealed similar knowledge about the most effective strategies for successful performance, but self-ratings indicated old and young persons had different rates of formulating and using plans.

Research relevant to planning in prospective remembering tasks goes back at least 100 years to when Colegrove (1898) queried some 1,600 people regarding how they remember to keep appointments. Many subsequent researchers (e.g., Ellis, 1988; Jackson, Bogers, & Kerstholt, 1988; Kreutzer et al., 1975; Maylor, 1990; Meacham & Singer, 1977; Moscovitch & Minde, cited in Moscovitch, 1982) also asked people how they remember to carry out future actions. In general, the findings have been that external aids are used more frequently than are internal aids (Kreutzer et al., 1975; Meacham & Singer, 1977), but that old adults are more likely than young adults to use external memory aids (Einstein & McDaniel, 1990; Jackson et al., 1988; Moscovitch & Minde, cited in Moscovitch, 1982). Because external prospective remembering aids are more effective than are internal ones (e.g., Meacham & Leiman, 1982; Moscovitch & Minde, cited in Moscovitch, 1982; Nazarian, Machuber, Charney, & Coulter, 1974; Shepard & Moseley, 1976), older adults are utilizing the better plans. This might explain why older adults often outperform younger adults in prospective memory tasks completed in the real world (e.g., Martin, 1986; Moscovitch & Minde, cited in Moscovitch, 1982; Poon & Schaffer, cited in West, 1988) where people are free to use their own system for remembering.

Planning also has played a central role in prospective remembering training studies (Anschutz, Camp, Markley, & Kramer, 1985; Furst, 1986; Mateer & Sohlberg, 1988; Stevens, Camp, & O'Hanlon, 1992). For example, Stevens et al., 1992, trained Alzheimer's disease patients to consult a calendar and then to perform the tasks entered for that day. The rationale in this type of intervention is that if people use a good strategy, they are more likely to remember to complete the future action. This may be especially important for persons showing one or another cognitive deficit in that an effective plan might alter the task to compensate for the deficit.

Almost all of the planning research has concerned what we have labeled the monitoring component of prospective remembering. In fact, the majority of studies on prospective remembering seem to focus on plans to aid monitoring. This research focus is probably due to the saliency of the monitoring component as a central feature of prospective remembering. However, plans pertaining to the other prospective remembering components can be observed in everyday life. For example, when we want to bring up many points during a meeting we usually write then down as an aid to content recall. And, if we check off or make notes regarding the items we discussed, this is an aid to output monitoring.

The recemt push toward preventive care resulted in many clinics inserting checklists into patient files or having patients bring them to appointments. The checklists typically record the preventive tests that would be appropriate for someone of that age and sex. The doctors can record if each test was given (or why not). These aids do not affect monitoring (because they are seen after the patient arrives) but they do influence content recall (for tests to give), output monitoring (for tests already given) and compliance (if notes were previously made as to why a test should not be given). Generally, the research indicates that providing doctors with such checklists increases the delivery of preventive care (e.g., Ornstein, Garr, Jenkins, Rust, & Arnon, 1991; Turner, Day, & Borenstein, 1989; Turner, Waivers, & O'Brien, 1990). Checklists of actions to be completed also are commonly used by pilots and astronauts. However, in spite of using a checklist, it is still possible for actions to be omitted or repeated (e.g., "Astronauts suffer effects," cited in Meacham, 1982). After all, the formulation of a good plan is only one step in the prospective remembering process. It is also important that the plan be utilized effectively, and this may require efficient monitoring for when to use the list and monitoring of output.

Monitoring

Successful monitoring in prospective remembering occurs when the person remembers at the appropriate time or event that something is to be done, even if the person cannot remember what has to be done. Conceptually, monitoring involves both the *monitoring behaviors* that occur while the person is awaiting the appropriate circumstances to perform the action, and the *accuracy* of the person in identifying those circumstances. Monitoring behaviors are those implicit and explicit checks of whether or not the appropriate circumstances to act have occurred. Monitoring accuracy is the accuracy with which the person identifies the appropriate circumstances to act, regardless of how much the person did or did not monitor (check) while they were awaiting those circumstances. Moreover, monitoring accuracy is knowing when to respond, regardless of whether or not the person can remember what to do or chooses not to comply and complete the action. Of course, the pattern and extent of monitoring behaviors that occur during the interval and the accuracy of the monitoring both depend on the person remembering the critical time or event. To our knowledge, this retrospective memory aspect of prospective remembering tasks has not been an explicit target of study. Instead, accurate recall of the critical time or event most often has been presumed. When it has been assessed, the goal has been to ensure that the person had the knowledge and to eliminate trials for which the appropriate knowledge was lacking, rather than to study task attributes that might affect the recallability of this information. Because of this, our discussion will be restricted to considerations of monitoring behaviors and monitoring accuracy. These two aspects of monitoring (behavior and accuracy) will be considered separately.

Monitoring Behavior.   A prospective memory task is usually considered to have been performed incorrectly if it is performed at the wrong time. Consequently, when a person is to perform a prospective memory task, it is important to monitor the environment so that when the right circumstances occur the action can be performed promptly. Harris and Wilkins (1982) proposed that people's behavior while waiting to perform a future action can be explained in terms of a test–wait–test–exit model. According to this model, there is a critical period during which the action of a prospective memory task must be completed. The size of this critical period varies between tasks, but if the designated action is performed outside the boundaries of its critical period, it is considered to have been performed incorrectly. While waiting to perform the action, a person can test to see if the critical period for responding has arrived. If it has, the person exits the waiting phase. Otherwise, the person must continue to wait and test for the arrival of the critical period.

The test–wait–test–exit model is a descriptive model of monitoring behavior. Monitoring should not, however, be thought of as a continuous sequence of test–wait cycles filling the interval between the beginning of the prospective task and the occasion for responding. Monitoring occurs as a background task with one or more other tasks being completed as foreground tasks. (Allowing the person to concentrate solely on monitoring for the occasion to respond makes the task a vigilance task.) Thus, monitoring is costly because it is disruptive to foreground task performance, but monitoring may not be as costly as performing the prospective memory task too early or too late. Because of this, an important question concerns the conditions that initiate a testing cycle.

It seems reasonable to presume that the conditions are either internal (e.g., an internal clock) or they are particular and definable aspects of the environment (cf., Harris & Wilkins, 1982). To our knowledge, this was not a focus of study except in the case of external memory aids, but investigation directed toward delineating the conditions that bring about an explicit monitoring test sequence clearly are needed. As a footnote to this, it should be noted that there is little study of the relationship between the type of foreground task (its importance, demands and relationship to the cue to respond) and monitoring. Although a discussion of this is beyond the scope of this chapter, monitoring does occur in the presence of other tasks and the choice of these tasks could strongly influence the monitoring behavior.

Monitoring behavior typically has been studied by observing when (over the waiting interval involving another, foreground, task) people check the time on a clock. Ceci and Bronfenbrenner (1985) reported three clock checking patterns—a U-shaped pattern, a linearly increasing pattern, and a linearly decreasing pattern. Both the U-shaped and linearly increasing patterns were associated with on-time performance, but the U-shaped pattern was more efficient because, overall, it was associated with fewer clock checks (and hence was least disruptive to performance on the foreground task). Ceci and Bronfenbrenner interpreted the U-shaped pattern as follows: During the beginning of the task, the participants looked frequently at the clock in order to get their internal clocks synchronized with the external clock. During the middle of the period they looked at the clock infrequently because they could rely largely on their internal clocks to keep track of the time. Finally, as the response time approached, they relied mainly on the external clock to ensure they were not late in performing the prospective memory task.

The strategic patterns produced by Ceci and Bronfenbrenner's participants are not limited to monitoring real time. Similar patterns are found when participants monitored with accelerated or decelerated clocks (Ceci, Baker, & Bronfenbrenner, 1988). Several of our own studies revealed similar monitoring patterns when people are not monitoring time, per se. The task, affectionately referred to as "the vile task," requires people to monitor a pebble falling in a fluid-filled vial simulated on a computer screen. When the pebble enters a colored band (demarcating the critical period) near the bottom of the vial, the participants are instructed to press a button that will reset the pebble's position to the top of the vial. Another button must be pressed whenever the participants want to see the position of the pebble. This "show" button provides a measure of overt monitoring behavior. This task is accomplished as a background task while the subjects are engaged in a continuous lexical decision task.

Using this task, we found that people display U-shaped monitoring patterns for monitoring intervals ranging from just over 1 min to 30 min (Chen, 1993; Reeves, 1992; Reeves, Dobbs, & Heller, 1995). These same types of monitoring patterns were produced regardless of whether people were performing one prospective memory task or three concurrent ones (i.e., monitoring one vial or three vials). We also found that both young and old adults produce these U-shaped monitoring patterns (Reeves, 1992; Reeves et al., 1995). However, when the pebble fell multiple times, the U-shaped pattern was produced only for the first time the pebble fell. After the first fall, the large number of checks associated with the beginning of the interval dropped off, presumably because people had already calibrated their internal clock and did not need to do so again (Reeves, et al., 1995).

Monitoring Accuracy. In distinguishing prospective from retrospective remembering, an emphasis is placed on monitoring accuracy. This is because it is essential that the person "remember to remember" at the appropriate time, or when the critical event occurs, in order to perform correctly. This requirement either is absent or trivialized in retrospective memory tasks. However, in spite of its theoretical importance, independent measures of monitoring accuracy are hard to find in the prospective remembering literature. An independent measure would require documenting whether or not the person knew at the appropriate time or event occurrence that something was to be done, independent of whether or not he or she could recall *what* (content) was to be done, and independent of whether or not the person was going to *comply* by performing the designated action. More commonly, the measure of monitoring accuracy is confounded by the accuracy with which the person is able to recall the action and his or her compliance. For example, in an earlier study from our laboratory (Dobbs & Rule, 1987), the task was to remember to ask for a red pen at the right time. Because the only performance measure was whether or not the person actually asked for the red pen at the right time, we could not ascertain whether failure to do the task was due to a monitoring failure (did not recognize when to complete the action), or a content failure (could not remember what was to be done), or knew when to do the action, knew what to do, but decided not to comply.

In contrast to many of the prospective remembering tasks described before, the red pen task is not temporally predictable. Therefore, for tasks of this type, the setting of an internal clock is not important to monitoring accuracy. Instead, the cue properties of the event signaling the critical period for responding are important. Current research shows that performance tends to be better with unfamiliar rather than familiar cues (Einstein & McDaniel, 1990; McDaniel & Einstein, 1993), specific rather than general cues (Einstein, McDaniel, Cunfer, & Guynn, 1991), distinctive rather than nondistinctive cues (McDaniel & Einstein, 1993), and elaborate rather than simple cues (Loftus, 1971). Occasionally (but not consistently), there are different effects of cues with different age groups. For example, Einstein, Holland, McDaniel, and Guynn (1992) found no age differences when the same cue was used repeatedly, but young adults were better than old adults when three distinct cues were used. In addition, West (1988) found that old participants performed better after a combined verbal and situational cue than after a verbal and visual cue. However, this manipulation had no effect on the young participants.

In one of our studies (reported in Dobbs & Reeves, 1991), two tasks were given on different days to assess the effect of the relationship between the cue and the content of the prospective task. For both tasks, we asked people to turn over their testing booklet and write their estimate of the current time on the back. In the related cue condition, there was a close relationship between the action to be performed (estimate the time) and the cue (draw a clock) for that action. In the unrelated condition, there was no obvious connection between the action and its signal (a booklet containing pictures of scenes). Performance was generally much better after a related rather than an unrelated cue. But the cue effects were qualified by age such that there was a greater age-related drop in performance with the unrelated cue. This is consistent with Craik's (1986) suggestion that the magnitude of the age-related decrement observed on a task is inversely related to the amount of environmental support inherent in the task.

In another study from our laboratory, Reeves (1991) looked at the influence of cue value on both prospective remembering and concurrent task performance by embedding different types of cues for a prospective task within an ongoing lexical decision task. In one trial, people were to perform the prospective task when the letter strings turned one of three colors. In the other trial, people were to perform the task when an item from one of three designated categories appeared in the lexical decision task. People never failed to perform the task after a perceptual cue (color change), but they did not always remember after a semantic cue (category member). In addition, monitoring for these two types of signals had different effects on the foreground task in that the overall mean lexical decision times were much slower when monitoring for a semantic cue as opposed to a perceptual cue.

Thus far, in discussing the accuracy of responding, we have ignored involvement of the critical period. The critical period is the region during which the person feels it is acceptable to perform the task. The size of a critical period, its shape, and the permeability of its beginning and ending boundaries vary between prospective memory tasks. In addition, it seems probable that the parameters of critical periods will vary between individuals. For example, in one study conducted in our laboratory, we found that, whereas most younger adults tended to arrive after the time booked for the testing session, older adults tended to arrive before it. Perhaps older and younger adults have a different concept of the acceptable time to arrive. This leads us to wonder if differences in the parameters of the critical period (the acceptable region for responding) might, in part, account for older adults' superior performance on real-world prospective remembering studies (e.g., Martin, 1986; Moscovitch & Minde, cited in Moscovitch, 1982; Poon & Schaffer, cited in West, 1988). Perhaps older adults are more likely to mail a postcard because they are less likely to consider it an error to mail it *before* the specified day. Group differences in critical periods would be a useful topic of research, but this topic has been almost completely ignored by researchers.

Monitoring in prospective memory tasks has been investigated in a variety of studies. Although the findings from these studies provide a substantive information base, there is still much to learn. Perhaps the most critical issues concern what it is that initiates a monitoring sequence and the trade-off between monitoring performance and performance on the foreground tasks.

Content Recall

For the purposes of this discussion, *content recall* refers the person's knowledge of the content of the action that is to be performed.[1] Within the framework presented here, content recall is an independent component in the sense that success in remembering the content of the action can be measured independent of the success with which the other components are completed. Thus, people might have accurate knowledge of the action that is to be performed even though they fail to monitor accurately or fail to respond because they do not comply.

Although content recall could be an important aspect of everyday prospective remembering tasks, most researchers have been more interested in the monitoring component than in content recall. As a result, the memory demands for the content of prospective remembering tasks are often minimized (e.g., mail one or more pre-addressed postcards, press a button).

When recall of content has been assessed directly there have been two approaches. The first has been to obtain measures of both content recall and monitoring within the context of a prescribed prospective task. Several researchers (Dobbs & Rule, 1987; Maylor, 1993; West, 1988) have attempted to examine age differences this way. Unfortunately, in all of these studies, the measure of content recall was confounded with the success of monitoring. If the monitoring failed, there was, of course, no response even though the person may have had perfect retention of the content.

Dobbs and Reeves (1991) attempted to minimize the confounding by scoring monitoring accuracy to be high if the participants indicated in any overt way that they knew they were to do something when the appropriate cue was presented, and by scoring content in terms of its accuracy, regardless of whether the information was recalled when the appropriate cue was presented or at any other time during the session. In our view, it is important that measures of content knowledge not be tied to monitoring accuracy or compliance, because the person may know full well what to do (content) independent of whether he or she monitors accurately for when to perform the action or comply with the task demands to accomplish the action. For this reason, we scored the person as having the correct content knowledge if the designated action

---

[1]Content recall includes knowledge about the time or event that signals when the action is to be performed. However, as mentioned in the previous section, neither the memory nor recallability of cue information was the subject of study.

was performed at the correct time, at an incorrect time, or the person later indicated having known what to do but then forgot or missed the signal for when to do it. All of the participants were better at content recall than at monitoring accuracy, and the younger participants outperformed the older participants on both measures. More interestingly, the Age × Component Type interaction was not reliable, indicating that at least with this task, older people were not differentially advantaged or disadvantaged on one as compared to the other component.

The second approach to studying content recall has been to study this component without requiring that a prospective remembering task be completed. As an example of this approach, Hitch and Ferguson (1991) investigated the memories of film society members for films they had seen and the films they intended to see during the year. Memory scores for "have-seen" and "intend-to-see" films were reliably correlated, leading the investigators to conclude that the retrieval of stored information about past events and future actions may follow similar laws.

Questionnaire rating studies provide another example of this approach. Some memory questionnaires (e.g., Bennett-Levy & Powell, 1980; Herrman & Neisser, 1978) contained items for which the person was to rate his or her ability to recall the content in prospective remembering tasks. One such item was "set off to do something, then can't remember what." Bennett-Levy and Powell (1980) reported that self-ratings of memory failures on this content item linearly increased with age.

The content recall component is the one that is most clearly linked to retrospective remembering. As such, it is likely that variables that alter the recallability of information in a cued recall situation would have similar effects when that same information serves as the content (action) in a prospective remembering task. Whether or not monitoring might alter these relationships (e.g., because the information might be retrieved on monitoring episodes that occur during the interval) has yet to be studied.

Compliance

Compliance is important to the completion of a prospective memory task because people sometimes know perfectly well what action they are to perform, and they may know when to perform it, and yet decide not to perform it. Thus compliance refers to a person's willingness to carry out a future action. It should be noted that this is different from how medical researchers refer to compliance. Since the mid-1970s, the medical professions have been concerned with why people may miss appointments or fail to take medications as prescribed. The result of this interest was hundreds of research papers, numerous books, and speciality conferences on this topic. These researchers were interested in any and all topics relevant to the completion of medical instructions (see Haynes, Taylor, Snow, & Sackett, 1979, for an extensive listing of research topics). Although much of this "compliance" research is directly relevant to prospective remembering as psychologists study it, its applicability goes beyond compliance as we defined it. In medical research, the label of *compliance* is equivalent to the cognitive psychologist's label of *prospective remembering*. Throughout this chapter, we included studies of medical compliance within the reviews of relevant components.

To the layperson, compliance is strongly associated with beliefs about the reasons for nonsuccessful performance on prospective remembering tasks. Munsat (1966) pointed out that when a person forgets something he or she learned in the past, other people attribute this failure to his or her memory, but when a person forgets to do something in the future, other people attribute this failure to character. The role of compliance in prospective remembering may be salient to laypeople because of the social obligations frequently inherent in prospective memory tasks (cf., Meacham, 1988). Much more so than with retrospective memory failures, failures in prospective remembering situations often result in another person feeling neglected, let down, slighted, and angry. In this vein a dentist recently wrote that a missed or cancelled appointment "is wasteful and expensive but more than either of these economic irritations it is straightforwardly frustrating" (Hancocks, 1993).

Information about the nature of compliance in prospective remembering is difficult to cull from the literature. This is because there are few studies that have measured compliance directly (e.g., by asking people if they did not perform an action because they chose not to). In a preliminary study, we attempted to provide information about the percentage of prospective memory task failures that are believed to be due to noncompliance. We asked undergraduates: "When you don't do something in the future that you said you would, what percentage of the time is it because you forgot and what percentage of the time is it because you didn't want to?" We also asked them the same question regarding other people. There were no reliable differences between self and other, but overall, people estimated that noncompliance was responsible for just under one half of the failures to complete the prospective tasks.

Several medical researchers (e.g., Alpert, 1964; Cooper, Love, & Raffoul, 1982; Cosgrove, 1990; Kellaway & McCrae, 1975; Rickels, Anderson, & Howard, 1968) also asked people why they failed to carry out medical directives. However, the authors' grouping of responses often made it difficult to tell how often compliance was intentional as opposed to unintentional. For example, Alpert (1964) lumped forgetting and indifference into one category and lack of a sitter, illness, lack of transportation, and inadequate finances into another. Some of the incidents in either of those categories could reflect intentional noncompliance. However, two groups of researchers explicitly categorized responses to questions about compliance in terms of intentional and unintentional noncompliance. Kellaway and McCrae (1975) contrasted noncompliant alteration of prescribed medication regimes (a decision with at least some degree of volitional intent) with simple errors (unintentional mistakes with no suggestion of volitional intent). Most people who deviated from their drug regimen did so intentionally. Cooper et al. (1982) found that a large majority of their nonadherent group also admitted that it was intentional.

Intentional noncompliance has been observed in other patient populations. In a training study with Alzheimer's disease patients, Stevens et al. (1992) reported that for those trained to look at a calendar and perform the actions recorded there, unappealing tasks were often not completed regardless of whether or not they looked at the calendar. Hendin and Haas (1988) reported that veterans suffering Post-Traumatic Stress Disorder will "forget" or consciously choose to miss appointments when the sessions become psychologically distressful.

In other studies, compliance has been related to personality variables (e.g., Lay, 1988; Orne, 1970; Searleman & Gaydusek, 1989; Wichman & Oyasato, 1983), task demands, such as discomfort (Meacham & Kushner, 1980), importance–interest in the task (Kvavilashvili, 1987; Somerville, Wellman, & Cultice, 1983), and reward for successful completion (Meacham & Singer, 1977; Orne, 1970; Poon & Schaffer, cited in West, 1988). Poon and Schaffer found that the size of monetary payments positively affected performance of older adults but not that of younger adults.

Compliance is of obvious importance to the completion of a prospective memory task. Unless an investigator can be assured of compliance, the measurement of successful monitoring or content recall is in jeopardy. For this reason alone, it is important that more knowledge be acquired regarding this component. For more broad goals, the study of compliance is important for understanding when an action is likely to be completed given that all other aspects are successful. Clearly, there must be increased study of this component if generalization to the natural environment is to be accomplished.

As a final comment about compliance, it should be noted that we have used compliance in a narrow way. We could have used compliance as an aspect of other components. That is, people could know that they should plan in order to maximize performance, but choose not to comply, or know that they should monitor at any particular moment but choose not to comply and concentrate instead on the foreground task. We chose to restrict the compliance component to refer to responding because this is the aspect for which compliance has been of greatest concern. Perhaps as we learn more about planning, monitoring and other components, it will become more apparent that compliance has a broader role and these restrictions should be lifted.

Output Monitoring

The final component of this conceptual framework is *output monitoring*. The term "output monitoring" came from Koriat and his colleagues (Koriat & Ben-

Zur, 1988; Koriat, Ben-Zur, & Nussbaum, 1990; Koriat, Ben-Zur, & Sheffer, 1988). Koriat and Ben-Zur referred to two types of error—*repetition errors* and *omission errors*. Both types of error result from erroneous knowledge about the completion status of the prospective memory task.

In Koriat and Ben-Zur's (1988) view, repetition errors occur in output monitoring when we fail to successfully erase the intention from memory or when we fail to tag an intention as completed. Omission errors result when a person inappropriately erases an intention or tags one as completed when it has not actually been performed. Omission errors might happen, for example, when we have to give a friend two different messages. After the first message was delivered we might, inadvertently, tag both prospective memory tasks as complete.

Although Koriat and Ben-Zur reported several studies on output monitoring (Koriat & Ben-Zur, 1988; Koriat et al., 1990; Koriat et al., 1988), none were accomplished within the context of prospective remembering. There are, however, prospective memory studies whose results can be interpreted in terms of output monitoring. For example, Wilkins and Baddeley (1978) had their participants simulate pill taking by pressing a button four times a day. They found that when their participants did press the button, they remembered they had done so, but if they failed to press it, they were often unaware of this failure. In terms of the drug regime, the omission errors would result in underdosing, a common finding in drug studies. Consistent with Wilkins and Baddeley's findings, taking too many pills (a repetition error) is less common. Both repetition and omission errors were measured in another simulation of pill taking (Leirer, Morrow, Tanke, & Pariante, 1991) and repetition errors were rare compared to omission errors. Finally, in contrast to Wilkins and Baddeley, Maylor (1990) reported that her middle- and older-aged participants were aware of when they had performed a prospective memory task and when they had failed to do so.

Many questionnaires also included measures of output monitoring (Bennett-Levy & Powell, 1980; Broadbent, Cooper, Fitzgerald, & Parkes, 1982; Lovelace & Twohig, 1990). In some cases, these questions were designed to assess action slips rather than output monitoring in a prospective memory task. However, several kinds of action slips can be thought of as output monitoring errors (e.g., *omissions* and *forgetting previous actions* in Reason's, 1979, classification). Lovelace and Twohig reported that most (80%) of their older respondents had sometimes been uncertain that a task was completed and 15% experienced this uncertainty on a weekly basis. Twenty percent of the respondents felt that their failures in output monitoring had increased with age.

Unfortunately, little research on output monitoring has been reported in the context of prospective memory tasks. More research is needed. Fortunately, there are several areas that are either directly or indirectly related, and the findings from these areas may provide clues about the avenues that may be most fruitful. For example, reality monitoring seems to be of direct relevance. The finding that older adults perform less well than younger adults in these studies (Cohen & Faulkner, 1989), probably has implications for age differences in output monitoring and hence for age differences in prospective remembering. Similarly, output monitoring seems to be involved when repetitions are found in free-recall and verbal fluency tasks, and findings from these studies may provide information about individual difference variables and situations that are important to study within the context of prospective memory tasks.

In the study of output monitoring, some cautions are worth noting. When an action is repeated, it seems clear that the person failed to monitor their output response successfully and "tag" the actions as completed. However, in the case of an omitted action, it is less clear that the omission was the result of a failure in output monitoring. This is because an action could be omitted due to disruptions in other components (e.g., inaccurate monitoring, forgetting the action to be performed, lack of compliance). Studies directed toward investigating output monitoring within the context of prospective remembering need to incorporate methodologies that can isolate the failure to respond as being due to faulty output monitoring.

The nature of the processes that enable knowing the completion status of a prospective memory are far from being well-understood. There are at least two possibilities. It could be that the intention is somehow erased or tagged as having been completed. Koriat and Ben-Zur (1988) referred to this as *online processing*. However, such explicit tagging or erasure may not occur or be typical. Instead, the person may have knowledge about the completion status only through explicit checking of the environmental consequences or for episodic memory of the act. Koriat and Ben-Zur termed this *retrospective* knowledge about the completion status. These are very different types of possibilities, in that erasing or tagging an intention as being completed implies an action on the part of the person. Necessarily relying on the environmental consequences or memory does not imply any special type of processing when the action is performed. Koriat and Ben-Zur discussed these possibilities, but there was not strong empirical support for one as compared to the other. This lack of knowledge continues, and research directed toward delineating the processes involved in enabling task completion knowledge could provide an important advancement. There may not be a simple answer. Perhaps both types of processing are available to the person. Surely, at least in some cases, the intention is erased and the person no longer monitors the environment for the signal to perform the act. In other cases, especially when the prospective task is an habitual one (see the taxonomy presented later), there may not be any explicit erasure or tagging and the person may have to rely on episodic memory of the action or survey the environment for evidence. Because of this, it may be that the research might be better directed toward delineating the circumstances under which intentions are erased or tagged as completed and when the person must rely on retrospective knowledge.

Summary

In the preceding sections we emphasized that prospective remembering involves a variety of qualitatively different components that interact to influence the final performance. Here we use the term *interact* to indicate that changes in one component can influence the way in which another component(s) is accomplished, or even alter the necessity of another component. This mutual influence underscores the importance of having some framework for analyzing the tasks.

The different aspects or components of prospective remembering tasks we discussed extend far beyond what we conventionally think of as memory. They are illustrative of why it is important to think about prospective remembering as being more than just memory. In fact, the most widely studied aspects of prospective remembering such as the setting of plans and monitoring are better thought of as outside the realm of memory. It is hoped that by identifying different aspects and by providing at least an initial working definition of these components, research can be expanded to encompass more of the interesting aspects of prospective remembering while being more focused toward specifying the diversity of processing that can occur. Again, despite our presentation being in terms of discussing the individual components, we are fully aware that the manner in which one component is completed could dramatically alter the processing involved in other components. It seemed more important at this point in time, however, to emphasize a differentiation between the components in order to justify the claim that prospective memory is more than just memory.

If it is accepted that there is a set of qualitatively different types of components that contribute to performance in prospective remembering tasks, then it is clear that a single outcome measure (e.g., the task was completed or not completed at the appropriate time or when the designated event occurred) may not be adequate. This is because the outcome could occur for a variety of reasons, as discussed in the earlier sections of this chapter. It is reasonable to ask, then, whether all aspects (components) need to be measured. It seems to us that this might be unduly cumbersome in many situations and probably unnecessary if the researcher appropriately attends to the multidimensionality of the task. For example, when the goal is to investigate the processing that occurs within one component, then the task and situation need to be designed such that other aspects of the task do not vary or vary only in the prescribed ways. For example, if one is interested in studying the effects of different plans on monitoring, then it is important that the appropriate plans are set, the action is equally memorable for the various conditions, compliance is optimal, and so on. If the different types of plan altered the memorability of the action to be performed or the signal to perform the action, then the performance differences could not be attributed to the effect of the different plans on monitoring. There are cases, however, where the investigator might be interested in measuring several or all components. This might occur when two groups are compared (e.g., young and old or normal and pathological) and the interest is in how the two groups complete the task. It might be of interest in how one group compensates for lost abilities by setting different plans or altering the processing in one or another component. In short, we do not think there is a single approach that is necessitated. We do believe that the field has advanced sufficiently that it now is imperative for researchers to recognize the multi-dimensionality of prospective remembering tasks and to accommodate that knowledge within their experimental designs. Our goal was to provide a frame-work that could be useful in guiding research, both for formulating the issues and problems to be studied, and for designing projects in terms of what needs to be controlled and measured.

TAXONOMY OF PROSPECTIVE MEMORY TASKS

Dimensions of Prospective Memory Tasks

As mentioned earlier, there is a wide variety of tasks that could be used to study prospective remembering. In fact, the diversity could be a barrier to advance-ment if either the commonalities or differences are overlooked. The framework we outline provides one way in which different tasks could be compared. For the goal of comparing between tasks it would be useful to compare the extent of planning, the type of monitoring, and so on, that are necessitated by differ-ent formats of prospective memory tasks.

Because of the potentially large number of tasks that could be devised, it would be helpful if there could be some limited set of dimensions along which different tasks could be categorized to minimize the necessity of task by task comparisons. To assist in this, our goal was to identify dimensions that at once differentiate between sets of tasks and at the same time delineate commonal-ities within sets that would imply similarities in processing. It most often has been the case that earlier considerations of categories of prospective remem-bering tasks have been in terms of dichotomies. In reviewing these dicho-tomies, we found ourselves identifying another dimension that had important implications for the types of processes that would be required. Although this may be inevitable no matter how detailed the taxonomy for differentiating between tasks, we suggest that four dimensions can go a long way toward cap-turing the distinctiveness of different categories of tasks while identifying significant attributes of the groupings. These four dimensions represent an amalgamation of those found in the literature and our own thinking. As will be evident, three (time vs. event, short- vs. long-term, step vs. pulses) of the four dimensions are most closely identified with what we have labelled as the *moni-*

toring component. This may not be unreasonable because monitoring is the component that is the most distinctive (although not necessarily the most important) attribute of prospective remembering. However, any or all components could be influenced by the dimensions of the taxonomy. Clearly, the type of metaknowledge that is relevant and the types of plans that are set may be quite different within the context of different tasks designated by the dimensions of the taxonomy. Although there will be no attempt to provide an exhaustive listing, we provide initial suggestions as to how other components might be altered by changes in these dimensions.

We restrict the consideration of a possible taxonomy to a discussion of the dimensions. An analysis of the categories of tasks that can be formed using these dimensions can be accomplished using the components we described earlier, but that analysis is beyond the scope and goals of this chapter.

Short- Versus Long-term

The first dimension is the length of the interval between the presentation of the task and when the action is to be performed. Here, either the specified time or event marking when the task is to be accomplished could occur within a relatively short time period after the task was defined, or days, weeks, or months later. Although a specific break point between short and long intervals is no more clear here than it is in the traditional memory areas, the type of plan that is formulated and the monitoring probably will be considerably different for short and long intervals. In addition, the role of retrospective memory variables may become more prominent with longer intervals, depending on the nature of the action and the use of memory aids. Not unimportantly, compliance may be a greater concern with long retention intervals, at least in research situations.

Episodic Versus Habitual

A second dimension is what Mcacham and Leiman (1982) termed *episodic versus habitual prospective memory tasks.* Episodic tasks ordinarily occur only once, and after the completion of the task they can be dropped from memory. Having to give someone a message is an example of an episodic task. Habitual tasks must be accomplished on repeated occasions. The checking of charts and charting by nurses provides a good example.

The episodic–habitual distinction is, we think, more interesting than it may appear. First, the type of plan that is set may be quite different for the two types of tasks. Second, prospective remembering tasks often require not one but a sequence of actions. Initially, the individual actions may be more or less independent, but with practice an action schema may develop. As the schema begins to develop, there may be a decrease in the output monitoring for individual action elements. Perhaps when the action schema is fully developed, there is no explicit knowledge about the completion of any individual element. In this case, interruptions during the execution of the action set could have very different consequences for content recall than would be found for actions typical of episodic tasks.

Step Versus Pulses

The third dimension is Ellis' (1988) distinction between steps and pulses. The distinction is based on the precision of the dating of the task. Some prospective tasks are precisely dated (e.g., "call Bob at 10:30"). Others are imprecisely dated (e.g., "call Bob before 12:00," or, "review your notes before class"). Ellis suggested that different monitoring processes are involved for the two types of dating, and large performance differences can be obtained for the two classes of tasks.

Time Versus Event

The final distinction concerns whether the task is time or event dated (Einstein & McDaniel, 1990). Time dated tasks specify a particular time or range of times for which the task must be accomplished (e.g., "call the travel agent at 10:00"). Event dated tasks define the occasion for when the task should be accomplished in terms of an event (e.g., deliver a message to a person the next time you see her).

This is an important distinction that has processing implications. It is a distinction between what is being monitored. Monitoring time is unquestionably different from monitoring the environment for an event. Although monitoring for time seems to involve calibration of an internal clock, this calibration is unimportant to monitoring for an event. When monitoring for an event, perceptual attributes of the cue become paramount. Here, what we know about problems in field dependence and other aspects of stimulus identification are relevant.

There may be other dimensions that are of importance in categorizing prospective remembering tasks that may become apparent as the analysis of the tasks moves forward. This analysis may be in terms of the components we suggest or another scheme, but such an analysis can be fruitful in defining the similarities in processing (and thus comparability) within categories of tasks. At present, the four dimensions presented seemed to capture the major distinctions between tasks and may allow for an effective categorization.

FINAL COMMENT

Throughout this chapter, we have endeavored to show why prospective memory tasks involve more than just memory. Although we suspect that this is not contentious, research often has been designed as though prospective remembering was a memory task, without attention to either the diversity of tasks or the multidimensionality of prospective remembering. In part, this may have been because there was no comprehensive framework that would enable an analysis and comparison of tasks. Our goal has been to suggest a beginning toward redressing this problem by providing an componential analysis of prospective remembering that can be used to compare among tasks, and as a guide to designing future research, defining response measures and interpreting findings. It may also serve as an heuristic for directed research efforts.

In this chapter, the components were presented sequentially with only suggestions as to how differences in one component may affect the nature and processing involved in another component. We hope that this will be considered as a limitation of a beginning effort. All components can be important determiners of performance and differences in the components resulting from task demands or individual performances need to be explored, measured, or accommodated. Because of this, explicit attention to the interaction among components is important to advancements in knowledge, and for avoiding misleading conclusions about the abilities of different groups.

REFERENCES

Alpert, J. J. (1964). Broken appointments. *Pediatrics, 34,* 127–132.

Anschutz, L., Camp, C. J., Markley, R. P., & Kramer, J. J. (1985). *Experimental Aging Research, 11,* 157–160.

Beal, C. R. (1985). Development of knowledge about the use of cues to aid prospective retrieval. *Child Development, 56,* 631–642.

Beal, C. R. (1988). The development of prospective memory skills. In M. M. Gruneberg, P. E. Morris, & R. N. Sykes (Eds.), *Practical aspects of memory: Current research and issues* (Vol. 1, pp. 366–370). Chichester, England: Wiley.

Bennett-Levy, J., & Powell, G. E. (1980). The Subjective Memory Questionnaire (SMQ). An investigation into the self-reporting of 'real-life' memory skills. *British Journal of Social and Clinical Psychology, 19,* 177–188.

Brandimonte, M. A., & Passolunghi, M. C. (1994). The effect of cue-familiarity, cue-distinctiveness and retention interval on prospective remembering. *The Quarterly Journal of Experimental Psychology, 47A,* 1–23.

Broadbent, D. E., Cooper, P. F., Fitzgerald, P., & Parkes, K. R. (1982). The cognitive failures questionnaire (CFQ) and its correlates. *British Journal of Clinical Psychology, 21,* 1–8.

Brown, A. L. (1978). Knowing when, where, and how to remember: A problem of metacognition. In R. Glaser (Ed.), *Advances in instructional psychology* (Vol. 1, pp. 77–165). Hillsdale, NJ: Lawrence Erlbaum Associates.

Brown, A. L., Bransford, J. D., Ferrara, R. A., & Campione, J. C. (1983). Learning, remembering, and understanding. In J. H. Flavell & E. M. Markman (Eds.), *Handbook of child psychology. Vol. 3: Cognitive development* (pp. 77–166). New York: Wiley.

Cavanaugh, J. C. (1989). The importance of awareness in memory aging. In L. W. Poon, D. C. Rubin, & B. A. Wilson (Eds.), *Everyday cognition in adulthood and late life* (pp. 416–436), Cambridge, England: Cambridge University Press.

Cavanaugh, J. C., & Perlmutter, M. (1982). Metamemory: A critical examination. *Child Development, 53,* 11–28.

Ceci, S. J., Baker, J. G., & Bronfenbrenner, U. (1988). Prospective remembering, temporal calibration, and context. In M. M. Gruneberg, P. E. Morris, & R. N. Sykes (Eds.), *Practical aspects of memory: Current research and issues* (Vol. 1, pp. 360–365). Chichester, England: Wiley.

Ceci, S. J., & Bronfenbrenner, U. (1985). "Don't forget to take the cupcakes out of the oven": Prospective memory, strategic time-monitoring, and context. *Child Development, 56,* 152–164.

Chen , S. H. (1993). *Monitoring behaviour in prospective memory.* Unpublished honors thesis, University of Alberta, Edmonton.

Cohen, G. (1989). *Memory in the real world.* Hillsdale, NJ: Lawrence Erlbaum Associates.

Cohen, G., & Faulkner, D. (1989). Age differences in source forgetting: Effects on reality monitoring and eyewitness testimony. *Psychology and Aging, 4,* 10–17.

Colegrove, F. W. (1898). Individual memories. *American Journal of Psychology, 10,* 228–255.

Cooper, J. K , Love, D. W., & Raffoul, P. R. (1982). Intentional prescription nonadherence (noncompliance) by the elderly. *Journal of the American Geriatrics Society, 30,* 329–333.

Cosgrove, M. P. (1990). Defaulters in general practice: Reasons for default and patterns of attendance. *British Journal of General Practice, 40,* 50–52.

Craik, F. I. M. (1986). A functional account of age differences in memory. In F. Klix & H. Hagendorf (Eds.), *Human memory and cognitive capabilities: Mechanisms and performances* (pp. 409–422). North Holland, Amsterdam: Elsevier.

Devolder, P. A., Brigham, M. C., & Pressley, M. (1990). Memory performance awareness in younger and older adults. *Psychology and Aging, 5*(2), 291–303.

Dixon, R. A. (1989). Questionnaire research on metamemory and aging: Issues of structure and function. In L. W. Poon, D. C. Rubin, & B. A. Wilson (Eds.), *Everyday cognition in adulthood and late life* (pp. 394–415). Cambridge, England: Cambridge University Press.

Dobbs, A. R., & Reeves, M. B. (1991, June). *Prospective memory, aging, and the workplace.* Paper presented at the annual convention of the Canadian Psychological Association, Calgary, Alberta.

Dobbs, A. R., Reeves, M. B., & Rule, B. G. (1995). *Prospective remembering in patients with whiplash or minor head injury.* Manuscript in preparation.

Dobbs, A. R., & Rule, B. G. (1987). Prospective memory and self-reports of memory abilities in older adults. *Canadian Journal of Psychology, 41*(2), 209–222.

Einstein, G. O., Holland, L. J., McDaniel, M. A., & Guynn, M. J. (1992). Age- related deficits in prospective memory: The influence of task complexity, *Psychology and Aging, 7,* 471–478.

Einstein, G. O., & McDaniel, M. A. (1990). Normal aging and prospective memory. *Journal of Experimental Psychology: Learning, Memory, & Cognition, 16*(4), 717–726.

Einstein, G. O., McDaniel, M. A., Cunfer, A. R., & Guynn, M. J. (1991). *Aging and prospective memory: Examining the influences of self-initiated retrieval processes and mind wandering.* Unpublished manuscript, Furman University.

Ellis, J. A. (1988). Memory for future intentions: Investigating pulses and steps. In M. M. Gruneberg, P. E. Morris, & R. N. Sykes (Eds.), *Practical aspects of memory: Current research and issues* (Vol. 1, pp. 371–376). Chichester, England: Wiley.

Flavell, J. H. (1971). First discussant's comments: What is memory development the development of? *Human Development, 14,* 272–278.

Flavell, J. H., & Wellman, H. M. (1977). Metamemory. In R. V. Kail, Jr., & J. W. Hagen (Eds.), *Perspectives on the development of memory and cognition* (pp. 3–33). Hillsdale, NJ: Lawrence Erlbaum Associates.

Furst, C. (1986). The memory derby: Evaluating and remediating intention memory. *Cognitive Rehabilitation, 4*(3), 24–26.

Hancocks, S. (1993). A turn up for the books? *British Dental Journal, 174*(9), 344.

Harris, J. E. (1984). Remembering to do things: A forgotten topic. In J. E. Harris & P. E. Morris

(Eds.), *Everyday memory, actions and absent-mindedness*, (pp. 71–91). New York: Academic Press.

Harris, J. E., & Wilkins, A. J. (1982). Remembering to do things: A theoretical framework and an illustrative experiment. *Human Learning, 1,* 123–136.

Haynes, R. B., Taylor, D. W., Snow, J. C., & Sackett, D. L. (1979). Annotated and indexed bibliography on compliance with therapeutic and preventive regimens. In R. B. Haynes, D. W. Taylor, & D. L. Sackett (Eds.), *Compliance in health care* (pp. 337–474). Baltimore: Johns Hopkins University Press.

Hendin, H., & Haas, A. P. (1988). Posttraumatic stress disorder. In C. G. Last & M. Hersen (Eds.), *Handbook of Anxiety Disorders* (pp. 127–142). New York: Pergamon.

Herrman, D. J., & Neisser, U. (1978). An inventory of everyday memory experiences. In M. M. Gruneberg, P. E. Morris, & R. N. Sykes (Eds.), *Practical aspects of memory* (pp. 35–51). New York: Academic Press.

Hitch, G. J., & Ferguson, J. (1991). Prospective memory for future intentions: Some comparisons with memory for past events. *European Journal of Cognitive Psychology, 3*(3), 285–295.

Istomina, Z. M. (1986). The development of voluntary memory in children of preschool age. In U. Neisser (Ed.), *Memory observed: Remembering in natural contexts* (pp. 349–365). San Fransico: Freeman.

Jackson, J. L., Bogers, H., & Kerstholt, J. (1988). Do memory aids aid the elderly in their day to day remembering? In M. M. Gruneberg, P. E. Morris, & R. N. Sykes (Eds.), *Practical aspects of memory: Current research and issues* (Vol. 2, pp. 137–142). Chichester, England: Wiley.

Kellaway, G. S. M., & McCrae, E. (1975). Non-compliance and errors of drug administration in patients discharged from acute medical wards. *New Zealand Medical Journal, 81,* 508–512.

Koriat, A., & Ben-Zur, H. (1988). Remembering that I did it: Processes and deficits in output monitoring. In M. M. Gruneberg, P. E. Morris, & R. N. Sykes (Eds.), *Practical aspects of memory: Current research and issues* (Vol. 1, pp. 203–208). Chichester, England: Wiley.

Koriat, A., Ben-Zur, H., & Nussbaum, A. (1990). Encoding information for future action: Memory for to-be-performed versus memory for to-be-recalled tasks. *Memory and Cognition, 18,* 568–578.

Koriat, A., Ben-Zur, H., & Sheffer, D. (1988). Telling the same story twice: Output monitoring and age. *Journal of Memory and Language, 27,* 23–29.

Kreutzer, M. A., Leonard, C., & Flavell, J. H. (1975). An interview study of children's knowledge about memory. *Monographs of the Society for Research in Child Development, 40* (1, Serial No. 159).

Kvavilashvili, L. (1987). Remembering intention as a distinct form of memory. *British Journal of Psychology, 78,* 597–518.

Lay, C. H. (1988). Procrastination and everyday memory. In M. M. Gruneberg, P. E. Morris, & R. N. Sykes (Eds.), *Practical aspects of memory: Current research and issues* (Vol. 1, pp. 453–458). Chichester, England: Wiley.

Leirer, V. O., Morrow, D. G., Tanke, E. D., & Pariante, G. M. (1991). Elders' nonadherence: Its assessment and medication reminding by voice mail. *The Gerontologist, 31*(4), 514–520.

Levy, R. L., & Loftus, G. R. (1984). Compliance and memory. In J. E. Harris & P. E. Morris (Eds.), *Everyday memory, actions, and absent-mindedness* (pp. 93–112). London: Academic Press.

Loftus, E. F. (1971). Memory for intentions: The effect of presence of a cue and interpolated activity. *Psychonomic Science, 23*(4), 315–316.

Lovelace, E. A., & Twohig, P. T. (1990). Healthy older adults perceptions of their memory functioning and use of mnemonics, *Bulletin of the Psychonomic Society, 28*(2), 115–118.

Martin, M. (1986). Ageing and patterns of change in everyday memory and cognition. *Human Learning, 5,* 63–74.

Mateer, C. A., & Sohlberg, M. M. (1988). A paradigm shift in rehabilitation. In H. Whitaker (Ed.), *Neuropsychological studies in non-focal brain damage* (pp. 202–225). New York: Springer-Verlag.

Maylor, E. A. (1990). Age and prospective memory. *The Quarterly Journal of Experimental Psychology, 42A,* 471–493.

Maylor, E. A. (1993). Aging and forgetting in prospective and retrospective memory tasks. *Psychology and Aging, 8,* 420–428.

McDaniel, M. A., & Einstein, G. O. (1993). The importance of cue familiarity and cue distinctiveness in prospective memory. *Memory, 1*(1), 23–41.

McMillan, T. M. (1984). Investigation of everyday memory in normal subjects using the subjective memory questionnaire (SMQ). *Cortex, 20,* 333–347.

Meacham, J. A. (1982). A note on remembering to execute planned actions. *Journal of Applied Developmental Psychology, 3,* 121–133.

Meacham, J. A. (1988). Interpersonal relations and prospective remembering. In M. M. Gruneberg, P. E. Morris, & R. N. Sykes (Eds.), *Practical aspects of memory: Current research and issues* (Vol. 1, pp. 354–359). Chichester, England: Wiley.

Meacham, J. A., & Kushner, S. (1980). Anxiety, prospective remembering, and performance of planned actions. *Journal of General Psychology, 103,* 203–209.

Meacham, J. A., & Leiman, B. (1982). Remembering to perform future actions. In U. Neisser (Ed.), *Memory observed: Remembering in natural contexts* (pp. 327–336). San Francisco: Freeman.

Meacham, J. A., & Singer, J. (1977). Incentive effects in prospective remembering. *The Journal of Psychology, 97,* 191–197.

Moscovitch, M. (1982). A neuropsychological approach to perception and memory in normal and pathological aging. In F. I. M. Craik & S. Trehub (Eds.), *Advances in the study of communication and affect. Vol. 8: Aging and cognitive processes* (pp. 55–78). New York: Plenum Press.

Munsat, S. (1966). *The concept of memory.* New York: Random House.

Nazarian, L. F., Machuber, J., Charney, E., & Coulter, M. D. (1974). Effects of a mailed appointment reminder on appointment keeping. *Pediatrics, 53,* 349–351.

Orne, M. T. (1970). Hypnosis, motivation and the ecological validity of the psychological experiment. In W. J. Arnold & M. M. Page (Eds.), *Nebraska symposium on motivation. Vol. 18: Current theory and research in motivation* (pp. 187–265). Lincoln: University of Nebraska Press.

Ornstein, S. M., Garr, D. R., Jenkins, R. G., Rust, P. F., & Arnon, A. (1991). Computer-generated physician and patient reminders: Tools to improve population adherence to selected preventative services. *The Journal of Family Practice, 32*(1), 82–90.

Reason, J. T. (1979). Actions not as planned: The price of automatization. In G. Underwood & R. Stevens (Eds.), *Aspects of consciousness* (Vol. 1, pp. 67- 89). New York: Academic Press.

Reeves, M. B. (1991). *All prospective memory tasks are not the same: The influence of processing demands on remembering to remember and remembering content.* Unpublished manuscript, University of Alberta, Edmonton.

Reeves, M. B. (1992). *Adult age differences in the components underlying prospective memory.* Unpublished master's thesis. University of Alberta, Edmonton.

Reeves, M. B., Dobbs, A. R., & Heller, R. B. (1995). *Adult age differences in the monitoring of a vial prospective memory task.* Manuscript in preparation.

Rickels, K., Anderson, J., & Howard, K. (1968). Dropout contact by mail: A useful research tool. *Diseases of the Nervous System, 29,* 545–548.

Searleman, A., & Gaydusek, K. A. (1989, November). *Relationship between prospective memory ability and selective personality variables.* Paper presented at the 30th annual meeting of the Psychonomic Society, Atlanta, GA.

Shepard, D. S., & Moseley, T. A. (1976). Mailed vs telephoned appointment reminders to reduce broken appointments in a hospital outpatient department. *Medical Care, 14,* 268–273.

Somerville, S. C., Wellman, H. M., & Cultice, J. C. (1983). Young children's deliberate reminding, *Journal of Genetic Psychology, 143,* 87–96.

Stevens, A. B., Camp, C. J., & O'Hanlon, A. M. (1992, April). *Strategy training for individuals with Alzheimer's Disease: The spaced-retrieval method.* Poster presented at the Cognitive Aging Conference, Atlanta, GA.

Turner, B. J., Day, S. C., & Borenstein, B. (1989). A controlled trial to improve delivery of preventive care: Physician or patient reminders? *Journal of General Internal Medicine, 4,* 403–409.

Turner, R. C., Waivers, L. E., & O'Brien, K. (1990). The effect of patient-carried reminder cards on the performance of health maintenance measures. *Archives of Internal Medicine, 150,* 645–647.

West, R. L. (1988). Prospective memory and aging. In M. M. Gruneberg, P. E. Morris, & R. N. Sykes (Eds.), *Practical aspects of memory: Current research and issues* (Vol. 2, pp. 119–125). Chichester, England: Wiley.

Wichman, H., & Oyasato, A. (1983). Effects of locus of control and task complexity on prospective remembering. *Human Factors, 25,* 583–591.

Wilkins, A. J., & Baddeley, A. D. (1978). Remembering to recall in everyday life: An approach to absent-mindedness. In M. M. Gruneberg, P. E. Morris, & R. N. Sykes (Eds.), *Practical aspects of memory* (pp. 27–34). London: Academic Press.

Zelinski, E., Gilewski, M., & Anthony-Bergstone, C. (1990). Memory functioning questionnaire: Concurrent validity with memory performances and self-reported memory failures. *Psychology and Aging, 5,* 388–399.

11

COMMENTARY

Prospective Memory, Aging, and Lapses of Intention

Fergus I. M. Craik
Sheila A. Kerr
University of Toronto

The chapters by Maylor and by Dobbs and Reeves are in good agreement about a variety of issues—crucially, perhaps, on the point that prospective memory is not so much a type of memory as it is a set of abilities that depend on a broad range of underlying processes. It is "more than memory" in the words of Dobbs and Reeves. In fact, prospective memory may be nothing more than a unifying label for a wide range of tasks involving the timely performance of planned actions. The decomposition of overall performance into its component processes is therefore essential, because so many factors can contribute to successful completion of the target task. As the authors of the two preceding chapters point out, some of these factors are not related to memory at all—for example, compliance and the ability to judge how much time has passed—whereas others are only marginally related, like the setting up of external cues, and the number of time checks carried out in a time-based task. Some of the factors are more related to personality than to cognitive variables, and perhaps to experience in the real world of carrying out planned actions, including experience of the penalties associated with failing to carry them out. This heightened sensitivity to the responsible execution of plans, and to the negative consequences of failing to execute the plans, is typically associated with the aging process. Older people were initially perceived as being better than their younger counterparts on prospective memory tasks (e.g. Moscovitch, 1982), although further work has made it clearer that the superiority is probably attributable to the greater attention paid to compensatory strategies by older participants, rather than to the maturation of cognitive abilities. The observed superiority may have less to do with the processes of aging than with the contrast between subjects who are still in school and those (even of the same age) who are employed, and are thus faced with harsher penalties for failure to carry out planned actions (cf. Loewen, Shaw, & Craik, 1990). One striking observation reported by Dobbs and Reeves is that noncompliance was responsible for almost one half of the failures to carry out prospective memory tasks in real-world settings. Presumably this proportion drops to almost zero in laboratory studies (there is nothing particularly aversive about pressing a key or asking for a red pen!), providing a further argument for bringing studies into the lab and focusing on the cognitive aspects of success and failure.

Dobbs and Reeves describe the stages of a prospective memory task through time as planning, monitoring, recalling the action, performing the action and remembering whether the action was completed. In addition, they postulate the necessity of some form of metaknowledge about the person's memory abilities that would influence the planning stage. Although dividing prospective memory tasks into such distinct categories is conceptually clarifying, we believe that the classification highlights the need to focus on the prospective memory component of prospective memory tasks. It could be argued, for instance, that all memory tasks require some metaknowledge of cognitive processes. Although a fuller understanding of such issues as metaknowledge, compliance, retrospective memory, and output monitoring is important, such insights are less relevant to the issue of defining the "prospectiveness" of prospective memory tasks. In our view, the critical components are the planning and monitoring stages—even the performance of a prospective memory task is merely the behavioral product of successful monitoring. In this chapter, we comment on some components of prospective remembering, on their relations to other forms of memory, and on their changes as a function of normal aging.

PROSPECTIVE AND RETROSPECTIVE MEMORY

How do the encoding, retention, and retrieval phases differ between prospective and retrospective memory? We deal with each aspect in turn.

Encoding

One difference between the two classes of task is that, whereas retrospective memory is typically for events, prospective memory usually deals with the encoding, storage, and retrieval of intentions. This difference makes comparisons difficult if we believe that intentions really are somehow different from other information. In the Einstein and McDaniel (1990) paradigm, the comparison is facilitated in that subjects are given targets and asked to respond when the targets occur later in the experiment. The evidence presented by Einstein and McDaniel here suggests that performance does improve as a function of the depth or elaborateness of processing at encoding, just as does performance in traditional episodic memory tasks (e.g. Craik & Tulving, 1975). Einstein and McDaniel (this volume) also describe the interesting experiment by Koriat, Ben-Zur, and Nussbaum (1990) in which better memory was found when subjects expected to perform a set of tasks as opposed to recall that same set of tasks. Einstein and McDaniel take this result as evidence for different encoding processes in prospective and retrospective memory, but we question this conclusion. Different orienting tasks during encoding are associated with large differences in subsequent episodic memory performance (Craik & Tulving, 1975), and it is likely that the extra visual and motor information encoded under "perform" conditions supported better prospective and retrospective performance. Much the same account was given of why "subject-performed tasks" support better memory than do verbal commands (Saltz & Donnenwerth-Nolan, 1981). Will deeper, richer, or more elaborate encodings of events or instructions improve their effectiveness in time-based, in addition to event-based, prospective memory tasks? If so, are deeper encodings somehow more "active" in the sense proposed by Goschke & Kuhl (1993, this volume)?

Encoding Retrieval Interactions

A major factor in retrospective memory is the similarity between encoding and retrieval operations. This factor is known as the *encoding specificity principle* (Tulving & Thomson, 1973) or as *transfer appropriate processing* (Morris, Bransford, & Franks, 1977), and it would be surprising if it did not also apply to prospective memory. In fact, an experiment by Robinson (1992) confirms this speculation. Prospective memory targets were presented at encoding and test as either pictures or words; extrapolating from the reported values, when presentation and test forms were compatible, performance was at the level of 79%, as compared to 59% for incompatible conditions. A second interesting result was the effectiveness of reinstating environmental context in a prospective memory task. As reported by Einstein and McDaniel (this volume), Robinson found a positive effect of reinstatement when the target was a word, but not when the target was a picture. This interaction is reminiscent of the results reported by Geiselman and Bjork (1980); they showed that reinstatement of a physical context (voice) boosted recognition performance when the word targets were encoded in a shallow fashion, but had no effect in combination with deep encoding. All of these results speak in favor of the similarity of encoding processes in prospective and retrospective memory

Retention

Although it appears that the encoding phases of the prospective and retrospective paradigms do not radically differ, the retention phases do appear to differ. In retrospective long-term memory, the retention phase is psychologically empty; that is, unless the subject is rehearsing the material surreptitiously, there are no cognitive processes associated with retention. In prospective memory, by way of contrast, the retention phase is cognitively active in varying degrees. At one end of the continuum a prospective memory task may be identical to a retrospective memory task, with a distinctive event cuing retrieval instead of an explicit request to remember. An intermediate case is one in which the subject remembers from time to time that an action must be performed at a certain time in the future. At the other end of the continuum, the retention interval may be filled with a large number of time checks, indicating that the prospective task is never far from conscious awareness. These cases illustrate low, moderate, and high degrees of cognitive activity, respectively, during the retention interval. If the task is in mind throughout retention, the paradigm becomes one of vigilance, as Dobbs and Reeves point out.

One of the distinctions proposed by researchers is that between short- and long-term retention intervals. This distinction is not a theoretically useful one, however, in our opinion. Our main reason for arguing against it is that it is rare that the planning of an intention is completed at a specific time whereupon the monitoring stage begins; rather, the plan is specified more fully with the approach of the target event in time. We believe the first planning stage is a "generalized intention" to do something, such as to send Christmas cards to England before December 1. It is now early October, so no action is required for 8 weeks. Eventually, we will decide where to purchase cards, and on which day and at which hour we will complete the task, but we do not make these specific plans 8 weeks in advance. The benefit of the increasing specificity of a plan as the task deadline approaches is similar to the cognitive benefits we find in other hierarchically organized tasks where the fine details are organized at the last minute and subject to current environmental constraints. The later we make specific plans to complete an intention, however, the fewer memory demands there are on the cognitive system, and the more likely it is that the task will be completed efficiently. For example, if we happen to be walking in a shopping mall tomorrow and see a card shop, this may stimulate us to take our generalized intention to buy Christmas cards before December 1 and turn it into a specific intention to "buy cards right now." This intention is more likely to be fulfilled if it is completed right away than if we decide to stop at the store on the way home from work. All prospective memory tasks thus end up being short-term—that is, no matter how much time elapsed since the first generalized intention was formed, in the end there is always a final specific plan that is or is not executed at the appropriate time.

Retrieval

The two classes of memory do appear to differ in the retrieval phase, notably with respect to the function of cues. As well as having the retrospective function of inducing or evoking the wanted information or action, prospective cues must have the quality of signaling that some switch from the ongoing behavior is required. This is why unusual events, such as a knotted handkerchief, and unusual words like *sone* or *bole,* are effective triggers for prospective action. More generally, an event will trigger prospective remembering either because it breaks the flow of current thought or activity and so initiates a search for the appropriate response, or the event evokes the prospective target directly. In the latter case, the event acts as a reminder and the resulting retrieval may be classified as *involuntary conscious memory* (Ebbinghaus, 1885/1964). In this second case, cues appear to work similarly in prospective and retrospective remembering.

Summary

It seems to us that although there are marked differences in the components involved in prospective and retrospective memory tasks, there is no reason to believe that prospective remembering relies on some different set of underlying processes. The components that do differ include the planning that goes on at encoding in prospective memory, the setting up of external cues, and also possibly the encoding of intentions rather than facts or events. During the retention phase there is the necessity to monitor, and there may also be trade-offs between the prospective intention and the foreground task. Finally, at retrieval, cues can act as triggers (to alert the subject that some special action is required) as well as reminders, self-initiation is required in time-based tasks, and performance is affected by the subject's degree of involvement (owing to well-practiced habits or to current interest) in the foreground task and in the prospective memory task itself.

MONITORING

Monitoring, everyone agrees, is one of the defining processes in prospective memory tasks. Perhaps the most critical issues concern what it is that initiates a monitoring sequence and the trade-off between monitoring performance and performance on the foreground task. One factor is the subject's degree of involvement or absorption in the foreground task; greater involvement should be associated with less effective monitoring or fewer time checks. Preliminary evidence in our laboratory showed that subjects were later in stopping a clock when reading interesting as opposed to boring material.

Prospective memory failures often occur when the foreground task is well-practiced and habitual (Reason, 1979)—although such failures are probably greatest when the prospective task conflicts with a habitual foreground task (e.g., making an unaccustomed deviation during a daily commuting trip) as opposed to being independent from it. Are these cases of competition for processing resources? Does keeping an intention in mind reduce performance on the foreground task, as Maylor (this volume) suggests? There is some evidence that this is the case (Brandimonte & Passolunghi, 1994; Ellis & Nimmo-Smith, 1993), although it may be that the "divided attention cost" of holding an intention to perform a future action depends on the extent to which the intention is held in conscious awareness during performance of the foreground task. It is unlikely, for example, that an intention to pick up groceries on the way home from work would reduce performance on a foreground task performed in the morning. If holding a prospective intention is disruptive only to the extent that it occupies some portion of current awareness, then prospective memory does not differ in any fundamental way from retrospective memory.

It is difficult to measure monitoring behavior. Although we can measure external behaviors such as checking a clock, it is hard to control for internal monitoring that induces a subject to decide if it is yet time to check the clock. It seems likely that the more often subjects are reminded of the upcoming prospective task, the more often they will complete it on time. In line with this suggestion, Einstein, McDaniel, Richardson, Guynn, and Cunfer (in press) found that the number of time checks correlates with successful performance on a time-based prospective memory task. It might also be predicted that the closer a reminder is to the time of the event-based prospective task, the better performance should be. However, some preliminary evidence presented by Kerr (1993) indicates that the proximity of a reminder to the time of event-based task performance is not a predictor of success unless the reminder is presented immediately before the target event appears.

Momentary Lapses of Intention

A distinction exists between information held in current awareness (*primary memory*) and information that must be retrieved before we are aware of it (*secondary memory*). Most prospective memory tasks involve secondary memory in this classification, but there is an interesting subcategory of tasks in which the person intends to execute an action almost immediately, and so carries the intention in conscious awareness. Despite the short retention intervals involved, such intentions often drop from awareness, especially if the foreground task is very absorbing. Kerr (1993) referred to these failures as *momentary lapses of intention* (MLIs). Such lapses can also occur during a time-based prospective memory task; if the subject carries out a time check and finds that he or she must respond after a further minute, he or she attempts to hold the intention in mind, but may miss the target interval. It seems that intentions are difficult to maintain in mind in the face of other ongoing mental activities, especially in the case of older people.

There are few studies of the phenomenon to date. Harris and Wilkins (1982) devised a task in which subjects were asked to hold up a series of cards with specific times on them (e.g., 2:44) while they were watching a film. The cards showed times that were either 3 or 9 min apart. A clock was placed behind the subjects and a video camera recorded when they looked at the clock. The task was scored successful if the subject responded within 15 sec of the target time. Remarkably, when subjects were late in responding by this criterion, they had checked the time within 30 sec of the target time on nearly one half of the occasions, and checked within 10 sec of the target time on over one quarter of the occasions. In an earlier study on aging, Schonfield and Shooter (reported in Welford, 1958) asked subjects to press a button before giving each verbal response in a perceptual judgment task. The researchers found dramatic age-related increases in forgetting to press the button before responding verbally, even though subjects were reminded after every trial to do so. Subjects were asked to respond as quickly as they could, so it is possible that the time pressure increased the incidence of MLIs—especially for older subjects.

The length of the critical period for successful execution of the prospective task is one of the major dimensions related to MLIs (Dobbs & Reeves, this volume). Some tasks, such as taking a tea bag out of your tea, must be performed within a relatively limited period, whereas others, such as buying your mother a present for her birthday sometime in the next week, have greater latitude. Ellis (1988) made a similar distinction between what she called *pulses* (tasks that are personally important and must be done at a specific point in time) and *steps* (tasks that are less important and can be completed with more leisure). This analysis, however, confounds the length of time available to perform a task with the motivational importance of the task. We wish to record some mild dissatisfaction with the terminology itself—largely because we can never remember which intervals are pulses and which are steps! We suggest instead that the descriptions *small time window* and *large time window* are more informative and motivationally neutral (Kerr, 1991).

In our opinion the further study of MLIs would be a profitable research venture. Interesting questions include the effects of other information held concurrently in mind, the subject's degree of interest in the other material, and the extent to which further processing operations must be carried out on the material. Again, we could ask whether intentions are more vulnerable to forgetting than are other types of information; and finally, the effects of aging on MLIs will form an interesting field of enquiry.

AGE DIFFERENCES IN PROSPECTIVE MEMORY

The chapters by Maylor and by Dobbs and Reeves make it clear that age-related decrements in prospective memory performance do exist; the question of interest concerns the locus or loci of these age differences. Maylor makes a good point when she observes that researchers must establish that the age-related difference is in the prospective memory component, and not in some associated component such as retrospective memory, compliance, or time perception. Two interesting cases of prospective memory failure that are attributable ultimately to inefficiencies of retrospective episodic memory are, first, a failure by older people to perform the prospective task because they think they have already carried it out, and second, a failure to remember that they have performed the action, with a consequent repetition of the prospective act (Maylor, this volume). These failures are presumably most likely to occur with small-scale routine activities (e.g. taking medicine, putting sugar in your coffee, mailing a letter) rather than with elaborate sequences of action. The second of the cases concerns an inefficiency of output monitoring (Koriat, Ben-Zur, & Sheffer, 1988) and may be traceable to an age-related decrement in the encoding formed by executing the action. For example, if the prospective task is carried out in a more routine fashion by older people, or with less attention to task details, memory for the action sequence will be less distinctive and less memorable. This type of age-related change in response execution may underlie Maylor's observation of more forgetting on the part of older subjects in later trials of repeated prospective memory tasks.

One of us (Craik, 1986) has suggested that memory tasks differ in the degree of self-initiation required, and that prospective memory tasks were particularly reliant on self-initiation.[1] However, Einstein and McDaniel point out in the present volume that prospective memory tasks also vary in the degree of self-initiation required, and this insight led to the useful distinction between time-based and event-based prospective memory tasks. If older people are less able to break away from their current activity and initiate a new processing sequence, the consequent decrement in prospective memory performance should be found in time-based tasks but not necessarily in event-based tasks, where the environmentally produced event serves to cue the prospective target. Recent experiments showed that the predicted interaction between age and type of test does indeed occur (Einstein, et al., in press). The distinction between time-based and event-based tasks has also led to the discovery that subjects prepare for these different tasks in different ways (Maylor, this volume); Maylor's work suggests that younger subjects complement time-based tasks with external cues and event-based tasks with internal cues, although with increasing age there is a growing tendency to rely on external cues in all cases.

The evidence discussed by Einstein and McDaniel (this volume) strongly suggests that age-related decrements occur more often in time-based than in event-based tasks. If this result is confirmed by further work, it will then be-

---

[1] John Harris suggested this idea to Craik after hearing the talk that resulted in an earlier publication (Craik, 1983).

come of interest to localize the loss. At encoding, older people may plan less effectively, or fail to set up external cues—although earlier work suggested the opposite, that older people were more effective than their younger counterparts in this respect (Moscovitch, 1982). It is possible, however, that intentions can be encoded in qualitatively different ways, just as words and other episodic events are (Craik & Tulving, 1975); this may be an interesting topic for further research.

During the retention (or monitoring) interval in a time-based task, older people may make fewer time checks. Kerr (1991) found this result in a computer-simulated task in which subjects "cooked" various breakfast foods (e.g., bacon, eggs, tea, toast) for various lengths of time. The cooking progress of each item had to be checked by accessing its special screen. Between checks, subjects performed a table-setting task on a further screen, and had to remember to interrupt this foreground task at various times to prevent the food items being overcooked. The main finding was that older people showed an alarming tendency to burn their breakfast! The older subjects checked their foods less often per minute of cooking time than did the younger subjects; the older people were apparently more reluctant to switch their attention from the ongoing table-setting task to the task of checking the food. This observation raises the possibility that older people become more absorbed in a current task, or perhaps are simply more reluctant to switch from one activity to another. This latter possibility would be in accordance with the suggestion that normal aging resembles mild cases of frontal impairment (Craik, Morris, Morris, & Loewen, 1990; Stuss & Benson, 1984). On the other hand, there is also evidence to suggest that older people are less efficient in inhibiting intrusive stimuli and are therefore more distractible (Hasher & Zacks, 1988). This factor would naturally lead to a greater liability to lapses of intention on the part of the elderly. Whether subjects show greater vulnerability to distraction, or greater absorption in the foreground task, is likely to depend on the subject's relative interest in the foreground and prospective tasks and on how habitual and routinized these tasks are (Dobbs & Reeves, this volume).

Finally, there may be age differences in the effectiveness of cues to act either as *triggers* (i.e., to signal that current behavior should be interrupted and that something else must be done) or as *reminders* (eliciting the required prospective action). Dobbs and Reeves (1991) made a start on this research topic. In the absence of cues, subjects must self-initiate a time check or switch to the prospective action, and older people seem to find such self-initiated behaviors harder to accomplish (Craik, 1986; Einstein & McDaniel, this volume; Kerr, 1991; Maylor, this volume).

The two preceding chapters perform a useful function by isolating and describing the various components of prospective remembering. It seems likely (as Dobbs and Reeves emphasize) that the components will interact in complex ways, depending on the subjects and on the specific tasks examined. A fuller understanding of the components and their interactions is of great interest, both theoretically and practically, and we see the topic providing a fruitful field for further research.

ACKNOWLEDGMENTS

Preparation of this chapter was supported by a grant from the Natural Sciences and Engineering Research Council of Canada to the first author.

REFERENCES

Brandimonte, M. A., & Passolunghi, M. C. (1994). The effect of cue-familiarity, cue-distinctiveness, and retention interval on prospective remembering. *The Quarterly Journal of Experimental Psychology, 47a,* 565–587.

Craik, F. I. M. (1983). On the transfer of information from temporary to permanent memory. *Philosophical Transactions of the Royal Society of London, Series B, 302,* 341–359.

Craik, F. I. M. (1986). A functional account of age differences in memory. In F. Klix & H. Hagendorf (Eds.), *Human memory and cognitive capabilities, mechanisms and performances* (pp. 409–422). Amsterdam: Elsevier North-Holland.

Craik, F. I. M., Morris, L. W., Morris, R. G., & Loewen, E. R. (1990). Relations between source amnesia and frontal lobe functioning in older adults. *Psychology and Aging, 5,* 148–151.

Craik, F. I. M., & Tulving, E. (1975). Depth of processing and the retention of words in episodic memory. *Journal of Experimental Psychology: General, 104,* 268–294.

Dobbs, A. R., & Reeves, M. B. (1991, June). *Prospective memory, aging, and the workplace.* Paper presented at the annual convention of the Canadian Psychological Association, Calgary, Alberta.

Ebbinghaus, H. (1964). *Memory.* New York: Dover. (Original work published 1885)

Einstein, G. O., & McDaniel, M. A. (1990). Normal aging and prospective memory. *Journal of Experimental Psychology: Learning, Memory, and Cognition, 16,* 717–726.

Einstein, G. O., McDaniel, M. A., Richardson, S. L., Guynn, M. J., & Cunfer, A. R. (in press) Aging and prospective memory: Examining the influences of self-initiated retrieval processes. *Journal of Experimental Psychology: Learning, Memory, and Cognition.*

Ellis, J. A. (1988). Memory for future intentions: Investigating pulses and steps. In P. E. Gruneberg, P. E. Morris, & R. N. Sykes (Eds.), *Practical aspects of memory: Current research and issues* (pp. 371–376). Chichester, England: Wiley.

Ellis, J. A., & Nimmo-Smith, I. (1993). Recollecting naturally-occurring intentions: A study of cognitive and affective factors. *Memory, 1*(2), 107–126.

Geiselman, R. E., & Bjork, R. A. (1980). Primary versus secondary rehearsal in imagined voices: Differential effects on recognition. *Cognitive Psychology, 12,* 188–205.

Goschke, T., & Kuhl, J. (1993). Representation of intentions: Persisting activation in memory. *Journal of Experimental Psychology: Learning, Memory, and Cognition, 19,* 1211–1226.

Harris, J. E., & Wilkins, A. J. (1982). Remembering to do things: A theoretical framework and an illustrative experiment. *Human Learning, 1,* 123–136.

Hasher, L., & Zacks, R. T. (1988). Working memory, comprehension, and aging: A review and a new view. In G. H. Bower (Ed.), *The Psychology of Learning and Motivation* (pp. 193–225). San Diego: Academic Press.

Kerr, S. A. (1991) *Prospective memory and aging*. Unpublished master's thesis, University of Toronto.

Kerr, S. A. (1993, July). *Momentary lapses of intention: Effects of reminders*. Presented at the Third Annual Meeting of the Canadian Society for Brain, Behaviour and Cognitive Science, Toronto, Ontario.

Koriat, A., Ben-Zur, H., & Nussbaum, A. (1990). Encoding information for future action: Memory for to-be-performed tasks versus memory for to-be-recalled tasks. *Memory & Cognition, 18,* 568–578.

Koriat, A., Ben-Zur, H., & Sheffer, D. (1988). Telling the same story twice: Output monitoring and age. *Journal of Memory and Language, 27,* 23–29.

Loewen, E. R., Shaw, R. J., & Craik, F. I. M. (1990). Age differences in components of metamemory. *Experimental Aging Research, 16,* 43–48.

Morris, C. D., Bransford, J. D., & Franks, J. J. (1977). Levels of processing versus transfer appropriate processing. *Journal of Verbal Learning and Verbal Behavior, 16,* 519–533.

Moscovitch, M. (1982). A neuropsychological approach to memory and perception. In F. I. M. Craik & S. Trehub (Eds.), *Aging and cognitive processes* (pp. 55–78). New York: Plenum.

Reason, J. T. (1979). Actions not as planned: The price of automatization. In G. Underwood & R. Stevens (Eds.), *Aspects of consciousness: Psychological issues* (pp. 67–89). London: Academic Press.

Robinson, M. B. (1992). *Contextual effects in prospective memory*. Unpublished master's thesis, Purdue University.

Saltz, E., & Donnenwerth-Nolan, S. (1981). Does motoric imagery facilitate memory for sentences? A selective interference test. *Journal of Verbal Learning and Verbal Behavior, 20,* 322–332.

Stuss, D. T., & Benson, D. F. (1984). Neuropsychological studies of the frontal lobes. *Psychological Bulletin, 95,* 3–28.

Tulving, E., & Thomson, D. M. (1973). Encoding specificity and retrieval processes in episodic memory. *Psychological Review, 80,* 352–373.

Welford, A. T. (1958). *Ageing and human skill*. London: Oxford University Press.

12

COMMENTARY

Why Are Studies of
"Prospective Memory" Planless?

Patrick Rabbitt
University of Manchester

Maylor's and Dobbs and Reeves' excellent reviews show that *prospective memory* has become a generic label for a narrow range of experimental paradigms, most of which tell us little about how memory is used to control behavior. Dobbs and Reeves acutely observe that this is partly because the literature is dominated by the unhelpful question as to whether an hypothetical "prospective" "memory system" is functionally distinct, or shares the "performance characteristics" attributed to "retrospective memory" by a century of research. Both reviews explicitly acknowledge, or implicitly illustrate, other weak questions that have distracted investigators from fruitful research on how people actually use their memories to predict and plan their future behaviour.

One distraction has been the idea that a distinguishing characteristic of prospective memory is that it involves purpose or intention (e.g., Meacham, 1988; Meacham & Singer, 1977). Observations that social demands or expected benefits may affect people's decisions about whether or not to remember to do things do not improve on common sense, nor clarify the epistemology of intentionality, nor add to our understanding of the functional bases of "purpose," nor tell us anything about the functional bases of memory. They are offered as evidence that functional models for memory will remain incomplete until they address some poorly defined quasiphilosophical issues. This distracts attention from more enlightening discussions of purpose in prospective memory that might be based on empirical distinctions made by Jacoby (1991) and others between explicit–purposive versus implicit–involuntary memory systems. Jacoby's (1991) work highlighted the intuitively important distinction between

239

the ability to recognize the general familiarity of scenarios that may instantiate automatic and only approximately appropriate behaviors and the explicit and consciously controlled identification of particular goals, comparison of alternative plans, and selection and detailed planning of sequences of actions.

The main impression left by these scholarly reviews is the variety and interest of the topics that have not been discussed under the generic label of prospective memory. Among these are (a) the objective task demands that are unique to prospective memory, (b) whether formal descriptions of the logical structures of plans can help us to recognize differences in the qualitative and quantitative demands they make on memory and attention, (c) how people manage to update or abandon plans and goals and to establish, act upon, and keep track of their current positions in the trajectories of each of a number of different, concurrent sequences of activity, (d) how people can carry out one plan while maintaining readiness to recognize and act upon opportunities abruptly to divert to others.

Maylor's charity suppresses direct criticisms, but her clarity exposes implicit weaknesses in two dichotomies she borrows as frameworks to review the literature. The first is a distinction made by McDaniel and Einstein (1992) and Einstein and McDaniel (1990) between *time-based* and *event-based* prospective memory tasks. The second is a logically related suggestion by Craik (1986), that a useful distinction between prospective and recollective memory tasks is that the former typically receive minimal environmental support. Both these ideas seem to derive from the assumption that the difficulty humans find in managing their behavior in relation to time is a central issue in prospective memory and that studies of time-keeping efficiency offer crucial insights into planning and control.

A voluminous literature testifies that humans are indeed inaccurate at estimating arbitrary intervals of time expressed in "clock units" of hours or minutes. This makes it unsurprising that when they are asked to respond at a precise future moment in an environment deliberately stripped of nearly all cues to the passage of time except for an inconveniently placed clock, they can only do so by turning to check this clock, and continuing to do so, increasingly often as the assigned moment approaches (described in McDaniel & Einstein, 1992). In the 1960s, studies of vigilance and sustained attention adequately established that people become less efficient at monitoring signals, such as the positions of the hands of a clock if they are distracted by a concurrent secondary task. I argue that the idea that people are especially poor at regulating their behavior in relation to time is false. It stems from observations that people can only imprecisely judge time units calibrated by an arbitrary external standard, "clock time," and ignores the ease and precision with which they tailor their behavior in relation to "living time"—the demands of ongoing processes, unfolding in time, in which they are continually involved. If people are deprived of what Gibson might have called the rich and convenient "temporal affordances" of their normal routines, they can only schedule their time-keeping with respect to precise external or fallible internal clocks, or by monitoring some regular metabolic process such as their own heart rate or breathing. They have no other options because, in this universe, the passage of time is only manifest as successive, perceptible changes in physical processes. It is inaccurate to say that people "estimate the durations of periods of time." People can only be aware of time by observing changes that must always take place in time. These changes are ubiquitous, because stasis is unobtainable in even the most scrupulously impoverished laboratory environment. Even a secondary task may offer coarse temporal affordances. For example, participants may tally recurrences of operations during a cyclical task and so, in effect, use their own information processing rates as coarse chronometers. Note, however, that because any demand for time-keeping necessarily entails monitoring some internal or external process, it always places an additional demand on limited information processing resources. Time-keeping always, in effect, must act as a secondary task that may interfere with the recollection or execution of activities, responses, and plans. This, rather than the dearth of environmental cues to the passage of time, may be the significant characteristic of time-based prospective memory tasks.

Craik's (1986) suggestion that, in everyday life, time-based prospective memory is unique because it receives minimal environmental support misses the point that knowledge of the passage of time is impossible without environmental support. This is not a trivial semantic quibble because, in everyday life, the changes that people continually experience or make to their environments, to themselves, or to their locations in space provide directly perceptible sequences of "self-updating" cues that mark the passage of time and also provide unambiguous agendas to schedule their actions. Clocks provide otherwise inaccessible precision of time estimation and a public reference base independent of individual cycles and patterns of activity (Clark, 1994). We consult clocks only when we cannot regulate our behavior by monitoring less precise, but much more urgently intrusive, patterns of change than the regular rotation of a pair of hands around a dial. Neither tribal peoples nor urban office workers need control their activities in terms of clock time because their lives are tightly constrained, or supported, by regular cycles of obtrusive environmental changes and by the unfolding of the consequences of their own intentions and actions. The powerful entrainments that guide us through most of our everyday activities may make more or less demand on memory. For example, to cook a stir fry, a person must precisely estimate relative heating times for different ingredients. Even a novice would not choose to heat all ingredients in separate pans, try to remember their various cooking times in minutes or seconds, and continuously consult a clock to get these right. He or she would, sensibly, ease task demands, including memory load, by putting ingredients successively into a single pan in inverse order of their optimal cooking durations. However, he or she might nervously consult memory, or a recipe book, for relative cooking times, and watch a clock to schedule the process. Confident cooks reduce their "wokking memory load" almost to zero and obtain total environmental support for "time-cued prospective memory" by observing critical changes in the ingredients as they are heated, thus using the cooking process itself as a reliable clock and as a self-updating sequence of reminders for each successive operation.

Fine-grained temporal management is usually tightly enforced through the unfolding of the causal structures of our everyday routines. It is only when we have to shift from one internally constrained behavior sequence to another that we may have to access wider contexts of temporal orientation. A touching illustration is that even patients who are so profoundly amnesic that they are completely disoriented in time may only intermittently realize this when they emerge from regular routines in which each step completely determines the next (Parkin, 1993).

Rather than considering how well people can manage to plan and execute activities in relation to clock time when we deprive them of as many cues as we can it may be more useful to consider what sequences of self-updating changes are offered by different tasks, and how these affect demands on long- and short-term memory. This would bring the study of prospective memory closer to four fruitful lines of research. One is Norman's (1981) and Reason's (1979) brilliant analyses of human errors to locate the points at which action slips are most likely to occur. A second is the attempt to derive functional, and eventually neurological, models for planning and control of behavior from studies of the loss of efficiency of the central executive system following frontal brain damage (Baddeley 1986; Shallice, 1982; Shallice & Burgess, 1991; Shimamura, Janowski, & Squire, 1991). A third is the clever and humane analyses of everyday tasks made by clinicians such as Cockburn (1993), to discover the particular demands with which their patients cannot cope, and to find ingenious ways of adapting tasks, environments, and memory aids to their surviving skills. A fourth is human factors research on complex software aids such as word processing and interactive information management systems, spreadsheets or computerized "organizers." To describe how people learn to use such complex systems it was necessary to develop abstract general models by Olsen and others for interactive planning and control such as GOMS. Models such as GOMS have been shown to make accurate and detailed predictions of which sequences of available operations people are likely to follow and of the relative times that these choices will require. Theoreticians such as Young and Mac-Lean (1988) suggested ways of quantitatively comparing the relative success of different models in describing different kinds of interactions between humans and complex systems.

Perhaps even simplistic structural models of situations requiring prospective memory can suggest new ways of empirically investigating how different task demands may impose or abolish qualitatively, as well as quantitatively different loads on prospective memory.

VARIETIES OF MEMORY LOAD IN SIMPLE LINEAR PLANS: "LOOPING AND DERAILMENT" ILLUSTRATED BY BROADBENT'S LAPSES

Laboratory studies of prospective memory seem unambitious because they typically only test memory for a single instruction or procedure. In the real world, complex organisms such as Deans of Science must identify and pursue multiple subgoals. These require conscious choices between different, and sometimes competing, sequences of behavior. A simplistic description of such a sequence might include a list of goals, or "things to do" (g^1 through g^N) and cues or conditions (c^1 through c^5), each appropriate to initiate one of a set of different procedures (p^1 through p^5) that may attain these goals. Each p may, in turn, specify a number of cues, or states, (t^1 to t^N) each prompting or initiating a corresponding action (a^1 to a^N). The model must also incorporate stop-rules for terminating procedures. These may be recognitions of one or other of a set of desired goal states s^1 through s^N.

Even this simplistic schematic shows that, in the worst case, different plans may require operators to hold different kinds, as well as amounts, of information in memory. Schematics also help us to recognize when we have poorly defined one or more of the hypothetical components in our model. In this case the concreteness of terms such as *cues, conditions,* or *states* masks the ambiguity that these may be the completion of a previous action (e.g., the immediately preceding a) or a change in the environment brought about by this action, or some environmental or internal change that must be actively sought or passively awaited before the next action or plan becomes appropriate. Initial conditions for plans that involve sequences of successive actions must be differentiated in memory from initial conditions for individual actions carried

$$g^1 \rightarrow c^1 \rightarrow p^1 \{t^1 - a^1 - t^2 - a^2 - t^3 - a^3\} \rightarrow S^1$$
$$g^2 \rightarrow c^2 \rightarrow p^2 \{t^1 - a^1 - t^2 - a^2 - t^3 - a^3\} \rightarrow S^2$$
$$g^3 \rightarrow c^3 \rightarrow p^3 \{t^1 - a^1 - t^2 - a^2 - t^3 - a^3\} \rightarrow S^3$$
$$g^4 \rightarrow c^4 \rightarrow p^4 \{t^1 - a^1 - t^2 - a^2 - t^3 - a^3\} \rightarrow S^4$$
$$g^5 \rightarrow c^5 \rightarrow p^5 \{t^1 - a^1 - t^2 - a^2 - t^3 - a^3\} \rightarrow S^5$$

FIG 11.1. Illustration of hypothetical sequence structures in which recognition of goal states (g^1 to g^n) initiate learned procedures, (p^1 to p^n) within each of which cues or states (t^1 to t^n) prompt corresponding actions, (a^1 to a^n). Sequences are terminated by recognition of stop rules or states (S^1 to S^n).

out during the course of particular plans. This distinction is crucial in practice because if one or more t states in a sequence are identical to each other, or to some c state, the only way we can know what to do next is to remember what we have just done. The definitions of t states may expand to include long sequences of temporally successive events with consequent increases in working memory load. Both the amount, and the nature of the memory load imposed by a plan will not only depend on the number of different a and t states that it specifies, but on whether or not each is unique. As a concrete illustration, consider the following sequences of cues or events, each of which requires a different response:

1. A – B – C – D – E – F-G – H – I – J – K
2. A – B – C – D – E – C – F – G – C – H-I
3. A – B – C – D – E – C – F – G – H – C – J – K
4. A – B – C – D – E – A – F – B – G – H – A – B – C – I – J – K – C

In case 1, each action or cue is unique. To know what to do next a person who learned this sequence need only remember what he or she last did. Although sequence 2 involves the same number of successive steps, and indeed contains two fewer unique elements, to know what to do after any C, a person must remember at least his or her last two actions to establish whether he or she is at the C after B, after E, or after H. Here the critical event is a sequence of two or more temporally successive cues or actions and discrimination between such temporally extended events makes proportionately greater demands on working memory. Sequence 4 shows that recognition of events may demand memory for even longer runs of events. Rabbitt (1982) found that participants running through highly practiced sequences of responses made most of their errors at points at which they had to cope with increased memory load to resolve such ambiguities. Errors at these points disproportionately increased when participants were elderly or were given a secondary task. The different kinds of errors they made suggested that performance on these simple tasks can offer insights into real-life failures. Individuals might *jump ahead* to the next-but-one occurrence of a repeated element, or *loop back* to repeat the sequence that followed its last occurrence. Jumping ahead in a plan provides a structural description for common slips of action such as forgetting to put tea in a teapot before filling it with hot water and looping back for slips such as reaching to change gear while driving, and finding that one has already done so. If two practiced action sequences incorporate identical runs of elements, *derailment* from one to another may occur. Analogous derailment between rival plans in real life was illustrated by Broadbent's charming anecdote that, when going into his bedroom to dress for a dinner party, he would sometimes find himself changing into his pyjamas and getting into bed. To illustrate that derailments also become more likely when we try to carry out simultaneous, interlocking plans, we use his claim that, at least once, he left some cabbage leaves out for the milkman and put the milk bottles that he was also holding into his rabbit hutch.

UPDATING, AND VARIATIONS IN MEMORY LOAD
WITHIN SIMPLE SERIAL PLANS:
THE DEAN'S DILEMMAS

In the simplest case, the environment provides a reliable set of cues, c^1 through c^5 that always occur separately, and all initiate the same single procedure, p, to reach the same goal. An example might be a Dean of Cognitive Science engaged in the routine administrative task of asking all of his or her colleagues the same question, for the same purpose. He or she need remember only the set of distinct cue-states (relevant colleagues) c^1 through c^5 and, for each, initiate the same procedure, (p^1) involving only a single action, (a^1). He or she need not worry about the temporal order of these interrogations. As a cognitive scientist, he or she may find a plausible laboratory analogue in the Sternberg (1966) *memory search paradigm*, in which participants make the same response to each of a set of symbols designated as targets and withhold a response, or make a different response, to all other nontarget symbols. His or her efficiency, whether indexed by decision speed or number of errors, declines as the sizes of the target and nontarget sets grow. The Dean's prospective memory load will increase with the numbers of colleagues and acquaintances. However, because repeatedly questioning the same colleagues may cause embarrassing speculation, he or she will be wise to self-impose an additional load of continual updating. The Dean will also have to remember the answers received. Thus, increases in memory load imposed by the c set will cause corresponding, and possibly much more troublesome, contingent increases in memory load imposed by updating and by remembering answers to questions. Sensitive clinicians such as Camp, Robertson, or Wilson, might advise a failing Dean that, unless he or she has some Machiavellian reason for sampling colleagues independently, he or she can reduce memory load almost to zero by raising the necessary question at a meeting at which they are all present and making careful notes of their replies.

The Sternberg task can incorporate updating by requiring participants to respond only to the first appearance of each target item, which, thereafter, becomes a nontarget. The memory load of remembering different answers to a question might plausibly be simulated by displaying each target with the additional word *YES* or *NO*, requiring participants to stop when all targets have been acknowledged, and then to report the "Yesses" and "Nos" corresponding to each. Unsurprisingly, when tasks of this kind were examined in our laboratory, decision times and errors markedly increased with demands on working memory load. These effects are disproportionately greater for elderly than for younger adults, and in individuals with lower IQs.

Our Dean's dilemmas may be complicated in other instructive ways. For example, if plotting a more complex political strategy, he or she may not only have to remember which colleagues to interrogate but may find it expedient to interrogate them in a particular order. With some creaking, the Sternberg paradigm can still model this case if c^2 through c^5 are treated as nontarget signals until a valid response has been made to c^1, and c^3 through c^5 as nontargets until a valid response has been made to c^2, . . . and so on. In real life, the Dean may perhaps find environmental support for his or her maneuvers by planning a cunning route through campus to consecutively sample colleagues. If one of those rare individuals who actually use, rather than merely research, mnemonic systems, he or she may employ the *method of loci*. If devious, the Dean may, according to a running evaluation of the responses received, choose to alter and update the order in which colleagues are consulted, the particular information that is given to each, and the questions asked of them. A laboratory analogue might be a paradigm in which participants have to remember to make new, different responses to some, but not to all, target items on their second appearances in a series. However the Dean may also choose to use the information progressively obtained to go back and reinform and reinterrogate some individuals that he or she has approached once, or more often. Although further elaborations of the Sternberg paradigm may no longer provide plausible simulations, simple structural descriptions still allow us to identify what and where increases in memory load occur and to notice how they are compounded by additional task demands such as updating. Even simple structural descriptions can be useful templates for designing new tasks and frameworks for analyzing observational data.

Structural descriptions of everyday tasks can also reveal interesting conceptual links across diverse research literatures. For example, an efficient, politically active Dean must cope with the simultaneous demands of many parallel, perhaps even competing, plans, often having to interrupt one chain of activity to capitalize on favorable opportunities to pursue another. He or she has to develop efficient stop-rules; that is, to recognize, as soon as possible, when goals or plans have become redundant or inaccessible and must be abandoned or superseded. These demands are structurally analogous to those imposed by use of stick and shift rules and extra- versus intradimensional shifts in paradigms such as the Wisconsin card sorting task, useful in the diagnosis of frontal brain damage. Recent structural decompositions of other "frontal sensitive" tasks such as the Tower of Hanoi, revealed that superficially identical problems can make different demands on memory load and that their difficulty can be predicted by simple structural descriptions.

Obviously, these simplistic structural descriptions do not provide a comprehensive description of how memory is involved in the planning and control of behavior. Neither do they invalidate many useful studies that Dobbs and Reeves and Maylor insightfully review. They only make the point that even complex behaviors can be captured by surprisingly simple structural descriptions and that use of structural descriptions alerts us when we are being obstructed by ambiguities of definition of terms. It also allows us to look beyond superficialities and to recognize when apparently disparate tasks are identical in terms of their deeper functional structures, and to compare the different kinds, and amounts, of demands that apparently similar tasks make on working memory. Elementary structural descriptions make it easier to design laboratory paradigms to study planning and control of behavior. They not only force us to accept Dobbs and Reeves' useful point that prospective memory is more than memory, but also help us to understand precisely how memory is involved in prospection.

REFERENCES

Baddeley, A. D. (1986). *Working memory*. Oxford, England: Oxford University Press.

Clark, G. (1994). *Space, time and man: A pre-historian's view*. Cambridge, England: Cambridge University Press.

Cockburn, J. (1993). Errors of prospective memory after head injury: Memory, information processing or awareness of time? *Clinical Rehabilitation, 7*, 86.

Craik, F. I. M. (1986). A functional account of age differences in memory. In F. Klix & H. Hagendorf (Eds). *Human Memory and Cognitive Capabilities: Mechanisms and Performances* (pp. 409–422). North Holland: Elsevier.

Einstein G. O., & McDaniel, M. A. (1990). Normal Aging and Prospective Memory, *Journal of Experimental Psychology, Learning, Memory & Cognition, 16*, 717–726.

Jacoby, L. L. (1991). A process disassociation framework: Separating automatic from intentional uses of memory. *Journal of Memory and Language, 30*, 513–541.

McDaniel, M. A., & Einstein, G. O. (1992). Aging and Prospective Memory: Basic findings and practical applications. *Advances in Learning and Behavioural Disabilities, Volume 7*. 87–105.

Meacham, J. A. (1988). Interpersonal relations and prospective remembering. In M. M. Gruneberg, P. E. Morris, & R. N. Sykes (Eds). *Practical Aspects of Memory: Current research and issues* (Vol. 1, pp 354–359). Chichester, England: Wiley.

Meacham, J. A., & Singer, J. (1977). Incentive effects in prospective remembering. *The Journal of Psychology, 97*, 191–197.

Norman, D. A. (1981). Categorisation of action slips. *Psychological Review, 88*, 1–5.

Parkin, A. J. (1993). *Memory: Phenomena, Experiment and Theory*. Oxford, England: Blackwell.

Rabbitt, P. M. A. (1982). How do old people know what to do next? In F. I. M. Craik & S. Trehub (Eds.), *Aging and cognitive processes*. New York: Plenum Press.

Reason, J. T. (1979). Actions not as planned: the price of automatisation. In G. Underwood & R. Stevens (Eds.), *Aspects of consciousness* (Vol. 1, pp. 67–89). New York: Academic Press.

Shallice, T. (1982). Specific impairments of planning. *Philosophical transactions of the Royal Society of London, 298*, 199–109.

Shallice, T., & Burgess, P. (1991). Deficits in strategy application following frontal lobe damage in man. *Brain, 114*, 727–741.

Shimamura, A. P., Janowski, J. S., & Squire, L. R. (1991). What is the role of frontal lobe damage in memory disorders? In H. S. Levin, H. M. Eisenberg, and A. L. Benton (Eds.), *Frontal Lobe Function and Dysfunction.* New York: Oxford University Press.

Sternberg, S. (1966). High speed scanning in human memory, *Science, 153,* 652–654.

Young, R. M., & MacLean, P. T. (1988). Choosing between methods: Analysing the user's decision space in terms of schemas and linear models. *Proceedings of the CHI '88 Conference on Human Factors in Computing Systems,* 139–143. New York, ACM.

PART III

Neuropsychology of Prospective Memory

13

Prospective Memory and the Frontal Lobes

Elizabeth L. Glisky
University of Arizona

Investigations of *retrospective memory*—memory for past events and experiences—led researchers to hypothesize that memory is not a unitary construct. Instead, it is composed of several kinds of memory systems or processes that are used differentially depending on task demands (for reviews, see Baddeley, 1990; Richardson-Klavehn & Bjork, 1988; Schacter, Chiu, & Ochsner, 1993). For example, we use short-term, primary, or working memory to maintain or manipulate information in consciousness for brief periods of time (Baddeley, 1986; Waugh & Norman, 1965), whereas we use long-term or secondary memory to store information permanently (Atkinson & Shiffrin, 1968). Episodic memory enables us to keep track of personally experienced events according to the time and place of their occurrence; semantic memory stores knowledge without reference to spatiotemporal context (Tulving, 1972). Declarative memory is concerned with memory for facts—propositions that have truth value—whereas procedural memory involves memory for skills or action sequences (Squire, 1987). We can retrieve past experiences consciously through explicit memory processes or we can express our knowledge of the past implicitly through changes in performance (Graf & Schacter, 1985).

Although many of these ideas concerning different kinds of memory were derived from studies of normal individuals, neuropsychological investigations of patients with memory disorders have confirmed the notion that memory is multidimensional and suggested that different components of memory may rely on different parts of the brain. For example, patients with bilateral damage to medial temporal lobe structures or diencephalic regions of the brain

249

often display an amnesic syndrome, characterized by an inability to acquire and retain new factual information or to remember recent experiences. At the same time, these individuals maintain their general knowledge of the world, are often able to learn new procedures, and may have normal short-term or working memory abilities (for reviews, see Kihlstrom & Glisky, 1994; Mayes, 1988; Shimamura, 1989; Squire, 1987). Such a disorder has been variably referred to as a deficit in long-term memory (Baddeley & Warrington, 1970), episodic memory (Kinsbourne & Wood, 1975), declarative memory (Cohen & Squire, 1980), or explicit memory (Graf & Schacter, 1985). Within the deficient domain, the amnesic deficit is usually global; that is, it affects memory for all kinds of materials (e.g., verbal, visual, spatial) and is reflected in all kinds of tests (e.g., recall, cued recall, recognition).

Unilateral lesions and damage to other regions of the brain, however, reveal further fractionation of memory processes such that some patients are more impaired in recall than in recognition (Hirst et al., 1986), are more or less impaired in memory for verbal than for visual information (Milner, 1966), for context than for item information (Janowsky, Shimamura, & Squire, 1989b), and so forth (see Squire & Butters, 1992). Selective deficits in short-term memory (Warrington & Shallice, 1969), semantic memory (Warrington, 1975), procedural memory (Heindel, Butters, & Salmon, 1988), and implicit memory (Gabrieli, Fleischman, Keane, Reminger, & Morrell, 1995) were also demonstrated and found to be associated with specific loci in the brain. Examination of individuals with disorders of memory helped to clarify the functions subserved by different brain regions and to enhance theoretical accounts of normal memory by identifying individual components of the memory process that might otherwise have been indistinguishable in normal subjects.

Prospective memory—memory for future actions—received less attention from memory theorists than its retrospective counterpart, probably because it is much less tractable in the laboratory. Investigations often occurred in naturalistic environments where researchers were able to exercise little control over the many variables influencing behavior (e.g., Moscovitch, 1982). It has been difficult to construct theories of prospective memory or even to determine the extent to which the processes involved in prospective memory are similar to or different from those involved in retrospective memory. Evidence from brain-damaged patients is also sparse, although clinical observation suggests that problems in prospective memory are commonly reported in conjunction with other disorders of retrospective memory (e.g., Mateer, Sohlberg, & Crinean, 1987). Complaints of prospective memory failure are also frequent among the elderly.

This chapter adopts the position that, like retrospective memory, prospective memory is not unitary. Instead, it relies on different processes depending on task demands, and these different processes depend on different underlying brain structures. Some of the processes are similar to those involved in retrospective memory; others may be unique to prospective memory. To the extent that different tasks share components, performance on the tasks should be correlated, whereas if the tasks require different processes, correlations should be reduced or absent. I argue that at least some of the processes that characterize prospective memory and distinguish it from retrospective memory depend on the integrity of the frontal lobes, but the extent to which the frontal lobes are involved in any particular prospective memory task will depend on the characteristics of that task.

To my knowledge, no work has been published concerning prospective memory performance in patients with circumscribed frontal lobe lesions. For that reason, my ideas concerning the contribution of the frontal lobes are necessarily speculative and are derived from theories of frontal lobe function, theories of cognitive and biological aging, and existing empirical work in prospective memory. I primarily rely on studies of prospective memory with older adults who acquire an increased likelihood of frontal system dysfunction as they age, and therefore may provide insights into the contribution of frontal lobe processes to prospective memory.

In the balance of this chapter, I (a) summarize the cognitive functions thought to be associated with the frontal lobes, (b) indicate the ways in which the frontal lobes might be involved in various kinds of retrospective memory, (c) outline the evidence for frontal lobe decline with age, (d) examine theories of cognitive aging and their relation to frontal system dysfunction, (e) analyze different prospective memory tasks with respect to their reliance on frontal lobe processes, and (f) indicate the extent to which the empirical literature on prospective memory and aging supports a role for the frontal lobes in prospective memory.

THE FRONTAL LOBES

The frontal lobes constitute the largest area of cortex in the human brain; they are evolutionarily the most recent structures to emerge and ontogenetically the latest to reach maturity. Although the prefrontal cortex (i.e., the regions anterior and mesial to the motor and speech areas) is thought to support the highest levels of cognitive functioning, the particular functions involved defy clear specification and precise localization. Because the frontal lobes are morphologically complex and richly connected to every other system in the brain (Weinberger, 1993), it is unlikely that they subserve a single function. At the same time, this extensive connectivity is consistent with a role for prefrontal cortex as the organizer of multiple behaviors across a range of cognitive domains, and many theorists propose that the overriding function of the frontal lobes is integrative or executive processing (e.g., Fuster, 1989; Luria, 1966; Moscovitch & Winocur, 1992; Petrides, 1989; Shallice, 1982; Stuss & Benson,

1987; Weinberger, 1993). The frontal lobes are required for formulating plans and supervising activities that are not routine, are embedded in novel situations, and involve cognitive and behavioral selectivity. They are responsible for initiating actions, monitoring ongoing behavior, and evaluating outcomes. They act as a kind of executive controller or overseer of a broad range of activities across a variety of tasks and situations, deciding what stimuli will be selected for processing at any one time and ensuring that multiple procedures are executed in an organized and timely fashion. They are sometimes thought of as the center for working memory (Baddeley, 1986; Goldman-Rakic, 1991)—a "place" where new information can be manipulated and integrated with prior knowledge in preparation for use in a range of tasks.

Damage to the frontal lobes often results in a *dysexecutive syndrome* (Baddeley, 1986; Baddeley & Wilson, 1988). Patients frequently have difficulty initiating or organizing new goal-directed behaviors; they often appear apathetic and distracted, perform in stereotyped ways, and routinely repeat or perseverate on old responses (e.g., Goldberg & Bilder, 1987; Luria, 1966; Stuss & Benson, 1984). Frontal dysfunction is revealed on a number of neuropsychological tests. For example, in the Wisconsin Card Sorting Test (WCST) (Heaton, 1981; Milner, 1964), subjects are required to respond to one of three relevant dimensions of stimuli that appear on cards (color, number, shape), maintain that response set across several trials, and then switch to a new dimension or category in accordance with feedback from the tester. Frontal lobe patients have problems with this test; they tend to perseverate on an initial response and have difficulty adapting to the changing demands of the task (e.g., Janowsky, Shimamura, Kritchevsky, & Squire, 1989). Frontally impaired patients also have problems on the Controlled Oral Word Association Test (Benton & Hamsher, 1976). This test requires the generation of words beginning with the letters F, A, and S (given 1 min per letter). The depressed performance of frontal patients appears to be attributable to difficulty in initiating the processes necessary to retrieve responses from the knowledge system (Lezak, 1983; Stuss & Benson, 1984) and in the tendency to repeat responses.

Although there is consensus concerning the importance of the prefrontal cortex for executive function, there is disagreement concerning the subprocesses or particular mechanisms required to carry out the job of a central executive, the localization of these component processes within the frontal system, or the several additional functions that also seem to rely on intact frontal lobes. Prefrontal cortex seems necessary for a diversity of specific functions that defy simple classification. The frontal lobes have been implicated in a range of problems in attention, language, memory, problem solving, personality, motivation, emotion, arousal, and awareness (for reviews, see Damasio & Anderson, 1993; Levin, Eisenberg, & Benton, 1991; Luria, 1966; Perecman, 1987; Stuss & Benson, 1984, 1986). Which functions are impaired in any individual patient depends on a number of factors including the locus and side of the lesion, the nature and extent of the lesion, the degree to which other nonfrontal regions of the brain are also compromised, and the etiology of the problem.

Much of the information concerning the functions of the frontal lobes was gleaned from patients who had frontal lobe resections or other surgeries for intractable epilepsy, psychiatric disturbance, or tumor. Head injury, vascular syndromes affecting the anterior cerebral artery or the anterior communicating artery, chronic alcoholism, and dementia also cause damage to areas of frontal cortex. Although in the case of surgical lesions the extent of brain damage may be known, pre-existing pathological conditions may also impact current behavior, further complicating interpretation of performance on "frontal lobe" tasks. For these and other reasons, neuropsychological studies of patients with frontal lobe damage did not always produce consistent findings. For example, perseveration (such as that revealed on the WCST), which in many ways is thought to be a classic symptom of frontal lobe dysfunction, is not always seen—even in patients with frank pathology of the frontal lobes observable on CT scan or MRI. On the other hand, impaired performance on the WCST was observed in patients without frontal damage (Anderson, Damasio, Jones, & Tranel, 1991; Lezak, 1983; Stuss & Benson, 1984). These inconsistencies suggest that not only are frontal lobe patients heterogeneous with respect to their functional deficits, but performance on many psychometric tests such as the WCST likely requires multiple processes, only some of which depend on frontal lobe structures.

The Frontal Lobes and Retrospective Memory

What might be said about the frontal processes involved in memory tasks? The *amnesic syndrome*, which represents a profound deficit in the ability to remember events that have occurred since trauma, has been associated with damage either to the hippocampus and surrounding medial temporal lobe structures, or to diencephalic structures including the mamillary bodies and the dorsomedial nucleus of the thalamus. Damage to the frontal lobes does not usually produce a global amnesia (e.g., Luria, 1973; Schacter, 1987). Nevertheless, patients with frontal damage often show highly specific memory deficits. For example, although normal on many tests of item or factual memory, frontal patients are frequently impaired in memory for the source of recently acquired information (Janowsky et al., 1989b), for temporal order (McAndrews & Milner, 1991; Milner, Petrides, & Smith, 1985; Shimamura, Janowsky, & Squire, 1990), for frequency of occurrence information (Smith & Milner, 1988), and, under some conditions, for spatial sequences (Vilkki & Holst, 1989). They also seem particularly susceptible to the effects of interference (e.g., Shimamura, 1994), performing poorly on tests such as the Brown–Peterson task, which requires memory for highly similar stimuli on successive trials (Brown, 1958; Peterson & Peterson, 1959; Stuss, 1991). In addition, they lack metamemory abilities: They have poor insight into their own memory capabilities and may have little awareness of appropriate memory strategies (Janowsky, Shimamura, & Squire, 1989a).

In various tests of memory for new information (including word lists, prose passages, complex figures and paired associates), patients with damage confined to the frontal lobes usually show no deficits, whether memory is tested in free recall, cued recall, or recognition (Shimamura, Janowsky, & Squire, 1991). However, there are a few isolated reports of impaired memory performance in frontal patients, particularly on tests of free recall. For example, Janowsky et al. (1989) showed that on a multitrial free-recall test for 15 unrelated words, patients with frontal lesions were significantly impaired across all trials, although they were normal on a comparable test of recognition memory. The authors suggested that multitrial free-recall tests might be particularly sensitive to frontal dysfunction because they require the planning and development of retrieval strategies across trials. Incisa della Rocchetta (1986) reported impaired performance of patients with unilateral frontal lobe lesions on a free-recall test of categorizable pictures. He argued that impaired performance was attributable to failure to use appropriate organizational strategies at either encoding or retrieval. Finally, Jetter, Poser, Freeman, & Markowitsch (1986) found frontally damaged patients to be impaired on free recall of a list of unrelated words after a single exposure, but not on tests of cued recall or recognition.

Although impairments in memory for item information among patients with frontal lesions are not consistently reported in the literature, the cases in which such deficits are found tend to be situations in which strategic processes might provide a memorial advantage, such as in the free recall of categorized material or in multitrial free recall. When cues are provided, as in tests of cued recall or recognition, demands on strategic processes are considerably less and deficits are rarely found. The frontal lobes thus seem to play an organizational or strategic role in memory tasks and perhaps are only important when cue information is insufficient to specify the target event (cf., Moscovitch & Winocur, 1992).

A similar analysis may be useful for the understanding of prospective memory. Although some theorists proposed that prospective memory generally places greater demands on the frontal lobes than does retrospective memory, involvement of the frontal lobes in prospective tasks may be confined to those situations in which cues are underspecified and strategies are required. No direct tests of this hypothesis have yet been conducted in frontal lobe patients, but studies of normal elderly subjects may be relevant. If the frontal lobes are particularly susceptible to the aging process, then older adults may show selective deficits on memory tests—both retrospective and prospective—that are particularly susceptible to frontal lobe dysfunction. The next sections consider this possibility.

The Frontal Lobes and Aging

Neurophysiological and neuroanatomical evidence suggests that prefrontal cortex is significantly and perhaps preferentially affected by aging. For example, Martin, Friston, Colebatch, and Frackowiak (1991) found age-related decreases in regional cerebral blood flow in limbic and association cortices including the prefrontal areas. Coffey et al. (1992), using MRI, found decreases in cortical volume with age that were substantially greater for the frontal lobes than for other regions. A reduction in the amplitude of some components of evoked potentials over the frontal areas has also been noted (Michalewski et al., 1980).

Although these neuroanatomical and neurophysiological changes were not linked directly to particular cognitive declines in the elderly (Ivy, MacLeod, Petit, & Marcus, 1992), neuropsychological data, although limited, supports a connection between age-related changes and declining frontal lobe function. For example, Daigneault, Braun, and Whitaker (1992) found significant age impairments on WCST, Petrides & Milner's (1982) self-ordered pointing task, Porteus (1965) mazes and the Stroop task (Golden, 1978)—tests designed to tap frontal lobe function. Mittenberg, Seidenberg, O'Leary, and Di Giulio (1989) reported age-related deficits in recency discrimination and nonverbal fluency. On a memory task, Craik and his colleagues (Craik, Morris, Morris, & Loewen, 1990; McIntyre & Craik, 1987) demonstrated that the degree to which older adults showed impaired memory for the source of newly acquired information (i.e., *source amnesia*) was correlated with performance on tasks sensitive to frontal lobe pathology—the WCST and verbal fluency (see also, Parkin & Walter 1992). Spencer and Raz (1994) reported significant correlations between perseverative errors on the WCST and poor contextual memory in elderly subjects.

Older adults are also more impaired in free recall than in cued recall or recognition (Craik & McDowd, 1987). They experience particular difficulties in memory for temporal information (Kausler, Lichty, & Davis, 1985), source information (McIntyre & Craik, 1987; Schacter, Kaszniak, Kihlstrom, & Valdiserri, 1991) and other aspects of context (Ferguson, Hashtroudi, & Johnson, 1992; Kausler & Puckett, 1981; Rabinowitz, Craik, & Ackerman, 1982). Working memory shows substantial decrements (Dobbs & Rule, 1989; Salthouse & Babcock, 1991) and some aspects of metamemory are also impaired (Cavanaugh, 1989; McGlynn, 1993). These selective memory deficits tend to occur, as previously noted, in conjunction with frontal lobe dysfunction.

Despite the evidence for frontal system decline in the elderly, there is also widespread reduction in the volume and metabolic rate in other cortical and subcortical regions of the brain (e.g., Jernigan et al., 1991; Marchal et al., 1992). Decrements in performance on any particular cognitive task may thus be attributable to several factors and subject to a variety of interpretations. The fact that older adults show episodic memory deficits that are strikingly similar to those found in amnesic patients (although considerably less marked), suggests that at least some memory declines with age may be attributable to declining hippocampal function—an impression that is supported by findings of neuronal loss in the hippocampus with age (Squire, 1987).

Theories of Cognitive Aging

Although many cognitive interpretations of memory decline have ignored the neuroanatomical structures or systems that underlie memory deficits (e.g., Craik, 1986; Jacoby, 1983; Roediger, Weldon, & Challis, 1989), many of the theories of cognitive aging easily lend themselves to frontal lobe interpretations. For example, Craik (1986, 1994) proposed that the principal deficiency underlying reduced memory performance in older adults is a problem with self-initiated encoding and retrieval processes. A number of empirical results are consistent with this view. For example, the finding of greater age deficits in free recall than in cued recall and recognition (Craik & McDowd, 1987) can be readily interpreted in terms of differences in the requirements for self-initiated retrieval processes. In cued recall and recognition, the test environment provides external support to guide search processes; in free recall, retrieval strategies have to be formulated and initiated by the individual. Similarly, if older adults are deficient in the initiation of appropriate encoding processes, they may fail to encode nonfocal aspects of an event and thus show relatively poor memory for context or source (cf., Craik & Jennings, 1992). Craik (1986; see also Craik & Byrd, 1982; Salthouse, 1988) proposed that a reduction in processing resources accounts for the difficulty that older adults experience in the self-initiation of encoding and retrieval processes.

The frontal lobe hypothesis proposed here is not incompatible with Craik's (1986) process account of memory deficits in aging, but it may have greater generality and parsimony. At the same time, it does not depend on the conceptually and empirically elusive construct of "processing resources" and may be more directly testable. It states simply that to the extent that performance on memory tasks requires or is facilitated by processes associated with the frontal lobes, such as planning, organization, and self-initiation, older adults will be impaired. The essential implication of this hypothesis for prospective memory and aging is that elderly adults should show deficits on prospective memory tasks if the tasks require significant frontal input. Although prospective memory may be more demanding of frontal lobe function than is retrospective memory, the involvement of the frontal lobes may also vary across prospective tasks.

PROSPECTIVE MEMORY

Prospective Memory and Retrospective Memory

Given the limited empirical base in prospective memory, it is not surprising that relatively few cognitive theories have been formulated to account for memory for future actions. Although most theorists agree that some aspects of prospective memory must involve retrospective remembering (e.g., Baddeley & Wilkins, 1984; Hitch & Ferguson, 1991; Huppert & Beardsall, 1993; Loftus, 1971), the extent of the overlap between the two tasks remains unclear. Several studies failed to find correlations between performance on retrospective and prospective memory tasks (Einstein & McDaniel, 1990; Huppert & Beardsall, 1993; Maylor, 1990; Meacham & Leiman, 1982), and some investigators (Wilkins & Baddeley, 1978) even reported negative correlations. These findings suggest that some of the processes required for the two tasks are different. On the other hand, certain variables such as retention interval, the presence of cues (Loftus, 1971), and the number of events to be remembered (Einstein, Holland, McDaniel, & Guynn, 1992; Hitch & Ferguson, 1991) were found to affect the two tasks similarly, implying shared components across tasks.

Intuitively, it is reasonable that prospective remembering requires retrospective memory plus some additional process that enables subjects to remember to perform an action at a particular time. Unlike retrospective memory in which subjects are prompted to search memory, in prospective remembering subjects must also "remember to remember." This distinction is expressed in the literature as a difference in the availability or salience of retrieval cues (Baddeley & Wilkins, 1984; Harris, 1984; Maylor, 1990; West, 1988). In retrospective remembering, cues are usually obvious, although variable in the degree to which they specify the to-be-remembered event; subjects are given the cues at time of retrieval and prompted to recall a prior event. In prospective remembering, external cues are often less identifiable and may fail to stand out against a background of similar stimuli. Subjects must first recognize the cue as a cue before using it to retrieve the associated event. Thus, although the two tasks share the requirement to retrieve previously stored information, prospective memory tasks also require identification of the appropriate cue.

Retrospective and prospective remembering may also differ in other respects. Some theorists suggest that to-be-performed tasks may be encoded more elaborately than to-be-recalled tasks. Findings of enhanced memory for prospective memories relative to retrospective memories are consistent with these views (Koriat, Ben-Zur, & Nussbaum, 1990). Others propose that, perhaps in anticipation of different retrieval requirements, prospective memories are held in a state of heightened activation to keep them accessible for imminent use (Baddeley & Wilkins, 1984; Goschke & Kuhl, 1993).

The two kinds of tasks may also differ in attentional requirements. In retrospective memory, full attention can usually be devoted to the retrieval task, whereas in prospective memory, remembering occurs while other activities are ongoing. Attention may therefore be divided between present and future tasks.

Different Kinds of Prospective Memory Tasks

Prospective memory tasks may also differ among themselves. They may be self-imposed or other-imposed, routine or novel, isolated or part of a network of related actions (Cohen, 1989), event-based or time-based (Einstein & McDaniel, 1990). They may vary with respect to difficulty of cue identification, complexity of the action to be encoded, time across which the intention must be maintained, and extent to which other activities demand attention. Research on prospective memory has focused primarily on manipulation of these task variables and on the identification of conditions under which performance may be enhanced or diminished. Little attention has been paid to the cognitive processes involved in the different tasks. Given the variability among tasks and the likelihood that different processes are involved in them, the inconsistent pattern of correlations with retrospective tasks is not surprising.

Prospective Memory and the Frontal Lobes

Prospective memory tasks may also vary in the extent to which they involve the frontal lobes. For example, frontal function may be particularly important when cue information is poorly specified or difficult to identify, thereby creating a need for self-initiated retrieval processing. The frontal lobes will likely be involved when demands on working memory are considerable, when preliminary planning is necessary, when tasks are not routine, when temporal tracking or time estimation is required, when ongoing behaviors have to be interrupted and when environmental or contextual stimuli need to be monitored. Most prospective memory tasks seem to require these frontal functions but to varying degrees.

As noted earlier in the chapter, most standard retrospective memory tasks, however, do not require frontal lobe input and may be expected not to correlate with prospective memory tasks, at least when the retrospective component of those tasks is minimal. If the retrospective component of the prospective task is complex, however, correlations between the two tasks are likely (e.g., Einstein et al., 1992).

Two further predictions can be derived from the frontal lobe hypothesis: First, correlations should exist between retrospective and prospective tasks when both tasks involve a significant frontal lobe component. We obtained preliminary support for this prediction from an experiment showing a correlation between prospective memory and source memory—a retrospective task that reputedly relies on the frontal lobes (McDaniel et al., 1994). Second, deficits in prospective remembering should be found for frontal patients and elderly subjects to the extent that the prospective task requires frontal control. An examination of the aging literature provides tentative support for a relation between impaired prospective memory performance and frontal lobe dysfunction.

Prospective Memory and Aging

In the aging domain, Craik (1986) hypothesized that prospective memory should be particularly susceptible to the effects of aging because of its demand on self-initiated retrieval processes. Because prospective memory tasks provide little in the way of environmental support or cue information, older subjects must initiate mnemonic activities spontaneously. According to Craik, the initiation of such processes requires considerable resource and elderly adults should therefore be impaired on prospective memory tasks.

In line with this prediction, several studies reported age-related impairments on prospective memory tasks (Dobbs & Rule, 1987; West, 1988). Other studies, however, failed to find age deficits or have found reverse age effects (Einstein & McDaniel, 1990; Maylor, 1990; Moscovitch, 1982; Patton & Meit, 1993; West, 1988). In several of these latter studies, external cues or aids were available as prompts for performance of the prospective task. The presence of such cues may well have reduced the need for self-initiated retrieval processes, thus eliminating age deficits.

Einstein and McDaniel (1990; McDaniel & Einstein, 1992) suggested a similar explanation to account for the lack of age differences in what they have termed *event-based prospective memory tasks*. These investigators, in an attempt to extend and test Craik's theoretical framework, developed two kinds of prospective memory tasks that they claim differ in the extent to which they rely on self-initiated retrieval processes. Event-based prospective tasks, in which subjects are required to respond to a particular cue, may demand little in the way of self-initiated retrieval processes; *time-based tasks*, on the other hand, in which subjects are required to monitor a clock in order to respond at a particular time, require subjects to initiate monitoring behavior on their own and to decide when to respond. According to Craik's (1986) formulation, age-related decrements should therefore be exhibited in time-based tasks but not in event-based tasks. That is exactly what was found (Einstein & McDaniel, 1990; Einstein, McDaniel, Richardson, Guynn, & Cunfer, in press).

Although event-based and time-based prospective memory tasks differ with respect to demands placed upon self-initiated retrieval processes, they also differ in their reliance on a number of other frontally based processes, any of which might account for the differential age effects across tasks. For example, time-based tasks require memory for temporal information, time estimation abilities, strategic planning, environmental monitoring and divided attention. Event-based tasks lack a temporal memory component or the need for time estimation, may require less in the way of strategic planning, and generally involve less division of attention because the cue is usually embedded in the primary task. Thus some event-based tasks may require less input from prefrontal cortex than do the time-based tasks, and thereby fail to show age-related deficits. If this analysis is correct, performance on time-based tasks should correlate with other measures of frontal lobe function and with tests of retrospective memory that rely on frontal control, whereas performance on event-based tasks may not.

Although Einstein and McDaniel (1990) did not find age differences in their event-based prospective memory task, other researchers did so. For example, West (1988) reported that older adults were impaired in prospective memory tasks despite available external cues (i.e., event-based tasks). The cues, however, may not have been particularly salient or distinctive so that subjects may have had to rely on other strategic processes in order to be successful. West suggested that cues must stand out against background context or have high "attention-grabbing" qualities in order for them to be useful for older adults. Consistent with this notion, Einstein and McDaniel (1990; McDaniel & Einstein, 1993) demonstrated that distinctive or salient cues substantially improved the performance of young and old subjects in an event-based task.

The inconsistent findings with older adults on prospective memory tasks may be attributable to the differential demands on frontal lobe functioning across tasks and to individual differences among the elderly with respect to integrity of the frontal lobes. If this is the case, older adults who show few signs of frontal deterioration should show little impairment on prospective memory tests. On the other hand, those individuals with significant frontal lobe decline should be impaired in prospective memory, particularly on those tasks that rely most heavily on frontal function. On tasks that have a minimal frontal component, deficits should be reduced.

CONCLUDING REMARKS

A good part of the remembering we do in everyday life is prospective, yet we know little about how people remember future actions or intentions. Research suggests that some of the processes involved in prospective memory differ from those used in retrospective remembering and may involve functions attributable to the frontal lobes. But prospective memory may be multidimensional and may engage the frontal lobes to a greater or lesser degree depending on task demands.

Because of declining frontal lobe function with age, many older adults experience difficulty with certain prospective memory tasks—those in which cues are limited or lack precision, that place heaviest demands on working memory, that require strategic processes at either encoding or retrieval, and that involve time monitoring. The fact that studies of prospective memory did not always find age differences may be attributable to the differences in tasks across studies and to the fact that not all older adults experience equivalent frontal decline.

Two research strategies may help to extend our understanding of memory for future actions and to link the cognitive processes involved to their underlying brain structures: First, studies of patients with circumscribed brain lesions, particularly in frontal and hippocampal regions, may be able to isolate components of prospective memory tasks and to clarify their relation to retrospective tasks. For example, documenting the performance of frontal patients on a variety of prospective tasks may reveal whether all prospective tasks rely on the same frontal function, or whether different tasks tap independent frontal processes. Studies of hippocampal patients may indicate whether there is an essential relation between retrospective and prospective memory. If hippocampal patients perform normally on most prospective tasks (given a minimal retrospective component), the likelihood of shared processes between the two classes of tasks is reduced. The few studies that investigated patient populations tested patients with diffuse damage, such as occurs in dementia (Huppert & Beardsall, 1993) and are therefore subject to various interpretations.

A second approach to establishing more direct links between brain regions and cognitive activities involves the use of neuroimaging techniques that allow us to see the brain in action. Two types of imaging studies could be useful: First, imaging data from normal young adults may enable more precise localization within frontal cortex of the various components of prospective and retrospective memory. Second, functional images of aging brains may provide more direct evidence of the relation between decline in frontal lobe functioning and particular components of memory.

Whether the retrospective–prospective memory dichotomy will be as theoretically important as many of the other dichotomies in memory remains to be seen. The importance of the dichotomy will depend in part on the development of prospective memory research programs that address theoretical questions. This book outlines initial attempts in this direction and suggests that an understanding of the mechanisms involved in prospective memory will contribute to a broader understanding of memory processes in general.

ACKNOWLEDGMENTS

Preparation of this chapter was supported by National Institute on Aging Grant AG 09195. I am grateful to Maria Brandimonte, Mark McDaniel, and Michael Polster for helpful discussion of the ideas contained in this chapter.

REFERENCES

Anderson, S. W., Damasio, H., Jones, R. D., & Tranel, D. (1991). Wisconsin Card Sorting Test performance as a measure of frontal lobe damage. *Journal of Clinical and Experimental Neuropsychology, 13,* 909–922.

Atkinson, R. C., & Shiffrin, R. W. (1968). Human memory: A proposed system and its control processes. In K. W. Spence & J. T. Spence (Eds.), *The psychology of learning and motivation: Vol. 2* (pp. 89–195). New York: Academic Press.

Baddeley, A. D. (1986). *Working memory.* Oxford, England: Oxford University Press.

Baddeley, A. D. (1990). *Human memory.* Boston: Allyn & Bacon.

Baddeley, A. D., & Warrington, E. K. (1970). Amnesia and the distinction between long- and short-term memory. *Journal of Verbal Learning and Verbal Behavior, 9,* 176–189.

Baddeley, A. D., & Wilkins, A. J. (1984). Taking memory out of the laboratory. In J. E. Harris & P. E. Morris (Eds.), *Everyday memory, actions and absentmindedness* (pp. 1–17). London: Academic Press.

Baddeley, A., & Wilson, B. (1988). Frontal amnesia and the dysexecutive syndrome. *Brain and Cognition, 7,* 212–230.

Benton, A. L., & Hamsher, K. de S. (1976). *Multilingual Aphasia Examination [manual].* Iowa City: University of Iowa.

Brown, J. (1958). Some tests of the decay theory of immediate memory. *Quarterly Journal of Experimental Psychology, 10,* 12–21.

Cavanaugh, J. C. (1989). The importance of awareness in memory aging. In L. W. Poon, D. C. Rubin & B. A. Wilson (Eds.), *Everyday cognition in adulthood and late life* (pp. 416–436). Cambridge, England: Cambridge University Press.

Coffey, C. E., Wilkinson, W. E., Parashos, I. A., Soady, S. A. R., Sullivan, R. J., Patterson, L. J., Figiel, G. S., Webb, M. C., Spritzer, C. E., & Djang, W. T. (1992). Quantitative cerebral anatomy of the aging human brain: A cross-sectional study using magnetic resonance imaging. *Neurology, 42,* 527- 536.

Cohen, G. (1989). *Memory in the real world.* Hillsdale, NJ: Lawrence Erlbaum Associates.

Cohen, N. J., & Squire, L. R. (1980). Preserved learning and retention of pattern-analyzing skill in amnesia: Dissociation of "knowing how" and "knowing that." *Science, 210,* 207–209.

Craik, F. I. M. (1986). A functional account of age differences in memory. In F. Klix & H. Hagendorf (Eds.), *Human memory and cognitive capabilities, mechanisms and performances* (pp. 409–422). Amsterdam: Elsevier.

Craik, F. I. M., (1994). Memory changes in normal aging. *Current Directions in Psychological Science, 3,* 155–158.

Craik, F. I. M., & Byrd, M. (1982). Aging and cognitive deficits: the role of attentional resources. In F. I. M. Craik & S. Trehub (Eds.), *Aging and cognitive processes* (pp. 191–211). New York: Plenum.

Craik, F. I. M., & Jennings, J. M. (1992). Human memory. In F. I. M. Craik & T. A. Salthouse (Eds.), *The handbook of aging and cognition* (pp. 51–110). Hillsdale, NJ: Lawrence Erlbaum Associates.

Craik, F. I. M., & McDowd, J. M. (1987). Age differences in recall and recognition. *Journal of Experimental Psychology: Learning, Memory, and Cognition, 13,* 474–479.

Craik, F. I. M., Morris, L. W., Morris, R. G., Loewen, E. R. (1990). Relations between source amnesia and frontal lobe functioning in older adults. *Psychology and Aging, 5,* 148–151.

Daigneault, S., Braun, C. M. J., & Whitaker, H. A. (1992). Early effects of normal aging on perseverative and non-perseverative prefrontal measures. *Developmental Neuropsychology, 8,* 99–114.

Damasio, A. R., & Anderson, S. W. (1993). The frontal lobes. In K. M. Heilman & E. Valenstein (Eds.), *Clinical neuropsychology* (pp. 409–460). New York: Oxford University Press.

Dobbs, A. R., & Rule, B. G. (1987). Prospective memory and self-reports of memory abilities in older adults. *Canadian Journal of Psychology, 41*, 209–222.

Dobbs, A. R., & Rule, B. G. (1989). Adult age differences in working memory. *Psychology and Aging, 4*, 500–503.

Einstein, G. O., Holland, L. J., McDaniel, M. A., & Guynn, M. J. (1992). Age-related deficits in prospective memory: The influence of task complexity. *Psychology and Aging, 7*, 471–478.

Einstein, G. O., & McDaniel, M. A. (1990). Normal aging and prospective memory. *Journal of Experimental Psychology: Learning, Memory, & Cognition, 16*, 717–726.

Einstein, G. O., McDaniel, M. A., Richardson, S. L., Guynn, M. J., & Cunfer, A. R. (in press). Aging and prospective memory: Examining the influences of self-initiated retrieval processes and mind wandering. *Journal of Experimental Psychology: Learning, Memory, and Cognition.*

Ferguson, S. A., Hashtroudi, S., & Johnson, M. K. (1992). Age differences in using source-relevant cues. *Psychology and Aging, 7*, 443–452.

Fuster, J. M. (1989). *The prefrontal cortex.* New York: Raven.

Gabrieli, J. D. E., Fleischman, D. A., Keane, M. M., Reminger, S. L., & Morrell, F. (1995). Double dissociation between memory systems underlying explicit and implicit memory in the human brain. *Psychological Science, 6*, 76–82

Goldberg, E., & Bilder, Jr., R. M. (1987). The frontal lobes and hierarchical organization of cognitive control. In E. Perecman (Ed.), *The frontal lobes revisited* (pp. 159–187). Hillsdale, NJ: Lawrence Erlbaum Associates.

Golden, C. J. (1978). *Stroop Color and Word Test.* Chicago: Stoelting.

Goldman-Rakic, P. S. (1991). The circuitry of working memory revealed by anatomy and metabolic imaging. In H. S. Levin, H. M. Eisenberg, & A. L. Benton (Eds.), *Frontal lobe function and dysfunction* (pp. 72–91). New York: Oxford University Press.

Goschke, T., & Kuhl, J. (1993). Representation of intentions: Persisting activation in memory. *Journal of Experimental Psychology: Learning, Memory, & Cognition, 19*, 1211–1226.

Graf, P., & Schacter, D. L. (1985). Implicit and explicit memory for new associations in normal and amnesic patients. *Journal of Experimental Psychology: Learning, Memory, and Cognition, 11*, 501–518.

Harris, J. E. (1984). Remembering to do things: a forgotten topic. In J. E. Harris & P. E. Morris (Eds.), *Everyday memory, actions and absentmindedness* (pp. 71–92). London: Academic Press.

Heaton, R. K. (1981). *Wisconsin Card Sorting Test [manual].* Odessa, FL: Psychological Assessment Resources.

Heindel, W. C., Butters, N., & Salmon, D. P. (1988). Impaired learning of a motor skill in patients with Huntington's disease. *Behavioral Neuroscience, 102*, 141–147.

Hirst, W., Johnson, M., Kim, J., Phelps, E., Risse, G., & Volpe, B. (1986). Recognition and recall in amnesics. *Journal of Experimental Psychology: Learning, Memory, and Cognition, 12*, 445–451.

Hitch, G. J., & Ferguson, J. (1991). Prospective memory for future intentions: Some comparisons with memory for past events. *European Journal of Cognitive Psychology, 3*(3), 285–295.

Huppert, F. A., & Beardsall, L. (1993). Prospective memory impairment as an early indicator of dementia. *Journal of Clinical and Experimental Neuropsychology, 15*(5), 805–821.

Incisa della Rocchetta, A. (1986). Classification and recall of pictures after unilateral frontal or temporal lobectomy. *Cortex, 22*, 189–211.

Ivy, G. O., MacLeod, C. M., Petit, T. L., & Marcus, E. J. (1992). A physiological framework for perceptual and cognitive changes in aging. In F. I. M. Craik & T. A. Salthouse (Eds.), *The handbook of aging and cognition* (pp. 273–314). Hillsdale, NJ: Lawrence Erlbaum Associates.

Jacoby, L. L. (1983). Remembering the data: Analyzing interactive processes in reading. *Journal of Verbal Learning and Verbal Behavior, 22*, 485–508.

Janowsky, J. S., Shimamura, A. P., Kritchevsky, M., & Squire, L. R. (1989). Cognitive impairment following frontal lobe damage and its relevance to human amnesia. *Behavioral Neuroscience, 103,* 548–560.

Janowsky, J. S., Shimamura, A. P., & Squire, L. R. (1989a). Memory and metamemory: Comparisons between patients with frontal lobe lesions and amnesic patients. *Psychobiology, 17*(1), 3–11.

Janowsky, J. S., Shimamura, A. P., & Squire, L. R. (1989b). Source memory impairment in patients with frontal lobe lesions. *Neuropsychologia, 27,* 1043–1056.

Jernigan, T. L., Archibald, S. L., Berhow, M. T., Sowell, E. R., Foster, D. S., & Hesselink, J. R. (1991). Cerebral structure on MRI, Part I: Localization of age-related changes. *Biological Psychiatry, 29,* 55–67.

Jetter, W., Poser, U., Freeman, Jr., R. B., & Markowitsch, H. J. (1986). A verbal long term memory deficit in frontal lobe damaged patients. *Cortex, 22,* 229–242.

Kausler, D. H., Lichty, W., & Davis, R. T. (1985). Temporal memory for performed activities: Intentionality and adult age differences. *Developmental Psychology, 21,* 1132–1138.

Kausler, D. H., & Puckett, J. M. (1981). Adult age differences in memory for sex of voice. *Journal of Gerontology, 36,* 44–50.

Kihlstrom, J. K., & Glisky, E. L. (1994). Amnesia. In V. S. Ramachandran (Ed.), *Encyclopedia of Human Behavior* (Vol. 1, pp. 113–123). San Diego, CA: Academic Press.

Kinsbourne, M., & Wood, F. (1975). Short term memory and the amnesic syndrome. In D. D. Deutsch & J. A. Deutsch (Eds.), *Short-term memory* (pp. 258–291). New York: Academic Press.

Koriat, A., Ben-Zur, H., & Nussbaum, A. (1990). Encoding information for future action: Memory for to-be-performed tasks versus memory for to-be-recalled tasks. *Memory & Cognition, 18,* 568–578.

Levin, H. S., Eisenberg, H. M., & Benton, A. L. (1991). *Frontal lobe function and dysfunction.* New York: Oxford University Press.

Lezak, M. D. (1983). *Neuropsychological assessment.* New York: Oxford University Press.

Loftus, E. (1971). Memory for intentions: The effect of presence of a cue and interpolated activity. *Psychonomic Science, 23*(4), 315–316.

Luria, A. R. (1966). *Higher cortical functions in man.* New York: Basic Books.

Luria, A. R. (1973). *The working brain.* New York: Basic Books.

Marchal, G., Rioux, P., Petit-Taboue, M. C., Sette, G., Travere, J. M., Le Poec, C., Courtheoux, P., Derlon, J. M., & Baron, J. C. (1992). Regional cerebral oxygen consumption, blood flow, and blood volume in healthy human aging. *Archives of Neurology, 49,* 1013–1020.

Martin, A. J., Friston, K. J., Colebatch, J. G., & Frackowiak, R. S. J. (1991). Decreases in regional cerebral blood flow with normal aging. *Journal of Cerebral Blood Flow and Metabolism, 11,* 684–689.

Mateer, C. A., Sohlberg, M. M., & Crinean, J. (1987). Focus on clinical research: Perceptions of memory function in individuals with closed-head injury. *Journal of Head Trauma Rehabilitation, 2,* 74–84.

Mayes, A. R. (1988). *Human organic memory disorders.* Cambridge, England: Cambridge University Press.

Maylor, E. A. (1990). Age and prospective memory. *The Quarterly Journal of Experimental Psychology, 42A,* 471–493.

McAndrews, M. P., & Milner, B. (1991). The frontal cortex and memory for temporal order. *Neuropsychologia, 29,* 849–859.

McDaniel, M. A., & Einstein, G. O. (1992). Aging and prospective memory: Basic findings and practical applications. In T. E. Scruggs & M. A. Mastropieri (Eds.), *Advances in learning and behavioral disabilities* (Vol. 8, pp. 87–105). Greenwich, CT: JAI Press.

McDaniel, M. A., & Einstein, G. O. (1993). The importance of cue familiarity and cue distinctiveness in prospective memory. *Memory, 1,* 23–41.

McDaniel, M. A., Glisky, E. L., Routhieaux, B. C., & Remers, L. (1994). The role of frontal lobe functioning in temporally-based and cue-based prospective remembering in older adults. Paper presented at the Cognitive Aging Conference, Atlanta, GA.

McGlynn, S. M. (1993). Metamemory and frontal lobe function in the elderly. *Dissertation Abstracts International, 53*(10–B), 5467.

McIntyre, J. S., & Craik, F. I. M. (1987). Age differences in memory for item and source information. *Canadian Journal of Psychology, 41,* 175–192.

Meacham, J. A., & Leiman, B. (1982). Remembering to perform future actions. In U. Neisser (Ed.), *Memory observed: Remembering in natural contexts* (pp. 327–336). San Francisco: Freeman.

Michalewski, H., Thompson, L., Smith, D., Patterson, J., Bowman, T., Litzelman, D., & Brent, G. (1980). Age differences in the contingent negative variation (CNV): Reduced frontal activity in the elderly. *Journal of Gerontology, 35*(4), 542–549.

Milner, B. (1964). Some effects of frontal lobectomy in man. In J. M. Warren & K. Akert (Eds.), *The frontal granular cortex and behavior* (pp. 313–334). New York: McGraw-Hill.

Milner, B. (1966). Amnesia following operation on the temporal lobes. In C. W. M. Whitty & O. L. Zangwill (Eds.), *Amnesia* (pp. 109–133). London: Butterworths.

Milner, B., Petrides, M., & Smith, M. L. (1985). Frontal lobes and the temporal organization of memory. *Human Neurobiology, 4,* 137–142.

Mittenberg, W., Seidenberg, M., O'Leary, D. S., & DiGiulio, D. V. (1989). Changes in cerebral functioning associated with normal aging. *Journal of Clinical and Experimental Neuropsychology, 11,* 918–933.

Moscovitch, M. (1982). A neuropsychological approach to perception and memory in normal and pathological aging. In F. I. M. Craik & S. Trehub (Eds.), *Aging and cognitive processes* (pp. 55–79). New York: Plenum.

Moscovitch, M., & Winocur, G. (1992). The neuropsychology of memory and aging. In F. I. M. Craik & T. A. Salthouse (Eds.), *The handbook of aging and cognition* (pp. 315–372). Hillsdale, NJ: Lawrence Erlbaum Associates.

Parkin, A. J., & Walter, B. M. (1992). Recollective experience, normal aging, and frontal dysfunction. *Psychology and Aging, 7,* 290–298.

Patton, G. W. R., & Meit, M. (1993). Effect of aging on prospective and incidental memory. *Experimental Aging Research, 19,* 165–176.

Perecman, E. (1987). *The frontal lobes revisited.* Hillsdale, NJ: Lawrence Erlbaum Associates.

Peterson, L. R., & Peterson, M. J. (1959). Short-term retention of individual verbal items. *Journal of Experimental Psychology, 58,* 193–198.

Petrides, M. (1989). In F. Boller & J. Grafman (Eds.), *Handbook of neuropsychology: Vol. 3* (pp. 75–90). Amsterdam: Elsevier.

Petrides, M., & Milner, B. (1982). Deficits on subject-ordered tasks after frontal- and temporal-lobe lesions in man. *Neuropsychologia, 20,* 249–262.

Porteus, S. D. (1965). *Porteus Maze Test, fifty years application.* Palo Alto, CA: Pacific.

Rabinowitz, J. C., Craik, F. I. M., & Ackerman, B. P. (1982). A processing resource account of age differences in recall. *Canadian Journal of Psychology, 36,* 325–344.

Richardson-Klavehn, A., & Bjork, R. A. (1988). Measures of memory. *Annual Review of Psychology, 39,* 475–543.

Roediger, H. L., III, Weldon, M. S., & Challis, B. H. (1989). Explaining dissociations between implicit and explicit measures of retention: A processing account. In H. L. Roediger III & F. I. M. Craik (Eds.), *Varieties of memory and consciousness: Essays in honor of Endel Tulving* (pp. 3–41). Hillsdale, NJ: Lawrence Erlbaum Associates.

Salthouse, T. A. (1988). Resource-reduction interpretations of cognitive aging. *Developmental Review, 8,* 238–272.

Salthouse, T. A., & Babcock, R. L. (1991). Decomposing adult age differences in working memory. *Developmental Psychology, 27,* 763–776.

Schacter, D. L. (1987). Memory, amnesia, and frontal lobe dysfunction. *Psychobiology, 15,* 21–36.

Schacter, D. L., Chiu, C. Y. P., & Ochsner, K. N. (1993). Implicit memory: A selective review. *Annual Review of Neuroscience, 16,* 159–182.

Schacter, D. L., Kaszniak, A. W., Kihlstrom, J. F., & Valdiserri, M. (1991). The relation between source memory and aging. *Psychology and Aging, 6,* 559–568.

Shallice, T. (1982). Specific impairments of planning. *Philosophical Transactions of the Royal Society of London, B, 298,* 199–209.

Shimamura, A. P. (1989). Disorders of memory: The cognitive science perspective. In F. Boller & J. Grafman (Eds.), *Handbook of neuropsychology: Vol. 3* (pp. 35–73). Amsterdam: Elsevier.

Shimamura, A. P. (1994). Memory and frontal lobe function. In M. S. Gazzaniga (Ed.), *The Cognitive Neurosciences* (pp. 803–813). Cambridge: MIT Press.

Shimamura, A. P., Janowsky, J. S., & Squire, L. R. (1990). Memory for temporal order in patients with frontal lobe lesions and patients with amnesia. *Neuropsychologia, 28,* 803–813.

Shimamura, A. P., Janowsky, J. S., & Squire, L. R. (1991). What is the role of frontal lobe damage in memory disorders? In H. S. Levin, H. M. Eisenberg, & A. L. Benton (Eds.), *Frontal lobe function and dysfunction* (pp. 173–195). New York: Oxford University Press.

Smith, M. L., & Milner, B. (1988). Estimation of frequency of occurrence of abstract designs after frontal or temporal lobectomy. *Neuropsychologia, 26,* 297–306.

Spencer, W. D., & Raz, N. (1994). Memory for facts, source and context: Can frontal lobe dysfunction explain age-related differences? *Psychology and Aging, 9,* 149–159.

Squire, L. R. (1987). *Memory and brain.* New York: Oxford University Press.

Squire, L. R., & Butters, N. (1992). *Neuropsychology of memory (2nd ed.).* New York: Guilford.

Stuss, D. T. (1991). Interference effects on memory functions in postleukotomy patients: An attentional perspective. In H. S. Levin, H. M. Eisenberg, & A. L Benton (Eds.), *Frontal lobe function and dsyfunction* (pp. 157–172). New York: Oxford University Press.

Stuss, D. T., & Benson, D. F. (1984). Neuropsychological studies of the frontal lobes. *Psychological Bulletin, 95,* 3–28.

Stuss, D. T., & Benson, D. F. (1986). *The frontal lobes.* New York: Raven.

Stuss, D. T., & Benson, D. F. (1987). The frontal lobes and control of cognition and memory. In E. Perecman (Ed.), *The frontal lobes revisited* (pp. 141–158). Hillsdale, NJ: Lawrence Erlbaum Associates.

Tulving, E. (1972). Episodic and semantic memory. In E. Tulving & W. Donaldson (Eds.), *Organization of memory* (pp. 381–403). New York: Academic Press.

Vilkki, J., & Holst, P. (1989). Deficient programming in spatial learning after frontal lobe damage. *Neuropsychologia, 27,* 971–976.

Warrington, E. K. (1975). The selective impairment of semantic memory. *Quarterly Journal of Experimental Psychology, 27,* 187–199.

Warrington, E. K., & Shallice, T. (1969). The selective impairment of auditory verbal short-term memory. *Brain, 92,* 885–896.

Waugh, N. C., & Norman, D. A. (1965). Primary memory. *Psychological Review, 72,* 89–104.

Weinberger, D. R. (1993). A connectionist approach to the prefrontal cortex. *Journal of Neuropsychiatry and Clinical Neurosciences, 5,* 241–253.

West, R. L. (1988). Prospective memory and aging. In M. M. Gruneberg, P. E. Morris & R. N. Sykes (Eds.), *Practical aspects of memory: Current research and issues* (Vol. 2, pp. 119–125). Chichester, England: Wiley.

Wilkins, A. J., & Baddeley, A. D. (1978). Remembering to recall in everyday life: an approach to absentmindedness. In M. M. Gruneberg, P. E. Morris & R. N. Sykes (Eds.), *Practical aspects of memory* (pp. 27–34). London: Academic Press.

14

A Preliminary Theory of the Interactions Between Prefrontal Cortex and Hippocampus that Contribute to Planning and Prospective Memory

Jonathan D. Cohen
Carnegie Mellon University
University of Pittsburgh

Randall C. O'Reilly
Carnegie Mellon University

This chapter addresses the neurobiological mechanisms that may underlie prospective memory. In our work, we have exploited the use of computational modeling techniques to help identify the role that specific brain structures play in cognition. In particular, we have used such techniques to characterize the function of prefrontal cortex and hippocampus in terms of specific processing mechanisms. This work suggests that an important function of prefrontal cortex is the representation and maintenance of *contextual information*—information that must be held in mind in such a form that it can be used to mediate an appropriate behavioral response. At the same time, our work supports the idea that an important function of the hippocampus is to rapidly establish novel associations, that can also be used to guide behavior. In our view, prospective memory reflects the interaction between these two systems, allowing established sequences of behavior to be associated with new conditions—in effect, providing a mechanism for planning.

Consider the following situation: You open the refrigerator one morning and discover that you are out of orange juice. You make a mental note to stop by the grocery store on the way home from work, and then "put it out of mind." Five o'clock rolls around, and as you are leaving your office, you think to yourself: "Right, the grocery store," and stop by to pick up the orange juice on your way home. The remarkable thing is that during the day you may not have thought about the errand at all. Somehow, you magically remember it, and manage to perform it at the appropriate time. We hypothesize that this reflects an interaction between the prefrontal cortex and hippocampal systems in the following way. When you first recognize that you need to go to the grocery store, you decide to do so within a particular context—after work. We assume this process involves the activation of representations of the action plan (going to the grocery store) as well as the context in which it is to take place (e.g., the end of the work day). We assume, furthermore, that prefrontal cortex is responsible for eliciting these representations, and that the hippocampus is responsible for encoding an association between them. Once this is done, the activity of the representations fades. As the end of the day comes, the environment elicits representations—darkness outside, clock striking 5:00, and so on—that are closely associated with "end of the work day." This activates the action plan by way of the hippocampal association that was established that morning. The action plan is then maintained by prefrontal cortex, and the behavior is executed.

This example illustrates how we believe that interactions between prefrontal cortex and hippocampus can support both the scheduling and elicitation of plans of action. Although planning is probably the most common reflection of the operation of the prefrontal cortex–hippocampal system in daily life, we believe this system is centrally involved in a number of standard laboratory tasks, which can be used to test hypotheses concerning this system's function. We will return to these in the general discussion.

In the sections that follow, we review both empirical and computational modeling work that bears on the function of prefrontal cortex and hippocampus. This work provides a basis for the assumptions, both implicit and explicit, present in the example. We begin by reviewing work that suggests prefrontal cortex plays an important role in representing and maintaining context representations. We then turn to the hippocampus, and review research indicating that it is responsible for encoding novel associations, and for using these to activate corresponding representations within association cortex. We conclude by considering how these two systems can be integrated to provide a mechanistic account of prospective memory, discuss how this account can shed light on traditional distinctions between controlled and automatic processes, and describe predictions our account makes for performance in a set of classical learning tasks.

FUNCTIONS OF PREFRONTAL CORTEX AND HIPPOCAMPUS

Functions of Prefrontal Cortex

Prefrontal cortex is the area of the human brain most significantly expanded relative to other animals. There is general consensus that prefrontal cortex is centrally involved in higher cognitive activities such as planning, problem solving and language. However, despite this consensus, there is little discussion of the specific information-processing mechanisms subserved by prefrontal cortex that contribute to these cognitive activities. Theorists have attributed many general functions to the frontal lobes, such as attention (Ferrier, 1886), abstract intelligence (Hitzig, 1874), and synthesis of percepts (Bianchi, 1922). Attention seems to have recently focused on two information-processing functions—inhibition and working memory (Fuster, 1989; Goldman-Rakic, 1987; Mishkin, 1964; Petrides & Milner, 1982). We briefly review the literature concerning these two functions of prefrontal cortex, and then describe recent work we have conducted using computational models of prefrontal cortex function, suggesting that these two functions reflect the operation of a single underlying information-processing mechanism that is responsible for representing and maintaining context information.

Inhibition. Traditionally, lesions of prefrontal cortex were associated with a clinical syndrome of behavioral disinhibition, in which subjects exhibit impulsive, socially inappropriate behavior (Hecaen & Albert, 1978; Stuss & Benson, 1984). Abnormalities of frontal cortex (mostly orbital) were implicated in clinical disorders involving forms of behavioral or cognitive disinhibition, such as attention deficit disorder with hyperactivity (Gorenstein, Mammato, & Sandy, 1989) and obsessive–compulsive disorder (Swedo et al., 1989). These phenomena were often cited as evidence that prefrontal cortex plays an important role in mediating socially appropriate behavior, by inhibiting compelling but inappropriate behaviors. Neuropsychological and neurodevelopmental data support this view: Patients with damage to prefrontal cortex exhibit perseverative behavior (i.e., a tendency toward prepotent but inappropriate responses) in tests such as the Wisconsin Card Sort Task (WCST; Grant & Berg, 1948) and Stroop Color–Word test (Stroop, 1935). Schizophrenics, who are believed to have deficits of prefrontal cortex, also exhibit prepotent response tendencies in a variety of tasks (see Cohen & Servan-Schreiber, 1992 for a review). Furthermore, Diamond and her colleagues (Diamond, 1990a; Diamond & Doar, 1989; Diamond & Goldman-Rakic, 1989) showed that human and monkey infants fail to inhibit prepotent response tendencies in developmental tasks such as the A-not-B. Diamond cited extensive data from lesion studies in adult monkeys and from developmental studies in human and monkey infants that use a variety of behavioral tasks (including object retrieval, visual paired comparisons, delayed response, and the A-not-B task). Results from these and many previous studies suggest that prefrontal cortex is directly involved in maintaining representations (e.g., the location of a hidden object) that are required to inhibit reflexive, dominant, or habitually reinforced behaviors (e.g., return to the most recently rewarded location) in order to attain a goal.

The performance deficits observed for infants and frontally lesioned monkeys on delay tasks are similar to those observed for adult frontal lobe patients on the WCST. In this task, subjects are presented with a series of cards containing figures that vary in shape, color, and number. They are asked to sort the cards into piles according to a rule that the experimenter has in mind (e.g., separate the cards by color). However, subjects are not told the rule for sorting; rather, they are given feedback for each card as to whether or not they sorted it properly. Normal subjects discover the rule quickly. Once they demonstrate they know it (i.e., by correctly sorting a certain number of cards in a row) the experimenter switches the rule, and the subject is required to discover the new rule. Patients with damage to the frontal lobes do poorly on this task (e.g., Milner, 1963; Nelson, 1976; Robinson, Heaton, Lehman, & Stilson, 1980). Although they are able to discover the first rule without much difficulty, they are unable to switch to a new one: They continue to sort according to the old rule. As in delay tasks, this is a failure to overcome a response pattern that was correct on previous trials. Furthermore, there are additional indications from these tasks that a specific failure to control behavior is involved in these tasks, as distinct from a disturbance in declarative, or short-term memory. In both the WCST and in delayed response tasks, some subjects show perseveratory behavior despite indications that they remember the relevant prior information. Thus, subjects in the WCST sometimes comment that they know their perseveratory response is incorrect even as it is carried out (Goldberg, Weinberger, Berman, Pliskin, & Podd, 1987). In the A-not-B task, some subjects look at the cued (new) location, while reaching for the old (incorrect) one (Diamond & Goldman-Rakic, 1989). These kinds of observations support a dissociation between declarative or short-term memory and the kinds of representations stored in prefrontal cortex that are needed to actually control the response. We return to this point in discussing the specific processing mechanisms subserved by prefrontal cortex.

In both the WCST and A-not-B task, subjects with poor prefrontal function are not impaired in their ability to learn the basic elements of the task. Rather, they are impaired in their ability to use an internal representation of context to override the effects of prior experience in the task. This characterization of frontal lobe function fits well with clinical descriptions of the *disinhibition syndrome* that often accompanies frontal lobe pathology (e.g., Stuss & Benson, 1984). It is also consistent with difficulties observed for frontal lobe patients in performing the Stroop task (Perret, 1974) and similar tasks in clinical use (e.g., the "go–no-go" paradigm) that require the subject to use task instructions to inhibit a dominant response tendency.

Working Memory.   Studies of nonhuman primates provide strong evidence that certain areas of prefrontal cortex are centrally involved in *working memory*. Working memory is typically defined as the maintenance of active representations of task-relevant information needed to mediate an appropriate response. Specific regions of prefrontal cortex have been implicated in memory for spatial and, more recently, object information. For example, in neurophysiological studies, Fuster (1980, 1985a, 1985b), Goldman-Rakic (1987) and others (e.g., Barone & Joseph, 1989) observed cells in prefrontal cortex that are specific to a particular stimulus and response, and that remain active during a delay between these. They argued that neural patterns of activity are maintained in prefrontal cortex that encode the temporary information needed to guide a response. Furthermore, structural and neuropharmacological lesions along the superior margin of the principal sulcus in the monkey produce spatially specific deficits in memory-guided, but not sensory-guided, performance. That is, deficits occur only when the animal must remember a target location over a delay prior to responding, but not when the location is marked by a continuous visual cue during the delay. Other regions of prefrontal cortex support memory for object-related information, such as the color or shape of a stimulus (Wilson et al., 1993). These authors and others (e.g., Damasio, 1979; Mishkin & Pribram, 1955; Passingham, 1985; Rosenkilde, 1979; Rosvold, Szwarcbart, Mirsky & Mishkin, 1961; Stuss & Benson, 1986) suggested that prefrontal cortex is needed to perform tasks involving delayed responses to stimuli.

Neuroimaging data from normal human subjects also provide support for the role of frontal cortex in working memory. A number of PET studies have shown activation of prefrontal cortex during a variety of tasks that appear to rely on working memory. Thus, studies of digit-span (Becker, Mintun, Diehl, DeKosky, & Dobkin, 1993; Grasby et al., 1993) and spatial stimuli (Jonides et al., 1993), of the ability to maintain information about the temporal order of sequential stimuli (Petrides et al., 1993), and of face recognition (Haxby et al., 1993) all demonstrate activation of prefrontal cortex—typically localized to Brodmann's area 46, which is one of the areas associated with working memory in nonhuman primates (e.g., Goldman-Rakic, 1987). Functional magnetic resonance imaging studies provide similar results, for both spatial (Blamire, McCarthy, Bloch, Rothman, & Shulman, 1993) and nonspatial (Cohen et al., 1994) stimuli.

Computer Simulation Models of Prefrontal Cortex Function: Processing of Context. We used computational models to address the function of prefrontal cortex. Based on this work, we proposed that inhibition and working memory reflect the operation of a single underlying processing mechanism that represents and maintains context information (Cohen & Servan-Schreiber, 1992). By context information, we mean information that must be held in mind in such a form that it can be used to mediate an appropriate behavioral response. By this definition, context information is relevant to but does not necessarily form part of the content of the actual response. This distinguishes context information from the kind of information traditionally thought to be stored in short-term memory (i.e., recently presented information, the specific identity of which must soon be retrieved). The role of context information is to enhance and/or maintain information relevant to task performance in the pathways responsible for processing that information. Another way of stating this, that we find useful further on, is that context representations serve to bias processing in favor of information relevant to the task at hand.

According to our hypothesis, memory and inhibition reflect the operation of the context processing mechanism under different task conditions. When strong competing response tendencies must be overcome for appropriate behavior, then context mechanisms play an inhibitory role by selectively enhancing processing in the task-relevant pathway relative to processing in the competing pathway. When there is a delay between information relevant to a response and the execution of that response, then context mechanisms play a memory role, by actively maintaining that information, and supporting it against the cumulative effects of noise. In both cases, the context mechanism is still performing the same basic function: supporting representations necessary to perform the task, and that may be stored elsewhere in cortex, against sources of interference. In the case of inhibition tasks, the interference is from an explicit, competing process; in memory tasks, interference comes from the degrading effects of noise.

We used computer simulation models to demonstrate how a single mechanism for representing context can perform both of these functions (Cohen & Servan-Schreiber, 1992). These models were developed within the parallel distributed processing (PDP) framework (Rumelhart & McClelland, 1986), in which information is represented as patterns of activation over simple processing units, and information processing takes place through the spread of activation between modules made up of such units. We used these models to simulate quantitative aspects of human performance in a variety of attention and language tasks that involve overcoming interference to respond appropriately. In each model, prefrontal cortex is represented by a module responsible for representing and maintaining context information, supporting the processing of task-relevant information over sources of interference.

For example, one model simulates human subjects' ability to interpret the meaning of ambiguous words (such as *pen*) given the context of the sentence in which they occur (e.g., "In order to keep chickens you need a pen"). This model (Fig. 14.1) contains modules for representing the individual words of the sentence (the *input* module), the meaning that the subject might report for each (the *output* module), and the topic, or overall meaning of the sentence (the *discourse* module). Words in the sentence are presented to the model one by one. Bottom-up connections in the model allow each word to contribute to the activation of an appropriate discourse representation. Top-down connections allow this representation to influence the interpretation of subsequent words. Thus, when words such as *chicken* or *farmer* are presented,

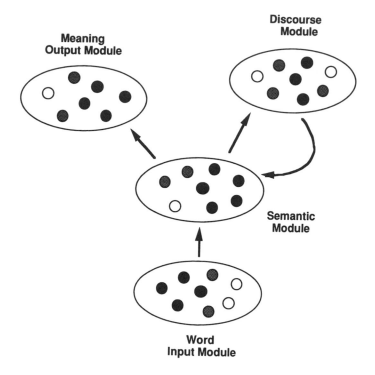

FIG. 14.1.   Simulation model of a lexical disambiguation task. Patterns of activation over the units in the input module are assumed to represent the current sensory stimulus (e.g., the orthographic code for a written word), whereas the output module is assumed to represent the information necessary to generate an overt response (e.g., the phonological code needed to pronounce the meaning of the word). Note that the connections between the semantic and discourse modules are bidirectional, allowing stimuli to help establish a discourse representation, acting as context that governs the processing of subsequent stimuli.

they activate a discourse representation related to farming, which then helps to select the weaker, but contextually appropriate meaning of an ambiguous word like *pen* (i.e., fenced enclosure), rather than its more frequent meaning (writing implement). The discourse module serves to represent and maintain context information, and so functions as the context processing mechanism. In models of delay tasks—in which the correct response to a target stimulus depends upon prior information—the module identified with prefrontal cortex is responsible for maintaining this information against the cumulative effects of noise. By introducing a specific lesion to this module, we were able to quantitatively account for the performance in these tasks of patients with schizophrenia, who are believed to have disturbances of frontal lobe function (Cohen & Servan-Schreiber, 1992). Most recently, we used the models to predict specific behavioral deficits that should arise in patients with differing degrees of disturbance to prefrontal cortex. These predictions were corroborated by a comparative study of first episode and multiepisode schizophrenics (Servan-Schreiber, Cohen, & Steingard, in submission).

In summary, neurophysiological and neuroimaging data suggest that prefrontal cortex plays an important role in both behavioral inhibition and working memory. Using computer simulation models, we showed that a single mechanism responsible for the representation and maintenance of context information can subserve both inhibition and memory in cognitive tasks. That is, rather than reflecting the operation of two separate mechanisms, memory and inhibition reflect the influence of two factors that characterize cognitive tasks—the relative dominance of task-relevant processes compared to competing ones, and the temporal extent over which these processes operate. The context processing mechanism is sensitive to both of these factors. Its primary function is to protect task relevant processes against the effects of interference, which can come either from competing, dominant processes, or from the effects of noise that accumulate over delays.

We suggest that prefrontal cortex may house such a context processing mechanism. This could account for the involvement of frontal cortex in goal-oriented activity; that is, the planning and sequencing of complex actions (e.g., Bianchi, 1922; Duncan, 1986; Luria, 1969; Shallice, 1982). The construction and maintenance of internal representations of context are an important component of these faculties. The actions associated with a particular goal may, in other situations, be relatively infrequent or weak behaviors. Such actions require the maintenance of an internal representation of the goal, or of goal-related knowledge to favor their execution (i.e., to suppress competing, possibly more compelling behaviors, or to sustain them over temporal delays). Thus, context representations maintained by prefrontal cortex can function as a plan that helps govern the execution of goal-directed behaviors. We think of plans as constituting just such sets of context representations, and wherever we use the term *plan* this is how we mean it—as a set of context representations maintained in prefrontal cortex that support the execution of actions directed toward a goal. We return to this point in a later section, when we discuss the interactions between prefrontal cortex and hippocampus that we believe underlie prospective memory.

In the section that follows, we discuss the information-processing functions of the hippocampus. Before we do so, it will be helpful to say one more thing about the use of the term context. We argue that the representation of context is an important, if not the central function of prefrontal cortex. However, those familiar with the animal learning literature on hippocampal function will know that hippocampus is thought to be necessary for context-sensitive learning.

This use of the term is slightly different than the way we use it. In this case, context refers to features of the environment, that can become associated with an identified stimulus and influence responses to it. As we use the term, with regard to prefrontal cortex function, it refers to internal representations that can influence processing. Of course, these are not unrelated concepts: In both cases, one source of information (whether external stimuli or internal representations) is influencing the processing of another. The relationship between these, and the involvement of hippocampus and prefrontal cortex in processing each will be taken up further on. For now, in order to be clear about which type of context we mean, we refer to external elements of context as the environment, whereas we continue to refer to internal context representations simply as context.

Complementary Memory Systems in Hippocampus and Neocortex

Evidence indicates that the hippocampus plays a unique role in the formation and retrieval of memories (see Squire, 1992 for a review). A theoretical perspective on the hippocampus proposed in McClelland, McNaugton, and O'Reilly (in press; also see McClelland, McNaughton, O'Reilly, & Nadel, 1992) provides a framework for understanding this unique role, especially in terms of the relationship between the hippocampus and the neocortex. This approach follows Marr (1971) and many others in proposing that the hippocampus is part of a dual memory system consisting of cortical and hippocampal components.

In brief, we propose that the cortex is responsible for developing a stable, efficient, and general framework for representing and encoding information, whereas the hippocampus is responsible for rapidly storing the contents of specific episodes or events, thought to correspond to particular states of the cortical system. The critical distinctions between these forms of learning are the temporal duration underlying the formation of the representations, and the relationship to other representations in the system. In the temporal dimension, the hippocampus must form and rapidly store its representations (in order to capture and bind together temporally coincident events in one memory), whereas the cortex must adapt slowly in order to capture the relevant general structure common to different samples of the environment.

How do representations relate to other memories or representations in the system? We assume that hippocampal representations must be kept distinct, so that specific events with many similar features (e.g., where you parked your car today as opposed to yesterday or the day before, etc.) can be recalled without undue interference from similar memories. For the cortex to exploit the shared structure present in ensembles of events and experiences it must assign similar internal representations to similar events, and to do so it must make the representations overlap. To summarize the differences between these two systems, we label the hippocampal system as performing *rapid, arbitrary learning,* where the term arbitrary denotes that the representation does not capture structural relationships between the components of the representation. Conversely, the neocortical system performs *long-term, integrative learning.*

Experimental data in support of the idea that the hippocampus is responsible for a particular kind of memory is vast and goes back to the seminal work of Scoville & Milner (1957) who described the severe anterograde amnesia produced by bilateral removal of the hippocampus in patient HM. Squire (1992) presented a review of the literature, and argued for understanding the difference between the hippocampus and neocortex in terms of declarative versus nondeclarative memory. Although we argue that this terminology does not capture precisely the distinctions described above, there is a great deal of overlap between them. In particular, Squire (1992) described the role of the hippocampus as one of rapidly binding together representations in the cortex. This view is consistent with the data showing an impairment in amnesic subjects for both *paired-associate* and *episodic memory tasks,* among others (see Squire, 1992). Paired-associate learning requires the subject to rapidly form an association between two words that are otherwise unrelated, so as to be able to recall one of the words when given the other as a cue. Episodic memory (Tulving, 1983) refers to the ability to remember particular episodes or events of daily life that due to their transient nature, must be learned rapidly and require the binding together of the individual features of the event (e.g., visual appearance of the place, representations of what was happening at the time, etc.).

Examples of forms of learning that are spared in amnesic subjects provide evidence consistent with our characterization of neocortical learning. These include gradually acquired skills that emerge over several sessions of practice, such as the skill of tracing a figure viewed in a mirror (Milner (1966), and reading mirror-reversed print (Cohen & Squire, 1980). At a more cognitive level, amnesic subjects reliably show repetition priming for familiar items such as known words (Graf, Squire, & Mandler, 1984), but not for completely novel items such as in the paired-associate task described (Shimamura & Squire, 1989). Although it was shown that priming can be obtained in hippocampal subjects for novel material of various forms, this is due to the priming of the low-level perceptual representations and not the novel semantic-level information (Schacter, Delaney, & Merikle, 1990). The neocortical representations of familiar things can be facilitated by recent exposure (priming), but the neocortex cannot rapidly form novel representations. Because the visual system is capable of representing novel material without forming new representations, priming is seen at this level but not at a higher level. These results support the characterization of the neocortex as a slow learning system.

Insights as to why the brain might have two complementary learning systems can be obtained from the successes and failures of neural-network or connectionist models of learning (Rumelhart, Hinton & Williams, 1986). For example, our view of cortical learning and representation is captured by models that develop representations of the overall structure of experience through a gradual learning process, relying on repeated samples of inputs drawn from an environment (White 1989). However, these same networks exhibit *catastrophic interference* (McCloskey & Cohen, 1989) with what is already stored in the system when they are forced to rapidly learn new associations. There are many reasons to think that this result reflects a fundamental trade-off between long-term integrative learning and rapid, arbitrary learning (see McClelland et al., in press).

One of the consequences of a dual memory system of this form is that certain kinds of information (conjunctive information that must be quickly learned) are learned and initially stored in the hippocampus. Consequently, this information must also be retrieved from the hippocampus. Thus, the storage and retrieval properties of the hippocampus will play a large role in tasks that require the rapid storage of conjunctive information. As we discuss in more detail later, prospective memory relies on storing novel conjunctions of various cortical representations, and is therefore partially dependent on the hippocampus. Thus, we consider the properties of storage and recall in the hippocampus.

Pattern Separation and Completion in the Hippocampus: A Trade-off. Pattern separation is the mechanism by which the hippocampus is able to store conjunctive representations rapidly and without undue interference, and pattern completion is the mechanism by which previously stored representations in the hippocampus are recalled. O'Reilly and McClelland (1994) examined these properties using an analytical model that incorporated the broad anatomical and physiological features of the hippocampus. In particular, we focused on the intrinsic trade-off that exists between separation and completion, arising because pattern separation causes similar input patterns to give rise to distinct, separated representations, whereas pattern completion causes similar input patterns to give rise to a common (recalled) representation. We cannot simultaneously perform separation and completion, and so a trade-off between these two processes must be made. In other words, when faced with a stimulus that is similar to, but not identical to some familiar stimulus, a decision must be made. Is the current stimulus a noisy or partial version of the familiar one, in which case completion is the appropriate choice, or is this a genuinely new stimulus, in which case separation is the appropriate choice?

Having a concrete computational framework for examining the performance characteristics of these processes, O'Reilly and McClelland (1994) were able to quantitatively evaluate the ways in which the hippocampus might avoid or minimize the effects of the trade-off. They hypothesized that the distinctive anatomical and physiological properties of the hippocampus exist so as to avoid (as much as possible) this intrinsic trade-off. The results indicate that indeed the structure of the hippocampus does make sense when viewed in terms of improving the characteristics of this trade-off.

Without going into the anatomical or computational details, we can use this data from O'Reilly and McClelland (1994) as a basis for understanding when patterns of activity over the neocortex will lead to the recall of representations from the hippocampus, and when new hippocampal representations will be stored. In general, the relevant dimension for deciding between storage and recall is the relative similarity of patterns of activity over the region of the brain that provides the primary cortical input into the hippocampus, known as the Entorhinal Cortex (EC). We assume that the EC activity reflects the activity patterns over wide areas of the neocortex. When an input pattern closely resembles a previously stored one, it will trigger the recall of that pattern. When it is sufficiently distinct from other patterns, a new representation will be formed. However, other factors are undoubtedly relevant, including emotional state and arousal level, attention, and task demands.

With the caveat that they form only part of the overall picture, we examine the pattern separation–completion trade-off results from O'Reilly and McClelland. Figure 14.2 shows pattern completion and separation for the best overall compromise between the two. Judging from these results, the hippocampus would be capable of taking a relatively small fragment (around 30% of the original pattern) and completing a substantial portion of the original pattern (around 80%), while being able to keep reasonably separate patterns that overlap to around 60%. These results are just for the feed-forward pathway from the EC to hippocampal area CA3, and it is widely thought that the recurrent collateral pathway within area CA3 would be capable of performing significant pattern completion on top of that performed by the feed-forward pathway (McNaughton & Morris, 1987). This CA3 completion would have the effect of introducing a threshold, above which the input pattern would get drawn into the nearest familiar attractor state. Estimates of the value of this threshold depend on various parameters, most of which are not sufficiently constrained by the known neurophysiology, but it is probably between 50% to 80%.

To summarize, the O'Reilly and McClelland (1994) results show that the hippocampus could be capable of either recalling a stored pattern with a reasonably small portion of the original pattern as a cue, or separating full input patterns that are similar so that they may be learned rapidly without interference. Although the precise numerical parameters governing these processes are not known, the qualitative relationship between completion and separation can be estimated from results such as those shown in Fig. 14.2. It is important to emphasize the following points. First, whether the system performs recall or storage of new patterns is determined by the properties of the pattern on the EC, and not by some other unspecified control system (i.e., a "homuncu-

Hippocampal Pattern Completion and Separation

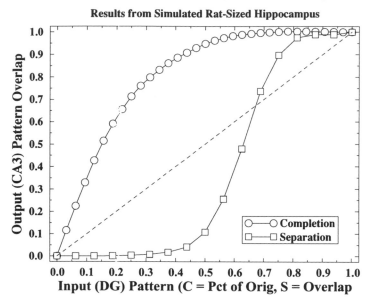

Results from Simulated Rat-Sized Hippocampus

FIG. 14.2.   Pattern completion and separation in the hippocampus as simulated in O'Reilly & McClelland (1994). For completion, the X axis represents the percent of the original pattern as a cue for retrieving the stored pattern. For separation, the X axis represents the degree to which a full input pattern overlaps with a stored one. In both cases, the Y axis represents the degree to which the output pattern matches the original stored one. This figure corresponds to the FMSEPO condition with WID learning of .2 from O'Reilly and McClelland (1994).

lus"). Second, separation is driven by parts of the input pattern that do not overlap with stored patterns, to which the system is very sensitive. Thus, it is important that recall cues be partial input patterns, whereas new patterns to be stored should be complete.

Relative Properties of and Interactions Between Prefrontal Cortex and Hippocampus

We previously discussed theories concerning the functioning of prefrontal cortex and hippocampus in detail. In Table 14.1 we compare and contrast their functions along two dimensions that we believe highlight their relative contributions to memory.

Memory Mechanisms: Activation Versus Weight Change.   Note first that Table 14.1 distinguishes between two types of memory mechanisms—activa-

TABLE 14.1.
Properties of Neocortex and Hippocampus

Structure	Activation	Weight Changes
Prefrontal Cortex	Sustained	Long-term, integrative
Nonprefrontal Neocortex	Transient	Long-term, integrative
Hippocampus	Transient	Rapid, arbitrary

tion and weight changes. We think of activation as corresponding to the concepts of short-term or working memory, whereas weight changes provide the basis for long-term memory. Thus, activation represents the current state of the system, whereas its connection weights represent its long-term knowledge. In other words, maintenance of activation offers one temporary way to "remember" a state, and weight changes offer another, more enduring way. Note, however, that the latter requires the activation of some cue state in order to retrieve the to-be-remembered one.

From our review of the literature concerning prefrontal cortex, it seems clear that this structure plays an important role in activation-based memory. A growing number of studies suggest that it is required for performance in tasks that rely on the maintenance of task-relevant representations, and thus is characterized by the ability for sustained activation. In contrast, hippocampus and nonprefrontal neocortex seem to be better characterized by transient activity: Lesions of prefrontal cortex impair performance on tasks requiring sustained activation, suggesting that other regions are incapable, on their own, of sustained activity (e.g., Barone & Joseph, 1989; Goldman-Rakic, 1987).

A second distinction that we make in Table 14.1 is between rapid versus long-term, integrative learning. As discussed in the section on the hippocampus, there is strong evidence that this structure is required for the encoding of episodic associations—that is, associations that have be observed only once or a limited number of times. Conversely, there is growing evidence to suggest that, even in the absence of a hippocampus, it is possible to learn new associations. We assume that this occurs through neocortical mechanisms, which require extensive, repeated experience. As discussed, this difference suggests that the hippocampus may be specialized for the rapid encoding of arbitrary new associations, whereas the neocortex is adapted to the encoding and integration of repeatedly observed associations over extended periods of time.

Dimensions of "Top-Down" Control: Bias and Binding. Although our discussions of prefrontal cortex and hippocampus suggest that both of these structures play an important role in the top-down control of behavior, it should also be obvious by now that their contributions are different. In considering how these structures contribute to the control of planful behaviors, such as prospective memory, we think it is helpful to further clarify these differences by identifying two dimensions of top-down control that reflect the two principles by which prefrontal cortex and hippocampus operate. The first, which we refer to as *bias,* has to do with top-down influences on the execution of and competition between learned, or familiar neocortical processes; the second, which we refer to as *binding,* has to do with mediation of the associations necessary for performing novel tasks.

As discussed earlier, we assume that prefrontal cortex is responsible for actively supporting context, or plan representations, and that these serve to support task-relevant processes over extended delays, and to adjudicate the competion between task-relevant and task-irrelevant processes. Thus, the prefrontal cortex comes into play when either a plan is associated with a temporally extended set of processes, or it must "inhibit" competing, more dominant processes. Again, these both reflect the operation of a single mechanism within prefrontal cortex—to actively support task-relevant processes against interference (i.e., from cumulative effects of noise, over time, or from direct competion). Conversely, we assume that tasks requiring only transient activation of a plan, or that involve only dominant sequences of actions, can be performed independently of prefrontal cortex. We refer to this dimension of control as the *bias dimension* to convey the ability of representations within prefrontal cortex to bias processing elsewhere within the system in favor of task-relevant information (see Cohen, Dunbar, & McClelland, 1990, for a detailed discussion and examples of how bias can have a modulatory influence in systems using nonlinear processing units).

Depending upon the circumstances in which a task is performed, it may require a greater or lesser degree of bias; that is, its reliance on prefrontal cortex may vary. Thus, a task relying on a sequence of dominant processes may ordinarily require little bias from prefrontal cortex (other than, perhaps, an initial prefrontal cortex representation to launch it). However, if it is interrupted, it may then rely on prefrontal cortex for completion. The fact that it was interrupted indicates that it has come into competition with another, more dominant process; it now requires top-down input from prefrontal cortex, or bias, to overcome this competition if it is to be completed.

The second dimension of top-down influence has to do with the degree of experience associated with a task. Thus, a task may be novel, it may be highly rehearsed, or somewhere in between. We believe this dimension is closely related to the role of the hippocampus. We assume that the hippocampus is necessary to mediate the performance of novel tasks. It does this by binding together the neocortical representations necessary to perform the task, for which associations have not yet formed. These may or may not include representations within prefrontal cortex, depending upon the task. Thus, a task that involves a simple response to a simple stimulus, even if it is novel, may require hippocampal binding of relatively simple representations, all of which are outside of prefrontal cortex. In contrast, execution of a novel task that involves a temporally extended sequence of processes, many or all of which are subject to competion from more dominant processes, will require hippocampal binding of representations within prefrontal cortex as well as nonprefrontal neocortex. Of course, with practice, weight changes within neocortex will progressively encode the appropriate associations, so that eventually the hippocampus will no longer be needed to bind together the representations needed to perform the task. We refer to this dimension of top-down control as the *binding dimension*, to convey the role that hippocampus plays in mediating new associations until these are encoded as weight changes within neocortex.

We consider bias and binding to be continuous dimensions along which processes vary by degree. Thus, processes differ by the extent to which they rely on control by prefrontal cortex and hippocampus, and may show different combinations of reliance on each. It is important to distinguish between and consider processes along each of these dimensions. This is particularly clear when considering the relationship between practice on a task and performance. The relationship between practice and binding is straightforward: With more practice, a task becomes less reliant on binding, consequently, increasingly independent of hippocampus. However, practice also affects the degree to which a task relies on bias. As a task becomes more practiced, it also becomes more dominant, and therefore relies less on bias, that is, on prefrontal cortex mediation. Because practice has effects along both the bias and binding dimensions, the patterns of performance that result from practice may be complex. We feel that dissociating these two dimensions can help clarify the effects of practice, particularly with regard to traditional psychological theories of automaticity and control.

Automaticity and Control in Terms of Binding and Bias

Automaticity is usually considered as either a dichotomous variable, or as a unitary dimension that is directly related to practice. The traditional definition of an automatic process is one that does not rely on and is not subject to attentional control, whereas controlled processes rely on the allocation of limited-capacity attention (Posner & Snyder, 1975; Shiffrin & Schneider, 1977). Some authors point out that this distinction should really be considered a continuum, with some processes being more automatic than others (e.g., Kahneman & Treisman, 1984), and with greater practice leading to greater automaticity (e.g., MacLeod & Dunbar, 1988). However, a careful consideration of learning phenomena suggests that there are still reasons to believe in a distinction between novel tasks and practiced ones that is qualitative and different from the variations that are observed among practiced tasks. That is, something different seems to be happening during the earliest stages of practice than during later stages. This is not a new idea. For example, Anderson (1983) distinguished between two procedural learning mechanisms in his ACT* theory—

compilation, which occurs during the initial stages of practice; and strengthening, which continues to occur even for very familiar procedures (and accounts for the power law of practice effects). Similarly, we argued that the mechanisms underlying performance during the earliest stages of practice may be qualitatively different than those involved after moderate amounts of practice (Cohen et al., 1990; Cohen, Servan-Schreiber, & McClelland, 1992). We distinguished between indirect, or mediated processes involved in the performance of novel tasks, and direct processes that underlie performance of more practiced tasks. We took care to point out the differences between this distinction and the more traditional one between controlled and automatic processes. Processes traditionally considered to be controlled include both indirect (i.e., truly novel) as well as weak, but direct processes (e.g., color naming in the Stroop task). We believe that we can now explain the overlap between these two distinctions (controlled vs. automatic, and direct vs. indirect) in terms of the relative contribution of prefrontal cortex and hippocampus; that is, according to the two dimensions introduced earlier—novelty and interference. Thus, the distinction between novelty versus familiarity reflects the influence of the binding dimension, whereas differences in the strength of direct processes reflects the influence of the bias dimension. Processes that are considered to be "controlled" in the traditional sense may be so either because they rely on binding (i.e., hippocampal mediation), or bias (i.e., prefrontal cortex mediation), or both. These relationships are illustrated in Fig. 14.3.

The dimensions of bias and binding make a number of predictions regarding performance on prospective memory tasks, specifically with respect to factors that affect task difficulty and types of errors. For example, the extent of delay over which items must be maintained or remembered and the number of novel associations (bindings) required to perform the task will contribute to task difficulty. There are some empirical findings consistent with such predictions (Einstein, Holland, McDaniel, & Guynn, 1992; Einstein & McDaniel, 1990).

Interactions Between Bottom-Up and Top-Down Influences in Neocortex. In the previous section, we considered the two ways in which prefrontal cortex and hippocampus can influence behavior through top-down mediation of nonprefrontal neocortical processes. Before we consider a full account of planful behavior, however, we need to consider how these top-down influences interact with the processing of bottom-up inputs within neocortex. We assume that different inputs to neocortex activate different representations, and that these are in relative competition. However, to the extent that no single representation is significantly more active than competing ones, then multiple representations can coexist. Under such circumstances, top-down influences become important: input to a representation from prefrontal cortex or the hippocampus will not only support that representation, but will allow it to compete more effectively, and suppress other representations. This suggests how

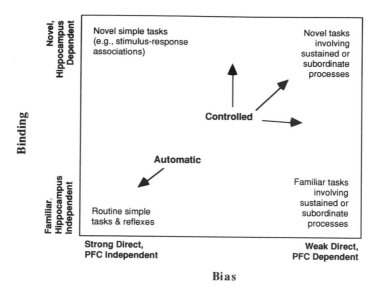

FIG. 14.3.   Theorized relationship among the several distinctions that have been used to describe the relationship between practice and underlying processing mechanisms. Automatic processes are assumed to be both familiar and highly practiced, relying neither on hippocampus nor on prefrontal cortex. Processes traditionally considered to be controlled rely either on binding (hippocampus) or bias (prefrontal cortex) or both.

top-down support for a representation can also appear to produce inhibition of competing ones (as with the inhibitory function of prefrontal cortex discussed earlier). Evidence from recent neurophysiological studies (Desimone & Duncan, 1995) supports our view of the interaction between prefrontal cortex and other neocortical areas; that is, that attentional effects occur by the top-down support of task-relevant representations, allowing them to compete more effectively with, and inhibit task-irrelevant ones.

DISCUSSION

In the remainder of this chapter, we consider how these concepts can be used to explain the processes underlying prospective memory, and how these ideas can be applied to performance in more traditional laboratory tasks used to empirically test them.

A Processing Account of Prospective Memory

Recall the example at the beginning of this chapter. You wake up and the environment (time of day, alarm clock going off) as well as internal cues (growling belly, foggy head) dictate that you get ready to go to work. This occurs via existing cortical associations; that is, you have long-standing experience waking up and going to work, and thus have developed "direct" associations between the environmental conditions and your actions. Although getting ready for work involves a sequence of relatively routine actions, as noted in the discussion of the bias dimension, this will still rely on a plan in prefrontal cortex because it is temporally extended, and may need to be supported in the face of distractions.

In the process of executing the plan, you notice the missing orange juice and the plan is violated. At this point, several things happen. First, the missing orange juice elicits a plan to address this—that is, go to grocery store. However, this plan conflicts with the already active plan of going to work. Attempting to carry both of these out would lead to conflicting sequences of actions. One of the general principles of neural network models is to solve problems (i.e., conflicts) through constraint satisfaction. We assume that this principle applies here. There is an attempt to find a state of activation that accommodates both the current plan (go to work) as well as the plan to get more orange juice. Constraint satisfaction operates by preferentially activating and stabilizing those features that are associated with both plans, or that are associated with one that do not conflict with the other. Through association, the plan to get more orange juice will activate the representation of the trip to the grocery store, sharing some activation with the trips to and from work. At the same time, the current plan to go to work will activate associated representations like "get to work on time." A plan to stop by the grocery store is likely to conflict with the current plan (and its associates, like getting to work on time) more than a plan for the trip home. Thus, the latter will be favored, and survive the competition. This will activate representations of the environment associated with the trip home (e.g., dark outside, clock strikes 5:00, etc.). Thus, the system is likely to stabilize in a state comprised of the following representations: go to work; go home; go to grocery store; 5:00, and so on. As noted earlier, the hippocampus acts to bind the components of such stable neocortical states.

This leads to the question: given the coactivation of both the current plan (get to work) and the plan to stop by the grocery store, why is it that the former prevails now whereas the latter prevails at the end of the day? The answer is that at present the environment strongly favors the go to work plan, through associations in the neocortex. There are strong associations between the morning environment and the plan to go to work. It is possible to activate the plan representation of (i.e., "imagine") going to the grocery store, without actually executing it. On the other hand, at 5:00, by the same mechanism, the environment strongly supports the going home plan. However, due to hippocampally bound associations, today this environment also elicits the go-to-grocery store plan. That is, the hippocampus reinstates the set of representations bound earlier that morning. Note that this also includes the then-current plan, go-to-work. However, the current environment strongly favors the go-home plan, and thus prevails. Finally, there is a conflict between the usual go-home plan elicited directly by the environment and the go-to-grocery store plan, elicited by the hippocampus (e.g., the usual trip home involves a left at the light, whereas the trip to the grocery involves a right). Here, both the hippo-campus and PFC play a role in controlling behavior: The hippocampus helps favor the go-to-grocery store representation over the usual go-straight-home representation within the PFC. This PFC representation acts to bias behavior toward the appropriate, but less habitual response of turning left at the light. Note that this predicts that, under conditions of distraction (i.e., prefrontal cor-tex failure), a particular type of error will be made, the elicitation of the more habitual response (going straight home). These types of habitual errors are well-documented (Reason & Mycielska, 1982).

The astute reader will notice at least one problem with this account: Why don't you go to the grocery store on the way home tomorrow as well? That is, the end of the day today may be similar to the end of the day tomorrow, so why doesn't the environment elicit the same set of representations encoded by the hippocampus this morning? There are a number of possible responses to this question. First, we should note that, at the very least, anecdotal evidence sug-gests that such errors do occur. We would predict, furthermore, that the more similar the environmental cues (e.g., the weather, the activities you are en-gaged in at the end of the day, etc.) the more likely such errors are to occur. However, even if these occur, they are not the norm. This suggests that the rep-resentations active when associations are encoded by the hippocampus are richer than we allowed. Specifically, there are likely to be feature dimensions that encode days of the week, recency, and so on. A combination of such fea-tures may help to identify and distinguish individual days. Finally, it is likely that hippocampally encoded associations are subject to decay, so that the over-all likelihood of retrieval is reduced with time.

Prefrontal Cortex-Hippocampus Interactions in Classical Learning Tasks

The previous section provides a narrative account of how prefrontal cortex and hippocampus may interact in the service of prospective memory. Such ac-counts are difficult to test. Here, we consider how our theory can be applied to performance in a set of laboratory tasks—blocking and latent inhibition. Ev-idence from animal studies suggests that these tasks are sensitive to hippo-campal function, and there are at least two computational accounts of the func-tions of hippocampus and neocortex in these learning tasks of which we are aware (Schmajuk & DiCarlo, 1992; Gluck & Meyers, in press). Schmajuk and DiCarlo hypothesized that hippocampus is responsible for error-based learn-ing in the service of predicting expected responses from sensory cues, whereas neocortex relies only on associate learning in such tasks. Gluck and Meyers (in press) argued that the hippocampus is responsible for recoding sensory representation; these recoded representations then govern the generation of associations between stimuli and responses in the neocortex. We offer an account that is different from both of these, that describes performance in such tasks in terms of hippocamplal–neocortex interactions similar to the ones we described earlier. We consider how out theory can account for findings in the blocking and latent inhibition paradigms.

Blocking. In the blocking paradigm (Kamin, 1969), subjects are first conditioned to respond to a particular stimulus (let us say, stimulus A), during a pretraining phase. During a subsequent training phase, stimulus A is paired with a second conditional stimulus (say, stimulus B). Finally, during a test phase, subjects are tested on the association between B and the unconditioned stimulus—that is, the ability of B to elicit the unconditioned response. Performance is compared with a control case in which there is no pretraining on A—that is, the subject is trained only on A and B together. The typical finding is that pretraining on A reduces conditioning to B during the A-and-B training phase. In other words, pretraining on A "blocks" the ability of B to acquire an association with the unconditioned stimulus. Lesions of the hippocampus were observed to reduce this effect, increasing conditioning to B in the face of pretraining on A (Solomon, 1977; Rickert et al., 1978).

Schmajuk & DiCarlo (1992) explained these findings by observing that, with an error-driven learning rule, pretraining on A will gradually reduce the error in predicting the unconditioned stimulus, thereby reducing the amount of error available for training during the A-and-B phase. As such, conditioning to B will be reduced. This effect is attributed to the hippocampus, presumed to use error-driven learning. Neorcortex, however, is assumed to use an associative learning rule; this is influenced only by the co-occurrence of stimuli, and not by the error in predicting them. As such, during the A-and-B phase, only the co-occurrence of B and the unconditioned stimulus is relevant, and not the fact that A is already associated with the unconditioned stimulus. Thus, in the absence of the hippocampus, conditioning of B is not influenced by pretraining on A.

Our theory suggests a different account of the findings. During the A-only phase, we assume that both the hippocampus and neocortex act in parallel to encode the association between A and the unconditioned stimulus. However, there are differences in how this is encoded by the two structures. The hippocampus encodes this as an association between the stimulus, the experimental context (including a representation of the task context in the prefrontal cortex), and the unconditioned stimulus. In the neocortex, however, the association is directly between the stimulus and the unconditioned stimulus. During the A-and-B phase, however, matters change. In the absence of the hippocampus, the neocortex continues to encode associations between the stimuli present, and would begin to form an association between B and the unconditioned stimulus. However, the hippocampus, if present, will cause the representation of B to be suppressed. This is because the presentation of A in the experimental context causes it to help reinstate the set of representations that were associated during the A-only pahse, which did not include B. Although there is no evidence tthat the hippocampus directly inhibits representations that do not form part of the recalled set (in this case, B), we assume that the additional input provided to the representations of A and to the experimental context allow these to copmete more aggressively with B, which is receiving only bottom-up support, and therefore the activation of B diminishes. This reduces the chance for new associations to form between B and the unconditioned stimulus. Again, evidence from neurophysiological studies support the existence of such competition within neocortex, and the importance of top-down influences on this competition (Desimone & Duncan, 1995).

Thus, our account, like the error–associative learning account (Schmajuk & DiCarlo, 1992), is consistent with the observation that blocking occurs in normal subjects and that it appears to be reduced in hippocampally lesioned animals (Solomon & Moore, 1975). The sensory-recoding theory (Gluck & Meyers, in press) seems to account for blocking in a parameter-dependent fashion, which may rely to greater or lesser extent upon hippocampal function. Therefore, the blocking paradigm does not provide a good test of this theory. However, it can be used to test our theory, which makes two predictions that differ from the Schmajuk & DiCarlo (1992) theory.

First, our theory predicts actual suppression of the representation of B during the A-and-B phase. The Schmajuk & DiCarlo theory does not make this prediction; it asserts that no association will occur between B and the response because A adequately predicts the response, not because B is suppressed. This could be tested. For example, activation of B could be assessed using a priming paradigm in concert with the blocking paradigm. We predict that there would be less priming of B than in an appropriate control condition, and that this reduction should correlate postively with the degree of blocking.

Second, because we assume that the neocortex has the capacity for error-based learning, but over a much longer time frame, we expect that even hippocampally lesioned subjects should show a blocking effect with sufficient training in the A-only phase. Over time, a cortical association would develop between A and the experimental context, obviating the need for the hippocampus to produce the top-down activation of A (during A-and-B phase) that inhibits B and produces the blocking effect. In contrast, the entire premise of the error-vs.-associative learning account is that neocortex is capable only of associative learning, and therefore should never show blocking on its own.

Latent Inhibition.   This refers to any reduction of conditioning to a stimulus that can be attributed to pre-exposure to that stimulus (Lubow, 1989).

Thus, in latent inhibition paradigms, subjects are exposed to a stimulus in a pretraining, or pre-exposure phase, without presentation of the unconditioned stimulus. This is followed by a conditioning phase, during which the stimulus is paired with the unconditioned stimulus. The rate of conditioning is slower when compared with that of subjects who have not been pre-exposed to the stimulus, using a wide variety of different stimuli and tasks (Lubow, 1989). Furthermore, lesions of the hippocampus appear to reduce the effect of stimulus pre-exposure, such that the rate of conditioning during the training phase is increased.

The traditional account of this phenomenon considers it in terms of selective attention (Lubow, 1989): It is assumed that subjects become familiar with and learn to ignore the uninformative stimulus during the pre-exposure phase, reducing its salience during subsequent conditioning. Schmajuk and DiCarlo (1992) and Gluck and Meyers (in press) offered closely related accounts in which associative resources are preferentially allocated to informative stimuli, and reduced for uninformative ones.

Our account is somewhat different from traditional ones. During the phase of pre-exposure to stimulus A, we assume that the hippocampus forms an association between this stimulus, the environmental context, and the representation active within prefrontal cortex. Although typically there is no experimentally determined task that the subject performs during the pre-exposure phase, we assume that subjects are engaged in some set of activities (such as exploration, grooming, etc.) that are associated with corresponding "state" (i.e., internal context) representations within prefrontal cortex. Thus, during the test phase, presentation of A causes the hippocampus to reactivate this set of representations. This set contrasts with the set of representations activated by presentation of the unconditioned stimulus. This stimulus is strongly associated with a specific behavior, the unconditioned response, that is different than the behaviors engaged in by the subject during the pre-exposure phase. Furthermore, we assume that the unconditioned stimulus and response activate a representation within prefrontal cortex (e.g., a state of alertness or anticipation), that differs from the representation within prefrontal cortex during the pre-exposure phase. Thus, stimulus A and the unconditioned stimulus favor the activation of different and conflicting sets of representations, or states. As we discussed in the orange juice example, we assume that constraint satisfaction, operating within the neocortex, favors one or the other of these two states, or an alternation between them. Conditioning of an association between two stimuli (in this case, stimulus A and the unconditioned stimulus) requires that these be coactivated. Thus, competition between incompatible states accounts for the latent inhibition effect. Finally, without pre-exposure to stimulus A, it will not be associated with any hippocampally mediated state, and therefore no competition will arise within the neocortex upon presentation of the unconditioned stimulus.

This account shares something in common with our account of the blocking phenomenon: Both assume that hippocampus is responsible for binding together representations during the initial phase, and that recall of this set of representations is mediated by hippocampus during subsequent phases of the experiment. In the blocking paradigm, this recall leads to the inhibition of the novel stimulus, interfering with conditioning on that stimulus. In the latent inhibition paradigm, the novel stimulus is salient, and thus is unlikely to be inhibited. However, as we suggested, it has strong associations with representations that conflict with those of the pre-exposure stimulus, and it is the competition between these sets of representations that interferes with conditioning.

As described, an important feature of our account of blocking and latent inhibition that ditinguishes it from others is that our suggests that the prefrontal cortex plays a significant role in these phenomena in addition to that played by the hippocampus. Another important difference between our account of latent inhibition and more traditional ones is that we do not assume that pre-exposure to a stimulus reduces its representation, or makes this less distinct. More fundamentally, we do not assume that subjects actively ignore the familiar stimulus, but simply that its representation—within the experimental context—has become incompatible with that of the unconditioned stimulus, and that this incompatibility interferes with conditioning.

Relationship of Blocking and LI to Prospective Memory Tasks

The specific laboratory tasks we discussed (blocking and LI) illustrate task dimensions, and the operation of processing mechanisms that are relevant for understanding the kinds of errors likely to occur under conditions in which prospective memory operates. We predict that pre-exposure to task variables and responses will affect subsequent planning and memory. For example, consider the possibility that, in the "missing orange juice" scenario, one discovers a second item during the day that needs to be purchased at the grocery store on the way home. We predict that this second item is more likely to be forgotten than if it had been the only one needed, due to a blocking-like effect. When the attempt is made to add the second item to the mental shopping list, we expect that reinstatement of the hippocampal "go to the grocery store on the way home" plan, and its prior association with orange juice will actually tend to interfere with the association of the new item with the plan.

We can also imagine a case in which latent inhibition will affect prospective memory performance. As was suggested (Mark McDaniel, personal communication, July, 1994), we can consider the case where the grocery store on the way home is actually an expensive convenience store that was avoided in the past. In this case, the plan to stop at the convenience store will have to overcome this prior "no response" association, and we predict that more failures to "stop and shop" would occur in this situation, as compared to one in which the store is a regular venue.

CONCLUSION

In this chapter, we review findings concerning the functions of prefrontal cortex and hippocampus, and their roles in information processing. We also describe computational mechanisms that were proposed to account for these, and describe how these may interact to give rise to the coordinated execution of planful behavior and prospective memory, in particular. We discuss how these ideas relate to more traditional concepts such as automaticity, and how they may apply to specific laboratory tasks that can be used to test them. At this stage, however, the interaction between the computational mechanisms we propose is conjectural. Our claims need to be substantiated, both in functioning simulations that implement these mechanisms, and in empirical validation of the predictions they make. These suggest future activities that, with time, we hope to be able to look back on as an example of prospective memory at work.

REFERENCES

Anderson, J. R. (1983). *The architecture of cognition.* Cambridge, MA: Harvard University Press.

Barone, P., & Joseph, J. P. (1989). Role of the dorsolateral prefrontal cortex in organizing visually guided behavior. *Brain Behavior and Evolution, 33,* 132–135.

Becker, J. T., Mintun, M. A., Diehl, D., DeKosky, S. T., & Dobkin, J. (1993). Functional neuroanatomy of verbal memory as revealed by word list recall during PET scanning. *Society for Neuroscience Abstracts, 19*(2), 1079.

Bianchi, L. (1922). *The mechanism of the brain and the function of the frontal lobes.* Edinburgh, Scotland: Livingstone.

Blamire, A. M., McCarthy, G., Bloch, G., Rothman, D. L., & Shulman, R. G. (1993). Functional magnetic resonance imaging of human pre-frontal cortex during a spatial working memory task. In *Proceedings of the Society for Magnetic Resonance in Medicine, 12th Annual Scientific Meeting, 3,* 1412.

Cohen, J. D., & Servan-Schreiber, D. (1992). Context, cortex and dopamine: A connectionist approach to behavior and biology in schizophrenia. *Psychological Review, 99,* 45–77.

Cohen, J. D., Dunbar, K., & McClelland, J. L. (1990). On the control of automatic processes: A parallel distributed processing model of the Stroop effect, *Psychological Review, 97*(3), 332–361.

Cohen, J. D., Forman, S. D., Braver, T. S., Casey, B. J., Servan-Schreiber, D., & Noll, D. C. (1994). Activation of prefrontal cortex in a non-spatial working memory task with functional MRI. *Human Brain Mapping, 1,* 293–304.

Cohen, J. D., Servan-Schreiber, D., & McClelland, J. L. (1992). A parallel distributed processing approach to automaticity. *American Journal of Psychology, 105,* 239–269.

Cohen, N. J., & Squire, L. R. (1980). Preserved learning and retention of pattern analyzing skill in amnesia: Dissociation of knowing how and knowing that. *Science, 210,* 207–209.

Damasio, A. R. (1979). The frontal lobes. In K.M. Heilman & E. Valenstein (Eds.), *Clinical neuropsychology* (pp. 3360–3411). New York: Oxford University Press.

Desimone, R., & Duncan, J. (1995). Neural mechanisms of selective visual attention. *Annual Review of Neuroscience, 18,* 193.

Diamond, A., & Doar, B. (1989). The performance of human infants on a measure of frontal cortex function, the delayed response task. *Developmental Psychobiology, 22*(3), 271–294.

Diamond, A., & Goldman-Rakic, P. S. (1989). Comparison of human infants and rhesus monkeys on Piaget's A B task: Evidence for dependence on dorsolateral prefrontal cortex. *Experimental Brain Research, 74,* 24–40.

Diamond, A. (1990). The development and neural bases of memory functions as indexed by the A B and delayed response tasks in human infants and infant monkeys. In A. Diamond (Ed.), *The development and neural bases of higher cognitive functions* (pp. 267–317). New York: New York Academy of Science Press.

Duncan, J. (1986). Disorganization of behavior after frontal lobe damage. *Cognitive neuropsychology, 3*(3), 271–290.

Einstein, G. O., Holland, L. J., McDaniel, M. A., & Guynn, M. J. (1992). Age-related deficits in prospective memory: The influence of task complexity. *Psychology and Aging, 7,* 471–478.

Einstein, G. O., & McDaniel, M. A. (1990). Normal aging and prospective memory. *Journal of Experimental Psychology: Learning, Memory and Cognition, 16,* 717–726.

Ferrier D. (1886). *Functions of the Brain.* London: Smith and Elder.

Fuster, J. M. (1980). *The prefrontal cortex.* New York: Raven.

Fuster, J. M. (1989). *The prefrontal cortex. Anatomy, physiology and neuropsychology of the frontal lobe.* New York: Raven.

Fuster, J. M. (1985a). The prefrontal cortex and temporal integration. In A. Peters & E. G. Jones (Eds.), *Cerebral cortex* (pp. 151–177). New York: Plenum.

Fuster, J. M. (1985b). The prefrontal cortex, mediator of cross-temporal contingencies. *Human Neurobiology, 4,* 169–179.

Gluck, M. A., & Meyers, C. E. (in press). Hippocampal mediation of stimulus representation: A computational theory. *Hippocampus.*

Goldberg, T. E., Weinberger, D. R., Berman, K. F., Pliskin, N. H., & Podd, M. H. (1987). Further evidence of dementia of the prefrontal type in schizophrenia? *Archives of General Psychiatry, 44,* 1008–1014.

Goldman-Rakic, P.S. (1987). Circuitry of primate prefrontal cortex and regulation of behavior by representational memory. *Handbook of Physiology—The Nervous System, 5,* 373–417.

Gorenstein, E. E., Mammato, C. A., Sandy, J. M. (1989). Performance of inattentive–overactive children on selected measures of prefrontal-type function. *Journal of Clinical Psychology, 45,* 619–632.

Graf, P., Squire, L. R., & Mandler, G. (1984). The information that amnesic patients do not forget. *Journal of Experimental Psychology: Learning Memory and Cognition, 10,* 164–178.

Grant, D. A., & Berg, E. A. (1948). A behavioral analysis of degree of reinforcement and ease of shifting to new responses in a Weigl type card sorting problem. *Journal of Experimental Psychology, 38,* 404–411.

Grasby, P. M., Frith, C. D., Friston, K. J., Bench, C., Frackowiak, R. S. J., & Dolan, R. J. (1993). Functional mapping of brain areas implicated in auditory-verbal memory function. *Brain, 116,* 1–20.

Haxby, J. V., Horwitz, B., Ungerleider, L. G., Maisog, J., Allen, D. G., Kurkijan, M., Schapiro, M. B., Rapoport, S. I., & Grady, C. L. (1993). Lateralization of frontal lobe activity associated with working memory for faces changes with retention interval: A parametric PET-rCBF study. *Society for Neurosciences Abstract, 19,* 1284.

Hecaen, H., & Albert, M. L. (1978). *Human neuropsychology.* New York: Wiley.

Hitzig, E. (1874). *Untersuchungen uber das Gehirn.* Berlin: Hirschwald.

Jonides, J., Smith, E. E., Koeppe, R. A., Awh, E., Minoshima, S., & Mintun, M. A. (1993). Spatial working memory in humans as revealed by PET. *Nature, 363,* 623–625.

Kahneman, D., & Treisman, A. (1984). Changing views of attention and automaticity. In R. Parasuraman, R. Davies, & J. Beatty (Eds.), *Varieties of attention* (pp. 29–61). New York: Academic Press.

Kamin, L. J. (1969). Predictability, surprise, attention and conditioning. In B. A. Campbell & R. M. Church (Eds.), *Punishment and Aversive Behavior* (pp. 279–296). New York: Appleton-Cenutry-Crofts.

Lubow, R. E. (1989). *Latent inhibition and conditioned attention theory.* Cambridge, England: Cambridge University Press.

Luria, A. R. (1969). Frontal lobe syndromes. In P. J. Vinken & G. W. Bruyn (Eds.), *Handbook of clinical neurology* (Vol. 2, pp. 725–757). New York: Elsevier.

MacLeod, C. M., & Dunbar, K. (1988). Training and Stroop-like interference: Evidence for a continuum of automaticity. *Journal of Experimental Psychology, 14,* 126–135.

Marr, D. (1971). Simple memory: A theory for archicortex. *Philosophical Transactions of the Royal Society of London, B, 262,* 23–81.

McClelland, J. L., McNaughton, B. L., & O'Reilly, R. C. (in press). Why there are complementary learning systems in the hippocampus and neocortex: Insights from the successes and failures of connectionist models of learning and memory. *Psychological Review.*

McClelland, J. L., McNaughton, B. L., O'Reilly, R. C., & Nadel, L. (1992). Complementary roles of hippocampus and neocortext in learning and memory. *Society for Neuroscience Abstracts, 18*(2), 1216.

McCloskey, M., & Cohen, N. J. (1989). Catastrophic interference in connectionist networks: The sequential learning problem. In G. H. Bower (Ed.), *The psychology of learning and motivation* (Vol. 24, pp. 109–164). San Diego: Academic Press.

McNaughton, B. L., & Morris, R. G. M. Hippocampal synaptic enhancement and information storage within a distributed memory system. *Trends in Neurosciences, 10*(10), 408–415.

Milner, B. (1963). Effects of different brain lesions on card sorting. *Archives of Neurology, 9,* 90–100.

Milner, B. (1966). Amnesia following operation on the temporal lobe. In C. W. M. Whitty & O. L. Zangwill (Eds.), *Amnesia* (pp. 109–133). London: Butterworth & Co.

Mishkin, M., & Pribram, K. H. (1955). Analysis of the effects of frontal lesions in monkeys. I. Variations on delayed alternation. *Journal of Comparative Physiological Psychology, 388,* 492–495.

Mishkin, M. (1964). Perseveration of central sets after frontal lesions in monkeys. In J. M. Warren & K. Akert (Eds.), *The frontal granual cortex and behavior* (pp. 219–241). New York: McGraw-Hill.

Nelson, H. E. (1976). A modified card sorting test sensitive to frontal lobe defects. *Cortex, 12,* 313–324.

O'Reilly, R. C., & McClelland, J. L. (1994). Hippocampal conjunctive encoding, storage, and recall: Avoiding a tradeoff. *Hippocampus, 6,* 661–682.

Passingham, R. E. (1985). Memory of monkeys (*Macaca mulatta*) with lesions in prefrontal cortext. *Behavioral Neuroscience, 99,* 3–21.

Perret, E. (1974). The left frontal lobe of man and the suppression of habitual responses in verbal categorical behavior. *Neuropsychologia, 12,* 323–330.

Petrides, M., & Milner, B. (1982). Deficits on subject-ordered tasks after frontal- and temporal-lobe lesions in man. *Neuropsychologia, 20,* 249–262.

Petrides, M. E., Alivisatos, B., Meyer, E., & Evans, A. C. (1993). Functional activation of the human frontal cortex during the performance of verbal working memory tasks. *Proceedings of the National Academy of Science, U.S.A., 90,* 878–882.

Posner, M. I., & Snyder, C. R. (1975). Attention and cognitive control. In R. L. Solso (Ed.), *Information processing and cognition*. Hillsdale, NJ: Lawrence Erlbaum Associates.

Reason, J. R., & Mycielska, K. (1982). *Absentminded? The psychology of mental lapses and everyday errors*. Englewood Cliffs, NJ: Prentice-Hall.

Rickert, E. J., Lorden, J. F., Smyly, E., & Callahan, M. (1978). Hippocampectomy and the attenuation of blocking. *Behavioral Biology, 22*, 147–160.

Robinson, A. L., Heaton, R. K., Lehman, R. A. W., & Stilson, D. W. (1980). The utility of the Wisconsin Card Sorting Test in detecting and localizing frontal lobe lesions. *Journal of Consulting Clinical Psychology, 48*, 605–614.

Rosenddkilde, K. E. (1979). Functional heterogeneity of the prefrontal cortext in the monkey: A review. *Behavioral Neural Biology, 25*, 301–345.

Rosvold, K. E., Szwarcbart, M. K., Mirsky, A. F., & Mishkin, M. (1961). The effect of frontal-lobe damage on delayed response performance in chimpanzees. *Journal of Comparative Physiological Psychology, 54*, 368–374.

Rumelhart, D. E., & McClelland, J. L. (1986). *Parallel Distributed Processing: Explorations in the microstructure of cognition* (Vols. 1 and 2). Cambridge, MA: MIT Press.

Rumelhart, D. E., Hinton, G. E., & Williams, R. J. (1986). Learning internal representations by error propagation. In D. E. Rumelhart, J. L. McClelland, & PDP Research Group (Eds.), *Parallel Distributed Processing. Volume 1: Foundations* (pp. 318–362). Cambridge, MA: MIT Press.

Schacter, D. L., Delaney, S. M., & Merikle, E. P. (1990). Priming of nonverbal information and the nature of implicit memory. In G. Bower (Ed.), *The psychology of learning and motivation* (Vol. 26, pp. 83–123). San Diego: Academic Press.

Schmajuk, N. A., & DiCarlo, J. J. (1992). Stimulus configuration, classical conditioning, and hippocampus function. *Psychological Review, 2*, 268–305.

Scoville, W., & Milner, B. (1957). Loss of recent memory after bilateral hippocampal lesions. *Journal of Neurology, Neurosurgery, and Psychiatry, 20*, 11–21.

Servan-Schreiber, D., Cohen, J. D., & Steingard, S. (1994). Schizophrenic performance in a variant of the CPT-AX: A test of theoretical predictions concerning the processing of context. Unpublished manuscript.

Shallice T. (1982). Specific impairments of planning. *Philosophical Transactions of the Royal Society of London, 298*, 199–209.

Shiffrin, R. M., & Schneider, W. (1977). Controlled and automatic human information processing: II. Perceptual learning, automatic attending, and a general theory. *Psychological Review, 84*, 127–190.

Shimamura, A. P., & Squire, L. R. (1989). Impaired priming of new associations in amnesia. *Journal of Experimental Psychology: Learning Memory and Cognition, 15*, 721–728.

Solomon, P. R. (1977). Role of the hippocampus in blocking and conditioned inhibition of the rabbit's nictitating membrane response. *Journal of Comparative and Physiological Psychology, 91*, 407–417.

Solomon, P. R., & Moore, J. W. (1975). Latent inhibition and stimulus generalization of the classically conditioned nictitating membrane response in rabbits (*Oryctolagus cuniculus*) following dorsal hippocampal ablation. *Journal of Comparative and Physiological Psychology, 89*, 1192–1203.

Squire, L. R. (1992). Memory and the hippocampus: A synthesis from findings with rats, monkeys, and humans. *Psychological Review, 99*, 195–231.

Stroop, J. R. (1935). Studies of interference in serial verbal reactions. *Journal of Experimental Psychology, 18*, 643–662.

Stuss, D. T., & Benson, D. F. (1984). Neuropsychological studies of the frontal lobes. *Psychological Bulletin, 95*, 3–28.

Stuss, D. T., & Benson, D. F. (1986). *The Frontal Lobes*. New York: Raven Press.

Swedo, S. E., Shapiro, M. B., Grady, C. L., Cheslow, D. L., Leonard, H. L., Kumar, A., Friedland, R., Rapoport, S. I., & Rapoport, J. L. (1989). Cerebral glucose metabolism in childhood-onset OCD. *Archives of General Psychiatry, 46,* 518–523

Tulving, E. (1983). *Elements of Episodic Memory.* Oxford: Clarendon Press.

White, H. (1989). Learning in artificial neural networks: A statistical perspective. *Neural Computation, 1,* 425–464.

Wilson, F. A. W., Scalaidhe, S. P. O., & Goldman-Rakic, P. S. (1993). Dissociation of object and spatial processing domains in primate prefrontal cortex. *Science, 260,* 1955–1957.

15

The Neuropsychological Approach in the Study of Prospective Memory

Patrizia S. Bisiacchi
Università Degli Studi Di Padova, Italy

The term *Prospective Memory* (PM) may seem to signal a new memory store, one additional box to add to the diagrams that explain memory processes. Indeed, some of the literature on PM that attempts to differentiate PM from other kinds of memory strengthens this attitude (Kvavilashvili, 1987). Probably the question is not clearly put. The problem is not to demonstrate that PM is different from short term memory (STM) or long term memory (LTM), but to define which processes are involved in PM, or which task requirements are present in a certain PM test. One way to achieve this goal is to utilize neuropsychological methodology.

The aim of the present chapter is to summarize the neuropsychological methodologies that may be helpful for a better specification of the processes underlying prospective memory. In the neuropsychological literature, there is no sign of a selective PM impairment. No observed neuropsychological deficit was classified as damage to a PM process. This may be due to the fact that there is always a delay between the progress in cognitive psychology and its confirmation from neuropsychological data, or to a still embryonic progress of the cognitive research in this field, or to inadequate search in the existing neuropsychological literature. In the intent to overcome this gap, I review some literature concerning deficits that may be considered involved in PM tasks such as planning, retrospective memory, time estimation, and control mechanisms.

The structure of the chapter is the following. A brief summary of neuropsychological methodologies is presented first, followed by some observations on the probable neuronal substrate for PM, and then some experimental neuropsychological data.

THE NEUROPSYCHOLOGICAL METHODOLOGY

A main goal of cognitive neuropsychology consists in finding relationships between theories (or models) of normal cognitive processes and the neural substrate (for a different opinion see Caramazza, 1986; Rapp & Caramazza, 1991). There are at least three different ways to attain this goal. The first concerns the study of people with impairments of cognitive processes related to brain lesions. The second regards the study of normal subjects with special methodologies (i.e., hemispheric specialization techniques, endogenous components of event related potentials, dual-task methodology, brain imaging, etc.). The third is centered on the study of cognitive processes in normal and pathological aging.

Common to all these approaches is the assumption that cognition is an information-processing system consisting of a number of modular, functionally distinct, and isolable components (the *functional architecture;* for a more detailed discussion on theoretical issues see Denes, Semenza & Bisiacchi, 1988; Fodor, 1983; Semenza, in press; Shallice, 1988).

Studies on Brain Damaged Subjects

The study of people with brain lesions is the most diffuse approach in cognitive neuropsychology and is mainly based on the observation of *dissociations* (Shallice, 1988).

A *double dissociation* occurs when, considering two patients (or group of patients), one performs poorly on one task (i.e., significatively worse than normal subjects) and at a normal level on another task, and the second presents the reverse pattern. The aim of double dissociation experiments is to show that loss of a particular function is associated with damage to a particular structure and is not the result of generalized neurological impairment that follows brain damage. This is accomplished by comparing subjects with circumscribed damage to different brain areas and showing that functional loss is directly related to the site of the lesion. In a successful double dissociation experiment, damage to area A produces deficits in function A while sparing function B, whereas the opposite occurs when area B is damaged. A classical example of double dissociation are the two major aphasic syndromes: *Broca's Aphasia* and *Wernicke's Aphasia*. In the former, there are impairments in the production of speech with a well preserved comprehension, whereas the reverse pattern is true for the latter.[1]

When double dissociation experiments are not possible because, for example, patients with reverse patterns of behavior are not available, *single disso-*

---

[1]Psycholinguistic research in aphasia is much more sophisticated than this simplistic sketch. However, a detailed discussion of aphasia is beyond the scope of this chapter.

ciation experiments may be conducted. In single dissociation experiments, the effects of lesions to only one region of the brain are examined. These experiments try to demonstrate that damage to a particular area affects performance in certain tasks, but not others. Single dissociation experiments present some problems in the interpretation of the findings because the observed deficit may arise from nonspecificity of the lesion, rather than from selective disruption of functions associated with the damaged region. In other words, the observed deficit on one experimental task may be due to other reasons than the specificity of the lesion (e.g., the two tasks might differ in difficulty level).

A further application of the dissociation logic is the *critical variable method* (Shallice, 1988, 1991). According to this approach, the performance of a certain type of task is affected in one patient by a change in variable x but not by a change in variable y, whereas the reverse is found in another patient.

Another important, often neglected, method is the study of *associations* (Semenza & Bisiacchi, in press). Associations are generally confounded with symptom complexes—i.e., the co-occurence of more than one deficit following a specific brain lesion. Associations are not to be considered synonymous with symptom complexes such as Gerstman's syndrome.[2] In this case, they would not have inferential value for the understanding of normal processes because Gerstman's syndrome components (acalculia, finger anomia, left–right confusion) are also observed in isolation and no common factor except anatomical contiguity can be advocated to explain the syndrome. If associations are interpreted within a theoretically valid model of human cognition, then they are extremely useful. One example will better specify the validity of the method.

Patient K. E., reported by Hillis, Rapp, Romani, and Caramazza (1990), makes semantic errors on various types of lexical processing tasks (reading, writing, naming, and comprehension) at virtually identical rates regardless of the modality of stimulus or response. K. E.'s homogenous pattern of semantic errors across modalities is interpreted as evidence of selective damage to a semantic system common to all lexical processes. The value of this finding, an association, is not hampered by the dissociation in the performance of the same tasks observed still by Caramazza and Hillis (1990) on patients R. G. B. and H. W. These patients show similar, high rates of semantic errors in oral naming and oral reading but not in comparable written tasks. Furthermore, they show unimpaired comprehension of printed or spoken words, including

---

[2]Patients with Gerstman syndrome are characterized by *left–right disorientation* (an inability to distinguish between left and right); *finger agnosia* (difficulty in locating the relative position of fingers when a specific finger is touched); *agraphia* (a writing disability despite the absence of motor or sensory deficits), *acalculia* (an inability to carry out mathematical calculations). This syndrome, widely accepted since the 1960s, is now attacked by cognitive neuropsychologists because the symptoms that characterize the syndrome are not exclusively observed as a syndrome-complex, but often are observed in isolation.

those words in which the patients produced semantic errors in oral presentation. Taken together, these findings, associations and a dissociation, allow Caramazza and colleagues to support a theoretical model that distinguishes a single, modality neutral, central semantic system, disturbed in K. E., from a more peripheral level of lexical representation, the phonological output lexicon, disturbed in R. G. B. and H. W.

Studies on Normal Subjects

Most of the neuropsychological studies with normal subjects (dichotic listening, lateralized tachistoscopic presentation, dihaptic stimulation, etc.) were developed with the aim of studying the different functioning of the two cerebral hemispheres—hemispheric specialization. This issue is not considered here because it is not heuristic in the study of PM.

Other methodologies, which are increasingly used in cognitive psychology and that may have potentially heuristic value in PM works, are the study of brain imaging (positron emission tomography, PET) and event-related potentials (ERPs).

These techniques seem extremely promising for studies of PM because their peculiarity allows the measurement of brain functioning during the execution of a cognitive task. This enables us to constrain inferences about the processes involved in a task and their cerebral involvement.

Positron emission tomography (PET) provides images of brain functioning. It combines the principles of computerized tomography and radioisotope imaging. Some limits to the use of such a technique on a vast scale are due to the high cost of the machine, and to the prohibition in some countries to test normal volunteers. Another limit of the technique is that the time available for cognitive testing is a few minutes for each behavioral response (the time corresponds to the period of activity of the injected isotope); it is therefore necessary to test a subject for hours in order to obtain sufficient data.

The other technique (ERPs) does not present such limits and may be easily used in cognitive psychology laboratories. ERPs represent changes in the ongoing brain electrical activity (measured by EEG) and these changes are time-locked to a stimulus event. ERPs arise from the synchronous activities of neural populations involved in information processing. The theoretical interest in ERPs for cognitive psychologists derives from the possibility that specific wave forms can be correlated with specific types of cognitive and subcognitive processing taking place in the brain, and that on the basis of confirmed correlations the nature of the processes can be investigated (Kutas & Hillyard, 1984). In contrast to most measures used in cognitive experiments, which are discrete and offline (i.e., delayed with respect to the cognitive process under investigation), ERPs (like PET) are recorded continuously and therefore provide an online record of brain activity associated with the presentation of a stimulus.

Many studies supported the sensitivity of late components of ERPs to cognitive variables. Changes in P300 (a wave form which appears 300 msec after the presentation of a stimulus) are found with stimulus repetition, lexical decision, word frequency, attentional shifting, and so on (for reviews see Hylliard & Picton, 1987; Roharbaugh, Parasuraman, & Johnson, 1990). If used in conjunction with behavioral measures, ERP data can be used to identify and classify perceptual, cognitive, and linguistic operations. The most commonly used technique for separating the ERP from the EEG background is *averaging*. The process of averaging requires repetition of the event to which the ERP is related and computer summation of the time-locked electrical activity. The basic procedure consists of the repetition of a large number of identical trials. Through averaging of the signal trials the constant psychophysiological response (ERP) to the stimulus remains constant, whereas the variability not consistently related to the external event averages to zero. This procedure might limit the use of ERPs in PM studies because it requires too many trials that are not obtainable in PM tasks. Another approach to ERP analysis is more convenient with a PM procedure. It involves correlational techniques to measure the degree of similarity between ERP waveforms recorded under different conditions. Discriminant functions can be employed to measure how well an ERP conforms to one or another of the classes being discriminated. These discriminant functions can even be used to classify unaveraged, single-trial ERPs.

Another interesting methodology mimics functional loss due to a focal brain lesion in normal subjects. This may be accomplished using a dual-task paradigm (Bisiacchi, 1990). The logic underlying such a procedure is that if we prevent one component (the same supposed to be damaged by brain lesion) from working, then we should have the same pattern of performance in normal subjects as in patients with that particular functional loss.

In a dual-task paradigm with normal subjects Shallice, McLeod, and Lewis (1985) studied to what extent two tasks can be combined if one of them requires an input component involvement of the input–output subsystem and the other the output component involvement. It was showed that the task of detecting an unspecified name in an auditory input stream can be combined with reading aloud visually presented words with relatively little task decrement. The fact that the two tasks can be effortlessly combined supports the view that the systems underlying reading aloud and listening are separated. This procedure succeeded in paralleling with normal subjects the dissociation found by other researchers in patients for speech and music processing (Basso & Capitani, 1985).

Bisiacchi (1990) reproduced in normal subjects a conduction aphasic patient's deficit in phonological short-term memory. When asked to repeat SVO

(subject–verb–object) sentences with an *anomalous* word (i.e., a word semantically not appropriate for the context: "In the long grass the horses were
flying quietly"), the patient normalized the sentence giving the most frequent
solution (i.e., "In the long grass the horses were grazing quietly"). The same
pattern of errors was found in a group of normal subjects who had to perform
a concurrent backward counting task, but not in other groups of subjects who
performed dual tasks that did not require an involvement of phonological short
term memory.

Studies of Cognitive Processes
in Normal and Pathological Aging

Many batteries of neuropsychological tests are now standardized with an adult
sample of the population. This offers the possibility to evaluate the performance of brain damaged patients and to evaluate aged subjects (both normal
and pathological) and specify the tasks in which there is an age- or pathology-
related decrement and those in which no decrement is present. Because each
neuropsychological task is linked to the functioning of some cerebral areas, we
may infer the cerebral zone more affected by aging.

Moscovitch and Winocur (1992) formalized this approach calling it a *functional analogue of double and single dissociations*. The underlying assumption is that scores on neuropsychological tasks are valid measures of localized
deterioration. For instance, if a subject performs worse in memory tasks than
in linguistic ones, the structures involved in memory are probably more damaged than the speech areas. However, this technique must be used with caution in the study of aging because standardized neuropsychological tasks were
developed in the study of patients with focal lesions. The study of normal and
pathological elderly people who have a diffuse cerebral impairment may be
misleading. As Moscovitch and Winocur observed:

> Failure to find a correlation among neuropsychological tests does not mean nec-
> essarily that the functions they measure are not mediated by a common struc-
> ture. It might imply, instead, that supportive functions are sufficiently different
> that they obscure the correlation that may exist between the principal compo-
> nents. Consequently, only significant correlations on functional double or single
> dissociation tests are informative. (p.320)

EVIDENCE FOR A NEURAL SUBSTRATE
OF PROSPECTIVE MEMORY

From a neuropsychological point of view, prospective memory is strongly associated with a highly studied research area—frontal lobe functioning. What
comes to mind at once is one experimental paradigm (i.e., the delayed re-

sponse task) and a set of still open questions concerning the role of frontal lobes (i.e., planning, sequencing, control mechanisms, etc.).

Delayed Response Task[3]

The *delayed response paradigm* consists in training the experimental subject to respond to the stimulus target after a certain delay. It requires the execution of specific motor acts in accordance with specific events in the recent past. For example, in the classical delayed response task, every trial requires the manual choice of one or two identical objects under which, a few seconds before, food has been placed in full view of the animal. The hidden food is the reward for making the correct choice between the two objects.

The first data in neurobiology using this paradigm were from Jacobsen (1935) and Jacobsen and Nissen (1937), who found a specific deficit in monkeys with ablations of the anterior frontal cortex. Since Jacobsen (1935), it has been firmly established that lesions of the prefrontal cortex cause deficits in learning and performance of delay tasks (for a review see Fuster, 1985). That is, the delay task deficit is strictly dependent on the presence of delays between cues or between cues and responses; it is not present when the delay is eliminated. Furthermore, the deficit is not present when the animal has a single response associated with a single stimulus. The deficit appears only if two or more conflicting stimuli are present. The most accepted explanation is that animals with prefrontal lesions are incapable of normally performing those tasks because they lack the ability to retain information over a short period of time, or to suppress interfering responses, or both.

A similar pattern of performance was shown in human subjects with frontal lesions. Prisko (1963, quoted in Milner, 1964) adapted the delayed-response paradigm to study patients with frontal lobotomy. The task consisted of two easily discriminable stimuli presented in succession. The subjects' task was to say whether the second stimulus was the same as, or different from, the first stimulus presented 60 secs earlier. Patients with frontal lobe lesions were impaired in those tasks in which a few stimuli recurred in different pairs throughout the test, but made few errors when new stimuli were used. The interpretation was that frontal-lobe lesions showed a heightened susceptibility to interference from the effects of preceding trials. Milner (1968) advanced the hypothesis that frontal lobotomy may interfere with the ability to structure and segregate events in memory. Milner and collaborators (Milner, Petrides, & Smith, 1985) demonstrated in such patients a specific deficit in visual recog-

---

[3]The delay tasks belong to a category of experimental short-term memory tasks. In addition to the delayed response task, they include the delayed alternation and the delayed matching to sample. They all require the subject to retain information over a period of time and the need to ignore the alternate response.

nition and delayed-matching tests. Patients also showed deficits in temporal order and card sorting tasks. According to the authors, most of the deficits may be attributed to a failure of the control of internal interference. Lewinsohn, Zieler, Libet, Eyeberg, & Nielson (1972) showed the modality nonspecific nature of the retention deficit by testing patients with delayed matching tasks with different sensory cues and consistently finding impaired performance.

Electrophysiological studies used a behavioral paradigm similar to that of the delay tasks. This paradigm requires that on every trial the subject makes a simple motor response (pressing a button) after presentation of two stimuli (one auditory and one visual) that are separated by a 1-sec delay. The most prominent ERP, a slow surface negative potential, observed during intervals of preparation and anticipation is termed the *contingent negativity variation* (CNV) or *expectancy wave*. The first to study CNV were Walter, Cooper, Aldridge, McCallum, and Winter (1964) who observed this component in a fixed foreperiod[4] reaction time task. During the interval between a warning cue (S1) and a cue for prompt motor action (S2), the CNV appeared in frontal regions and remained until the response was executed. The first interpretation proposed was that this cortical electronegativity reflected the priming of the frontal lobe for efficient action. Subsequent research on the CNV demonstrated that it also occurs in the foreperiod of decision tasks that do not involve an overt motor response and that may require delays longer that 1 sec (up to 15 sec). What is essential for observing the CNV is the decision to take any kind of action, including the inhibition of movement (McCallum, 1979). Rugg et al. (1989) found CNV abnormalities in head injury patients. In these patients, at difference from controls, the early frontal CNV wave did not differentiate GO (execution of a response) and NO-GO (inhibition of a response) trials. These data were interpreted as reflecting impairments in selectively orienting to salient stimuli, and in differential response preparation. Such impairments were ascribed to damage to the frontal lobes or their connections.

Another source of evidence for a neural substrate of a-to-be-performed action comes from Fuster and collaborators' work on cell discharge (Fuster, 1973; Fuster, Bauer, & Jervery, 1982). They undertook a series of studies on cell discharge in the prefrontal cortex of monkeys performing delay tasks. They noted that a large proportion of cells reacted with increasing activity to the presentation of the cue. The magnitude of the increase depended on the cell, the nature of the cue, and the region of prefrontal cortex involved. The duration of the reactions varied widely. As soon as the cue disappeared, some cells returned to a baseline rate of firing, whereas others continued to fire during the delay period. This demonstrated that the cells in question were involved in retention in STM. On the other hand, the delay activity of some prefrontal cells by virtue of its temporally accelerating course or its relationship to im-

---

[4]It refers to the period between the ready signal and the presentation of the stimulus.

pending motor responses, seemed to be "looking forward" to the coming motor act (Fuster, 1985). It can therefore be considered as a preparation for anticipated action—one of the probable necessary components of a prospective task.

From the above exposition, it seems there are many similarities between the delayed response tasks and PM tasks—the need of a delay between the cue and the performance of the action (the longer the delay, the worse the performance of the action), the retention in STM of the intention (or at least the presence of a marker for the intention) to perform the action, the preparation for the action during the delay, and the monitoring of all of the activity. However, there is at least one important difference between delayed-response tasks and PM tasks. It concerns the self-initiating aspects of most PM tasks. Although external cues (such as the boxes with the hidden reward, or the overt requirement to execute the action at the end of the delay) are always present in delayed tasks, these cues are not always present in PM tasks.

According to Craik's (1986) view on memory, prospective memory is the memory task that requires the greatest degree of self-initiation. One aspect of the frontal-lobe syndrome consists of an inability to spontaneously initiate an action. It seems therefore plausible to suppose a deficit in self-initiating tasks. Incisa della Rocchetta & Milner (1993) stress the importance of frontal-lobe integrity in recall, especially when the search for stored items depends on strategies generated by the subject, rather than being guided by externally provided cues. However, the self-initiating aspect might be altered in other neurological diseases, such as lesions in basal ganglia like in Parkinson's disease. Unfortunately, there are no studies that address such questions with Parkinson's patients.

From Temporal Organization to Control Mechanisms

Milner et al. (1985), Fuster (1985, 1989), and Ingvar (1985) agreed in assigning to prefrontal and frontal cortex an important role in handling *temporal organization* of behavior and cognition.

Many different sequential forms of behavioral or cognitive performance give rise to an activation of frontal–prefrontal cortical areas as evident by studies on two- and three- dimensional metabolic rates and blood flow (Ingvar, 1985). The task varies from motor ideation (i.e., the willed conceptualization of a rhythmic movement of one hand) to silent speech, and all present an activation in frontal/prefrontal regions. According to Ingvar, cognitive action plans underlying memorization, recall, reasoning, and various types of problem solving have a neuronal substrate with a wide distribution in the prefrontal cortex.

A large body of empirical evidence (some of which is summarized in the previous section) supports the notion of a critical role of the prefrontal cortex in the temporal organization of goal-directed behavior sequences. The main feature of such a role is the adjustment of the actions of the organism to temporally distant events and goals.

Some data (Becker, Wess, Hunkin, & Parkin, 1993; Kopelman, 1989; Parkin, Leng, & Hunkin, 1990) showed that the temporal organization of behavior is not exclusively a function of frontal–prefrontal regions.

Parkin et al. (1990) and Becker et al. (1993) evaluated the ability of patients with memory deficits to encode and use information about temporal context. Subjects were taught to recall a set of four target objects and then were given a recognition test for those four objects. On Trial 1, both targets and distractors were novel, but on subsequent trials, objects that were previously used as targets were used as foils. By virtue of this procedure, the subjects were required not only to remember that they had seen an object, but when an object had been presented. They found that patients with Korsakoff's syndrome and Alzheimer's disease were impaired only in the temporal organization, whereas patients with temporal-lobe amnesia did not present such an impairment.

The authors concluded that the neural substrate of the ability to remember when a stimulus is presented is not necessarily in the frontal lobe but involves the midline diencephalic structures. It still might be the case, however, that the frontal lobes are primarily involved in temporal organization for stimuli that will happen in the future, whereas diencephalic structures are concerned with the temporal organization of past events.

Clarke, Assal, and de Tribolet (1993) described a young patient whose cerebral lesion was in the posterior part of the right hemisphere. She presented a deficit in time planning, accompanied by retrospective memory disorders, severe topographical disorientation, and mild apperceptive agnosia. The time-planning deficit consisted in extreme slowness and occasional inability to tell about activities planned for the following days. The authors attributed the impairment to the deficiency of an inner representation of her projects.

One process that directly derives from temporal organization of actions is *planning*. Planning is the ability to organize behavior in order to achieve some goal. It is a mental simulation that envisages circumstances and runs through possible actions, evaluating the consequences and selecting the optimal actions and the optimal order for executing them.

Two cognitive processes involved in planning are *memory* and *monitoring*. Knowledge derived from past experience and stored in long-term memory must be retrieved and used in formulating possible plans, and in constructing representations of hypothetical events. A working memory buffer store is needed to hold tentative or incomplete plans while these are being evaluated or revised.

The second process involved in planning is a *control mechanism* that enables verifying, almost online, the correct execution of the plan and allows switching between different actions, permitting the inhibition of one task in favor of another.

Luria (1966, 1973) described patients with frontal-lobe lesions who showed impairments in tasks that required planning and organization over a time period, such as following recipes and scheduling appointments. He called such disorders *frontal apraxia* and defined them as a breakdown in programming, regulation, and verification of activity.

Schwartz et al. (1991) described a case of intellectual decline and persistent action disorder following a subarachnoid haemorrhage involving the frontal lobes, the anterior part of corpus callosum, and the basal ganglia. A detailed analysis of everyday action disorders (using their action coding system) led the authors to show that the disruption of performance may be a consequence of a deficit in the intentional control of action.

Shallice (1982, 1988, 1994) and Norman and Shallice's (1986) model of attentional control of action furnished a theoretical background for planning and control mechanisms. The model involves three levels. The lowest level consists of a psychological processing structure whose operation is controlled by action or thought schemas. Then the model distinguishes between two modes of action control: an automatic one via a *contention scheduling* mechanism, and a deliberate attentional control via a *supervisory attentional system* (SAS), operating by biasing the contention scheduling selection process. Shallice and Burgess (1991) tested this model with three patients who had sustained traumatic injures involving prefrontal structures. The patients performed mainly in the normal range in a variety of neuropsychological tests. Two patients performed within normal range on tests requiring an involvement of frontal lobes. Their main problems were in tasks that required the performance of multiple activities. One task involved the creation of a simple plan, the scheduling of subtests, and the checking of time. The second involved the performance of a sequence of actions in a real-life situation. The authors attributed the observed impairment in one case to errors in the marker creation that permits the triggering of the appropriate action and in another case to disturbances in goal articulation, plan formulation, and evaluation. These findings suggest the possibility of a fractionation of the component processes undertaken by the SAS and a main involvement of frontal lobes in such processes.

Another critical aspect for control mechanisms is the ability to switch between two or more different tasks or responses. This ability is also called *cognitive flexibility*. Neuropsychological studies demonstrated that impairments in cognitive flexibility are predominantly associated with frontal lobe pathology (Stuss & Benson, 1986). Eslinger and Grattan (1993) found that cognitive flexibility may be disrupted in frontal-lobe and in basal ganglia lesions. They differentiated two types of flexibility—*reactive flexibility* (i.e., shifting response set) from *spontaneous flexibility* (i.e., producing a diversity of ideas). They found that frontal-lobe lesions markedly disturbed spontaneous flexibility, whereas basal ganglia lesions produced a poor performance, similar to frontal lesions, in reactive flexibility. These findings suggest that frontal lobe and basal

ganglia are both involved in the response-shifting aspect of cognitive flexibility. Indeed, anatomical connections from frontal lobe to basal ganglia were
found in primates (Goldman & Nauta, 1977), supporting the hypothesis of a
strong connection between the two cerebral structures.

NEUROPSYCHOLOGICAL APPROACH TO PM:
SOME EXPERIMENTAL EVIDENCE

Bearing in mind the points discussed, we used a neuropsychological methodology to address the question of which processes are involved in PM tasks. One
study (Bisiacchi & Sgaramella, 1993) concerned the use of the functional analogue of double dissociation, and the other was a study of single cases using
the dissociation approach (Sgaramella, Zettin, Bisiacchi, Verné, & Rago, 1993).

A Neuropsychological Study of Normal Aging

A battery of neuropsychological tests was administered to 131 persons ranging in age from 50 to 92 (75 women, 56 men). All the subjects were self-suffi-
cient and performed in the normal range on an assessment scale for dementia.

Subjects were divided into four groups according to their age: 50–60, 60–
70, 70–80, > 80.

Each group was engaged in a series of neuropsychological tasks, during
which they were asked to perform some prospective memory tasks. The tasks
consisted of the following:

Memory Tasks (Both Short- and Long-Term). Digit span, either forward
and backward; spatial span (Corsi test); span for short and long names; free
recall.

Frontal Lobe Tasks. A reduced version of the Wisconsin Card Sorting Test
(WCST; Wechsler, 1981) (Nelson, 1976); story arrangements and maze tests
from the Wechsler Adult Intelligence Scale (WAIS); and a planning task. In the
planning task, subjects were presented with a map of a town and asked to move
around this hypothetical town. They were asked to produce a plan for completing as many as possible of ten errands proposed in the instructions, using
the shortest way. The subjects' task was to sequence errands, to time actions,
and to logically order goals (Cohen, 1988; Hayes-Roth & Hayes-Roth, 1979).
Some constraints were given—the time of starting, and the return (9:00 a.m.
and 12:30 a.m., respectively); the opening hours of shops, public offices (from
9:00 a.m. to 12:30 a.m.), and the hospital (from 11:00 a.m. to 1:00 p.m.). The
score (max. 100) was calculated considering both the number of errands performed and the errors made. Errors were categorized in several types—omis-

sions, logical errors (rule breaking, i.e., going to post office before taking the money from the bank); perseverations (i.e., going more than once in the same place); intrusions (i.e., executions of errands not proposed in the instructions) either related or not to everyday routines referred by the subject; and planning errors (i.e., choosing a longer way to reach the target or losing time).

Intelligence Level. Raven Matrices.

Prospective Memory Tasks. Event- or time-based actions. The prospective memory tasks were either time- or event-related actions. For the time-based action, on the ongoing tasks subjects were asked to inform the experimenter when they estimated that 10 min had passed. For the event-based task, subjects were required to write a cross on a list at the end of each task.

A clock was always visible to the subjects in the room, however no subject (in all conditions) looked at the clock more than twice in a session. At the beginning of the session, subjects were informed about task requirements, which were never mentioned again. The two PM tasks differed in the extent to which subjects relied on an external cue, which consisted of the pronunciation of the utterance, "now the task is finished," at the end of each task. It was a cue for the event-related action and was almost neutral in the time-based action.

The score consisted in the percentage of correct executions.

As shown in Figs. 15.1, 15.2, and 15.3, all tests showed a decline with increasing age. Different patterns of decline seemed to emerge for different tasks; in some cases the declines appeared after 60 (digit-span forward, free recall, short names span, Raven Matrices, planning task); in other cases after 70 (spatial span, Maze test, story arrangements, PM tasks as a whole); and in other cases, the difference was significant only when comparing the youngest group with the oldest (digit backward and long names span, WCST).

However, the most interesting result comes from a factor analysis. Two dif-

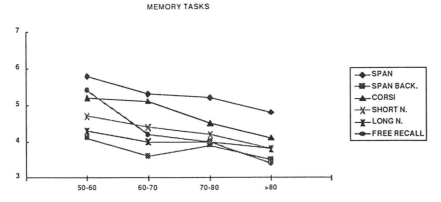

FIG. 15.1.   Scores on memory tasks for the four groups.

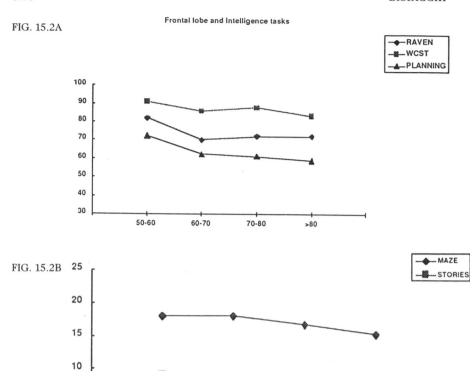

FIGS. 15.2A and 15.2B.   Performance of the four groups on Raven matrices,
WCST and Planning; standarized score on WAIS stories and Porteus maze.

ferent factor analyses were performed, the first with subjects under 70 and the
second with subjects over 70.

For the youngest group, three factors emerged. The first factor was saturated by all memory tasks, Raven matrices, maze test, and stories arrange-
ment. The second factor consisted of WSCT and Planning; the third factor was
saturated only by prospective memory tasks. The presence of a factor devoted
to PM tasks outlines the peculiarities and the independence of this "memory"
regarding retrospective memory and other processes.

However, if we consider the other factor analysis (with subjects over 70) a
different pattern of results emerges. The first factor is saturated by all of the
STM tasks; the second factor by planning, free recall and PM tasks; the third
factor by WSCT, Raven Matrices, story arrangements, and maze test.

In the elderly, the decline of some retrospective memory abilities is more influential within the different PM components. It might be that the performance in planning and prospective memory tasks is differently achieved according to the subject's age. The different strategies utilized in performing might strongly depend on subjects' retrospective memory abilities (and mainly short-term memory abilities). The observed impairment with aging may be due to a differential influence of the PM components. The well-documented decline with age in retrospective memory induces a rearrangement of the relative importance of each subcomponent required in a PM task. This pattern of behavior is a compensation effect often observed in brain-damaged patients (Bisiacchi, 1987, 1990; Semenza et al., 1988) who overuse the intact abilities to solve a task that requires a damaged process. The performance of brain-damaged patients reflects a reorganization that highlights the regularities of the residual system in its regular functions and in its hidden potentialities. Frequently, neuropsychological reorganization results in overusing unimpaired processes in order to compensate for a deficiency in other processes. For instance, the paralexic errors of deep dyslexics arise because no interactions with the process of visual segmentation of the script take place. Elderly subjects might rely on everyday routines in performing the planning and PM tasks because they are limited in working memory capacities required, as mentioned before, by both tasks.

The Study of Single Cases

The literature on PM states that following components are involved: It seems necessary to form and organize an intention, to remember the intention over

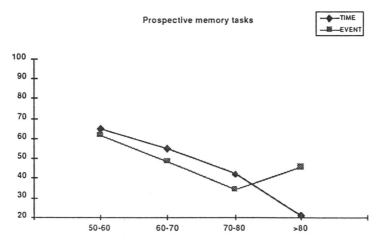

FIG. 15.3.　Percentage of correct remembering in the two conditions of prospective memory tasks.

a period of time, to monitor when and how to execute the action and, finally, to perform the action and remember to have done it (see Ellis, this volume). In such an analysis there is the more or less implicit agreement about the utilization of some retrospective abilities that permit, over a certain delay, memory for the content of the action to be performed in the future. The possibility to study patients who may present a deficit in one of the components hypothesized to play a role in PM is a further confirmation of the validity of the componential analysis.

In a pilot work, three patients with closed head injury and a major involvement of frontal lobe(s) were studied (Sgaramella et al., 1993).

Table 15.1 reports patients' neuropsychological screening.

From a rapid inspection of the results of neuropsychological tests, intelligence level (tested by WAIS and Raven matrices) is in the normal range for all patients; the performance of frontal-lobe tasks involving concept formation, selection, and shifting of rules (Weigl, WCST) is also in the normal range; memory span (verbal and spatial) is in the inferior limits; memory abilities tested with Wechsler Memory Scale (WMS) are within normal limits; the ability to learn a suvraspan list of words is preserved in all subjects except one (LIN). Only patient LIN presented a mild impairment in long-term memory, for the other two, the neuropsychological evaluation did not show any impairment.

The choice of these patients was due to common observations in clinical neuropsychology that neuropsychological testing does not predict the serious problems that these patients encounter in everyday life (e.g., scheduling appointments, following time-tables, preparing meals, etc.). Often the neuropsychological tests suggest that the cognitive abilities are mostly conserved. Despite this favorable diagnosis, patients are unable to deal with their normal life —their jobs, housekeeping, and so on.

TABLE 15.1A
Neuropsychological Data, Levels of Instruction,
Age and Side of the Lesion of the Three Patients

	Age	Scholarity	IQ	WCST	Raven	Weigl	Lesion
AL	18	10	113	60/77	42/48	12/15	Frontal Bilateral
CAB	16	10	120	60/70	43/48	15/15	Frontal Left
LIN	33	10	118	60/72	36/48	13/15	Front-Temp. Right

	WMS	Span	Learning	Primacy	Recency
AL	129	5	4.4	+	+
CAB	101	4	7.7	+	+
LIN	84	5	19.6*	+	+

*out of normal range
– absence   + presence

TABLE 15.2
Scores on Planning Task (maximum 100) and
Percentage of Correct Execution in PM Tasks of the Three Patients

	Planning	PM Time	PM Event
AL	90	0	0
CAB	20	100	100
LIN	50	0	0

PM tasks seemed to us a useful tool for studying their abilities in some everyday problems. We tested the same tasks used with the elderly—the planning task and two recursive PM tasks, both event- and time-based (described in the preceding section) together with a neuropsychological assessment.

The pattern of results for the planning task and prospective memory tasks is different, as shown in Table 15.2.

In this case, the patients show some interesting dissociations. Patient AL performs well in planning (90 is a score within the normal range for his age[5]), but performs poorly on the PM tasks (the score is 0). Conversely, patient CAB performs poorly in planning (20) but perfectly well in PM tasks (100). Patient LIN displays a poor performance both in planning (50) and in the PM tasks (0). Considering the performance of these patients in retrospective memory tasks, impairments in planning or prospective memory may be independent from memory abilities because patients CAB and AL perform within the normal range in all the memory tests. However, patient LIN who presents deficits in retrospective memory, is also affected in planning and PM performances. The data are insufficient to make strong inferences. In fact, good retrospective memory is insufficient to predict good PM performance, as shown by CAB and AL who had a performance within normal range in all the retrospective memory tasks, but presented selective deficit in planning (CAB) or in PM tasks (AL).

The results from the research with the elderly and the study of single cases with specific impairment in PM abilities present some converging elements. Both planning abilities and performance of an action in the future may be impaired in subjects with no other cognitive impairments. The factor analyses in the study of the elderly and the presence of a selective deficit for planning, present in one patient we studied, suggest an independence of these two tasks. This finding supports the idea of the presence of different processes in PM tasks. This is not an exhaustive list of processes (others such as monitoring were not tested), but the guess is that control mechanisms play an important role in PM tasks.

---

[5]The normative data for the planning task are from Bisiacchi and Sgaramella (1992) and from Sgaramella, Bisiacchi, & Falchero (in press).

CONCLUDING REMARKS

The findings in this chapter support the idea, advanced by Hitch and Ferguson's (1991) theoretical analysis, that PM is a multicomponent process. Hitch and Ferguson pointed out three different stages in prospective remembering—forming a future intention, remembering the intention during an intervening period, and performing the intention at the right moment. Neuropsychological data provide empirical evidence concerning PM organization. According to Hitch and Ferguson the first stage consists in *forming a future intention*. We rarely form a single future intention; what generally happens is that we have to fit one (or more) future intention(s) into an already existing plan. This plan has to be kept in a short-term buffer until an external or, more often, an internal marker triggers action execution. Correct performance requires an intact temporal organization and a control mechanism that permits continuous checking of the chaining of activities and inhibits the ongoing activity when the marker prompts action execution.

As a consequence of PM's multicomponent process, it is unlikely that only a lesion to a specific cerebral area will produce disorders in PM. It is more plausible that depending on the side and the size of the lesion, some processes involved in PM will be damaged, whereas others will be spared.

Most findings support the idea of a major involvement of frontal and prefrontal cerebral areas in practically all of the components of PM (Fuster, 1985; Ingvar, 1985, Shallice & Burgess, 1991). Exceptions to this trend are the results by Bisiacchi and Sgaramella (1993) and McDaniel, Glisky, Routhieaux, and Remers (1994), who showed that performance of older adults under age 70 on neuropsychological tests related to frontal functioning does not correlate with prospective memory performance.

Some of the data reported suggest that diencephalic and basal ganglia structures are involved in processes underlying PM. Parkin et al. (1990) and Becker et al. (1993) found a diencephalic involvement in temporal organization. Schwartz, Reed, Montgomery, Palmer, & Mayer's (1991) patient with action disorder presented a large lesion involving both frontal lobe and basal ganglia. Eslinger and Grattan (1993) found a dissociation between frontal-lobe lesions and basal ganglia lesions in spontaneous flexibility, but not in reactive flexibility. This seems to suggest an involvement of basal ganglia in control mechanisms.

Furthermore the retrospective memory requirements of PM tasks may cause patients with memory deficits, but no lesion in the frontal lobes, to fail to remember a PM action (Bisiacchi & Sgaramella, 1992, 1993).

The neuropsychological study of normal subjects and patients with PM disorders is just beginning, but it promises to be an heuristic field of research leading to a better comprehension of this multicomponent activity.

REFERENCES

Basso, A., & Capitani, E. (1985). Spared musical abilities in a conductor with global aphasia and ideomotor apraxia. *Journal of Neurology, Neurosurgery and Psychiatry, 48,* 407–412.

Becker, J. T., Wess, J., Hunkin, N. M., & Parkin A. J. (1993). Use of temporal context information in Alzheimer disease, *Neuropsychologia, 2,* 137–143.

Bisiacchi, P. S. (1987, January). *Knowledge and processing of semantic relations in aphasia.* Paper presented at the Fifth European Workshop on Cognitive Neuropsychology, Bressanone, Italy.

Bisiacchi, P. S., & Sgaramella, M. T. (1993, November). *A neuropsychological approach to prospective memory.* Paper presented at the 34th annual meeting of the Psychonomic Society, Washington, DC.

Bisiacchi, P. S., & Sgaramella, M. T. (1992). La memoria prospettica negli anziani. *Psicologia e società. Rivista di Psicologia Sociale, XVII(XXXIX), 1–2,* 77–94.

Bisiacchi, P. S. (1990). Lo studio del singolo caso in neuropsicologia cognitiva: una diversa prospettiva nella valutazione del cambiamento [Single case study in cognitive neuropsychology: A different view in changing evaluation]. In M. Sambin (Ed.), *La misura del cambiamento* (pp. 33–47). Milano: Franco Angeli.

Caramazza, A., & Hillis, A. E. (1990). Where do lexical errors come from? *Cortex, 1,* 95–122.

Caramazza, A. (1986). On drawing inferences about the structure of normal cognitive systems from the analysis of patterns of impaired performance: The case for single-patient studies. *Brain and Cognition, 5,* 41–66.

Clarke, S., Assal, G., & de Tribolet, N. (1993). Left hemisphere strategies in visual recognition, topographical orientation and time planning, *Neuropsychologia, 31(2),* 99–113.

Cohen, G. (1988). *Memory in the real world.* London: Lawrence Erlbaum Associates.

Craik, F. I. M. (1986). A functional account of age differences in memory. In F. Klix & H. Hagendorf (Eds.), *Human memory and cognitive capabilities: mechanisms and performances* (pp. 409–422). North Holland: Elsevier Science.

Denes, G., Semenza, C., & Bisiacchi, P. S. (1988). *Perspectives on Cognitive neuropsychology,* London: Lawrence Erlbaum Associates.

Eslinger, P. J., & Grattan, L. M. (1993). Frontal lobe and frontal-striatal substrates for different forms of human cognitive flexibility, *Neuropsychologia, 31,(1),* 17–28.

Fodor, J. A. (1983). *The modularity of mind.* Cambridge, MA: MIT Press.

Fuster, J. M. (1973). Unit activity in prefrontal cortex during delayed-response performance: neuronal correlates of transient monkey. *Journal of Neurophysiology, 36,* 61–78.

Fuster, J. M. (1985). The prefrontal cortex, mediator of cross-temporal contingencies, *Human Neurobiology, 4,* 169–179.

Fuster, J. M. (1989). *The prefrontal cortex.* New York: Raven.

Fuster, J. M., Bauer, R. H., & Jervery, J. P. (1982). Cellular discharge in the dorsolateral prefrontal cortex of the monkey in cognitive tasks. *Experimental Neurology, 77,* 679–694.

Goldman, P. S., & Nauta, W. J. H. (1977). An intricately patterned prefrontal-caudal projection in the rhesus monkey, *Journal of Comparative Neurology, 171,* 369–386.

Hayes-Roth, B., & Hayes-Roth, F. (1979). A cognitive model of planning, *Cognitive Science, 3,* 275–310.

Hillis, A. E., Rapp, B. C., Romani, C., & Caramazza, A. (1990). Selective impairment of semantics in lexical processing. *Cognitive Neuropsychology, 7,* 191–244.

Hitch, G. J., & Ferguson, J. (1991). Prospective memory for future intentions: some comparisons with memory for past events, *European Journal of Cognitive Psychology, 3(3),* 285–295.

Hylliard, S. A., & Picton, T. W. (1987). Electrophysiology of cognition. In V. Mountcastle (Ed.), *Handbook of physiology* (Vol. 6, pp. 519–584). Amsterdam, Netherlands: Elsevier.

Incisa della Rocchetta, A., & Milner, B. (1993). Strategic search and retrieval inhibition: the role of the frontal lobes. *Neuropsychologia, 31*(6), 503–524.

Ingvar, D. H. (1985). "Memory of the future": an essay on the temporal organization of conscious awareness, *Human Neurobiology, 4,* 127–136.

Jacobsen, C. F. (1935). Functions of the frontal association area in primates. *Arch. Neurol. Psychiatr., 33,* 558–569.

Jacobsen, C. F., & Nissen, H. W. (1937). Studies of cerebral functions in primates. The effects of frontal lobe lesions on the delayed alternation habit in monkeys. *Journal of Comparative Physiological Psychology, 23,* 101–112.

Kopelman, M. D. (1989). Remote and autobiographical memory, temporal context memory and frontal atrophy in Korsakoff and Alzheimer patients. *Neuropsychologia, 27,* 437–460.

Kutas, M., & Hillyard, S. A. (1984). Brain potentials during reading reflect word expectancy and semantic association, *Nature, 307,* 161–163.

Kvavilashvili, L. (1987). Remembering intentions as a distinct form of memory. *British Journal of psychology, 78,* 507–518.

Lewinsohn, P., Zieler, R., Libet, J., Eyeberg, S., & Nielson, G. (1972). Short term memory—a comparison between frontal and non frontal right- and left-hemisphere brain-damaged patients. *Journal of Comparative Physiological Psychology, 81,* 248–255.

Luria, R. (1966). *Higher cortical functions in man.* New York: Basic Books.

Luria, R. (1973). *The working brain.* New York: Basic Books.

McCallum, W. C. (1979). Cognitive aspects of slow potentials changes. In J. E. Desmedt (Ed.), *Cognitive components in cerebral event related potentials and selective attention* (pp. 151–171). Basel, Switzerland: Krager.

McDaniel, M. A., Glisky, E. L., Routhieaux, B. C., & Remers, L. A. (1994, April). *The role of frontal lobe in temporally-based and cue-based prospective remembering in older adults.* Paper presented at Cognitive Aging Conference, Atlanta, GA.

Milner, B. (1964). Some effects of frontal lobectomy in man. In J. M. Warren & K. Albert (Eds.), *The frontal granular cortex and behaviour* (pp. 313–339). New York: McGraw-Hill.

Milner, B. (1968). Memory. In L. Weiskrantz (Ed.), *Analysis of behavioural changes* (pp. 328–356). New York: Harper & Row.

Milner, B., Petrides, M., & Smith, L. (1985). Frontal lobes and the temporal organization of memory. *Human Neurobiology, 4,* 137–142.

Moscovitch M., & Winocur G. (1992). The neuropsychology of memory and aging. In T. A. Salthouse & F. I. M. Craik (Eds.), *The handbook of aging and cognition* (pp. 315–372). Hillsdale, NJ: Lawrence Erlbaum Associates.

Nelson, H. E. (1976). A modified card sorting test sensitive to frontal lobe defect. *Cortex, 12,* 313–324.

Norman, D. A., & Shallice, T. (1986). Attention to Action: Willed and automatic control of behaviour. In R. J. Davidson, G. E. Schwartz, & D. Shapiro (Eds.), *Consciousness and self regulation* (Vol. 4, pp. 1–18). New York: Plenum.

Parkin, A. J., Leng, N. R. C., & Hunkin, N. M. (1990). Differential sensitivity to context in diencephalic and temporal lobe amnesia. *Cortex, 26,* 373–380.

Prisko, L. (1963). *Short term memory in focal cerebral damage.* Unpublished doctoral dissertation, McGill University, Montreal.

Rapp, B. C., & Caramazza, A. (1991). Cognitive neuropsychology: From impaired performance to normal cognitive structure. In R. G. Lister & H. J. Weingartner (Eds.), *Perspective on cognitive neuroscience* (pp. 389–504). Oxford, England: Oxford University Press.

Roharbaugh, J. W., Parasuraman, R., & Johnson, R. (1990). *Event related potentials.* New York: Oxford University Press.

Rugg, M. D., Cowan, C. P., Nagy, M. E., Milner, A. D., Jacobson, I., & Brooks, D. N. (1989). CNV abnormalities following closed head injury. *Brain, 112,* 489–506.

Schwartz, M. F., Reed, E. S., Montgomery, M., Palmer, C., & Mayer, N. H. (1991). The quantitative description of action disorganisation after brain damage case study. *Cognitive Neuropsychology, 8*(5), 381–414.

Semenza, C. (in press). Methodological issues. In G. Beaumont & J. Sergent (Eds.), *Dictionary of Neuropsychology*, Oxford, England: Basil Blacknell.

Semenza, C., & Bisiacchi, P. S. (in press). Warrington & Shallice's (1984). category specific case JBR. In C. Code, K. Wallesh, I. Jouanette, & J. Lecours (Eds.), *Classical cases in Neuropsychology*. Hillsdale, NJ: Lawrence Erlbaum Associates.

Semenza, C., Bisiacchi, P. S., & Rosenthal, V. (1988). A function for Cognitive Neuropsychology. In G. Denes, C. Semenza, & P. S. Bisiacchi (Eds.), *Perspectives on Cognitive Neuropsychology* (pp. 1–24). Hillsdale, NJ: Lawrence Erlbaum Associates.

Sgaramella, T. M., Bisiacchi, P. S., & Falchero, S. (in press). Il ruolo dell'età nell'abilità di pianificazione [The role of age in spatial planning], *Ricerche di psicologia*.

Sgaramella, T. M., Zettin, M., Bisiacchi, P. S., Verné, D., & Rago, R. (1993, June). *Retrospective memory and planning components in prospective remembering: Evidence from a neuropsychological study*. Paper presented at the Workshop on Memory and Mental Representations, Roma, Italy.

Shallice, T. (1982). Specific impairments of planning, *Philosophical Transcripts of the Royal Society of London, B 298*, 199–209.

Shallice, T. (1988). *From Neuropsychology to mental structure*. Cambridge, England: Cambridge University Press.

Shallice, T. (1991). Précis of From Neuropsychology to mental structure. *Behavioural and Brain Sciences, 14*, 429–469.

Shallice, T. (1994). Multiple levels of control processes, In C. A. Umilta' & M. Moskovitch (Eds.), *Attention & Performance XV*. Hillsdale, NJ: Lawrence Erlbaum Associates.

Shallice, T., & Burgess, P. W. (1991). Deficits in strategy application following frontal lobe damage in man. *Brain, 114*, 727–741.

Shallice, T., McLeod, P., & Lewis, K. (1985). Isolating cognitive modules with the dual task paradigm: are speech perception and production two separate processes? *Quarterly Journal of Experimental Psychology, 37A*, 507–532.

Stuss, D. T., & Benson, D. F. (1986). *The frontal lobes*. New York: Raven.

Walter, W. G. R., Cooper, R., Aldridge, V. J., McCallum, W. C., & Winter, A. L. (1964). Contingent negativity variation: an electric sign of sensorimor association and expectancy in the human brain. *Nature Lond., 203*, 380–384.

Wechsler, D. (1987). Wechsler Adult Intelligent Scale–Revised. Ohio: The Psychological Corporation.

16

COMMENTARY

The Neuropsychology of
Prospective Memory

Tim Shallice
University College London

The neuropsychology of prospective memory is poorly understood. A brief look at the practical difficulties involved in the area makes it clear why this is the case. Following Bisiacchi I consider the standard human neuropsychological approaches, namely single-case studies and group studies.

Effective single-case studies in the area are presented with a number of problems. First, appropriate patients for single-case studies are normally detected in clinical testing. However, a standard clinical neuropsychological work-up of a patient will contain one or more sets of tests on retrospective memory, but no clinical tests batteries contain any whole subtests directly relevant to the area.[1] Moreover, problems in the realization of intentions, although clinically apparent when the patient's everyday behavior is known (see Shallice & Burgess, 1991), do not present floridly in the clinical examination, unlike, say, confabulation following anterior communicating artery aneurysms or classical amnesia in the retrospective memory domain. An equally critical problem is that the experimental paradigms are both fewer in number and have a much lower output in information for the time invested than those in the retrospective memory domain. Thus, the design of an effective single-case study in the area is especially difficult.

---

[1] Two new executive test batteries will contain clinical versions of the Six Elements Test on which the patients that Burgess and I argue had a selective deficit in the realization of intentions (see Bisiacchi's chapter) performed poorly. They are being developed by Wilson and colleagues from the Applied Psychology Unit, Cambridge, and Levine, Stuss, and Milberg from the Rotman Research Unit, Toronto.

For group studies, the contrast with the situation in the retrospective memory domain is equally poor. Classical amnesia within the retrospective memory domain is one of the few selective disorders where functionally based group studies are highly valuable (see Shallice, 1988, for discussion). This occurs because a variety of disease processes can produce relatively specific lesions of the structures responsible for episodic memory (e.g., hippocampus, mamilliary bodies, thalamus). No equivalent disease-to-structure-to-process mappings occur in the prospective memory domain as far as is known with the doubtful exception of frontal head injury. This leaves the lesion-location-based group study, which is very costly in time and resources. No one to my knowledge has yet carried out such a study in the prospective memory domain.

The three authors adopted shrewd and complementary approaches to this somewhat discouraging state of affairs. Bisiacchi provides a thorough review of the sketchy literature currently available on the topic. In addition, she presents a brief account of the work by herself and her colleagues, which may well prove to be the most relevant studies yet carried out. Glisky takes a more indirect approach reviewing the literature on frontal lobe function and retrospective memory and on normal ageing and prospective memory. This is appropriate, given that the frontal lobes are critical for prospective memory function and that the normal ageing process most typically produces greater impairments in functions based in the frontal lobes than in other cortical structures. Cohen and O'Reilly take a more panoramic perspective, placing prospective memory in the context of a more general theory of frontal lobe and hippocampal functions.

A consistent theme throughout all three chapters is that the prefrontal cortex is likely to prove a critical area of the cortex for the processes underlying prospective memory. However, Bisiacchi points out that in the study of Bisiacchi and Sgamarella, the performance of older adults under 70 on neuropsychological tests related to frontal functioning does not correlate with planning and prospective memory performance. Unfortunately, the correlation matrices related to these factor analyses have yet to be published. However, for only one task used that is held to be related to frontal functioning—the Wisconsin—is the relation solidly established (e.g., Milner, 1963; Nelson, 1976), but even in this case other structures also seem to be involved (Anderson et al., 1991). More critically correlations between tasks known to be frontally loaded can be low in some groups (e.g., Kopelman, 1991) and the correlations that exist can disappear when IQs are partialled out (e.g., Shallice & Burgess, 1993).

There are at least four reasons why these low correlations may be found, other than that prospective memory does not involve processes located in prefrontal structures. The degree of variability in frontal function in the particular relatively intact group—older adults under 65—may not be critical for one or other test performance. One or other test may have low reliability or may also be heavily loaded on processes located elsewhere in the brain. Most critically, there may be fractionation within frontal lobe functions (e.g., Shallice & Burgess, 1993). Factor analytic studies of tests loaded on frontal functions are beginning to be carried out in a variety of populations and are producing intriguing results. At present, however, it is most unclear how these results should be interpreted. I believe that direct investigations of neurological patients with frontal lesions such as the tantalizingly brief account of patient AL who appears to have a selective prospective memory problem, are more likely to provide clear results.

Glisky, of course, makes frontal involvement in memory tasks a central plank of her chapter. Much of her argument as far as prospective memory is concerned is based on her anatomically orientated adaptation of Craik's (1986) position about the effects of aging on prospective memory performance. The general position that aging affects executive functions more than the specific processing resources they control, seems eminently plausible. Thus Craik, Morris, and Gick (1990), in noting the relative lack of age differences on primary memory tasks, argued that most vulnerable to the effects of age are the "flexibility and computational abilities" of Baddeley's (1986) central executive system, which Baddeley identified with a frontally located supervisory system.

Glisky finishes by suggesting that functional imaging studies may elucidate the involvement of the prefrontal cortex in memory tasks. As far as retrospective memory tasks are concerned, her suggestion is prescient. Thus, Grasby et al. (1993) showed greater involvement of both left and right prefrontal cortices (areas 9/10 and 46) in secondary compared with primary memory in (verbal) free recall.[2] For verbal material, encoding seems to involve the left dorsolateral prefrontal region (area 46) (Kapur et al., 1994; Shallice et al., 1994). However, retrieval involves primarily the right dorsolateral prefrontal (areas 10, 46 and 47; Shallice et al., 1994; Tulving et al., 1994 [see also Squire et al., 1992 where, however, the paradigm involved priming]). Glisky suggests that functional imaging may also be useful for localizing processes involved in prospective memory. However, the recall of intentions is a process that is not precisely localizable in time and not under direct stimulus control. As effective PET scanning, for instance, requires the occurrence of multiple relevant events within

---

[2]It should be noted with respect to Cohen and O'Reilly's statement that digit span involves activation of prefrontal cortex, that only processing of supra span lists in the Grasby et al. study led to greater activation than rest of left dorsolated prefrontal cortex. Processing subspan lists, which has essentially the same phonological buffer requirements as digit span, involves left parietotemporal cortex (see also Paulesu, Frith, & Frackowiak, 1993; Warrington, Logue, & Pratt, 1971). This indicates that it is dangerous to characterize certain processes carried out in the left dorsolateral prefrontal cortex by the broad term *working memory,* which has a complex information-processing referent (see Baddeley, 1986).

a 40 to 60 sec window, there would be considerable technical difficulty in applying the technique to the processes underlying prospective memory retrieval.

The third chapter—that of Cohen and O'Reilly—is highly original if much more speculative. It is assumed that prospective memory requires an interaction between processes localized in the prefrontal cortex and those in the hippocampus. Task-relevant bias is the responsibility of the processes localized in prefrontal cortex and the novel binding of memory elements that of processes in the hippocampus. Separate models of the two types of process are described.

That the realization of intentions involves interactions between the prefrontal cortex and the hippocampus is most plausible. In addition, the two models provide theoretically powerful ways of accounting for a range of findings. However, I find the extension of the ideas proposed to prospective memory rather difficult to follow.

Consider the retrieval of intentions, and in particular, the example discussed of the elicitation of the go-to-grocery plan. Processes localized in the hippocampus are held to favor the go-to-grocery plan over the "usual go-straight-home representation within the PFC." Cohen and O'Reilly argue that distraction could lead to a "prefrontal cortex failure" and so "the elicitation of the more habitual response (going straight home)," which they point out is a well-documented lapse shown in normal subjects (e.g., Reason, 1984). The presupposition that distraction leads to a weakening of the control over supervisory processes localized in prefrontal cortex seems appropriate (see Shallice, 1982). However, it is unclear on their model why the weakening of prefrontal influences should not strengthen rather than weaken the tendency to go to the currently appropriate place because the prefrontal cortex is where the go-straight-home plan is held to be localized. The currently appropriate representation is stored in the hippocampus, not held to be affected by distraction.

We can confront this problem by assuming that executing a routine plan requires neither the PFC nor the hippocampus, but is controlled at the level of what Norman and I (Norman & Shallice, 1980) called *contention scheduling*. A novel plan would be held at the supervisory system level, but the hippocampus would be one of the structures that is activated when initiating the plan involves the realization of a prior intention. Thus, the hippocampus would be the servant of frontal processes and not an independent actor.

Cohen and O'Reilly, however, appear to view the supervisory level processes as passive and one-dimensional. This is illustrated by their approach to two other issues. The first is why in their illustrative example, one does not go to the grocery the following day, too. They argue that this may be because the representation coded in the hippocampus is richer than their initial account might suggest. In my view, it is more plausible to see the supervisory system as containing an explicit representation for future action including its goal or goals, which can be checked. Thus if the go-to-grocery alternative were to be retrieved from structures in the hippocampus, on the next day it would be rejected at the supervisory system level. This is an analogous position for prospective memory to that provided for retrospective memory by Shallice (1988) and Moscovitch (1989).

Secondly, what happens when the missing orange juice is discovered in the example? It is argued that this "elicits a plan to address this." Representation of plans are elicited and compared and the process "is likely to stabilize in a state comprised of the following representations: go to work; go home; go to grocery store; 5:00, etc." Many questions are posed by this account. Does the temporal organization of the day not have a special status (see Ellis, this volume). How are "go home" — "at 5:00" represented and do they have equivalent status? Under what circumstances would an output be produced to the processes taking place in the hippocampus and how would that be decided? Most critically, what sort of processing structure would be powerful enough to carry out the computation? Would it not need to have a complex structure?

It is possible to explain different and even seemingly opposing tendencies shown after prefrontal lesions by assuming that the damaged system modulates a lower level process, with different states of the unmodulated lower level system giving rise to the apparently contradictory types of behavior (Shallice, 1982). Cohen and O'Reilly's model provides a most elegant example of this type of argument. They, however, summarize their position by saying that "we proposed that inhibition and working memory reflect the operation of a single underlying processing mechanism," namely, "supporting representations necessary to perform the task against sources of interference." This can be read as implying that the different parts of prefrontal cortex are equipotential or differ only in the representations they support. However, a task like Stroop (a prototypic inhibition task), involves activation of the right anterior cingulate and right frontal polar (area 10) regions (Bench et al., 1993, Exp. 2; Pardo, J.V., Pardo, P. J., Janer, & Raichle, 1990), whereas working memory tasks are held by Cohen and O'Reilly to involve sulcus principalis (area 46). Moreover the purest patient of Shallice and Burgess (1991) who we argue had a selective inability to realize intentions (AP), had a lesion of the orbital frontal cortex, a different part of the prefrontal cortex.

In my view the single underlying processing mechanism that Cohen and O'Reilly consider the prefrontal cortex to contain needs to be viewed as a complex system. One of its subsystems seems likely to have a specific role in the realization of intentions (Shallice & Burgess, 1991). Cohen and O'Reilly's argument that any such system must interact with the hippocampus seems plausible. However, it seems likely to be more than a mere passive repository of the representation of context.

REFERENCES

Anderson, S. W., Damasio, H., Jones, R. D., & Tranel, D. (1991). Wisconsin Card Sorting Test performance as a measure of frontal lobe damage. *Journal of Clinical and Experimental Neuropsychology, 13*, 909–922.

Baddeley, A. D. (1986). *Working Memory.* Oxford, England: Clarendon Press.

Bench, C. J., Frith, C. D., Grasby, P. M., Friston, K. J., Paulesu, E., Frackowiak, R. S. I., & Dolan, R. J. (1993). Investigations of the frontal anatomy of attention using the Stroop test. *Neuropsychologia, 31*, 907–922.

Craik, F. I. M. (1986). A functional account of age differences in memory. In F. Klix & H. Hagendorf (Eds.), *Human memory and cognitive capabilities, mechanisms and performances* (pp. 409–422). Amsterdam: Elsevier.

Craik, F. I. M., Morris, R. G., & Gick, M. L. (1990). Adult age differences in working memory. In G. Vallar & T. Shallice (Eds.), *Neuropsychological Impairments in Working Memory.* Cambridge, England: Cambridge University Press.

Grasby, P. M., Frith, C. D., Friston, K. J., Bench, C., Frackowiak, R. S. J., & Dolan, R. J. (1993). Functional mapping of brain areas implicated in audiotry-verbal memory function. *Brain, 116,* 1–20.

Kapur, S., Craik, F. I. M., Tulving, E., Wilson, A. W., Houle, S., & Brown, G. M. (1994). Neuroanatomical correlates of encoding in episodic memory: Levels of processing effect. *Proceedings of the National Academy of Science, 91,* 2008–2011.

Kopelman, M. D. (1991). Frontal dysfunction and memory deficits in the alcoholic Korsakoff syndrome and Alzheimer-type dementia. *Brain, 114,* 117–137.

Milner, B. (1963). Effects of different brain lesion on card sorting. *Archives of Neurology, 9,* 90–100.

Moscovitch, M. (1989). Confabulation and the frontal system. In H. L. Roediger & F. I. M. Craik (Eds.), *Varieties of Memory and Consciousness: Essays in honor of Endel Tulving.* Hillsdale, NJ: Lawrence Erlbaum Associates.

Nelson, H. E. (1976). A modified card sorting test sensitive to frontal lobe defects. *Cortex, 12,* 313–324.

Norman, D. A., & Shallice, T. (1980). Attention to action: Willed and automatic control of behavior. Center for Human Information Processing (Tech. Rep. No. 99). Reprinted in revised form in R. J. Davidson, C. E. Schwartz, & D. Shapiro (Eds.), *Consciousness and Self-Regulation* (Vol. 4). New York: Plenum Press.

Pardo, J. V., Pardo, P. J., Janer, K. W., & Raichle, M. E. (1990). The anterior cingulate cortex mediates processing selection in the Stroop attentional conflict paradigm. *Proceedings of the National Academy of Sciences, 87,* 256–259.

Paulesu, E., Frith, C. D., & Frackowiak, R. S. J. (1993). The neural correlates of the verbal component of working memory. *Nature, 362,* 342–344.

Reason, J. T. (1984). Lapses of attention. In R. Parasuraman, R. Davies, & J. Beatty (Eds.), *Varieties of Attention.* Orlando, FL: Academic Press.

Shallice, T. (1982). Specific impairment of planning. *Philosophical Transactions of the Royal Society of London B, 298,* 199–209.

Shallice, T. (1988). *From neuropsychology to mental structure.* Cambridge: Cambridge University Press.

Shallice, T. & Burgess, P. (1993). Supervisory control of action and thought selection. In A. Baddeley & L. Weiskrantz (Eds.), *Attention: Selection, awareness and control.* Oxford, England: Clarendon Press.

Shallice, T., Fletcher, P., Frith, C. D., Grasby, P. M., Frackowiak, R. S. J., & Dolan, R. J. (1994). Brain regions associated with acquisition and retrieval of verbal episodic memory. *Nature, 368,* 633–635.

Squire, L. R., Ojemann, J. C., Miezin, F. M., Peterson, S. E., Videen, T. O., & Raichle, M. E. (1992). *Proceedings of the National Academy of Sciences, 89,* 1837–1841.

Tulving, E., Kapur, S., Markowitsch, H. J., Craik, F. I. M, Habib, R., & Houle, S. (1994). Neuroanatomical correlates of retrieval in episodic memory: Auditory sentence recognition. *Proceedings of the National Academy of Sciences, 91,* 2012–2015.

Warrington, E. K., Logue, V., & Pratt, R. T. C. (1971). The anatomical localisation of selective impairment of auditory verbal short-term memory. *Neuropsychologia, 9,* 377–387.

PART IV

Applications: Using and Improving Prospective Memory in Real World Settings

17

Assessment and Treatment of Prospective Memory Deficits

Janet Cockburn
*University of Reading and Rivermead
Rehabilitation Centre, Oxford*

Consideration of deficits of prospective memory can only be made in the light of an appreciation of "normal" prospective memory. We all forget to do things from time to time, with consequences of varying degrees of severity. Much of the interest for the neuropsychologist or gerontologist lies in failures that fall outside the bounds of normal forgetting, their relationship to impaired performance in other cognitive domains and, possibly, their amenability to remediation. Approaches to identification of constituents of prospective memory are outside the scope of this chapter, but are considered insofar as they contribute to the determination of what is a deficit and to the establishment of a rationale for attempts at remediation. This chapter aims to examine currently available tools for assessing prospective memory and to evaluate the pitifully few published remediation programs. Some attempt is made to provide a reason for the absence of successful treatment for impaired prospective memory, and suggestions are provided for future directions.

Knowledge of how prospective memory is used in the real world, and suggestions for improving skills of remembering to do things, are derived partially from studies in naturalistic settings and partially from theory-driven analogues under experimental control. It is necessary to understand an individual's beliefs about memory functions and how these may relate to or influence their lifestyle, but it is also necessary to examine potentially influential variables and their interactions under controlled conditions to identify types of failure or reasons for failure. As with any other form of remediation, techniques for remediation of failures of prospective memory need both initial establishment in carefully controlled situations and later generalization to the real-world environment in which the skills learned will need to be used.

In this chapter, I explore the contribution of questionnaire and checklist studies to understanding of self-belief about the role of prospective memory in everyday life and to the relationship between self- and observer-awareness of failures of prospective memory. This information is compared with that obtained from objective assessments following brain injury and among elderly people. A discussion of approaches to remediation of prospective memory after brain injury follows and the chapter concludes with suggestions for directions of future development in assessment and remediation.

SELF-ASSESSMENT OF PROSPECTIVE MEMORY

Questionnaire Studies

Much of what we know about what memory means to nonpsychologists was obtained from subjective memory or metamemory questionnaires. The information received is constrained by the content of the questions asked, reflecting psychologists' interpretations of the concept of memory. For example, Bennett-Levy and Powell (1980) derived the content of their Subjective Memory Questionnaire (SMQ) from suggestions made by colleagues regarding forgetting in everyday life. Nevertheless, analysis of responses gives an indication of the relative role of different components of memory in the daily lives of respondents and the importance credited to them. Common or related factors can be identified through comparative study of questionnaires that measure beliefs about memory or ask about observed memory failures. Prospective memory as a distinct entity is rarely named, although a number of items with a prospective memory component can be identified in the different scales.

Herrmann (1984) carried out a systematic review of 10 metamemory questionnaires in order to evaluate their potential usefulness for assessing memory performance in the natural environment and to examine the relationship between beliefs about memory and memory performance. The questionnaires differed considerably in length, detail of response criteria, direction of question (whether remembering or forgetting was emphasized) and specificity of each question. Despite differences in general content and format for responding, Hermann was able to classify the majority of items under one of five main headings—common work and tasks, specific episodes, semantic information, skill memory, and memory vulnerability. The majority of memory tasks could be listed under the heading of common events and tasks, with memory for appointments investigated in seven questionnaires and memory for errands in four. The relationship between subjective reports and objective memory test score was low (rarely exceeding $r = 0.5$). However, tests on which there is a direct match with everyday actions, such as remembering names (Bennett-Levy & Powell, 1980) or recalling a story (Sunderland, Harris, Baddeley, 1983) or that were designed to simulate everyday memory, such as the Rivermead Behavioural Memory Test (RBMT; Wilson, Cockburn, & Baddeley, 1985) correlated better with self-reported memory failures (Lincoln & Tinson, 1989; Schwartz & McMillan, 1989).

Further evidence to support the validity of subjective questionnaires when matched with everyday actions, and with particular relevance to prospective memory, was provided by Martin (1986) who used an everyday memory questionnaire to compare self-reports of memory in everyday situations by old and young subjects. This study found that older adults reported themselves to be good at remembering appointments, paying bills, and taking medication (all of which tap some aspect of prospective memory), and poor at remembering names. Young people reported the opposite pattern. Martin was able to check comparative accuracy of appointment-keeping against records of attendance as research subjects, which confirmed her respondents' self-evaluation. The older people were more assiduous at keeping appointments to participate in research projects. She suggested that tasks that improve with age, such as keeping appointments, require higher order cognitive control, whereas those that decline, such as remembering names or telephone numbers, are more dependent on elementary processes of rote memory that may be most sensitive to deterioration of the central nervous system. She likened changes in memory performance with aging that favored tasks using prospective memory to an improvement in software engineering (or processing strategies) to compensate for deterioration in efficiency of the hardware (or central nervous system). However, this finding of apparent age-related superiority in some activities tapping prospective memory was not universally supported by subsequent research (Cockburn & Smith, 1988, 1991; Dobbs & Rule, 1987), but see Einstein and McDaniel (1990) for evidence that older adults can use processing strategies in prospective memory tasks as effectively as can younger adults.

Attempts were also made to identify the underlying construct of everyday memory by factor analysis of the content of metamemory questionnaires. Bennett-Levy and Powell (1980) hypothesized that responses to their SMQ would load on a large general factor because people tend to comment on memory in general terms, such as "I have a terrible memory." However, they found a very fragmented structure, with 16 components having eigenvalues greater than 1.0, that together accounted for 74.8% of the total variance. The largest of these, accounting for 12.4% of the variance, they termed an *Organization of Behavior* factor. As it contained such items as remembering appointments, returning borrowed items, passing on messages, it appears to include at least some aspects of prospective memory. Bennett-Levy and Powell compared it with the *Absent-mindedness* factor identified by Herrmann and Neisser (1978) and found a number of parallels. They identified a linear trend with age on the *Organization of Behavior* factor that led them to postulate better organization among older people than younger—a suggestion subsequently supported by empirical evidence from Martin (1986).

The perceived role of prospective memory in everyday life, was explored in comparison with other hypothesized components of memory (Mateer, Sohlberg, & Crinean, 1987) in a questionnaire study. The purpose was to examine response patterns of brain-injured subjects alongside those of normal controls. The questions were chosen to probe six hypothesized essential components of memory—anterograde episodic and semantic memory, retrograde episodic and semantic memory, working memory, and prospective memory. Responses to the 30-item questionnaire from 337 subjects, approximately one half of whom had sustained brain injury of varying degrees of severity, were subjected to factor analysis. Four factors were isolated instead of the hypothesized six— Attention–Prospective Memory, Retrograde Memory, Anterograde Memory, Historic–Overlearned Memory. No item loaded on more than one factor and only two items, which were subsequently dropped from the questionnaire, failed to load on any of the factors. Items loading on the Attention–Prospective memory factor related to immediate memory, working memory, mental control, and carrying out intended actions. The authors interpreted this clustering of items as indicating that the ability to carry out intended actions relies heavily on attention, perhaps in the form of vigilance relative to temporal and situational cues. The dissociation identified in this study between attention and anterograde memory appears to cut across the content of the Absentmindedness factor identified by Herrmann and Neisser (1978) and the Organization of Behavior factor of Bennett-Levy and Powell (1980) that contain both items relating to memory for what to do and what has recently been done. One major source of difference may be that Mateer et al. (1987) surveyed both normal and brain-injured people, whereas both Herrmann and Neisser and Bennett-Levy and Powell derived their factor structures from only responses of nonbrain-injured subjects. Mateer et al. suggested that heightened emotional responsiveness to head injury, especially minor trauma, and its consequences might have the greatest impact on processes involved in attending and remembering prospectively. One important conclusion drawn from this study was that most individuals were more concerned with their ability to remember to perform future actions than with other types of memory. This may be because, as Winograd (1988) noted, if retrospective memory fails, the memory is seen as unreliable, but if prospective memory fails, the person is seen as unreliable. Identification of the relative prominence of prospective memory in self-assessment of memory after brain injury is important to the design of therapeutic programs for memory remediation, which are more likely to succeed if perceived by the recipient to match their needs.

Checklist or Diary Studies

One criticism of questionnaires as indices of behavior is that the respondents, especially those whose memories are poor or who lack insight into their actions, will fail to acknowledge lapses made and will report their memories to be better than they actually are (Sunderland, Watts, Baddeley, & Harris, 1986). Checklist or diary studies that require a more immediate response to actions or omissions, have been used with a variety of populations in attempts to obtain a more accurate record of lapses. Some of these also provided useful information on the perceived role of prospective memory in everyday life. In their study of incidence of forgetting among elderly people, Sunderland et al. (1986) compared self-report and report by a relative of everyday memory lapses with performance on a battery of tests that specifically incorporated prospective memory tasks. Responses were made both to a questionnaire on frequency of memory lapses and a checklist of errors noted. Low positive correlations were found between prospective memory errors and self-report of memory failures, both on questionnaire and checklist, but no correlation with relatives' observations of memory lapses. This may indicate that, although we may not always be aware of our memory lapses, there are also situations in which it is easier to know ourselves that we have forgotten to do something than for someone else to know that we intended to do something but failed to carry out the action.

In a study that used a small and disparate sample, Crovitz, Cordoni, Daniel, and Perlman (1984) collected self-reported incidences of forgetting over a 1-week period by young, old, and amnesic subjects. They identified categories of intended actions and absent-mindedness as two of the nine types of forgetting recorded in the diaries, and found that forgetting intended actions had the highest mean frequency of occurrence among young normal subjects, although there were large individual variations. Both memory-impaired and elderly subjects recorded memory lapses within the range of the young subjects but, again, there were wide differences in the number of incidences reported. One elderly subject reported 73% of lapses occurring for intended actions, whereas a memory-impaired patient recorded only 12.5% for intended actions, with 50% for failures in retrieval of known data. Of interest for later studies of cue specificity and distinctiveness in prospective memory (McDaniel & Einstein, 1993), was the finding that the physical presence of something was most often reported as cueing awareness of having forgotten.

Questionnaires, checklists, and diary records of memory lapses have provided important information concerning the role of prospective memory in everyday life. However, they lack the rigor of objective assessments and can only give a partial indication of the processes involved.

AWARENESS OF FUTURE INTENTIONS

Naturally Occurring Intentions

Reports by people of what they have or have not done are open to falsification, whether or not intentional. We may forget to do something and forget that we have forgotten. We may also never have intended to perform a particular task but not wish to admit that. In a novel exploration of the extent to which people are aware of their future intentions between formulation and execution, Ellis and Nimmo-Smith (1993) asked eight subjects to keep a record of all occasions over 5 consecutive days on which they recalled future intentions and the context surrounding recall. Although in everyday life, enactment may not occur until months after formulation of the intention, responses in this study were constrained to activities to be enacted later the same day. They were compared with a control condition that sampled subjects' behavior and its surrounding context at pseudorandom intervals during the day. Results suggested that performance of a concurrent activity requiring little concentration was most conducive to recollection of intention. Differences in context between recollection and control conditions were, however, small. There was some indication that relatively low levels of attentional load of the intervening task were more conducive to recollection of tasks that came under the heading of *pulses* (Ellis, 1988), for example, keep an appointment at 3:00 p.m. Tasks that Ellis described as *Step* tasks that did not have, in themselves, a precise temporal target for performance, such as "phone to book a holiday sometime today," or tasks intermediate between pulses and steps, were most likely to be recalled during times when subjects were concentrating less on the ongoing activity, but the level of attention demanded by the ongoing task was not rated as significantly different from the control condition. The authors also noted that frequency of interim recall between formulating and executing the intention was not a predictor of successful eventual performance. Recall during the time period immediately preceding the moment for execution of the intention, however, appeared an important prerequisite of task completion. Because in this study subjects were asked to list at the start of the day the activities for execution during that day, it was possible to match intention against later action and note omissions, of which there were few (a gross incidence of 3.8% unsatisfied intentions). The restricted time-scale of this study, although reducing the realism, may be of minor importance to interpretation of the results. Information about the effect of different time-scales on accuracy of performance of prospective memory actions suggests that there is little difference in reliability of performance over short or long intervals between a few days and 1 month (Meacham & Leiman, 1982).

Experimental Manipulation of Intention

Better control of subject behavior, as well as of intervening activities, can be obtained by simulating a natural action in a laboratory setting. Kvavilashvili (1987) manipulated the relative importance of both the intended action and the intervening task to investigate accuracy of performance. Subjects were required to replace a telephone receiver on the rest at the end of a 5-min period that was either empty or filled with a boring or an interesting activity. They were either merely asked to replace the receiver at the end or to do so because an important call was expected. The interaction shown in the analysis of results indicated that, if the intention was important, remembering was not dependent on the character of the intervening period but, if unimportant, then the interest level of the intervening period would substantially influence remembering. This study does not, however, shed much light on how people remember to perform such a task. Fewer than one third of the subjects reported at debriefing that they had thought about the intended action during the intervening period. However, it is possible that the nondirective method of questioning needed to conceal the true purpose of the study may have failed to elicit acknowledgment from subjects that they had thought about the intended action during the intervening time. Ellis and Nimmo-Smith (1993) suggested, in the conclusion to their more naturalistic study, that occasions on which subjects report recollecting a future intention may only be a subset of the occasions on which recollection has actually occurred. In particular, when current tasks are demanding, recollections may only be fleeting and insufficient to strengthen the memory trace of the intention. There is clearly scope for more work on discriminating the conditions in which people reinforce their encoded intention prior to timely retrieval from those in which they fail to do so. There is potential importance in extending this study to other populations, such as the brain-injured or the very old, for whom demands placed on information-processing capacities by concurrent activities may be greater, thus compromising the timely executing of the intention.

Although there are relatively few studies of self-assessment that have concentrated on pathologically impaired memory, it is important to have guidelines of the range of behaviors that are found in naturally occurring and artificially contrived situations. Information obtained from volunteer subjects provides an essential starting point from which to investigate the nature and prevalence of abnormal failures of prospective memory.

OBJECTIVE ASSESSMENT OF PROSPECTIVE MEMORY

Assessment of Prospective Memory in Older People

Perhaps unsurprisingly, in the light of an extensive literature on changes in memory abilities with age, a number of studies focused on assessment of prospective memory in older people. Some contrasted performance of old with young subjects (e.g., Einstein & McDaniel, 1990; West, 1988) whereas others measured differences within a sample of older people (Cockburn & Smith, 1991; Maylor, 1990). West compared performance of old and young subjects in two separate studies. In the first, she found little difference between young and old subjects in accuracy of remembering to make a telephone call or mail a postcard from their home when they had the opportunity to use external cues if they wished. Instructions were given at the end of an interview and the time between instruction and action covered 2 days. In the second study, elderly participants were found to be less accurate at delivering a message on cue, either during or at the end of a 1-hr interview, when the instruction was embedded in the overall structure of the interview. West refuted the possibility of external cues being the salient difference between the two studies, but suggested distinctiveness of cue in relation to surrounding context, particularly for older adults, may be of critical importance. However, analysis of these results did not take into account the possible influence of making or providing one's own cue. My observations suggest that it is rare for either older people or neurological patients to make spontaneous use of cues when prospective memory tasks are built into a test or interview. Control of the situation in such circumstances appears is perceived by the subjects as in the hands of the experimenter/interviewer rather than their own. Additionally, the relative familiarity of the target action to the situation in which it is embedded may influence accuracy of responding. West's subjects in the second experiment had to respond to the appearance of a visual cue that was part of an ongoing task, or to interpret an apparently unrelated statement, such as "now we have come to the end of the test" as the target context for retrieving an encoded intention and carrying out the related action. Both of these represent unfamiliar targets in unfamiliar situations.

In contrast, a study that found a high degree of accuracy in performance of a laboratory-based prospective memory task (Einstein & McDaniel, 1990) used a design in which tasks were driven by experimental conditions. Subjects had to respond to a visual cue on a computer screen that was part of the ongoing task. One half of the old and one half of the young subjects were allowed to create and use an external memory aid and one half were not. There was no evidence for deterioration in performance with age but presence of an aid enhanced prospective remembering in both age groups. A second experiment varied the familiarity of the target event relative to the familiarity of the filler activity. Their results supported West's argument for effectiveness of target events that stand out from the context. However, Einstein and McDaniel again found no significant difference in performance between old and young. It may be that neither of their studies represented prospective memory in everyday life, but rather investigated learning a routine, because performance of the same prospective memory task was repeated at intervals during the experimental session. Subjects may perform more accurately because they are able to set up a program to expect a target to occur, although they do not know when or how frequently. However, the laboratory-based design used by Sunderland et al. (1986) in which elderly subjects had to respond in the same way on eight occasions throughout the session, produced a high error rate. It is not known how younger people would have performed on this task because the study did not include a young group.

Woolf (1994) started from the assumption that errors of prospective memory would be made and investigated tasks and conditions that might assist prospective remembering of old and young people. She interviewed 25 community-dwelling young (18 to 40 years) and 25 old (60+ years) people in their homes, using an experimental design that compared performance across task, time, and cue conditions. Four tasks were included that covered a time-span between 5 min and 48 hr. One half of the young and one half of the old subjects were encouraged to discuss and subsequently use aids to remember what they had to do, whereas the others were not specifically encouraged, although all subjects were given paper on which they were free to make notes if they wished. Results suggest an overall superiority of younger people if the criterion was spontaneous and timely accuracy of response. However, if a more generous scoring criterion was used of response either spontaneously or after a reminder such as "is there something you had to do?," there was no significant difference between young and old in retrieval of the content of the instruction. Presence of a cue helped older people more but this could be a function of the overall better spontaneous performance of the younger subjects, so that a visual aid was redundant. There was no indication of a differential effect of time-span over which tasks had to be remembered. The overall results from the study suggest that older people in particular were assisted to remember by engaging in conversation about the tasks and by the visible and distinctive presence of a cue related to the task. As these appear to be strategies that are simple to implement, this study is worth replicating with other samples of subjects and other conditions.

Although it appears that timely provision of a salient and distinctive cue is a factor in successful prospective memory performance of older people, there are still a number of questions to be answered, for example concerning the supplier of the cue, and the nature of the relationship between cue, context, and to-be-performed-action.

Dissociations Between Prospective and Retrospective Memory Among Older People

Cockburn and Smith (1988, 1991) used the RBMT, which contains items testing retrospective and prospective memory in verbal and nonverbal conditions, to investigate relative performances of community-dwelling elderly people. Findings in the first study of age-related deficits of prospective memory that were independent of current intelligence, but none of retrospective memory, with a small, well-educated sample led to a replication with a larger sample of people aged at least 70 years. Although current intelligence was now found to be a significant predictor of prospective memory, there were still significant independent effects of age for the prospective memory tasks but for only one retrospective memory task—gist recall of a story. Cockburn and Smith (1991) interpreted their results in terms of reduction in information-processing resources with age that manifests as failure to remember what to do or failure to organize incoming material for subsequent output, neither of which is wholly attributable to changes measurable by tests of current intelligence.

Huppert and Beardsall (1993) proposed that selective impairment of prospective memory may be less a function of aging than an early indicator of dementia. They examined performance on tests of retrospective and prospective memory of four groups of people—normal elderly, subjects who were normal on clinical examination but scored below the cut-off for dementia on the Mini Mental State Examination (Folstein, Folstein, & McHugh, 1975), subjects with minimal dementia, subjects with mild or moderate dementia. They found significant differences between groups on both retrospective and prospective memory tests. Both dementia groups performed significantly more poorly than the normal group on all measures of prospective memory, but not significantly differently from one another. In contrast the scores of the minimal dementia group were intermediate between those of the low-scoring normals and the mild/moderate dementia group on the retrospective memory measures. Huppert and Beardsall were able to make a direct comparison between performance on two measures of memory taken from the RBMT, one retrospective and one prospective. Examination of scores on the items remembering a route around the room and remembering to deliver a message while following the route indicated little difference between scores on the two items by either normal group, but substantially poorer scores in the immediate recall condition for the message and a greater drop over a delay by the two dementia groups. Results also indicated that the discrepancy between prospective and retrospective memory performance was particularly marked in the minimal dementia group. However, the authors acknowledged the need to examine performance on tasks of prospective and retrospective memory that are exacting comparable cognitive demands on the performers. They suggest that, as prospective memory typically requires holding one set of information in mind while carrying out another set of activities, an element of dual-task information processing is involved. It may therefore be necessary to compare performance against retrospective memory tasks that also incorporate dual-task processing. Nevertheless, these results are of considerable interest and potential value in understanding both the breakdown of cognitive processes in early dementia and the role of prospective memory in everyday life of the older person.

These findings of Huppert and Beardsall again highlight the question of whether there is a critical difference between normal lapses of prospective memory and the impairments seen in people with acquired or progressive brain damage, or whether the difference is merely one of degree.

Assessment of Prospective Memory in Neurological Patients

Impairment of prospective memory after brain damage received little attention in contrast to the extensive literature on retrospective memory impairments. However, interest is growing in relating behavioral anomalies seen after certain forms of brain damage to models of the hypothesized essential components of prospective memory. If successful prospective memory depends on the formulation of an intention to perform an action in response to the occurrence of a target and the subsequent timely performance of that action, failures at any stage of the process that can be associated with known damage may provide important information about the neural substrates of prospective memory. Shimamura, Janowsky, and Squire (1991) suggested that the definition of prospective memory should be widened to include processes and strategies involved in planning, organizing and monitoring memory. They noted shared features between impaired prospective memory, the dysexecutive syndrome (Baddeley, 1986) and forms of disinhibited behavior that may reflect selective sensitivity to damage to the frontal lobes of the cerebral cortex, although they gave no experimental evidence to support the comparison. However, Shallice and Burgess (1991), in an ingenious series of experiments, showed a relationship between skills of planning, decision making and executive control and remembering to carry out tasks appropriately in three subjects with documented frontal-lobe lesions.

Another area of behavior shown to be selectively impaired in some patients after frontal-lobe damage is the ability to interrupt an ongoing activity, especially one that incorporates a sequence of familiar, overlearned behaviors, in order to perform a nonroutine task (Cockburn, 1995). The person may be aware of what they should be doing and may demonstrate a dissociation between verbal and action output, for example, saying, "I am going to put this chocolate away until tea-time" while unwrapping and eating the chocolate. Deficits of this nature are, however, difficult to demonstrate experimentally and there is some indication that such behavior is but an extreme example of a common lapse of everyday memory, similar to the slips of action described by Reason (1979). Nevertheless, because the ability to remember to do something at the end of another task may remain unimpaired, the possibility is raised that different prospective memory tasks are differentially sensitive to attentional control mechanisms mediated by the frontal lobes.

In the questionnaire study described earlier, Mateer et al. (1987) sought to identify similarities and differences in subjective awareness of memory function of brain-injured and nonbrain-injured people. They obtained a similar pattern of relative level of self-reported impairment in different categories of memory function from people with mild or more severe head injury and non-injured control subjects, with failures of attention and prospective memory being reported most frequently by all groups. A relatively greater incidence of errors was reported by people with mild than more severe head injury. The authors suggested this pattern may have occurred because people with mild head injury often consider themselves to be gravely impaired cognitively or because the heightened emotional responsiveness to mild head injury manifests itself in reduced levels of attention and prospective memory. However, it is also possible that, as Sunderland et al. (1983) suggested, people with more severe head injury are more likely to forget what they have to do and whether or not they have carried out the activities correctly. Self-reporting, unless backed by objective measures of lapses of attention and prospective memory, may not give a reliable estimate of level of functioning.

Mateer and colleagues (Sohlberg & Mateer, 1989a; Sohlberg, White, Evans, & Mateer, 1992a, 1992b) took the information obtained from responses to their memory questionnaire (Mateer et al., 1987) as a starting point for developing a screening assessment to quantify prospective memory ability of brain-injured patients. They provided a structured situation in which to measure accuracy of carrying out a task at a future moment in time and to assess different parameters of performance along dimensions of time and cue type. The time span ranged from 60 sec to 24 hr and subjects either had to keep track of the time and respond after a certain interval or associate the instruction to respond with a cue, such as the sound of a timer. These types of cue are similar to the time-based and event-based conditions described by Einstein and McDaniel (1990). Assessment of length of time over which the patient could remember to perform an action was linked to treatment with the aim of training to remember over progressively longer intervals. The program either utilized a single-task paradigm, in which the subject was merely required to sit quietly until it was time to perform the future action, or a dual-task situation, such as solving mental arithmetic puzzles while waiting, which places a heavier demand on memory capacity but is more representative of real-life conditions. Examples of the training procedure with individual subjects were described in two papers (Sohlberg et al., 1992a, 1992b) and are discussed in more detail later in this chapter.

IDENTIFYING AND CLASSIFYING ERRORS OF PROSPECTIVE MEMORY

Slips of Action and Errors of Prospective Memory

In order to make appropriate plans to remediate deficits of prospective memory, it is necessary to know the form such deficits take. It is not sufficient to know that an action has not been carried out. When responses are not made, or are not made correctly, what happens? Cohen (1989) distinguished between *slips of action,* such as putting the empty milk bottle in the refrigerator instead of outside the back door, and *errors of prospective memory,* such as failing to keep an appointment or pass on a message. One essential difference appears to be the level of intention that is generated. Reason (1979, 1984a, 1984b) made an extensive and detailed study of self-reported action slips, their nature, and the circumstances in which they occurred. He found the majority could be categorized under one of four main headings: *repetition errors*—forgetting an action has already been performed; *goal switches*—forgetting a goal and substituting a different one, possibly more familiar or more practiced; *omissions and reversals*—wrongly ordering elements in a sequence; and *confusions/blends*—interchanging elements from other action sequences. Although an intention may have been formulated to carry out an action sequence, in situations where slips tend to occur, the component steps of the sequence will probably be highly practiced or overlearned and not under conscious control. Reason (1984b) argued that slips of action result from faulty deployment of attention and occur when the allocation of attention is insufficient to ensure both accurate progression of actions in the sequence and accurate recording of steps that were taken. Similarly, Norman (1981) proposed that slips of action occur when a person does an action that was not intended. This can be contrasted with not doing an action that was intended, which may more properly come under the heading of *errors of prospective memory.* However, this is not a dichotomy. There is a continuum of behaviors from the habitual daily tasks that are part of our knowledge base, or *semantic prospective memory* (lock the door at night), via the less frequent action (water the flowers each week) and the task to be done at some time (reply to a letter), to the task of *episodic prospective memory* that occurs in response to a single, specific set of circumstances (attend my child's school concert this evening), that must be carried out at a precise time. Each category of behaviors places different demands on skills of memory, attention, and planning, and may be differentially affected by personal (e.g., illness, stress, age) or extrapersonal (e.g., number of competing activities) variables.

Factors Involved in Failure of Prospective Memory

We are all familiar with the situation in which we intended to do something that interrupts our routine but found ourselves instead continuing the routine sequence. Baddeley (1990) described an occasion on which he should have participated in an early morning radio program and was cued, too late, by looking at details of the evening's television programs, to remember his intended activity. He identified certain features in his lapse that were characteristic of prospective remembering and forgetting: The time and place were out of the structure of the normal working day, but not so far out as to generate an entirely separate intention–action–context map; the cue that eventually triggered activation of the intention was related to the target event; and, finally, the incident caused him considerable embarrassment. Differences between normal lapses such as this and abnormal failures sometimes seen after frontal-lobe damage may pivot on frequency of occurrence, disruption caused to daily life and the extent of the embarrassment generated by failure.

Incidents of this type are common in everyday life, in which much prospective memory is self-initiated, even though plans may be made at the behest of or to meet the needs of others. Failure to implement planned action may occur because too little time has been allocated for all plans in the sequence, for example needing to go to the bank and supermarket before meeting a train at 3:00 p.m., or because a plan is low in the order of priorities. Motivation to perform an action may then become influential. We know we should telephone the dentist for an appointment and plan to do so, but dislike of visiting the dentist may be a stronger influence. Although the intention is there, the plan does not become translated into action and the telephone call is not made. Meacham and Kushner (1980) investigated self-reports of occasions on which actions had been planned but not performed. They asked subjects to distinguish between occasions on which they had forgotten to perform a task and occasions on which they had remembered but not carried out the task. Analysis of responses suggested that successful prospective remembering depends on a balance between the importance of the task and the extent to which it generates feelings of discomfort. Anxiety over an activity was associated with remembering but not performing it, whereas forgetting was associated with perceived lack of importance of the activity.

Meacham and Kushner's study, however, relied on subjective report and retrieval of memories of behavior in past situations. Studies that sought to impose some degree of experimental constraint on performance of prospective memory tasks in order to measure comparable rates of success and failure of a number of subjects used a wide range of materials and situations. Evidence was obtained from studies conducted in natural or pseudonatural settings, in which subjects were asked to make telephone calls (Maylor, 1990) or return postcards (Meacham & Leiman, 1982) to the experimenter. Although these tasks have some real-world validity—we all carry out such activities at some time—the conditions under which they are performed impose a number of artificial conditions at the encoding stage. Accuracy of performance may be higher than in a true real-life situation, because the subject is aware of the experimental nature of the task and is motivated to succeed. However, when failure does occur it is not always possible to identify reasons for noncompliance with experimenter's instructions. Did the subjects forget altogether, did they forget to respond at the precise time and think it was too late when they did remember, or did they decide not to comply? Reasons for failure to carry out an intended action are not always evident, and failures themselves may not be registered. Wilkins and Baddeley (1978) found that 30% of their subjects not only failed to carry out a simulation of a pill-taking task at the designated time but were unaware they failed to do so. Although this was an experimental situation, in which a certain degree of imagination is needed to associate pressing a button on a box with taking medication, an important corollary of the results is that self-report of memory lapses may not be a very reliable indicator of the extent and frequency of omissions. This suggests a plausible reason for not relying wholly on information obtained from questionnaires or checklists and an argument for further experimental investigation of the nature of lapses

Errors of Prospective Memory Under Experimental Conditions

There has been little systematic study of errors of prospective memory and the conditions in which they occur. The nature of the error made when people fail to carry out an intended action may vary with the situation, the task, and the performer. It may be necessary to investigate them in controlled experimental situations where the differences between people who do or do not make errors and the situations in which they do or do not occur are under the control of the experimenter. Failure can occur as a consequence of breakdown of encoding–storage or as a failure of retrieval. If the intention is inadequately encoded there will be no record that the activity should be performed. If the intention is there but the planned action has not been encoded adequately, it is likely that the target context will trigger the response that something should be done but what should be done is not recalled. Failure to retrieve the appropriate action for the context will result in the wrong action being performed for the encoded intention. Failure to recognize or respond to the target context will result in the task not being performed spontaneously, even though a cue may reactivate memory of the planned action. This last error pattern is evident in Baddeley's (1990) example cited earlier. The nature of the errors may indicate whether spontaneous but incorrect responses arise from encoding or from retrieval failures and may also provide further identification of the processes involved in successful prospective memory.

Cockburn and Smith (1994) examined errors made by elderly people on a measure of prospective memory that was performed at or near ceiling level by younger people. The task, one item of the RBMT, was to remember that the ringing of a timer 20 min after the instruction was given was the signal to ask the examiner about the date of their next appointment. Over one half the sample of community-dwelling older people made errors on the task, and these could be classified into one of four categories—spontaneously asking about another, temporally contiguous, test item; spontaneously remembering that they had to ask something, but not being able to say what that something was; failing to respond until prompted, then making the correct response; failing to respond even after being prompted or making an incorrect response after a prompt. Identification of these error types led Cockburn and Smith to examine the relationship between type of error made and other cognitive and behavioral variables. They hypothesized a difference between *blocking errors*—spontaneously knowing that something should be asked, or failing to respond until prompted—and *nonblocking errors*—no recall or spontaneously incorrect recall. Blocking errors can be defined as errors that result from failure to retrieve either action or intention. The information is stored but cannot be accessed spontaneously. Nonblocking errors result from faulty encoding or storage, possibly resulting from insufficient attention to the information at the encoding stage. Within this sample, there was a complex relationship between age, current level of general intelligence, self-reported anxiety measured on a 100mm visual analogue scale, and type of error made. Nonblocking errors, resulting from faulty encoding or storage, tended to be associated with low anxiety and blocking errors with high anxiety.

Cockburn and Smith suggested that higher levels of anxiety may lead to increased monitoring or rehearsal of the to-be-performed tasks. These behaviors ensure distinctive encoding, but the processes themselves place demands on working memory, leading to reduced capacity being available for retrieval of previously stored information. Thus, a block is created in the retrieval process, which may be removed by appropriate cueing. Conversely, the lower the reported level of anxiety the less likely the respondent may be to initiate rehearsal processes necessary to ensure distinctive encoding. Nonblocking errors will then be made that are not responsive to appropriate cueing. As prevalence of blocking errors increases with age, functional improvement in prospective memory efficiency of elderly people may be achieved by reducing the load on working memory, for example by structuring activities into discrete, consecutively performed tasks.

REMEDIATION OF DEFICITS
OF PROSPECTIVE MEMORY

Much of the information available on strategies for remediation of deficits of prospective memory is anecdotal or relies on recommendation of common-sense strategies, such as using a diary or making a list of things-to-do. Such strategies can be adopted relatively easily by the nonbrain-injured person who may discover the need, with advancing age or increasing workload, to supplement internal resources with external aids. There is little or no evidence to suggest that people with impaired prospective memory after brain injury will spontaneously adopt strategies to improve their performance. Rehabilitation of memory disorders has not been shown to have a high success rate, possibly because of the labor-intensive nature of the programs. However, some successes were reported from teaching usage of memory aids and strategies to improve prospective memory in early and late stage rehabilitation.

Utilizing Procedural Learning to Improve Prospective Memory

Furst (1986) suggested the possibility of a specific deficit in the ability to lay down a memory trace and initiate future retrieval of it after closed-head-injury as a consequence of associated frontal-lobe damage. Using the ecologically valid task of remembering to punch a card in a time clock at set times, he devised a 6-week training program for 12 brain-injured adults. They were encouraged to use written reminders or other self-cueing strategies and were given weekly feedback of their performance. Results suggested an improvement in accuracy of response. However, given the considerable variability in initial level of cognitive function of the subjects and the reported variation in degree of success achieved, no valid conclusions as to the effectiveness of the program can be drawn. Nevertheless, the exercise was reported to generate a high degree of involvement by the patients and so may be a technique that should be investigated with a more rigorous experimental design.

Following the findings from their questionnaire study (Mateer et al., 1987), Mateer and colleagues published reports of memory training programs that had direct or indirect bearing on remediation of prospective memory deficits. Two studies were reported that focused specifically on training to improve prospective memory. These used an intensive program of 4 to 6 hr of training per week that depended heavily on interdisciplinary collaboration from those treating the patient. Training involved repetitive administration of prospective memory tasks requiring the patient to initiate an action at a future designated time. The initial time-scale was selected on the basis of the patient's own span of remembering. The first study (Sohlberg et al., 1992a) described training of a patient who, at 6 years post-injury, was unable to retain any instruction for as much as 60 seconds. Training took the form of instruction to carry out a one-step motor command (such as "clench your right fist") after a set time interval, with 5 to 10 trials being inserted into a 1-hour treatment session. Cueing was initially given at 15-sec intervals and progressively reduced. If the subject failed to initiate the task at the correct time, cueing returned to its original level for the subsequent trial. During the interval between instruction and performance the subject sat quietly, with no experimenter distraction, to allow concentration on the task. This subject was reported to have progressed from no accuracy at 1 min to 40 to 80% accuracy over 8 min during a 4.5-month treatment program. No attempt was made to generalize to an untrained task or to more realistic situations. However, reports from the spouse and from therapists suggested an improvement in ability to retain information, such as telephone messages, over a short period. A second patient was trained using a dual-task condition of solving mathematical problems during the interval between instruction and action. This study commenced when the patient was 8 months post-injury, and so possibly still at a stage of making spontaneous recovery. Improvement was noted in ability to retain instructions and respond appropriately for longer periods. However, because there was a concomitant improvement in others areas of memory and attention, the question of whether improvement was due to specific training or to spontaneous recovery remains to be answered.

An associated paper (Sohlberg et al, 1992b) described training under more rigorous experimental conditions, employing a within-subject, single-case research design. Measures of generalization to more realistic activities were also incorporated. Training consisted of repetitive administration of prospective memory tasks to be performed at a specific future time, with the time interval systematically lengthened. Simulations of real-life activities included such tasks as making a telephone call or taking a dish out of the oven. The patient selected for this study was severely amnesic, with no delayed recall on the logical memory subtest of the Wechsler Memory Scale, who also scored poorly on tests of attention and executive function. At the start of the program, effective prospective memory span was determined by working backwards from a 10-min interval until an interval was reached when the subject could remember to perform the task. Each prospective memory task during training took the form of a two-stage motor command, such as "close your eyes and clap your hands." Training again utilized a dual-task situation, in which mathematical problems were solved during the interval between instruction and target response time. Results indicated that the subject made greater improvement at remembering when something should be done than at remembering what should be done. This suggests that separate elements of processes involved in prospective memory are dissociable and different strategies may be needed for remediation. Accuracy of performance was also noted to decrease during the treatment session, which the authors interpreted as suggesting elements of boredom or reduced vigilance. Some element of proactive interference from previously presented instructions might, however, be expected to occur. Little evidence was reported for generalization to more naturalistic tasks, nor was there any sustained improvement on standard tests of recall memory. One of the major weaknesses of these studies was that reliance on repetitive programs, akin to utilizing procedural memory, introduces a degree of inflexibility, reducing the likelihood of the subject achieving independence or the ability spontaneously to generalize to other settings.

Training to use a Diary as a Prospective Memory Aid

Results from a single-case study of training to use a compensatory memory notebook (Sohlberg & Mateer, 1989b) suggest that an intensive, individually based systematic approach can be an effective form of memory remediation. Considerable emphasis was placed on the ability to record and carry out future actions as this was perceived to be a crucial element in return to independent living. However, 6 months of intensive training, with at least five structured sessions per day, were needed for the subject to achieve independent use of the system, making it unlikely to be replicated in many clinical settings.

A study currently in progress in the clinical psychology department at Rivermead uses a similar method to that of Sohlberg and Mateer, but with less intensive input, to train patients to use a memory diary both retrospectively and prospectively. In Stage 1, the therapist and patient review the patient's memory deficits, the reason for using a diary–organizer and discuss techniques needed for the program to work, such as selecting section headings or color coding to differentiate the days of the week in the diary. The first task is to copy the daily timetable into the diary, with prompting or cueing from the therapist that is gradually faded out over following days. The level of intervention required is recorded on a 3-point scale: (1) *major help*, (2) *minor help*, (3) *independent*, for both initiation and implementation of the activity. This forms the main training session of the day. The patient is encouraged throughout the day by staff members to use the dairy to check where he or she should be rather than to ask for the information. Specific targets, such as "use information in diary to improve spatial and temporal orientation" or "take independent responsibility for getting to therapy on time" are set in accordance with the patient's needs and goals. At a later stage in the program, the patient is taught to use the diary independently to record other relevant prospective information, such as planning what to take home for the weekend. This leads to generalization to use in settings outside the rehabilitation center. Preliminary results suggest that these techniques are of considerable benefit to some patients, but others, with similar neuropsychological test profiles, have made no significant progress despite several months of training. Further work is in progress to refine the program and identify variables that predict success.

Generalization of use of Aids to Improve Prospective Memory in the Real World

This is an area where objective evidence of success is weak and where much work needs to be done if remediation of deficits of prospective memory is to be shown to be both cost- and time-effective.

Wilson (1991), reporting results of a long-term follow-up of severely memory-impaired brain-injured subjects, noted that although 60% of subjects showed no change in formal memory test score over a 6 to 10 year period, the majority had learned to use aids and strategies to bypass or compensate for their memory deficits. The study did not specifically seek information about remembering to do things, but most frequently reported aids used were a notebook, a list, or a calendar, suggesting that people had developed strategies for reminding themselves of what they had to do and when to do it. It remains to be seen whether training on an individual basis to use memory aids and strategies may be a more effective means of improving prospective memory in the real world than repetitive practice of motor actions of the sort employed by Sohlberg et al. (1992a, 1992b).

Evans and Wilson (1992) described a group that met weekly for 11 months, with the stated aim of helping participants to find ways of utilizing memory aids to overcome their everyday memory problems. This was an open group, with a fluctuating membership, but results are reported for the progress of 5 participants who attended most of the sessions during the 11 months. They were between 1 and 35 months post-injury at the start of the study and all had been in coma for at least 48 hr. The RBMT was used as an objective measure of memory ability and a brief questionnaire on frequency of use of different memory aids was administered at the beginning and end of the study. All aids included in the questionnaire were external, such as a wall chart, an alarm watch, or putting an item in a special place so it acted as a cue. These are similar to the examples given by Maylor (1990) of external cues spontaneously used by her elderly subjects to remind them to make a telephone call at the given time, and so have relevance for everyday actions.

Results demonstrated a significant increase by the group as a whole in use of memory aids over the first 7 months of the study, as reported by relatives, although there were considerable differences in frequency of use of aids. Scores on the RBMT also improved for some individual members but no division of scores into prospective and retrospective memory items was made. Feedback from relatives indicated only that some patients made increased use of aids, not whether or not the use was effective in cueing appropriate actions, and so the extent to which training improved independent functioning is not wholly evident. The authors suggested the absence of a significant improvement overall on the objective measure lends support to the argument that the most effective use of group therapy for memory-impaired individuals is to teach use of aids and strategies for augmenting memory, rather than to seek to improve memory function.

REMEDIATION OF DEFICITS OF PROSPECTIVE MEMORY: WHERE NEXT?

Although none of the studies of remediation reported here presented conclusive evidence for the efficacy of prospective memory training, they suggest opportunities for replication and extension with other subjects and in other settings. More information is needed about effectiveness of different methods of presentation of instructions. One approach that has potential relevance is described in the experiments of Koriat, Ben-Zur, and Nussbaum (1990). These indicated a substantial advantage of motor over verbal encoding for subsequent retrieval of a to-be-performed action among student subjects. The effectiveness of this procedure does not yet appear to have been systematically investigated with brain-injured subjects, but if encouraging motor encoding influences appropriate retrieval of the correct response, training that utilizes more than one modality at encoding may lead to improvement in remembering what to do as well as when.

It may be particularly difficult to demonstrate improvement and generalization of specific prospective memory training in a subject with severe amnesia and numerous other deficits—although these form a substantial proportion of referrals for neuropsychological rehabilitation. However, for prospective memory training to become widely accepted as an effective form of treatment, it is necessary to show that training will generalize beyond the ability to perform a meaningless motor activity on one or two occasions during a 1-hr therapy session and beyond the confines of the rehabilitation center into an environment where demands are often unpredictable and there may be no one available to prompt if spontaneous initiation is not achieved.

There are inevitable difficulties in introducing remediation techniques at a stage when natural recovery may still be taking place. However, if strategies such as learning to use a diary or a personal organizer are to be effective, they may need to be introduced and built into the rehabilitation program at an early stage so that ineffectual strategies do not have to be unlearned. Successful techniques may vary with the needs of the individual as well as with their residual learning ability. Amnesic persons who have difficulty remembering what they have already done or what they have decided to do will require different strategies from those who can remember accurately what they have done and what they should do but who are unable to break spontaneously into any ongoing activity to initiate a new action sequence. The first may need to rely on procedural memory of an unvaried program, whereas the second may benefit from a program of activities structured in a series of discrete but consecutively performed tasks. This latter is similar to the proposals made by Cockburn and Smith (1994) for improving prospective memory efficiency of elderly people. Both types of subject, however, are likely to benefit from a structure initially provided by an external source (e.g., the therapist), individually tailored to meet the needs of their daily life.

CONCLUSION

The evidence to date for effectiveness of therapeutic techniques and strategies to improve prospective memory functioning of older or brain-injured people is still sparse. Although differences between old and young appear not to be large and only to be evident in certain conditions, objective measures of performance of people after brain injury have only been reported for subjects who have severe deficits of memory and often of other cognitive abilities. This not only impedes identification of the most likely underlying cause of any deficit of prospective memory, it also reduces the likelihood of successful treatment and generalization to other activities. One major practical difficulty underlying the scarcity of reports of successful remediation programs is the amount of time needed to design, implement, and establish them. This requires the dedication of therapists and cohesive interdisciplinary cooperation if the program is to be systematically reinforced throughout the day. In a busy clinical or rehabilitation setting, the patient with memory problems may have to compete for scarce resources with others whose problems are primarily motor, linguistic, or perceptual. However, given the importance to everyday life of remembering what to do, when, and where, further exploration into factors affecting breakdown and remediation of prospective memory skills is a valuable aspect of neuropsychological rehabilitation. The insights afforded by controlled investigation of deficits will enhance understanding of the essential components of prospective memory, which may lead to improvements in training strategies for remediation of the identified deficits.

ACKNOWLEDGMENTS

The author was funded by a research fellowship with the McDonnell-Pew Centre for Cognitive Neuroscience, Oxford, at the time of writing this chapter.

REFERENCES

Baddeley, A. D. (1986). *Working memory*. Oxford, England: Oxford Medical Publications.

Baddeley, A. D. (1990) *Human memory*. Hillsdale, NJ: Lawrence Erlbaum Associates.

Bennett-Levy, J., & Powell, G. E. (1980). The subjective memory questionnaire: An investigation into the self-reporting of real-life memory skills. *British Journal of Social and Clinical Psychology, 19*, 177–188.

Cockburn, J. (1995). Task interruption in prospective memory: A frontal lobe function? (*Cortex, 31*, 87–97.

Cockburn, J., & Smith, P. T. (1988). Effects of age and intelligence on everyday memory tasks. In M. M. Gruneberg, P. E. Morris, & R. N. Sykes (Eds.), *Practical aspects of memory: Current research and issues* (Vol. 2, pp. 132–136). Chichester, England: Wiley.

Cockburn, J., & Smith, P. T. (1991). The relative influence of intelligence and age on everyday memory. *Journal of Gerontology, 46*, 31–36.

Cockburn, J., & Smith, P. T. (1994). Anxiety and errors of prospective memory among elderly people. *British Journal of Psychology, 85*, 273–282.

Cohen, G. (1989). *Memory in the real world*. Hillsdale, NJ: Lawrence Erlbaum Associates.

Crovitz, H. F., Cordoni, C. N., Daniel, W. F., & Perlman, J. (1984). Everyday forgetting experiences:

Real-time investigations with implications for the study of memory management in brain-damaged patients. *Cortex, 20,* 349–359.

Dobbs, A. R., & Rule, B. G. (1987). Prospective memory and self-report of memory abilities in older adults. *Canadian Journal of Psychology, 41,* 209–222.

Einstein, G. O., & McDaniel, M. A. (1990). Normal aging and prospective memory. *Journal of Experimental Psychology: Learning, Memory and Cognition, 16,* 717–726.

Ellis, J. A. (1988). Memory for future intentions: Investigating pulses and steps. In M. M. Gruneberg, P. E. Morris, & R. N. Sykes (Eds.), *Practical aspects of memory: Current research and issues* (Vol. 1, pp. 371–376). Chichester, England: Wiley.

Ellis, J. A., & Nimmo-Smith, I. (1993). Recollecting naturally-occurring intentions: A study of cognitive and affective factors. *Memory, 1,* 107–126.

Evans, J., & Wilson, B. A. (1992). A memory group for individuals with brain injury. *Clinical Rehabilitation, 6,* 75–81.

Folstein, M. F., Folstein, S. E., & McHugh, P. R. (1975). "Mini-mental state": A practical method for grading the cognitive state of patients for the clinician. *Journal of Psychiatric Research, 12,* 189–198.

Furst, C. (1986). The Memory Derby: Evaluating and remediating intention memory. *Cognitive Rehabilitation, 4,* 24–26.

Herrmann, D. J. (1984). Questionnaires about memory. In J. E. Harris & P. E. Morris (Eds), *Everyday Memory, Actions and Absentmindedness* (pp. 133–151). London: Academic Press.

Herrmann, D. J., & Neisser, U. (1978). An inventory of everyday memory experiences. In M. M. Gruneberg, P. E. Morris, & R. N. Sykes (Eds.), *Practical aspects of memory* (pp. 35–42). London: Academic Press.

Huppert, F. A., & Beardsall, L. (1993). Prospective memory impairment as an early indicator of dementia. *Journal of Clinical and Experimental Neuropsychology, 15,* 805–821.

Koriat, A., Ben-Zur, H., & Nussbaum, A. (1990). Encoding information for future actions: Memory for to-be-performed tasks versus to-be-recalled tasks. *Memory and Cognition, 18,* 568–578.

Kvavilashvili, L. (1987). Remembering intention as a distinct form of memory. *British Journal of Psychology, 78,* 507–518.

Lincoln, N. B., & Tinson, D. (1989). The relation between subjective and objective memory impairment after stroke. *British Journal of Clinical Psychology, 28,* 61–65.

Martin, M. (1986). Ageing and patterns of change in everyday memory and cognition. *Human Learning, 5,* 63–74.

Mateer, C. A., Sohlberg, M. M., & Crinean, J. (1987). Perceptions of memory functions in individuals with closed head injury. *Journal of Head Trauma Rehabilitation, 2,* 74–84.

Maylor, E. A. (1990). Age and prospective memory. *Quarterly Journal of Experimental Psychology, 42A,* 471–493.

McDaniel, M. A., & Einstein, G. O. (1993). The importance of cue familiarity and cue distinctiveness in prospective memory. *Memory, 1,* 23–41.

Meacham, J. A., & Kushner, S. (1980). Anxiety, prospective remembering and performance of planned actions. *Journal of General Psychology, 103,* 203–209.

Meacham, J. A., & Leiman, B. (1982). Remembering to perform future actions. In U. Neisser (Ed.), *Memory observed: Remembering in natural contexts* (pp. 327–336). San Francisco: Freeman.

Norman, D. A. (1981). Categorization of action slips. *Psychological Review, 88,* 1–15.

Reason, J. (1979). Actions not as planned: The price of automatisation. In G. Underwood & R. Stevens (Eds.), *Aspects of consciousness* (pp. 67–89). London: Academic Press.

Reason, J. T. (1984a). Absentmindedness and cognitive control. In J. E. Harris & P. E. Morris (Eds.), *Everyday memory, action and absentmindedness* (pp. 113–132). London: Academic Press.

Reason, J. T. (1984b). Lapses of attention in everyday life. In R. Paraswaman & D. R. Davies (Eds.), *Varieties of attention* (pp. 515–549). Orlando, FL: Academic Press.

Schwartz, A. F., & McMillan, T. M. (1989). Assessment of everyday memory after severe head injury. *Cortex, 25,* 665–671.

Shallice, T., & Burgess, P. (1991). Deficits in strategy application following frontal lobe damage in man. *Brain, 114,* 727–741.

Shimamura, A. P., Janowsky, J. S., & Squire, L. R. (1991). What is the role of frontal lobe damage in memory disorders? In H. S. Levin, H. M. Eisenberg, & A. L. Benton (eds): *Frontal lobe function and dysfunction* (pp. 173–195). New York: Oxford University Press.

Sohlberg, M. M., & Mateer, C. A. (1989a). *Introduction to cognitive rehabilitation.* New York: Guilford Press.

Sohlberg, M. M., & Mateer, C. A. (1989b). Training use of compensatory memory books: A three stage behavioural approach. *Journal of Clinical and Experimental Neuropsychology, 11,* 871–891.

Sohlberg, M. M., White, O., Evans, E., & Mateer, C. A. (1992a). Background and initial case studies into the effects of prospective memory training. *Brain Injury, 6,* 129–138.

Sohlberg, M. M., White, O., Evans, E., & Mateer, C. A. (1992b). An investigation of the effects of prospective memory training. *Brain Injury, 6,* 139–154.

Sunderland, A., Harris, J. E., & Baddeley, A. D. (1983). Do laboratory tests predict everyday memory? A neuropsychological study. *Journal of Verbal Learning and Verbal Behaviour, 22,* 341–357.

Sunderland, A., Watts, K., Baddeley, A. D., & Harris, J. E. (1986). Subjective memory assessment and test performance in elderly adults. *Journal of Gerontology, 41,* 376–384.

West, R. L. (1988). Prospective memory and aging. In M. M. Gruneberg, P. E. Morris, & R. N. Sykes (Eds.), *Practical aspects of memory: Current research and issues* (Vol. 2, pp. 119–125). Chichester, England: Wiley.

Wilkins, A. J., & Baddeley, A. D. (1978). Remembering to recall in everyday life: An approach to absent-mindedness. In M. M. Gruneberg, P. E. Morris, & R. N. Sykes (Eds.), *Practical aspects of memory* (pp. 27–34). London: Academic Press.

Wilson, B. A. (1991). Long-term prognosis of patients with severe memory disorders. *Neuropsychological Rehabilitation, 1,* 117–134

Wilson, B. A., Cockburn, J., & Baddeley, A. D. (1985). *The Rivermead Behavioural Memory Test.* Bury St. Edmunds, England: Thames Valley Test Co.

Winograd, E. (1988). Some observations on prospective remembering. In M. M. Gruneberg, P. E. Morris, & R. N. Sykes (Eds.), *Practical aspects of memory: Current research and issues* (Vol. 1, pp. 348–353). Chichester, England: Wiley.

Woolf, M. J. (1994). Age difference in prospective memory. *The Psychologist, 2,* 55.

18

Improving Prospective Memory Task Performance in Persons with Alzheimer's Disease

Cameron J. Camp
Jean W. Foss
Alan B. Stevens
Ann M. O'Hanlon
University of New Orleans

Persons with mild to moderate cognitive impairment due to Alzheimer's disease (AD) were trained to perform prospective memory (PM) tasks in two experiments using a technique called *spaced-retrieval* (SR). SR training involves practicing retrieval of specific information over expanding intervals. In Experiment 1, over 70% of the 30 participants displayed the ability to redeem a coupon after a 1-week interval. In Experiment 2, 87% of the 23 participants learned the strategy "look at the calendar" to remember what to do each day, and could remember this strategy over a 1-week delay. Of these, 75% were able to use the calendar effectively as a means of performing PM tasks. Measures of SR training speed and effectiveness were, in most cases, not related to mental status measures or demographics. Thus, SR training can improve PM task performance in persons with AD across a wide range of cognitive impairment. We describe a line of research involving ways of improving the performance of PM tasks in persons with AD. We begin with a brief review of the cognitive impairments associated with AD, especially as they impact memory performance. This is followed by a review of memory intervention research for older adults involving PM and AD. Highlighted will be the use of the SR intervention technique. This intervention served as the focus of a growing line of research, and is the basis for the PM research conducted by the authors detailed here.

COGNITIVE IMPAIRMENTS IN AD

AD is a degenerative disease that produces a variety of symptoms associated with dementia. These include memory loss for recent events, impaired consolidation of new information, and a severe impairment in tasks requiring delayed recall of information (see Bäckman, 1992; Camp & McKitrick, 1992; McKitrick, Camp, & Black, 1992). These memory impairments are pervasive in their disruption of the lives of persons with AD and may contribute to the stress of caregivers dealing with AD. Camp and McKitrick (1992) wrote:

> Afflicted individuals forget locations of objects; routes to follow; to keep appointments; to pay bills; the names of friends and relatives; how often they have asked the same question; whether or not they have eaten; and so on. It is very common for these people to write notes to themselves (including statements such as "My name is Joe") and forget where they placed the notes. Such problems are the everyday behavioral manifestations of the memory deficits seen in both research settings and neuropsychological examinations. (pp. 155–156)

Extremely poor performance for delayed recall is, in fact, one of the best diagnostic markers of early AD (Larrabee, Youngjohn, Sudilovsky, & Crook, 1993; Reisberg, et al., 1989). Under such circumstances, it would seem that PM would be severely impaired in AD. This "obvious" conclusion might explain the general lack of research conducted on PM performance in AD. Most information concerning PM performance in this population is anecdotal, such as for caregivers who complained to the authors that the person with AD fails "to remember to do the simplest tasks when they should." Persons with AD who fail at PM tasks complain about not being given instructions by caregivers or forgetting where their reminder messages were written down.

Memory Interventions for Older Adults Involving PM and AD

Memory Interventions Involving PM. Although a variety of memory improvement techniques were suggested for improving PM performance in normal aging populations (see Maylor, 1993; McDaniel & Einstein, 1992), some of these techniques might not work for persons with AD. Bäckman (1992) listed the following memory manipulations as having little impact in AD populations—organizational instructions, verbal mediators, level-of-processing, organizational structure, item familiarity, item richness, self-generation activity, and category cues. McDaniel and Einstein (1992) suggested the use of internal mnemonics such as the peg–word system as aids to PM performance in older adults. However, the use of mental imagery appears to be ineffective in persons with AD (e.g., Bäckman, 1992; Bäckman, Josephsson, Herlitz, Stigsdotter, & Vittanen, 1991).

Two findings from the PM literature, however, proved most useful in the current line of research. The first is the suggestion that external memory aids can substantially improve prospective memory task performance (e.g., McDaniel

& Einstein, 1992). This can be especially true for AD populations, in which internal storage of information is so severely compromised. The problem with using external aids alone as an intervention for persons with AD is that the location, purpose, or need to seek out such aids can be forgotten. (This is especially true if the aid was implemented after onset of the disease.)

A second finding from this literature is that PM task performance is related to indirect tests of retrospective memory (McDaniel & Einstein, 1993). One implication of such findings is that the unconscious memory system (i.e., implicit memory) assumed to underlie indirect memory tests (see Jacoby, Lindsay, & Toth, 1992; Schacter, 1992) may play a part in PM task performance. If so, and if unconscious learning could be accessed in persons with AD, interventions based on unconscious learning might be developed to enhance PM performance for these populations.

Memory Interventions in AD.   In a related context, Bäckman (1992) reviewed memory interventions for persons with AD that yielded gains. He listed these features as characteristics for successful intervention in AD: The training is based on skills that are preserved in AD, rather than on impaired skills; training programs are fairly extensive; caregivers are involved in training; and the retrieval process is strongly supported. (See Bäckman, 1992; and Camp & McKitrick, 1992, for reviews of memory intervention research in AD). Next, a specific memory intervention in AD, the SR technique, is discussed.

SR Training.   SR is a method of learning and retaining information by recalling that information over increasingly longer periods of time. It is a shaping paradigm applied to memory (Bjork, 1988; Camp & McKitrick, 1992; Landauer & Bjork, 1978). When a retrieval is successful, the interval preceding the next recall test is increased. If a recall failure occurs, the participant is told the correct response and asked to repeat it. Then the following interval length returns to the last one at which retrieval was successful. An example of a SR training session is shown in Fig. 18.1.

Data indicate that the participant failed to remember the information at Trial 1 (a 20-sec interval), remembered the information at Trials 2–5 (recall intervals increase to 90 sec), failed at the 120-sec interval (Trial 6), was tested at 90 sec on the next trial (Trial 7), and was given successively longer recall intervals with each new success (Trials 7–12), culminating with a recall interval of 240 sec.

We engaged in a series of studies training older adults with dementia to remember specific pieces of information using the SR method. These include names of common objects (Abrahams & Camp, 1993; McKitrick & Camp, 1993), a PM task (remembering to perform a future action; McKitrick et al., 1992), face–name associations (Camp & Schaller, 1989; Camp & Stevens, 1990), and object–location associations (Camp & Stevens, 1990). We wit-

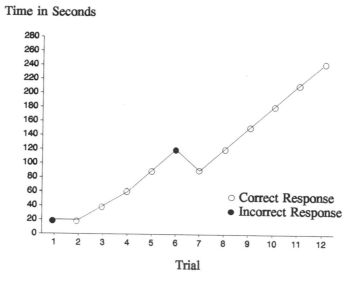

FIG. 18.1.   Hypothetical performance during an initial spaced-retrieval training session.

nessed retention of new information across weeks in individuals who could not
retain new information for 60 sec without training.

Arkin (1991) reported a case study in which she utilized SR to train her
mother to retain information over long time periods. McKitrick and Camp
(1993) and Riley (1992) demonstrated that caregivers could utilize this technique to train individuals with AD. In fact, Riley documented that a man in the
early stages of AD could train himself to remember new associations using SR.
There is mounting evidence, therefore, that SR training can improve memory
performance in AD.

The SR technique has several aspects that make it especially applicable to
AD subjects and their caregivers. Camp (1989) noted that the intervals between recall trials can be filled with conversation, playing games, looking over
photo albums, and so on. Thus, the intervention takes on the form of a social
visit or pleasant social interaction rather than a testing or training session. Due
to the use of shaping procedures, individuals with AD experience high rates of
successful recall with SR training. This contrasts with most other attempts to
remember recent information. Finally, the learning seems to take place with
little or no expenditure of cognitive effort on the part of the learner. Current
theoretical speculation on the reasons SR is successful in AD populations are
reviewed next.

Theoretical Basis of SR.   Spacing effects in recall were shown to improve memory performance in a number of studies with normal populations, and as a result, researchers such as Landauer and Bjork (1978) and Dempster (1988) called for expansion of its use in a variety of real world settings. There is substantial evidence that retrieval itself enhances memory, more than additional study (McDaniel & Masson, 1985). But why should this be the case? Is it because spacing of retrieval is simply a more effective technique than other commonly used mnemonics, or is it that spacing effects are qualitatively different?

Camp and his colleagues (Camp et al., 1993; see also Bäckman, 1992) proposed that SR engages a memory system known as *implicit memory*. Implicit memory, as defined by Schacter (1992), is ". . . an unconscious form of retention that . . . is assessed with tasks that do not require conscious recollection of specific episodes" (p. 559). This is in contrast to the conscious, effortful information processing associated with the explicit memory system. Mitchell (1993) suggested that ". . . it is clear that children and the elderly remember less information (than young adults) when asked to engage in conscious recollection. In marked contrast, memory tested implicitly appears to be asymptotic and remains stable from at least age 3 to 83" (p. 171).

Bäckman (1992) noted that in AD, there is evidence that ". . . implicit memory may be relatively intact in this disease" (p. 87), at least under some testing conditions. SR training appears to require little cognitive effort (Camp & Stevens, 1990; Schacter, Rich, & Stampp, 1985). For example, target information is learned in SR without the need for active rehearsal or other mnemonic strategies. Lack of conscious recollection and effortless learning are often associated with implicit memory. Research is underway to provide more direct evidence that SR engages implicit memory, but such an explanation would fit with current theory regarding memory in both normal and pathological aging. As a result, SR seemed to be a likely intervention technique for improving PM task performance in AD populations. In addition, individuals without memory deficits may also benefit from spaced-retrieval ". . . for retention of information that cannot be conveniently recorded . . . in practical settings" (Landauer & Bjork, 1978, p. 631). Having an intact explicit memory would not exclude acquiring information through implicit memory.

In this chapter, we report the results from two experiments involving training persons with AD to perform PM tasks. The emphasis in our research is on improving PM task performance, not on improving or impacting PM itself. To the extent that PM relies on explicit memory, the devastation wrought to this memory system even in the earlier stages of AD renders attempts to improve PM futile. As we noted earlier, most memory interventions attempted for persons with AD have not worked. Such interventions generally required cognitive effort–conscious processing–explicit memory. We try to find some combination of external supports and training regimens targeted at implicit memory that serve as a prosthesis for persons with AD, enabling them to successfully complete PM tasks.

DESCRIPTION OF THE RESEARCH SAMPLES

Thirty-four participants constituted the subject pool for this research. The participants in these two experiments represent samples from this pool of 34 persons. As a result, there is substantial (but not total) overlap in the makeup of the participants in the two experiments. This pool (62% females) was recruited from the Greater New Orleans Metropolitan Area meeting the National Institute of Neurological and Communicative Disorders and Stroke and Alzheimer's Disease and Related Disorders Association (NINCDS–ADRDA; McKhann et al., 1984) criteria for this diagnosis. All participants were characterized as having mild to moderate dementia using DSM III–R criteria and were at Stage 3 to Stage 5 on the Global Deterioration scale (Reisberg, Ferris, DeLeon, & Crook, 1982). Primary caregivers for these participants included spouses (53%), children or sons–daughters-in-law (27%), paid caregivers (3%), and no primary caregiver or nursing home resident (17%).

Baseline Measures

Baseline measures taken for this subject pool included the Folstein Mini-Mental Status Examination (MMSE; Folstein, Folstein, & McHugh, 1975) and Logical Memory I, Logical Memory II, Digit Span Forward, and Digit Span Backwards from the Wechsler Memory Scale–Revised (WMS–R; Wechsler, 1987). Demographic information and scores on baseline measures for the samples from the pool taking part in the two experiments are presented in Table 18.1.

TABLE 18.1
Subject Demographics and Mental Status Measures
in Experiments 1 and 2

Demographics	Experiment 1 (n = 30)		Experiment 2 (n = 23)	
	M	SD	M	SD
Age (years)	74.2	9.3	74.8	9.0
Years of education	12.9	3.3	12.2	3.0

Mental Status Measures				
	Median	Range	Median	Range
MMSE	20	9–26	18	9–26
Digit Span Forward[1]	6	4–8	5	4–8
Digit Span Backward[1]	4	0–6	3	0–5
Logical Memory I	4	0–18	3	0–18
Logical Memory II	0	0–5	0	0–5

[1] Raw Score

FIG. 18.2.   Example of coupon used in Experiment 1.

EXPERIMENT 1

The first experiment in this project was based on materials and procedures developed by McKitrick, Camp, and Black (1992). We wished to replicate their initial findings with a much larger sample. This would demonstrate that persons with AD could be trained to perform a PM task using the SR technique. As part of this procedure, participants had to learn, vocalize, and later utilize a strategy—to redeem a coupon for $1 by handing it to the experimenter after a 1-week delay.

Method

Thirty participants (67% female) from the subject pool described earlier participated. Demographics and mental status measures associated with these participants are shown in Table 18.1. All demonstrated the ability to distinguish the colors used in the training materials.

Participants were tested individually in their places of residence. The experiment was conducted in two phases—screening and training. In the first phase, screening measures were taken in one to two sessions, each of approximately 30 min duration. The second phase of the experiment involved three sessions, each occurring 1 week apart. In the first two sessions of this phase, the SR procedure was used to train the PM task. The last session was used to assess the effects of the previous SR training.

Coupon Training.   At the start of the first training session, a 3 × 3 array of coupons was placed before the participant. Each coupon was a 3″ × 6½″ colored card with the word *COUPON* printed in large letters in the center (See Fig. 18.2).

Each coupon was a different color, with the yellow designated as the target coupon. The experimenter then requested that the participant remember to give the experimenter the yellow coupon upon the experimenter's return the following week. This initiated a training sequence designed to enable the participant to successfully fulfill this request. This practice of the task required that the participant provide an appropriate response to the experimenter's question, "What are you going to do when I come back next week?" The subject's response consisted of a verbal and a motor component. The verbal component required the subject to respond with the statement, "I'm going to hand–give you the yellow coupon." After the verbal response, the subject was then required to select the yellow coupon from the array of coupons and hand it to the experimenter.

Both the verbal and motor component of the response were required to achieve a correct response. Presentation of recall trials utilized the SR method (described earlier) beginning with an interval of 20 sec, and intervals between responses continued to increase when training was successful. Presentation of SR recall intervals was controlled by a microcomputer utilizing software designed by the first author. This software also enabled the participant's responses to be recorded in a data file. The position of the target coupon was changed in the 3 × 3 matrix after each SR trial to control for location learning.

At the beginning of the second session (the following week), the participant was tested for spontaneous recall of the verbal component of the target response. If the participant did not say that he or she was to hand the experimenter the yellow coupon, he or she was given the verbal prompt, "What were you going to do when I came back this week?"

If the participants responded correctly either spontaneously or to the verbal prompt, they were awarded $1 (the redemption value of the coupon) and training was begun for a new color coupon (blue), to be redeemed on the third visit. If the participant did not respond correctly, either spontaneously or after the verbal prompt, the coupon array was placed before the participant and training reinstated for the yellow (first color) coupon.

The third session began with another test for spontaneous recall of the verbal component of the target response (the color coupon trained during the second session). If spontaneous recall did not occur, a verbal prompt was again administered, and the participant's response was recorded. A correct recall (spontaneous or following the verbal prompt) allowed the participant to receive $1 for coupon redemption.

Note that a correct recall of the statement "I'm going to hand–give you the (target color) coupon" constituted a correct response at the beginning of Sessions 2 and 3 without the requirement that the target coupon be physically handed to the experimenter. Pilot research demonstrated that persons with AD who were able to execute the verbal component of the response had no difficulty in actually handing a coupon to researchers afterwards. (They were recalling the verbal response after a 1-week delay from the previous session). In addition, we were interested in determining if persons with AD could be trained to learn and recall a verbal strategy using only a verbal prompt. This would serve as a central focus for a later study (Experiment 2, to be discussed later).

Results

Number of Coupons Redeemed.   After two training sessions, 12 participants (40%) redeemed one coupon, and 10 (33%) redeemed two coupons. Only eight participants (27%) failed to redeem a coupon after a 1-week delay. Thus, after only two 30 min training sessions, over 70% of these participants exhibited the ability to execute a prospective memory task after a delay of 7 days.

Recall Intervals Associated with Coupon Redemption.   We were also interested in determining the recall intervals achieved during SR training that would be predictive of successful PM task performance. Results from past research (e.g., McKitrick et al., 1992) indicated that if AD participants could retain target information for approximately 5 min within a training session, longterm retention of the information (across several days) was then possible. In this study, data from participants who redeemed one coupon were compared with data of participants who redeemed two coupons. For participants who redeemed only one coupon, a mean recall interval of 244 sec (*SD* = 52) within a SR training session was associated with the successful PM task performance of redeeming the yellow coupon 1 week later. For participants who redeemed two target coupons, the mean recall intervals during training before redemption of the first and second coupons were 267 sec (*SD* = 84) and 249 sec (*SD* = 28), respectively. Taken in combination with the findings of McKitrick, Camp, and Black (1992), these results indicate that if SR training can produce within-session recall intervals of 4 to 5 min, long-term retention of target information can be achieved. This, in turn, can lead to successful execution of prospective memory tasks over a relatively long (1-week) time period.

Correlations Between Coupon Learning and Other Measures.   Do demographic or mental status measures predict ability to learn coupons? Correlations between the number of coupons learned and the measures shown in Table 18.1 were computed. These results are shown in Table 18.2.

None of these correlations reached significance. The pattern of results clearly indicates that standard mental status measures did not relate well to PM task performance after receiving SR training, at least for the range of mental status scores obtained for this sample.

EXPERIMENT 2

Given that persons with AD can be trained with SR to execute PM tasks, what might be the best way to maximize the impact of interventions in the everyday environments of such individuals? We reasoned that a good way to proceed

TABLE 18.2
Correlations between # of Coupons Learned and
Demographics/Mental Status Measures

	# of Coupons Learned
Age	−.04
Years of Education	.01
MMSE	.29
Digit Span Forward[1]	.12
Digit Span Backward[1]	−.02
Logical Memory I	.10
Logical Memory II	.10

[1]Raw Score
Note: For all correlations, $p > .05$.

would be to use SR to train persons with AD to learn a strategy, and to link that strategy to the use of an external memory aid. In this case, we attempted to train persons with AD to look at a calendar, on which PM tasks would be listed. If successful, persons with AD would be able to use the calendar to execute a variety of PM tasks, the contents of which could change on a daily basis.

Method

Twenty-three participants (56% female) from the subject pool described earlier participated. Demographics and mental status measures associated with these participants are shown in Table 18.1. Note that some participants in Experiment 1 were excluded from Experiment 2 because they either demonstrated an ability to utilize a calendar before training (during a baseline period described here), or did not have a primary caregiver to assist with maintaining calendars during the experiment.

All training sessions took place in the participant's place of residence. A 1-day-per-page calendar was especially developed for use in this study (see Fig. 18.3).

The calendar pages were legal-size and fastened on a clipboard for easy removal and refilling. Distracting information often seen on commercial calendars was eliminated. The format featured the date predominantly in large print, leaving ample space for writing daily tasks and appointments.

In Session 1, a calendar with 7 days of pages was left with the participant and a location for the calendar was selected. Each page of the calendar contained a line with the instruction "sign your name" and another task for the participant to perform that day. These additional tasks were selected through discussions with the participant and his or her caregiver, and changed daily. The caregiver was asked to remove the calendar pages daily and put the pages in an envelope attached to the back of the clipboard. The caregiver was also instructed not to remind the participant of the calendar or the tasks written on its pages.

The first session was considered part of a 1-week baseline period, and no training was conducted. This was done to determine if the participant could spontaneously use the calendar effectively prior to training. As stated earlier, any participants who successfully used the calendar during the baseline period were excluded. On the second and all other weekly return visits, the experimenter would supply 7 days of calendar pages and collect the pages from the previous week. In addition, if spontaneous calendar usage had not occurred during the baseline, spaced-retrieval training was begun in the second session.

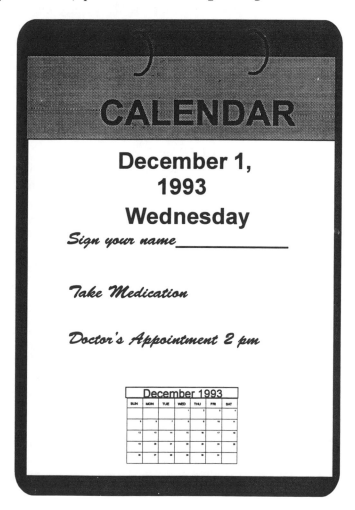

FIG. 18.3.   Example of calendar used in Experiment 2.

At the beginning of the next (third) session and the beginning of all subsequent sessions, participants were probed with the question "How are you going to remember what to do each day?" This was done to determine if participants were retaining the strategy across training sessions.

Calendar Training. Effective calendar usage by the participant was defined a priori as signing at least four of the seven calendar pages in 1 week, and performing at least four of the seven tasks listed on the calendar pages during the week. If the participant was unable to utilize the calendar without training, the SR technique was initiated on the second weekly visit.

Again, timing of recall intervals was controlled by a laptop microcomputer using the same software as that described in Experiment 1. Beginning with a 20-sec interval that increased when recall was successfull, the participant was instructed to respond to the experimenter's question, "How are you going to remember what to do each day?" with the response "Look at my calendar." SR training was implemented in the manner described earlier for the duration of the 30- to 45-min visit. As stated earlier, on return visits (beginning with Week 3), the experimenter began each session by asking the participant the question "How are you going to remember what to do each day?" A correct response (i.e., "look at my calendar") on 2 consecutive weeks constituted successful strategy learning and concluded SR training for the strategy. If successful strategy learning was not achieved after 10 weekly sessions, SR training was terminated.

If a participant demonstrated effective calendar usage for 2 consecutive weeks after initiation of SR training, the sessions were concluded. Learning the strategy did not necessarily assure effective calendar usage. For participants who had demonstrated strategy learning but who were not completing PM tasks, weekly sessions continued until either effective calendar usage was obtained or a maximum of 15 weeks after the initial baseline session was reached.

To enhance the likelihood of successful task performance in those instances when strategy learning was not accompanied by effective calendar usage, a number of informal interventions were attempted. For example, in one instance a woman began to use the calendar when she was encouraged to write down the calendar tasks herself. Recognition of her own handwriting increased the personal relevance of the calendar and its daily tasks for her.

With a few other participants, within-session training, called *task training,* was implemented. In task training, individuals were asked to perform a task that was written on the calendar (e.g., "Give Joe [the experimenter] the pencil from the green box") at expanding intervals *during* the 30-min session. SR training for this task helped the participant became familiar with reading tasks written on the calendar and then performing them. Thus, learning the strategy "look at the calendar" proved to be necessary though not sufficient for effective calendar usage. Additional training to personalize and familiarize participants with the mechanics of calendar usage sometimes proved helpful.

Results

Learning the Target Strategy. Fourteen participants (61%) met the criteria for long-term retention of the strategy after only three SR training sessions or less (i.e. showed retention of the strategy when probed at the beginning of Sessions 3 and 4 or Sessions 4 and 5. Note that Session 1 did not involve SR training, but was used as a baseline measure of spontaneous calendar usage. SR training began in Session 2.) Another six (26%) learned the strategy after four to seven training sessions. Three participants (13%) did not learn the strategy.

Recall Intervals Associated with Learning the Strategy. For the 20 participants who learned the strategy, the mean within-training-session recall interval immediately preceding 1-week retention of the strategy was 268 sec (*SD* = 90 sec). As was the case in Experiment 1, successful recall of target information over an interval of 4 to 5 min was predictive of long-term retention of the information.

Correlations Between Strategy Learning and Other Measures. Correlations between the number of training sessions needed to learn the strategy and the measures shown in Table 18.1 were computed. These results are shown in Table 18.3.

Only the correlation with age reached statistical significance ($r = .45$), with increased age associated with increased number of trials to learn the strategy.

Completing Calendar Tasks. For those participants who learned the strategy, seven (35%) were able to meet criteria for effective calendar task per-

TABLE 18.3
Correlations between # of Training Sessions for Strategy Learning–Meeting
Task Criteria and Demographics–Mental Status Measures

| | # of Training Sessions to | |
	Learn Strategy	Meet Task Criteria
Age	.45*	.33
Years of Education	−.30	.10
MMSE	−.24	.29
Digit Span Forward[1]	−.12	.59*
Digit Span Backward[1]	−.12	.02
Logical Memory I	−.30	−.13
Logical Memory II	−.19	−.25

[1] Raw Score.
*Correlation is significant at $p < .05$.

formance (described earlier) after two training sessions. Four (20%) demonstrated effective calendar usage in from 4 to 7 sessions and another four (20%) in from 8 to 11 sessions. Five participants who had learned the strategy (25%) were not able to effectively utilize the calendar. Examining these five cases, there were several instances in which caregivers failed to play their assigned role in the study (e.g., did not assist in changing calendar pages). Thus, successful usage of the calendar required both strategy learning as well as an active, involved caregiver.

Correlations Between Number of Sessions Needed to Achieve Calendar Usage and Other Measures. Correlations between the number of training sessions needed to achieve effective calendar usage and demographic–mental status measures are shown in Table 18.3. The only correlation to reach statistical significance was a positive correlation involving digit span forward scores ($r = .59$). The two participants who took 11 training sessions to achieve effective calendar usage had the longest forward digit spans (6 and 8 digits). They also had the highest MMSE scores of those who learned the strategy. We discuss the implications of these interesting results in the summary.

SUMMARY

Persons with AD can be trained using SR techniques to execute PM tasks. By teaching persons with AD a strategy involving the use of an external memory aid, the number and variety of PM tasks that can be successfully completed is substantial. This represents an improvement over results that could be obtained if training were limited to completion of specific PM tasks.

As was the case in previous research, it appears that the ability to retain new information for a 4 to 5 min interval enables such information to enter the long-term memory of persons with AD, at least in the case where such information is presented via SR training. But why should SR training be effective in AD populations? What are the predictors of its success?

In a small sample ($n = 4$), McKitrick et al., (1992) noted that the ordinal rank of participants with regard to coupon learning ability was not clearly related to any demographic or mental status measures other than age, with increasing age associated with decreased coupon learning speed. In our Experiment 1, no measures were significantly correlated with the number of coupons learned. In Experiment 2, similar to the results of McKitrick, Camp, and Black, increasing age was related to an increase in the number of training sessions needed to learn the strategy.

We would like to reiterate that the only instance of a significant correlation between a mental status measure and a PM performance measure involved a positive relationship between digit span forward and the number of training sessions needed to effectively execute calendar tasks. Perhaps this outcome is simply not reliable, and will fail to replicate. However, it may be that persons with AD who have high forward digit spans attempt to use an impaired explicit memory to execute PM tasks to a greater extent than persons with AD with lower forward digit spans, at least under conditions such as those in Experiment 2.

The lack of a strong relationship between mental status measures and the success of SR training supports the contention that SR appears to access implicit memory systems, as opposed to the explicit–declarative memory system generally accessed by mental status measures. In this lab, we recently gathered evidence to directly address this issue, and initial results provide strong evidence that SR training involves effortless learning that occurs independent of explicit memory functioning (Foss, 1994). As discussed earlier in this chapter and elsewhere (see Camp et al., 1993), implicit memory can provide an important basis for the design of a successful interventions in persons with AD. Such interventions may serve normal elderly adults, as well.

ACKNOWLEDGMENTS

Preparation of this chapter and the research described in it, were supported by Grant 1 R01 MH45389–01A1 from the National Institutes of Mental Health to the first author.

We gratefully acknowledge the assistance of Amy Mandella in the preparation of this article.

REFERENCES

Abrahams, J. P., & Camp, C. J. (1993). Maintenance and generalization of object naming training in anomia associated with degenerative dementia. *Clinical Gerontologist, 12*(3), 57–72.

Arkin, R. M. (1991). Memory training in early Alzheimer's disease: An optimistic look at the field. *American Journal of Alzheimer's Care and Related Disorders & Research, 6*(4), 17–25.

Bäckman, L. (1992). Memory training and memory improvement in Alzheimer's disease: Rules and exceptions. *Acta Neurologica Scandinavica, 84*, 84–89.

Bäckman, L., Josephsson, S., Herlitz, A., Stigsdotter, A., & Vittanen, M. (1991). The generalizability of training gains in dementia: Effects of an imagery-based mnemonic on face-name retention duration. *Psychology and Aging, 6*, 489–492.

Bjork, R. A. (1988). Retrieval practice and the maintenance of knowledge. In M. M. Gruneberg, P. Morris, & R. Sykes (Eds.), *Practical aspects of memory* (Vol. 2, pp. 396–401). London: Academic Press.

Camp, C. J. (1989). Facilitation of new learning in Alzheimer's disease. In G. C. Gilmore, P. J. Whitehouse, & M. L. Wykle (Eds.), *Memory and aging: Research, theory, and practice* (pp. 212–225). New York: Springer.

Camp, C. J., Foss, J. W., Stevens, A. B., Reichard, C. C., McKitrick, L. A., & O'Hanlon, A. M.

(1993). Memory training in normal and demented elderly populations: The E-I-E-I-O model. *Experimental Aging Research, 19,* 277–290.

Camp, C. J., & McKitrick, L. A. (1992). Memory interventions in Alzheimer's-type dementia populations: Methodological and theoretical issues. In R. L. West & J. D. Sinnott (Eds.), *Everyday memory and aging: Current research and methodology* (pp. 155–172). New York: Springer-Verlag.

Camp, C. J., & Schaller, J. R. (1989). Epilogue: Spaced-retrieval memory training in an adult day-care center. *Educational Gerontologist, 15,* 641–648.

Camp, C. J., & Stevens, A. B. (1990). Spaced-retrieval: A memory intervention for dementia of the Alzheimer's type (DAT). *Clinical Gerontologist, 10,* 58–61.

Dempster, F. N. (1988). The spacing effect: A case study in the failure to apply the results of psychological research. *American Psychologist, 43,* 627–634.

Folstein, M. F., Folstein, S. E., & McHugh, P. R. (1975). "Mini-mental state" a practical method for grading the cognitive state of patients for the clinician. *Journal of Psychiatric Research, 12,* 189–198.

Foss, J. W. (1994). *Cognitive effort: Effects of Spaced Retrieval on learning in AD.* Unpublished master's thesis, University of New Orleans.

Jacoby, L. L., Lindsay, D. S., & Toth, J. P. (1992). Unconscious influences revealed. *American Psychologist, 47,* 802–809.

Landauer, T. K., & Bjork, R. A. (1978). Optimum rehearsal patterns and name learning. In M. M. Grunenberg, P. E. Morris, & R. N. Sykes (Eds.), *Practical aspects of memory* (pp. 625–632). New York: Academic Press.

Larrabee, G. J., Youngjohn, J. R., Sudilovsky, A., & Crook, T. H., III. (1993). Accelerated forgetting in Alzheimer-type dementia. *Journal of Clinical and Experimental Neuropsychology, 15*(5), 701–712.

Maylor, E. A. (1993). Minimized prospective memory loss in old age. In J. Cerella, J. Rybash, W. Hoyer, & M. L. Commons (Eds.), *Adult information processing: Limits on loss* (pp. 529–551). San Diego: Academic Press.

McDaniel, M. A., & Einstein, G. O. (1992). Aging and prospective memory: Basic findings and practical applications. In T. E. Scruggs & M. A. Mastropieri (Eds.), *Advances in learning and behavioral disabilities* (Vol. 7, pp. 87–105). Greenwich, CT: JAI Press.

McDaniel, M. A., & Einstein, G. O. (1993). The importance of cue familiarity and cue distinctiveness in prospective memory. *Memory, 1*(1), 23–41.

McDaniel, M. A., & Masson, M. E. J. (1985). Altering memory representation through retrieval. *Journal of Experimental Psychology: Learning, Memory, & Cognition, 11,* 371–385.

McKhann, G., Drachman, D., Folstein, M., Katzman, R., Price, D., & Stadlan, E. (1984). Clinical diagnosis of Alzheimer's disease: Report of the NINCDS–ADRDA work group. *Neurology, 34,* 939–949.

McKitrick, L. A., & Camp, C. J. (1993). Relearning the names of things: The spaced-retrieval intervention implemented by caregivers. *Clinical Gerontologist, 14,* 60–62.

McKitrick, L. A., Camp, C. J., & Black, F. W. (1992). Prospective memory intervention in Alzheimer's disease. *Journal of Gerontology: Psychological Sciences, 47*(5), 337–343.

Mitchell, D. B. (1993). Implicit and explicit memory for pictures: Multiple views across the lifespan. In P. Graf & M. E. J. Masson (Eds.), *Implicit memory: New directions in cognition, development, and neuropsychology* (pp. 171–190). Hillsdale, NJ: Lawrence Erlbaum Associates.

Reisberg, B., Ferris, S. H., DeLeon, M. J., & Crook, T. H., III (1982). The Global Deterioration Scale for assessment of primary dementia. *American Journal of Psychiatry, 139,* 1136–1139.

Reisberg, B., Ferris, S. H., Kluger, A., Franssen, E., deLeon, M. S., Mittelman, M., Borenstein, J., Rameshwar, K., & Alba, R. (1989). Symptomatic changes in CNS aging and dementia of the Alzheimer-type: Cross-sectional, temporal, and remediable concomitants. In M. Bergener &

B. Reisberg (Eds.), *Diagnosis and treatment of senile dementia* (pp. 193–223). New York: Springer.

Riley, K. P. (1992). Bridging the gap between researchers and clinicians: Methodological perspectives and choices. In R. L. West & J. D. Sinnott (Eds.), *Everyday memory and aging: Current research and methodology* (pp. 182–189). New York: Springer-Verlag.

Schacter, D. L. (1992). Understanding implicit memory: A cognitive neuroscience approach. *American Psychologist, 47*(4), 559–569.

Schacter, D. L., Rich, S. A., & Stampp, M. S. (1985). Remediation of memory disorders: Experimental evaluation of the spaced-retrieval technique. *Journal of Clinical and Experimental Neuropsychology, 7*(1), 79–96.

Wechsler, D. (1987). *Wechsler Memory Scale-Revised.* New York: Harcourt Brace Jovanovich.

19

Prospective Memory and Medication Adherence

Denise C. Park
Daniel P. Kidder
University of Georgia

In almost every scientific article written on prospective memory, the importance of remembering to take medication is cited an example of an important, ecologically valid prospective memory task (Einstein & McDaniel, 1990; Winograd, 1988). Despite the salience of medication-taking behavior to prospective memory researchers, little research actually examines the prospective aspects of this behavior. This may be a result of the complexity of medication adherence behavior and the accompanying tangle of theoretical and methodological issues associated with this area of research. The act of remembering to take a medication at the appointed time represents only the final point in a complex chain of cognitive and psychosocial behaviors that begins when an individual is prescribed a medication. Wilkins and Baddeley (1988) presented the opposite point of view and suggested that ". . . the task of taking medication at scheduled times each day . . . is simpler than most memory tasks in that the person has nothing to recall other than that he must take his medication" (p. 28). Winograd (1988) presented a contrasting view and conceptualized medication adherence as a complex, multifaceted behavior, a view that is more compatible with the approach taken in this chapter.

Winograd (1988) noted in his discussion of prospective memory and medication adherence that "prospective remembering is not an isolable act of pure cognition. It is part of ongoing action and such factors as attention, motivation, compliance, vigilance, reward, conflicting goals, and the like are all involved to a greater or lesser extent in acts of prospective remembering" (p. 350). Extrapolating from Winograd's statement, whether or not an individual "remembers" to take his or her medication is related to a complex array of variables, including beliefs about his or her illness and about the medication's efficacy and side effects, the ability of the individual to comprehend and to remember the medication instructions, as well as availability of and sensitivity to internal and external cues reminding the individual to take the medication. Thus, one important but frequently ignored aspect of medication adherence research is that an adequate understanding of it requires an integration of theoretical constructs from several domains of psychology. Merely understanding the cognitive events of how an individual comprehends and remembers to take medication will not account for the individual who fails to take medication because of the perception that he or she is not ill or that the medication has unacceptable side effects.

In this chapter, we examine the implications of theoretical models and empirical findings associated with laboratory studies of prospective memory for medication adherence behaviors. Embedded within this analysis is a recognition of the complexity of the behavior under discussion. We begin with a review of methods for measuring adherence behavior. This is followed by a brief discussion of the relationship of important constructs from the domains of health psychology and behavioral medicine to an understanding of medication adherence. Following this, the role of retrospective memory in medication adherence is briefly reviewed, and prospective memory issues are discussed in detail. Cognitive intervention techniques to improve medication adherence are then described. We close with recommendations for future directions of research in this area that emphasize an integration of cognitive research with other domains of psychology in order to address this problem of practical significance.

Defining and Measuring Medication Adherence

Medication adherence is using medication correctly, as prescribed by a physician. It requires that the individual take medication at the right time, in the correct amount, and that he or she follows special instructions associated with the medication (e.g., "Take with food"). Typically, measurement of nonadherence focused on accurately recording the medication event—the time at which a medication is taken and the amount that is taken, rather than on whether or not special instructions are followed or noted and the context in which the adherence occurs.

One initial problem encountered by researchers in the study of medication adherence behaviors is how to measure accurately adherence behavior. Some researchers relied on verbal reports and diary techniques (Folkman, Bernstein, & Lazarus, 1987), others conducted pill counts (Deyo, Inui, & Sullivan, 1981; Rudd et al., 1989), and a few studies looked at biological markers present in blood or urine (Beck et al., 1988; Hecht, 1974). Each of these techniques has problems. Wilkins and Baddeley (1988), for example, asked subjects to press a button in a device four times a day, mimicking the prospective component of a medication adherence task. They also had subjects keep a diary of when they forgot to press the button. Wilkins and Baddeley reported that 36% of all omissions were not recorded, suggesting that diary data provide underestimates of adherence errors, a finding also reported by Rand et al., (1992). Pill counts are a more systematic measurement of adherence. A major disadvantage, however, is that they do not allow the experimenter to determine the times at which medications were taken, providing only a crude estimate of adherence behaviors. Data from biological markers like blood and urine have a similar problem, generally providing only presence or absence data for a medication, particularly given the variability in rates in which individuals metabolize drugs. In addition, these tests can be expensive and are somewhat invasive.

Recently, microelectronic devices were used to monitor medication events more precisely, providing an important tool for memory researchers. With the use of microelectronic devices, researchers can get a window into the precise times when medications are taken outside of the laboratory. Two techniques have been used. One is the Videx time wand system and the other is the Medication Event Monitoring System (MEMS), both of which are described in more detail in Park, Morrell, Frieske, Gaines, and Lautenschlager (1993) and Park, Willis, Morrow, Diehl, and Gaines (1994). Briefly, the Videx time wand system relies on bar coding technology and a small scanner subjects use to scan a bar code associated with each medication they are taking. The date, time, and identity of the medication are stored in the scanning device, providing researchers with a detailed, accurate record of when medications were taken. The MEMS system is a bottle cap system, wherein the date and time are recorded every time the cap is removed from the medication bottle, so that detailed information about when the medication was used is available for as long as 6 months. The advent of these systems greatly increased the accuracy with which acts of prospective memory such as medication-taking behaviors can be measured.

Once a medication-taking event has been recorded, another issue that emerges is how to quantify the behavior of medication adherence. This is not a straightforward issue, as decisions must be made as to what constitutes an adherence error as well as how to aggregate the behavior of adherence across time and types of medication for a given individual subject. Generally, measures of omission and commission are easy to quantify, as an *omission* occurs when a prescribed dosage is omitted and a *commission* occurs when extra medication events occur. Omission errors are most common (Park, Morrell, Frieske, & Kincaid, 1992), and within a prospective memory framework, represent a *slip of action* as described by Cohen (1989). Using the Cohen framework, a medication adherence schedule would represent a prospective action plan and a slip of action would occur when an individual omitted a component of the plan—something Cohen suggested is more likely to occur with a highly routine plan. In contrast, the much rarer commission error would appear to represent a failure in reality monitoring and would be described as a *repetition error*, using the Cohen classification schema. In this case, an individual would make a commission error because he or she could not remember whether or not he or she had taken a medication yet and so opts to take a dose, when in fact it had already been taken earlier. An omission could also represent a failure in reality monitoring, except in this case the individual would decide incorrectly that he or she had already taken the medication and elect not to take a dose.

Both omission and commission errors can be reliably measured with the Videx and MEMS systems, although the cause of the error cannot be isolated. Both omission and commission behaviors may not be errors at all and can occur intentionally, because a subject elects not to take a medication or because a subject feels that it is to his or her benefit to take extra doses, such as in the case of pain killers. Although this behavior represents nonadherence, it is not due to memory function, an issue that is discussed later.

Another type of error is a *quantity error*, occurring when a subject takes too many or too few tablets within a dosing event. These can be quantified with the Videx system, as a subject can scan the bar code once for each tablet that is taken. Quantity errors cannot be quantified with the MEMS system, as it is never clear how many tablets are removed from a vial when it is opened. Evidence from our work suggests quantity errors occur rarely with the Videx system (or that Videx is not a viable means of measuring these errors), so we no longer record them in our research protocols.

One other kind of adherence error, particularly relevant to prospective research, is the issue of *time errors*—a subject takes a medication in the right amount but at the wrong time. In quantifying adherence behaviors, it is not easy to define what is meant by the "wrong time." Ellis (1988) presented a useful prospective memory framework for classifying time errors in medication adherence. She stated that it is important to know whether or not a prospective act must be performed within a very narrow window at a very precise time (e.g., catching a train) or whether the prospective act can be accurately completed within a larger window of time (e.g., stopping at the store to buy some bread some time before you get home for dinner). She called the former events *pulses* and the latter events *steps*. Generally, medication adherence events are described more accurately as steps, but there may be situations where a medication must be taken at a relatively precise time such as to regulate the heart, to prevent pain, or to maintain breathing. Because many medications require that they be taken with food or drink, although the general event of taking this medication may be a step, it may be transformed to a pulse due to the requirement that the medication be taken at the time a meal is consumed. Thus, as these examples illustrate, merely knowing that a medication is to be taken three times a day and at what time does not provide sufficient information to classify errors as time errors. The window for describing when a time error occurs for medications with the same schedule could be different as a function of type of medication and special instructions.

A final issue in quantifying adherence behaviors is how to aggregate the behaviors over time and medication. Park et al. (1993a) discussed this issue in some detail. Generally, it appears that adherence is not a stable behavior even within subjects. That is, subjects may reliably take one medication accurately but not another, a behavior described by Park et al. as *selective nonadherence*. Thus, assessing a general measure of adherence within a single subject across all of the medications that subject is taking may not provide an accurate picture of what is occurring within a given subject. Aggregating behaviors across days and weeks may also be problematic, even when a medication × medication approach is taken, unless measures of variability are also examined. In other words, a subject who is 25% nonadherent across an aggregated period of 1 week or 1 month might be relatively consistent in the behavior, regularly missing the evening dose of a four dose per day medication. Alternatively, subjects could be missing all doses on certain days and taking all of their medications on others, averaging a rate of 25% nonadherence over 1 week or 1 month. There are different clinical implications for these behaviors; it is important to develop measurement techniques that capture the dynamic nature of the behavior over time. The high variability we observed suggests that prospective memory is not a stable behavior within an individual. This judgment, however, is likely erroneous, as the variability exhibited by subjects in adherence behaviors is not due to memory difficulties but rather to differential beliefs subject hold about the efficacy and importance of different medications within their individual regimen.

Nonmemory Variables and Medication Adherence

It is critically important to recognize that when we attempt to understand the relationship between medication adherence and memory there is a substantial component to the behavior that is noncognitive, a point also noted by Winograd (1988). In fact, dominant views of medication adherence view the behavior as being embedded more within a social–psychological context than a cognitive context. The *self-regulatory model of medication adherence* (Leventhal & Cameron, 1987) emphasizes the role of patient values, beliefs, and construction of illness as the predictors of how an individual regulates medication-taking behavior. The patient is viewed as an intelligent problem-solver who will utilize and adjust medication dosages based on experience. The self-regulatory model suggests that in order to understand adherence behavior, it is important to determine first if an individual has an illness representation that is consonant with accurate adherence to a prescribed medication regimen. If the response to that question is negative, then the study of the cognitive–prospective aspects of medication-taking behavior should not proceed because the failure to take medications accurately is almost certainly not a prospective failure.

If an individual's illness representation is consistent with accurate use of medications, it may then become important to determine how distressing the individual finds his or her medical condition and how critical the individual believes the use of the medication is in either alleviating symptoms or curing the disease. If an individual has a deeply distressing disorder for which they believe a medication to be highly effective, they should be more likely to take that medication accurately than one where the individual perceives the illness to be more trivial or the treatment to be less effective. Both Cohen (1989) and Kvavilashvili (1987) emphasized that an important aspect of whether or not a prospective intention is acted on may be how important completion of the action is to the individual. The perceived side effects associated with medication usage are also important. Are there adjunct negative consequences for the performance of the prospective act of taking a medication? The importance of illness representation in predicting adherence behaviors was discussed in more detail in Park (1994) and a model of adherence that integrates both cognitive and psychosocial variables was presented in Park (1992a).

Finally, individuals likely possess an illness representation for each condition for which they are being treated. As a result, they may have different plans and intentions to adhere to medication regimens. For example, an individual who had a mildly uncomfortable skin allergy as well as a serious heart condition would have different representations of these illnesses and assign markedly different values to the importance of adherence to medications associated with each of these conditions.

Although the issues presented here are certainly complex, they are amenable to experimental study. This discussion helps delineate the dimensions that must be assessed to understand any real world prospective memory event. Prospective memories in the real world are value laden and embedded in a complex socioemotional as well as physical context that must be addressed in order to understand significant amounts of variance in prospective behaviors.

RETROSPECTIVE MEMORY
AND MEDICATION ADHERENCE

Prospective memories of all types have a retrospective component, a point emphasized by Einstein, Holland, McDaniel, and Guynn (1992) and by Einstein and McDaniel (this volume). An individual in a prospective situation must remember not only when to perform a future action, he or she must also remember the content of that future action—the retrospective component. The retrospective content could be simple (e.g., go to the doctor's at an appointed time) or it could be complex (e.g., on your way home from work, pick up a number of items at the grocery store, pick up one of your children at a friend's house, and retrieve the other child from swimming practice). In addition to remembering this series of actions, within each action an additional retrospective component is embedded (e.g., the exact groceries to be purchased, at which friend's house the child is, what time they expect you, at which sports practice the other child is, etc.). A memorable prospective failure of one of the authors occurred when she arrived at exactly the right time to pick up her daughter at swimming practice. When the child was not there and no one had seen her, the mother prepared to call the police, only to find that the child had been waiting with great anxiety for 1 hour at gymnastics practice that particular day, not swimming practice. Thus, the prospective aspect of the memory was intact, but the retrospective content was faulty, resulting in what would typically be considered a prospective failure.

Retrospective memory is of particular importance in medication adherence because of the complexity of the information associated with each medication, as well as the absolute number of medications an individual may have in a regimen, with each medication increasing the retrospective load. The retrospective aspect of medication-taking is not trivial; we commonly see older adults in our laboratory who are using eight or more medications, and the World Health Organization (1981) reported that 34% of older adults take three or more prescription drugs. Park (1992a) presented a model of medication cognition that includes four components, only the last of which is prospective. Park suggested that in order to take medication correctly, an individual must comprehend the instructions; he or she must use working memory to integrate the instructions across medications to form an overall adherence plan; then the individual must either remember the plan or write it down. Finally, the individual must remember to perform the prospective act of taking the medication. The first three components of medication cognition are comprised of nonprospective components, and the working memory and long-term memory components are clearly retrospective. Park reviewed the role that comprehension, working memory, and long-term memory might play in medication adherence.

A point of particular importance is that older adults may be particularly disadvantaged on the comprehension and retrospective aspects of medication cognition. Older adults showed lower comprehension and memory for medication information in a lab setting (Morrell, Park, & Poon, 1989) even when given unlimited study time. When older subjects were given organizational devices that supported the comprehension, working memory, and long-term memory aspects of medication cognition, the adherence behaviors of a subset of subjects were facilitated. Young–old adults in the study (those aged 60–70) were not facilitated by organizational devices, largely because they were adherent. In contrast, old–old adults (aged 71 and older) evidenced higher levels of nonadherence and were significantly improved by the organizational devices (Park et al., 1992). This finding may have occurred because the young–old adults had sufficient cognitive resources to accurately handle the comprehension and retrospective aspects of medication cognition, so that the devices did not provide any useful support. Because cognitive decline, however, is particularly pronounced in the seventh decade and later (see figures in Salthouse, 1991), very old adults may not have sufficient cognitive resources to function adequately with respect to the retrospective aspects of medication adherence. Thus, the organizational devices provided a useful support for this aspect of medication adherence, resulting in an improvement in adherence.

The notion that older adults are particularly at risk for difficulties with the retrospective aspects of medication cognition is consistent with the findings of Einstein et al. (1992), who hypothesized that age deficits on a prospective memory task in the laboratory were a result of poor function on the retrospective aspect of the task. More work is needed on the role that retrospective aspects of medication adherence play in global medication adherence behaviors. Individuals with low levels of education and poor reading ability, as well as the very old, may be at risk of failing to take medications correctly, not because they cannot remember when to do it, but because they have difficulty comprehending and remembering the instructions. Research that emphasizes the use of comprehension and retrospective memory function as individual differences variables to predict cognition would be welcome, as would research that examines types of external aids that provide appropriate cognitive support.

Another variable of importance in this context is complexity, as it is likely that complexity of medication regimen will interact with individual differences variables. The prediction would be that the most complex, resource-demanding regimens result in the greatest difficulty for subjects with limited cognitive resources. This is a particular concern because frail elderly are likely to be in the old–old category and thus may have more limited cognitive resources. They are also most likely to be on complex medication regimens as a direct result of frailty. They are at greatest risk for developing adverse reactions if medications are misused, so that this vulnerable population is of particular concern with respect to comprehension and retrospective aspects of adherence and complexity of regimen.

MEDICATION ADHERENCE
AND PROSPECTIVE MEMORY

The development of laboratory paradigms for the study of prospective memory (Einstein & McDaniel, 1990) greatly increased our theoretical understanding of prospective memory. The theoretical constructs and models derived from the laboratory work provide a useful framework to guide research in medication adherence. The laboratory work helps to highlight aspects of medication adherence that may be of particular importance in understanding and enhancing the behavior. The focus in this section, then, is on exploring the implications of laboratory-based constructs for the prospective aspects of medication adherence. Constructs to be discussed include the distinction between time-based and event-based prospective memory, the effect of concurrent activities on prospective memory, the role of number of events to be monitored on prospective performance, and the effects of aging on prospective memory.

Time-Based Versus Event-Based Prospective Memory

Perhaps the most basic distinction in the prospective literature that is of importance for understanding medication adherence behavior is whether a prospective memory is event-based or time-based. Einstein and McDaniel (1990) distinguished between event-based and time-based prospective memory in terms of task demands and the associated processing requirements. A laboratory version of an event-based task requires that a subject who is studying a series of words respond by pressing a key when a particular word appears. A laboratory version of a time-based task would require the subject to make a response at a specific time. Thus, as Einstein and McDaniel noted, the two types of tasks differ in terms of the amount of external cognitive support provided for the prospective memory. In the event-based task, the word itself is an external cue or cognitive support to remember to perform the prospective task of key pressing. In the time-based task, there are no external cues readily provided, and subjects must engage in a considerable amount of what Craik (1986) described as self-initiated processing. Craik suggested that prospective tasks were high in requirements for self-initiated processing, and predicted that age effects would be particularly pronounced for prospective tasks. Einstein and McDaniel (1990) were initially surprised to find that no age differences occurred in the event-based task they studied in the laboratory. They suggested that the age invariance occurred because the event-based task that they used was high in environmental support, as the target item served as a supportive cue to perform the prospective act. Thus processing demands in the event-based task were low and resulted in age invariance. In fact, Einstein and McDaniel (this volume) argue that event-based tasks have more or less the same properties as a cued-recall task—a task that exhibits smaller age differences than free recall.

A time-based task, however, has properties that are different from the event-based, as there are no obvious external cues to perform a time-based task. Therefore the task is high in self-initiated processing requirements and Einstein and McDaniel (1990) suggested that age differences would be found in a time-based task, a result they report in their chapter of this volume.

The prospective aspects of medication adherence would appear to be time-based, as medications are prescribed to be taken on some type of time-based schedule (e.g., three times a day). This time-based nature of medication-taking behavior suggests that it should be a difficult behavior for individuals to perform, due to the high processing requirements associated with time-based prospective tasks. Older adults would also be expected to be particularly disadvantaged in the performance of this type of task, due to the high self-initiated processing demands (Craik, 1986). Einstein and McDaniel (this volume), however, make an important point. They (as well as Maylor, 1990) note that although a task may initially be time-based, subjects may use techniques to transform it into an event-based task. For example, Maylor conducted a study where subjects were required to make telephone calls on a daily basis to the experimenter at a prescribed time. The time to call was either very specific (a pulse, as describe by Ellis, 1988) or was to occur within a 4-hour time band. The subjects who exhibited the best and most accurate behavior were those who attempted to remember to make the phone call by changing the task from a time-based to an event-based task. They did this by linking the initiation of the phone call to some other routine aspect of their life that occurred at the time the phone call was to be made.

Maylor's (1990) findings have obvious implications for the prospective component of medication adherence. The prediction is that subjects who link medication-taking to some specific routine event such as meals or brushing teeth, should evidence higher rates of adherence for that medication than subjects who do not engage in such linkage. There are little data on this topic, but there are several hypotheses that could be explored in order to determine if converting an adherence regimen to an event-based schedule might be an effective strategy. One example of such an hypothesis is that one would expect that the more doses per day required, the poorer adherence might be, a finding reported by Kruse, Eggert-Kruse, Rampmaier, Runnebaum, and Weber (1991), who used precise electronic monitors to measure adherence. The basis for this finding, in addition to the increased memory load that occurs with more medication events, may be that a high number of events (e.g., four per day was used in Kruse et al., as is common with antibiotics) might make it difficult to come up with routine events that are equally spaced—resulting in some difficulty in converting the time-based task into an event-based one. A second hypothesis is that medications that are explicitly prescribed to be event-based (e.g., "take three times a day with meals") should have a higher adherence rate than those not explicitly linked.

Another important issue regarding cues associated with the prospective aspect of medication adherence is that event-based cues need not necessarily be external. Internal physical state may serve as a powerful event that can convert a time-based adherence task into an event-based one. In other words, the experience of a heart beating too rapidly, chest pain, joint pain, or itchy, inflamed skin could all be internal cues that would remind the symptomatic individual to take medication. Thus, medications that treat silent conditions might have a lower adherence rate than medications for which failure to adhere results in negative physical consequences. One would expect lower adherence rates for medications for a silent disorder like hypertension, compared to another cardiovascular condition where failure to adhere resulted in heart palpitations. We found in preliminary data that the adherence rate for thyroid medications, which cause physiological cues if not taken as prescribed, is higher than for hypertension medications, which do not produce such cues.

Relevant to the issue of physical symptoms as cues for adherence is the Harris and Wilkins (1982) Test-Wait-Test-Exit (TWTE) model, proposed to understand time-based prospective behavior. The model suggests that the subject monitors or checks how close the interval is when the prospective task is to be performed. Depending on the results of the test, the subject either continues to wait to perform the prospective behavior if the window is not appropriate, or when the test indicates the prospective response is appropriate, the subject will make the response and exit the behavioral sequence. Internal cues of pain, fatigue, scratchy throat, and so on, could serve as reminders to initiate a test behavior in the TWTE sequence, and may play an important role in maintaining accurate medication adherence. Physiological state and internal cues may play a unique and important role in the prospective aspect of medication adherence.

In summary, the time-based–event-based distinction based on laboratory studies of prospective memory is an important construct in helping to understand the prospective aspects of medication adherence behavior, although predictions have not yet been tested. Research is needed to determine what techniques subjects use to remember to take medications, whether or not internal cues sometimes serve as a reminder to take medication for a particular disorder, and how these behaviors relate to adherence behavior.

Competing Activities and Medication Adherence

Another dimension besides the time-based–event-based distinction that is important for prospective memory in the laboratory are the competing activities in which the individual is engaged during periods when prospective memory tasks are to be performed. Perhaps the defining feature of prospective memories is that they occur against a background of other cognitive activity. This may be an important dimension for medication adherence behaviors, with the hypothesis being that extremely busy people have difficulty adhering to a medication regimen, particularly in the absence of internal illness cues. The reason for the poor adherence would be that the highly engaged primary behavior of their daily lives limits the cognitive effort devoted to the TWTE sequence described by Harris and Wilkins (1982). If the subject is too engaged to enter the testing sequence, time-monitoring behavior will not occur so that forgetting of the prospective behavior will be evidenced.

Einstein and McDaniel (this volume) make this point, and also suggest that highly engaged individuals may be too busy to notice event-based cues that would normally signal a prospective event like taking medication. Most of us have had the experience of realizing at the end of a highly engaged, stressful day that you feel ill, but that you were too busy all day to even notice all of the physiological cues signaling this "event" to which you might normally have attended. Thus the prediction of poorer prospective memory for busier people conceivably applies to both time-based and event-based medication adherence tasks.

Relative Importance of Medication Adherence

Another aspect that is of particular importance for medication adherence is how important it is that this prospective task be performed and what the consequences of not performing it are. Kvavilashvili (1987) elegantly demonstrated that subjects were more likely to remember to perform a more important prospective task than a less important one. She took the phone off the hook while subjects participated in an experiment so they would not be disturbed during the experiment, but instructed each subject to replace the receiver after they were done with the experiment. Importance of intention was manipulated by telling one half of the subjects to be sure to remember to hang up the receiver because a professor was expecting a phone call from Moscow. The other subjects were not given an important reason for hanging up the phone. Kvavilashvili also manipulated whether or not the interval was filled with a demanding cognitive task and also subtly queried subjects as to whether or not they thought about hanging up the phone during the interval.

Kvavilashvili reported a substantial effect of intention—that is, subjects were much more likely to remember to hang up the phone in the Moscow condition where there was considerable consequence associated with their forgetting. In addition, she also found that when subjects performed a trivial or uninteresting primary task *and* were in the condition where the prospective task was of lower importance, a great deal of forgetting to hang up the phone occurred. For the more important task, subjects were more likely to remember regardless of how engaging the primary task. In line with the finding of Kvavilashvili, Meacham and Singer (1977) also presented evidence that incentive affected college students' remembering to mail postcards to the experimenter.

These findings illustrate an important point about medication adherence. It is of critical importance to understand a subject's illness representation if one is to understand the prospective act of taking medications correctly. In other words, one strong predictor of whether or not we take medication may be how worried or concerned we are about the illness with which the medication is associated. If we are highly concerned about an illness perceived to be serious, it is likely that a great deal of internal musing about the disorder will occur, leading to many more entries into the TWTE sequence described by Harris and Wilkins (1982). The actual musings regarding the illness as well as symptoms from the illness can serve as event-based cues that trigger an evaluation of whether or not it is an appropriate time to take medication.

Medication adherence is an individual's routine plan that is imbedded in a series of other plans, all of which have a certain probability of being implemented. Cohen (1989) suggested that novel, high priority plans are more likely to be implemented. She stated that:

> Busy people have whole sets of prospective plans that are stacked up like planes over an airport, waiting to be implemented. Some will be postponed, some will be truncated, and some will be discarded altogether. . . . Both theoretical and common sense considerations suggest that novel, high-priority plans that are part of a network of related plans are more likely to be remembered. (pp. 25–26)

Because medication-taking is a repetitive, routine event, it is not likely to be a novel or distinctive plan. Thus, success in carrying the plan out may relate to how important it is to the individual and where it is placed in the queue of prospective tasks the individual is planning to perform, so vividly described by Cohen. Items higher up in the queue may receive more monitoring behavior, thus increasing the probability that the prospective task will be performed. The individual may also spend more cognitive effort to transform an important time-based task into a distinctive event-based task to increase the probability that it will be performed if it is a task high in the hierarchy of prospective intentions. A routine prospective event may become so imbedded in a routine behavior (e.g., after brushing teeth every morning, medication is taken), that it has a high probability of being performed, but that the probability is high precisely because the medication-taking has become so automatized that it no longer exists within the individual's hierarchy or queue of prospective tasks that need to be performed.

Complexity of Medication Adherence Regimen

Another construct of importance for medication adherence that affected prospective memory in laboratory research is complexity of the prospective task. Einstein, Holland, McDaniel, and Guynn (1992) manipulated the number of target words (one vs. four) to which subjects were to make a key press as their prospective task, while subjects performed a primary working memory task. Einstein et al. reported an interaction of complexity with age, such that old adults were more disadvantaged when the prospective component of the task had a high memory load compared to young subjects. The investigators interpreted this finding to be due to the higher retrospective load created by requiring subjects to respond prospectively to multiple targets. The implications of this work for medication adherence are straightforward. Medication adherence schedules can be extraordinarily complex. It is not uncommon for individuals with multiple chronic diseases like arthritis, hypertension, and diabetes to be on 10 or more medications. Many of the medications have multiple dosing events required each day as well as special instructions. The retrospective load of these tasks is high. Organizing the information across medications into a coherent medication plan and then remembering or writing the plan down are required in order for the prospective component of the task to be performed accurately. Interventions have been developed to assist with the retrospective aspect of medication adherence and their effectiveness are discussed shortly.

Age and Medication Adherence

A final issue to consider before turning to interventions in adherence is the relationship of age to medication adherence behaviors. The prospective literature suggests that age effects do not generally occur on event-based tasks (Einstein & McDaniel, 1990), unless the retrospective load of the task is high (Einstein et al., 1992). Time-based tasks typically do show age effects due to the self-initiated processing requirements associated with the task. Although there is disagreement as to whether or not there is a relationship of age to medication adherence, Park et al. (1992) did report such an effect when the behavior of young–old adults (in this case, adults below the age of 70) was contrasted with old–old adults. Deficits manifested by the old–old are primarily due to deficits in the retrospective component of medication adherence, particularly because interventions which supported working memory and long-term memory improved adherence behaviors in the old–old. However, it may also be that with very complex medication schedules that require frequent monitoring, that age deficits in the prospective act of monitoring could be manifested. This issue could best be addressed by determining if adherence deficits still exist when the retrospective burden of an adherence task is entirely relieved via memory aids so that monitoring becomes the primary aspect of the task, as in the Park et al. study.

One point that was not made in the literature with respect to age and adherence is that it may be a general misconception to suggest that older adults make many adherence errors compared to young adults. In two separate studies, we found that young–old elderly (generally individuals aged 60–75) have the lowest error rates of any age group—lower than the old–old (Park et al., 1992) and even lower than middle-aged adults (Park, 1992b). We believe that this is the case because young–old adults possess the appropriate cognitive skills, life style, and illness representation that would result in a high level of adherence. Adults in the 60- to 75-year-old range likely perceive that they are physically vulnerable and thus have an illness representation conducive to adherence and are motivated to take medications as prescribed. The majority of individuals in this age range do not work and so they may also have more time available to organize and monitor their prospective behavior. Finally, they appear to have the cognitive skills necessary to organize the retrospective aspects of their adherence regimen. Middle-aged adults who are somewhat less adherent than young-old adults almost certainly have appropriate cognitive abilities, but they may either not have an illness representation consistent with taking medications or they may experience prospective failure due to a high degree of personal and professional engagement, resulting in a higher level of nonadherence than young–old adults. The oldest–old's high rate of nonadherence would appear to be based in the retrospective component of the adherence task. The oldest–old generally have an illness representation that is consonant with taking medications correctly but they may have experienced sufficient decline in cognitive abilities that they have difficulty with the retrospective aspects of medication adherence, particularly a complex regimen.

Although these hypotheses have not been directly tested to date, studies are in progress in our lab that address the interaction effects of age, illness representation, and cognitive abilities on medication adherence. Park and colleagues (Park et al., 1993b) have developed multiple measures of illness representation and of retrospective and prospective cognitive function and are relating these measures to medication adherence in an age-stratified population.

INTERVENTIONS TO IMPROVE MEDICATION ADHERENCE

There is a large literature on techniques to improve medication adherence that is quite diverse and cuts across many disciplines. One literature focuses on the role of patient education and doctor–patient communication on improving adherence (Garnett, Davis, McKenney, & Steiner, 1981; MacDonald, MacDonald, & Phoenix, 1977; Peck & King, 1982; Zola, 1986). Such education programs are largely focused on modifying the individual's illness representation so that the representation is consistent with a desire to adhere. Because the emphasis in this chapter is on memory, education programs are not discussed here. There are a subset of studies in the literature that examined the role of cognitive supports on medication adherence and these are discussed within the context of what cognitive aspects of medication adherence they support.

There is a lengthy literature on improving subjects' comprehension of medication information and instructions. Based on the finding that picture recognition is age invariant (Park, Puglisi, & Smith, 1986), Morrell, Park, and Poon (1990) designed pictorially based medication labels and measured comprehension and memory for the medication information presented. They reported that young adults' memory was facilitated by the pictorial design, but older adults did somewhat better with the verbally based labels. These data suggest that without extensive training, it appears that the more familiar, verbally based labels are more supportive for older adults. Morrow, Leirer, and Sheikh (1988) proposed a series of specific rules for designing prescription instructions for the elderly who are more likely to experience declines in the comprehension and retrospective aspects of medication cognition. The recommendations were based on empirical findings in both the perception and cognitive aging literature. Suggestions include using large, high contrast print on the labels as well as simple language and explicit descriptions of when the medications should be taken. They also recommend providing patients with a complete summary of the medication information, including possible side effects, the purpose of the medication and how it works, warnings, and so on. Morrow, Leirer, Altieri, and Tanke (1991) reported that they were able to measure subjects' schemata or cognitive plans for taking medications and that memory for medication information was better when subjects received instructions compatible with these schemata.

There are a number of studies that focused on the working memory–long term memory (retrospective) aspect of medication adherence. Most of these studies examined how some type of external aid that provides organizational support for medication-taking can improve adherence behaviors. Perhaps the most readily available, commonly used external aids are the various types of medication organizers available to customers at most pharmacies. These devices are designed to improve adherence behaviors by providing organization of the medications across a 1 day or 1 week time period, relieving some of the retrospective burden of medication-taking. Medications are placed in labeled slots and removed as needed. These devices also support another retrospective aspect of medication adherence—the reality-monitoring component. If, for example, an individual is not certain if he or she has already taken a medication dose for the morning, the individual can be certain that the act was completed if the medication is missing from the organizer for the morning dose. Finally, some devices also have time-based programmable beepers supportive of the purely prospective aspect of adherence.

It is essential that over-the-counter memory aids be loaded correctly if they are to be useful in facilitating medication adherence. Park, Morrell, Frieske, Blackburn, and Birchmore (1991) examined whether or not arthritis patients on three or more medications could correctly load a week's supply of medications into three different types of organizers. They reported a high degree of accuracy for an organizer with 28 compartments—four compartments for morning, noon, dinner, and evening for each of the days of the week. Somewhat more errors were made with a wheel device that had a compartment for each hour of the day, and the most errors were made with an organizer that had seven compartments—one for each day of the week, with no discrimination among which medications were to be taken at what times across the day.

Thus, the prospects of such a device improving adherence seem remote, given that subjects had difficulty in loading it correctly and all of the information about dosing schedule and medication identity are lost once the information is placed into the organizer.

In a later study, Park et al. (1992) measured adherence when older adults were given over-the-counter organizers. They provided young–old and old–old adults with the 7-day-with-times (28 compartment) organizer, as well as an organizational chart with an hour-by-hour account of how they were to take medications, providing substantial retrospective support for complex adherence behavior. Either device alone did not improve adherence, but the two together significantly improved adherence in old–old adults. In a similar vein, Rehder, McCoy, Blackwell, Whitehead, and Robinson (1980) found that the use of a 7-day-with-times organizer improved adherence in hypertensive patients. Medication adherence can be improved by providing individuals with memory aids that support the organization of the memory load associated with the substance of the task.

It is possible, however, that the memory aids worked not because they helped reduce the complexity of the memory load associated with the medication regimen, but because they provided subjects with clear feedback regarding whether or not they had performed the act of taking the medication. In other words, this argument suggests that there is yet another retrospective component to medication cognition in addition to the working memory and long-term memory components discussed earlier in the chapter and also suggested by Park (1992a). Besides memory for the content of the regimen (what is to be done and when it is to be done), there is also an episodic–retrospective component—memory for the episodic act of whether the medication was taken. Because of the highly repetitive, routine nature of taking medication, multiple acts of medication taking can become readily confused with one another over hours and days. There are a few studies that focus only on the effect of providing subjects with information about whether or not the episodic act of taking the medication was completed. In these studies, subjects were presented with devices attached to individual medication bottles that provided time and date information about when the medication was last used. If subjects were not sure if they had completed a medication dose, they could examine the record on the bottle cap of the individual medication to determine if it was taken. Such devices provide no support for the content aspects of a medication regimen, they only provide information about when medication episodes have occurred. In one study, cigarette smokers were instructed to use an inhaler and received a nebulizer chronolog that provided them with detailed information about whether or not they had used it (Nides et al., 1993). In another study, hypertensives received caps on their blood pressure medication that provided them with feedback about when they had last removed the cap (McKenney, Munroe, & Wright, 1992). Both studies provided evidence that adherence rates were higher when subjects received feedback about when individual medications had last been taken, suggesting that poor reality monitoring is a substantial component in failure to adhere correctly. Future studies are needed that separate the two retrospective aspects of medication adherence — memory for the adherence regimen and memory for the act of adherence — from one another. In other studies that provided reality-monitoring assistance, MacDonald et al., (1977) found that a tear-off calendar enhanced adherence, and Gabriel, Gagnon, and Bryan (1977) found that a check-off chart enhanced adherence. In these cases, the retrospective aspect of support was confounded with the prospective act of remembering to tear off the page or make a check when a medication was taken. Nevertheless, the studies suggest that this issue of remembering if one took a medication may be a more important aspect of nonadherence than was previously recognized.

There are a surprisingly small number of studies that directly investigate the role of reminders that act primarily on the prospective aspects of medication adherence. Prospective reminders for medication adherence would generally take the form of programmed alarms, telephone calls, or other external time-based signals that act much like an alarm clock, signalling an individual that it is time to get up and have a decent breakfast. In one study that focused on the prospective aspect of medical adherence, Leirer, Morrow, Tanke, and Pariante (1991) used a voice mail system to remind subjects that it was time to take their medication. Subjects who received phone calls did improve their adherence. In a related study, Leirer, Morrow, Pariante, and Doksum (1988) also found that telephone reminders improved the subjects' attending appointments made to get an influenza vaccine. Thus, telereminding appears to be an effective supportive device, but it is cumbersome in that it can only be effective if a subject is near a telephone, and can also be intrusive on daily events.

An alternative strategy is to attach reminding devices to the medications themselves. There are commercially available, inexpensive devices that sound an alarm at a fixed interval to be determined by the purchaser. These devices are designed to support only the prospective aspects of medication adherence and we are investigating their effectiveness in improving adherence for subjects who meet a nonadherence criterion after a period of monitoring. Research by Azrin and Powell (1969) suggests that such prospective reminders may be effective. They designed an apparatus that sounded a tone when it was time to take a medication. The tone could only be terminated by turning a knob, and when this was done, the pill was dispensed into the person's hand. This apparatus was compared to an alarm timer and a control container that made no sound. Azrin and Powell reported a significant increase in adherence for subjects assigned to the pill dispenser condition relative to the other conditions.

A discussion of prospective reminders for taking medication would not be complete without a mention of the importance of social support in medication adherence, and the role that knowledgable family members can play in serving as reminders for the prospective act of taking medications, as well as for organizing the retrospective aspects of the adherence task. Although there is no direct evidence that social support acts on the cognitive component of adherence (it could function to shape an illness representation consonant with adherence), Schwartz, Wand, Zeitz, and Goss (1962) reported that nonadherent patients were more likely to be widowed, divorced, or separated and Doherty, Schrott, Metcalf, and Iasiello-Vailas (1983) found that men recovering from coronaries who were adherent were characterized by highly supportive wives. The role that family members and significant others can play in shaping adherence behaviors is poorly understood but likely important and worthy of future investigation.

DIRECTIONS FOR FUTURE RESEARCH

There are two major points presented in this chapter that should help direct future research. The first is that theoretical constructs from laboratory research provide an important foundation for understanding related behaviors in the everyday environment. This chapter illustrates that laboratory constructs can provide significant insight into salient dimensions of real-world behavior that are amenable to investigation. All of the hypotheses advanced in this chapter are easily testable with the technology, psychological instruments, and analytic tools available today. The second point of importance is that in order to successfully characterize the complexity of an individual's real-world behavior, it is necessary to integrate across subfields within the psychological sciences. In the present chapter, we drew heavily upon social psychology and health psychology, as well as cognitive psychology, in an effort to accurately represent the role of cognitive function and cognitive abilities on medication adherence within an appropriate context.

These two points converge to provide clear directions for future research in medication adherence. Research will result in advances in understanding this important behavior only to the extent that it is both theoretically guided and the aspect of the behavior under study is examined within a broad contextual framework that addresses many aspects of psychological functioning. At present, there are hundreds of studies in the literature that focus on medication adherence, but because nearly all of these studies have been atheoretical, they do not provide us with a coherent corpus of knowledge on the topic. Comprehensive, large-scale studies able to address simultaneously the role of cognitive factors, illness variables, and psychosocial factors are needed. What especially needs to be recognized is that the most salient component of adherence behaviors will vary greatly as a function of individual difference variables and across illnesses. We have come a long way in developing technology in determining who is nonadherent. Such technology could easily be implemented in a physician's office to determine who is using medications incorrectly and how often. What is less clear is how to determine what intervention would be effective for the nonadherent individual. We hope that the constructs and ideas in this chapter serve as a basis for understanding not only prospective memory failure in medication adherence, but also the interaction of prospective failure with other cognitive, psychosocial, and disease variables.

ACKNOWLEDGMENTS

The authors gratefully acknowledge the support of the National Institute on Aging for this work. Support was provided by grants to the first author including AGO6265–08, AGO9868–02, and P50 AG11715–01.

REFERENCES

Azrin, N. H., & Powell, J. (1969). Behavioral engineering: The use of response priming to improve prescribed self-medication. *Journal of Applied Behavior Analysis, 2,* 39–42.

Beck, N. C., Parker, J. C., Frank, R. G., Geden, E. A., Kay, D. R., Gamache, M., Shivvers, N., Smith, E., & Anderson, S. (1988). Patients with rheumatoid arthritis at high risk for noncompliance with salicylate treatment regimens. *Journal of Rheumatology, 15,* 1081–1084.

Cohen, G. (1989). *Memory in the Real World.* Hove, England: Lawrence Erlbaum Associates.

Craik, F. I. M. (1986). A functional account of age differences in memory. In F. Klix & H. Hagendorf (Eds.), *Human memory and cognitive capabilities: Mechanisms and performance* (pp. 409–442). New York: Elsevier Science.

Deyo, R. A., Inui, T. S., & Sullivan, B. (1981). Compliance with arthritis drugs: Magnitude, correlates, and clinical implications. *Journal of Rheumatology, 8,* 931–936.

Doherty, W. J., Schrott, H. B., Metcalf, L., & Iasiello-Vailas, L. (1983). Effects of spouse support and health beliefs on medication adherence. *Journal of Family Practice, 17,* 837–841.

Einstein, G. O., Holland, L. J., McDaniel, M. A., & Guynn, M. J. (1992). Age related deficits in prospective memory: The influence of task complexity. *Psychology and Aging, 7*(3), 471–478.

Einstein, G. O., & McDaniel, M. A. (1990). Normal aging and prospective memory. *Journal of Experimental Psychology: Learning, Memory, Cognition, 16,* 717–726.

Ellis, J. A. (1988). Memory for future intentions: Investigating pulses and steps. In M. M. Gruneberg, P. E. Morris, & R. N. Sykes (Eds.), *Practical Aspects of Memory* (pp. 372–376). London: Academic Press.

Folkman, S., Bernstein, L., & Lazarus, R. S. (1987). Stress processes and the misuse of drugs in older adults. *Psychology and Aging, 2,* 366–374.

Gabriel, M., Gagnon, J. P., & Bryan, C. K. (1977). Improved patient compliance through use of a daily drug reminder chart. *American Journal of Public Health, 67,* 968–969.

Garnett, W. R., Davis, L. J., McKenney, J. M., & Steiner, K. C. (1981). Effect of telephone follow-up on medication compliance. *American Journal of Hospital Pharmacy, 38,* 676–679.

Harris, J. E. & Wilkins, A. J. (1982). Remembering to do things: a theoretical framework and an illustrative experiment. *Human Learning, 1,* 123–136.

Hecht, A. (1974). Improving medication compliance by teaching outpatients. *Nursing Forum, 13,* 112–129.

Kruse, W., Eggert-Kruse, W., Rampmaier, J., Runnebaum, B., & Weber, E. (1991). Dosage frequency and drug-compliance behaviour—A comparative study on compliance with a medication to be taken twice or four times daily. *European Journal of Clinical Pharmacology, 41,* 589–592.

Kvavilashvili, L. (1987). Remembering intention as a distinct form of memory. *British Journal of Psychology, 78,* 507–518.

Leirer, V. O., Morrow, D. G., Pariante, G. M., & Doksum, T. (1988). Increasing influenza vaccination adherence through voice mail. *Journal of the American Geriatric Society, 37,* 1147–1150.

Leirer, V. O., Morrow, D. G., Tanke, E. D., Pariante, G. M. (1991). Elders' nonadherence: Its assessment and medication reminding by voice mail. *The Gerontologist, 31,* 514–520.

Leventhal, H. & Cameron, L. (1987). Behavioral theories and the problem of compliance. *Patient Education and Counseling, 10,* 117–138.

MacDonald, E. T., MacDonald, J. B., & Phoenix, M. (1977). Improving drug compliance after hospital discharge. *British Medical Journal, 2,* 618–621.

Maylor, E. A. (1990). Age and prospective memory. *The Quarterly Journal of Experimental Psychology, 42A,* 471–493.

McKenney, J. M., Munroe, W. P., & Wright, J. T. (1992). Impact of an electronic medication compliance aid on long-term blood pressure control. *Journal of Clinical Pharmacology, 32,* 277–283.

Meacham, J. A., & Singer, J. (1977). Incentive effects in prospective remembering. *Journal of Psychology, 97,* 191–197.

Morrell, R. W., Park, D. C., & Poon, L. W. (1989). Quality of instruction on prescription drug labels: Effects on memory and comprehension in young and old adults. *The Gerontologist, 29,* 345–353.

Morrell, R. W., Park, D. C., & Poon, L. W. (1990). Effects of labeling techniques on memory and comprehension of prescription information in young and old adults. *Journals of Gerontology: Psychological Sciences, Special Issue, 45,* 166–172.

Morrow, D. G., Leirer, V. O., Altieri, P., & Tanke, E. D. (1991). Elders' schema for taking medication: Implications for instruction design. *Journals of Gerontology: Psychological Sciences, 46,* 378–385.

Morrow, D. G., Leirer, V. O., & Sheikh, J. I. (1988). Adherence and medication instructions: Review and recommendations. *Journal of the American Geriatric Society, 36,* 1147–1160.

Nides, M. A., Tashkin, D. P., Simmons, M. S., Wise, R. A., Li, V. C., & Rand, C. S. (1993). Improving inhaler adherence in a clinical trial through the use of the nebulizer chronolog. *Chest, 104,* 501–507.

Park, D. C. (1992a, August). *Applications of basic research in memory and aging.* Invited address presented at the National Institute on Aging Conference on Applied Gerontology, Bethesda, MD.

Park, D. C. (1992b). Applied cognitive aging research. In F. I. M. Craik & T. A. Salthouse (Eds.), *The handbook of aging and cognition* (pp. 449–493). Hillsdale, NJ: Lawerence Erlbaum Associates.

Park, D. C. (1994). Self-regulation and control of rheumatic disorders. In S. Maes, H. Leventhal, & M. Johnston (Eds.), *International Review of Health Psychology.* New York: Wiley.

Park, D. C., Morrell, R. W., Frieske, D., Blackburn, A. B., & Birchmore, D. (1991). Cognitive factors and the use of over-the-counter medication organizers by arthritis patients. *Human Factors, 33,* 57–67.

Park, D. C., Morrell, R. W., Frieske, D., Gaines, C. L., & Lautenschlager, G. (1993a). Measurement techniques and level of analysis of medication adherence behaviors across the life span. *Proceedings of the Human Factors and Ergonomics Society 37th Annual Meeting,* 188–192.

Park, D. C., Morrell, R. W., Frieske, D., & Kincaid, D. (1992). Medication adherence behaviors in older adults: Effects of external cognitive supports. *Psychology and Aging, 7,* 252–256.

Park, D. C., Morrell, R. W., Hertzog, C., Leventhal, H., Leventhal, E., Birchmore, D., & Kidder, D. (1993b). *Psychosocial instrument package for the assessment of osteoarthritis and rheumatoid arthritis patients.* Unpublished manuscript.

Park, D. C., Puglisi, J. T., & Smith, A. D. (1986). Memory for pictures: Does an age-related decline exist? *Psychology and Aging, 1,* 11–17.

Park, D. C., Willis, S. L., Morrow, D. G., Diehl, M., & Gaines, C. L. (1994). Cognitive function and medication usage in older adults. *The Journal of Applied Gerontology, 13,* 39–57.

Peck, C. L., & King, N. (1982). Increasing patient compliance with prescriptions. *Journal of the American Medical Association, 248,* 2874–2877.

Rand, C. S., Wise, R. A., Nides, M. A., Simmons, M. S., Bleecker, E. R., Kusek, J. W., Li, V. C., & Tashkin, D. P. (1992). Metered-dose inhaler adherence in a clinical trial. *American Review of Respiratory Disease, 146,* 1559–1564.

Rehder, T. L., McCoy, L. K., Blackwell, B., Whitehead, W., & Robinson, A. (1980). Improving medication compliance by counseling and special prescription container. *American Journal of Hospital Pharmacy, 37,* 379–384.

Rudd, P., Byyny, R. L., Zachary, V., LoVerde, M. E., Titus, C., Mitchell, W. D., & Marshall, G. (1989). The natural history of medication compliance in a drug trial: Limitations of pill counts. *Clinical Pharmacology Therapy, 46,* 169–176.

Salthouse, T. A. (1991). *Theoretical perspectives on cognitive aging.* Hillsdale, NJ: Lawerence Erlbaum Associates.

Schwartz, D., Wand, M., Zeitz, L., & Goss, M. E. (1962). Medication errors made by elderly chronically ill patients. *American Journal of Public Health, 52,* 2018–2029.

Wilkins, A. J., & Baddeley, A. D. (1988). Remembering to recall in everyday life: An approach to absentmindedness. In M. M. Gruneberg, P. E. Morris, & R. N. Sykes (Eds.), *Practical Aspects of Memory* (pp. 27–34). New York: Academic Press.

Winograd, E. (1988). Some observations on prospective remembering. In M. M. Gruneberg, P. E. Morris, & R. N. Sykes (Eds.), *Practical Aspects of Memory* (pp. 349–353). London: Academic Press.

World Health Organization. (1981). Health care in the elderly: Report of the Technical Group on use of medications by the elderly. *Drugs, 22,* 279–294.

Zola, I. K. (1986). Thoughts on improving compliance in elderly arthritics. *Geriatrics, 41,* 81–85.

20

COMMENTARY

Improving Prospective Memory

Douglas Herrmann
National Center for Health Statistics,
Hyattsville, Maryland

Prospective memory can be enhanced by a variety of methods. Probably the best known method is to provide some potential rememberers with an external aid, such as a tag or an alarm set to go off when an intended act is to be carried out. Another well known method is to imagine ourselves performing the intended act amidst salient cues that are expected to occur in the context where the act is to be performed.

The degree of enhancement provided by a method may be assessed by comparing the remembering of subjects who are provided with an external or internal aid with the remembering of subjects who are not so aided. Typically, performance was found to be enhanced by such aids, with the effectiveness of an aid dependent on the quality of the cues provided by it (McDaniel & Einstein, 1993).

Almost all previous research sought to facilitate prospective memory performance rather than to improve prospective memory skills (Herrmann & Palmisano, 1992). The three chapters in this section contrast with previous research in that these chapters are concerned with changing a person's prospective memory ability for the better. These chapters address the remediation of prospective memory deficits and offer suggestions about how a person's characteristic prospective memory may be improved.

In this chapter, I summarize what the preceding three chapters say about the improvement or remediation of prospective memory. Next, building upon the conclusions of these chapters and that of the literature, I propose a general framework for the improvement–rehabilitation of prospective memory.

RECENT DEVELOPMENTS IN IMPROVING
PROSPECTIVE MEMORY CAPABILITY

Cockburn (this volume) reviews the self-report literature, using question-naires, diaries, and monitoring, as well as experimental investigations that bear on losses in prospective memory functioning resulting from neurological im-pairment. She proposes that prospective errors consist of slips of action that are due to such factors as interruptions to one's daily routine and blocking. Cockburn concludes that training at arranging and using cues and the keep-ing a diary appears to improve prospective memory skills.

Camp, Foss, Stevens, and O'Hanlon (this volume) report a series of exper-iments in which Alzheimer's disease (AD) patients are trained to use spaced rehearsal to remember intentions. This research indicated that patients who have good working memory capacity may be inclined to rely on their own memory and not use external aids. Camp et al. conclude that that spaced re-hearsal enhances the prospective performance of AD patients because this kind of rehearsal affects implicit memory.

Park and Kidder (this volume) review the literature on methods for im-proving medication adherence. They note that medication adherence is pri-marily time-based, although some medication is event-based because it is taken as symptoms arise. For medication that is time-based, the use of timing devices (such as alarm clocks, pill cap alarms, and reminding services) is recom-mended because memory for time is generally poor. Both time and event tasks benefit from use of pill organizers because they make it visually apparent when a pill was not taken (given that the patient remembers the number of pills to be taken). Park and Kidder conclude that the problem of medication adher-ence is a complex function of memory and nonmemory factors (such as social context and motivation) and of individual differences in prospective memory ability.

TOWARD A TECHNOLOGY
OF IMPROVING PROSPECTIVE MEMORY

The improvement or rehabilitation methods addressed by the preceding three chapters are diverse. The improvement or rehabilitation of prospective mem-ory requires a multifaceted approach, one that capitalizes on all *modes* (sub-systems) of the human psychological system. In the past several years, my colleagues and I took such an approach to memory improvement and rehabil-itation for both retrospective and prospective memory. I review the theoretical basis of this approach in general and then describe how it applies to prospec-tive memory performance.

The Multimodal Approach

The multimodal approach is based on the assumption that memory performance can be influenced by other systems or modes of psychological processing (e.g., physiological, perceptual, emotional, motivational, social, and environmental). According to this approach, memory improvement or memory rehabilitation will achieve the greatest improvement in a person's memory functioning by training a person to use better control processes and methods that enhance other modes. Support for the multimodal approach to improving prospective memory has come from both research (Bendiksen & Bendiksen, 1992, in press; Herrmann & Searleman, 1990; Herrmann, Weingartner, Searleman, & McEvoy, 1992; McEvoy, 1992; Mullin & Herrmann, 1994; Mullin, Herrmann, & Searleman, 1993) and from the independent development of new methods of memory improvement (Herrmann, Rea, & Andrezejewski, 1988; Herrmann & Searleman, 1990; McEvoy & Moon, 1988; Parenté & Anderson-Parenté, 1991; West, 1985).

In our most recent theorizing (Mullin & Herrmann, 1994), the multimodal model assumes that there are three kinds of processing modes. The three kinds of modes are *cognitive* modes, *physiological* modes, and *emotive* modes. Each kind of mode includes three categories. The functions of these modes and how they affect memory performance is discussed next.

Cognitive Modes. The three cognitive modes include *mental* manipulations, manipulations of the *physical environment,* and manipulations of the *social environment* (Herrmann & Searleman, 1990). Mental manipulations consist of the mental processes that enhance encoding or that cue retrieval. These manipulations are the mainstay of memory training and rehabilitation. Physical manipulations use physical records or other stimuli for information storage or for retrieval cueing. For example, notes can be taken, objects can be positioned, or alarms can be set in order to help an individual remember (Park & Kidder, this volume). Social manipulations consist of behaviors and conversational ploys that lead to successful memory performance (Best, 1992). For example, individuals can defer questions to others to gain time for retrieval or to listen for additional retrieval cues, or can make facial expressions and gestures that buy time to learn what is being said.

Physiological State Modes. These modes modulate memory processing (McGaugh, 1989). They include *physical, chemical,* and *health* states. They affect a person's strength for engaging in cognitive processing. For example, strenuous exercise reduces a person's physiological readiness for continued activity. Some medications may make a person sleepy and unable to pay attention. Ill health also can reduce a person's physiological readiness for mental activity.

Emotive State Modes.   The emotive state modes consist of the *emotional, attitudinal,* and *motivational* states. The emotional, attitudinal, and motivational states also affect a person's strength but, in addition, they influence a person's priorities regarding what tasks to perform and which cognitive processes to apply to a memory task. For example, a person who has just become emotionally upset, will often be physically and attitudinally less able to perform a memory task.

A Multimodal Account of Prospective Memory Performance

The multimodal view of prospective memory failures rests on the assumption that retrieval occurs differently for prospective memory than it does for retrospective memory. Retrospective memory tasks call for explicit retrieval. Prospective memory tasks require an intention to be held retrospectively in memory (McDaniel & Einstein, 1992), but typically these tasks do not involve explicit retrieval. Instead, the intention emerges implicitly into consciousness, without explicit retrieval attempts (Dorner, 1987; Herrmann, 1991; Searleman & Herrmann, 1994; see Camp et al., this volume). In some cases, a person may experience a feeling of knowing that something is to be done; this feeling may then give rise to an explicit search to retrieve the intention. However, prospective memory tasks tend to rely only on the process of emergence.

Cognitive Interventions.   Any mental manipulation of the intention that strengthens or elaborates the memory for the intention may be expected to increase the likelihood of emergence (Camp et al., this volume). However, attempts to improve prospective memory by studying an intention are sometimes ineffective because the emergence of an intention does not always occur. Preparation for a prospective memory task is typically most effective if the encoding method is fashioned to specifically address the task and to sensitize the rememberer to cues that will remind one of the act to be performed (Cockburn, this volume). For example, imaging a clock with the hands positioned at the time the act is to be performed may lead to remembering but not always; imagining the clock with the person to be met alongside works better; imagining the clock with the person in the room where the rememberer will be just prior to the time to carry out the intention works better yet.

Research showed that the emergence of an intention depends on the method of encoding and on the attributes of an intention. Time-based intentions are more difficult than event-based intentions (McDaniel & Einstein, 1992). Intentions that require an act to be performed at a certain time are more difficult than acts that can be performed within an interval; intentions are remembered less often as the retention period increases; and recurring intentions are sometimes easier to forget than unique intentions (Andrzejewski,

Moore, Corvette, & Herrmann, 1991). Accordingly, greater preparation for remembering is needed for intended acts that recur after long periods and that must be executed at a precise time. Because intentions vary according to how easily they are remembered, some memory training provides instruction about how the attributes of an intention affect the likelihood the intention will be remembered (Herrmann & Searleman, 1990).

The uncertain nature of emergence led researchers and practitioners to try cognitive modes to enhance prospective memory. External aids are used to improve the cueing of an intention (Intons-Peterson, 1993; Leirer, Tanke, & Morrow, 1993; Park & Kidder, this volume). Alarms are more effective reminders than notes (Harris, 1984) but alarms are often not enough; they work best if a note accompanies the alarm that tells the person the nature of the act to be performed. Commercial memory aids are popular because they usually provide specific cues that are effective and are appropriate to the individual (Petro, Herrmann, Burrows, & Moore, 1991). Research showed that training to use external aids enhances subsequent remembering of intentions (McEvoy & Moon, 1988).

The uncertainty of the emergence process also leads people to use social manipulations to ensure the presence of cues to remember. For example, people often ask others to remind them of things to do (Herrmann & Searleman, 1992). The use of someone else as a memory aid carries with it the risk that this person may have a bad prospective memory.

Physiological and Emotive Modes. Even when a person has made a good effort to encode an intention, poor physiological and emotive states can make memory failure inevitable. If a person's current physical condition is poor, prospective remembering is less likely (Herrmann & Parenté, 1994). A poor emotional state, such as anxiety, has been found to affect prospective memory (Meacham & Kushner, 1980). A person's motivation for an appointment will affect the likelihood of it being met (Parenté & Stapleton, 1993). For example, prospective memory failures were found to be considerably lower (from 5% to 60%) when the task was regarded by subjects as important than when it was regarded as as unimportant (Andrzejewski et al., 1991).

Individual Differences. People vary in their capability for dealing with prospective memory. One reason for such variation is personality. For example, people with a Type B personality tend to be less able to remember intentions than those with a Type A personality (Searleman & Gaydusek, 1989). Also people differ in their capability for remembering intentions as a function the amount of experience they have at remembering a certain kind of intention. People who have had experience with recurring appointments are better at remembering this kind of appointment than people who have not had such experience (Andrzejewski et al., 1991).

A Multimodal Program for Improving or Rehabilitating Prospective Memory. A multimodal program for improving or rehabilitating prospective memory will be most successful if it is designed to address the particular kind of intention that troubles a person. Mental manipulations, external aids, and social skills should be appropriate to the kind of intention to be remembered. In addition, the person may be directed to avoid substances that interfere with cognition, to cope with stress, and to take account of their motivation to remember an intended act. Training should take into account of certain individual differences, such as whether individuals have a Type A or B personality, and their experience with the intention that is the object of training.

CONCLUSION

Research that examines how prospective memory performance is facilitated by stimuli and task variables provides the foundation for a theory of prospective memory (Morris, 1992). However, in everyday life, prospective memory performance is based on a broad array of knowledge and skills pertaining not only to memory but also to other psychological systems. Thus, research on new methods of training, aiding, and enhancing prospective memory offers society new modes for coping with memory in daily life. In addition, such research provides a basis—in conjunction with research concerning the facilitation of prospective memory—for developing more complete theories of prospective memory.

REFERENCES

Andrzejewski, S. J., Moore, C. M., Corvette, M., & Herrmann, D. (1991). Prospective memory skill. *Bulletin of the Psychonomic Society, 29,* 304–306.

Bendiksen, M., & Bendiksen, I. (in press). Multi-modal memory rehabilitation for the toxic solvent injured population. In D. Herrmann, M. Johnson, C. McEvoy, C. Hertzog, & P. Hertel (Eds.), *Basic and Applied Memory Research: New Findings.* Hillsdale, NJ: Lawrence Erlbaum Associates.

Bendiksen, M., & Bendiksen, I. (1992). A multidimensional intervention program solvent injured population. *Cognitive Rehabilitation, 10,* 20–27.

Best, D. (1992). The role of social interaction in memory improvement. In D. Herrmann, H. Weingartner, A. Searleman, & C. McEvoy (Eds.), *Memory Improvement: Implications for Memory Theory* (pp. 122–149). New York: Springer Verlag.

Dorner, D. (1987). Memory systems and the regulation of behavior. In E. van der Meer & J. Hoffmann (Eds.), *Knowledge Aided Information Processing* (pp. 929–939). Amsterdam: North-Holland.

Harris, J.E. (1984). Methods of improving memory. In B. A. Wilson & N. Moffatt (Eds.), *Clinical Management of Memory Problem* (pp. 46–62). Croon Helm, England: Beckenham.

Herrmann, D. J. (1991) *SuperMemory.* Emmaus, PA: Rodale.

Herrmann, D. J., & Palmisano, M. (1992). The facilitation of memory. In M. Gruneberg & P. Morris (Eds.), *Aspects of Memory* (2nd ed.) (pp. 147–167). Chichester, England: Wiley.

Herrmann, D., & Parenté, R. (1994). The multi-modal approach to cognitive rehabilitation. *Journal of Head Trauma Rehabilitation, 4,* 133–142.

Herrmann, D. J., Rea, A., & Andrzejewski, S. J. (1988). The need for a new approach to memory improvement. In M. Gruneberg, P. Morris, & R. Sykes (Eds.), *Practial Aspects of Memory: Current Research and Issues* (Vol. 21, pp. 415–420). Chichester, England: Wiley.

Herrmann, D. J., & Searleman, A. (1990). A multi-modal approach to memory improvement. In G. H. Bower (Ed.), *Advances in Learning and Motivation* (pp. 147–206). New York: Academic Press.

Herrmann, D., & Searleman, A. (1992). Memory improvement and memory theory in historical perspective. In D. Herrmann, H. Wingartner, A. Searleman, & C. McEvoy (Eds.), *Memory Improvement: Implications for memory theory.* New York: Springer Verlag.

Herrmann, D., Weingartner, H., Searleman, A., and McEvoy, C. L. (Eds.) (1992). *Memory Improvement: Implications for Memory Theory.* New York: Springer-Verlag.

Intons-Peterson, M. J. (1993). External memory aids and their relation to memory. In C. Izawa (Ed.), *Cognitive Psychology Applied* (pp. 142–166). Hillsdale, NJ: Lawrence Erlbaum Associates.

Leirer, V. O., Tanke, E. D., & Morrow, D. G. (1993). Commercial cognitive/memory systems: A case study. *Applied Cognitive Psychology, 7,* 675–689.

McDaniel, M. A., & Einstein, G. O. (1992). Aging and prospective memory: Basic findings and applications. In T. E. Scruggs & M. A. Mastropieri (Eds.), *Advances in Learning and Behavioral Disabilities.* (Vol. 7, pp. 87–105). Greenwich, CT: JAI Press.

McDaniel, M. A., & Einstein, G. O. (1993). The importance of cue familiarity and cue distinctiveness in prospective memory. *Memory, 1,* 23–41.

McEvoy, C. L. (1992). Memory improvement in context: Implications for the development of memory improvement theory. In D. Herrmann, H. Weingartner, A. Searleman, & C. McEvoy (Eds.), *Memory Improvement: Implications for Memory Theory* (pp. 210–231). New York: Springer Verlag.

McEvoy, C. L., & Moon, J. R. (1988). Assessment and treatment of everyday memory problems in the elderly. In M. M. Gruneberg, P. E. Morris, & R. N. Sykes (Eds.), *Practical Aspects of memory: Current research and issues* (Vol. 2, pp. 155–160). Chichester, England: Wiley.

McGaugh, J. L. (1989) Modulation of memory processes. In P. R. Solomon, G. R. Goethals, C. M. Kelley, & B. R. Stephens (Eds.), *Memory: Interdisciplinary Approaches* (pp. 33–64). New York: Springer-Verlag.

Meacham, J. A., & Kushner, S. (1980) Anxiety, prospective remembering, and performance of planned actions. *Journal of General Psychology, 103,* 203–209.

Morris, P. E. (1992). Prospective memory: Remembering to do things. *Aspects of Memory, 1,* 196–222. London: Metheun.

Mullin, P., & Herrmann, D. J. (1994, August). *Interface Constructs in a Multimodal Approach to Memory Improvement.* Paper presented at the third Practical Aspects of Memory Conference, University of Maryland University College, College Park.

Mullin, P., Herrmann, D. J., & Searleman, A. (1993). Forgotten variables in memory research. *Memory, 15,* 43.

Parenté, R., & Anderson-Parenté, J. (1991). *Retraining memory: Techniques and applications.* Houston, TX: CSY Publishing.

Parenté, R., & Stapleton, M. (1993). An empowerment model of memory training. *Applied Cognitive Psychology, 7,* 585–602.

Petro, S., Herrmann, D., Burrows, D., & Moore, C. M. (1991). Usefulness of commercial memory aids as a function of age. *International Journal of Aging and Human Development, 33,* 295–309.

Searleman, A., & Gaydusek, K. A. (1989, November). *Relationship between prospective memory ability and selective personality variables.* Paper presented at the annual meeting of the Psychonomic Society, Atlanta, GA.

Searleman, A., & Herrmann, D. J. (1994). *Memory from a Broader Perspective.* New York: McGraw Hill.

West, R. L. (1985). *Memory Fitness Over Forty.* Gainesville, FL: Triad Publishing Company.

Author Index

A

Abrahams, J. P., 353, *365*
Abson, V., 182, *193, 197*
Ach, N., 55, 56, 59, 66, 67, 72, 81, *85*
Ackerman, B. P., 255, *265*
Ajzen, I., 26, *48*
Alba, R., 352, *366*
Albert, M. L., 269, *292*
Aldridge, V. J., 304, *317*
Alivisatos, B., 271, *293*
Allen, D. G., 271, *292*
Allen, L. G., 164, *171*
Alpert, J. J., 213, *221*
Altieri, P., 384, *389*
Anderson, D. C., 135, 136, *140*
Anderson, J. R., 10, *20*, 55, 59, 60, 62, 79, *85*, 100, *110*, 122, 123, *138*, 282, *291*
Anderson, J., 213, *224*
Anderson, S. W., 252, 253, *262*, 320, *324*
Anderson, S., 370, *388*
Anderson-Parenté, J., 393, *397*
Andrzejewski, S. J., 24, 32, 34, 39, 40, 41, *47*, 393–395, *396, 397*
Anschutz, L., 205, *221*
Anthony-Bergstone,, 204

B

Baars, B. J., 33, *47*
Babcock, R. L., 255, *266*
Bäckman, L., 95, 96, *110*, 179, *194*, 352, 353, 355, *365*
Baddeley, A. D., 8, 9, 18, 19, *20*, 24, 25, 34, 45, 46, *47*, *51*, 58, *86*, 94, 102, 104, 110, *110, 113*, 176, 178, *194, 197*, 199, 215, *225*, 242, *247*, 249, 250, 252, 257, *262, 266*, 321, *324*, 328, 329, 331, 334, 337, 338, 339, 341, *348, 350*, 369, 371, *390*
Bahrick, H. P., 8, *20*, 110, *110*
Baker, J. G., 24, *47*, 63, 82, *86*, 184, *194*, 208, *222*
Banaji, M. R., 23, *47*

Archibald, S. L., 256, *264*
Arkin, R. M., 354, *365*
Arnon, A., 206, *224*
Assal, G., 306, *315*
Atkinson, J. W., 57, *85*
Atkinson, R. C., 249, *262*
Awh, E., 271, *293*
Azrin, N. H., 386, *388*

Subject Index

A

Action
activation, 6, 159 (*see also* Intentions, level of activation)
complexity, 3, 4 (*see also* Prospective memory tasks, complexity)
evaluation of outcome, 2, 14–16
execution, 2, 14, 146
time of, 41, 42
inhibition, 12
initiation, 2, 14
intentional, 54, 100
interruption, 36–37 (*see also* Task interruption)
mental representation of actions, *see* representation of intentions
nonroutine, 11 (*see also* Intentions, episodic)
and self-initiation, 94
routine, 3, 9, 11, 13 (*see also* Intentions, habitual)
schema, 6, 16–17, 55
automatic activation of, 55
selection of, 6, 8, 57
slips, 242, 244, 371
stages (number of), 42

to-be-performed vs. to-be-recalled, 95, 96, 117, 159
Action Control Scale (ACS), 73
ACT* theory, 79, 100, 282
Action Trigger Schema (ATS), 6, 9
Aging
age-related changes, 177–178
age-related deficits, 117–118, 178–179, 186
and effectiveness of cues, 235
and memory, 117–118
and output monitoring, 179, 193 (*see also* Monitoring)
and prospective memory, 125, 175, 227, 233–236, 259
age differences in prospective memory, 98–99, 131–134, 182, 183, 233–236, 260, 329, 334
and reality monitoring, 179, 193
and self-initiation, 94, 134, 177, 178, 234
and the use of cues, 180, 181, 183, 334
Alzheimer's disease (AD) (*see also* Dementia)
and explicit memory, 355, 365
and implicit memory, 355, 365
cognitive impairments in, 351, 352
Amnesic Syndrome, 250, 253

413